"The *Confessions* of Augustine  read in Latin. This *Reader's E* to this marvelous text while s _____ will enjoy the experience and come away prepared to go farther faster."

JAMES J. O'DONNELL
Arizona State University

"In his *Confessions*, Augustine of Hippo sought to give his readers a language in which to speak to God. To this end he crafted a work using all his skill as a student of rhetoric, and all the fruits of his life as a monk and bishop imbued with the language of Scripture—and especially with that of the Psalms. Something vital of Augustine's vision may certainly be seen through a translation, but only in Latin are the curtains fully drawn back. This *Latin Reader's Edition* will provide vital assistance for someone venturing on Augustine's great work for the first time. The glossary of key terms and the many vocabulary footnotes form an invaluable aid and encouragement for the reader. Kevin Bergdorf has provided a resource for which teachers and students of Augustine will be extremely grateful."

LEWIS AYRES
Abbey House, Durham
Pontifical University of Saint Thomas Aquinas
Australian Catholic University

"Language matters as more than a way to communicate ideas; it is also an experience that carries meaning in the way that words interrelate and persuade. This book is a very good tool for delving more deeply into the experience that Augustine wanted to share with us. Kevin Bergdorf has presented the text with several kinds of reading aids, allowing this book to show how Augustine uses language to build relationships with his readers and with God as well. His feelings continue to inspire. I clearly and highly recommend it to anyone who wants to be part of his deeper adventure—a beautiful chance to get in touch with Augustine's mind in a direct way."

ALLAN FITZGERALD, O.S.A.
Villanova University

"Texts for classical authors with running vocabularies have long been the staple of students of pagan authors. Here finally we have the beginnings of a similar facility for those who wish to read St. Augustine without constant recourse to dictionaries or translations. I wish I had had such a tool in my hands during the several years I have been learning and teaching Latin, and I am delighted that it is now available."

TAMSIN GEACH, O.P.
Blackfriars Priory and Studium
University of Oxford

"In his masterful presentation of the *Confessions*, Kevin Bergdorf has opened up this fundamental text of Western civilization for a whole new generation of philosophers, theologians, seminarians, clergy, and religious, as well as students of literature, classics, linguistics, and, above all, to all those who wish to 'know' Augustine and his own meditative account of his conversion and continuing search for Christ and for the meaning of perfection.

"For skilled Latinists, the edition enables the reader to encounter the text anew, but ponderously and meditatively, reflecting again, or indeed for the first time, on the meaning behind familiar words and phrases and to appreciate the skill of Augustine as a writer and wordsmith. For those approaching for the first time, Bergdorf provides the key into what has so often proved to be a life-changing text for readers over sixteen centuries. The main glossary allows the reader and student to recall and revise vocabulary and grammar which will already be familiar, as well as to make use of extensive tables and examples. Running alongside the central text are words which the reader will perhaps be encountering for the first time, and these are presented not only with an easy-to-grasp meaning, so as to facilitate uninterrupted reading, but also informative indications of origin and grammar.

"Bergdorf's text is a delight to use for both study and personal reflection. Well-thumbed copies of this work will, I am sure, be a feature of many libraries and bookshelves for many years to come."

RUPERT ALLEN, C.O.
The Oxford Oratory

THE
CONFESSIONS
OF
SAINT AUGUSTINE

THE

CONFESSIONS

OF

SAINT AUGUSTINE

A Latin Reader's Edition

BOOKS I–IX

Edited by

K. A. BERGDORF

EMMAUS
ACADEMIC

Steubenville, Ohio
www.emmausacademic.com

EMMAUS
ACADEMIC

Steubenville, Ohio
www.emmausacademic.com
A Division of The St. Paul Center for Biblical Theology
Editor-in-Chief: Scott Hahn
1380 University Blvd
Steubenville, Ohio 43952

Library of Congress Cataloging-in-Publication Data applied for
ISBNs: 978-1-64585-388-6 paperback | 978-1-64585-389-3 ebook

Cover design and layout by Allison Merrick
Cover painting by Jessica Coe, The Living Heart Co.

"magna spes oborta est:

non docet Catholica fides quod putabamus et uani accusabamus"

Confessions, 6.11.18

CONTENTS

Introduction   xi

How to Use This Book   xiii

Acknowledgments   xvii

A Note on the Text   xix

Abbreviations   xxi

References   xxv

THE CONFESSIONS

BOOK 1: *Childhood and Elementary School*   3

BOOK 2: *Toxic Friendships*   31

BOOK 3: *Higher Education*   47

BOOK 4: *Teacher of Rhetoric and Manichee*   69

BOOK 5: *Lucky Faustus*   95

BOOK 6: *Ambrose, Alypius, and Ambition*   121

BOOK 7: *Neoplatonism and the Incarnation*   153

BOOK 8: *"Tolle, lege"*   185

BOOK 9: *Saint Monica*   219

Main Glossary   255

Appendix A: Common Latin Words   273

Appendix B: People and Places   277

INTRODUCTION

The *Confessions* of St. Augustine has enjoyed a continuous readership for over sixteen centuries. It has been read and appreciated by students, scholars, philosophers, historians, theologians, Catholics, Protestants, atheists, and the merely curious. In the process it has become an acknowledged classic of both Christian spirituality and world literature. But more importantly, it is a work that still moves people deeply. It is unique among classical or even other early Christian texts in that it has never lost any of that original energy. Augustine's spiritual odyssey still possesses the power to affect the reader aesthetically, emotionally, spiritually. This is hardly surprising, as Augustine himself was profoundly sensitive to beauty, human feelings, and the interior life.

Augustine tells the story of the heart's journey to God with an artistry that practically defies explanation. I hope that the reader discovers that the aesthetic effect is greatly amplified when encountered in the original. It has been my experience that a heightened aesthetic awareness increases rather than diminishes the emotional and spiritual impact of the book. Until now there has not been available to readers an unabridged Latin text of the *Confessions* designed specifically with their needs in mind. While this publication contains only the first nine books, it should nonetheless provide ample material for classroom use. Ideally, this first release would have included my work on all thirteen books, but constraints of time and space now require this hope to be deferred to a second edition. It remains my conviction that Augustine produced the *Confessions* as a unified whole, and it is only in books x–xiii that we discover the destination largely unimagined in books i–ix. For now, students and teachers can begin the journey with Augustine, a journey so very much like and unlike "the wanderings of some fellow named Aeneas."

HOW TO USE THIS BOOK

This *Latin Reader's Edition* is designed to make reading authentic, unabridged Latin as enjoyable and rewarding as possible for both students and teachers. The present edition of Augustine's *Confessions* contains a Main Glossary, running glossary, a system of references in-text, and a few useful appendices.

The Main Glossary in the back of the book contains the most frequently occurring words within *Confessions*. The first 20 words presented in the glossary each occur more than 500 times and account for one out of every three words in the book! This is a list that should be memorized on day one, although there is probably nothing here that is unfamiliar. The rest of the glossary contains the other 500 words that occur 20 times or more, and should be learned as a work in progress. About half of these are among the most common words in the Latin language. Words that are otherwise very common in Latin but appear infrequently in *Confessions* are in Appendix A. Words that are found in the Main Glossary or in Appendix A are not contained in the running glossary.

Words that occur less than 20 times are glossed below the main text (in the running glossary) every time they occur unless they occur more than once in the same section with the same sense. When a more remote sense of a word is to be understood it is indicated by > following the primary sense. The gloss given in **bold** is the contextual sense. The running glossary contains the appropriate lexical abbreviations to make conjugation and declension easy. For verbs, all four principal parts are given in their abbreviated form. Nouns are given in standard lexical format and are further identified by grammatical gender. Adjectives and all other parts of speech are identified using standard lexical and grammatical abbreviations (see Abbreviations).

Late Latin is deemed to begin where the *Oxford Latin Dictionary* leaves off, and all words not found therein are tagged as LATE. Late

Latin vocabulary has been identified and glossed primarily on the basis of Hrdlicka (1931) and Souter (1997). Words that appeared originally or exclusively in Christian writers, or are the result of Latin translation of the Bible, are tagged ECCL. When Augustine coins a word or uses a word that appears to be first attested in Latin in his writings, it is tagged AUG. For words that underwent a change of meaning from the classical to the late period, both senses are usually given.

While Augustine frequently writes in a way that could allow him to be mistaken for one of our contemporaries, he inhabited a world rather remote from our own and routinely makes reference to people and places that are probably unfamiliar. All people and places (basically all proper nouns capitalized in the text, regardless of frequency) are explained in detail in the People and Places appendix located at the end of the book. Proper nouns are not included in the running glossary.

Late Latin literature and especially Ecclesiastical literature is characterized by the frequent inclusion of outside material. This occurs by way of references to the vast inheritance of classical literature, but even more so to the Old Latin Bible known as the *Vetus Latina* (*VL*). Most of these references are transparent, others are somewhat opaque, but rarely does Augustine provide a direct identification of his source. For his original audience familiarity with these works could be assumed from a shared *paideia*, so that the echoes and resonance of everything from the *Aeneid* to the Gospel of Luke contributed to the overall rhetorical effect.

This edition attempts to document every time Augustine incorporates a reference from another work of literature into *Confessions* and identifies these by placing them in italics followed by an in-text citation. The goal is to help the reader to appreciate the enormous synthesis in Augustine's artistry, and to make plain where certain words and phrases are coming from that do not occur in classical Latin. For the most part, identifying a citation involves establishing direct verbal reliance on a source, rather than merely establishing a similarity of idea. The citations from the Psalms (numbered according to the LXX) and St. Paul are overwhelming; these two sources essentially create the language from which Augustine describes his spiritual progress and state. In the majority of cases these references are rather obvious, even when Augustine is recalling a translation of the Bible from memory that we no longer possess in its entirety. When a citation more closely follows readings know from the *VL,* it is indicated as such. This happens most frequently with the Psalms and Job. Likewise, it has to be understood that every citation from Genesis chapter one derives from a version of the text that differs appreciably from the Vulgate. A hypothetical reconstruction of Augustine's text of Genesis can be found in O'Donnell (1992), vol. 3, at 13.1.1.

ACKNOWLEDGMENTS

I owe a debt of gratitude to the Department of Greek and Latin at the Catholic University of America where I was first introduced to the Latin text of *Confessions* by Sarah Moravsik, and was encouraged in my earliest efforts to lemmatize a classical text by William McCarthy. A century ago, members of religious orders studied at CUA under the direction of Roy J. Deferrari and wrote pioneering PhD dissertations on a host of philological topics related to Augustine's Latinity. These were reviewed favorably by scholars at the time and continue to appear in the bibliographies of serious scholarship on *Confessions*. My own debt to them is substantial.

The presentation of the results of lemmatization has been greatly enhanced based on suggestions received from Prof. Guiseppe "Beppe" Pezzini, Corpus Christi College, Oxford.

A project like this would have been inconceivable even a generation ago. It has been made possible by individuals and organizations who have made academic resources available electronically for the first time. I would especially like to mention the text and commentary of *Confessions* by Jim O'Donnell hosted by the author (https://faculty.georgetown.edu/jod/conf), the complete works of Augustine in Latin hosted by Nuova Biblioteca Agostiniana (https://www.augustinus.it), and the Loeb Classical Library (https://www.loebclassics.com). At an early stage in the project the tools developed by Alpheios (https://alpheios.net) were invaluable. At every stage of the project Verbum software (https://verbum.com) was essential.

A NOTE ON THE TEXT

The text of Professor J. J. O'Donnell (Oxford, 1992) is used with kind permission, here gratefully acknowledged, and is substantially unchanged except to facilitate reading in this format. Specifically, capitalization follows the usage of the *Oxford Latin Dictionary*, and for Ecclesiastical Latin, the Vulgate. The first word of each paragraph is capitalized as well. Personification is capitalized throughout, whether pertaining to the Godhead or otherwise. Additional paragraph divisions within sections as well as the formatting of poetical material and inner dialogue generally follow the lead of Boulding (2012). The section headings are my own.

ABBREVIATIONS

Lexical

adj.	adjective
adv.	adverb
colloq.	colloquial
compar.	comparative
conj.	conjunction
dim.	diminutive
f.	feminine
impers.	impersonal
indecl.	indeclinable
interj.	interjection
intr.	intransitive
m.	masculine
neut.	neuter
pl.	plural
ppl.	participial
pron.	pronoun
prep.	preposition
sg.	singular
superl.	superlative

Grammatical

abl.	ablative	lit.	literally
acc.	accusative	neg.	negative
dat.	dative	onomat.	onomatopoeic
esp.	especially	pass.	passive
euphem.	euphemism	perf.	perfect
expr.	expressing	qu.	question
fig.	figuratively	refl.	reflexive
gen.	genitive	rel.	relative
hort.	horticultural	rhet.	rhetorical
hyperb.	hyperbole	spec.	specifically
inf.	infinitive	transf.	in a transferred sense
infreq.	infrequent	usu.	usually
imp.	imperative	w.	with

Scriptural

Gen	Genesis	Mt	Matthew
Ex	Exodus	Lk	Luke
Num	Numbers	Jn	John
Deut	Deuteronomy	Acts	Acts
Josh	Joshua	Rom	Romans
1 Kgs	1 Kings	1 Cor	1 Corinthians
2 Kgs	2 Kings	2 Cor	2 Corinthians
Tob	Tobit	Gal	Galatians
Jdt	Judith	Eph	Ephesians
Job	Job	Phil	Philippians
Ps	Psalms	Col	Colossians
Prov	Proverbs	1 Thess	1 Thessalonians
Eccl	Ecclesiastes	2 Thess	2 Thessalonians
Cant	Canticle	1 Tim	1 Timothy
	(Song of Solomon)	2 Tim	2 Timothy
Wis	Wisdom	Tit	Titus
Sir	Sirach (Ecclesiasticus)	Heb	Hebrews
Isa	Isaiah	Jas	James
Jer	Jeremiah	1 Pet	1 Peter
Lam	Lamentations	2 Pet	2 Peter
Ezek	Ezekiel	1 Jn	1 John
Dan	Daniel	Rev	Revelation
Mic	Micah		
Hab	Habakuk		
Mal	Malachi		
2 Macc	2 Maccabees		

Ecclesiastical

Augustine makes very few references to other Ecclesiastical writers and does not quote from any of his own works. There is a passing reference to a few of his letters (*epp.*) at 9.4.7, and his dialogue with his son, *de Magistro*, at 9.6.14. Based on his *Reconsiderations* (*retr.*), written at the end of his life, he wished a correction to be noted at both 4.6.11 and 13.32.47.

dom. orat.	Cyprian *On the Lord's Prayer*
Hymn 2	Ambrose *Deus creator omnium*
Hymn 7	Ambrose *Splendor paternae gloriae*
Vita	Evagrius *Life of Antony by St. Athanasius*

Classical

Classical references follow the standard abbreviations as described in the Bibliographical Guide of the *Oxford Latin Dictionary*, and *Liddell, Scott, Jones Ancient Greek Lexicon* in the single instance of Plotinus.

Ac.	Cicero *Academica*
Ad.	Terence *Adelphi*
A.	Vergil *Aeneis*
Amic.	Cicero *de Amicitia*
An.	Terence *Andria*
Carm.	Horace *Carmina*
Cat.	Sallust *Catilina*
Ecl.	Vergil *Eclogae*
Ep.	Horace *Epodi*
Eu.	Terence *Eunuchus*
Fast.	Ovid *Fasti*
Fin.	Cicero *de Finibus Bonorum et Malorum*
G.	Vergil *Georgica*
Hort. fr.	Cicero *Hortensius* (fragments of a lost work)
L.	Varro *de Lingua Latina*
Met.	Ovid *Metamorphoses*
N.D.	Cicero *de Natura Deorum*
Off.	Cicero *de Officiis*
Ph.	Terence *Phormio*
Plot.	Plotinus *Enneads*
Rep.	Cicero *de Republica*
Tr.	Ovid *Tristia*
Tusc.	Cicero *Tusculanae Disputationes*

REFERENCES

Editions

Augustinus Hipponensis. (n.d.) *Confessionum Libri XIII*. http://www.augustinus.it/latino/ confessioni/index.htm.

Campbell, J. M., & McGuire, M. R. P., eds. (1931) *The Confessions of Saint Augustine: Books 1–9 (Selections)*. New York: Prentice-Hall.

Gibb, J., & W. Montgomery. (1908) *The Confessions of Augustine*. Cambridge: Cambridge University Press. With commentary.

O'Donnell, J. J. (1992) *Confessions*. Three volumes. Oxford: Oxford University Press. Available online at https://faculty.georgetown.edu/jod/conf/index.html.

Skutella, M., Juergens, H., & Schaub, W. (2009) *S. Aureli Augustini Confessionum Libri XIII*. Berlin: Walter de Gruyter.

Solignac, A. (1997) *Les Confessions. Texte de l'editione de M. Skutella; introduction et notes par A. Solignac; traducion de E. Tréhorel et G. Bouissou*. Two volumes (BA 13–14). Paris: Institut d'Études Augustiniennes.

Translations

Boulding, M. (2012) *The Confessions (The Works of Saint Augustine: A Translation for the 21st Century)*. 2nd ed. New York: New City Press.

Chadwick, H. (1991) *Saint Augustine. Confessions. Translated with an Introduction and Notes*. Oxford: Oxford University Press.

Hammond, C. J.-B. (2014) *Confessions, Volume I: Books 1–8*. Loeb Classical Library 26. Cambridge, MA: Harvard University Press.

Hammond, C. J.-B. (2016) *Confessions, Volume II: Books 9–13* Loeb Classical Library 27. Cambridge, MA: Harvard University Press.

Pusey, E. B. (1838) *The Confessions of Saint Augustine*. Oxford: J. H. Parker. Available online at https://faculty.georgetown.edu/jod/Englishconfessions.html.

Reference Works

Biblia Sacra Juxta Vulgatam Clementinam. Ed. Electronica. (2005) Bellingham, WA: Logos Bible Software.

Glare, P. G. W., ed. (2012) *Oxford Latin Dictionary*. Vol. I & II. Oxford: Oxford University Press.

Lewis, C. T., & Short, C. (1891) *A New Latin Dictionary [Founded on Andrew's Edition of Freund's Latin Dictionary]*. Oxford: Clarendon Press.

Souter, A. (1997) *A Glossary of Later Latin to 600 A. D.* Oxford: Oxford University Press.

References

Thesaurus linguae Latinae. (1900–). Berlin (formerly Leipzig): De Gruyter (formerly Teubner). Open Access online https://publikationen.badw.de/en/thesaurus.

Books

Arts, M. R. (1927) *The Syntax of the Confessions of Saint Augustine* Washington, DC: Catholic University of America.

Augustinus Hipponensis. (n.d.) *Ennarationes in Psalmos* http://www.augustinus.it/latino/esposizioni_salmi/index2.htm.

Barry, M. I. (1924) *St. Augustine, the Orator. A Study of the Rhetorical Qualities of St. Augustine's Sermones ad Populum.* Washington, DC: Catholic University of America.

Burton, P. (2007) *Language in the Confessions of Augustine.* [Online]. Oxford: Oxford University Press.

Fitzgerald, A., & Cavadini, J. (2009) *Augustine through the Ages: an Encyclopedia.* Grand Rapids, MI: William B. Eerdmans Publishing Company.

Grilli, A. (1962) *Hortensius.* Industrie Grafiche A. Nicola & C.: Varese-Milano.

Hagendahl, H. (1967) *Augustine and the Latin Classics.* Two volumes. Gothenburg: Acta Universitatis Gothoburgensis.

Hrdlicka, C. L. (1931) *A Study of the Late Latin Vocabulary and the Prepositions and Demonstrative Pronouns in the Confessions of St. Augustine.* Washington, DC: Catholic University of America.

Ladouceur, D. (2005) *The Latin Psalter: Introduction, Selected Text and Commentary.* Bristol: Bristol Classical Press.

Palmer, L. R. (1977) *The Latin Language.* London: Faber and Faber.

Plater W. E., & White, H. J. (1926) *A Grammar of the Vulgate. An Introduction to the Study of the Latinity of the Vulgate Bible.* Oxford: Oxford University Press.

Quinn, J. M. (2007) *A Companion to the "Confessions" of St. Augustine.* New York: Peter Lang.

Walpole, A. S. (1922) *Early Latin Hymns* Cambridge: Cambridge University Press.

Articles

Broeniman, C. S. (1993) "The Resurrection of a Latin Classic: The 'Confessions' of St. Augustine." *The Classical World* 86, no. 3: 209–13.

Bull, W. E. (1949) "Natural Frequency and Word Counts." *The Classical Journal* 44, no. 8: 469–84.

Major, W. E. (2008) "It's Not the Size, It's the Frequency: The Value of Using a Core Vocabulary in Beginning and Intermediate Greek." *CPL Online* 4, no. 1.

THE
CONFESSIONS
OF
SAINT AUGUSTINE

Books I–IX

1

CHILDHOOD AND
ELEMENTARY SCHOOL

Thagaste (Souk Ahras, Algeria), 354–368

Restless hearts

1.1.1 *Magnus es, Domine, et laudabilis*[1] *ualde. magna uirtus tua et sapientiae tuae non est numerus*[2] (Ps 47:2; 95:4; 146:5). et laudare te uult homo, aliqua portio[3] creaturae tuae, et homo circumferens[4] mortalitatem[5] suam, circumferens testimonium[6] peccati sui et testimonium quia *superbis resistis* (1 Pet 5:5); et tamen laudare te uult homo, aliqua portio creaturae tuae. tu excitas[7] ut laudare te delectet, quia fecisti nos ad te et inquietum[8] est cor nostrum donec requiescat in te.

Da mihi, Domine, scire et intellegere utrum sit prius inuocare te an laudare te, et scire te prius sit an inuocare te. sed quis te inuocat nesciens te? aliud enim pro alio potest inuocare nesciens. an potius inuocaris ut sciaris? *quomodo autem inuocabunt, in quem non crediderunt? aut quomodo credent sine praedicante?*[9] (Rom 10:14). *et laudabunt Dominum qui requirunt*[10] *eum* (Ps 21:27): *quaerentes enim inueniunt* (Mt 7:7) eum et inuenientes laudabunt eum. quaeram te, Domine, inuocans te et inuocem te credens in te: praedicatus enim es nobis.

---

[1]laudabilis ~is, ~e *adj.* **praiseworthy** [2]numerus ~i *m.* number > **reckoning** [3]portio ~onis *f.* **part** [4]circumfero ~ferre, ~tuli, ~latum **to carry about** [5]mortalitas ~atis *f.* **mortality** [6]testimonium ~ii *neut.* testimony > **evidence** [7]excito ~are, ~aui, ~atum **to stir up** [8]inquietus ~a, ~um *adj.* **restless** [9]praedico ~are, ~aui, ~atum to proclaim; ECCL **to preach** [10]requiro ~rere, ~siui, ~situm **to seek**

3

inuocat te, Domine, fides mea, quam dedisti mihi, quam inspirasti[11] mihi per humanitatem[12] Filii tui, per ministerium[13] praedicatoris[14] tui.

[11]inspiro ~are, ~aui, ~atum to breathe in > **to inspire supernaturally;** (LATE w. dat.) [12]humanitas ~atis *f.* **humanity** [13]ministerium ~ii *neut.* **ministry** [14]praedicator ~oris *m.* ECCL **preacher**

The paradox of invocation

1.2.2 Et quomodo inuocabo Deum meum, Deum et Dominum meum, quoniam utique in me ipsum eum uocabo, cum inuocabo eum? et quis locus est in me quo ueniat in me Deus meus, quo Deus ueniat in me, *Deus* qui *fecit caelum et terram*? (Gen 1:1). itane, Domine Deus meus? est quicquam in me quod capiat te? an uero caelum et terra, quae fecisti et in quibus me fecisti, capiunt te? an quia sine te non esset quidquid est, fit ut quidquid est capiat te? quoniam itaque et ego sum, quid peto ut uenias in me, qui non essem nisi esses in me? non enim ego iam inferi,[1] et tamen etiam ibi es, *nam etsi descendero*[2] *in infernum,*[3] *ades* (Ps 138:8). non ergo essem, Deus meus, non omnino essem, nisi esses in me. an potius non essem nisi essem in te, *ex quo omnia, per quem omnia, in quo omnia*? (Rom 11:36, 1 Cor 8:6). etiam sic, Domine, etiam sic. quo te inuoco, cum in te sim? aut unde uenias in me? quo enim recedam extra[4] caelum et terram, ut inde in me ueniat Deus meus, qui dixit, *Caelum et terram ego impleo*? (Jer 23:24).

[1]inferus ~a, ~um *adj.* infernal; ECCL **Hell** [2]descendo ~dere, ~di, ~sum **to descend** [3]infernus ~i *m.* underworld; ECCL **Hell** [4]extra *prep. acc.* **outside**

What can contain God?

1.3.3 Capiunt ergone te caelum et terra, quoniam tu imples ea? an imples et restat,[1] quoniam non te capiunt? et quo refundis[2] quidquid impleto caelo et terra restat ex te? an non opus habes ut quoquam continearis, qui contines omnia, quoniam quae imples continendo imples? non enim uasa[3] quae te plena sunt stabilem[4] te faciunt, quia etsi frangantur non effunderis.[5] et cum *effunderis super* nos (Acts 2:17–18), non tu iaces sed

[1]resto ~are, ~iti **to be left over** [2]refundo ~undere, ~udi, ~usum **to pour back** [3]uas uasis *neut.* **vessel** [4]stabilis ~is, ~e *adj.* **stable** [5]effundo ~undere, ~udi, ~usum **to pour out**

erigis[6] nos, nec tu dissiparis[7] sed conligis nos. sed quae imples omnia, te toto imples omnia. an quia non possunt te totum capere omnia, partem tui capiunt et eandem partem simul omnia capiunt? an singulas singula et maiores maiora, minores minora capiunt? ergo est aliqua pars tua maior, aliqua minor? an ubique[8] totus es et res nulla te totum capit?

[6]erigo ~igere, ~exi, ~ectum **to lift** [7]dissipo ~are, ~aui, ~atum **to disintegrate** [8]ubique *adv.* **everywhere**

What is God?

1.4.4 Quid es ergo, Deus meus? quid, rogo,[1] nisi Dominus Deus? *quis enim Dominus praeter Dominum? aut quis Deus praeter Deum nostrum?* (Ps 17:32). summe, optime,[2] potentissime, omnipotentissime,[3] misericordissime[4] et iustissime, secretissime[5] et praesentissime, pulcherrime et fortissime, stabilis[6] et incomprehensibilis,[7] immutabilis[8] mutans omnia, numquam nouus numquam uetus, innouans[9] omnia et *in uetustatem*[10] *perducens*[11] *superbos et nesciunt* (Job 9:5). semper agens semper quietus,[12] conligens et non egens,[13] portans[14] et implens et protegens,[15] creans et nutriens[16] et perficiens, quaerens cum nihil desit tibi. amas nec aestuas,[17] zelas[18] et securus[19] es, paenitet[20] te et non doles, irasceris[21] et tranquillus[22] es, opera mutas nec mutas consilium, recipis quod inuenis et numquam amisisti. numquam inops[23] et gaudes lucris,[24] numquam auarus[25] et usuras[26] exigis, *supererogatur*[27] *tibi* (Lk 10:35) ut debeas: et *quis habet quicquam non tuum?* (1 Cor 4:7). reddis debita nulli debens, donas[28] debita nihil perdens.

[1]rogo ~are, ~aui, ~atum **to ask** [2]optimus ~a, ~um *superl. adj.* **best** [3]omnipotens ~ntis *adj.* **omnipotent** [4]misericors ~rdis *adj.* **merciful** [5]secretus ~a, ~um *adj.* **remote** [6]stabilis ~is, ~e *adj.* **stable** [7]incomprehensibilis ~is, ~e *adj.* **incomprehensible** [8]immutabilis ~is, ~e *adj.* **immutable** [9]innouo ~are, ~aui, ~atum **to renew** [10]uetustas ~atis *f.* **old age** [11]perduco ~cere, ~xi, ~ctum **to bring** [12]quietus ~a, ~um *adj.* **at rest** [13]egens ~ntis *adj.* **needy** [14]porto ~are, ~aui, ~atum **to carry** [15]protego ~gere, ~xi, ~ctum **to protect** [16]nutrio ~ire, ~iui or ~ii, ~itum **to nourish** [17]aestuo ~are, ~aui, ~atum **to burn fiercely** [18]zelo ~are **to love ardently; ECCL to be jealous** [19]securus ~a, ~um *adj.* **untroubled** [20]paeniteo ~ere, ~ui **to cause regret** (w. acc. of person) [21]irascor ~i, iratus sum **to be angry** [22]tranquillus ~a, ~um *adj.* **calm > undisturbed** [23]inops ~pis *adj.* **lacking wealth** [24]lucrum ~i *neut.* **profit** [25]auarus ~a, ~um *adj.* **avaricious** [26]usura ~ae *f.* **usury** (interest on a loan) [27]supererogo ~are, ~aui, ~atum LATE **to pay beyond what is owed** [28]dono ~are, ~aui, ~atum **to forgive**

Et quid diximus, Deus meus, uita mea, dulcedo[29] mea sancta, aut quid dicit aliquis cum de te dicit? et uae[30] tacentibus de te, quoniam loquaces[31] muti[32] sunt.

[29]dulcedo ~inis *f.* **sweetness** [30]uae *interj.* [a cry of pain, anger, sorrow] **woe!** [31]loquax ~acis *adj.* **loquacious** [32]mutus ~a, ~um *adj.* **mute**

What are you to me?

1.5.5 Quis mihi dabit adquiescere[1] in te? quis dabit mihi ut uenias in cor meum et inebries[2] illud, ut obliuiscar mala mea et unum bonum meum amplectar,[3] te? quid mihi es? miserere ut loquar. quid tibi sum ipse, ut amari te iubeas a me et, nisi faciam, irascaris[4] mihi et mineris[5] ingentes[6] miserias? paruane ipsa est si non amem te? ei mihi![7] dic mihi per miserationes[8] tuas, Domine Deus meus, quid sis mihi. *dic animae meae, salus tua ego sum* (Ps 34:3): sic dic ut audiam. ecce aures cordis mei ante te, Domine. aperi eas et *dic animae meae, salus tua ego sum.* curram[9] post uocem hanc et apprehendam[10] te. noli abscondere[11] a me faciem tuam: moriar, ne moriar, ut eam uideam.

[1]adquiesco ~escere, ~ei **to find rest** [2]inebrio ~are, ~aui, ~atum **to intoxicate** [3]amplector ~cti, ~xus **to embrace with affection** [4]irascor ~i, iratus sum **to be angry** (w. dat.) [5]minor ~ari, ~atus **to threaten** (w. dat.) [6]ingens ~ntis *adj.* **vast** [7]'ei mihi' **ah me!** (expr. anguish) [8]miseratio ~onis *f.* **mercy** [9]curro ~rere, cucurri, ~sum **to run** [10]apprehendo ~dere, ~di, ~sum **to lay hold of** [11]abscondo ~ere, ~i, ~itum **to hide**

The dilapidated house of my soul

1.5.6 Angusta[1] est domus animae meae quo uenias ad eam: dilatetur[2] abs te. ruinosa[3] est: refice[4] eam. habet quae offendant[5] oculos tuos: fateor[6] et scio. sed quis mundabit[7] eam? aut cui alteri praeter te clamabo, *Ab occultis meis munda me, Domine, et ab alienis parce seruo tuo* (Ps 18:13–14)? *credo, propter quod et loquor* (2 Cor 4:13, Ps 115:10), *Domine: tu scis* (Jn 21:16). nonne tibi prolocutus[8] sum *aduersum me delicta[9]*

[1]angustus ~a, ~um *adj.* **narrow** [2]dilato ~are, ~aui, ~atum **to make wider** [3]ruinosus ~a, ~um *adj.* **in ruins** [4]reficio ~icere, ~eci, ~ectum **to restore** [5]offendo ~dere, ~di, ~sum to stumble upon > **to give offense to** [6]fateor ~eri, fassus **to confess** [7]mundo ~are, ~aui, ~atum **to make clean** [8]proloquor ~qui, ~cutus **to declare** [9]delictum ~i *neut.* offense; ECCL sin

mea, Deus meus, *et tu dimisisti impietatem*[10] *cordis mei?* (Ps 31:5) non *iudicio contendo*[11] *tecum* (Job 9:3), qui ueritas es, et ego nolo fallere me ipsum, ne *mentiatur*[12] *iniquitas mea sibi* (Ps 26:12). *non* ergo *iudicio contendo tecum,* quia, *si iniquitates obseruaueris,*[13] *Domine, Domine, quis sustinebit?*[14] (Ps 129:3).

[10]impietas ~atis *f.* impiety [11]contendo ~dere, ~di, ~tum to contend [12]mentior ~iri, ~itus to deceive [13]obseruo ~are, ~aui, ~atum to make note [14]sustineo ~ere, ~ui to sustain > to withstand

Where did I come from?

1.6.7 Sed tamen sine me loqui apud misericordiam tuam, me *terram et cinerem*[1] (Job 42:6 VL) sine tamen loqui. quoniam ecce misericordia tua est, non homo, inrisor[2] meus, cui loquor. et tu fortasse[3] *inrides me* (Ps 36:13), sed conuersus misereberis mei. quid enim est quod uolo dicere, Domine, nisi quia nescio unde uenerim huc, in istam dico uitam mortalem[4] an mortem uitalem?[5] nescio. et susceperunt[6] me *consolationes*[7] *miserationum*[8] *tuarum* (Ps 93:19; 68:17), sicut audiui a parentibus carnis meae, ex quo et in qua me formasti in tempore: non enim ego memini. Exceperunt[9] ergo me consolationes lactis[10] humani, nec mater mea uel nutrices[11] meae sibi ubera[12] implebant, sed tu mihi per eas dabas alimentum[13] infantiae[14] secundum institutionem[15] tuam et diuitias[16] usque ad fundum[17] rerum dispositas.[18] tu etiam mihi dabas nolle amplius quam dabas, et nutrientibus[19] me dare mihi uelle quod eis dabas: dare enim mihi per ordinatum[20] affectum uolebant quo abundabant[21] ex te. nam bonum erat eis bonum meum ex eis, quod ex eis non sed per eas erat. ex te quippe bona omnia, Deus, et ex Deo meo salus mihi uniuersa. quod animaduerti[22] postmodum,[23] clamante

[1]cinis ~eris *m.* ashes [2]inrisor ~oris *m.* mocker [3]fortasse *adv.* perhaps [4]mortalis ~is, ~e *adj.* dying [5]uitalis ~is, ~e *adj.* living [6]suscipio ~ipere, ~epi, ~eptum to support [7]consolatio ~onis *f.* consolation [8]miseratio ~onis *f.* mercy [9]excipio ~ipere, ~epi, ~eptum to receive > to greet [10]lac lactis *neut.* milk [11]nutrix ~icis *f.* wet nurse [12]uber ~ris *neut.* breast (as source of milk) [13]alimentum ~i *neut.* food [14]infantia ~ae *f.* infancy (0–2 years old) [15]institutio ~onis *f.* arrangement [16]diuitiae ~arum *f. pl.* riches [17]fundus ~i *m.* bottom > foundation (transf.) [18]dispositus ~a, ~um *adj.* properly arranged [19]nutrio ~ire, ~iui or ~ii, ~itum to nurse [20]ordino ~are, ~aui, ~atum to arrange > to ordain [21]abundo ~are, ~aui, ~atum to overflow [22]animaduerto ~tere, ~ti, ~sum to pay attention > to realize [23]postmodum *adv.* later

te mihi per haec ipsa quae tribuis²⁴ intus et foris.²⁵ nam tunc sugere²⁶ noram et adquiescere²⁷ delectationibus,²⁸ flere autem offensiones²⁹ carnis meae, nihil amplius.

²⁴tribuo ~uere, ~ui, ~utum **to bestow** ²⁵foris *adv.* **outwardly** ²⁶sugo ~gere, ~xi **to suck(le)** ²⁷adquiesco ~escere, ~ei to rest > **to be satisfied with** ²⁸delectatio ~onis *f.* **pleasure** ²⁹offensio ~onis *f.* stumbling > **discomfort**

Infancy

1.6.8 Post et ridere¹ coepi, dormiens² primo,³ deinde uigilans.⁴ hoc enim de me mihi indicatum est et credidi, quoniam sic uidemus alios infantes:⁵ nam ista mea non memini. et ecce paulatim⁶ sentiebam ubi essem, et uoluntates meas uolebam ostendere eis per quos implerentur, et non poteram, quia illae intus erant, foris⁷ autem illi, nec ullo suo sensu ualebant introire⁸ in animam meam. itaque iactabam⁹ membra et uoces, signa similia uoluntatibus meis, pauca¹⁰ quae poteram, qualia poteram: non enim erant uere similia. et cum mihi non obtemperabatur,¹¹ uel non intellecto uel ne obesset,¹² indignabar¹³ non subditis¹⁴ maioribus et liberis¹⁵ non seruientibus, et me de illis flendo uindicabam.¹⁶ tales esse infantes didici quos discere potui, et me talem fuisse magis mihi ipsi indicauerunt nescientes quam scientes nutritores¹⁷ mei.

¹rideo ~dere, ~si, ~sum **to smile** ²dormio ~ire, ~iui, ~itum **to sleep** ³primo *adv.* **at first** ⁴uigilo ~are, ~aui, ~atum **to be awake** ⁵infans ~ntis *m. f.* **infant** ⁶paulatim *adv.* **gradually** ⁷foris *adv.* **outwardly** ⁸introeo ~ire, ~iui or ~ii, ~itum **to enter in** ⁹iacto ~are, ~aui, ~atum **to hurl** ¹⁰paucus ~a, ~um *adj.* **few** ¹¹obtempero ~are, ~aui, ~atum **to submit** (w. dat.) ¹²obsum ~esse, ~fui **to harm** ¹³indignor ~ari, ~atus **to be indignant** (w. dat.) ¹⁴subdo ~ere, ~idi, ~itum **to place under > to subordinate** ¹⁵liber ~era, ~erum *adj.* **free** ¹⁶uindico ~are, ~aui, ~atum **to take one's revenge on** (refl. w. 'de') ¹⁷nutritor ~oris *m.* **nurse**

Where was I before my infancy?

1.6.9 Et ecce infantia¹ mea olim² mortua est et ego uiuo. tu autem, Domine, qui et semper uiuis et nihil moritur in te, quoniam ante primordia³ saeculorum, et ante omne quod uel "ante" dici potest, tu es, et Deus es Dominusque omnium quae creasti, et apud te rerum omnium

¹infantia ~ae *f.* **infancy** (0–2 years old) ²olim *adv.* **a long time ago** ³primordium ~ii *neut.* **beginnings** (*pl.*)

instabilium[4] stant causae, et rerum omnium mutabilium immutabiles[5]
manent origins,[6] et omnium inrationalium[7] et temporalium[8] sempi-
ternae[9] uiuunt rationes, dic mihi supplici[10] tuo, Deus, et misericors[11]
misero tuo dic mihi, utrum alicui iam aetati meae mortuae successerit[12]
infantia mea. an illa est quam egi intra[13] uiscera[14] matris meae? nam et
de illa mihi nonnihil[15] indicatum est et praegnantes[16] ipse uidi feminas. quid ante hanc etiam, dulcedo[17] mea, Deus meus? fuine alicubi[18]
aut aliquis? nam quis mihi dicat ista, non habeo; nec pater nec mater
potuerunt, nec aliorum experimentum[19] nec memoria mea. an *inrides
me* (Ps 36:13) ista quaerentem teque de hoc quod noui laudari a me
iubes et confiteri me tibi?

[4]instabilis ~is, ~e *adj.* **unstable** [5]immutabilis ~is, ~e *adj.* **immutable** [6]origo ~inis *f.* **origin** [7]inra-
tionalis ~is, ~e *adj.* **unreasoning** [8]temporalis ~is, ~e *adj.* **temporal** [9]sempiternus ~a, ~um *adj.*
eternal [10]supplex ~icis *adj.* **suppliant** (as noun) [11]misericors ~rdis *adj.* **merciful** [12]succedo ~dere,
~ssi, ~ssum **to come after** (w. dat.) [13]intra *prep. acc.* **inside** [14]uiscus ~eris *neut.* **womb** [15]nonnihil
indecl. neut. **not a little** [16]praegnans ~ntis *adj.* **pregnant** [17]dulcedo ~inis *f.* **sweetness** [18]alicubi *adv.*
anywhere at all [19]experimentum ~i *neut.* experiment > **experience**

Your "today"

1.6.10 *Confiteor tibi, Domine caeli et terrae* (Mt 11:25), laudem dicens
tibi de primordiis[1] et infantia[2] mea, quae non memini. et dedisti ea
homini ex aliis de se conicere[3] et auctoritatibus etiam muliercularum[4]
multa de se credere. eram enim et uiuebam etiam tunc, et signa quibus
sensa mea nota aliis facerem iam in fine infantiae quaerebam. unde hoc
tale animal[5] nisi abs te, Domine? an quisquam se faciendi erit artifex?[6]
aut ulla uena[7] trahitur[8] aliunde[9] qua esse et uiuere currat[10] in nos, praeterquam quod[11] tu facis nos, Domine, cui esse et uiuere non aliud atque
aliud, quia summe[12] esse ac summe uiuere idipsum[13] est? summus enim
es et non mutaris, neque peragitur[14] in te "hodiernus dies,"[15] et tamen

[1]primordium ~ii *neut.* **beginnings** (*pl.*) [2]infantia ~ae *f.* **infancy** (0–2 years old) [3]conicio ~icere,
~ieci, ~iectum to put together > **to figure out** [4]muliercula ~ae *f.* **little woman** [5]animal ~alis *neut.*
living creature [6]artifex ~ficis *m.* **maker** [7]uena ~ae *f.* **vein** [8]traho ~here, ~xi, ~ctum to draw > **to
derive** [9]aliunde *adv.* **from another place** [10]curro ~rere, cucurri, ~sum to run > **to flow swiftly**
[11]'praeterquam quod' **apart from the fact that** [12]summe *adv.* **in the highest degree** [13]idipsum
pron. ECCL **self-same** [14]perago ~agere, ~egi, ~actum **to come to an end** [15]'hodiernus dies' **today**

in te peragitur, quia in te sunt et ista omnia: non enim haberent uias transeundi, nisi contineres eas. et quoniam anni tui non deficient,[16] anni tui "Hodiernus Dies." et quam multi iam dies nostri et patrum nostrorum per "Hodiernum"[17] tuum transierunt et ex illo acceperunt modos et utcumque[18] extiterunt,[19] et transibunt adhuc alii et accipient et utcumque existent.[20] *tu autem idem ipse es* (Ps 101:28) et omnia crastina[21] atque ultra[22] omniaque hesterna[23] et retro[24] Hodie[25] facies, Hodie fecisti.

Quid ad me, si quis non intellegat? gaudeat et ipse *dicens: Quid est hoc?* (Sir 39:26). gaudeat etiam sic, et amet non inueniendo inuenire potius quam inueniendo non inuenire te.

[16]deficio ~icere, ~eci, ~ectum **to fail** [17]hodiernus ~a, ~um *adj.* **today** (*m.* as noun) [18]utcumque *adv.* **as far as possible** [19]exto ~are, extiti **to exist** [20]exsisto ~ere, extiti to appear > **to arise** [21]crastinus ~a, ~um *adj.* **tomorrow** (*neut.* as noun) [22]ultra *adv.* **beyond** [23]hesternus ~a, ~um *adj.* **yesterday** (*neut.* as noun) [24]retro *adv.* **behind** [25]hodie *adv.* **today**

Infant selfishness

1.7.11 *Exaudi, Deus* (Ps 54:2). *uae*[1] *peccatis* (Isa 1:4) hominum! et homo dicit haec, et misereris eius, quoniam tu fecisti eum et peccatum non fecisti in eo. quis me commemorat peccatum infantiae[2] meae, quoniam *nemo mundus*[3] a peccato coram te, nec infans[4] cuius est *unius diei uita super terram* (Job 14:4–5 VL)? quis me commemorat? an quilibet[5] tantillus[6] nunc paruulus, in quo uideo quod non memini de me? quid ergo tunc peccabam? an quia uberibus[7] inhiabam[8] plorans?[9] nam si nunc faciam, non quidem uberibus sed escae[10] congruenti[11] annis meis ita inhians, deridebor[12] atque reprehendar[13] iustissime.[14] tunc ergo reprehendenda faciebam, sed quia reprehendentem intellegere non poteram, nec mos reprehendi me nec ratio sinebat: nam extirpamus[15] et eicimus[16] ista crescentes. nec uidi quemquam scientem,

[1]uae *interj.* [a cry of pain, anger, sorrow] **woe!** (w. dat.) [2]infantia ~ae *f.* **infancy** (0–2 years old) [3]mundus ~a, ~um *adj.* **clean** [4]infans ~ntis *m. f.* **infant** [5]quilibet, quae-, quod- *adj.* **any whatever** [6]tantillus ~a, ~um *adj.* **so small** [7]uber ~ris *neut.* **breast** (as the source of milk) [8]inhio ~are, ~aui, ~atum **to greedily open one's mouth** [9]ploro ~are, ~aui, ~atum **to weep aloud** [10]esca ~ae *f.* **food** [11]congruens ~ntis *adj.* **fitting** [12]derideo ~dere, ~si, ~sum **to deride** [13]reprehendo ~dere, ~di, ~sum **to reprehend** [14]iuste *adv.* **justifiably** [15]extirpo ~are, ~aui, ~atum to dig up > **to eradicate impulses** (transf.) [16]eicio eicere, eieci, eiectum **to throw out**

cum aliquid purgat,[17] bona proicere.[18] an pro tempore[19] etiam illa bona erant, flendo petere etiam quod noxie[20] daretur, indignari[21] acriter[22] non subiectis[23] hominibus liberis[24] et maioribus hisque, a quibus genitus[25] est, multisque praeterea[26] prudentioribus[27] non ad nutum[28] uoluntatis obtemperantibus[29] feriendo[30] nocere[31] niti[32] quantum potest, quia non oboeditur[33] imperiis quibus perniciose[34] oboediretur?

Ita inbecillitas[35] membrorum infantilium[36] innocens[37] est, non animus infantium. uidi ego et expertus sum zelantem[38] paruulum: nondum loquebatur et intuebatur pallidus[39] amaro[40] aspectu[41] conlactaneum[42] suum. quis hoc ignorat? expiare[43] se dicunt ista matres atque nutrices[44] nescio quibus remediis.[45] nisi uero[46] et ista innocentia[47] est, in fonte lactis[48] ubertim[49] manante[50] atque abundante[51] opis egentissimum[52] et illo adhuc uno alimento[53] uitam ducentem consortem[54] non pati. sed blande[55] tolerantur[56] haec, non quia nulla uel parua, sed quia aetatis accessu[57] peritura sunt. quod licet probes,[58] cum ferri aequo[59] animo eadem ipsa non possunt quando in aliquo annosiore[60] deprehenduntur.[61]

[17]purgo ~are, ~aui, ~atum **to purge** [18]proicio ~icere, ~ieci, ~iectum **to discard** [19]'pro tempore' **at the time** [20]noxie *adv.* LATE **injuriously** [21]indignor ~ari, ~atus **to be indignant** (w. dat.) [22]acriter *adv.* **bitterly** [23]subicio ~icere, ~ieci, ~iectum **to make subject** [24]liber ~era, ~erum *adj.* **free** [25]gigno ~ere, genui, genitum **to be born** (pass.) [26]praeterea *adv.* **in addition to that** [27]prudens ~ntis *adj.* **prudent** [28]nutus ~us *m.* nod > **gesture** [29]obtempero ~are, ~aui, ~atum **to submit** [30]ferio ~ire **to strike with the hand** [31]noceo ~ere, ~ui, ~itum **to injure** [32]nitor ~ti, ~xus or ~sus to lean on > **to struggle** [33]oboedio ~ire, ~iui, ~itum **to obey** (w. dat.) [34]perniciose *adv.* **harmfully** [35]inbecillitas ~atis *f.* **weakness** [36]infantilis ~is, ~e *adj.* **infantile** [37]innocens ~ntis *adj.* **innocent** [38]zelo ~are **to love ardently**; ECCL **to be jealous** [39]pallidus ~a, ~um *adj.* **pallid** [40]amarus ~a, ~um *adj.* **bitter** [41]aspectus ~us *m.* seeing > **facial expression** [42]conlactaneus ~i *m.* **fellow nursling** [43]expio ~are, ~aui, ~atum to expiate > **to avert** [44]nutrix ~icis *f.* **child's nurse** [45]remedium ~ii *neut.* **remedy** [46]'nisi uero' **unless of course** [47]innocentia ~ae *f.* **innocence** [48]lac lactis *neut.* **milk** [49]ubertim *adv.* **plentifully** [50]mano ~are, ~aui **to flow** [51]abundo ~are, ~aui, ~atum **to overflow** [52]egens ~ntis *adj.* **needy** [53]alimentum ~i *neut.* **food** [54]consors ~tis *m. f. adj.* co-heir > **sharer** [55]blande *adv.* **affectionately** [56]tolero ~are, ~aui, ~atum **to tolerate** [57]accessus ~us *m.* **arrival** [58]probo ~are, ~aui, ~atum to approve > **to agree** [59]aequus ~a, ~um *adj.* smooth > **calm** [60]annosus ~a, ~um *adj.* **full of years** [61]deprehendo ~dere, ~di, ~sum to catch > **to detect**

No memory of infancy

1.7.12 Tu itaque, Domine Deus meus, qui dedisti uitam infanti[1] et corpus, quod ita, ut uidemus, instruxisti[2] sensibus, compegisti[3] membris,

[1]infans ~ntis *m. f.* **infant** [2]instruo ~ere, ~xi, ~ctum **to furnish** [3]compingo ~ingere, ~egi, ~actum **to bind together**

figura[4] decorasti[5] proque eius uniuersitate[6] atque incolumitate[7] omnes conatus[8] animantis[9] insinuasti,[10] iubes me laudare te in istis et *confiteri tibi et psallere*[11] *nomini tuo, Altissime* (Ps 91:2), quia Deus es omnipotens[12] et bonus, etiamsi sola ista fecisses, quae nemo alius[13] potest facere nisi tu, une, a quo est omnis modus, formosissime,[14] qui formas omnia et lege tua ordinas[15] omnia.

Hanc ergo aetatem, Domine, quam me uixisse non memini, de qua aliis credidi et quam me egisse ex aliis infantibus conieci,[16] quamquam ista multum fida[17] coniectura[18] sit, piget[19] me adnumerare[20] huic uitae meae quam *uiuo in hoc saeculo* (Tit 2:12). quantum enim attinet[21] ad obliuionis[22] meae tenebras, par illi est quam uixi in matris utero.[23] quod si et *in iniquitate conceptus*[24] *sum et in peccatis mater mea me in utero aluit*[25] (Ps 50:7), ubi, oro[26] te, Deus meus, ubi, Domine, *ego, seruus tuus* (Ps 115:16), ubi aut quando innocens[27] fui?

Sed ecce omitto[28] illud tempus: et quid mihi iam cum eo est,[29] cuius nulla uestigia[30] recolo?

[4]figura ~ae *f.* shape > **outward appearance** [5]decoro ~are, ~aui, ~atum **to add beauty** [6]uniuersitas ~atis *f.* the whole > **the overall aspect** [7]incolumitas ~atis *f.* **safety** [8]conatus ~us *m.* attempt > **instinctive impulse** [9]animans ~ntis *m. f. neut.* **living creature** [10]insinuo ~are, ~aui, ~atum **to instill** [11]psallo ~ere, ~i **to make music** [12]omnipotens ~ntis *adj.* **omnipotent** [13]'nemo alius' **no one else** [14]formosus ~a, ~um *adj.* **fair** (beautiful) [15]ordino ~are, ~aui, ~atum **to set out in order** [16]conicio ~icere, ~ieci, ~iectum to put together > **to guess** [17]fidus ~a, ~um *adj.* **reliable** [18]coniectura ~ae *f.* **conjecture** [19]piget ~ere, ~uit, ~itum *impers.* **it is irksome** [20]adnumero ~are, ~aui, ~atum to include in a total > **to count among** (w. dat.) [21]attineo ~ere, ~ui, attentum to hold > **to affect** (w. 'ad') [22]obliuio ~onis *f.* **oblivion of forgetting** [23]uterum ~i *neut.* **womb** [24]concipio ~ipere, ~epi, ~eptum **to conceive** [25]alo ~ere, ~ui, ~tum **to nourish** [26]oro ~are, ~aui, ~atum **to beseech** [27]innocens ~ntis *adj.* **innocent** [28]omitto ~ittere, ~isi, ~issum to release > **to leave off** [29]'quid mihi iam cum eo est' **what have I to do with that now?** [30]uestigium ~ii *neut.* track > **trace**

Speech acquisition: infancy to boyhood

1.8.13 Nonne ab infantia[1] huc pergens[2] ueni in pueritiam?[3] uel potius ipsa in me uenit et successit[4] infantiae? nec discessit[5] illa: quo enim abiit?[6] et tamen iam non erat. non enim eram infans[7] qui non farer,[8]

[1]infantia ~ae *f.* **infancy** (0–2 years old) [2]pergo ~gere, ~rexi, ~rectum **to proceed** [3]pueritia ~ae *f.* **boyhood** (2–15 years old) [4]succedo ~dere, ~ssi, ~ssum **to come after** (w. dat.) [5]discedo ~dere, ~ssi, ~ssum **to depart** [6]abeo ~ire, ~ii, ~itum **to go away** [7]infans ~ntis *m. f.* **infant** [8]for fari, fatus **to talk**

sed iam puer loquens eram. et memini hoc, et unde loqui didiceram post aduerti.[9] non enim docebant me maiores homines, praebentes[10] mihi uerba certo aliquo ordine doctrinae sicut paulo[11] post litteras, sed ego ipse mente quam dedisti mihi, Deus meus, cum gemitibus[12] et uocibus uariis[13] et uariis membrorum motibus edere[14] uellem sensa cordis mei, ut uoluntati pareretur,[15] nec ualerem quae uolebam omnia nec quibus uolebam omnibus, prensabam[16] memoria. cum ipsi appellabant rem aliquam et cum secundum eam uocem corpus ad aliquid mouebant, uidebam et tenebam hoc ab eis uocari rem illam quod sonabant cum eam uellent ostendere. hoc autem eos uelle ex motu corporis aperiebatur tamquam uerbis naturalibus[17] omnium gentium, quae fiunt uultu et nutu oculorum[18] ceterorumque membrorum actu[19] et sonitu[20] uocis indicante affectionem[21] animi in petendis, habendis, reiciendis[22] fugiendisue rebus.

Ita uerba in uariis sententiis locis suis posita et crebro[23] audita quarum rerum signa essent paulatim[24] conligebam measque iam uoluntates edomito[25] in eis signis ore per haec enuntiabam.[26] sic cum his inter quos eram uoluntatum enuntiandarum signa communicaui,[27] et uitae humanae procellosam[28] societatem[29] altius[30] ingressus[31] sum, pendens[32] ex parentum auctoritate nutuque[33] maiorum hominum.

[9]aduerto ~tere, ~ti, ~sum to turn towards > **to realize** [10]praebeo ~ere, ~ui, ~itum **to put forward** [11]paulo *adv.* **somewhat** [12]gemitus ~us *m.* **inarticulate utterance** [13]uarius ~a, ~um *adj.* **various** [14]edo ~ere, ~idi, ~itum **to produce** [15]pareo ~ere, ~ui, ~itum **to submit to** *or* **to make evident** (w. dat.) [16]prenso ~are, ~aui, ~atum **to try to grasp** [17]naturalis ~is, ~e *adj.* natural > **instinctual** [18]'nutu oculorum' **wink** [19]actus ~us *m.* driving > **motion** [20]sonitus ~us *m.* sound > **inflection** [21]affectio ~onis *f.* **mood** [22]reicio ~icere, ~ieci, ~iectum **to reject** [23]crebro *adv.* **repeatedly** [24]paulatim *adv.* **gradually** [25]edomo ~are, ~ui, ~itum to subdue > **to bring under control** [26]enuntio ~are, ~aui, ~atum **to make known** [27]communico ~are, ~aui, ~atum **to communicate** [28]procellosus ~a, ~um *adj.* **stormy** [29]societas ~atis *f.* **society** [30]alte *adv.* **deeply** [31]ingredior ~di, ~ssus to go on foot > **to enter in and take part** [32]pendeo ~ere, pependi **to depend on** (w. 'ex') [33]nutus ~us *m.* **nod of approval**

Intolerable school days

1.9.14 Deus, Deus meus, *quas ibi miserias* (Ad. 867) expertus sum et ludificationes,[1] quandoquidem[2] recte mihi uiuere puero id proponebatur,[3]

[1]ludificatio ~onis *f.* **trifling** [2]quandoquidem *adv.* **inasmuch as** [3]propono ~onere, ~osui, ~ositum **to place before**

obtemperare[4] monentibus,[5] ut in hoc saeculo florerem[6] et excellerem[7] linguosis[8] artibus ad honorem hominum et falsas diuitias[9] famulantibus.[10] inde in scholam[11] datus sum ut discerem litteras, in quibus quid utilitatis[12] esset ignorabam miser. et tamen, si segnis[13] in discendo essem, uapulabam.[14] laudabatur enim hoc a maioribus, et multi ante nos uitam istam agentes praestruxerant[15] aerumnosas[16] uias, per quas transire cogebamur multiplicato[17] labore et dolore *filiis Adam* (Sir 40:1)

Inuenimus autem, Domine, homines rogantes[18] te et didicimus ab eis, sentientes te, ut poteramus, esse magnum aliquem qui posses etiam non apparens sensibus nostris exaudire nos et subuenire[19] nobis. nam puer coepi rogare te, *auxilium[20] et refugium[21] meum* (Ps 93:22), et in tuam inuocationem[22] rumpebam nodos[23] linguae meae et rogabam te paruus non paruo affectu, ne in schola uapularem. et cum me *non exaudiebas, quod non erat ad insipientiam[24] mihi* (Ps 21:3), ridebantur[25] a maioribus hominibus usque ab ipsis parentibus, qui mihi accidere[26] mali nihil uolebant, plagae[27] meae, magnum tunc et graue malum meum.

[4]obtempero ~are, ~aui, ~atum **to obey** (w. dat.) [5]moneo ~ere, ~ui, ~itum **to admonish** [6]floreo ~ere, ~ui **to flourish** [7]excello ~ere **to excel** [8]linguosus ~a, ~um *adj.* **wordy** [9]diuitiae ~arum *f. pl.* **riches** [10]famulor ~ari, ~atus **to be a servant to** [11]schola, scola ~ae *f.* **school** [12]utilitas ~atis *f.* **utility** [13]segnis ~is, ~e *adj.* **lazy** [14]uapulo ~are, ~aui, ~atum **to be beaten** [15]praestruo ~ere, ~xi, ~ctum to obstruct > **to contrive beforehand** [16]aerumnosus ~a, ~um *adj.* **distressing** [17]multiplico ~are, ~aui, ~atum **to multiply** [18]rogo ~are, ~aui, ~atum to ask; ECCL **to pray** [19]subuenio ~enire, ~eni, ~entum **to bring relief** [20]auxilium ~ii *neut.* **help** [21]refugium ~ii *neut.* **refuge** [22]inuocatio ~onis *f.* **invocation** [23]nodus ~i *m.* **knot** [24]insipientia ~ae *f.* **folly** [25]rideo ~dere, ~si, ~sum to laugh > **to treat as a laughing matter** (hyperb.) [26]accido ~ere, ~i to fall upon > **to happen to** [27]plaga ~ae *f.* **blow** (received violently)

The "business" of grown-ups

1.9.15 Estne quisquam, Domine, tam magnus animus, praegrandi[1] affectu tibi cohaerens,[2] estne, inquam, quisquam (facit enim hoc quaedam etiam stoliditas:[3] est ergo), qui tibi pie[4] cohaerendo ita sit affectus[5] granditer,[6] ut eculeos[7] et ungulas[8] atque huiuscemodi[9] uaria[10] tormenta[11]

[1]praegrandis ~is, ~e *adj.* enormous; LATE **intense** [2]cohaereo ~rere, ~si, ~sum **to cling to** (w. dat.) [3]stoliditas ~atis *f.* **brutish insensibility** [4]pie *adv.* **piously** [5]affectus ~a, ~um *adj.* **possessed of** [6]granditer *adv.* LATE **strongly** [7]eculeus ~i *m.* **wooden rack** (for torture) [8]ungula ~ae *f.* claw; LATE **iron claw** (for torture) [9]huiuscemodi *m.* **of such a kind** [10]uarius ~a, ~um *adj.* **various** [11]tormentum ~i *neut.* **torture**

(pro quibus effugiendis[12] tibi per uniuersas terras cum timore[13] magno supplicatur[14]) ita parui aestimet,[15] diligens eos qui haec acerbissime[16] formidant,[17] quemadmodum parentes nostri ridebant[18] tormenta quibus pueri a magistris affligebamur?[19] non enim aut minus ea metuebamus aut minus te de his euadendis[20] deprecabamur.[21]

Et peccabamus tamen minus scribendo aut legendo aut cogitando de litteris quam exigebatur a nobis. non enim deerat, Domine, memoria uel ingenium, quae nos habere uoluisti pro illa aetate satis, sed delectabat ludere[22] et uindicabatur[23] in nos ab eis qui talia utique agebant. sed maiorum nugae[24] "negotia"[25] uocantur, puerorum autem talia cum sint, puniuntur[26] a maioribus, et nemo miseratur pueros uel illos uel utrosque. nisi uero[27] approbat[28] quisquam bonus rerum arbiter[29] uapulasse[30] me, quia ludebam pila[31] puer et eo ludo[32] impediebar[33] quominus[34] celeriter[35] discerem litteras, quibus maior deformius[36] luderem. aut aliud faciebat idem ipse a quo uapulabam, qui si in aliqua quaestiuncula[37] a condoctore[38] suo uictus esset, magis bile[39] atque inuidia[40] torqueretur[41] quam ego, cum in certamine[42] pilae a conlusore[43] meo superabar?[44]

[12]effugio ~ugere, ~ugi **to escape from** [13]timor ~oris *m.* **fear** [14]supplico ~are, ~aui, ~atum **to beg for mercy** (pass. *impers.* w. dat.) [15]aestimo ~are, ~aui, ~atum **to value** (w. gen. of price) [16]acerbe *adv.* **bitterly** [17]formido ~are, ~aui, ~atum **to dread** [18]rideo ~dere, ~si, ~sum to laugh > **to treat as a laughing matter** (hyperb.) [19]affligo ~gere, ~xi, ~ctum **to afflict** [20]euado ~dere, ~si, ~sum **to escape from** [21]deprecor ~ari, ~atus **to beg in prayer** [22]ludo ~dere, ~si, ~sum **to play** (a game) [23]uindico ~are, ~aui, ~atum **to exact punishment** (*impers.* w. 'in' + acc.) [24]nugae ~arum *f. pl.* **frivolities** [25]negotium ~ii *neut.* **business** [26]punior, poenior ~iri, ~itus. **to punish** [27]'nisi uero' **unless of course** [28]approbo ~are, ~aui, ~atum **to approve** [29]arbiter ~tri *m.* **judge** [30]uapulo ~are, ~aui, ~atum **to be beaten** [31]pila ~ae *f.* **ball game** [32]ludus ~i *m.* **game** [33]impedio ~ire, ~iui or ~ii, ~itum **to hinder** [34]quominus *conj.* **by which the less** [35]celeriter *adv.* **quickly** [36]deformis ~is, ~e *adj.* **disfigured** [37]quaestiuncula ~ae *f.* **trivial argument** [38]condoctor ~is *m.* LATE **fellow teacher** [39]bilis ~is *f.* **ill temper** [40]inuidia ~ae *f.* **envy** [41]torqueo ~quere, ~si, ~tum to twist > **to torment mentally** [42]certamen ~inis *neut.* **contest** [43]conlusor ~oris *m.* **playmate** [44]supero ~are, ~aui, ~atum to rise above > **to outdo** (w. abl.)

Grown-up hypocrisy

1.10.16 Et tamen peccabam, Domine Deus, ordinator[1] et creator rerum omnium naturalium,[2] peccatorum autem tantum ordinator, Domine Deus meus, peccabam faciendo contra praecepta[3] parentum et magistrorum

[1]ordinator ~oris *m.* **orderer** [2]naturalis ~is, ~e *adj.* **natural** [3]praeceptum ~i *neut.* **precept**

illorum. poteram enim postea bene uti litteris, quas uolebant ut discerem quocumque animo illi mei. non enim meliora eligens[4] inoboediens[5] eram, sed amore ludendi,[6] amans in certaminibus[7] superbas uictorias[8] et scalpi[9] aures meas falsis fabellis,[10] quo prurirent[11] ardentius,[12] eadem curiositate[13] magis magisque per oculos emicante[14] in spectacula,[15] ludos[16] maiorum — quos tamen qui edunt,[17] ea dignitate[18] praediti[19] excellent,[20] ut hoc paene[21] omnes optent paruulis suis, quos tamen caedi[22] libenter[23] patiuntur, si spectaculis talibus impediantur[24] ab studio quo eos ad talia edenda cupiunt peruenire.

Vide ista, *Domine* (Ps 9:15), misericorditer,[25] *et libera*[26] *nos* (Ps 78:9, Mt 6:13) iam inuocantes te, libera etiam eos qui nondum te inuocant, ut inuocent te et liberes eos.

[4]*eligo* ~igere, ~egi, ~ectum **to choose** [5]*inoboediens* ~ntis *ppl. adj.* ECCL **disobedient** [6]*ludo* ~dere, ~si, ~sum **to play** [7]*certamen* ~inis *neut.* **competition** [8]*uictoria* ~ae *f.* **victory** [9]*scalpo* ~pere, ~psi, ~ptum **to scratch** [10]*fabella* ~ae *f.* **story** [11]*prurio* ~ire **to itch** [12]*ardenter adv.* **ardently** [13]*curiositas* ~atis *f.* **curiosity** (usu. in a bad sense) [14]*emico* ~are, ~ui, ~atum **to flash forth** [15]*spectaculum* ~i *neut.* **public shows** [16]*ludus* ~i *m.* **game** [17]*edo* ~ere, ~idi, ~itum **to produce** [18]*dignitas* ~atis *f.* **dignity** [19]*praeditus* ~a, ~um *adj.* **endowed with** (w. abl.) [20]*excello* ~ere **to be pre-eminent** [21]*paene adv.* **practically** [22]*caedo* ~dere, cecidi, ~sum **to beat** [23]*libenter adv.* **willingly** [24]*impedio* ~ire, ~iui or ~ii, ~itum **to hinder** [25]*misericorditer adv.* **with pity** [26]*libero* ~are, ~aui, ~atum **to set free** (a slave)

Baptism deferred

1.11.17 Audieram enim ego adhuc puer de uita aeterna promissa[1] nobis per humilitatem[2] Domini Dei nostri descendentis[3] ad superbiam[4] nostram, et signabar[5] iam signo crucis[6] eius, et condiebar[7] eius sale[8] iam inde ab utero[9] matris meae, quae multum sperauit[10] in te. uidisti, Domine, cum adhuc puer essem et quodam die pressu[11] stomachi[12] repente[13] aestuarem[14] paene[15] moriturus, uidisti, Deus meus, quoniam custos[16] meus iam eras, quo motu animi et qua fide baptismum[17] Christi tui, *Dei et Domini mei* (Jn 20:28), flagitaui[18] a pietate matris meae et

[1]*promitto* ~ittere, ~isi, ~issum **to promise** [2]*humilitas* ~atis *f.* **humility** [3]*descendo* ~dere, ~di, ~sum **to descend** [4]*superbia* ~ae *f.* **pride** [5]*signo* ~are, ~aui, ~atum **to mark with a sign** [6]*crux* ~ucis *f.* **cross** [7]*condio* ~ire, ~iui, ~itum **to season** [8]*sal salis m.* **salt** [9]*uterum* ~i *neut.* **womb** [10]*spero* ~are, ~aui, ~atum **to hope in** [11]*pressus* ~us *m.* **pressure** [12]*stomachus* ~i *m.* **stomach** [13]*repente adv.* **without warning** [14]*aestuo* ~are, ~aui, ~atum **to burn** (with fever) [15]*paene adv.* **almost** [16]*custos* ~odis *m. f.* **guardian** [17]*baptismus* ~i *m.* (~um ~i *neut.*) ECCL **baptism** [18]*flagito* ~are, ~aui, ~atum **to ask repeatedly**

matris omnium nostrum, Ecclesiae tuae. et conturbata[19] mater carnis meae, quoniam et sempiternam[20] salutem meam carius[21] parturiebat[22] corde casto[23] in fide tua, iam curaret festinabunda[24] ut sacramentis salutaribus[25] initiarer[26] et abluerer,[27] te, Domine Iesu, confitens in remissionem[28] peccatorum, nisi statim[29] recreatus[30] essem.

Dilata[31] est itaque mundatio[32] mea, quasi necesse[33] esset ut adhuc sordidarer[34] si uiuerem, quia uidelicet[35] post lauacrum[36] illud maior et periculosior[37] in sordibus[38] delictorum[39] reatus[40] foret. ita iam credebam et illa et omnis domus, nisi pater solus, qui tamen non euicit[41] in me ius maternae[42] pietatis, quominus[43] in Christum crederem, sicut ille nondum crediderat. nam illa satagebat[44] ut tu mihi pater esses, Deus meus, potius quam ille, et in hoc adiuuabas[45] eam, ut superaret[46] uirum, cui melior seruiebat, quia et in hoc tibi utique id iubenti seruiebat.

[19]conturbo ~are, ~aui, ~atum **to dismay** [20]sempiternus ~a, ~um *adj.* **eternal** [21]care *adv.* **lovingly** [22]parturio ~ire, ~iui **to be in labor** (giving birth) [23]castus ~a, ~um *adj.* **chaste** [24]festinabundus ~a, ~um *adj.* **hurrying** [25]salutaris ~is, ~e *adj.* **life-giving** [26]initio ~are, ~aui, ~atum **to initiate** (with rites) [27]abluo ~uere, ~ui, ~utum **to wash away** [28]remissio ~onis *f.* **remission** [29]statim *adv.* **at that moment** [30]recreo ~are, ~aui, ~atum **to recover** (from illness) [31]differo ~rre, distuli, dilatum **to postpone** [32]mundatio ~onis *f.* LATE physical cleansing; ECCL **spiritual cleansing** [33]necesse *adv.* **it would be inevitable** (w. 'esset') [34]sordido ~are, ~aui, ~atum ECCL **to stain** [35]uidelicet *adv.* **no doubt** [36]lauacrum ~i *neut.* bath; ECCL **baptism** [37]periculosus ~a, ~um *adj.* **dangerous** [38]sordes ~is *f.* **stain** [39]delictum ~i *neut.* offense; ECCL **sin** [40]reatus ~us *m.* accused; LATE **guilt** [41]euinco ~incere, ~ici, ~ictum **to prevail over** [42]maternus ~a, ~um *adj.* **maternal** [43]quominus *conj.* **by which the less** [44]satago ~agere, ~egi, ~actum **to be anxious for** [45]adiuuo ~iuuare, ~iuui, ~iutum **to help** [46]supero ~are, ~aui, ~atum to rise above > **to gain the upper hand**

Why postpone my baptism?

1.11.18 Rogo[1] te, Deus meus: uellem scire, si tu etiam uelles, quo consilio dilatus[2] sum ne tunc baptizarer,[3] utrum bono meo mihi quasi laxata[4] sint lora[5] peccandi. an non laxata sunt? unde ergo etiam nunc de aliis atque aliis sonat undique[6] in auribus nostris: "Sine illum, faciat — nondum enim baptizatus est"? et tamen in salute corporis non dicimus: "Sine uulneretur[7] amplius — nondum enim sanatus est." quanto ergo melius et cito[8] sanarer et id ageretur mecum meorum meaque diligentia,[9] ut

[1]rogo ~are, ~aui, ~atum **to ask** [2]differo ~rre, distuli, dilatum **to delay** [3]baptizo ~are, ~aui, ~atum ECCL **to baptize** [4]laxo ~are, ~aui, ~atum **to relax** [5]lorum ~i *neut.* **reins** [6]undique *adv.* **from all directions** [7]uulnero ~are, ~aui, ~atum **to wound** [8]cito *adv.* **quickly** [9]diligentia ~ae *f.* **diligence**

recepta salus animae meae tuta esset tutela[10] tua, qui dedisses eam. melius uero. sed quot[11] et quanti fluctus impendere[12] temptationum post pueritiam[13] uidebantur, nouerat eos iam illa mater et terram per eos, unde postea formarer, quam ipsam iam effigiem[14] committere[15] uolebat.

[10]tutela ~ae *f.* **protection** [11]quot *indecl. adj.* **how many** [12]impendeo ~dere, ~sum **to hang over** > **to threaten** [13]pueritia ~ae *f.* **boyhood** (2–15 years old) [14]effigies ~ei *f.* image; ECCL **the image of Christ** [15]committo ~ittere, ~isi, ~issum **to commit** x (acc.) **to** y (acc.) w. 'per'

Disordered soul its own punishment

1.12.19 In ipsa tamen pueritia, de qua mihi minus quam de adulescentia[1] metuebatur,[2] non amabam litteras et me in eas urgeri[3] oderam, et urgebar tamen et bene mihi fiebat. nec faciebam ego bene (non enim discerem nisi cogerer; nemo autem inuitus[4] bene facit, etiamsi bonum est quod facit), nec qui me urgebant bene faciebant, sed bene mihi fiebat abs te, Deus meus. illi enim non intuebantur quo referrem[5] quod me discere cogebant, praeterquam[6] ad satiandas[7] insatiabiles[8] cupiditates copiosae[9] inopiae[10] et ignominiosae[11] gloriae. tu uero, cui *numerati sunt capilli*[12] *nostri* (Mt 10:30), errore omnium qui mihi instabant[13] ut discerem utebaris ad utilitatem[14] meam, meo autem, qui discere nolebam, utebaris ad poenam meam, qua plecti[15] non eram indignus,[16] tantillus[17] puer et tantus peccator.[18] ita de non bene facientibus tu bene faciebas mihi et de peccante me ipso iuste[19] retribuebas[20] mihi. iussisti enim et sic est, ut poena sua sibi sit omnis inordinatus[21] animus.

[1]adulescentia ~ae *f.* **young adulthood** (age 16–30) [2]metuo ~ere, ~i, metutum **to fear** (pass. *impers.*) [3]urgeo ~ere, ursi **to compel** [4]inuitus ~a, ~um *adj.* **unwilling** [5]refero ~rre, rettuli, relatum **to refer;** LATE **to put to use** [6]praeterquam *conj.* **beyond** [7]satio ~are, ~aui, ~atum **to satiate** [8]insatiabilis ~is, ~e *adj.* **insatiable** [9]copiosus ~a, ~um *adj.* **copious** [10]inopia ~ae *f.* **lack of resources** [11]ignominiosus ~a, ~um *adj.* **ignominious** [12]capillus ~i *m.* **hair of the head** [13]insto ~are, ~iti **to insist** [14]utilitas ~atis *f.* **advantage** [15]plecto ~ere **to punish** [16]indignus ~a, ~um *adj.* **undeserving** [17]tantillus ~a, ~um *adj.* **so small** [18]peccator ~oris *m.* ECCL **sinner** [19]iuste *adv.* **justly** [20]retribuo ~uere, ~ui, ~utum **to repay** [21]inordinatus ~a, ~um *adj.* **disordered**

I hated Greek, loved Latin

1.13.20 Quid autem erat causae cur Graecas litteras oderam, quibus puerulus[1] imbuebar?[2] ne nunc quidem mihi satis exploratum[3] est. adamaueram[4] enim Latinas, non quas primi magistri sed quas docent qui "grammatici"[5] uocantur. nam illas primas, ubi legere et scribere et numerare discitur, non minus onerosas[6] poenalesque[7] habebam quam omnes Graecas. unde tamen et hoc nisi de peccato et uanitate uitae, qua *caro eram et spiritus ambulans[8] et non reuertens[9]* (Ps 77:39)? nam utique meliores, quia certiores, erant primae illae litterae quibus fiebat in me et factum est et habeo illud ut et legam, si quid scriptum inuenio, et scribam ipse, si quid uolo, quam illae quibus tenere cogebar Aeneae nescio cuius errores, oblitus errorum meorum, et plorare[10] Didonem mortuam, quia se occidit[11] ab amore, cum interea[12] me ipsum in his a te morientem, Deus, uita mea, siccis[13] oculis ferrem miserrimus.

[1]puerulus ~i *m.* **little boy** [2]imbuo ~uere, ~ui, ~utum **to immerse** [3]exploratus ~a, ~um *adj.* **certain** [4]adamo ~are, ~aui, ~atum **to come to love** [5]grammaticus ~i *m.* **grammar teacher** [6]onerosus ~a, ~um *adj.* **onerous** [7]poenalis ~is, ~e *adj.* punitive; LATE **painful** [8]ambulo ~are, ~aui, ~atum **to walk** [9]reuertor, reuor- ~ti, ~sus **to return** [10]ploro ~are, ~aui, ~atum **to weep aloud** [11]occido ~dere, ~di, ~sum **to kill** [12]interea *adv.* **meanwhile** [13]siccus ~a, ~um *adj.* **dry**

The death of Dido

1.13.21 Quid enim miserius misero non miserante se ipsum et flente Didonis mortem, quae fiebat amando Aenean, non flente autem mortem suam, quae fiebat non amando te, Deus, lumen cordis mei et panis[1] oris intus animae meae et uirtus maritans[2] mentem meam et sinum cogitationis meae? non te amabam, et fornicabar[3] abs te, et fornicanti sonabat undique:[4] *Euge! euge!*[5] (Ps 39:16) *amicitia[6] enim mundi huius* (Jas 1:4) fornicatio[7] est abs te et *Euge! euge!* dicitur ut pudeat,[8] si non ita homo sit. et haec non flebam, et flebam Didonem *extinctam[9] ferroque extrema secutam* (Aen. 6.457), sequens ipse extrema condita[10] tua

[1]panis ~is *m.* **bread** [2]marito ~are, ~aui, ~atum **to marry** [3]fornico ~are, ~aui, ~atum ECCL **to commit adultery/idolatry** [4]undique *adv.* **from all directions** [5]euge *interj.* **well done!** [6]amicitia ~ae *f.* **friendship** [7]fornicatio ~onis *f.* ornamental arch; ECCL **adultery/idolatry** [8]pudeo ~ere, ~ui **to make ashamed** [9]extinguo ~guere, ~xi, ~ctum **to extinguish** (life) [10]condo ~ere, ~idi, ~itum **founding** (*neut. pl.*); ECCL **creation**

19

relicto te et *terra iens in terram* (Gen 3:19). et si prohiberer[11] ea legere, dolerem, quia non legerem quod dolerem. tali dementia[12] honestiores[13] et uberiores[14] litterae putantur quam illae quibus legere et scribere didici.

[11]prohibeo ~ere, ~ui, ~itum **to forbid** [12]dementia ~ae *f.* **craziness** [13]honestus ~a, ~um *adj.* **respectable** [14]uber ~ris *adj.* **productive**

Elementary lessons better than AP literature

1.13.22 Sed nunc in anima mea clamet Deus meus, et ueritas tua dicat mihi, "Non est ita, non est ita. melior est prorsus[1] doctrina illa prior." nam ecce paratior[2] sum obliuisci errores Aeneae atque omnia eius modi quam scribere et legere. at enim uela[3] pendent[4] liminibus[5] grammaticarum scholarum,[6] sed non illa magis honorem secreti[7] quam tegimentum[8] erroris significant.[9] non clament aduersus me quos iam non timeo, dum confiteor tibi quae uult anima mea, Deus meus, et adquiesco[10] in reprehensione[11] malarum uiarum mearum, ut diligam bonas uias tuas, non clament aduersus me uenditores[12] grammaticae[13] uel emptores,[14] quia, si proponam[15] eis interrogans, utrum uerum sit quod Aenean aliquando Carthaginem uenisse poeta[16] dicit, indoctiores[17] nescire se respondebunt, doctiores autem etiam negabunt uerum esse. at si quaeram quibus litteris scribatur "Aeneae" nomen, omnes mihi qui haec didicerunt uerum respondent secundum id pactum[18] et placitum quo inter se homines ista signa firmarunt.[19] item[20] si quaeram quid horum maiore uitae huius incommodo[21] quisque obliuiscatur, legere et scribere an poetica[22] illa figmenta,[23] quis non uideat quid responsurus sit, qui non est penitus[24] oblitus sui?

Peccabam ergo puer cum illa inania[25] istis utilioribus[26] amore praeponebam,[27] uel potius ista oderam, illa amabam. iam uero[28] "Unum

[1]prorsus *adv.* **in every respect** [2]paratus ~a, ~um *adj.* **prepared** [3]uelum ~i *neut.* **curtain** [4]pendeo ~ere, pependi **to hang** [5]limen ~inis *neut.* **entrance** [6]'grammaticarum scholarum' **schools of literature** [7]secretum ~i *neut.* **secrecy > privacy** [8]tegimentum ~i *neut.* **cloak** [9]significo ~are, ~aui, ~atum **to signify** [10]adquiesco ~escere, ~ei **to acquiesce** [11]reprehensio ~onis *f.* **finding fault** [12]uenditor ~oris *m.* **vender** [13]grammatica ~ae *f.* **literature** [14]emptor ~oris *m.* **buyer** [15]propono ~onere, ~osui, ~ositum **to put forward** [16]poeta ~ae *m.* **poet** [17]indoctus ~a, ~um *adj.* **uneducated** [18]pactum ~i *neut.* **agreement** [19]firmo ~are, ~aui, ~atum **to establish** [20]item *adv.* **similarly** [21]incommodum ~i *neut.* **disadvantage** [22]poeticus ~a, ~um *adj.* **poetic** [23]figmentum ~i *neut.* **fiction** [24]penitus *adv.* **entirely** [25]inanis ~is, ~e *adj.* **empty** [26]utilis ~is, ~e *adj.* **profitable** [27]praepono ~onere, ~osui, ~ositum **to prefer** x (acc.) **over** y (dat.) [28]'iam uero' **what is more**

et unum duo, duo et duo quattuor,"[29] odiosa[30] cantio[31] mihi erat, et dulcissimum spectaculum[32] uanitatis, equus ligneus[33] plenus armatis[34] et Troiae incendium[35] *atque ipsius umbra Creusae* (Aen. 2.772).

[29]quattuor *indecl. adj.* four [30]odiosus ~a, ~um *adj.* hateful [31]cantio ~onis *f.* song; LATE sing-song [32]spectaculum ~i *neut.* spectacle [33]ligneus ~a, ~um *adj.* wooden [34]armatus ~i *m.* soldiers [35]incendium ~ii *neut.* burning

Coercion checks curiosity

1.14.23 Cur ergo Graecam etiam grammaticam[1] oderam talia cantantem? nam et Homerus peritus[2] texere[3] tales fabellas[4] et dulcissime[5] uanus est, mihi tamen amarus[6] erat puero. credo etiam Graecis pueris Vergilius ita sit, cum eum sic discere coguntur ut ego illum. uidelicet[7] difficultas,[8] difficultas omnino ediscendae[9] linguae peregrinae,[10] quasi felle[11] aspergebat[12] omnes suauitates[13] Graecas fabulosarum[14] narrationum.[15] nulla enim uerba illa noueram, et saeuis terroribus[16] ac poenis ut nossem instabatur[17] mihi uehementer.[18] nam et Latina aliquando infans[19] utique nulla noueram, et tamen aduertendo[20] didici sine ullo metu atque cruciate,[21] inter etiam blandimenta[22] nutricum[23] et ioca[24] adridentium[25] et laetitias adludentium.[26] didici uero illa sine poenali[27] onere[28] urgentium,[29] cum me urgeret cor meum ad parienda[30] concepta[31] sua, et qua[32] non esset, nisi aliqua uerba didicissem non a docentibus sed a loquentibus, in quorum et ego auribus parturiebam[33] quidquid sentiebam. hinc satis elucet[34] maiorem habere uim ad discenda ista liberam[35] curiositatem[36] quam meticulosam[37] necessitate.[38]

[1]grammatica ~ae *f.* literature [2]peritus ~a, ~um *adj.* skilled [3]texo ~ere, ~ui, ~tum to weave [4]fabella ~ae *f.* story [5]dulciter *adv.* sweetly [6]amarus ~a, ~um *adj.* bitter [7]uidelicet *adv.* clearly [8]difficultas ~atis *f.* difficulty [9]edisco ~ere, edidici to learn thoroughly [10]peregrinus ~a, ~um *adj.* foreign [11]fel ~llis *neut.* gall [12]aspergo ~gere, ~si, ~sum to sprinkle (w. abl.) [13]suauitas ~atis *f.* charm [14]fabulosus ~a, ~um *adj.* fantastical [15]narratio ~onis *f.* tale [16]terror ~oris *m.* terror [17]insto ~are, ~iti to threaten (*impers.* pass. w. dat.) [18]uehementer *adv.* vehemently [19]infans ~ntis *m. f.* infant [20]aduerto ~tere, ~ti, ~sum to pay attention [21]cruciatus ~us *m.* torment [22]blandimentum ~i *neut.* coddling [23]nutrix ~icis *f.* child's nurse [24]iocus ~i *m.* joke [25]adrideo ~dere, ~si, ~sum to smile at [26]adludo ~dere, ~si, ~sum to play with [27]poenalis ~is, ~e *adj.* punitive; LATE painful [28]onus ~eris *neut.* encumbrance [29]urgeo ~ere, ursi to compel [30]pario ~ere, peperi, ~tum to give birth to [31]conceptum ~i *neut.* thought [32]qua *adv.* up to that point or in any way [33]parturio ~ire, ~iui to be in labor giving birth (fig.) [34]eluceo ~cere, ~xi to shine; LATE to be apparent (*impers.*) [35]liber ~era, ~erum *adj.* free [36]curiositas ~atis *f.* curiosity (usu. in a bad sense) [37]meticulosus ~a, ~um *adj.* fear-inducing [38]necessitas ~atis *f.* compulsion

sed illius fluxum[39] haec restringit[40] legibus tuis, Deus, legibus tuis a magistrorum ferulis[41] usque ad temptationes martyrum,[42] ualentibus legibus tuis miscere salubres[43] amaritudines[44] reuocantes[45] nos ad te a iucunditate[46] pestifera[47] qua recessimus a te.

[39]fluxus ~us *m.* **flow** *or* **flux** [40]restringo ~ngere, ~nxi, ~ctum **to restrain** [41]ferula ~ae *f.* **rod** (**for discipline**) [42]martyr ~is *m. f.* ECCL **martyr** [43]saluber ~bris, ~bre *adj.* **healthy** [44]amaritudo ~inis *f.* **bitterness** [45]reuoco ~are, ~aui, ~atum **to call upon to return** [46]iucunditas ~atis *f.* **charm** [47]pestifer ~era, ~erum *adj.* **deadly**

Useful lessons

1.15.24 *Exaudi*, Domine, *deprecationem*[1] *meam* (Ps 60:2), ne deficiat[2] anima mea sub disciplina[3] tua neque deficiam in confitendo tibi miserationes[4] tuas, quibus eruisti[5] me *ab omnibus uiis meis pessimis*[6] (2 Kgs 17:13), ut dulcescas[7] mihi super omnes seductiones[8] quas sequebar, et amem te ualidissime,[9] et amplexer[10] manum tuam totis praecordiis[11] meis, et *eruas me ab* omni *temptatione* (Ps 17:30) *usque in finem* (Ps 37:7, 1 Cor 1:8). ecce enim tu, Domine, *rex meus et Deus meus* (Ps 5:3), tibi seruiat quidquid utile[12] puer didici, tibi seruiat quod loquor et scribo et lego et numero, quoniam cum uana discerem tu disciplinam dabas mihi, et in eis uanis peccata delectationum[13] mearum dimisisti mihi. didici enim in eis multa uerba utilia, sed et in rebus non uanis disci possunt, et ea uia tuta est in qua pueri ambularent.[14]

[1]deprecatio ~onis *f.* **plea** [2]deficio ~icere, ~eci, ~ectum **to fail** [3]disciplina ~ae *f.* **discipline** [4]miseratio ~onis *f.* **mercy** [5]eruo ~uere, ~ui, ~utum **to pluck out**; ECCL **to rescue** [6]pessimus ~a, ~um *superl. adj.* **most wicked** [7]dulcesco ~ere **to become sweet** [8]seductio ~onis *f.* **leading astray**; ECCL **seduction** [9]ualide *adv.* **intensely** [10]amplexor ~ari, ~atus **to clasp** [11]praecordia ~orum *neut. pl.* **depths of the heart** [12]utilis ~is, ~e *adj.* **profitable** [13]delectatio ~onis *f.* **delight** [14]ambulo ~are, ~aui, ~atum **to walk**; ECCL **to live**

Cicero on Homer

1.16.25 Sed uae[1] tibi, flumen moris humani! *quis resistet tibi?* (Ps 75:8). Quamdiu[2] non siccaberis?[3] quousque[4] uolues[5] Euae filios in mare

[1]uae *interj.* [a cry of pain, anger, sorrow] **woe!** [2]quamdiu *adv.* **for how long?** [3]sicco ~are, ~aui, ~atum **to dry up** [4]quousque *adv.* **how far?** [5]uoluo ~uere, ~ui, ~utum **to tumble**

magnum et formidulosum,[6] quod uix transeunt qui lignum[7] conscenderint?[8] nonne ego in te legi et tonantem[9] Iouem et adulterantem?[10] et utique non posset haec duo, sed actum est ut haberet auctoritatem ad imitandum[11] uerum adulterium[12] lenocinante[13] falso tonitru.[14] quis autem paenulatorum[15] magistrorum audit aure sobria[16] ex eodem puluere[17] hominem clamantem et dicentem: *Fingebat*[18] *haec Homerus et humana ad deos transferebat:*[19] *diuina*[20] *mallem*[21] *ad nos?* (Tusc. 1.65). sed uerius dicitur quod fingebat haec quidem ille, sed hominibus flagitiosis[22] diuina tribuendo,[23] ne flagitia[24] flagitia putarentur et ut, quisquis ea fecisset, non homines perditos[25] sed caelestes[26] deos uideretur imitatus.

[6]formidulosus ~a, ~um *adj.* **dangerous** [7]lignum ~i *neut.* **wood**; ECCL the cross (transf.) [8]conscendo ~dere, ~di, ~sum **to embark** [9]tono ~are, ~ui **to thunder** [10]adultero ~are, ~aui, ~atum **to commit adultery** [11]imitor ~ari, ~atus **to imitate** [12]adulterium ~ii *neut.* **adultery** [13]lenocinor ~ari, ~atus **to serve one's interests**; LATE **to pander** [14]tonitrus ~us *m.* **thunder** [15]paenulatus ~a, ~um *adj.* **hooded** [16]sobrius ~ia, ~ium *adj.* **sober** > **sensible** [17]puluis ~eris *m.* **dust (of an arena—implying a contest)** [18]fingo ~ngere, ~nxi, ~ctum **to fashion** [19]transfero ~ferre, ~tuli, ~latum **to transfer** [20]diuinus ~a, ~um *adj.* **divine** [21]malo ~lle, ~lui **to prefer** [22]flagitiosus ~a, ~um *adj.* **indecent** [23]tribuo ~uere, ~ui, ~utum **to attribute** [24]flagitium ~ii *neut.* **indecency (of sexual misconduct)** [25]perditus ~a, ~um *adj.* **abandoned** (morally) [26]caelestis ~is, ~e *adj.* **celestial**

Terence's *Eunuchus*

1.16.26 Et tamen, o flumen Tartareum, iactantur[1] in te filii hominum cum mercedibus,[2] ut haec discant, et magna res agitur cum hoc agitur publice[3] in foro,[4] in conspectu legum supra[5] mercedem salaria[6] decernentium,[7] et saxa tua percutis[8] et sonas dicens: "Hinc uerba discuntur, hinc adquiritur[9] eloquentia,[10] rebus persuadendis[11] sententiisque explicandis[12] maxime necessaria."[13] ita uero non cognosceremus uerba haec, "imbrem[14] aureum"[15] et "gremium"[16] et "fucum"[17] et "templa caeli" et alia uerba quae in eo loco scripta sunt, nisi Terentius induceret[18] nequam[19] adulescentem[20] proponentem[21] sibi Iouem ad exemplum[22] stupri,[23] dum

[1]iacto ~are, ~aui, ~atum **to toss** [2]merces ~edis *f.* **fee** [3]publice *adv.* **at the public expense** [4]forum ~i *neut.* **public square** [5]supra *prep. acc.* **beyond** [6]salarium ~ii *neut.* **government salary** [7]decerno ~ernere, ~reui, ~retum **to decree** [8]percutio ~tere, ~ssi, ~ssum **to crash upon** [9]adquiro ~rere, ~siui, ~situm **to acquire** [10]eloquentia ~ae *f.* **eloquence** [11]persuadeo ~dere, ~si, ~sum **to persuade** [12]explico ~are, ~aui or ~ui, ~atum **to set out in words** [13]necessarius ~a, ~um *adj.* **necessary** [14]imber ~bris *m.* **shower** [15]aureus ~a, ~um *adj.* **golden** [16]gremium ~ii *neut.* **lap** [17]fucus ~i *m.* **disguise** [18]induco ~cere, ~xi, ~ctum **to bring (on stage)** [19]nequam *indecl. adj.* **depraved** [20]adulescens ~ntis *m.* **young man** [21]propono ~onere, ~osui, ~ositum **to hold up (as a model)** [22]exemplum ~i *neut.* **example** [23]stuprum ~i *neut.* **illicit sexual conduct**

spectat tabulam quandam pictam[24] in pariete[25] ubi inerat[26] pictura[27]
haec, Iouem quo pacto[28] Danae misisse aiunt in gremium quondam[29]
imbrem aureum (Eu. 584–85)...
...fucum factum[30] mulieri[31] (Eu. 589)?

et uide quemadmodum se concitat[32] ad libidinem quasi caelesti[33] magisterio:[34]

at quem deum! inquit *qui templa caeli summo sonitu[35] concutit.[36]*
ego homuncio[37] id non facerem?
ego uero illud feci ac libens[38] (Eu. 590–91).

Non omnino per hanc turpitudinem[39] uerba ista commodius[40] discuntur, sed per haec uerba turpitudo ista confidentius[41] perpetratur.[42] non accuso[43] uerba quasi uasa[44] electa[45] atque pretiosa,[46] sed uinum[47] erroris quod in eis nobis propinabatur[48] ab ebriis[49] doctoribus,[50] et nisi biberemus[51] caedebamur,[52] nec appellare ad aliquem iudicem[53] sobrium[54] licebat. et tamen ego, Deus meus, in cuius conspectu iam secura[55] est recordatio[56] mea, libenter[57] haec didici, et eis delectabar miser, et ob hoc bonae spei puer appellabar.

[24]'tabulam pictam' **painting** [25]paries ~etis *m.* **wall** [26]insum inesse, infui **to be in or on** [27]pictura ~ae *f.* **picture** [28]'quo pacto' **by what means** [29]quondam *adv.* **once upon a time** [30]'fucum factum' **played a trick** [31]mulier ~eris *f.* **woman** [32]concito ~are, ~aui, ~atum **to stir up (feelings)** [33]caelestis ~is, ~e *adj.* **celestial** [34]magisterium ~ii *neut.* **teacher** [35]sonitus ~us *m.* **noise** [36]concutio ~tere, ~ssi, ~ssum **to shake** [37]homuncio ~onis *m.* **puny human** [38]libens ~ntis *adj.* **gladly** (*quasi-adv.*) [39]turpitudo ~inis *f.* **indecency** [40]commode *adv.* **easily** [41]confidenter *adv.* **audaciously** [42]perpetro ~are, ~aui, ~atum **to put into practice** [43]accuso ~are, ~aui, ~atum **to blame** [44]uas uasis *neut.* **vessel** [45]electus ~a, ~um *adj.* **choice** [46]pretiosus ~a, ~um *adj.* **precious** [47]uinum ~i *neut.* **wine** [48]propino ~are, ~aui, ~atum **to give to drink** [49]ebrius ~a, ~um *adj.* **intoxicated** [50]doctor ~oris *m.* **teacher** [51]bibo ~ere, ~i **to drink** [52]caedo ~dere, cecidi, ~sum **to beat** [53]iudex ~icis *m.* **judge** [54]sobrius ~ia, ~ium *adj.* **sober** [55]securus ~a, ~um *adj.* **untroubled** [56]recordatio ~onis *f.* **recollection** [57]libenter *adv.* **willingly**

The prize-winning speech of Juno

1.17.27 Sine me, Deus meus, dicere aliquid et de ingenio meo, munere tuo, in quibus a me deliramentis[1] atterebatur.[2] proponebatur[3] enim mihi

[1]deliramentum ~i *neut.* **nonsense** [2]attero ~terere, ~triui, ~tritum **to waste** [3]propono ~onere, ~osui, ~ositum **to set out > to assign**

negotium,[4] animae meae satis inquietum[5] praemio[6] laudis et dedecoris[7] uel plagarum[8] metu, ut dicerem uerba Iunonis *irascentis*[9] *et dolentis* (Aen. 1.8–11) quod non posset *Italia Teucrorum auertere*[10] *regem* (Aen. 1.38), quae numquam Iunonem dixisse audieram. sed figmentorum[11] poeticorum[12] uestigia[13] errantes sequi cogebamur, et tale aliquid dicere solutis uerbis[14] quale poeta[15] dixisset uersibus.[16] et ille dicebat laudabilius[17] in quo pro dignitate[18] adumbratae[19] personae[20] irae ac doloris similior affectus eminebat,[21] uerbis sententias congruenter[22] uestientibus.[23] ut quid mihi illud,[24] o uera uita, Deus meus, quod mihi recitanti[25] adclamabatur[26] prae multis coaetaneis[27] et conlectoribus[28] meis? nonne ecce illa omnia fumus[29] et uentus? itane aliud non erat ubi exerceretur[30] ingenium et lingua mea? laudes tuae, Domine, laudes tuae per scripturas tuas suspenderent[31] *palmitem*[32] (Jn 15:4) cordis mei, et non raperetur per inania[33] nugarum[34] *turpis praeda*[35] (G. 2.60) uolatilibus.[36] non enim uno modo sacrificatur[37] transgressoribus[38] angelis.

[4]negotium ~ii *neut.* work > **task** [5]inquietus ~a, ~um *adj.* restless > **disquieting** [6]praemium ~ii *neut.* **prize** [7]dedecus ~oris *neut.* **disgrace** [8]plaga ~ae *f.* **beating** [9]irascor ~i, iratus sum **to be angry** [10]auerto ~tere, ~ti, ~sum **to divert** [11]figmentum ~i *neut.* **fiction** [12]poeticus ~a, ~um *adj.* **poetic** [13]uestigium ~ii *neut.* **footprint** [14]'solutis uerbis' words free from meter, i.e., **prose** [15]poeta ~ae *m.* **poet** [16]uersus ~us *m.* **verse** [17]laudabiliter *adv.* **laudably** [18]dignitas ~atis *f.* **dignity** [19]adumbratus ~a, ~um *adj.* **pretended** [20]persona ~ae *f.* **character in a play** [21]emineo ~ere, ~ui **to be pre-eminent** [22]congruenter *adv.* **aptly** [23]uestio ~ire, ~iui, ~itum **to clothe** (fig.) [24]'ut quid mihi illud' ECCL = 'quid mihi illud' **what does it matter to me?** [25]recito ~are, ~aui, ~atum **to recite** [26]adclamo ~are, ~aui, ~atum **to applaud** (pass. *impers.*) [27]coaetaneus ~i *m.* **one of the same age** [28]conlector ~oris *m.* AUG **fellow-reader** [29]fumus ~i *m.* **smoke** [30]exerceo ~ere, ~ui, ~itum **to train by practice** [31]suspendo ~dere, ~di, ~sum **to hold up** [32]palmes ~itis *m.* **vine branch** [33]inane ~is *neut.* **emptiness** [34]nugae ~arum *f. pl.* **absurdities** [35]praeda ~ae *f.* **prey** [36]uolatilis ~is, ~e *adj.* flying; **bird** (as noun) [37]sacrifico ~are, ~aui, ~atum **to offer a sacrifice** (pass. *impers.*) [38]transgressor ~oris *m.* ECCL **rebel** (as. *adj.*)

The Prodigal Son

1.18.28 Quid autem mirum, quod in uanitates ita ferebar et a te, Deus meus, ibam foras,[1] quando mihi imitandi[2] proponebantur[3] homines qui aliqua facta sua non mala, si cum barbarismo[4] aut soloecismo[5]

[1]foras *adv.* **abroad** [2]imitor ~ari, ~atus **to imitate** [3]propono ~onere, ~osui, ~ositum **to hold up** (as a model) [4]barbarismus ~i *m.* barbarism i.e., **mispronunciation** [5]soloecismus ~i *m.* solecism i.e., **grammatical mistake**

enuntiarent,[6] reprehensi[7] confundebantur,[8] si autem libidines suas inte-
gris[9] et rite[10] consequentibus uerbis[11] *copiose*[12] *ornateque*[13] (Tusc. 1.7)
narrarent, laudati gloriabantur?[14] uides haec, Domine, et taces, *longa-
nimis*[15] *et multum misericors*[16] *et uerax*[17] (Ps 102:8). numquid semper
tacebis? et nunc eruis[18] de hoc immanissimo[19] profundo[20] quaerentem
te animam et sitientem[21] delectationes[22] tuas, et cuius *cor dicit tibi:
quaesiui uultum tuum; uultum tuum, Domine, requiram*[23] (Ps 26:8),
nam longe a uultu tuo in affectu tenebroso.[24] non enim pedibus aut
a spatiis locorum itur abs te aut reditur ad te, aut uero *filius ille tuus
minor* (Lk 15:11–32) equos uel currus uel naues quaesiuit, aut auolauit[25]
pinna[26] uisibili, aut moto poplite[27] iter egit, ut in longinqua[28] regione[29]
uiuens prodige[30] dissiparet[31] quod dederas proficiscenti,[32] dulcis pater
quia dederas, et egeno[33] redeunti dulcior: in affectu ergo libidinoso,[34]
id enim est tenebroso, atque id est longe a uultu tuo.

[6]enuntio ~are, ~aui, ~atum **to pronunce** [7]reprehendo ~dere, ~di, ~sum **to censure a mistake**
[8]confundo ~undere, ~udi, ~usum to confuse > **to embarrass** [9]integer ~gra, ~grum *adj.* unimpaired;
LATE **grammatically correct** [10]rite *adv.* **correctly** [11]'consequentibus uerbis' **well-ordered speech**
[12]copiose *adv.* **richly** [13]ornate *adv.* **elaborately** [14]glorior ~ari, ~atus **to boast** [15]longanimis ~is, ~e
adj. ECCL **patient** [16]misericors ~rdis *adj.* **merciful** [17]uerax ~acis *adj.* **truthful** [18]eruo ~uere, ~ui,
~utum **to pluck out**; ECCL **to rescue** [19]immanis ~is, ~e *adj.* **immense** [20]profundum ~i *neut.* **depths**
[21]sitiens ~ntis *adj.* **thirsty** [22]delectatio ~onis *f.* **delight** [23]requiro ~rere, ~siui, ~situm **to look for**
[24]tenebrosus ~a, ~um *adj.* **dark** [25]auolo ~are, ~aui, ~atum **to fly away** [26]pinna ~ae *f.* **wing** [27]poples
~itis *m.* **knee** [28]longinquus ~a, ~um *adj.* **far off** [29]regio ~onis *f.* **land** [30]prodige *adv.* **extravagantly**
[31]dissipo ~are, ~aui, ~atum **to squander** [32]proficiscor ~icisci, ~ectus **to depart** [33]egenus ~a, ~um
adj. **destitute** [34]libidinosus ~a, ~um *adj.* **lustful**

Loving humanities, hating humans

1.18.29 *Vide, Domine* Deus (Ps 9:14), et patienter,[1] ut uides, uide
quomodo diligenter[2] obseruent[3] filii hominum pacta[4] litterarum et syllabarum[5] accepta a prioribus locutoribus,[6] et a te accepta aeterna pacta
perpetuae[7] salutis neglegant,[8] ut qui illa sonorum uetera placita teneat
aut doceat, si contra disciplinam[9] grammaticam[10] sine adspiratione[11]
primae syllabae "hominem" dixerit, magis displiceat hominibus quam

[1]patienter *adv.* **patiently** [2]diligenter *adv.* **carefully** [3]obseruo ~are, ~aui, ~atum **to give attention
to** [4]pactum ~i *neut.* **what is agreed upon** [5]syllaba ~ae *f.* **syllable** [6]locutor ~oris *m.* **speaker** [7]per-
petuus ~a, ~um *adj.* **unending** [8]neglego ~gere, ~xi, ~ctum **to neglect** [9]disciplina ~ae *f.* **practice**
[10]grammatica ~ae *f.* **grammar** [11]asspiratio ~onis *f.* **aspiration**

si contra tua praecepta[12] hominem oderit, cum sit homo. quasi uero quemlibet[13] inimicum hominem perniciosius[14] sentiat quam ipsum odium[15] quo in eum inritatur,[16] aut uastet[17] quisquam persequendo[18] alium grauius[19] quam cor suum uastat inimicando.[20] et certe non est interior litterarum scientia quam *scripta conscientia*,[21] (Rom 2:15) id se alteri facere quod nolit pati.

Quam tu secretus[22] es, *habitans*[23] *in excelsis*[24] (Isa 33:5 VL) in silentio,[25] Deus solus magnus, lege infatigabili[26] spargens[27] poenales[28] caecitates[29] supra[30] inlicitas[31] cupiditates, cum homo eloquentiae[32] famam quaeritans ante hominem iudicem[33] circumstante[34] hominum multitudine[35] inimicum suum odio immanissimo[36] insectans[37] uigilantissime[38] cauet,[39] ne per linguae errorem dicat, "inter hominibus," et ne per mentis furorem hominem auferat ex hominibus, non cauet.

[12]praeceptum ~i *neut.* **precept** [13]quilibet, quae-, quod- *adj.* **any** [14]perniciosus ~a, ~um *adj.* **destructive** [15]odium ~i *neut.* **hatred** [16]inrito ~are, ~aui, ~atum **to provoke anger** [17]uasto ~are, ~aui, ~atum **to lay waste** [18]persequor ~qui, ~cutus **to pursue punitively** [19]grauiter *adv.* **grievously** [20]inimico ~are, ~aui, ~atum **to feel hostile** [21]conscientia ~ae *f.* **conscience** [22]secretus ~a, ~um *adj.* **existing apart** [23]habito ~are, ~aui, ~atum **to dwell** [24]excelsum ~i *neut.* **height**; ECCL **heavens** (*neut. pl.*) [25]silentium ~ii *neut.* **silence** [26]infatigabilis ~is, ~e *adj.* **indefatigable** [27]spargo ~gere, ~si, ~sum **to sprinkle** [28]poenalis ~is, ~e *adj.* **penal** [29]caecitas ~atis *f.* **blindness** [30]supra *prep. acc.* **over** [31]inlicitus ~a, ~um *adj.* **illicit** [32]eloquentia ~ae *f.* **eloquence** [33]iudex ~icis *m.* **judge** [34]circumsto ~are, ~eti (~iti) **to surround with hostility** [35]multitudo ~inis *f.* **multitude** [36]immanis ~is, ~e *adj.* **savage** [37]insector ~ari, ~atus **to pursue with hostility** [38]uigilanter *adv.* **vigilantly** [39]caueo ~ere, caui, ~tum **to be careful**

We are (not) born innocent

1.19.30 Horum ego puer morum in limine[1] iacebam miser, et huius harenae[2] palaestra[3] erat illa, ubi magis timebam barbarismum[4] facere quam cauebam,[5] si facerem, non facientibus inuidere.[6] dico haec et confiteor tibi, Deus meus, in quibus laudabar ab eis quibus placere tunc mihi erat honeste[7] uiuere. non enim uidebam uoraginem[8] turpitudinis[9] in quam *proiectus*[10] eram *ab oculis tuis* (Ps 30:23). nam in illis iam quid me

[1]limen ~inis *neut.* **entrance** [2]harena ~ae *f.* **arena** [3]palaestra ~ae *f.* **wrestling** > **rhetorical exercise** (fig.) [4]barbarismus ~i *m.* **mispronunciation** [5]caueo ~ere, caui, ~tum **to beware** [6]inuideo ~idere, ~idi, ~isum **to be jealous of** (w. dat. of person) [7]honeste *adv.* **respectably** [8]uorago ~inis *f.* **quagmire** [9]turpitudo ~inis *f.* **turpitude** [10]proicio ~icere, ~ieci, ~iectum **to cast off**

foedius[11] fuit, ubi etiam talibus displicebam fallendo innumerabilibus[12] mendaciis et paedagogum[13] et magistros et parentes amore ludendi,[14] studio spectandi nugatoria[15] et imitandi[16] ludicra[17] inquietudine?[18]

Furta[19] etiam faciebam de cellario[20] parentum et de mensa,[21] uel gula[22] imperitante[23] uel ut haberem quod darem pueris ludum[24] suum mihi quo pariter[25] utique delectabantur tamen uendentibus.[26] in quo etiam ludo fraudulentas[27] uictorias[28] ipse uana excellentiae[29] cupiditate uictus saepe aucupabar.[30] quid autem tam nolebam pati atque atrociter,[31] si deprehenderem,[32] arguebam,[33] quam id quod aliis faciebam? et, si deprehensus arguerer, saeuire[34] magis quam cedere libebat.[35] istane est innocentia[36] puerilis?[37] non est, Domine, non est. oro[38] te, Deus meus: nam haec ipsa sunt quae a paedagogis et magistris, a nucibus[39] et pilulis[40] et passeribus,[41] ad praefectos[42] et reges, aurum, praedia,[43] mancipia,[44] haec ipsa omnino succedentibus[45] maioribus aetatibus transeunt, sicuti ferulis[46] maiora supplicia[47] succedunt. Humilitatis[48] ergo signum in statura[49] pueritiae,[50] rex noster, probasti,[51] cum aisti, *talium est regnum caelorum* (Mt 19:14).

[11]foede *adv.* **foul** [12]innumerabilis ~is, ~e *adj.* **innumerable** [13]paedagogus ~i *m.* **slave who escorts a child to school** [14]ludo ~dere, ~si, ~sum **to play games** [15]nugatorius ~ia, ~ium *adj.* **worthless** [16]imitor ~ari, ~atus **to imitate** [17]ludicrum ~i *neut.* **public entertainment** [18]inquietudo ~inis *f.* disturbance; LATE **restlessnes** [19]furtum ~i *neut.* **theft** [20]cellarium ~ii *neut.* **cellar** [21]mensa ~ae *f.* **table** [22]gula ~ae *f.* gullet > **appetite** [23]imperito ~are, ~aui, ~atum **to be in control** [24]ludus ~i *m.* **play** [25]pariter *adv.* **equally as much** [26]uendo ~ere, ~idi, ~itum **to sell** [27]fraudulentus ~a, ~um *adj.* **fraudulent** [28]uictoria ~ae *f.* **victory in a contest** [29]excellentia ~ae *f.* excellence > **superiority** [30]aucupor ~ari, ~atus to catch > **to snatch** [31]atrociter *adv.* **acrimoniously** [32]deprehendo ~dere, ~di, ~sum **to catch** [33]arguo ~uere, ~ui, ~utum to prove > **to accuse** [34]saeuio ~ire, ~ii, ~itum **to rage** [35]libet ~ere, ~uit or ~itum est *impers.* **it is desirable** [36]innocentia ~ae *f.* **innocence** [37]puerilis ~is, ~e *adj.* **childish** [38]oro ~are, ~aui, ~atum **to beseech** [39]nux ~cis *f.* **nut** (used in games) [40]pilula ~ae *f.* **little ball** [41]passer ~eris *m.* **sparrow** (as a pet) [42]praefectus ~i *m.* **governor** [43]praedium ~ii *neut.* **estate** [44]mancipium ~ii *neut.* **property** *or* **slave** [45]succedo ~dere, ~ssi, ~ssum **to come after** (w. dat.) [46]ferula ~ae *f.* **rod** (for discipline) [47]supplicium ~ii *neut.* **punishment** [48]humilitas ~atis *f.* **humility** [49]statura ~ae *f.* **stature** [50]pueritia ~ae *f.* **childish nature** [51]probo ~are, ~aui, ~atum **to approve**

Your gifts to me

1.20.31 Sed tamen, Domine, tibi excellentissimo[1] atque optimo conditori[2] et rectori[3] uniuersitatis,[4] Deo nostro gratias, etiamsi me

[1]excellens ~ntis *adj.* **excellent** [2]conditor ~oris *m.* founder; ECCL **creator** [3]rector ~oris *m.* **ruler** [4]uniuersitas ~atis *f.* **the universe**

puerum tantum esse uoluisses. eram enim etiam tunc, uiuebam atque sentiebam meamque incolumitatem,[5] uestigium[6] secretissimae[7] unitatis[8] ex qua eram, curae habebam, custodiebam[9] interiore sensu integritatem[10] sensuum meorum inque ipsis paruis paruarumque rerum cogitationibus ueritate delectabar. falli nolebam, memoria uigebam,[11] locutione[12] instruebar,[13] amicitia[14] mulcebar,[15] fugiebam dolorem, abiectionem,[16] ignorantiam.[17]

> Quid in tali animante[18]
> non mirabile[19] atque laudabile?[20]
> at ista omnia Dei mei dona sunt.
> non mihi ego dedi haec,
> et bona sunt, et haec omnia ego.
> bonus ergo est qui fecit me, et ipse est bonum meum,
> et illi exulto[21] bonis omnibus
> quibus etiam puer eram.
> hoc enim peccabam,
> quod non in ipso sed in creaturis eius me atque ceteris
> uoluptates, sublimitates,[22] ueritates quaerebam,
> atque ita inruebam[23] in dolores, confusiones,[24] errores.
> gratias tibi, dulcedo[25] mea et honor meus et fiducia[26] mea,
> Deus meus, *gratias tibi de donis tuis* (1 Cor 9:15):
> sed tu mihi ea serua. ita enim seruabis me,
> et augebuntur[27] et perficientur quae dedisti mihi,
> et ero ipse tecum, quia et ut sim tu dedisti mihi.

[5]incolumitas ~atis *f.* **soundness** [6]uestigium ~ii *neut.* trace > **imprint** [7]secretus ~a, ~um *adj.* **hidden** [8]unitas ~atis *f.* **unity** [9]custodio ~ire, ~iui, ~itum **to keep safe** [10]integritas ~atis *f.* **wholeness** [11]uigeo ~ere, ~ui **to be vigorous** (mentally) [12]locutio ~onis *f.* **speech** [13]instruo ~ere, ~xi, ~ctum **to equip** [14]amicitia ~ae *f.* **friendship** [15]mulceo ~ere, mulsi, mulsum to soothe > **to affect in an agreeable way** [16]abiectio ~onis *f.* dejection; LATE **abjection** [17]ignorantia ~ae *f.* **ignorance** [18]animans ~ntis *m.* **living creature** [19]mirabilis ~is, ~e *adj.* **marvelous** [20]laudabilis ~is, ~e *adj.* **praiseworthy** [21]exulto ~are, ~aui **to exult** [22]sublimitas ~atis *f.* **sublimity** [23]inruo ~uere, ~ui **to run headlong** [24]confusio ~onis *f.* **confusion** [25]dulcedo ~inis *f.* **sweetness** [26]fiducia ~ae *f.* **confidence** [27]augeo ~gere, ~xi, ~ctum **to increase**

2

TOXIC FRIENDSHIPS

Home from Madauros (near M'daourouch, Algeria),

Nov. 369–Nov. 370

My disintegrated self

2.1.1 Recordari uolo transactas[1] foeditates[2] meas et carnales[3] corruptiones[4] animae meae, non quod eas amem, sed ut amem te, Deus meus. amore amoris tui[5] facio istuc,[6] recolens uias meas nequissimas[7] in amaritudine[8] recogitationis[9] meae, ut tu dulcescas[10] mihi, dulcedo[11] non fallax,[12] dulcedo felix et secura,[13] et *conligens me a dispersione,*[14] (Isa 11:12) in qua frustatim[15] discissus[16] sum dum ab uno te auersus[17] in multa euanui.[18] exarsi[19] enim aliquando satiari[20] inferis[21] in adulescentia,[22] et siluescere[23] ausus sum uariis[24] et umbrosis[25] amoribus, et contabuit[26] species mea, et computrui[27] coram oculis tuis placens mihi et placere cupiens oculis hominum.

---

[1]transigo ~igere, ~egi, ~actum **to spend time doing** [2]foeditas ~atis *f.* **foulness** [3]carnalis ~is, ~e *adj.* ECCL **carnal** [4]corruptio ~onis *f.* **corruption** [5]tuus ~a, ~um *adj.* or tu *pron.* [6]istic ~aec, ~uc *pron.* **this very thing** [7]nequam *adj.* **worthless** (morally) [8]amaritudo ~inis *f.* **bitterness** [9]recogitatio ~onis *f.* LATE **thinking over with regret** [10]dulcesco ~ere **to become sweet** [11]dulcedo ~inis *f.* **sweetness** [12]fallax ~acis *adj.* **deceitful** [13]securus ~a, ~um *adj.* **untroubled** [14]dispersio ~onis *f.* ECCL **dispersion** [15]frustatim *adv.* **in little pieces** [16]discindo ~ndere, ~di, ~ssum **to tear apart** [17]auersus ~a, ~um *adj.* **turned back** [18]euanesco ~escere, ~ui **to fade away** [19]exardesco ~descere, ~si **to burn** (with desire) [20]satio ~are, ~aui, ~atum **to gratify** (desires) [21]inferi ~orum *m. pl.* **the underworld;** ECCL **Hell** [22]adulescentia ~ae *f.* **young adulthood** (age 16–30) [23]siluesco ~ere **to grow wildly** (of plants) [24]uarius ~a, ~um *adj.* **various** [25]umbrosus ~a, ~um *adj.* **shadowy** [26]contabesco ~escere, ~ui **to waste away** [27]computresco ~escere, ~ui **to rot**

Fog of lust

2.2.2 Et quid erat quod me delectabat, nisi amare et amari? sed non tenebatur modus ab animo usque ad animum quatenus[1] est luminosus[2] limes[3] amicitiae,[4] sed exhalabantur[5] nebulae[6] de limosa[7] *concupiscentia*[8] *carnis* (1 Jn 2:16) et scatebra[9] pubertatis,[10] et obnubilabant[11] atque obfuscabant[12] cor meum, ut non discerneretur serenitas[13] dilectionis[14] a caligine[15] libidinis. utrumque in confuso[16] aestuabat[17] et rapiebat inbecillam[18] aetatem per abrupta[19] cupiditatum atque mersabat[20] gurgite[21] flagitiorum.[22] inualuerat[23] super me ira tua, et nesciebam. obsurdueram[24] stridore[25] catenae[26] mortalitatis[27] meae, poena superbiae[28] animae meae, et ibam longius a te et sinebas, et iactabar[29] et effundebar[30] et difflue-bam[31] et ebulliebam[32] per fornicationes[33] meas, et tacebas. o tardum[34] gaudium meum! tacebas tunc, et ego ibam porro[35] longe a te in plura et plura sterilia[36] semina[37] dolorum superba deiectione[38] et inquieta[39] lassitudine.[40]

[1]quatenus *adv.* **so far as** [2]luminosus ~a, ~um *adj.* **luminous** [3]limes ~itis *m.* **boundary** [4]amicitia ~ae *f.* **friendship** [5]exhalo, exal- ~are, ~aui, ~atum **to belch** [6]nebula ~ae *f.* **cloud** [7]limosus ~a, ~um *adj.* **muddy** [8]concupiscentia ~ae *f.* ECCL **concupiscence** [9]scatebra ~ae *f.* **bubbling spring** [10]pubertas ~atis *f.* **puberty** [11]obnubilo ~are, ~aui, ~atum **to overcloud** [12]obfusco ~are, ~aui, ~atum ECCL **to darken** [13]serenitas ~atis *f.* **clear sky** [14]dilectio ~onis *f.* ECCL **love** [15]caligo ~inis *f.* **smog** [16]confusus ~a, ~um *adj.* **confusion** (*neut. sg.* as noun) [17]aestuo ~are, ~aui, ~atum **to boil up** [18]inbecillus ~a, ~um *adj.* **feeble** [19]'per abrupta' **by rough, dangerous ways** [20]merso ~are, ~aui, ~atum **to submerge** [21]gurges ~itis *m.* **whirlpool** [22]flagitium ~ii *neut.* **indecency** (of sexual misconduct) [23]inualesco ~escere, ~ui **to grow in intensity** [24]obsurdesco ~escere, ~ui **to become deaf** [25]stridor ~oris *m.* **grating** [26]catena ~ae *f.* **fetters** [27]mortalitas ~atis *f.* **mortality** [28]superbia ~ae *f.* **pride** [29]iacto ~are, ~aui, ~atum **to toss about** [30]effundo ~undere, ~udi, ~usum **to pour out** [31]diffluo ~ere, ~xi, ~ctum **to melt away** [32]ebullio ~ire, ~ii or ~iui **to boil over** [33]fornicatio ~onis *f.* ornamental arch; ECCL **sexual sin** [34]tardus ~a, ~um *adj.* **tardy** [35]porro *adv.* **further** [36]sterilis ~is, ~e *adj.* **sterile** [37]semen ~inis *neut.* **seed** [38]deiectio ~onis *f.* **ejection**; LATE **dejectedness** [39]inquietus ~a, ~um *adj.* **restless** [40]lassitudo ~inis *f.* **weariness**; LATE **busyness**

Marriage: a cure?

2.2.3 Quis mihi modularetur[1] aerumnam[2] meam et nouissimarum[3] rerum fugaces[4] pulchritudines[5] in usum uerteret earumque suauitatibus[6] metas[7] praefigeret,[8] ut usque ad coniugale[9] litus exaestuarent[10] fluctus aetatis

[1]modulor ~ari, ~atus **to regulate**; LATE **to mitigate** [2]aerumna ~ae *f.* **distress** [3]nouissimus ~a, ~um *superl. adj.* **lowest** [4]fugax ~acis *adj.* **fleeting** [5]pulchritudo ~inis *f.* **beauty** [6]suauitas ~atis *f.* **charm** [7]meta ~ae *f.* **limit** [8]praefigo ~gere, ~xi, ~xum **to stick** [9]coniugalis ~is, ~e *adj.* **conjugal** [10]exaestuo ~are, ~aui, ~atum **to surge**

meae? si tranquillitas[11] in eis non poterat esse fine procreandorum[12] liberorum[13] contenta (sicut praescribit[14] lex tua, Domine, qui formas etiam propaginem[15] mortis nostrae, potens imponere lenem[16] manum ad temperamentum[17] spinarum[18] a paradiso[19] tuo seclusarum;[20] non enim longe est a nobis omnipotentia[21] tua, etiam cum longe sumus a te) — aut certe[22] sonitum[23] nubium[24] tuarum uigilantius[25] aduerterem:[26] *tribulationem[27] autem carnis habebunt huius modi;[28] ego autem uobis parco* (1 Cor 7:28); et *bonum est homini mulierem[29] non tangere[30]* (1 Cor 7:1); et *qui sine uxore[31] est, cogitat ea quae sunt Dei, quomodo placeat Deo; qui autem matrimonio[32] iunctus[33] est, cogitat ea quae sunt mundi, quomodo placeat uxori* (1 Cor 7:32–33). has ergo uoces exaudirem uigilantior, et abscisus[34] *propter regnum caelorum* (Mt 19:12) felicior expectarem amplexus[35] tuos.

[11]tranquillitas ~atis *f.* **tranquility** [12]procreo ~are, ~aui, ~atum **to procreate** [13]liberi ~orum *m. pl.* **children** [14]praescribo ~bere, ~psi, ~ptum **to prescribe** [15]propago ~inis *f.* **offspring** [16]lenis ~is, ~e *adj.* **gentle** [17]temperamentum ~i *neut.* **restraint** [18]spina ~ae *f.* **thorn** [19]paradisus ~i *m.* ECCL **paradise** (i.e., Garden of Eden) [20]secludo ~dere, ~si, ~sum **to shut out** [21]omnipotentia ~ae *f.* LATE **omnipotence** [22]'aut certe' **this much is certain** [23]sonitus ~us *m.* **voice** [24]nubes ~is *f.* **cloud** [25]uigilanter *adv.* **vigilantly** [26]aduerto ~tere, ~ti, ~sum to turn towards > **to pay attention** [27]tribulatio ~onis *f.* ECCL **trouble** [28]'huius modi' **(they) of this sort** (i.e., married people) [29]mulier ~eris *f.* **woman** [30]tango ~ere, tetigi, tactum **to touch** [31]uxor ~oris *f.* **wife** [32]matrimonium ~ii *neut.* **marriage** [33]iungo ~gere, ~xi, ~ctum **to join** [34]abscido ~dere, ~di, ~sum **to cut off**; ECCL **to castrate** [35]amplexus ~us *m.* **embrace**

God mercifully angry

2.2.4 Sed efferbui[1] miser, sequens impetum fluxus[2] mei relicto te, et excessi[3] omnia legitima[4] tua nec euasi[5] flagella[6] tua. quis enim hoc mortalium?[7] nam tu semper aderas misericorditer[8] saeuiens,[9] et amarissimis[10] aspergens[11] offensionibus[12] omnes inlicitas[13] iucunditates[14] meas, ut ita quaererem sine offensione iucundari,[15] et ubi hoc possem, non inuenirem quicquam praeter te, Domine, praeter te, *qui fingis[16]*

[1]efferuesco ~ere, efferbui **to boil over** [2]fluxus ~a, ~um *adj.* **dissolute** [3]excedo ~dere, ~ssi, ~ssum **to go beyond** [4]legitimus ~a, ~um *adj.* **lawful**; ECCL **laws** (*neut. pl.*) [5]euado ~dere, ~si, ~sum **to evade** [6]flagellum ~i *neut.* **whip** (fig.) [7]mortalis ~is *m.* **mortal** [8]misericorditer *adv.* **with pity** [9]saeuio ~ire, ~ii, ~itum **to vent one's rage** [10]amarus ~a, ~um *adj.* **bitter** [11]aspergo ~gere, ~si, ~sum **to sprinkle** [12]offensio ~onis *f.* **setback** > **disappointment** [13]inlicitus ~a, ~um *adj.* **illicit** [14]iucunditas ~atis *f.* **pleasure** [15]iucundo ~are, ~aui, ~atum ECCL **to gladden** [16]fingo ~ngere, ~nxi, ~ctum **to fashion**

dolorem in praecepto[17] (Ps 93:20 VL) et percutis[18] ut sanes et occidis[19] nos ne moriamur abs te. ubi eram? et quam longe exulabam[20] a deliciis[21] domus tuae anno illo sexto decimo[22] aetatis carnis meae, cum accepit in me sceptrum[23] (et totas manus ei dedi[24]) uesania[25] libidinis, licentiosae[26] per dedecus[27] humanum, inlicitae autem per leges tuas? non fuit cura meorum ruentem[28] excipere[29] me matrimonio,[30] sed cura fuit tantum ut discerem sermonem facere quam optimum et persuadere[31] dictione.[32]

[17]praeceptum ~i *neut.* **precept** [18]percutio ~tere, ~ssi, ~ssum **to strike forcibly** [19]occido ~dere, ~di, ~sum **to kill** [20]exulo ~are, ~aui, ~atum **to live in exile** [21]delicia ~ae *f.* **delights** [22]'sexto decimo' **sixteenth** [23]sceptrum ~i *neut.* **sceptre** (lit.); **control** (fig.) [24]'manus dedi' **I surrendered** [25]uesania ~ae *f.* **frenzy** [26]licentiosus ~a, ~um *adj.* **unrestrained** [27]dedecus ~oris *neut.* **shame** [28]ruo ~ere, ~i **to rush headlong** [29]excipio ~ipere, ~epi, ~eptum **to extract** > **to catch from falling** [30]matrimonium ~ii *neut.* **marriage** [31]persuadeo ~dere, ~si, ~sum **to persuade** [32]dictio ~onis *f.* **public speaking**

Studies interrupted

2.3.5 Et anno quidem illo intermissa[1] erant studia mea, dum mihi reducto[2] a Madauris, in qua uicina[3] urbe iam coeperam litteraturae[4] atque oratoriae[5] percipiendae[6] gratia peregrinari,[7] longinquioris[8] apud Carthaginem peregrinationis[9] sumptus[10] praeparabantur[11] animositate[12] magis quam opibus patris, municipis[13] Thagastensis admodum[14] tenuis.[15] cui narro haec? neque enim tibi, Deus meus, sed apud te narro haec generi meo, generi humano, quantulacumque[16] ex particula[17] incidere[18] potest in istas meas litteras. et ut quid hoc?[19] ut uidelicet[20] ego et quisquis haec legit cogitemus *de* quam *profundo*[21] *clamandum sit ad te* (Ps 129:1). et quid propius[22] auribus tuis, si cor confitens et uita ex fide est?

Quis enim non extollebat[23] laudibus tunc hominem, patrem meum, quod ultra[24] uires rei familiaris[25] suae impenderet[26] filio quidquid etiam

[1]intermitto ~ittere, ~isi, ~issum **to interrupt** [2]reduco ~cere, ~xi, ~ctum **to bring home** [3]uicinus ~a, ~um *adj.* **neighboring** [4]litteratura ~ae *f.* **literature** [5]oratoria ~ae *f.* **oratory** [6]percipio ~ipere, ~epi, ~eptum **to acquire** [7]peregrinor ~ari, ~atus **to be away from home** [8]longinquus ~a, ~um *adj.* **prolonged** [9]peregrinatio ~onis *f.* **living away from home** [10]sumptus ~us *m.* **resources** (to cover an expense) [11]praeparo ~are, ~aui, ~atum **to prepare beforehand** [12]animositas ~tatis *f.* animosity; LATE **enthusiasm** [13]municeps ~ipis *m.* **citizen of a town** [14]admodum *adv.* **rather** [15]tenuis ~is, ~e *adj.* **of limited resources** [16]quantuluscumque ~a-, ~um- *adj.* **however few** [17]particula ~ae *f.* **little part** [18]incido ~ere, ~i **to come by chance** [19]'ut quid hoc' ECCL = 'quid hoc' **why (do I write) this?** [20]uidelicet *adv.* **no doubt** [21]profundum ~i *neut.* **depths** [22]propior ~ior, ~ius *compar. adj.* **nearer** [23]extollo ~ere **to praise** (w. 'laudibus') [24]ultra *prep. acc.* **beyond** [25]'rei familiaris' **household finances** [26]impendo ~dere, ~di, ~sum **to spend**

longe peregrinanti studiorum causa opus esset? multorum enim ciuium longe opulentiorum[27] nullum tale negotium[28] pro liberis[29] erat, cum interea[30] non satageret[31] idem pater qualis crescerem tibi aut quam castus[32] essem, dummodo[33] essem disertus,[34] uel desertus potius a cultura[35] tua, Deus, qui es unus uerus et bonus dominus agri tui, cordis mei.

[27]opulentus ~a, ~um *adj.* **wealthy** [28]negotium ~ii *neut.* **pains** [29]liberi ~orum *m. pl.* **children** [30]interea *adv.* **meanwhile** [31]satago ~agere, ~egi, ~actum **to be anxious for** [32]castus ~a, ~um *adj.* **chaste** [33]dummodo *conj.* **so long as** [34]disertus ~a, ~um *adj.* **skilled in speaking** [35]cultura ~ae *f.* **cultivation**

Enforced leisure

2.3.6 Sed ubi sexto illo et decimo[1] anno, interposito[2] otio[3] ex necessitate[4] domestica,[5] feriatus[6] ab omni schola[7] cum parentibus esse coepi, excesserunt[8] caput meum uepres[9] libidinum, et nulla erat eradicans[10] manus. quin immo[11] ubi me ille pater in balneis[12] uidit pubescentem[13] et inquieta[14] indutum[15] adulescentia,[16] quasi iam ex hoc in nepotes[17] gestiret,[18] gaudens matri indicauit, gaudens uinulentia[19] in qua te iste mundus *oblitus est creatorem suum et creaturam tuam pro te amauit* (Rom 1:25), de uino[20] inuisibili peruersae[21] atque inclinatae[22] in ima[23] uoluntatis suae. sed matris in pectore iam inchoaueras[24] *templum tuum* (1 Cor 3:16) et exordium[25] *sanctae habitationis*[26] *tuae* (Sir 24:14), nam ille adhuc catechumenus[27] et hoc recens[28] erat. itaque illa exiliuit[29] pia trepidatione[30] ac tremore[31] et, quamuis mihi nondum fideli, timuit tamen uias distortas[32] in quibus ambulant[33] qui ponunt *ad te tergum et non faciem* (Jer 2:27).

[1]'sexto et decimo' **sixteenth** [2]interpono ~ponere, ~posui, ~positum **to interpose** [3]otium ~ii *neut.* **leisure** [4]necessitas ~atis *f.* **difficulty** (financial) [5]domesticus ~a, ~um *adj.* **family** [6]feriatus ~a, ~um *adj.* **on holiday** [7]schola ~ae *f.* **school** [8]excedo ~dere, ~ssi, ~ssum **to grow thickly over** [9]uepris ~is *m.* **thorn bush** [10]eradico ~are, ~aui, ~atum **to tear up by the roots** [11]'quin immo' **and furthermore** [12]balneum ~i *neut.* **public bath house** [13]pubesco ~ere **to reach puberty** [14]inquietus ~a, ~um *adj.* **restless** [15]induo ~uere, ~ui, ~utum **to clothe** [16]adulescentia ~ae *f.* **young adulthood** (age 16–30) [17]nepos ~otis *m.* **grandson** [18]gestio ~ire, ~iui or ~ii **to eagerly expect** [19]uinulentia ~ae *f.* **excessive drinking** [20]uinum ~i *neut.* **wine** [21]peruersus ~a, ~um *adj.* **perverse** [22]inclino ~are, ~aui, ~atum **to sink** [23]imus ~a, ~um *adj.* **lowest things** (*neut.* as noun) [24]inchoo ~are, ~aui, ~atum **to start work on** [25]exordium ~i *neut.* **beginning** [26]habitatio ~onis *f.* **habitation** [27]catechumenus ~i *m.* ECCL **catechumen** [28]recens ~ntis *adj.* **recent** [29]exilio ~ire, ~ui **to move excitedly (from fear)** [30]trepidatio ~onis *f.* **trepidation** [31]tremor ~oris *m.* **trembling** [32]distortus ~a, ~um *adj.* **twisted** [33]ambulo ~are, ~aui, ~atum **to walk**

Abandoned youths

2.3.7 Ei mihi![1] et audeo dicere tacuisse te, Deus meus, cum irem abs te longius? itane tu tacebas tunc mihi? et cuius erant nisi tua uerba illa per matrem meam, fidelem tuam, quae cantasti in aures meas? nec inde quicquam descendit[2] in cor, ut facerem illud. uolebat enim illa, et secreto[3] memini ut monuerit[4] cum sollicitudine[5] ingenti,[6] ne fornicarer[7] maximeque ne adulterarem[8] cuiusquam uxorem.[9] qui mihi monitus[10] muliebres[11] uidebantur, quibus obtemperare[12] erubescerem.[13] illi autem tui erant et nesciebam, et te tacere putabam atque illam loqui per quam mihi tu non tacebas, et in illa contemnebaris[14] a me, a me, filio eius, *filio ancillae*[15] *tuae, seruo tuo* (Ps 115:16). sed nesciebam et praeceps[16] ibam tanta caecitate[17] ut inter coaetaneos[18] meos puderet[19] me minoris dedecoris,[20] quoniam audiebam eos iactantes[21] flagitia[22] sua et tanto gloriantes[23] magis, quanto magis turpes essent, et libebat[24] facere non solum libidine facti uerum etiam laudis. quid dignum est uituperatione[25] nisi uitium? ego, ne uituperarer,[26] uitiosior[27] fiebam, et ubi non suberat[28] quo admisso[29] aequarer[30] perditis,[31] fingebam[32] me fecisse quod non feceram, ne uiderer abiectior[33] quo eram innocentior,[34] et ne uilior[35] haberer quo eram castior.[36]

---

[1]'ei mihi' **ah me!** (expr. anguish) [2]descendo ~dere, ~di, ~sum **to go down** [3]secreto *adv.* **in private** [4]moneo ~ere, ~ui, ~itum **to warn** [5]sollicitudo ~inis *f.* **anxiety** [6]ingens ~ntis *adj.* **intense** [7]fornicor ~ari, ~atus ECCL **to sin sexually** [8]adultero ~are, ~aui, ~atum **to commit adultery** [9]uxor ~oris *f.* **wife** [10]monitus ~us *m.* **advice** [11]muliebris ~is, ~e *adj.* **womanly** [12]obtempero ~are, ~aui, ~atum **to obey** (w. dat.) [13]erubesco ~escere, ~ui **to feel ashamed** [14]contemno ~nere, ~psi, ~ptum **to show contempt** [15]ancilla ~ae *f.* **handmaid** [16]praeceps *adv.* **plunging headlong** [17]caecitas ~atis *f.* **blindness** [18]coaetaneus ~i *m.* **one of the same age** [19]pudeo ~ere, ~ui **to make ashamed** [20]dedecor ~ris *adj.* **disgraceful** [21]iacto ~are, ~aui, ~atum **to brag** [22]flagitium ~ii *neut.* **indecency (of sexual misconduct)** [23]glorior ~ari, ~atus **to boast** [24]libet ~ere, ~uit or ~itum est *impers.* **it is pleasing** [25]uituperatio ~onis *f.* **censure** [26]uitupero ~are, ~aui, ~atum **to censure** [27]uitiosus ~a, ~um *adj.* **depraved** [28]subsum ~esse, suffui **to be under > to have a basis** [29]admitto ~ittere, ~isi, ~issum **to admit to** [30]aequo ~are, ~aui, ~atum **to be equal to** [31]perditus ~a, ~um *adj.* **abandoned person (as noun)** [32]fingo ~ngere, ~nxi, ~ctum **to make > to fabricate** (a story) [33]abiectus ~a, ~um *adj.* **unimportant** [34]innocens ~ntis *adj.* **innocent** [35]uilis ~is, ~e *adj.* **contemptible** [36]castus ~a, ~um *adj.* **chaste**

Streets of Babylon

2.3.8 Ecce cum quibus comitibus iter agebam platearum[1] Babyloniae, et uolutabar[2] in caeno[3] eius tamquam in cinnamis[4] et unguentis[5] pretiosis.[6] et in umbilico[7] eius quo tenacius[8] haererem,[9] calcabat[10] me inimicus inuisibilis et seducebat[11] me, quia ego seductilis[12] eram. non enim et illa quae iam *de medio*[13] *Babylonis fugerat* (Jer 51:6), sed ibat in ceteris eius tardior,[14] mater carnis meae, sicut monuit[15] me pudicitiam,[16] ita curauit quod de me a uiro suo audierat, iamque pestilentiosum[17] et in posterum[18] periculosum[19] sentiebat cohercere[20] termino[21] coniugalis[22] affectus, si resecari[23] ad uiuum non poterat. non curauit hoc, quia metus erat ne impediretur[24] spes mea compede[25] uxoria,[26] non spes illa quam in te futuri saeculi habebat mater, sed spes litterarum, quas ut nossem nimis uolebat parens uterque, ille quia de te prope nihil cogitabat, de me autem inania,[27] illa autem quia non solum nullo detrimento[28] sed etiam nonnullo[29] adiumento[30] ad te adipiscendum[31] futura existimabat[32] usitata[33] illa studia doctrinae. ita enim conicio,[34] recolens ut possum mores parentum meorum.

Relaxabantur[35] etiam mihi ad ludendum[36] habenae[37] ultra[38] temperamentum[39] seueritatis[40] in dissolutionem[41] affectionum[42] uariarum,[43] et in omnibus erat caligo[44] intercludens[45] mihi, Deus meus, serenitatem[46] ueritatis tuae, *et prodiebat*[47] *tamquam ex adipe*[48] *iniquitas mea* (Ps 72:7).

[1]platea ~ae *f.* **street** [2]uoluto ~are, ~aui, ~atum **to roll** (pass. in middle sense) [3]caenum ~i *neut.* **filth** [4]cinnamum ~i *neut.* **cinnamon** [5]unguentum ~i *neut.* **ointment** [6]pretiosus ~a, ~um *adj.* **precious** [7]umbilicus ~i *m.* (city) **center** [8]tenaciter *adv.* **tenaciously** [9]haereo ~rere, ~si, ~sum **to stick** [10]calco ~are, ~aui, ~atum **to trample** [11]seduco ~cere, ~xi, ~ctum to draw aside; ECCL **to seduce** [12]seductilis ~is, ~e *adj.* AUG **easily seduced** [13]medium ~ii *neut.* **center** [14]tardus ~a, ~um *adj.* **slow** [15]moneo ~ere, ~ui, ~itum **to urge** [16]pudicitia ~ae *f.* **sexual purity** [17]pestilentiosus ~a, ~um *adj.* **diseased** [18]'in posterum' **for the future** [19]periculosus ~a, ~um *adj.* **dangerous** [20]coherceo ~ere, ~ui, ~itum **to restrain** [21]terminus ~i *m.* **limit** [22]coniugalis ~is, ~e *adj.* **conjugal** [23]reseco ~care, ~ctum **to prune back** [24]impedio ~ire, ~iui, ~itum **to hinder** [25]compes ~edis *f.* **fetters** [26]uxorius ~a, ~um *adj.* **wifely** [27]inane ~is *neut.* **vanities** [28]detrimentum ~i *neut.* **detriment** [29]nonnullus ~a, ~um *adj.* **not a little** [30]adiumentum ~i *neut.* **inducement** [31]adipiscor ~ipisci, ~eptus **to reach** [32]existimo ~are, ~aui, ~atum **to think** [33]usitatus ~a, ~um *adj.* **usual** [34]conicio ~icere, ~ieci, ~iectum to put together > **to conjecture** [35]relaxo ~are, ~aui, ~atum **to relax** [36]ludo ~dere, ~si, ~sum **to play (amorously)** [37]habena ~ae *f.* **rein** [38]ultra *prep. acc.* **beyond** [39]temperamentum ~i *neut.* **moderation** [40]seueritas ~atis *f.* **severity** [41]dissolutio ~onis *f.* **dissolution** [42]affectio ~onis *f.* **affection** [43]uarius ~a, ~um *adj.* **various** [44]caligo ~inis *f.* **smog** [45]intercludo ~dere, ~si, ~sum **to cut off from** [46]serenitas ~atis *f.* **clear sky** [47]prodeo ~ire, ~ii, ~itum **to come forth** [48]adips ~ipis *m. f.* **fat**

Robbing the pear tree

2.4.9 *Furtum*[1] *certe punit*[2] *lex tua* (Ex 20:15), Domine, et *lex scripta in cordibus hominum* (Rom 2:15), quam ne ipsa quidem delet[3] iniquitas. quis enim fur[4] aequo[5] animo furem patitur? nec copiosus[6] adactum[7] inopia.[8] et ego furtum facere uolui et feci, nulla compulsus[9] egestate[10] nisi penuria[11] et fastidio[12] iustitiae et sagina[13] iniquitatis. nam id furatus[14] sum quod mihi abundabat[15] et multo melius, nec ea re uolebam frui[16] quam furto appetebam,[17] sed ipso furto et peccato.

Arbor erat pirus[18] in uicinia[19] nostrae uineae[20] pomis[21] onusta[22] nec forma nec sapore[23] inlecebrosis.[24] ad hanc excutiendam[25] atque asportandam[26] nequissimi[27] adulescentuli[28] perreximus[29] nocte intempesta[30] (quousque[31] ludum[32] de pestilentiae[33] more in areis[34] produxeramus[35]) et abstulimus inde onera[36] ingentia,[37] non ad nostras epulas[38] sed uel proicienda[39] porcis,[40] etiamsi aliquid inde comedimus,[41] dum tamen fieret a nobis quod eo[42] liberet[43] quo non liceret.

Ecce cor meum, Deus, ecce cor meum, quod miseratus es in imo[44] abyssi. dicat tibi nunc, ecce cor meum, quid ibi quaerebat, ut essem gratis malus et malitiae[45] meae causa nulla esset nisi malitia. foeda[46] erat, et amaui eam. amaui perire, amaui defectum[47] meum, non illud ad quod deficiebam,[48] sed defectum meum ipsum amaui, turpis anima et dissiliens[49] a firmamento tuo *in exterminium*[50] (Sir 39:36), non dedecore[51] aliquid, sed dedecus appetens.

---

[1]furtum ~i *neut.* **theft** [2]punior, poenior ~iri, ~itus. **to punish** [3]deleo ~ere, ~eui, ~etum **to erase** [4]fur ~ris *m.* **thief** [5]aequus ~a, ~um *adj.* **calm** (of the mind) [6]copiosus ~a, ~um *adj.* **rich** [7]adigo ~igere, ~egi, ~actum **to force** [8]inopia ~ae *f.* **poverty** [9]compello ~ellere, ~uli, ~ulsum **to compel** [10]egestas ~atis *f.* **extreme poverty** [11]penuria ~ae *f.* **deficiency** (of an abstract thing) [12]fastidium ~ii *neut.* **aversion** [13]sagina ~ae *f.* **getting fat** [14]furor ~ari, ~atus **to steal** [15]abundo ~are, ~aui, ~atum **to be abundant** [16]fruor ~i, ~ctus **to enjoy** [17]appeto ~ere, ~iui or ~ii, ~itum **to seek** (to do something) [18]pirus ~i *f.* **pear** (tree) [19]uicinia ~ae *f.* **vicinity** [20]uinea ~ae *f.* **vineyard** [21]pomum ~i *neut.* **fruit** (from an orchard) [22]onustus ~a, ~um *adj.* **weighed down** [23]sapor ~oris *m.* **flavor** [24]inlecebrosus ~a, ~um *adj.* **enticing** [25]excutio ~tere, ~ssi, ~ssum **to shake off** [26]asporto ~are, ~aui, ~atum **to carry off** [27]nequam *adj.* **worthless** [28]adulescentulus ~i *m.* **young man** [29]pergo ~gere, ~rexi, ~rectum **to set off** [30]'nocte intempesta' **in the dead of night** [31]quousque *adv.* **up till then** [32]ludus ~i *m.* **game** [33]pestilentia ~ae *f.* **disease** [34]area ~ae *f.* **playground** [35]produco ~cere, ~xi, ~ctum **to prolong** [36]onus ~eris *neut.* **load** [37]ingens ~ntis *adj.* **enormous** [38]epulae ~arum *f. pl.* **feast** [39]proicio ~icere, ~ieci, ~iectum **to throw away** [40]porcus ~i *m.* **pig** [41]comedo ~edere, ~edi, ~esum **to eat** [42]eo... quo' **for the reason that** [43]libet ~ere, ~uit or ~itum est *impers.* **it is pleasing** [44]imus ~a, ~um *adj.* **bottom of** (as noun) [45]malitia ~ae *f.* **malicious act/malice** [46]foedus ~a, ~um *adj.* **foul** [47]defectus ~us *m.* **defect** (of character) [48]deficio ~icere, ~eci, ~ectum **to fall** [49]dissilio ~ire, ~ui **to fly apart**; LATE **to leap down** [50]exterminium ~i *neut.* ECCL **destruction** [51]dedecus ~oris *neut.* **disgrace**

Sin enters through the lowest goods

2.5.10 Etenim[1] species est pulchris corporibus et auro et argento[2] et omnibus, et in contactu[3] carnis congruentia[4] ualet plurimum,[5] ceterisque sensibus est sua cuique adcommodata[6] modificatio[7] corporum. habet etiam honor temporalis[8] et imperitandi[9] atque superandi[10] potentia[11] suum decus,[12] unde etiam uindictae[13] auiditas[14] oritur,[15] et tamen in cuncta haec adipiscenda[16] non est egrediendum[17] abs te, Domine, neque deuiandum[18] a lege tua. et uita quam hic[19] uiuimus habet inlecebram[20] suam propter quendam modum decoris[21] sui et conuenientiam[22] cum his omnibus infimis[23] pulchris. amicitia[24] quoque hominum caro[25] nodo[26] dulcis est propter unitatem[27] de multis animis. propter uniuersa haec atque huius modi[28] peccatum admittatur,[29] dum immoderata[30] in ista inclinatione,[31] cum extrema bona sint, meliora et summa deseruntur, tu, Domine Deus noster, et ueritas tua, et lex tua. habent enim et haec ima[32] delectationes,[33] sed non sicut Deus meus, qui fecit omnia, quia in ipso delectatur iustus, et ipse est deliciae[34] *rectorum*[35] *corde* (Ps 63:11).

[1]etenim *conj.* **for** [2]argentum ~i *neut.* **silver** [3]contactus ~us *m.* **sense of touch** [4]congruentia ~ae *f.* **connection** [5]plurimum *adv.* **most of all** [6]adcommodatus ~a, ~um *adj.* **appropriate** [7]modificatio ~onis *f.* **mode of operation** [8]temporalis ~is, ~e *adj.* **temporal** [9]imperito ~are, ~aui, ~atum **to be in charge** [10]supero ~are, ~aui, ~atum **to be superior** [11]potentia ~ae *f.* **power** [12]decus ~oris *neut.* **honor** [13]uindicta ~ae *f.* **vengeance** [14]auiditas ~atis *f.* **inordinate desire** [15]orior ~iri, ~tus **to arise** [16]adipiscor ~ipisci, ~eptus **to acquire** [17]egredior ~edi, ~essus **to depart** [18]deuio ~are, ~aui, ~atum LATE **to deviate** [19]hic *adv.* **here** [20]inlecebra ~ae *f.* **enticement** [21]decor ~oris *m.* **beauty** [22]conuenientia ~ae *f.* **harmony** [23]infimus ~a, ~um *superl. adj.* **lowest** (in order) [24]amicitia ~ae *f.* **friendship** [25]carus ~a, ~um *adj.* **affectionate** [26]nodus ~i *m.* **knot** (fig. for bond of friendship) [27]unitas ~atis *f.* **unity** [28]'huius modi' **of this kind** [29]admitto ~ittere, ~isi, ~issum **to allow to enter** [30]immoderatus ~a, ~um *adj.* **immoderate** [31]inclinatio ~onis *f.* **inclination** [32]imus ~a, ~um *adj.* **lowest** (in order) [33]delectatio ~onis *f.* **source of delight** [34]delicia ~ae *f.* **delight** [35]rectus ~a, ~um *adj.* **upright**

Catiline: evil a means to an end

2.5.11 Cum itaque de facinore[1] quaeritur qua causa factum sit, credi non solet, nisi cum appetitus[2] adipiscendi[3] alicuius illorum bonorum quae "infima"[4] diximus esse potuisse apparuerit aut metus amittendi. pulchra sunt enim et decora,[5] quamquam prae bonis superioribus[6] et

[1]facinus ~oris *neut.* **deed** > **crime** [2]appetitus ~us *m.* **appetite** [3]adipiscor ~ipisci, ~eptus **to gain** [4]infimus ~a, ~um *superl. adj.* **lowest** (in order) [5]decorus ~a, ~um *adj.* **fair** (in appearance) [6]superior ~or, ~us *compar. adj.* **higher** (in order)

beatificis[7] abiecta[8] et iacentia. Homicidium[9] fecit. cur fecit? adamauit[10] eius coniugem aut praedium,[11] aut uoluit depraedari[12] unde uiueret, aut timuit ab illo tale aliquid amittere, aut laesus[13] ulcisci[14] se exarsit.[15] num[16] homicidium sine causa faceret ipso homicidio delectatus? quis crediderit? nam et de quo dictum est, uaecordi[17] et nimis crudeli[18] homine, quod *gratuito*[19] *potius*[20] *malus atque crudelis erat* (Cat. 16.3), praedicta[21] est tamen causa: *Ne per otium,*[22] inquit, *torpesceret*[23] *manus aut animus* (Cat. 16.3). quaere id quoque: "Cur ita?" ut scilicet[24] illa exercitatione[25] scelerum[26] capta urbe honores, imperia, diuitias[27] adsequeretur[28] et careret[29] metu legum et difficultate[30] rerum propter *inopiam*[31] *rei familiaris*[32] *et conscientiam*[33] *scelerum* (Cat. 5.7). nec ipse igitur Catilina amauit facinora sua, sed utique aliud cuius causa illa faciebat.

[7]beatificus ~a, ~um *adj.* **beatific** [8]abiectus ~a, ~um *adj.* **abject** [9]homicidium ~ii *neut.* **homicide** [10]adamo ~are, ~aui, ~atum to come to love > **to covet** [11]praedium ~ii *neut.* **estate** [12]depraedor ~ari **to pillage** [13]laedo ~dere, ~si, ~sum **to wrong** [14]ulciscor ~cisci, ~tus **to revenge oneself** (w. refl.) [15]exardesco ~descere, ~si (~sum) **to blaze** (with desire) [16]num *particle (expects a negative answer)* **can it be possible that..?** (rhet. qu.) [17]uaecors uaecordis *adj.* **demented** [18]crudelis ~is, ~e *adj.* **cruel** [19]gratuito *adv.* **gratuitously** [20]potius *adv.* **more gladly** [21]praedico ~cere, ~xi, ~ctum **to state earlier** (in the text) [22]otium ~ii *neut.* **idleness** [23]torpesco ~escere, ~ui **to become lethargic** [24]scilicet *adv.* **evidently** [25]exercitatio ~onis *f.* exercise > **proficiency** [26]scelus ~eris *neut.* **villainous crime** [27]diuitiae ~arum *f. pl.* **riches** [28]adsequor ~qui, ~cutus **to win** [29]careo ~ere, ~ui, ~itum **to be free from** [30]difficultas ~atis *f.* **difficulty** [31]inopia ~ae *f.* **lack** [32]rei familiaris' **personal fortune** [33]conscientia ~ae *f.* **guilty conscience**

The condiment was crime

2.6.12 Quid ego miser in te amaui, o furtum[1] meum, o facinus[2] illud meum nocturnum[3] sexti decimi[4] anni aetatis meae? non enim pulchrum eras, cum furtum esses. aut uero aliquid es, ut loquar ad te?

Pulchra erant poma[5] illa quae furati[6] sumus, quoniam creatura tua erat, pulcherrime omnium, *creator omnium* (Hymn 2.1), Deus bone, Deus summum bonum et bonum uerum meum. pulchra erant illa poma, sed non ipsa concupiuit[7] anima mea miserabilis.[8] erat mihi enim meliorum copia, illa autem decerpsi[9] tantum ut furarer. nam decerpta

[1]furtum ~i *neut.* **theft** [2]facinus ~oris *neut.* deed > **crime** [3]nocturnus ~a, ~um *adj.* **nocturnal** [4]'sexti decimi' **sixteenth** [5]pomum ~i *neut.* **fruit** (from an orchard) [6]furor ~ari, ~atus **to steal** [7]concupisco ~iscere, ~iui, ~itum **to desire ardently** [8]miserabilis ~is, ~e *adj.* **miserable** [9]decerpo ~ere, ~si, ~tum **to pluck**

proieci,[10] epulatus[11] inde solam iniquitatem qua laetabar[12] fruens.[13] nam et si quid illorum pomorum intrauit in os meum, condimentum[14] ibi facinus erat. et nunc, Domine Deus meus, quaero quid me in furto delectauerit, et ecce species nulla est: non dico sicut in aequitate[15] atque prudentia,[16] sed neque sicut in mente hominis atque memoria et sensibus et uegetante[17] uita, neque sicut speciosa[18] sunt sidera et decora[19] locis suis et terra et mare plena fetibus,[20] qui succedunt[21] nascendo decedentibus[22] — non saltem[23] ut est quaedam defectiua[24] species et umbratica[25] uitiis fallentibus.

[10]proicio ~icere, ~ieci, ~iectum **to throw away** [11]epulor ~ari, ~atus **to feast** [12]laetor ~ari, ~atus **to be glad** [13]fruor ~i, ~ctus **to enjoy** [14]condimentum ~i *neut.* condiment [15]aequitas ~atis *f.* **equity** [16]prudentia ~ae *f.* **prudence** [17]uegeto ~are **to invigorate** [18]speciosus ~a, ~um *adj.* **brilliant** [19]decorus ~a, ~um, ~issimus *adj.* **glorious** [20]fetus ~us *m.* **embryonic life** [21]succedo ~dere, ~ssi, ~ssum **to replace** (w. dat.) [22]decedo ~dere, ~ssi, ~ssum **to pass away** [23]saltem *adv.* **even** [24]defectiuus ~a, ~um *adj.* LATE **defective** [25]umbraticus ~a, ~um *adj.* living in the shade; LATE **shadowy** (unreal)

Vice is defective virtue

2.6.13 Nam et superbia[1] celsitudinem[2] imitatur,[3] cum tu sis unus super omnia *Deus excelsus*[4] (Ps 77:35). et ambitio[5] quid nisi honores quaerit et gloriam, cum tu sis prae cunctis honorandus[6] unus et gloriosus[7] in aeternum? et saeuitia[8] potestatum timeri uult: quis autem timendus nisi unus Deus, cuius potestati eripi aut subtrahi[9] quid potest, quando aut ubi aut quo uel a quo potest? et blanditiae[10] lasciuientium[11] amari uolunt: sed neque blandius[12] est aliquid tua caritate nec amatur quicquam salubrius[13] quam illa prae cunctis formosa[14] et luminosa[15] ueritas tua. et curiositas[16] affectare[17] uidetur studium scientiae, cum tu omnia summe[18] noueris. Ignorantia[19] quoque ipsa atque stultitia[20] simplicitatis[21] et innocentiae[22] nomine tegitur, quia te simplicius[23] quicquam non

[1]superbia ~ae *f.* **pride** [2]celsitudo ~inis *f.* height; LATE **loftiness** [3]imitor ~ari, ~atus **to imitate** [4]excelsus ~a, ~um *adj.* **highly elevated** [5]ambitio ~onis *f.* **ambition** [6]honoro ~are, ~aui, ~atum **to honor** [7]gloriosus ~a, ~um *adj.* **glorious** [8]saeuitia ~ae *f.* **cruelty** [9]subtraho ~here, ~xi, ~ctum **to drag off** [10]blanditia ~ae *f.* **flirtation** [11]lasciuio ~ire, ~ii, ~itum **to be wanton** [12]blandus ~a, ~um *adj.* **attractive** [13]salubriter *adv.* **salubriously** [14]formosus ~a, ~um *adj.* **beautiful** [15]luminosus ~a, ~um *adj.* **luminous** [16]curiositas ~atis *f.* **curiosity** (usu. in a bad sense) [17]affecto ~are, ~aui, ~atum **to affect or feign** [18]summe *adv.* **in the highest degree** [19]ignorantia ~ae *f.* **ignorance** [20]stultitia ~ae *f.* **stupidity** [21]simplicitas ~atis *f.* **simplicity** [22]innocentia ~ae *f.* **innocence** [23]simplex ~icis *adj.* **simple**

reperitur.[24] quid te autem innocentius,[25] quandoquidem[26] opera sua malis inimica sunt? et ignauia[27] quasi quietem[28] appetit:[29] quae uero quies certa praeter Dominum? luxuria[30] satietatem[31] atque abundantiam[32] se cupit uocari: tu es autem plenitudo[33] et indeficiens[34] copia incorruptibilis[35] suauitatis.[36] effusio[37] liberalitatis[38] obtendit[39] umbram: sed bonorum omnium largitor[40] affluentissimus[41] tu es. auaritia[42] multa possidere[43] uult: et tu possides omnia. Inuidentia[44] de excellentia[45] litigat:[46] quid te excellentius?[47] ira uindictam[48] quaerit: te iustius[49] quis uindicat?[50] timor[51] insolita[52] et repentina[53] exhorrescit[54] rebus quae amantur aduersantia,[55] dum praecauet[56] securitati:[57] tibi enim quid insolitum? quid repentinum? aut quis a te separat[58] quod diligis? aut ubi nisi apud te firma[59] securitas? tristitia[60] rebus amissis contabescit[61] quibus se oblectabat[62] cupiditas, quia ita sibi nollet, sicut tibi auferri nihil potest.

[24]reperio ~ire, repperi, ~tum **to discover** [25]innocens ~ntis *adj.* **innocent** [26]quandoquidem *adv.* **inasmuch as** [27]ignauia ~ae *f.* **idleness** [28]quies ~etis *f.* **rest** [29]appeto ~ere, ~iui or ~ii, ~itum **to try to imitate** [30]luxuria ~ae *f.* **luxury** [31]satietas ~atis *f.* **satiety** [32]abundantia ~ae *f.* **abundance** [33]plenitudo ~inis *f.* **plenitude** [34]indeficiens ~ntis *adj.* ECCL **unfailing** [35]incorruptibilis ~is, ~e *adj.* ECCL **incorruptible** [36]suauitas ~atis *f.* **sweetness** [37]effusio ~onis *f.* **lavish expenditure** [38]liberalitas ~atis *f.* **liberality** [39]obtendo ~dere, ~di, ~tum **to cover over** [40]largitor ~oris *m.* **bestower** [41]affluens ~ntis, ~ntior *adj.* **affluent** [42]auaritia ~ae *f.* **avarice** [43]possideo ~idere, ~edi, ~essum **to possess** [44]inuidentia ~ae *f.* **envy** [45]excellentia ~ae *f.* **excellence** (as superiority) [46]litigo ~are, ~aui, ~atum **to dispute** [47]excellens ~ntis *adj.* **excellent** [48]uindicta ~ae *f.* **vengenance** [49]iuste *adv.* **justly** [50]uindico ~are, ~aui, ~atum **to avenge** [51]timor ~oris *m.* **fear** [52]insolitus ~a, ~um *adj.* **unfamiliar** [53]repentinus ~a, ~um *adj.* **sudden** [54]exhorresco ~escere, ~ui **to shudder** [55]aduersor ~ari, ~atus **to have an adverse effect upon** (w. dat.) [56]praecaueo ~auere, ~aui, ~autum **to take precaution** [57]securitas ~atis *f.* **safety** [58]separo ~are, ~aui, ~atum **to separate** [59]firmus ~a, ~um *adj.* **firm** [60]tristitia ~ae *f.* **despondency** [61]contabesco ~escere, ~ui **to waste away** [62]oblecto ~are, ~aui, ~atum **to amuse**

What did I love in the theft?

2.6.14 Ita *fornicatur*[1] anima, cum auertitur[2] *abs te* (Ps 72:27) et quaerit extra[3] te ea quae pura[4] et liquida[5] non inuenit, nisi cum redit ad te. peruerse[6] te imitantur[7] omnes qui longe se a te faciunt et extollunt[8] se aduersum te. sed etiam sic te imitando indicant creatorem te esse omnis naturae, et ideo non esse quo a te omni modo recedatur.

[1]fornicor ~ari, ~atus ECCL **to commit adultery/idolatry** [2]auerto ~tere, ~ti, ~sum **to turn away** [3]extra *prep. acc.* **outside** [4]purus ~a, ~um *adj.* **pure** [5]liquidus ~a, ~um *adj.* **clear** [6]peruerse *adv.* **perversely** [7]imitor ~ari, ~atus **to imitate** [8]extollo ~ere **to raise up** (refl.)

Quid ergo in illo furto[9] ego dilexi, et in quo Dominum meum uel uitiose[10] atque peruerse imitatus sum? an libuit[11] facere contra legem saltem[12] fallacia,[13] quia potentatu[14] non poteram ut mancam[15] libertatem captiuus[16] imitarer, faciendo impune[17] quod non liceret tenebrosa[18] omnipotentiae[19] similitudine?[20] ecce est ille *seruus fugiens Dominum suum et consecutus*[21] *umbram* (Gen 3:8–10). o putredo,[22] o monstrum[23] uitae et mortis profunditas![24] potuitne libere quod non licebat, non ob aliud nisi quia non licebat?

[9]furtum ~i *neut.* **theft** [10]uitiose *adv.* **defectively** [11]libet ~ere, ~uit or ~itum est *impers.* **it is pleasing** [12]saltem *adv.* **even** [13]fallacia ~ae *f.* **deceit** [14]potentatus ~us *m.* **political authority; LATE power** [15]mancus ~a, ~um *adj.* **maimed** [16]captiuus ~ i *m.* **captive** [17]impune *adv.* **with impunity** [18]tenebrosus ~a, ~um *adj.* **darkened** [19]omnipotentia ~ae *f.* LATE **omnipotence** [20]similitudo ~inis *f.* **similitude or imitation** [21]consequor ~qui, ~cutus **to pursue** [22]putredo ~inis *f.* **putridness** [23]monstrum ~i *neut.* **monstrosity** [24]profunditas ~tatis *f.* LATE **depth**

One doctor, many patients

2.7.15 *Quid retribuam*[1] *Domino* (Ps 115:12) quod recolit haec memoria mea et anima mea non metuit inde? diligam te, Domine, et gratias agam et confitear nomini tuo, quoniam tanta dimisisti mihi mala et nefaria[2] opera mea. gratiae tuae deputo[3] et misericordiae tuae quod *peccata mea tanquam glaciem*[4] *soluisti*[5] (Sir 3:17). gratiae tuae deputo et quaecumque non feci mala. quid enim non facere potui, qui etiam gratuitum[6] facinus[7] amaui? et omnia mihi dimissa esse fateor,[8] et quae mea sponte[9] feci mala et quae te duce non feci.

Quis est hominum qui suam cogitans infirmitatem[10] audet uiribus suis tribuere[11] castitatem[12] atque innocentiam[13] suam, ut minus amet te, quasi minus ei necessaria[14] fuerit misericordia tua, qua donas[15] peccata conuersis ad te? qui enim uocatus a te secutus est uocem tuam et uitauit[16] ea quae me de me ipso recordantem et fatentem legit, non me

[1]retribuo ~uere, ~ui, ~utum **to repay** [2]nefarius ~a, ~um *adj.* **nefarious** [3]deputo ~are, ~aui, ~atum **to regard; LATE to attribute** [4]glacies ~ei *f.* **ice** [5]soluo ~uere, ~ui, ~utum **to melt** [6]gratuitus ~a, ~um *adj.* **gratuitous** (unprovoked/unprofitable) [7]facinus ~oris *neut.* **deed > crime** [8]fateor ~eri, fassus **to confess** [9]spons ~ntis *f.* (abl. only) **volition** [10]infirmitas ~atis *f.* **infirmity** [11]tribuo ~uere, ~ui, ~utum **to attribute** [12]castitas ~atis *f.* **chastity** [13]innocentia ~ae *f.* **innocence** [14]necessarius ~a, ~um *adj.* **necessary** [15]dono ~are, ~aui, ~atum **to forgive** [16]uito ~are, ~aui, ~atum **to avoid**

derideat[17] ab eo medico[18] aegrum[19] sanari a quo sibi praestitum[20] est ut non aegrotaret,[21] uel potius ut minus aegrotaret, et ideo te tantundem,[22] immo uero[23] amplius diligat, quia per quem me uidet tantis peccatorum meorum languoribus[24] exui,[25] per eum se uidet tantis peccatorum languoribus non implicari.[26]

[17]derideo ~dere, ~si, ~sum **to deride** [18]medicus ~i *m.* **physician** [19]aegrum ~i *neut.* **having a disease** [20]praesto ~are, ~iti, ~itum **to do better** [21]aegroto ~are, ~aui, ~atum **to be ill** [22]tantusdem ~adem, ~undem *adj.* **as much** [23]'immo uero' **no, in fact...** [24]languor ~oris *m.* faintness > **illness** [25]exuo ~uere, ~ui, ~utum **to set free** [26]implico ~are, ~aui, ~atum or ~itum to entangle > **to get a disease**

The thrill of conspiracy

2.8.16 *Quem fructum habui* miser aliquando *in his quae nunc* recolens *erubesco*[1] (Rom 6:21), maxime in illo furto[2] in quo ipsum furtum amaui, nihil aliud, cum et ipsum esset nihil et eo[3] ipso ego miserior? et tamen solus id non fecissem (sic recordor animum tunc meum), solus omnino id non fecissem. ergo amaui ibi etiam consortium[4] eorum cum quibus id feci. non ergo nihil aliud quam furtum amaui? immo uero[5] nihil aliud, quia et illud nihil est. quid est re uera? (quis est qui doceat me, nisi Qui *inluminat cor meum* (Sir 2:10) et discernit umbras eius?) quid est? quod mihi uenit in mentem quaerere et discutere[6] et considerare, quia si tunc amarem poma[7] illa quae furatus[8] sum et eis frui[9] cuperem, possem etiam solus; si satis esset committere[10] illam iniquitatem qua peruenirem ad uoluptatem meam, nec confricatione[11] consciorum[12] animorum accenderem[13] pruritum[14] cupiditatis meae. sed quoniam in illis pomis uoluptas mihi non erat, ea erat in ipso facinore[15] quam faciebat consortium simul peccantium.

[1]erubesco ~escere, ~ui **to feel ashamed** [2]furtum ~i *neut.* **theft** [3]eo *adv.* **because** [4]consortium ~ii *neut.* **sharing** (an experience) [5]'immo uero' **no, in fact...** [6]discutio ~tere, ~ssi, ~ssum to break up; LATE **to examine** [7]pomum ~i *neut.* **fruit** (from an orchard) [8]furor ~ari, ~atus **to steal** [9]fruor ~i, ~ctus **to enjoy** (w. abl.) [10]committo ~ittere, ~isi, ~issum **to commit** [11]confricatio ~onis *f.* AUG **friction** [12]conscius ~a, ~um *adj.* **conscious of guilt** [13]accendo ~dere, ~di, ~sum **to set on fire** [14]pruritus ~us *m.* **itch** [15]facinus ~oris *neut.* deed > **crime**

I would not steal alone

2.9.17 Quid erat ille affectus animi? certe enim plane[1] turpis erat nimis, et *uae*[2] *mihi erat* (Job 10:15) qui habebam illum. sed tamen quid erat? *Delicta*[3] *quis intellegit?* (Ps 18:13). risus[4] erat quasi titillato[5] corde, quod fallebamus eos qui haec a nobis fieri non putabant et uehementer[6] nolebant. cur ergo eo me delectabat quo id non faciebam solus? an quia etiam nemo facile solus ridet?[7] nemo quidem facile, sed tamen etiam solos et singulos homines, cum alius nemo[8] praesens, uincit risus aliquando, si aliquid nimie[9] ridiculum[10] uel sensibus occurrit uel animo. at ego illud solus non facerem, non facerem omnino solus. ecce est coram te, Deus meus, uiua recordatio[11] animae meae. solus non facerem furtum[12] illud, in quo me non libebat[13] id quod furabar[14] sed quia furabar: quod me solum facere prorsus[15] non liberet, nec facerem.

O nimis inimica amicitia,[16] seductio[17] mentis inuestigabilis,[18] ex ludo[19] et ioco[20] nocendi[21] auiditas[22] et alieni damni[23] appetitus[24] nulla lucri[25] mei, nulla ulciscendi[26] libidine! sed cum dicitur, "Eamus, faciamus," et pudet[27] non esse impudentem.[28]

[1]plane *adv.* **plainly** [2]uae *interj.* [a cry of pain, anger, sorrow] **woe!** [3]delictum ~i *neut.* offense; ECCL **sin** [4]risus ~us *m.* **laughter** [5]titillatus ~us *m.* **tickling** [6]uehementer *adv.* **vehemently** [7]rideo ~dere, ~si, ~sum **to have a laugh** [8]'alius nemo' **no one else** [9]nimie *adv.* LATE **exceedingly** [10]ridiculus ~a, ~um *adj.* **ridiculous** [11]recordatio ~onis *f.* **recollection** [12]furtum ~i *neut.* **theft** [13]libet ~ere, ~uit or ~itum est *impers.* **it is pleasing** [14]furor ~ari, ~atus **to steal** [15]prorsus *adv.* **entirely** [16]amicitia ~ae *f.* **friendship** [17]seductio ~onis *f.* leading astray; ECCL **seduction** [18]inuestigabilis ~is, ~e *adj.* ECCL **unsearchable** [19]ludus ~i *m.* **game** [20]iocus ~i *m.* **joke** [21]noceo ~ere, ~ui, ~itum **to injure** [22]auiditas ~atis *f.* **greedy desire** [23]damnum ~i *neut.* **loss** [24]appetitus ~us *m.* **appetite** [25]lucrum ~i *neut.* **profit** [26]ulciscor ~cisci, ~tus **to take revenge** [27]pudeo ~ere, ~ui **to make ashamed** [28]impudens ~ntis *adj.* **shameless**

The Prodigal in the land of famine

2.10.18 Quis exaperit[1] istam tortuosissimam[2] et implicatissimam[3] nodositatem?[4] foeda[5] est; nolo in eam intendere, nolo eam uidere. te uolo, iustitia et innocentia[6] pulchra et decora,[7] honestis[8] luminibus et

[1]exaperio ~ire, ~ui, ~tum AUG **to disentangle** [2]tortuosus ~a, ~um *adj.* **tortuous** [3]implicatus ~a, ~um *adj.* **intricate** [4]nodositas ~tatis *f.* LATE **knottiness** [5]foedus ~a, ~um *adj.* **disgusting** [6]innocentia ~ae *f.* **innocence** [7]decorus ~a, ~um *adj.* **graceful** [8]honestus ~a, ~um *adj.* **worthy**

insatiabili[9] satietate.[10] quies[11] est apud te ualde et uita imperturbabilis.[12] qui intrat in te, *intrat in gaudium Domini sui* (Mt 25:21) et non timebit et habebit se optime[13] in optimo.[14] defluxi[15] abs te ego et erraui, Deus meus, nimis deuius[16] ab stabilitate[17] tua in adulescentia,[18] et factus sum mihi regio[19] egestatis.[20]

[9]insatiabilis ~is, ~e *adj.* insatiable [10]satietas ~atis *f.* satiety [11]quies ~etis *f.* rest [12]imperturbabilis ~is, ~e *adj.* AUG imperturbable [13]optime *superl. adv.* supremely [14]optimus ~a, ~um *superl. adj.* supremely good (as noun) [15]defluo ~ere, ~xi, ~xum to sink away [16]deuius ~a, ~um *adj.* out-of-the-way [17]stabilitas ~atis *f.* stability [18]adulescentia ~ae *f.* young adulthood (age 16–30) [19]regio ~onis *f.* land [20]egestas ~atis *f.* destitution

3

HIGHER EDUCATION

Carthage (Greater Tunis, Tunisia), 371–374

In love with love

3.1.1 Veni Carthaginem, et circumstrepebat[1] me undique[2] sartago[3] flagitiosorum[4] amorum. nondum amabam, et amare amabam, et secretiore[5] indigentia[6] oderam me minus indigentem.[7] quaerebam quid amarem, amans amare, et oderam securitatem[8] et uiam sine muscipulis,[9] quoniam fames[10] mihi erat intus ab interiore cibo, te ipso, Deus meus, et ea fame non esuriebam,[11] sed eram sine desiderio alimentorum[12] incorruptibilium,[13] non quia plenus eis eram, sed quo inanior,[14] fastidiosior.[15] et ideo non bene ualebat anima mea et ulcerosa[16] proiciebat[17] se foras,[18] miserabiliter[19] scalpi[20] auida[21] contactu[22] sensibilium.[23] sed si non haberent animam, non utique amarentur. amare et amari dulce mihi erat, magis si et amantis[24] corpore fruerer.[25] uenam[26] igitur amicitiae[27]

[1]circumstrepo ~ere, ~ui, ~itum **to surround with a din and clamor of noise** [2]undique *adv.* **from all directions** [3]sartago ~inis *f.* **frying pan** [4]flagitiosus ~a, ~um *adj.* **scandalous** [5]secretus ~a, ~um *adj.* secret > **intimate** [6]indigentia ~ae *f.* **feeling of indigence** [7]indigeo ~ere, ~ui **to be indigent** [8]securitas ~atis *f.* **security** [9]muscipulum ~i *neut.* mouse-trap; ECCL **pitfall** [10]fames ~is *f.* **famine** [11]esurio, ess- ~ire, ~itum **to feel hungry** [12]alimentum ~i *neut.* **food** [13]incorruptibilis ~is, ~e *adj.* ECCL **incorruptible** [14]inanis ~is, ~e *adj.* **empty** [15]fastidiosus ~a, ~um *adj.* **nauseated** [16]ulcerosus ~a, ~um *adj.* **ulcerous** [17]proicio ~icere, ~ieci, ~iectum **to fling forth** (refl.) [18]foras *adv.* **outwards** [19]miserabiliter *adv.* **miserably** [20]scalpo ~pere, ~psi, ~ptum **to scratch an itch** [21]auidus ~a, ~um *adj.* avaricious > **hungry** [22]contactus ~us *m.* **contact** [23]sensibilis ~is, ~e *adj.* **what appeals to the senses** (*neut. pl.* as noun) [24]amans ~ntis *m. f.* **lover** [25]fruor ~i, ~ctus **to enjoy** (w.abl.) [26]uena ~ae *f.* vein > **underground stream** [27]amicitia ~ae *f.* **friendship**

coinquinabam[28] sordibus[29] concupiscentiae[30] candoremque[31] eius obnu-
bilabam[32] de Tartaro libidinis, et tamen foedus[33] atque inhonestus,[34]
elegans[35] et urbanus[36] esse gestiebam[37] abundanti[38] uanitate. rui[39] etiam
in amorem, quo cupiebam capi. *Deus meus, misericordia mea* (Ps 58:18),
quanto felle[40] mihi suauitatem[41] illam et quam bonus aspersisti,[42] quia et
amatus sum, et perueni occulte[43] ad uinculum[44] fruendi, et conligabar
laetus aerumnosis[45] nexibus,[46] ut caederer[47] uirgis[48] ferreis[49] ardentibus[50]
zeli[51] et suspicionum[52] et timorum[53] et *irarum atque rixarum*[54] (Gal 5:20).

[28]coinquino ~are, ~aui, ~atum **to pollute** [29]sordes ~is *f.* **filth** [30]concupiscentia ~ae *f.* ECCL **concupiscence** [31]candor ~oris *m.* **radiance** [32]obnubilo ~are, ~aui, ~atum **to cloud over** [33]foedus ~a, ~um
adj. **foul** [34]inhonestus ~a, ~um *adj.* **disgraceful** [35]elegans ~ntis *adj.* **elegant** [36]urbanus ~a, ~um *adj.*
urbane [37]gestio ~ire, ~iui or ~ii **to carry on (obnoxiously)** [38]abundans ~ntis *adj.* **abounding** [39]ruo
~ere, ~i **to rush headlong** [40]fel ~llis *neut.* **bitterness** [41]suauitas ~atis *f.* **sweetness** [42]aspergo ~gere,
~si, ~sum **to sprinkle** [43]occulte *adv.* **furtively** [44]uinculum ~i *neut.* **chain** [45]aerumnosus ~a, ~um *adj.*
distressing [46]nexus ~us *m.* **entanglement** [47]caedo ~dere, cecidi, ~sum **to strike** [48]uirga ~ae *f.* **rod**
(for punishment, torture) [49]ferreus ~a, ~um *adj.* **iron** [50]ardens ~ntis *adj.* burning > **glowing red hot**
[51]zelus ~i *m.* **jealousy** [52]suspicio ~onis *f.* **suspicion** [53]timor ~oris *m.* **fear** [54]rixa ~ae *f.* **noisy quarrel**

The theater

3.2.2 Rapiebant me spectacula[1] theatrica,[2] plena imaginibus miseriarum
mearum et fomitibus[3] ignis mei. quid est quod[4] ibi homo uult dolere
cum spectat luctuosa[5] et tragica,[6] quae tamen pati ipse nollet? et tamen
pati uult ex eis dolorem spectator[7] et dolor ipse est uoluptas eius. quid
est nisi mirabilis[8] insania?[9] nam eo magis eis mouetur quisque, quo
minus[10] a talibus affectibus sanus[11] est, quamquam, cum ipse patitur,
"miseria," cum aliis compatitur,[12] "misericordia" dici solet. sed qualis
tandem misericordia in rebus fictis[13] et scenicis?[14] non enim ad subue-
niendum[15] prouocatur[16] auditor[17] sed tantum ad dolendum inuitatur,[18]
et actori[19] earum imaginum amplius fauet[20] cum amplius dolet. et si
calamitates[21] illae hominum, uel antiquae[22] uel falsae, sic agantur ut

[1]spectaculum ~i *neut.* **spectacle** [2]theatricus ~a, ~um *adj.* AUG **of the theater** [3]fomes ~itis *m.* **kindling**
[4]'quid est quod' **why is it that..?** [5]luctuosus ~a, ~um *adj.* **sorrowful** [6]tragicus ~a, ~um *adj.* **tragic**
[7]spectator ~oris *m.* **spectator** [8]mirabilis ~is, ~e *adj.* **wondrous** [9]insania ~ae *f.* **insanity** [10]quominus
conj. **so much the less** [11]sanus ~a, ~um *adj.* **unimpaired** [12]compatior ~i, ~assum LATE **to relieve
another's suffering** [13]fictus ~a, ~um *adj.* **fictitious** [14]scenicus ~a, ~um *adj.* **on stage** [15]subuenio
~enire, ~eni, ~entum **to bring relief** [16]prouoco ~are, ~aui, ~atum **to provoke** [17]auditor ~oris *m.*
audience member [18]inuito ~are, ~aui, ~atum **to invite** [19]actor ~oris *m.* **stage actor** [20]faueo ~ere,
faui, ~tum *intr. w. dat.* **to admire** [21]calamitas ~atis *f.* **calamity** [22]antiquus ~a, ~um *adj.* **ancient**

qui spectat non doleat, abscedit[23] inde fastidiens[24] et reprehendens;[25] si autem doleat, manet intentus et gaudens lacrimat.[26]

[23]abscedo ~dere, ~ssi, ~ssum **to go away** [24]fastidio ~ire, ~iui or ~ii, ~itum **to be disgusted** [25]reprehendo ~dere, ~di, ~sum **to reprehend** [26]lacrimo ~are, ~aui, ~atum **to shed tears**

Loving theatrical sorrow

3.2.3 Ergo amantur et dolores. certe omnis homo gaudere uult. an cum miserum esse neminem libeat,[1] libet tamen esse misericordem,[2] quod quia non sine dolore est, hac una causa amantur dolores? et hoc de illa uena[3] amicitiae[4] est. sed quo uadit?[5] quo fluit?[6] ut quid[7] decurrit[8] in torrentem[9] picis[10] bullientis,[11] aestus[12] immanes[13] taetrarum[14] libidinum, in quos ipsa mutatur et uertitur per nutum[15] proprium[16] de caelesti[17] serenitate[18] detorta[19] atque deiecta?[20] repudietur[21] ergo misericordia? nequaquam.[22] ergo amentur dolores aliquando, sed caue[23] immunditiam,[24] anima mea, sub tutore[25] Deo meo, *Deo patrum nostrorum et laudabili[26] et superexaltato[27] in omnia saecula* (Dan 5:32), caue immunditiam.

Neque enim nunc non misereor, sed tunc in theatris[28] congaudebam[29] amantibus[30] cum sese fruebantur[31] per flagitia,[32] quamuis haec imaginarie[33] gererent in ludo spectaculi.[34] cum autem sese amittebant, quasi misericors[35] contristabar,[36] et utrumque delectabat tamen. nunc uero magis misereor gaudentem in flagitio quam uelut dura perpessum[37] detrimento[38] perniciosae[39] uoluptatis et amissione[40] miserae felicitatis.[41]

[1]libet ~ere, ~uit or ~itum est *impers.* **it is pleasing** [2]misericors ~rdis *adj.* **compassionate** [3]uena ~ae *f.* **stream** [4]amicitia ~ae *f.* **friendship** [5]uado ~ere **to go one's way** [6]fluo ~ere, ~xi, ~xum **to flow** [7]'ut quid' ECCL = quid (*adv.*) **why?** [8]decurro ~rrere, ~rri, ~rsum **to rush down** [9]torrens ~ntis *m.* **torrent** [10]pix picis *f.* **pitch** (tar) [11]bullio ~ire **to boil** [12]aestus ~us *m.* **heat** [13]immanis ~is, ~e *adj.* **enormous** [14]taeter ~tra, ~trum *adj.* **monstrous** [15]nutus ~us *m.* (nod of) **consent** [16]proprius ~a, ~um *adj.* **one's own** [17]caelestis ~is, ~e *adj.* **celestial** [18]serenitas ~atis *f.* **serenity** [19]detorqueo ~quere, ~si, ~tum **to distort** [20]deicio ~icere, ~ieci, ~iectum **to degrade** [21]repudio ~are, ~aui, ~atum **to repudiate** [22]nequaquam *adv.* **not at all** [23]caueo ~ere, caui, ~tum **to beware** [24]immunditia ~ae *f.* **uncleanness** [25]tutor ~oris *m.* **protector** [26]laudabilis ~is, ~e *adj.* **praiseworthy** [27]superexalto ~are, ~aui, ~atum **to highly exalt** [28]theatrum ~i *neut.* **theatre** [29]congaudeo ~ere, ~isi, ~isus ECCL **to share joy** [30]amans ~ntis *m. f.* **lover** [31]fruor ~i, ~ctus **to enjoy** (w. abl.) [32]flagitium ~ii *neut.* **indecency** (of sexual misconduct) [33]imaginarie *adv.* AUG **in an imaginary way** [34]'ludo spectaculi' **theatrical show** [35]misericors ~rdis *adj.* **moved to pity** [36]contristo ~are, ~aui, ~atum **to make one sad** [37]perpetior ~ti, ~ssus **to undergo to the full** [38]detrimentum ~i *neut.* **diminishment** [39]perniciosus ~a, ~um *adj.* **pernicious** [40]amissio ~onis *f.* **loss** [41]felicitas ~atis *f.* **happiness**

haec certe uerior misericordia, sed non in ea delectat dolor. nam etsi approbatur[42] officio[43] caritatis qui dolet miserum, mallet[44] tamen utique non esse quod doleret qui germanitus[45] misericors[46] est. si enim est maliuola[47] beniuolentia,[48] quod fieri non potest, potest et ille qui ueraciter[49] sinceriterque[50] misereretur cupere esse miseros, ut misereatur.

Nonnullus[51] itaque dolor approbandus,[52] nullus amandus est. hoc[53] enim tu, Domine Deus, qui animas amas, longe alteque[54] purius[55] quam nos et incorruptibilius[56] misereris, quod nullo dolore sauciaris.[57] *et ad haec quis idoneus?*[58] (2 Cor 2:16).

---

[42]approbo ~are, ~aui, ~atum **to approve** [43]officium ~ii *neut.* **duty** [44]malo ~lle, ~lui **to prefer** [45]germanitus *adv.* brotherly; LATE **genuinely** [46]misericors ~rdis *adj.* **merciful** [47]maliuolus ~a, ~um *adj.* **malevolent** [48]beniuolentia ~ae *f.* **benevolence** [49]ueraciter *adv.* LATE **truly** [50]sinceriter *adv.* **sincerely** [51]nonnullus ~a, ~um *adj.* **a certain amount** [52]approbo ~are, ~aui, ~atum **to commend** [53]hoc *adv.* **in this matter** [54]alte *adv.* **deeply** [55]pure *adv.* **purely** [56]incorruptibiliter *adv.* AUG **incorruptibly** [57]saucio ~are, ~aui, ~atum **to wound** [58]idoneus ~a, ~um *adj.* **sufficient**

Disfigured by fictitious tragedies

3.2.4 At ego tunc miser dolere amabam, et quaerebam ut esset quod dolerem, quando mihi in aerumna[1] aliena et falsa et saltatoria[2] ea magis placebat actio[3] histrionis[4] meque alliciebat[5] uehementius[6] qua mihi lacrimae excutiebantur.[7] quid autem mirum, cum *infelix*[8] *pecus*[9] (Ecl. 3.3) aberrans[10] a grege[11] tuo et impatiens[12] custodiae[13] tuae turpi scabie[14] foedarer?[15] et inde erant dolorum amores, non quibus altius[16] penetrarer[17] (non enim amabam talia perpeti[18] qualia spectare), sed quibus auditis et fictis[19] tamquam in superficie[20] raderer.[21] quos tamen quasi ungues[22] scalpentium[23] feruidus[24] tumor[25] et tabes[26] et sanies[27] horrida[28] consequebatur.[29] talis uita mea numquid uita erat, Deus meus?

---

[1]aerumna ~ae *f.* **distress** [2]saltatorius ~a, ~um *adj.* represented by dancers; LATE **theatrical** [3]actio ~onis *f.* **action** [4]histrio ~onis *f.* **actor** [5]allicio ~icere, ~exi, ~ectum **to attract** [6]uehementer *adv.* **vehemently** [7]excutio ~tere, ~ssi, ~ssum to shake off > **to elicit** [8]infelix ~icis *adj.* **unhappy** [9]pecus ~oris *neut.* **sheep** [10]aberro ~are, ~aui, ~atum **to wander away** [11]grex ~egis *m.* **flock** [12]impatiens ~ntis *adj.* **impatient** (of) [13]custodia ~ae *f.* **protection** [14]scabies ~ei *f.* **scab, mange** [15]foedo ~are, ~aui, ~atum **to disfigure** [16]alte *adv.* **deeply** [17]penetro ~are, ~aui, ~atum **to penetrate** [18]perpetior ~ti, ~ssus **to undergo to the full** [19]fictus ~a, ~um *adj.* **fictitious** [20]superficies ~iei *f.* **surface** (of the skin) [21]rado ~dere, ~si, ~sum **to scratch** [22]unguis ~is *m.* **fingernail** [23]scalpo ~pere, ~psi, ~ptum **to scratch** [24]feruidus ~a, ~um *adj.* **inflamed** [25]tumor ~oris *m.* **morbid swelling** [26]tabes ~is *f.* **putrefaction** [27]sanies (~ei) *f.* **foul-smelling discharge** [28]horridus ~a, ~um *adj.* **horrible** [29]consequor ~qui, ~cutus **to follow** (as a necessary consequence)

Sacrilegious sexual sin

3.3.5 Et circumuolabat[1] super[2] me fidelis a longe misericordia tua. in quantas iniquitates distabui[3] et sacrilegam[4] curiositatem[5] secutus sum, ut deserentem te deduceret[6] me ad ima[7] infida[8] et circumuentoria[9] obsequia[10] *daemoniorum,*[11] *quibus immolabam*[12] (1 Cor 10:20) facta mea mala! et in omnibus flagellabas[13] me. ausus sum etiam in celebritate[14] sollemnitatum[15] tuarum, intra[16] parietes[17] ecclesiae tuae, concupiscere[18] et agere negotium[19] procurandi[20] *fructus mortis* (Rom 7:5). unde me uerberasti[21] grauibus poenis, sed nihil ad culpam[22] meam, o tu praegrandis[23] *misericordia mea, Deus meus, refugium*[24] *meum* (Ps 58:18, 143:2) a terribilibus[25] nocentibus,[26] in quibus uagatus[27] sum praefidenti[28] collo[29] ad longe recedendum a te, amans uias meas et non tuas, amans fugitiuam[30] libertatem.

[1]circumuolo ~are, ~aui **to encircle in flight** [2]super *adv.* **over** [3]distabesco ~escere, ~ui **to melt away** [4]sacrilegus ~a, ~um *adj.* **sacrilegious** [5]curiositas ~atis *f.* **curiosity** (usu. in a bad sense) [6]deduco ~cere, ~xi, ~ctum **to lead away** [7]imus ~a, ~um *adj.* **lowest levels** (*neut. pl.* as noun) [8]infidus ~a, ~um *adj.* faithless; ECCL **unbelief** [9]circumuentorius ~a, ~um *adj.* AUG **fraudulent** [10]obsequium ~ii *neut.* **obsequiousness** [11]daemonium ~i *neut.* ECCL **demon** [12]immolo ~are, ~aui, ~atum **to offer as sacrifice** [13]flagello ~are, ~aui, ~atum **to flog** [14]celebritas ~atis *f.* **celebration** [15]sollemnitas ~atis *f.* ritual observance; ECCL **solemnity** (Eucharist) [16]intra *prep. acc.* **inside** [17]paries ~etis *m.* **wall** [18]concupisco ~iscere, ~iui, ~itum **to desire lustfully** [19]negotium ~ii *neut.* business > **affair** [20]procuro ~are, ~aui, ~atum **to take care of;** LATE **to procure** [21]uerbero ~are, ~aui, ~atum **to strike repeatedly** [22]culpa ~ae *f.* **guilt** [23]praegrandis ~is, ~e *adj.* **exceptionally great** [24]refugium ~ii *neut.* **refuge** [25]terribilis ~is, ~e *adj.* **terrifying** [26]nocens ~ntis *adj.* **guilty** [27]uagor ~ari, ~atus **to wander aimlessly** [28]praefidens ~ntis *adj.* **overconfident** [29]collum ~i *neut.* **neck** (fig.) [30]fugitiuus ~a, ~um *adj.* **fugitive** (of runaway slaves)

The "Wreckers"

3.3.6 Habebant et illa studia quae "honesta"[1] uocabantur ductum[2] suum intuentem *fora*[3] *litigiosa*[4] (Fast. 4.188), ut excellerem[5] in eis, hoc laudabilior,[6] quo fraudulentior.[7] tanta est caecitas[8] hominum de caecitate etiam gloriantium.[9] et maior etiam eram in schola[10] rhetoris,[11] et gaudebam superbe[12] et tumebam[13] typho,[14] quamquam longe sedatior,[15] *Domine,*

[1]honestus ~a, ~um *adj.* **respectable** [2]ductus ~us *m.* line; LATE **purpose** [3]forum ~i *neut.* **court of law** [4]litigiosus ~a, ~um *adj.* **litigious** [5]excello ~ere **to excel** [6]laudabilis ~is, ~e *adj.* **praiseworthy** [7]fraudulentus ~a, ~um *adj.* **fraudulent** [8]caecitas ~atis *f.* **blindness** [9]glorior ~ari, ~atus **to glory** [10]schola, scola ~ae *f.* **school** [11]rhetor ~oris *m.* **rhetorician** [12]superbe *adv.* **haughtily** [13]tumeo ~ere, ~ui **to be swollen** [14]typhus ~i *m.* ECCL **proud vanity** [15]sedatus ~a, ~um *adj.* **sedate**

tu scis (Jn 21:15), et remotus[16] omnino ab euersionibus[17] quas faciebant "euersores"[18] (hoc enim nomen scaeuum[19] et diabolicum[20] uelut insigne[21] urbanitatis[22] est), inter quos uiuebam pudore[23] impudenti,[24] quia talis non eram. et cum eis eram et amicitiis[25] eorum delectabar aliquando, a quorum semper factis abhorrebam,[26] hoc est ab euersionibus quibus proterue[27] insectabantur[28] ignotorum[29] uerecundiam,[30] quam proturbarent[31] gratis inludendo[32] atque inde pascendo maliuolas[33] laetitias suas. nihil est illo actu[34] similius actibus daemoniorum.[35] quid itaque uerius quam "euersores" uocarentur, euersi[36] plane[37] prius ipsi atque peruersi,[38] deridentibus[39] eos et seducentibus[40] fallacibus[41] occulte[42] spiritibus in eo ipso quod alios inridere amant et fallere?

[16]remotus ~a, ~um *adj.* removed [17]euersio ~onis *f.* wrecking (havoc) [18]euersor ~oris *m.* wrecker [19]scaeua ~ae *f.* left-handed; LATE sinister [20]diabolicus ~a, ~um *adj.* ECCL diabolical [21]insigne ~is *neut.* insignia [22]urbanitas ~atis *f.* urbanity [23]pudor ~oris *m.* feeling of shame [24]impudens ~ntis *adj.* shameless [25]amicitia ~ae *f.* friendship [26]abhorreo ~ere, ~ui to abhor [27]proterue *adv.* impudently [28]insector ~ari, ~atus to chase > to haze [29]ignotus ~a, ~um *adj.* complete stranger (as noun) [30]uerecundia ~ae *f.* sensitivity [31]proturbo ~are, ~aui, ~atum to drive away; LATE to deliberately agitate [32]inludo ~dere, ~si, ~sum to make fun of [33]maliuolus ~a, ~um *adj.* malevolent [34]actus ~us *m.* behavior [35]daemonium ~i *neut.* ECCL demon [36]euerto ~tere, ~ti, ~sum to wreck [37]plane *adv.* plainly [38]peruerto ~tere, ~ti, ~sum to pervert [39]derideo ~dere, ~si, ~sum to deride [40]seduco ~cere, ~xi, ~ctum to draw aside; ECCL to seduce [41]fallax ~acis *adj.* deceitful [42]occulte *adv.* invisibly

Cicero's *Hortensius*

3.4.7 Inter hos ego inbecilla[1] tunc aetate discebam libros eloquentiae,[2] in qua eminere[3] cupiebam fine damnabili[4] et uentoso[5] per gaudia uanitatis humanae. et usitato[6] iam discendi ordine perueneram in librum cuiusdam Ciceronis, cuius linguam fere[7] omnes mirantur, pectus non ita. sed liber ille ipsius exhortationem[8] continet ad philosophiam[9] et uocatur *Hortensius*. ille uero liber mutauit affectum meum, et ad te ipsum, Domine, mutauit preces[10] meas, et uota ac desideria mea fecit alia. uiluit[11] mihi repente[12] omnis uana spes, et immortalitatem[13] sapientiae concupiscebam[14] aestu[15] cordis incredibili,[16] et *surgere*[17] *coeperam*

[1]inbecillus ~a, ~um *adj.* weak > vulnerable [2]eloquentia ~ae *f.* eloquence [3]emineo ~ere, ~ui to be pre-eminent [4]damnabilis ~e, *adj.* LATE damnable [5]uentosus ~a, ~um *adj.* puffed up [6]usitatus ~a, ~um *adj.* usual [7]fere *adv.* almost [8]exhortatio ~onis *f.* exhortation [9]philosophia ~ae *f.* philosophy [10]preces ~um *f. pl.* prayers [11]uilesco ~ere, ~ui LATE to become worthless [12]repente *adv.* suddenly [13]immortalitas ~atis *f.* immortality [14]concupisco ~iscere, ~iui, ~itum to conceive a desire [15]aestus ~us *m.* passion [16]incredibilis ~is, ~e *adj.* incredible [17]surgo ~rgere, ~rrexi, ~rrectum to rise

ut ad te redirem (Lk 15:18). non enim ad acuendam[18] linguam, quod uidebar emere[19] maternis[20] mercedibus,[21] cum agerem annum aetatis undeuicensimum[22] iam defuncto[23] patre ante[24] biennium,[25] non ergo ad acuendam linguam referebam[26] illum librum, neque mihi locutio[27] sed quod loquebatur persuaserat.[28]

[18]acuo ~uere, ~ui, ~utum **to sharpen** [19]emo emere, emi, emptum **to buy** [20]maternus ~a, ~um *adj.* **mother's** [21]merces ~edis *f.* **payment** [22]undeuicensimus ~a, ~um *adj.* **nineteenth** [23]defunctus ~a, ~um *adj.* **dead** [24]ante *adv.* **earlier** [25]biennium ~ii *neut.* **two years** [26]refero ~rre, rettuli, relatum **to refer**; LATE **to employ** [27]locutio ~onis *f.* **locution** [28]persuadeo ~dere, ~si, ~sum **to persuade** (w. dat. of person)

Missing the name of Christ

3.4.8 Quomodo ardebam,[1] Deus meus, quomodo ardebam reuolare[2] a terrenis[3] ad te, et nesciebam quid ageres mecum! *apud te est enim sapientia* (Job 12:13). amor autem sapientiae nomen Graecum habet "philosophiam,"[4] quo me accendebant[5] illae litterae. sunt qui seducant[6] per philosophiam magno et blando[7] et honesto[8] nomine colorantes[9] et fucantes[10] errores suos, et prope[11] omnes qui ex illis et supra[12] temporibus tales erant notantur[13] in eo libro et demonstrantur,[14] et manifestatur[15] ibi salutifera[16] illa admonitio[17] Spiritus tui per seruum tuum bonum et pium: *uidete, ne quis uos decipiat[18] per philosophiam et inanem[19] seductionem[20] secundum traditionem[21] hominum, secundum elementa[22] huius mundi et non secundum Christum, quia in ipso inhabitat[23] omnis plenitudo[24] diuinitatis[25] corporaliter[26]* (Col 2:8–9). et ego illo tempore, scis tu, lumen cordis mei, quoniam nondum mihi haec apostolica[27] nota erant, hoc tamen solo delectabar in illa exhortatione,[28] quod non

[1]ardeo ~dere, ~si **to burn** > **to burn with desire** [2]reuolo ~are, ~aui **to fly back** [3]terrenus ~a, ~um *adj.* **terrestrial** [4]philosophia ~ae *f.* **philosophy** [5]accendo ~dere, ~di, ~sum **to set on fire** > **to kindle feelings** [6]seduco ~cere, ~xi, ~ctum **to lead astray** [7]blandus ~a, ~um *adj.* **winsome** [8]honestus ~a, ~um *adj.* **honorable** [9]coloro ~are, ~aui, ~atum **to color** [10]fuco ~are, ~aui, ~atum **to apply cosmetics** [11]prope *adv.* **practically** > **pretty well** (hyperb.) [12]supra *prep. acc.* **further back** (in time) [13]noto ~are, ~aui, ~atum **to note** [14]demonstro ~are, ~aui, ~atum **to explain** [15]manifesto ~are, ~aui, ~atum **to manifest** [16]salutifer ~era, ~erum *adj.* **salutary** [17]admonitio ~onis *f.* **admonition** [18]decipio ~ipere, ~epi, ~eptum **to deceive** [19]inanis ~is, ~e *adj.* **empty** [20]seductio ~onis *f.* **leading astray**; ECCL **seduction** [21]traditio ~onis *f.* **tradition** [22]elementum ~i *neut.* **element** [23]inhabito ~are, ~aui, ~atum **to inhabit** [24]plenitudo ~inis *f.* **plenitude** [25]diuinitas ~atis *f.* **divinity** [26]corporaliter *adv.* **bodily** [27]apostolicus ~a, ~um ECCL **apostolic** [28]exhortatio ~onis *f.* **exhortation**

illam aut illam sectam,[29] sed ipsam quaecumque esset sapientiam ut diligerem et quaererem et adsequerer[30] et tenerem atque amplexarer[31] fortiter,[32] excitabar[33] sermone illo et accendebar et ardebam, et hoc solum me in tanta flagrantia[34] refrangebat,[35] quod nomen Christi non erat ibi, quoniam hoc nomen *secundum misericordiam tuam, Domine* (Ps 24:7), hoc nomen Saluatoris[36] mei, Filii tui, in ipso adhuc lacte[37] matris tenerum cor meum pie[38] biberat[39] et alte[40] retinebat,[41] et quidquid sine hoc nomine fuisset, quamuis litteratum[42] et expolitum[43] et ueridicum,[44] non me totum rapiebat.

[29]secta ~ae *f.* **school of philosophy** [30]adsequor ~qui, ~cutus **to follow after** [31]amplexor ~ari, ~atus **to embrace** [32]fortiter *adv.* **with zeal and determination** [33]excito ~are, ~aui, ~atum **to excite** [34]flagrantia ~ae *f.* **ardor** [35]refrango ~ngere, fregi, ~ctum AUG **to lessen** [36]saluator ~oris *m.* ECCL **Savior** [37]lac lactis *neut.* **milk** [38]pie *adv.* **piously** [39]bibo ~ere, ~i **to drink** [40]alte *adv.* **deeply** [41]retineo ~ere, ~ui, retentum **to retain** [42]litteratus ~a, ~um *adj.* lettered > **cultured** [43]expolitus ~a, ~um *adj.* **polished** [44]ueridicus ~a, ~um *adj.* **conveying the truth**

Scripture is not very Cicero-like

3.5.9 Itaque institui[1] animum intendere in scripturas sanctas et uidere quales essent. et ecce uideo rem non compertam[2] superbis neque nudatam[3] pueris, sed incessu[4] humilem,[5] successu[6] excelsam[7] et uelatam[8] mysteriis.[9] et non eram ego talis ut intrare in eam possem aut inclinare[10] ceruicem[11] ad eius gressus.[12] non enim sicut modo loquor, ita sensi, cum attendi ad illam scripturam, sed uisa est mihi indigna[13] quam Tullianae dignitati[14] compararem.[15] tumor[16] enim meus refugiebat[17] modum eius et acies[18] mea non penetrabat[19] interiora eius. uerum autem illa erat quae cresceret cum paruulis, sed ego dedignabar[20] esse *paruulus* (Mt 11:25) et turgidus[21] fastu[22] mihi grandis uidebar.

[1]instituo ~uere, ~ui, ~utum **to set to work on** [2]comperio ~ire, ~i, ~tum **to find** [3]nudo ~are, ~aui, ~atum **to lay open to view** [4]incessus ~us *m.* **access** [5]humilis ~is, ~e *adj.* **humble** [6]successus ~us *m.* approach; LATE **progress** [7]excelsus ~a, ~um *adj.* **elevated** [8]uelo ~are, ~aui, ~atum **to veil** [9]mysterium ~iorum *neut. pl.* **mysteries** (to which only the initiates are admitted) [10]inclino ~are, ~aui, ~atum **to incline** [11]ceruix ~icis *f.* **neck** [12]gressus ~us *m.* **step** [13]indignus ~a, ~um *adj.* **undignified** [14]dignitas ~atis *f.* **dignity** [15]comparo ~are, ~aui, ~atum **to compare** (w. dat.) [16]tumor ~oris *m.* swelling > **arrogance** [17]refugio ~ugere, ~ugi **to recoil from** [18]acies ~ei *f.* **gaze** [19]penetro ~are, ~aui, ~atum **to penetrate** [20]dedignor ~ari, ~atus **to scorn** [21]turgidus ~a, ~um *adj.* **swollen** [22]fastus ~us *m.* **feeling of superiority**

Manichee madness

3.6.10 Itaque incidi[1] in homines superbe[2] delirantes,[3] carnales[4] nimis et loquaces,[5] in quorum ore *laquei*[6] *diaboli*[7] (1 Tim 3:7, 2 Tim 2:26) et uiscum[8] confectum[9] commixtione[10] syllabarum[11] nominis tui et Domini Iesu Christi et Paracleti consolatoris[12] nostri Spiritus Sancti. haec nomina non recedebant de ore eorum, sed tenus[13] sono et strepitu[14] linguae; ceterum cor inane[15] ueri. et dicebant, "Veritas et ueritas," et multum eam dicebant mihi, et nusquam[16] erat in eis, sed falsa loquebantur, non de te tantum, qui uere ueritas es, sed etiam de istis elementis[17] huius mundi, creatura tua, de quibus etiam uera dicentes philosophos[18] transgredi[19] debui prae amore tuo, mi Pater summe bone, pulchritudo[20] pulchrorum omnium.

O Veritas, Veritas, quam intime[21] etiam tum medullae[22] animi mei suspirabant tibi, cum te illi sonarent mihi frequenter[23] et multipliciter[24] uoce sola et libris multis et ingentibus![25] et illa erant fercula[26] in quibus mihi esurienti[27] te inferebatur[28] pro te sol et luna,[29] pulchra opera tua, sed tamen opera tua, non tu, nec ipsa prima. priora enim spiritalia opera tua quam ista corporea, quamuis lucida[30] et caelestia.[31] at ego nec priora illa, sed te ipsam, Veritas, in qua *non est commutatio*[32] *nec momenti*[33] *obumbratio*[34] (Jas 1:17), esuriebam[35] et sitiebam.[36] et apponebantur[37] adhuc mihi in illis ferculis phantasmata[38] splendida,[39] quibus iam melius erat amare istum solem saltem[40] istis oculis uerum quam illa falsa animo decepto[41] per oculos. et tamen, quia te putabam, manducabam,[42] non

---

[1]incido ~ere, ~i **to fall** [2]superbe *adv.* **haughtily** [3]deliro ~are **to be delirious** [4]carnalis ~is, ~e *adj.* ECCL **carnal** [5]loquax ~acis *adj.* **loquacious** [6]laqueus ~i *m.* **snare** [7]diabolus ~i *m.* ECCL **the Devil** [8]uiscum ~i *neut.* **birdlime** [9]conficio ~icere, ~eci, ~ectum **to manufacture** [10]commixtio ~onis *f.* **mixture** [11]syllaba ~ae *f.* **syllable** [12]consolator ~oris *m.* **consoler** [13]tenus *prep. abl.* **only as far as** [14]strepitus ~us *m.* **din** [15]inanis ~is, ~e *adj.* **empty** [16]nusquam *adv.* **in no place** [17]elementum ~i *neut.* **elements** [18]philosophus ~i *m.* **philosopher** [19]transgredior ~di, ~ssus **to bypass** [20]pulchritudo ~inis *f.* **beauty** [21]intime *adv.* **inwardly** [22]medulla ~ae *f.* **marrow** (*pl.*) [23]frequenter *adv.* **frequently** [24]multipliciter *adv.* **in many different ways** [25]ingens ~ntis *adj.* **enormous** [26]ferculum ~i *neut.* **food tray** [27]esuriens, ess- ~ntis *adj.* **starving** [28]infero ~re, intuli, illatum **to bring in** [29]luna ~ae *f.* **moon** [30]lucidus ~a, ~um *adj.* **lucid** [31]caelestis ~is, ~e *adj.* **celestial** [32]commutatio ~onis *f.* **turning** [33]momentum ~i *neut.* **movement** [34]obumbratio ~onis *f.* **shadowing** [35]esurio, ess- ~ire, ~itum **to be hungry** [36]sitio ~ire **to be thirsty** [37]appono ~ere, apposui, appositum **to serve food** [38]phantasma ~atis *neut.* **phantom**; LATE **figment of the imagination** [39]splendidus ~a, ~um *adj.* **splendid** [40]saltem *adv.* **at least** [41]decipio ~ipere, ~epi, ~eptum **to deceive** [42]manduco ~are, ~aui, ~atum **to eat**

auide[43] quidem, quia nec sapiebas[44] in ore meo sicuti es (neque enim tu eras illa figmenta[45] inania) nec nutriebar[46] eis, sed exhauriebar[47] magis. cibus in somnis[48] simillimus est cibis uigilantium,[49] quo tamen dormientes[50] non aluntur;[51] dormiunt enim. at illa nec similia erant ullo modo tibi, sicut nunc mihi locuta es, quia illa erant corporalia phantasmata, falsa corpora, quibus certiora sunt uera corpora ista quae uidemus uisu[52] carneo,[53] siue caelestia siue terrestria,[54] cum pecudibus[55] et uolatilibus.[56] uidemus haec, et certiora sunt quam cum imaginamur[57] ea. et rursus certius[58] imaginamur ea quam ex eis suspicamur[59] alia grandiora et infinita, quae omnino nulla sunt. qualibus ego tunc pascebar inanibus,[60] et non pascebar.

At tu, amor meus, in quem deficio[61] ut fortis sim, nec ista corpora es quae uidemus quamquam in caelo, nec ea quae non uidemus ibi, quia tu ista condidisti[62] nec in summis tuis conditionibus[63] habes. quanto ergo longe es a phantasmatis illis meis, phantasmatis corporum quae omnino non sunt! quibus certiores sunt phantasiae[64] corporum eorum quae sunt, et eis certiora corpora, quae tamen non es. sed nec anima es, quae uita est corporum (ideo melior uita corporum certiorque quam corpora), sed tu uita es animarum, uita uitarum, uiuens te ipsa, et non mutaris, uita animae meae.

[43]auide *adv.* **eagerly** [44]sapio ~ere, ~ii **to taste of** [45]figmentum ~i *neut.* **fiction** [46]nutrio ~ire, ~iui or ~ii, ~itum **to nourish** [47]exhaurio ~rire, ~si, ~stum **to drain** [48]somnus ~i *m.* sleep > **dream** [49]uigilans ~ntis *adj.* **awake** [50]dormio ~ire, ~iui, ~itum **to sleep** [51]alo ~ere, ~ui, ~tum **to feed** [52]uisus ~us *m.* **vision** [53]carneus ~a, ~um *adj.* ECCL **carnal** [54]terrestris ~is, ~e *adj.* **terrestrial** [55]pecus ~dis *f.* **beast** [56]uolatilis ~is, ~e *adj.* flying; **bird** (as noun) [57]imaginor ~ari, ~atus **to imagine** [58]certo *adv.* **certainly** [59]suspicor ~ari, ~atus **to form an idea of** [60]inane ~is *neut.* **illusory things** [61]deficio ~icere, ~eci, ~ectum to faint; ECCL **to pine for** [62]condo ~ere, ~idi, ~itum to found; ECCL **to create** [63]conditio ~onis *f.* ECCL **created object** [64]phantasia ~ae *f.* fantasy; LATE **mental image**

Medea better than Manichee myth

3.6.11 Ubi ergo mihi tunc eras et quam longe? et longe peregrinabar[1] abs te, exclusus[2] et a *siliquis*[3] *porcorum*[4] (Lk 15:16) quos de siliquis pascebam. quanto enim meliores grammaticorum[5] et poetarum[6] fabellae[7]

[1]peregrinor ~ari, ~atus to travel abroad > **to range or rove** (in thought) [2]excludo ~dere, ~si, ~sum **to exclude** [3]siliqua ~ae *f.* **husk** [4]porcus ~i *m.* **pig** [5]grammaticus ~i *m.* **grammar teacher** [6]poeta ~ae *m.* **poet** [7]fabella ~ae *f.* **fable**

quam illa decipula![8] nam uersus[9] et carmen et *Medea uolans*[10] (Met. 7.217–236) utiliores[11] certe quam quinque[12] elementa[13] uarie[14] fucata[15] propter quinque antra[16] tenebrarum, quae omnino nulla sunt et occidunt[17] credentem. nam uersum et carmen etiam ad uera pulmenta[18] transfero;[19] uolantem autem Medeam etsi cantabam, non adserebam,[20] etsi cantari audiebam, non credebam. illa autem credidi — uae, uae![21] quibus gradibus[22] deductus[23] in profunda[24] inferi,[25] quippe laborans[26] et aestuans[27] inopia[28] ueri, cum te, Deus meus (tibi enim confiteor, qui me miseratus es et nondum confitentem), cum te non secundum intellectum[29] mentis, quo me praestare[30] uoluisti beluis,[31] sed secundum sensum carnis quaererem. tu autem eras interior intimo[32] meo et superior[33] summo meo.

Offendi[34] illam mulierem[35] audacem,[36] inopem[37] prudentiae,[38] aenigma[39] Salomonis, sedentem[40] super sellam[41] in foribus[42] et dicentem: *panes[43] occultos libenter[44] edite,[45] et aquam dulcem furtiuam[46] bibite[47]* (Prov 9:13–17). quae me seduxit,[48] quia inuenit foris[49] habitantem[50] in oculo carnis meae et talia ruminantem[51] apud me qualia per illum uorassem.[52]

[8]decipula ~ae *f.* trap [9]uersus ~us *m.* verse [10]uolo ~are, ~aui, ~atum to fly [11]utilis ~is, ~e *adj.* useful [12]quinque *indecl. adj.* five [13]elementum ~i *neut.* element (of nature) [14]uarie *adv.* variating with colors [15]fuco ~are, ~aui, ~atum to color [16]antrum ~i *neut.* cave [17]occido ~dere, ~di, ~sum to kill [18]pulmentum ~i *neut.* large savory meal [19]transfero ~ferre, ~tuli, ~latum to transform [20]adsero ~ere, ~ui, ~tum to assert (as true) [21]uae *interj.* [a cry of pain, anger, sorrow] woe! [22]gradus ~us *m.* step [23]deduco ~cere, ~xi, ~ctum to draw downward [24]profundum ~i *neut.* depths [25]inferus ~a, ~um *adj.* the underworld; ECCL Hell [26]laboro ~are, ~aui, ~atum to labor [27]aestuo ~are, ~aui, ~atum to burn > to be feverish [28]inopia ~ae *f.* lack (of) [29]intellectus ~us *m.* intellection [30]praesto ~are, ~iti, ~itum to be superior (w. dat.) [31]belua ~ae *f.* beast [32]intimus ~a, ~um *superl. adj.* inmost [33]superior ~or, ~us *compar. adj.* higher [34]offendo ~dere, ~di, ~sum to stumble upon [35]mulier ~eris *f.* woman [36]audax ~acis *adj.* audacious [37]inops ~pis *adj.* lacking (in) [38]prudentia ~ae *f.* prudence [39]aenigma ~atis *neut.* enigma [40]sedeo ~ere, sedi, sessum to be seated [41]sella ~ae *f.* stool [42]in foribus' in the doorway [43]panis ~is *m.* bread [44]libenter *adv.* with pleasure [45]edo esse, edi, esum to eat [46]furtiuus ~a, ~um *adj.* stolen [47]bibo ~ere, ~i to drink [48]seduco ~cere, ~xi, ~ctum to draw aside; ECCL to seduce [49]foris *adv.* outside [50]habito ~are, ~aui, ~atum to dwell [51]rumino ~are, ~aui, ~atum to ruminate [52]uoro ~are, ~aui, ~atum to devour

I did not know God is spirit

3.7.12 Nesciebam enim aliud uere quod est, et quasi acutule[1] mouebar ut suffragarer[2] stultis[3] deceptoribus,[4] cum a me quaererent unde malum,

[1]acutule *adv.* AUG rather cleverly (contemptuous) [2]suffragor ~ari, ~atus to give one's support [3]stultus ~a, ~um *adj.* foolish [4]deceptor ~oris *m.* deceiver

et utrum forma corporea deus finiretur et haberet capillos[5] et ungues,[6] et utrum iusti existimandi[7] essent qui haberent uxores[8] multas simul et occiderent[9] homines et sacrificarent[10] de animalibus.[11] quibus rerum ignarus[12] perturbabar,[13] et recedens a ueritate ire in eam mihi uidebar, quia non noueram malum non esse nisi priuationem[14] boni usque ad quod omnino non est. (quod unde uiderem, cuius uidere usque ad corpus erat oculis, et animo usque ad phantasma?[15])

Et non noueram *Deum esse spiritum* (Jn 4:24), non cui membra essent per longum et latum[16] nec cui esse moles esset, quia moles in parte minor est quam in toto suo, et si infinita sit, minor est in aliqua parte certo spatio definita[17] quam per infinitum, et non est tota ubique[18] sicut spiritus, sicut Deus. et quid in nobis esset secundum quod essemus et recte[19] in scriptura diceremur *ad imaginem Dei* (Gen 1:27), prorsus[20] ignorabam.

[5]capillus ~i *m.* hair [6]unguis ~is *m.* fingernail [7]existimo ~are, ~aui, ~atum to think [8]uxor ~oris *f.* wife [9]occido ~dere, ~di, ~sum to kill [10]sacrifico ~are, ~aui, ~atum to offer sacrifice [11]animal ~alis *neut.* animal [12]ignarus ~a, ~um *adj.* ignorant [13]perturbo ~are, ~aui, ~atum to trouble [14]priuatio ~onis *f.* privation [15]phantasma ~atis *neut.* phantom; LATE figment of the imagination [16]latus ~a, ~um *adj.* breadth (as noun) [17]definitus ~a, ~um *adj.* definite [18]ubique *adv.* everywhere [19]recte *adv.* rightly [20]prorsus *adv.* entirely

Critiquing the Old Testament

3.7.13 Et non noueram iustitiam ueram interiorem, non ex consuetudine iudicantem sed ex lege rectissima[1] Dei omnipotentis,[2] qua formarentur mores regionum[3] et dierum pro regionibus et diebus, cum ipsa ubique[4] ac semper esset, non alibi[5] alia nec alias[6] aliter, secundum quam iusti essent Abraham et Isaac et Iacob et Moyses et Dauid et illi omnes laudati ore Dei. sed eos ab imperitis[7] iudicari iniquos,[8] *iudicantibus ex humano die* (1 Cor 4:3) et uniuersos mores humani generis ex parte moris sui metientibus, tamquam si quis nescius[9] in armamentis[10] quid cui membro

[1]rectus ~a, ~um *adj.* right (morally) [2]omnipotens ~ntis *adj.* omnipotent [3]regio ~onis *f.* land [4]ubique *adv.* everywhere [5]alibi *adv.* in another place [6]alias *adv.* at another time [7]imperitus ~a, ~um *adj.* unskilled [8]iniquus, ~os ~a *adj.* unfair; ECCL unrighteous [9]nescius ~a, ~um *adj.* ignorant [10]armamenta ~orum *neut. pl.* gear, rigging; LATE weapons

adcommodatum[11] sit ocrea[12] uelit caput contegi[13] et galea[14] calciari[15] et murmuret,[16] quod non apte[17] conueniat;[18] aut in uno die indicto[19] a promeridianis[20] horis iustitio[21] quisquam stomachetur[22] non sibi concedi[23] quid uenale[24] proponere,[25] quia mane[26] concessum est; aut in una domo uideat aliquid tractari[27] manibus a quoquam seruo quod facere non sinatur qui pocula[28] ministrat,[29] aut aliquid post praesepia[30] fieri quod ante mensam[31] prohibeatur,[32] et indignetur,[33] cum sit unum habitaculum[34] et una familia,[35] non ubique atque omnibus idem tribui.[36] sic sunt isti qui indignantur, cum audierint illo saeculo licuisse iustis aliquid quod isto non licet iustis, et quia illis aliud praecepit[37] Deus, istis aliud pro temporalibus[38] causis, cum eidem iustitiae utrique seruierint, cum in uno homine et in uno die et in unis aedibus[39] uideant aliud alii membro congruere,[40] et aliud iam dudum[41] licuisse, post horam non licere, quiddam in illo angulo[42] permitti[43] aut iuberi, quod in isto iuxta[44] uetetur[45] et uindicetur.[46] numquid iustitia *uaria*[47] *est et mutabilis* (Aen. 4.569)? sed tempora, quibus praesidet,[48] non pariter[49] eunt; tempora enim sunt. homines autem, quorum uita super terram breuis est, quia sensu non ualent causas conexere[50] saeculorum priorum aliarumque gentium, quas experti non sunt, cum his quas experti sunt, in uno autem corpore uel die uel domo facile possunt uidere quid cui membro, quibus momentis,[51] quibus partibus personisue[52] congruat, in illis offenduntur,[53] his seruiunt.

---

[11]adcommodatus ~a, ~um *adj.* **appropriate** [12]ocrea ~ae *f.* **shin guard** [13]contego ~gere, ~xi, ~ctum **to cover** [14]galea ~ae *f.* **helmet** [15]calcio ~are, ~aui, ~atum **to put shoes on** [16]murmuro ~are, ~aui, ~atum **to murmur or mutter** [17]apte *adv.* **aptly** [18]conuenio ~enire, ~eni, ~entum **to fit together** [19]indico ~cere, ~xi, ~ctum to make known > **to give public notice** [20]promeridianus ~a, ~um *adj.* **afternoon** [21]iustitium ~ii *neut.* **halt to business activity** [22]stomachor ~ari, ~atus **to be furious** [23]concedo ~dere, ~ssi, ~ssum **to allow or permit** [24]uenalis ~is, ~e *adj.* **for sale** [25]propono ~onere, ~osui, ~ositum **to put out** [26]mane *adv.* **in the morning** [27]tracto ~are, ~aui, ~atum **to handle** [28]poculum, -clum ~i *neut.* **drinks** (pl.) [29]ministro ~are, ~aui, ~atum **to serve** [30]praesepe, -saepe ~is *neut.* **horse stable** [31]mensa ~ae *f.* **dinner table** [32]prohibeo ~ere, ~ui, ~itum **to prohibit** [33]indignor ~ari, ~atus **to be indignant** [34]habitaculum ~i *neut.* **dwelling** [35]familia ~ae *f.* **family** [36]tribuo ~uere, ~ui, ~utum **to grant** [37]praecipio ~ipere, ~epi, ~eptum **to enjoin** [38]temporalis ~is, ~e *adj.* **temporary** [39]aedes, aedis ~is *f.* **house** [40]congruo ~ere, ~ui **to be appropriate** [41]'iam dudum' *adv.* **after all this time** [42]angulus ~i *m.* **corner** [43]permitto ~ittere, ~isi, ~issum **to permit** [44]iuxta *adv.* **side by side** [45]ueto ~are, ~ui, ~itum **to forbid** [46]uindico ~are, ~aui, ~atum **to punish** [47]uarius ~a, ~um *adj.* **variable** [48]praesideo ~idere, ~edi **to preside** [49]pariter *adv.* **alike** [50]conecto ~ctere, ~xui, ~xum **to connect** [51]momentum ~i *neut.* **moment** [52]persona ~ae *f.* **role** [53]offendo ~dere, ~di, ~sum **to take offense** (pass.)

Poetry like justice is constant

3.7.14 Haec ergo tunc nesciebam et non aduertebam,[1] et feriebant[2] undique[3] ista oculos meos, et non uidebam. et cantabam carmina et non mihi licebat ponere pedem quemlibet[4] ubilibet,[5] sed in alio atque alio[6] metro[7] aliter atque aliter[8] et in uno aliquo uersu[9] non omnibus locis eundem pedem. et ars ipsa qua canebam[10] non habebat aliud alibi,[11] sed omnia simul. et non intuebar iustitiam, cui seruirent boni et sancti homines, longe excellentius[12] atque sublimius[13] habere simul omnia quae praecipit[14] et nulla ex parte uariari[15] et tamen uariis[16] temporibus non omnia simul, sed propria[17] distribuentem[18] ac praecipientem. et reprehendebam[19] caecus[20] pios patres non solum, sicut Deus iuberet atque inspiraret,[21] utentes praesentibus uerum quoque, sicut Deus reuelaret,[22] futura praenuntiantes.[23]

[1]aduerto ~tere, ~ti, ~sum **to pay attention** [2]ferio ~ire **to assail** [3]undique *adv.* **from all directions** [4]quilibet, quae-, quod- *adj.* **whatever I please** [5]ubilibet *adv.* **wherever I please** [6]'alio atque alio' **different** [7]metrum, ~on ~i *neut.* **meter** [8]'aliter atque aliter' **differently** [9]uersus ~us *m.* **verse** [10]cano ~ere, cecini to sing > **to compose a poem** [11]'aliud alibi' **one in one place, another in another** [12]excellenter *adv.* **excellently** [13]sublimiter *adv.* **sublimely** [14]praecipio ~ipere, ~epi, ~eptum **to enjoin** [15]uario ~are, ~aui, ~atum **to vary** [16]uarius ~a, ~um *adj.* **various** [17]proprius ~a, ~um *adj.* **appropriate to each** [18]distribuo ~uere, ~ui, ~utum **to distribute** [19]reprehendo ~dere, ~di, ~sum **to find fault** [20]caecus ~a, ~um *adj.* **blind** [21]inspiro ~are, ~aui, ~atum to breathe in > **to inspire supernaturally** [22]reuelo ~are, ~aui, ~atum **to reveal** [23]praenuntio ~are, ~aui, ~atum **to predict**

Human laws conditioned by time and place

3.8.15 Numquid aliquando aut alicubi[1] iniustum[2] est diligere Deum *ex toto corde et ex tota anima et ex tota mente, et diligere proximum[3] tamquam te ipsum* (Lk 10:27)? itaque flagitia[4] quae sunt contra naturam ubique[5] ac semper detestanda[6] atque punienda[7] sunt, qualia Sodomitarum fuerunt. quae si omnes gentes facerent, eodem criminis reatu[8] diuina[9] lege tenerentur, quae non sic fecit homines ut se illo uterentur modo. uiolatur[10] quippe ipsa societas[11] quae cum Deo nobis esse debet cum eadem natura cuius ille auctor[12] est libidinis peruersitate[13] polluitur.[14]

[1]alicubi *adv.* **anywhere (at all)** [2]iniustus ~a, ~um *adj.* **unjust**; ECCL **unrighteous** [3]proximus ~a, ~um *superl. adj.* **neighbor** (*neut.* as noun) [4]flagitium ~ii *neut.* **indecency (of sexual misconduct)** [5]ubique *adv.* **everywhere** [6]detestor ~ari, ~atus **to detest** [7]punior, poenior ~iri, ~itus **to punish** [8]reatus ~us *m.* accused; LATE **guilt** [9]diuinus ~a, ~um *adj.* **divine** [10]uiolo ~are, ~aui, ~atum **to violate** [11]societas ~atis *f.* **fellowship** [12]auctor ~oris *m.* **author** [13]peruersitas ~atis *f.* **perversity** [14]polluo ~uere, ~ui, ~utum **to pollute**

Quae autem contra mores hominum sunt flagitia pro morum diuersi-tate[15] uitanda[16] sunt, ut pactum[17] inter se ciuitatis aut gentis consuetudine uel lege firmatum[18] nulla ciuis aut peregrini[19] libidine uioletur. turpis enim omnis pars uniuerso suo non congruens.[20] cum autem Deus ali-quid contra morem aut pactum quorumlibet[21] iubet, etsi numquam ibi factum est, faciendum est, et si omissum,[22] instaurandum,[23] et si institutum[24] non erat, instituendum est. si enim regi licet in ciuitate cui regnat[25] iubere aliquid quod neque ante illum quisquam nec ipse umquam iusserat, et non contra societatem ciuitatis eius obtempera-tur,[26] immo[27] contra societatem non obtemperatur (generale[28] quippe pactum est societatis humanae oboedire[29] regibus suis), quanto magis Deo Regnatori[30] uniuersae creaturae suae ad ea quae iusserit sine dubi-tatione[31] seruiendum est. sicut enim in potestatibus societatis humanae maior potestas minori ad oboediendum praeponitur,[32] ita Deus omnibus.

[15]diuersitas ~atis *f.* **diversity** [16]uito ~are, ~aui, ~atum **to avoid** [17]pactum ~i *neut.* **agreement** [18]firmo ~are, ~aui, ~atum **to establish** [19]peregrinus ~i *m.* **foreigner** [20]congruens ~ntis *adj.* **in keeping** [21]quilibet, quae-, quod- *pron.* **any (people) whatever** [22]omitto ~ittere, ~isi, ~issum **to discontinue** [23]instauro ~are, ~aui, ~atum **to resume** [24]instituo ~uere, ~ui, ~utum **to institute** [25]regno ~are, ~aui, ~atum **to reign** [26]obtempero ~are, ~aui, ~atum **to obey** (pass. *impers.*) [27]immo *particle* **rather** [28]generalis ~is, ~e *adj.* **in general** (abl.) [29]oboedio ~ire, ~iui, ~itum **to obey** (w. dat.) [30]regnator ~oris *m.* **ruler** [31]dubitatio ~onis *f.* **hesitation** [32]praepono ~onere, ~osui, ~ositum **to set in authority** x (acc.) **over** y (abl.)

The "ten-stringed" harp

3.8.16 Item[1] in facinoribus,[2] ubi libido est nocendi[3] siue per contume-liam[4] siue per iniuriam et utrumque uel ulciscendi[5] causa, sicut inimico inimicus, uel adipiscendi[6] alicuius extra[7] commodi,[8] sicut latro[9] uiatori,[10] uel euitandi[11] mali, sicut ei qui timetur, uel inuidendo,[12] sicut feliciori miserior aut in aliquo prosperatus[13] ei quem sibi aequari[14] timet aut aequalem[15] dolet, uel sola uoluptate alieni mali, sicut spectatores[16] gladiatorum[17] aut irrisores[18] aut inlusores[19] quorumlibet.[20]

[1]item *adv.* **similarly** [2]facinus ~oris *neut.* **deed > crime** [3]noceo ~ere, ~ui, ~itum **to injure** [4]contumelia ~ae *f.* **abusive language** [5]ulciscor ~cisci, ~tus **to inflict retribution** [6]adipiscor ~ipisci, ~eptus **to acquire** [7]extra *adv.* **beyond** [8]commodum ~i *neut.* **wages** [9]latro ~onis *m.* **robber** [10]uiator ~oris *m.* **traveler** [11]euito ~are, ~aui, ~atum **to evade** [12]inuideo ~idere, ~idi, ~isum **to be jealous of** [13]pro-spero ~are **to prosper** [14]aequo ~are, ~aui, ~atum **to be equal** [15]aequalis ~is *m.* **an equal in rank** [16]spectator ~oris *m.* **spectator** [17]gladiator ~oris *m.* **gladiator** [18]irrisor ~oris *m.* **scoffer** [19]inlusor ~oris *m.* ECCL **mocker** [20]quilibet, quae, quod- *pron.* **anyone whatever**

Haec sunt capita iniquitatis quae pullulant[21] principandi[22] et spectandi et sentiendi libidine aut una aut duabus earum aut simul omnibus, et uiuitur male[23] aduersus "tria et septem,"[24] *psalterium*[25] *decem*[26] *chordarum*[27] (Ps 32:2), decalogum[28] tuum, Deus altissime et dulcissime.

Sed quae flagitia[29] in te, qui non corrumperis?[30] aut quae aduersus te facinora, cui noceri non potest? sed hoc uindicas[31] quod in se homines perpetrant,[32] quia etiam cum in te peccant, impie[33] faciunt in animas suas, *et mentitur*[34] *iniquitas sibi* (Ps 26:12) siue corrumpendo ac peruertendo[35] naturam suam, quam tu fecisti et ordinasti,[36] uel immoderate[37] utendo concessis[38] rebus, uel in non concessa flagrando[39] *in eum usum qui est contra naturam* (Rom 1:26). aut rei tenentur[40] animo et uerbis saeuientes[41] aduersus te et *aduersus stimulum*[42] *calcitrantes*[43] (Acts 9:5), aut cum diruptis[44] limitibus[45] humanae societatis[46] laetantur[47] audaces[48] priuatis[49] conciliationibus[50] aut diremptionibus,[51] prout[52] quidque delectauerit aut offenderit.[53] et ea fiunt cum tu derelinqueris,[54] fons uitae, qui es unus et uerus creator et rector[55] uniuersitatis,[56] et priuata superbia[57] diligitur in parte "unum" falsum.

Itaque pietate humili[58] reditur in te, et purgas[59] nos a consuetudine mala, et propitius[60] es peccatis confitentium, et *exaudis gemitus*[61] *compeditorum*[62] (Ps 101:21), et soluis[63] a uinculis[64] quae nobis fecimus, si

[21]pullulo ~are, ~aui **spring forth** [22]principor ~ari, ~atum LATE **to rule over** [23]male *adv.* **badly** [24]septem *indecl. adj.* **seven** [25]psalterium ~i, *neut.* ECCL **psalter** [26]decem *indecl. adj.* **ten** [27]chorda ~ae *f.* **string** [28]decalogus ~i, *m.* ECCL **decalogue,** i.e., the ten commandments [29]flagitium ~ii *neut.* **indecency** [30]corrumpo ~umpere, ~upi, ~uptum **to corrupt** [31]uindico ~are, ~aui, ~atum **to avenge** [32]perpetro ~are, ~aui, ~atum **to perpetrate** [33]impie *adv.* **impiously** [34]mentior ~iri, ~itus **to deceive** [35]peruero ~tere, ~ti, ~sum **to pervert** [36]ordino ~are, ~aui, ~atum **to ordain** [37]immoderate *adv.* **immoderately** [38]concessus ~a, ~um *adj.* **permitted** [39]flagro ~are, ~aui **to burn with desire** [40]'rei tenentur' **found guilty** [41]saeuio ~ire, ~ii, ~itum **to rage** [42]stimulus ~i *m.* **goad** [43]calcitro ~are, ~aui, ~atum **to kick with the heels** [44]dirrumpo ~umpere, ~upi, ~uptum **to burst** [45]limes ~itis *m.* **limit** [46]societas ~atis *f.* **society** [47]laetor ~ari, ~atus **to take pleasure** [48]audax ~acis *adj.* **audacious** [49]priuatus ~a, ~um *adj.* **private** [50]conciliatio ~onis *f.* **alliance** [51]diremptio ~onis *f.* **division** [52]prout *conj.* **according as** [53]offendo ~dere, ~di, ~sum **to cause pain** [54]derelinquo ~inquere, ~iqui, ~ictum **to abandon** [55]rector ~oris *m.* **ruler** [56]uniuersitas ~atis *f.* **the universe** [57]superbia ~ae *f.* **pride** [58]humilis ~is, ~e *adj.* **humble** [59]purgo ~are, ~aui, ~atum **to purge** [60]propitius ~a, ~um *adj.* **propitious** [61]gemitus ~us *m.* **groaning** [62]compeditus ~a, ~um *adj.* **slave in fetters** (*m.* as noun) [63]soluo ~uere, ~ui, ~utum **to release** [64]uinculum ~i *neut.* **chain**

iam non erigamus[65] aduersus te cornua[66] falsae libertatis, auaritia[67] plus habendi et damno[68] totum amittendi, amplius amando proprium[69] nostrum quam te, omnium bonum.

[65]erigo ~igere, ~exi, ~ectum **to lift up** [66]cornu ~us *neut.* **horn** (fig. for defiance) [67]auaritia ~ae *f.* **avarice** [68]damnum ~i *neut.* **loss** [69]proprius ~a, ~um *adj.* **one's own** (*neut.* as noun)

Apparent but not actual sins

3.9.17 Sed inter flagitia[1] et facinora[2] et tam multas iniquitates sunt peccata proficientium,[3] quae a bene iudicantibus et uituperantur[4] ex regula[5] perfectionis[6] et laudantur spe frugis[7] sicut herba[8] segetis.[9] et sunt quaedam similia uel flagitio uel facinori et non sunt peccata, quia nec te offendunt,[10] Dominum Deum nostrum, nec sociale[11] consortium,[12] cum conciliantur[13] aliqua in usum uitae,[14] congrua[15] et tempori, et incertum[16] est an libidine habendi, aut puniuntur[17] corrigendi[18] studio potestate ordinata,[19] et incertum est an libidine nocendi.[20] multa itaque facta quae hominibus improbanda[21] uiderentur testimonio[22] tuo approbata[23] sunt, et multa laudata ab hominibus te teste[24] damnantur,[25] cum saepe se aliter habet species facti et aliter facientis animus atque articulus[26] occulti temporis.

Cum uero aliquid tu repente[27] inusitatum[28] et improuisum[29] imperas, etiamsi hoc aliquando uetuisti,[30] quamuis causam imperii tui pro tempore[31] occultes[32] et quamuis contra pactum[33] sit aliquorum hominum societatis,[34] quis dubitet[35] esse faciendum, quando ea iusta est societas

[1]flagitium ~ii *neut.* **indecency (of sexual misconduct)** [2]facinus ~oris *neut.* **deed > crime** [3]proficio ~icere, ~eci, ~ectum **to make progress** (morally) [4]uitupero ~are, ~aui, ~atum **to censure** [5]regula ~ae *f.* **rule** [6]perfectio ~onis *f.* **perfection** [7]frux ~ugis *f.* **fruit** (fig.) [8]herba ~ae *f.* **blade** (of corn) [9]seges ~etis *f.* **corn field** [10]offendo ~dere, ~di, ~sum **to give offense (to)** [11]socialis ~is, ~e *adj.* **fellowship** (as noun) [12]consortium ~ii *neut.* **community** [13]concilio ~are, ~aui, ~atum **to procure** [14]'in usum uitae' **in ordinary life** [15]congruus ~a, ~um *adj.* **appropriate** [16]incertus ~a, ~um *adj.* **uncertain** [17]punior, poenior ~iri, ~itus **to punish** [18]corrigo ~igere, ~exi, ~ectum **to chastise** [19]ordino ~are, ~aui, ~atum **to appoint** [20]noceo ~ere, ~ui, ~itum **to injure** [21]improbo ~are, ~aui, ~atum **to disapprove** [22]testimonium ~ii *neut.* **testimony** [23]approbo ~are, ~aui, ~atum **to approve** [24]testis ~is *m.* **witness** [25]damno ~are, ~aui, ~atum **to condemn** [26]articulus ~i *m.* **critical juncture** [27]repente *adv.* **suddenly** [28]inusitatus ~a, ~um *adj.* **unusual** [29]improuisus ~a, ~um *adj.* **unforeseen** [30]ueto ~are, ~ui, ~itum **to forbid** [31]'pro tempore' **at the time** [32]occulto ~are, ~aui, ~atum **to keep hidden** [33]pactum ~i *neut.* **convention** [34]societas ~atis *f.* **society** [35]dubito ~are, ~aui, ~atum **to doubt**

hominum quae seruit tibi? sed beati qui te imperasse sciunt. fiunt enim omnia a seruientibus tibi, uel ad exhibendum[36] quod ad praesens opus est, uel ad futura praenuntianda.[37]

[36]exhibeo ~ere, ~ui, ~itum **to reveal** [37]praenuntio ~are, ~aui, ~atum **to foreshadow**

Manichean liberation theology: burping out God

3.10.18 Haec ego nesciens inridebam illos sanctos seruos et prophe-tas[1] tuos. et quid agebam cum inridebam eos, nisi ut inriderer abs te sensim[2] atque paulatim[3] perductus[4] ad eas nugas[5] ut crederem ficum[6] plorare[7] cum decerpitur[8] et matrem eius arborem lacrimis lacteis?[9] quam tamen ficum si comedisset[10] aliquis sanctus, alieno sane[11] non suo scelere[12] decerptam, misceret uisceribus[13] et anhelaret[14] de illa angelos, immo uero[15] particulas[16] Dei gemendo[17] in oratione[18] atque ructando.[19] quae particulae summi et ueri Dei ligatae[20] fuissent in illo pomo,[21] nisi electi[22] sancti dente[23] ac uentre[24] soluerentur.[25] et credidi miser magis esse misericordiam praestandam[26] fructibus terrae quam hominibus propter quos nascerentur. si quis enim esuriens[27] peteret qui Manichaeus non esset, quasi capitali[28] supplicio[29] damnanda[30] buccella[31] uideretur si ei daretur.

[1]propheta ~ae *m.* ECCL **prophet** [2]sensim *adv.* **gradually** [3]paulatim *adv.* **by degrees** [4]perduco ~cere, ~xi, ~ctum **to lead** [5]nugae ~arum *f. pl.* **absurdities** [6]ficus ~i *m.* **fig** [7]ploro ~are, ~aui, ~atum **to weep** [8]decerpo ~ere, ~si, ~tum **to pluck off** (fruit from a tree) [9]lacteus ~a, ~um *adj.* **milky** [10]comedo ~edere, ~edi, ~esum **to eat up** [11]sane *adv.* **doubtless** (w. ironic force) [12]scelus ~eris *neut.* **guilt** [13]uiscus ~eris *neut.* **internal organs** [14]anhelo ~are, ~aui, ~atum **to exhale** [15]'immo uero' **no, in fact...** [16]particula ~ae *f.* **particle** [17]gemo ~ere, ~ui, ~itum **to groan** [18]oratio ~onis *f.* **speech**; ECCL **prayer** [19]ructo ~are, ~aui, ~atum **to belch out** [20]ligo ~are, ~aui, ~atum **to bind** [21]pomum ~i *neut.* **fruit** (from an orchard) [22]electus ~a, ~um *adj.* **"elect"** (high ranking Manichee) [23]dens ~ntis *m.* **tooth** [24]uenter ~tris *m.* **stomach** [25]soluo ~uere, ~ui, ~utum **to set free** [26]praesto ~are, ~iti, ~itum **to make available** [27]esuriens, ess- ~ntis *adj.* **starving** [28]capitalis ~is, ~e *adj.* **capital** [29]supplicium ~ii *neut.* **punishment** [30]damno ~are, ~aui, ~atum **to condemn** [31]buccella ~ae *f.* **morsel**

Monica's vision: the ruler

3.11.19 Et *misisti manum tuam ex alto*[1] (Ps 143:7) et de hac profunda[2] caligine[3] *eruisti*[4] *animam meam* (Ps 85:13), cum pro me fleret ad te

[1]altum ~i *neut.* **on high** [2]profundum ~i *neut.* **depths** [3]caligo ~inis *f.* **darkness** [4]eruo ~uere, ~ui, ~utum **to pluck out**; ECCL **to rescue**

mea mater, fidelis tua, amplius quam flent matres corporea funera.[5]
uidebat enim illa mortem meam ex fide et spiritu quem habebat ex te,
et exaudisti eam, Domine. exaudisti eam nec despexisti[6] lacrimas eius;
cum profluentes[7] rigarent[8] terram sub oculis eius in omni loco orationis[9]
eius, exaudisti eam. nam unde illud somnium[10] quo eam consolatus[11] es,
ut uiuere mecum cederet et habere mecum eandem mensam[12] in domo?
(quod nolle coeperat auersans[13] et detestans[14] blasphemias[15] erroris mei.)
uidit enim se stantem in quadam regula[16] lignea[17] et aduenientem[18] ad
se iuuenem splendidum[19] hilarem[20] atque arridentem[21] sibi, cum illa
esset maerens[22] et maerore[23] confecta.[24] qui cum causas ab ea quaesisset
maestitiae[25] suae cotidianarumque[26] lacrimarum, docendi, ut adsolet,[27]
non discendi gratia, atque illa respondisset perditionem[28] meam se
plangere,[29] iussisse illum (quo secura[30] esset) atque admonuisse,[31] ut
attenderet et uideret, ubi esset illa, ibi esse et me. quod illa ubi attendit,
uidit me iuxta[32] se in eadem regula stantem.

Unde hoc, nisi quia erant aures tuae ad cor eius, o tu bone Omnipotens,[33]
qui sic curas unumquemque[34] nostrum tamquam solum cures, et sic
omnes tamquam singulos?

[5]funus ~eris *neut.* **death** [6]despicio ~icere, ~exi, ~ectum **to despise** [7]profluo ~uere, ~uxi **to stream down** [8]rigo ~are, ~aui, ~atum **to soak** [9]oratio ~onis *f.* speech; ECCL **prayer** [10]somnium ~ii *neut.* **dream** [11]consolor ~ari, ~atus **to comfort** [12]mensa ~ae *f.* **dinner table** [13]auersor ~ari, ~atus **to turn away in disgust** [14]detestor ~ari, ~atus **to detest** [15]blasphemia ~ae *f.* ECCL **blasphemy** [16]regula ~ae *f.* **ruler** [17]ligneus ~a ~um *adj.* **wooden** [18]aduenio ~uenire, ~ueni, ~uentum **to approach** [19]splendidus ~a, ~um *adj.* **shining** [20]hilaris ~is, ~e. *adj.* **cheerful** [21]arrideo ~dere, ~si, ~sum **to smile at** [22]maerens ~ntis *adj.* **grieving** [23]maeror ~oris *m.* **grief** [24]conficio ~icere, ~eci, ~ectum **to complete** > **to overwhelm** [25]maestitia ~ae *f.* **sorrow** [26]cotidianus ~a, ~um *adj.* **daily** [27]adsoleo ~ere **to be in the habit of doing** [28]perditio ~onis *f.* ruin; ECCL **perdition** [29]plango ~gere, ~xi, ~ctum **to mourn for** [30]securus ~a, ~um *adj.* **untroubled** [31]admoneo ~ere, ~ui, ~itum **to admonish** [32]iuxta *prep. acc.* **by one's side** [33]omnipotens ~ntis *adj.* **omnipotent** [34]unusquisque *pron.* **each one**

Monica's interpretation

3.11.20 Unde illud etiam, quod cum mihi narrasset ipsum uisum, et
ego ad id trahere[1] conarer ut illa se potius non desperaret[2] futuram esse
quod eram, continuo[3] sine aliqua haesitatione:[4] "Non," inquit, "non

[1]traho ~here, ~xi, ~ctum to draw together > **to ascribe a meaning** [2]despero ~are, ~aui, ~atum **to despair** [3]continuo *adv.* **immediately** [4]haesitatio ~onis *f.* **hesitation**

enim mihi dictum est, 'Ubi ille, ibi et tu,' sed, 'Ubi tu, ibi et ille.'"
confiteor tibi, Domine, recordationem[5] meam, quantum recolo, quod
saepe non tacui, amplius me isto per matrem uigilantem[6] responso tuo,
quod tam uicina[7] interpretationis[8] falsitate[9] turbata[10] non est et tam
cito[11] uidit quod uidendum fuit (quod ego certe, antequam dixisset,
non uideram), etiam tum fuisse commotum[12] quam ipso somnio[13] quo
feminae piae gaudium tanto post[14] futurum ad consolationem[15] tunc
praesentis sollicitudinis[16] tanto ante[17] praedictum[18] est. nam nouem[19]
ferme[20] anni secuti sunt quibus ego *in illo limo*[21] *profundi*[22] (Ps 68:3)
ac tenebris falsitatis, cum saepe surgere[23] conarer et grauius[24] alliderer,[25]
uolutatus[26] sum, cum tamen illa uidua[27] casta,[28] pia et sobria,[29] quales
amas, iam quidem spe alacrior,[30] sed fletu[31] et gemitu[32] non segnior,[33]
non desineret[34] horis omnibus orationum[35] suarum de me plangere[36] ad
te, et *intrabant in conspectum tuum preces*[37] (Ps 87:3) eius, et me tamen
dimittebas adhuc uolui[38] et inuolui[39] illa caligine.[40]

[5]recordatio ~onis *f.* **recollection** [6]uigilans ~ntis *adj.* **vigilant** [7]uicinus ~a, ~um *adj.* **close** [8]interpretatio ~onis *f.* **interpretation** [9]falsitas ~atis *f.* LATE **error** [10]turbo ~are, ~aui, ~atum **to disturb** [11]cito *adv.* **easily** [12]commoueo ~ouere, ~oui, ~otum **to affect** [13]somnium ~ii *neut.* **dream** [14]'tanto post' **so much later** [15]consolatio ~onis *f.* **consolation** [16]sollicitudo ~inis *f.* **concern** [17]'tanto ante' **so long in advance** [18]praedico ~cere, ~xi, ~ctum **to predict** [19]nouem *indecl. adj.* **nine** [20]ferme *adv.* **nearly** [21]limus ~i *m.* **mire** [22]profundum ~i *neut.* **deep pit** [23]surgo ~rgere, ~rrexi, ~rrectum **to rise up** [24]grauiter *adv.* **grievously** [25]allido ~dere, ~si, ~sum **to strike down** [26]uoluto ~are, ~aui, ~atum **to roll** > **to wallow** (*pass. in middle sense*) [27]uiduus ~a, ~um *adj.* **widow** (*f.* as noun) [28]castus ~a, ~um *adj.* **chaste** [29]sobrius ~ia, ~ium *adj.* **sober** [30]alacer ~cris, ~cre *adj.* **lively** [31]fletus ~us *m.* **weeping** [32]gemitus ~us *m.* **groaning** [33]segnis ~is, ~e *adj.* **sluggish** [34]desino ~inere, ~iui, ~itum **to desist** [35]oratio ~onis *f.* **speech**; ECCL **prayer** [36]plango ~gere, ~xi, ~ctum **to bewail** [37]preces ~um *f. pl.* **prayers** [38]uoluo ~uere, ~ui, ~utum to roll > **to fall headlong** [39]inuoluo ~uere, ~ui, ~utum **to keep rolling** [40]caligo ~inis *f.* **darkness**

"Son of Tears"

3.12.21 Et dedisti alterum responsum interim[1] quod recolo. nam et
multa praetereo, propter quod propero[2] ad ea quae me magis urguent[3]
confiteri tibi, et multa non memini. dedisti ergo alterum per sacerdotem[4] tuum, quendam episcopum[5] nutritum[6] in ecclesia et exercitatum[7]

[1]interim *adv.* **meanwhile** [2]propero ~are, ~aui, ~atum **to be eager** [3]urgeo ~ere, ursi **to urge** [4]sacerdos ~otis *m.* **priest** [5]episcopus ~i *m.* ECCL **bishop** [6]nutrio ~ire, ~iui or ~ii, ~itum **to nurture** [7]exercitatus ~a, ~um *adj.* **proficient**

in libris tuis. quem cum illa femina rogasset[8] ut dignaretur[9] mecum conloqui[10] et refellere[11] errores meos et dedocere[12] me mala ac docere bona (faciebat enim hoc, quos forte idoneos[13] inuenisset), noluit ille, prudenter[14] sane,[15] quantum sensi postea. respondit enim me adhuc esse indocilem,[16] eo quod[17] inflatus[18] essem nouitate[19] haeresis[20] illius et nonnullis[21] quaestiunculis[22] iam multos imperitos[23] exagitassem,[24] sicut illa indicauerat ei. "Sed" inquit "sine illum ibi. tantum roga[25] pro eo Dominum. ipse legendo reperiet[26] quis ille sit error et quanta impietas."[27] simul etiam narrauit se quoque paruulum a seducta[28] matre sua datum fuisse Manichaeis, et omnes paene[29] non legisse tantum uerum etiam scriptitasse[30] libros eorum, sibique apparuisse nullo contra disputante[31] et conuincente[32] quam esset illa secta[33] fugienda: itaque fugisse.

Quae cum ille dixisset atque illa nollet adquiescere,[34] sed instaret[35] magis deprecando[36] et ubertim[37] flendo, ut me uideret et mecum dissereret,[38] ille iam substomachans[39] taedio,[40] "Vade"[41] inquit "a me. ita uiuas:[42] fieri non potest, ut filius istarum lacrimarum pereat." quod illa ita se accepisse inter conloquia[43] sua mecum saepe recordabatur, ac si de caelo sonuisset.

---

[8]rogo ~are, ~aui, ~atum **to ask** [9]digno ~are, ~aui, ~atum **to deign (to)** [10]conloquor ~qui, ~cutus **to talk together** [11]refello ~ere, ~i **to refute** [12]dedoceo ~ere, ~ui, ~tum **to disabuse** [13]idoneus ~a, ~um *adj.* **able** > **well-disposed** [14]prudenter *adv.* **prudently** [15]sane *adv.* **quite** (w. another *adv.*) [16]indocilis ~is, ~e *adj.* **unteachable** [17]'eo quod' **inasmuch as** [18]inflatus ~a, ~um *adj.* **inflated** [19]nouitas ~atis *f.* **novelty** [20]haeresis ~is *f.* **philosophical sect;** ECCL **heresy** [21]nonnullus ~a, ~um *adj.* **no few** [22]quaestiuncula ~ae *f.* **trifling question** [23]imperitus ~a, ~um *adj.* **inexperienced** [24]exagito ~are, ~aui, ~atum **to disturb continually** [25]rogo ~are, ~aui, ~atum **to ask;** ECCL **to pray** [26]reperio ~ire, repperi, ~tum **to discover** [27]impietas ~atis *f.* **impiety** [28]seduco ~cere, ~xi, ~ctum **to draw aside;** ECCL **to seduce** [29]paene *adv.* **practically** [30]scriptito ~are, ~aui, ~atum **to routinely copy out** [31]disputo ~are, ~aui, ~atum **to argue** [32]conuinco ~incere, ~ici, ~ictum **to convince** [33]secta ~ae *f.* **school of philosophy;** ECCL **sect** [34]adquiesco ~escere, ~ei **to acquiesce** [35]insto ~are, ~iti **to insist** [36]deprecor ~ari, ~atus **to beg** [37]ubertim *adv.* **copiously** [38]dissero ~ere, ~ui, ~tum **to discuss** [39]substomachor ~ari, ~atus AUG **to be somewhat annoyed** [40]taedium ~ii *neut.* **weariness** [41]uado ~ere **to go** [42]'ita uiuas' **as sure as you live!** [43]conloquium ~ii *neut.* **conversation**

4

TEACHER OF RHETORIC
AND MANICHEE

Carthage and Thagaste, 375–383

Publicly brilliant, privately silly

4.1.1 Per idem tempus annorum nouem,[1] ab undeuicensimo[2] anno aetatis meae usque ad duodetricensimum,[3] seducebamur[4] et seducebamus, falsi atque fallentes in uariis[5] cupiditatibus, et palam[6] per doctrinas quas "liberales"[7] uocant, occulte[8] autem falso nomine religionis,[9] hic[10] superbi, ibi superstitiosi,[11] ubique[12] uani, hac[13] popularis[14] gloriae sectantes[15] inanitatem,[16] usque ad theatricos[17] plausus[18] et contentiosa[19] carmina et agonem[20] coronarum[21] faenearum[22] et spectaculorum[23] nugas[24] et intemperantiam[25] libidinum, illac[26] autem purgari[27] nos ab istis sordibus[28] expetentes,[29] cum eis qui appellarentur[30] "electi[31] et sancti" afferremus[32] escas[33] de quibus nobis in officina[34] aqualiculi[35] sui

[1]nouem *indecl. adj.* **nine** [2]undeuicensimus ~a, ~um *adj.* **nineteenth** [3]duodetricensimus ~a, ~um *adj.* **twenty-eighth** [4]seduco ~cere, ~xi, ~ctum **to lead astray** [5]uarius ~a, ~um *adj.* **various** [6]palam *adv.* **openly** [7]liberalis ~is, ~e *adj.* **liberal** (of arts, studies, education) [8]occulte *adv.* **secretly** [9]religio ~onis *f.* **religion** [10]hic *adv.* **here** [11]superstitiosus ~a, ~um *adj.* **superstitious** [12]ubique *adv.* **everywhere** [13]hac *adv.* **on the one hand** [14]popularis ~is, ~e *adj.* **popular** [15]sector ~ari, ~atus **to pursue** [16]inanitas ~atis *f.* **emptiness** [17]theatricus ~a, ~um *adj.* AUG **of the theater** [18]plausus ~us *m.* **applause** [19]contentiosus ~a, ~um *adj.* **competitive** [20]agon ~onos *m.* **contest** [21]corona ~ae *f.* **crown** [22]faeneus ~a, ~um *adj.* **grass** [23]spectaculum ~i *neut.* **spectacle** [24]nugae ~arum *f. pl.* **frivolities** [25]intemperantia ~ae *f.* **intemperance** [26]illac *adv.* **on the other hand** [27]purgo ~are, ~aui, ~atum **to purge** [28]sordes ~is *f.* **stain** [29]expeto ~ere, ~iui, ~itum **to seek** [30]appello ~ellere, ~uli, ~ulsum **to call** (by a proper name) [31]electus ~a, ~um *adj.* **"elect"** (high ranking Manichee) [32]affero ~rre, attuli, allatum **to bring** [33]esca ~ae *f.* **food** [34]officina ~ae *f.* **workshop** [35]aqualiculus ~i *m.* **paunch**

fabricarent[36] angelos et deos per quos liberaremur.[37] et sectabar[38] ista atque faciebam cum amicis meis per me ac mecum deceptis.[39]

Inrideant me arrogantes[40] et nondum salubriter[41] prostrati[42] et elisi[43] a te, Deus meus, ego tamen confitear tibi dedecora[44] mea *in laude tua* (Ps 105:47). sine me, obsecro,[45] et da mihi circuire[46] praesenti memoria praeteritos circuitus[47] erroris mei et *immolare*[48] *tibi hostiam*[49] *iubilationis*[50] (Ps 26:6 VL). quid enim sum ego mihi sine te nisi dux in praeceps?[51] aut quid sum, cum mihi bene est, nisi sugens[52] lac[53] tuum aut fruens[54] te, *cibo qui non corrumpitur*[55] (Jn 6:27)? et quis homo est quilibet[56] homo, cum sit homo? sed inrideant nos fortes et potentes, nos autem infirmi[57] et inopes[58] confiteamur tibi.

[36]fabrico ~are, ~aui, ~atum **to forge** [37]libero ~are, ~aui, ~atum **to liberate** [38]sector ~ari, ~atus **to follow habitually** [39]decipio ~ipere, ~epi, ~eptum **to deceive** [40]arrogans ~ntis *adj.* **arrogant** [41]salubriter *adv.* **in a health giving way** [42]prosterno ~ernere, ~raui, ~ratum **to lay prostrate** [43]elido ~dere, ~si, ~sum **to crush**; ECCL **to cast down** [44]dedecus ~oris *neut.* **shameful act** [45]obsecro ~are, ~aui, ~atum **to beseech** [46]circueo ~ire, ~ii, ~iui, ~itum **to survey** [47]circuitus ~us *m.* **roving** [48]immolo ~are, ~aui, ~atum **to offer a sacrifice** [49]hostia ~ae *f.* **sacrifice** [50]iubilatio ~onis *f.* **jubilation** [51]praeceps ~ipitis *neut.* **headlong fall** [52]sugo ~gere, ~xi **to suck(le)** [53]lac lactis *neut.* **milk** [54]fruor ~i, ~ctus **to enjoy > to avail oneself of** [55]corrumpo ~umpere, ~upi, ~uptum **to spoil** [56]quilibet, quae-, quod- *adj.* **any whatever** [57]infirmus ~a, ~um *adj.* **weak** [58]inops ~pis *adj.* **poor**

Selling rhetoric... and the unnamed girl

4.2.2 Docebam in illis annis artem rhetoricam,[1] et uictoriosam[2] loqua-citatem[3] uictus cupiditate uendebam.[4] malebam[5] tamen, *Domine, tu scis* (Jn 21:15), bonos habere discipulos,[6] sicut appellantur[7] boni, et eos sine dolo[8] docebam dolos, non quibus contra *caput*[9] *innocentis*[10] (Off. 2.14.51) agerent sed aliquando pro capite nocentis.[11] et Deus, uidisti de longinquo[12] lapsantem[13] in lubrico[14] et in multo fumo[15] scintillan-tem[16] fidem meam, quam exhibebam[17] in illo magisterio[18] *diligentibus*[19] *uanitatem et quaerentibus mendacium* (Ps 4:3), socius eorum.

[1]rhetoricus ~a, ~um *adj.* **rhetorical** [2]uictoriosus ~a, ~um *adj.* **conducive to victory** [3]loquacitas ~atis *f.* **talkativeness** [4]uendo ~ere, ~idi, ~itum **to sell** (goods or services) [5]malo ~lle, ~lui **to prefer** [6]discipulus ~i *m.* **student** [7]appello ~ellere, ~uli, ~ulsum **to call** [8]dolus ~i *m.* **deception** [9]caput ~itis *neut.* **life** (endangered) [10]innocens ~ntis *adj.* **innocent** [11]nocens ~ntis *adj.* **guilty** [12]longinquo *adv.* **a long way off** [13]lapso ~are **to slip** [14]lubricus ~a, ~um *adj.* **slippery** [15]fumus ~i *m.* **smoke** [16]scintillo ~are **to send out sparks** [17]exhibeo ~ere, ~ui, ~itum **to exhibit** [18]magisterium ~ii *neut.* **office of teacher** [19]diligo ~igere, ~exi, ~ectum **to love**

In illis annis unam habebam non eo quod legitimum[20] uocatur coniugio[21] cognitam, sed quam indagauerat[22] uagus[23] ardor[24] inops[25] prudentiae,[26] sed unam tamen, ei quoque seruans tori[27] fidem, in qua sane[28] experirer exemplo meo[29] quid distaret[30] inter coniugalis[31] placiti modum, quod foederatum[32] esset generandi[33] gratia, et pactum[34] libidinosi[35] amoris, ubi proles[36] etiam contra uotum nascitur, quamuis iam nata cogat se diligi.

[20]legitimus ~a, ~um *adj.* **legitimate** (lawful) [21]coniugium ~ii *neut.* **marriage** [22]indago ~are, ~aui, ~atum **to find** [23]uagus ~a, ~um *adj.* **wandering** [24]ardor ~oris *m.* **passionate desire** [25]inops ~pis *adj.* **destitute** [26]prudentia ~ae *f.* **prudence** [27]torus ~i *m.* **bed** > **sexual relationship** (transf.) [28]sane *adv.* **to be sure** [29]'exemplo meo' **in my own case** [30]disto ~are **to be different** [31]coniugalis ~is, ~e *adj.* **conjugal** [32]foedero ~are, ~aui, ~atum **to seal** (an agreement) [33]genero ~are, ~aui, ~atum **to procreate** [34]pactum ~i *neut.* **agreement** [35]libidinosus ~a, ~um *adj.* **lustful** [36]proles ~is *f.* **offspring**

Animal sacrifice for the win

4.2.3 Recolo etiam, cum mihi theatrici[1] carminis certamen[2] inire[3] placuisset, mandasse[4] mihi nescio quem haruspicem,[5] quid ei dare uellem mercedis[6] ut uincerem, me autem foeda[7] illa sacramenta detestatum[8] et abominatum[9] respondisse, nec si corona[10] illa esset immortaliter[11] aurea[12] muscam[13] pro uictoria[14] mea necari[15] sinere. necaturus enim erat ille in sacrificiis[16] suis animantia,[17] et illis honoribus inuitaturus[18] mihi suffragatura[19] daemonia[20] uidebatur. sed hoc quoque malum non ex tua castitate[21] repudiaui,[22] *Deus cordis mei* (Ps 72:26). non enim amare te noueram, qui nisi fulgores[23] corporeos cogitare non noueram. talibus enim figmentis[24] suspirans anima *nonne fornicatur*[25] *abs te* (Ps 72:27) et *fidit*[26] *in falsis et pascit uentos* (Prov 10:4)? sed uidelicet[27] sacrificari[28]

[1]theatricus ~a, ~um *adj.* AUG **of the theater** [2]certamen ~inis *neut.* **competition** [3]ineo ~ire, ~ii, ~itum **to enter** [4]mando ~are, ~aui, ~atum **to message** [5]haruspex ~icis *m.* **soothsayer** [6]merces ~edis *f.* **fee** [7]foedus ~a, ~um *adj.* **loathsome** [8]detestor ~ari, ~atus **to detest** [9]abominor ~ari, ~atus **to loathe** [10]corona ~ae *f.* **crown** [11]immortaliter *adv. colloq.* **eternally** [12]aureus ~a, ~um *adj.* **golden** [13]musca ~ae *f.* **fly** [14]uictoria ~ae *f.* **victory in a contest** [15]neco ~are, ~aui, ~atum **to kill** [16]sacrificium ~ii *neut.* **sacrificial offering** [17]animans ~ntis *neut.* **animal** [18]inuito ~are, ~aui, ~atum **to invite** [19]suffragor ~ari, ~atus **to lend support** [20]daemon ~onis *m.* ECCL **demon** [21]castitas ~atis *f.* **purity** [22]repudio ~are, ~aui, ~atum **to reject** [23]fulgor ~oris *m.* **radiance** [24]figmentum ~i *neut.* **fiction** [25]fornico ~are, ~aui, ~atum ECCL **to commit adultery/idolatry** [26]fido ~ere, fisus **to place trust** (w. abl.) [27]uidelicet *adv.* **no doubt** (expr. irony) [28]sacrifico ~are, ~aui, ~atum **to offer as sacrifice**

pro me nollem daemonibus,[29] quibus me illa superstitione[30] ipse sacrificabam. quid est enim aliud "uentos pascere" quam ipsos pascere, hoc est errando[31] eis esse uoluptati atque derisui?[32]

[29]daemonium ~i *neut.* ECCL **demon** [30]superstitio ~onis *f.* **superstition** [31]erro ~are, ~aui, ~atum **to err > to be deluded** [32]derisus ~us *m.* **derision**

The fault in the stars

4.3.4 Ideoque illos planos[1] quos "mathematicos"[2] uocant plane[3] consulere[4] non desistebam,[5] quod quasi[6] nullum eis esset sacrificium[7] et nullae preces[8] ad aliquem spiritum ob diuinationem[9] dirigerentur.[10] quod tamen Christiana et uera pietas consequenter[11] repellit[12] et damnat.[13] *bonum est enim confiteri tibi, Domine* (Ps 91:2), et dicere, *Miserere mei: cura animam meam, quoniam peccaui tibi* (Ps 40:5), neque ad licentiam[14] peccandi abuti[15] indulgentia[16] tua, sed meminisse Dominicae[17] uocis: *Ecce sanus[18] factus es; iam noli peccare, ne quid tibi deterius[19] contingat[20]* (Jn 5:14). quam totam illi salubritatem[21] interficere[22] conantur cum dicunt, "De caelo tibi est ineuitabilis[23] causa peccandi" et "Venus hoc fecit aut Saturnus aut Mars," scilicet[24] ut homo sine culpa[25] sit, *caro et sanguis* (1 Cor 15:50) et superba putredo,[26] culpandus[27] sit autem caeli ac siderum creator et ordinator.[28] et quis est hic nisi Deus noster, suauitas[29] et origo[30] iustitiae, qui *reddes unicuique[31] secundum opera eius* (Mt 16:27, Rom 2:6) et *cor contritum[32] et humilatum[33] non spernis[34]* (Ps 50:19 VL)?

[1]planus ~i *m.* **fraud** [2]mathematicus ~i *m.* **astrologer** [3]plane *adv.* **utterly** [4]consulo ~ere, ~ui, ~tum **to consult** [5]desisto ~istere, ~titi **to leave off** [6]quod quasi' **because ostensibly** (w. subj.) [7]sacrificium ~ii *neut.* **sacrificial offering** [8]preces ~um *f. pl.* **prayer** [9]diuinatio ~onis *f.* **divination** (foreseeing the future) [10]dirigo ~igere, ~exi, ~ectum **to direct** [11]consequenter *adv.* **consequently** [12]repello ~ere, reppuli, repulsum **to reject** [13]damno ~are, ~aui, ~atum **to condemn** [14]licentia ~ae *f.* **license** [15]abutor ~ti, ~sus **to misuse** [16]indulgentia ~ae *f.* **leniency** [17]dominicus ~a, ~um *adj.* ECCL **of the LORD** [18]sanus ~a, ~um *adj.* **well** [19]deterior ~ior, ~ius *compar. adj.* **worse** [20]contingo ~ingere, ~igi, ~actum **to happen** (w. dat.) [21]salubritas ~atis *f.* **wholesomeness** [22]interficio ~ficere, ~feci, ~fectum **to destroy** [23]ineuitabilis ~is, ~e *adj.* **inevitable** [24]scilicet *adv.* **one may be sure** [25]culpa ~ae *f.* **blame** [26]putredo ~inis *f.* **putrefaction** [27]culpo ~are, ~aui, ~atum **to blame** [28]ordinator ~oris *m.* **orderer** [29]suauitas ~atis *f.* **sweetness** [30]origo ~inis *f.* **origin** [31]unusquisque *pron.* **each individual** [32]contero ~terere, ~triui, ~tritum **to crush, grind;** ECCL *ppl. adj.* **contrite** [33]humilo ~are, ~aui, ~atum ECCL **to humble** [34]sperno ~ere, spreui, spretum **to spurn**

Vindicianus helps but can't heal

4.3.5 Erat eo tempore[1] uir sagax,[2] medicinae[3] artis peritissimus[4] atque in ea nobilissimus, qui proconsul[5] manu sua coronam[6] illam agonisticam[7] imposuerat non sano[8] capiti meo, sed non ut medicus.[9] nam illius morbi[10] tu sanator,[11] qui *resistis superbis, humilibus*[12] *autem das gratiam* (Jas 4:6). numquid tamen etiam per illum senem[13] defuisti[14] mihi aut destitisti[15] mederi[16] animae meae? quia enim factus ei eram familiarior[17] et eius sermonibus (erant enim sine uerborum cultu[18] uiuacitate[19] sententiarum iucundi[20] et graues) adsiduus[21] et fixus[22] inhaerebam,[23] ubi cognouit ex conloquio[24] meo libris genethliacorum[25] esse me deditum,[26] benigne[27] ac paterne[28] monuit[29] ut eos abicerem[30] neque curam et operam[31] rebus utilibus[32] necessariam[33] illi uanitati frustra[34] impenderem,[35] dicens ita se illa didicisse ut eius professionem[36] primis annis aetatis suae deferre[37] uoluisset qua uitam degeret[38] et, si Hippocraten intellexisset, et illas utique litteras potuisse intellegere; et tamen non ob aliam causam[39] se postea illis relictis medicinam[40] adsecutum,[41] nisi quod eas falsissimas comperisset[42] et nollet uir grauis decipiendis[43] hominibus uictum[44] quaerere. "At tu" inquit "quo te in hominibus sustentas,[45] rhetoricam[46] tenes, hanc autem fallaciam[47] libero[48] studio, non necessitate[49] rei familiaris,[50] sectaris.[51] quo magis mihi te oportet[52] de illa credere, qui eam tam perfecte[53] discere elaboraui,[54] quam ex ea sola uiuere uolui."

[1]'eo tempore' **at that time** [2]sagax ~acis *adj.* **perceptive** [3]medicinus ~a, ~um *adj.* **medicinal** [4]peritus ~a, ~um *adj.* **skilled** [5]proconsul ~lis *m.* **proconsul** (governor of a province) [6]corona ~ae *f.* **crown** [7]agonisticus ~a, ~um *adj.* LATE **of a contest** [8]sanus ~a, ~um *adj.* **well** [9]medicus ~i *m.* **physician** [10]morbus ~i *m.* **disease** [11]sanator ~oris *m.* LATE **healer** [12]humilis ~is, ~e *adj.* **humble** [13]senex ~is, senior *m. adj.* **old man** [14]desum ~esse, ~fui **to fail** (w. dat. of person) [15]desisto ~istere, ~titi **to leave off** [16]medeor ~eri **to heal** [17]familiaris ~is, ~e *adj.* **familiar** [18]cultus ~us *m.* **polished** [19]uiuacitas ~atis *f.* vitality; LATE **liveliness** [20]iucundus ~a, ~um *adj.* **congenial** [21]adsiduus ~a, ~um *adj.* **continually** [22]fixus ~a, ~um *adj.* **fixed** [23]inhaereo ~rere, ~si, ~sum **to be utterly absorbed in** [24]conloquium ~ii *neut.* **conversation** [25]genethliacus ~i *m.* **caster of horoscopes** [26]deditus ~a, ~um *adj.* **devoted (to)** [27]benigne *adv.* **kindly** [28]paterne *adv.* AUG **fatherly** [29]moneo ~ere, ~ui, ~itum **to advise** [30]abicio ~cere, ~eci, ~ectum **to throw away** [31]opera ~ae *f.* **effort** [32]utilis ~is, ~e *adj.* **profitable** [33]necessarius ~a, ~um *adj.* **necessary** [34]frustra *adv.* **to no purpose** [35]impendo ~dere, ~di, ~sum **to expend** [36]professio ~onis *f.* **profession** [37]defero ~rre, detuli, delatum to transfer > **to switch** [38]dego ~ere **to spend (one's life)** [39]'non ob aliam causam' **for no other reason** [40]medicina ~ae *f.* **medicine** [41]adsequor ~qui, ~cutus **to pursue** [42]comperio ~ire, ~i, ~tum **to find out** [43]decipio ~ipere, ~epi, ~eptum **to deceive** [44]uictus ~us *m.* **living** [45]sustineo ~ere, ~ui **to sustain** [46]rhetoricus ~a, ~um *adj.* **rhetorical skill** (*f.* as noun) [47]fallacia ~ae *f.* **deceit** [48]liber ~era, ~erum *adj.* **free** [49]necessitas ~atis *f.* **necessity** [50]'rei familiaris' **personal finance** [51]sector ~ari, ~atus **to pursue** [52]'te oportet' it is right for you, i.e., **you should** [53]perfecte *adv.* **perfectly** [54]elaboro ~are, ~aui, ~atum **to take pains**

A quo ego cum quaesissem quae causa ergo faceret ut multa inde uera pronuntiarentur,[55] respondit ille ut potuit, uim sortis[56] hoc facere in rerum natura usquequaque[57] diffusam.[58] si enim de paginis[59] poetae[60] cuiuspiam[61] longe aliud canentis[62] atque intendentis, cum forte quis consulit,[63] mirabiliter[64] consonus[65] negotio[66] saepe uersus[67] exiret,[68] mirandum non esse dicebat si ex anima humana superiore[69] aliquo instinctu[70] nesciente quid in se fieret, non arte sed sorte, sonaret aliquid quod interrogantis rebus factisque concineret.[71]

[55]pronuntio ~are, ~aui, ~atum to announce; ECCL **to predict** [56]sors ~rtis *f.* **chance** [57]usquequaque *adv.* **everywhere** [58]diffundo ~undere, ~udi, ~usum **to diffuse** [59]pagina ~ae *f.* **page** [60]poeta ~ae *m.* **poet** [61]quispiam quae-, quod- *adj.* **one or other** [62]cano ~ere, cecini **to compose verse** [63]consulo ~ere, ~ui, ~tum **to consult** [64]mirabiliter *adv.* **extraordinarily** [65]consonus ~a, ~um *adj.* **in accord** [66]negotium ~ii *neut.* **the matter at hand** [67]uersus ~us *m.* **verse** [68]exeo ~ire, ~iui, ~itum **to turn out** [69]superior ~or, ~us *compar. adj.* **higher** [70]instinctus ~us *m.* **instinct** [71]concino ~ere, ~ui **to be in harmony**

Nebridius ridicules astrology

4.3.6 Et hoc quidem ab illo uel per illum procurasti[1] mihi, et quid ipse postea per me ipsum quaererem, in memoria mea deliniasti.[2] tunc autem nec ipse nec carissimus meus Nebridius, adulescens[3] ualde bonus et ualde cautus,[4] inridens totum illud diuinationis[5] genus, persuadere[6] mihi potuerunt ut haec abicerem,[7] quoniam me amplius ipsorum auctorum[8] mouebat auctoritas et nullum certum quale quaerebam documentum[9] adhuc inueneram, quo mihi sine ambiguitate[10] appareret, quae ab eis consultis[11] uera dicerentur, forte uel sorte[12] non arte inspectorum[13] siderum dici.

[1]procuro ~are, ~aui, ~atum to take care of; LATE **to cause to be done** [2]delinio ~are, ~aui, ~atum **to sketch** [3]adulescens ~ntis *m.* **young man** [4]cautus ~a, ~um *adj.* **circumspect** [5]diuinatio ~onis *f.* **divination** (foreseeing the future) [6]persuadeo ~dere, ~si, ~sum **to persuade** [7]abicio ~cere, ~eci, ~ectum **to throw away** [8]auctor ~oris m. **author** [9]documentum ~i *neut.* **example** [10]ambiguitas ~atis *f.* **ambiguity** [11]consultum ~i *neut.* **oracular response** [12]sors ~rtis *f.* **at random** [13]inspicio ~icere, ~exi, ~ectum **to observe**

An unnamed friend dies

4.4.7 In illis annis quo primum tempore[1] in municipio[2] quo natus sum docere coeperam, comparaueram[3] amicum societate[4] studiorum nimis

[1]'quo tempore' **at that time** [2]municipium ~ii *neut.* municipality (**town**) [3]comparo ~are, ~aui, ~atum to place together > **to pair up** (with a friend) [4]societas ~atis *f.* association > **affinity**

carum, coaeuum[5] mihi et conflorentem[6] flore[7] adulescentiae.[8] mecum
puer creuerat et pariter[9] in scholam[10] ieramus pariterque luseramus.[11] sed
nondum erat sic amicus, quamquam ne tunc quidem sic, uti[12] est uera
amicitia,[13] quia non est uera nisi cum eam tu agglutinas[14] inter haeren-
tes[15] tibi *caritate diffusa*[16] *in cordibus nostris per Spiritum Sanctum, qui
datus est nobis* (Rom 5:5). sed tamen dulcis erat nimis, cocta[17] feruore[18]
parilium[19] studiorum. nam et a fide uera, quam non germanitus[20] et
penitus[21] adulescens[22] tenebat, deflexeram[23] eum in superstitiosas[24]
fabellas[25] et perniciosas,[26] propter quas me plangebat[27] mater. mecum
iam errabat in animo ille homo, et non poterat anima mea sine illo. et
ecce tu imminens[28] dorso[29] fugitiuorum[30] tuorum, *Deus ultionum*[31] (Ps
93:1) et fons misericordiarum simul, qui conuertis nos ad te miris modis,
ecce abstulisti hominem de hac uita, cum uix expleuisset[32] annum in
amicitia mea, suaui[33] mihi super omnes suauitates[34] illius uitae meae.

[5]coaeuus ~a, ~um *adj.* ECCL **of the same age** [6]confloreo ~ere, ~ui AUG **to blossom together** [7]flos ~oris *m.* **blossom** [8]adulescentia ~ae *f.* **youth** [9]pariter *adv.* **together** [10]schola ~ae *f.* **school** [11]ludo ~dere, ~si, ~sum **to play** [12]'uti' = ut *adv.* **as** [13]amicitia ~ae *f.* **friendship** [14]agglutino ~are, ~aui, ~atum **to solder** [15]haereo ~rere, ~si, ~sum **to cling** [16]diffundo ~undere, ~udi, ~usum **to diffuse** [17]coctus ~a, ~um *adj.* **smelted** [18]feruor ~oris *m.* **heat, i.e., enthusiasm** [19]parilis ~is, ~e *adj.* **like in character** [20]germanitus *adv.* brotherly; LATE **genuinely** [21]penitus *adv.* **inwardly** [22]adulescens ~ntis *m.* **young man** [23]deflecto ~ctere, ~xi, ~xum **to turn aside** [24]superstitiosus ~a, ~um *adj.* **superstitious** [25]fabella ~ae *f.* **fable** [26]perniciosus ~a, ~um *adj.* **pernicious** [27]plango ~gere, ~xi, ~ctum **to mourn for** [28]immineo ~ere **to be almost upon** [29]dorsum ~i *neut.* **back** [30]fugitiuus ~i *m.* **fugitive** (esp. runaway slave) [31]ultio ~onis *f.* **vengeance** [32]expleo ~ere, ~eui, ~etum **to reach the end** [33]suauis ~is, ~e *adj.* **sweet** [34]suauitas ~atis *f.* **sweetness**

Unconscious baptism, unexpected result

4.4.8 Quis laudes tuas enumerat[1] unus in se uno quas expertus est?
quid tunc fecisti, Deus meus, et quam inuestigabilis[2] *abyssus iudiciorum
tuorum* (Ps 35:7)? cum enim laboraret[3] ille febribus,[4] iacuit diu sine
sensu in sudore[5] laetali[6] et, cum desperaretur,[7] baptizatus[8] est nesciens,
me non curante et praesumente[9] id retinere[10] potius animam eius quod a
me acceperat, non quod in nescientis corpore fiebat. longe autem aliter

[1]enumero ~are, ~aui, ~atum **to enumerate** [2]inuestigabilis ~is, ~e *adj.* ECCL **unsearchable** [3]laboro ~are, ~aui, ~atum **to suffer** [4]febris ~is *f.* **attack of fever** [5]sudor ~oris *m.* **sweat** [6]letalis ~is, ~e *adj.* **deathly** [7]despero ~are, ~aui, ~atum **to despair** [8]baptizo ~are, ~aui, ~atum ECCL **to baptize** [9]praesumo ~ere, ~si, ~ptum **to assume**; ECCL **to presume** [10]retineo ~ere, ~ui, retentum **to retain**

erat. nam recreatus[11] est et saluus[12] factus, statimque,[13] ut primo[14] cum eo loqui potui (potui autem mox ut[15] ille potuit, quando non discedebam[16] et nimis pendebamus[17] ex inuicem[18]), temptaui[19] apud illum inridere, tamquam et illo inrisuro mecum baptismum[20] quem acceperat mente atque sensu absentissimus, sed tamen iam se accepisse didicerat. at ille ita me exhorruit[21] ut inimicum admonuitque[22] mirabili[23] et repentina[24] libertate ut, si amicus esse uellem, talia sibi dicere desinerem.[25] ego autem stupefactus[26] atque turbatus[27] distuli[28] omnes motus meos, ut conualesceret[29] prius essetque idoneus[30] uiribus ualetudinis,[31] cum quo agere possem quod uellem. sed ille abreptus[32] dementiae[33] meae, ut apud te seruaretur consolationi[34] meae. post paucos[35] dies me absente repetitur[36] febribus et defungitur.[37]

[11]recreo ~are, ~aui, ~atum **to revive** [12]saluus ~a, ~um *adj.* **alive and well** [13]statim *adv.* **immediately** [14]'ut primo' **as soon as** [15]'mox ut' **as soon as** [16]discedo ~dere, ~ssi, ~ssum **to leave** [17]pendeo ~ere, pependi **to depend on** (w. 'ex') [18]inuicem *adv.* **mutually** [19]tempto ~are, ~aui, ~atum **to attempt** [20]baptismus ~i *m.* ECCL **baptism** [21]exhorresco ~escere, ~ui **to shudder** [22]admoneo ~ere, ~ui, ~itum **to warn** [23]mirabilis ~is, ~e *adj.* **astonishing** [24]repentinus ~a, ~um *adj.* **sudden** [25]desino ~inere, ~iui, ~itum **to leave off** [26]stupefacio ~facere, ~feci, ~factum **to stupefy** [27]turbo ~are, ~aui, ~atum **to throw into confusion** [28]differo ~rre, distuli, dilatum **to postpone** [29]conualesco ~escere, ~ui **to convalesce** [30]idoneus ~a, ~um *adj.* **fit** > **well-disposed** [31]'uiribus ualetudinis' **in good health** [32]abripio ~ipere, ~ipui, ~eptum **to snatch away** [33]dementia ~ae *f.* **insanity** [34]consolatio ~onis *f.* **consolation** [35]paucus ~a, ~um *adj.* **a few** [36]repeto ~ere, ~iui or ~ii, ~itum **to attack again** (of disease) [37]defungor ~gi, ~ctus **to die**

Black grief

4.4.9 Quo dolore *contenebratum*[1] *est cor meum* (Lam 5:17), et quidquid aspiciebam mors erat. et erat mihi patria supplicium[2] et paterna[3] domus mira infelicitas,[4] et quidquid cum illo communicaueram,[5] sine illo in cruciatum[6] immanem[7] uerterat. Expetebant[8] eum undique[9] oculi mei, et non dabatur. et oderam omnia, quod non haberent eum, nec mihi iam dicere poterant, "Ecce ueniet," sicut cum uiueret, quando absens erat. factus eram ipse mihi magna quaestio,[10] et interrogabam animam

[1]contenebro ~are, ~aui, ~atus ECCL **to darken** [2]supplicium ~ii *neut.* **torment** [3]paternus ~a, ~um *adj.* **father's** [4]infelicitas ~atis *f.* **unhappiness** [5]communico ~are, ~aui, ~atum **to share** [6]cruciatus ~us *m.* **form of torture** [7]immanis ~is, ~e *adj.* **brutal** [8]expeto ~ere, ~iui, ~itum **to look for** [9]undique *adv.* **all around** [10]quaestio ~onis *f.* **puzzle**

meam quare[11] tristis esset et quare conturbaret[12] me ualde, et nihil nouerat respondere mihi. et si dicebam, *Spera*[13] *in Deum* (Ps 41:6), iuste[14] non obtemperabat,[15] quia uerior erat et melior homo quem carissimum amiserat quam phantasma[16] in quod sperare iubebatur. solus fletus[17] erat dulcis mihi et successerat[18] amico *meo in deliciis*[19] animi *mei* (Ps 138:11).

[11]quare *adv.* **why?** [12]conturbo ~are, ~aui, ~atum **to dismay** [13]spero ~are, ~aui, ~atum **to hope in** [14]iuste *adv.* **justifiably** [15]obtempero ~are, ~aui, ~atum **to obey** [16]phantasma ~atis *neut.* **phantom;** LATE **figment of the imagination** [17]fletus ~us *m.* **weeping** [18]succedo ~dere, ~ssi, ~ssum **to succeed** > **to replace** (w. dat.) [19]delicia ~ae *f.* **delight**

Why does crying help?

4.5.10 Et nunc, Domine, iam illa transierunt, et tempore lenitum[1] est uulnus meum. possumne audire abs te, qui ueritas es, et admouere[2] aurem cordis mei ori tuo, ut dicas mihi cur fletus[3] dulcis sit miseris? an tu, quamuis ubique[4] adsis, longe abiecisti[5] a te miseriam nostram, et tu in te manes, nos autem in experimentis[6] uoluimur?[7] et tamen nisi ad aures tuas ploraremus,[8] nihil residui[9] de spe nostra fieret. unde igitur suauis[10] fructus de amaritudine[11] uitae carpitur,[12] gemere[13] et flere et suspirare et conqueri?[14] an hoc ibi dulce est, quod speramus[15] exaudire te? recte[16] istuc[17] in precibus,[18] quia desiderium peruemendi[19] habent. num[20] in dolore amissae rei et luctu,[21] quo tunc operiebar?[22] neque enim sperabam reuiuescere[23] illum aut hoc petebam lacrimis, sed tantum dolebam et flebam. miser enim eram et amiseram gaudium meum. an et fletus res amara[24] est et, prae fastidio[25] rerum quibus prius fruebamur[26] et tunc ab eis abhorremus,[27] delectat?

[1]lenio ~ire, ~iui or ~ii, ~itum **to becomes less intense** (*pass.*) [2]admoueo ~mouere, ~moui, ~motum **to bring near** [3]fletus ~us *m.* **weeping** [4]ubique *adv.* **everywhere** [5]abicio ~cere, ~eci, ~ectum **to push away** [6]experimentum ~i *neut.* **trial** [7]uoluo ~uere, ~ui, ~utum **to fall headlong** [8]ploro ~are, ~aui, ~atum **to weep aloud** [9]residuus ~a, ~um *adj.* **remnant** (*neut.* as noun) [10]suauis ~is, ~e *adj.* **sweet** [11]amaritudo ~inis *f.* **bitterness** [12]carpo ~ere, ~si, ~tum **to pick** [13]gemo ~ere, ~ui, ~itum **to groan** [14]conqueror ~ri, ~stus **to lament** [15]spero ~are, ~aui, ~atum **to hope that** (w. acc. and inf.) [16]recte *adv.* **rightly** [17]istic ~aec, ~uc *pron.* **this sort of thing** [18]preces ~um *f. pl.* **prayer** [19]peruenio ~enire, ~eni, ~entum **to reach** (the ears of a person) [20]num *particle* (*expects a negative answer*) **surely not..?** [21]luctus ~us *m.* **grief** [22]operio ~ire, ~ui, ~tum **to cover** > **to envelop** [23]reuiuesco ~escere, reuixi, reuictum **to revive** [24]amarus ~a, ~um *adj.* **bitter** [25]fastidium ~ii *neut.* **aversion** [26]fruor ~i, ~ctus **to enjoy** [27]abhorreo ~ere, ~ui **to recoil (from)**

Horace: a friend is half one's soul

4.6.11 Quid autem ista loquor? non enim tempus quaerendi nunc est, sed confitendi tibi. miser eram, et miser est omnis animus uinctus[1] amicitia[2] rerum mortalium,[3] et dilaniatur[4] cum eas amittit, et tunc sentit miseriam qua miser est et antequam amittat eas. sic ego eram illo tempore et flebam amarissime[5] et requiescebam in amaritudine.[6] ita miser eram et habebam cariorem illo amico meo uitam ipsam miseram. nam quamuis eam mutare uellem, nollem tamen amittere magis quam illum, et nescio an uellem uel pro illo, sicut de *Oreste et Pylade* (Amic. 7.24, Fin. 5.63) traditur, si non fingitur,[7] qui uellent pro inuicem[8] uel simul mori, qua[9] morte peius eis erat non simul uiuere. sed in me nescio quis affectus nimis huic contrarius[10] ortus[11] erat, et taedium[12] uiuendi erat in me grauissimum et moriendi metus. credo, quo magis illum amabam, hoc magis mortem, quae mihi eum abstulerat, tamquam atrocissimam[13] inimicam oderam et timebam, et eam repente[14] consumpturam[15] omnes homines putabam, quia illum potuit. sic eram omnino, memini.

Ecce cor meum, Deus meus, ecce intus. uide, quia memini, *spes mea* (Ps 70:5), qui me mundas[16] a talium affectionum[17] immunditia,[18] dirigens[19] oculos meos ad te et *euellens*[20] *de laqueo*[21] *pedes meos* (Ps 24:15). mirabar enim ceteros mortales[22] uiuere, quia ille, quem quasi non moriturum dilexeram, mortuus erat, et me magis, quia ille alter eram, uiuere illo mortuo mirabar. bene quidam dixit de amico suo: *dimidium*[23] *animae suae* (Carm. 1.3.8). nam ego sensi animam meam et animam illius *unam fuisse animam in duobus corporibus* (Tr. 4.4.72), et ideo mihi horrori[24] erat uita, quia nolebam dimidius uiuere, *et ideo forte mori metuebam, ne totus ille moreretur quem multum amaueram* (retr. 2.6.2).

---

[1]uincio ~cire, ~xi, ~ctum **to chain** [2]amicitia ~ae *f.* **friendship** [3]mortalis ~is, ~e *adj.* **mortal** [4]dilanio ~are, ~aui, ~atum **to tear to pieces** [5]amare *adv.* **bitterly** [6]amaritudo ~inis *f.* **bitterness** [7]fingo ~ngere, ~nxi, ~ctum **to invent** [8]inuicem *adv.* **each other** [9]qua *adv.* **inasmuch as** [10]contrarius ~a, ~um *adj.* **contrary** [11]orior ~iri, ~tus **to rise** [12]taedium ~ii *neut.* **tired (of)** [13]atrox ~ocis, ~ocior, ~ocissimus *adj.* **ruthless** [14]repente *adv.* **suddenly** [15]consumo ~ere, ~psi, ~ptum **to devour** [16]mundo ~are, ~aui, ~atum **to make clean** [17]affectio ~onis *f.* **affection** [18]immunditia ~ae *f.* **uncleanness** [19]dirigo ~igere, ~exi, ~ectum **to direct** [20]euello ~ellere, ~elli, ~ulsum **to pluck** [21]laqueus ~i *m.* **snare** [22]mortalis ~is *m.* **mortal** [23]dimidius ~a, ~um *adj.* **half** [24]horror ~oris *m.* **horror**

Loving people as more than people

4.7.12 O dementiam[1] nescientem diligere homines humaniter![2] o stultum[3] hominem immoderate[4] humana patientem! quod ego tunc eram. itaque aestuabam,[5] suspirabam, flebam, turbabar,[6] nec requies[7] erat nec consilium. Portabam[8] enim concisam[9] et cruentam[10] animam meam impatientem[11] portari a me, et ubi eam ponerem non inueniebam. non in amoenis[12] nemoribus, non in ludis[13] atque cantibus, nec in suaue[14] olentibus[15] locis, nec in conuiuiis[16] apparatis,[17] neque in uoluptate cubilis[18] et lecti,[19] non denique[20] in libris atque carminibus[21] adquiescebat.[22] horrebant[23] omnia et ipsa lux, et quidquid non erat quod ille erat improbum[24] et odiosum[25] erat praeter gemitum[26] et lacrimas: nam in eis solis aliquantula[27] requies. ubi autem inde auferebatur anima mea, onerabat[28] me grandi sarcina[29] miseriae. *ad te, Domine, leuanda[30] erat* (Ps 24:1) et curanda, sciebam, sed nec uolebam nec ualebam, eo magis[31] quia non mihi eras aliquid solidum[32] et firmum,[33] cum de te cogitabam. non enim tu eras, sed uanum phantasma[34] et error meus erat deus meus. si conabar eam ibi ponere ut requiesceret, per inane[35] labebatur[36] et iterum[37] ruebat[38] super me, et ego mihi remanseram[39] infelix[40] locus, ubi nec esse possem nec inde recedere. quo enim cor meum fugeret a corde meo? quo a me ipso fugerem? quo non me sequerer? et tamen fugi de patria. minus enim eum quaerebant oculi mei ubi uidere non solebant, atque a Thagastensi oppido[41] ueni Carthaginem.

---

[1]dementia ~ae *f.* insanity [2]humaniter *adv.* **humanly** [3]stultus ~a, ~um *adj.* **foolish** [4]immoderate *adv.* **immoderately** [5]aestuo ~are, ~aui, ~atum **to surge** (with emotion) [6]turbo ~are, ~aui, ~atum **to upset** [7]requies ~etis *f.* **rest** [8]porto ~are, ~aui, ~atum **to carry** [9]concido ~dere, ~di, ~sum **to cut to pieces** [10]cruentus ~a, ~um *adj.* **bleeding** [11]impatiens ~ntis *adj.* **impatient (of)** [12]amoenus ~a, ~um *adj.* **charming** [13]ludus ~i *m.* **game** [14]suauis ~is, ~e *adj.* **fragrant** [15]olens ~ntis *adj.* **aromatic** [16]conuiuium ~ii *neut.* **feast** [17]apparatus ~a, ~um *adj.* **sumptuous** [18]cubile ~is *neut.* **bed** [19]lectus ~i *m.* **couch** [20]denique *adv.* **lastly** [21]carmen ~inis *neut.* **incantation** [22]adquiesco ~escere, ~ei **to find rest** [23]horreo ~ere, ~ui **to have a gloomy appearance** [24]improbus ~a, ~um *adj.* **inferior** [25]odiosus ~a, ~um *adj.* **hateful** [26]gemitus ~us *m.* **groaning** [27]aliquantulum ~i *neut.* **small amount** [28]onero ~are, ~aui, ~atum **to weigh down** [29]sarcina ~ae *f.* **load** [30]leuo ~are, ~aui, ~atum **to lift up** [31]eo magis' **so much the more** [32]solidus ~a, ~um *adj.* **solid** [33]firmus ~a, ~um *adj.* **firm** [34]phantasma ~atis *neut.* phantom; LATE **figment of the imagination** [35]inane ~is *neut.* **emptiness** [36]labor ~bi, ~psus **to sink down** [37]iterum *adv.* **again** [38]ruo ~ere, ~i **to rush** [39]remaneo ~ere, ~si **to remain** [40]infelix ~icis *adj.* **unhappy** [41]oppidum ~i *neut.* **town**

Time and friends ease the pain

4.8.13 Non uacant[1] tempora nec otiose[2] uoluuntur[3] per sensus nostros: faciunt in animo mira opera. ecce ueniebant et praeteribant *de die in diem* (Ps 60:9), et ueniendo et praetereundo inserebant[4] mihi spes alias et alias memorias, et paulatim[5] resarciebant[6] me pristinis[7] generibus delectationum,[8] quibus cedebat dolor meus ille; sed succedebant[9] non quidem dolores alii, causae tamen aliorum dolorum. nam unde me facillime et in intima[10] dolor ille penetrauerat,[11] nisi quia fuderam[12] in harenam[13] animam meam diligendo moriturum acsi[14] non moriturum? maxime quippe me reparabant[15] atque recreabant[16] aliorum amicorum solacia,[17] cum quibus amabam quod pro te amabam, et hoc erat ingens fabula[18] et longum mendacium, cuius adulterina[19] confricatione[20] corrumpebatur[21] mens nostra *pruriens*[22] *in auribus* (2 Tim 4:3). sed illa mihi fabula non moriebatur, si quis amicorum meorum moreretur.

Alia erant quae in eis amplius capiebant animum, conloqui[23] et conridere[24] et uicissim[25] beniuole[26] obsequi,[27] simul legere libros dulciloquos,[28] simul nugari[29] et simul honestari,[30] dissentire[31] interdum[32] sine odio[33] tamquam ipse homo secum atque ipsa rarissima[34] dissensione[35] condire[36] consensiones[37] plurimas,[38] docere aliquid inuicem[39] aut discere ab inuicem, desiderare absentes cum molestia,[40] suscipere[41] uenientes cum laetitia: his atque huius modi[42] signis a corde amantium et redamantium[43]

---

[1]uaco ~are, ~aui, ~atum **to be idle** [2]otiose *adv.* **in a leisurely way** [3]uoluo ~uere, ~ui, ~utum **to roll along** [4]insero ~erere, ~eui, ~itum **to implant** (fig.) [5]paulatim *adv.* **gradually** [6]resarcio ~cire, ~sum **to restore** [7]pristinus ~a, ~um *adj.* **previous** [8]delectatio ~onis *f.* **delight** [9]succedo ~dere, ~ssi, ~ssum **to come after** [10]intimus ~a, ~um *superl. adj.* **inmost self** (*neut. pl.* as noun) [11]penetro ~are, ~aui, ~atum **to penetrate** [12]fundo ~ere, fudi, fusum **to pour out** [13]harena ~ae *f.* **sand** [14]acsi *conj.* = ac si **as if** [15]reparo ~are, ~aui, ~atum **to recover** [16]recreo ~are, ~aui, ~atum **to revive** [17]solacium ~ii *neut.* **solace** [18]'ingens fabula' **enormous mythology** (i.e. the Manichee system) [19]adulterinus ~a, ~um *adj.* **adulterous** [20]confricatio ~onis *f.* AUG **stimulus** [21]corrumpo ~umpere, ~upi, ~uptum **to corrupt** [22]prurio ~ire **to itch** [23]conloquor ~qui, ~cutus **to discuss** [24]conrideo ~ere **to laugh together** [25]uicissim *adv.* **in turn** [26]beniuole *adv.* **in a spirit of goodwill** [27]obsequor ~qui, ~cutus **to defer to another** [28]dulciloquus ~a, ~um *adj.* **worded sweetly** [29]nugor ~ari **to quibble** [30]honesto ~are, ~aui, ~atum to show respect; LATE **to be earnest** [31]dissentio ~tire, ~si, ~sum **to differ in opinion** [32]interdum *adv.* **now and then** [33]odium ~i *neut.* **antipathy** [34]rarus ~a, ~um *adj.* **infrequent** [35]dissensio ~onis *f.* **disagreement** [36]condio ~ire, ~iui, ~itum **to give zest to** [37]consensio ~onis *f.* **agreement** [38]plurimus ~a, ~um *superl. adj.* **very numerous** [39]inuicem *adv.* **each in turn** [40]molestia ~ae *f.* **distress** [41]suscipio ~ipere, ~epi, ~eptum **to receive** [42]'huius modi' **of this kind** [43]redamo ~are **to love in return**

procedentibus⁴⁴ per os, per linguam, per oculos et mille motus gratissimos, quasi fomitibus⁴⁵ conflare⁴⁶ animos et ex pluribus unum facere.

⁴⁴procedo ~dere, ~ssi, ~ssum **to proceed** ⁴⁵fomes ~itis *m.* **kindling** ⁴⁶conflo ~are, ~aui, ~atum
to blow on a fire

The source of grief

4.9.14 Hoc est quod diligitur in amicis, et sic diligitur ut rea¹ sibi sit humana conscientia² si non amauerit redamantem³ aut si amantem non redamauerit, nihil quaerens ex eius corpore praeter indicia⁴ beniuolentiae.⁵ hinc ille luctus⁶ si quis moriatur, et tenebrae dolorum, et uersa dulcedine⁷ in amaritudinem⁸ cor madidum,⁹ et ex amissa uita morientium mors uiuentium. beatus qui amat te et amicum in te et inimicum propter te. solus enim nullum carum amittit cui omnes in illo cari sunt qui non amittitur. et quis est iste nisi Deus noster, *Deus, qui fecit caelum et terram* (Gen 1:1) et *implet ea* (Jer 23:24), quia implendo ea fecit ea? te nemo amittit nisi qui dimittit, et quia dimittit, quo it aut *quo fugit* (Ps 138:7) nisi a te placido¹⁰ ad te iratum?¹¹ nam ubi non inuenit legem tuam in poena sua? et *lex tua ueritas* (Ps 118:142) et *ueritas tu* (Jn 14:6).

¹rea ~ae *f.* **guilty one** ²conscientia ~ae *f.* **conscience** ³redamo ~are **to love in return** ⁴indicium ~ii
neut. **indication** ⁵beniuolentia ~ae *f.* **goodwill** ⁶luctus ~us *m.* **grief** ⁷dulcedo ~inis *f.* **sweetness**
⁸amaritudo ~inis *f.* **bitterness** ⁹madidus ~a, ~um *adj.* **steeped** ¹⁰placidus ~a, ~um *adj.* **kindly**
¹¹iratus ~a, ~um *adj.* **angry**

No rest in transient things: a poem

4.10.15 *Deus uirtutum,*¹ *conuerte nos et ostende faciem tuam, et salui*² *erimus* (Ps 79:8). nam quoquouersum³ se uerterit anima hominis, ad dolores figitur⁴ alibi⁵ praeterquam⁶ in te, tametsi⁷ figitur in pulchris extra⁸ te et extra se. quae tamen nulla essent, nisi essent abs te. quae oriuntur⁹ et occidunt¹⁰ et oriendo quasi esse incipiunt, et crescunt ut

¹'Deus uirtutum' ECCL **God of hosts** ²saluus ~a, ~um *adj.* **safe** ³quoquouersum *adv.* **in whatever
direction** ⁴figo ~gere, ~xi, ~xum **to fix in** (place) ⁵alibi *adv.* **elsewhere** ⁶praeterquam *conj.* **apart
from** ⁷tametsi *conj.* **even though** ⁸extra *prep. acc.* **outside** ⁹orior ~iri, ~tus **to rise** ¹⁰occido ~idere,
~idi, ~asum **to fall**

perficiantur, et perfecta senescunt[11] et intereunt:[12] et non omnia senescunt, et omnia intereunt. ergo cum oriuntur et tendunt[13] esse, quo
magis celeriter[14] crescunt ut sint, eo magis[15] festinant[16] ut non sint:
sic est modus eorum. tantum dedisti eis, quia partes sunt rerum, quae
non sunt omnes simul, sed decedendo[17] ac succedendo[18] agunt omnes
uniuersum, cuius partes sunt. (ecce sic peragitur[19] et sermo noster per
signa sonantia. non enim erit totus sermo, si unum uerbum non decedat,
cum sonuerit partes suas, ut succedat aliud.)

> Laudet te ex illis anima mea,
> *Deus, creator omnium* (Hymn 2.1),
> sed non in eis figatur glutine[20] amore per sensus corporis.
> eunt enim quo ibant,
> ut non sint,
> et conscindunt[21] eam desideriis pestilentiosis,[22]
> quoniam ipsa esse uult et requiescere amat in eis quae amat.
> in illis autem non est ubi,
> quia non stant:
> fugiunt, et quis ea sequitur sensu carnis?
> aut quis ea comprehendit, uel cum praesto[23] sunt?
> tardus[24] est enim sensus carnis, quoniam sensus carnis est:
> ipse est modus eius.
> sufficit[25] ad aliud, ad quod factus est,
> ad illud autem non sufficit, ut teneat transcurrentia[26]
> ab initio[27] debito usque ad finem debitum.
> in Verbo enim tuo, per quod creantur,
> ibi audiunt,
> *Hinc et huc usque*[28] (Job 38:11).

[11]senesco ~escere, ~ui **to grow old** [12]intereo ~ire, ~ii, ~itum **to die** [13]tendo ~dere, tetendi, ~tum or ~sum **to tend towards** [14]celeriter *adv.* **quickly** [15]'eo magis' **so much the more** [16]festino ~are, ~aui, ~atum **to hasten** [17]decedo ~dere, ~ssi, ~ssum **to pass away** [18]succedo ~dere, ~ssi, ~ssum **to come after** [19]perago ~agere, ~egi, ~actum **to complete** [20]gluten ~inis *neut.* glue; LATE **bond** [21]conscindo ~indere, ~idi, ~issum **to tear in pieces** [22]pestilentiosus ~a, ~um *adj.* **pestilential** [23]praesto *adv.* **near at hand** [24]tardus ~a, ~um *adj.* **slow** [25]sufficio ~icere, ~eci, ~ectum **to be sufficient** [26]transcurro ~currere, ~curri, ~cursum **to run a course** [27]initium ~ii *neut.* **beginning** [28]'huc usque' **thus far**

The Word calls to a place of quiet

4.11.16 Noli esse uana, anima mea, et obsurdescere[1] in aure cordis tumultu[2] uanitatis tuae. audi et tu: Verbum ipsum clamat ut redeas, et ibi est locus quietis[3] imperturbabilis,[4] ubi non deseritur amor si ipse non deserat. ecce illa discedunt[5] ut alia succedant,[6] et omnibus suis partibus constet[7] infima[8] uniuersitas.[9] "Numquid ego aliquo[10] discedo?" ait Verbum Dei. ibi fige[11] mansionem[12] tuam, ibi commenda[13] quidquid inde habes, anima mea; saltem[14] fatigata[15] fallaciis,[16] Veritati commenda quidquid tibi est a ueritate, et non perdes aliquid, *et reflorescent*[17] *putria*[18] *tua* (Ps 27:7), et *sanabuntur omnes languores*[19] *tui* (Ps 102:3 VL), et fluxa[20] tua reformabuntur[21] et renouabuntur[22] et constringentur[23] ad te, et non te deponent[24] quo descendunt,[25] sed stabunt tecum et permanebunt[26] ad semper stantem ac permanentem Deum.

[1]obsurdesco ~escere, ~ui **to become deaf** [2]tumultu ~us *m.* **confused uproar** [3]quies ~etis *f.* **rest** [4]imperturbabilis ~is, ~e *adj.* AUG **imperturbable** [5]discedo ~dere, ~ssi, ~ssum **to pass away** [6]succedo ~dere, ~ssi, ~ssum **to succeed** [7]consto ~are, ~iti **to stand together** [8]infimus ~a, ~um *superl. adj.* **lowest** [9]uniuersitas ~atis *f.* **universe** [10]aliquo *adv.* **anywhere** [11]figo ~gere, ~xi, ~xum **to fix** [12]mansio ~onis *f.* **dwelling** [13]commendo ~are, ~aui, ~atum **to entrust** [14]saltem *adv.* **at least** [15]fatigo ~are, ~aui, ~atum **to wear down** [16]fallacia ~ae *f.* **deceit** [17]refloresco ~escere, ~ui **to flower again** [18]puter ~tris, ~tre *adj.* putrid > **disintegrated with age** [19]languor ~oris *m.* **sickness** [20]fluxus ~a, ~um *adj.* flowing > **crumbling** [21]reformo ~are, ~aui, ~atum **to restore** [22]renouo ~are, ~aui, ~atum **to renew** [23]constringo ~ngere, ~nxi, ~ctum **to hold together** [24]depono ~onere, ~osui, ~ostum **to set down** [25]descendo ~dere, ~di, ~sum **to descend** [26]permaneo ~ere, ~si, ~sum **to continue to be**

Experience: partial and passing away

4.11.17 Ut quid[1] peruersa[2] sequeris carnem tuam? ipsa te sequatur conuersam. quidquid per illam sentis in parte est, et ignoras totum cuius hae partes sunt, et delectant te tamen. sed si ad totum comprehendendum esset idoneus[3] sensus carnis tuae, ac non et ipse in parte uniuersi accepisset pro tua poena iustum modum, uelles ut transiret quidquid existit[4] in praesentia,[5] ut magis tibi omnia placerent. nam et quod loquimur per eundem sensum carnis audis, et non uis utique stare syllabas[6] sed transuolare,[7] ut aliae ueniant et totum audias. ita semper

[1]'ut quid' ECCL = quid (*adv.*) **why?** [2]peruerto ~tere, ~ti, ~sum **to pervert** [3]idoneus ~a, ~um *adj.* **adequate** [4]exsisto ~ere, extiti **to exist** [5]praesentia ~ae *f.* **presence** [6]syllaba ~ae *f.* **syllable** [7]transuolo ~are, ~aui, ~atum **to fly through the air**

omnia, quibus unum aliquid constat[8] (et non sunt omnia simul ea quibus constat): plus delectant omnia quam singula, si possint sentiri omnia. sed longe his melior qui fecit omnia, et *ipse est Deus* (Ps 99:3) noster, et non discedit,[9] quia nec succeditur[10] ei.

[8]consto ~are, ~iti **to stand together** [9]discedo ~dere, ~ssi, ~ssum **to pass away** [10]succedo ~dere, ~ssi, ~ssum **to succeed** (*impers.* w. dat.)

Speak to the others

4.12.18 Si placent corpora, Deum ex illis lauda et in artificem[1] eorum retorque[2] amorem, ne in his quae tibi placent tu displiceas. si placent animae, in Deo amentur, quia et ipsae mutabiles sunt et in illo fixae[3] stabiliuntur:[4] alioquin[5] irent et perirent. in illo ergo amentur, et rape ad eum tecum quas potes et dic eis:

"Hunc amemus: ipse fecit haec et *non est longe* (Acts 17:27). non enim fecit atque abiit,[6] sed ex illo in illo sunt. ecce ubi est, ubi sapit[7] ueritas: intimus[8] cordi est, sed cor errauit ab eo. *redite, praeuaricatores,*[9] *ad cor* (Isa 46:8) et inhaerete[10] illi qui fecit uos. state cum eo et stabitis, requiescite in eo et quieti[11] eritis. quo itis in aspera?[12] quo itis? bonum quod amatis ab illo est: sed quantum est ad illum, bonum est et suaue;[13] sed amarum[14] erit iuste,[15] quia iniuste[16] amatur deserto illo quidquid ab illo est. quo uobis adhuc et adhuc *ambulare*[17] *uias difficiles*[18] (Wis 5:7) et laboriosas?[19] non est requies[20] ubi quaeratis eam. quaerite quod quaeritis, sed ibi non est ubi quaeritis. beatam uitam quaeritis in regione[21] mortis: non est illic. quomodo enim beata uita, ubi nec uita? **[19]** Et descendit[22] huc ipsa uita nostra, et tulit mortem nostram et occidit[23] eam de abundantia[24] uitae suae, et tonuit,[25] clamans ut redeamus hinc

[1]artifex ~ficis *m.* **maker** [2]retorqueo ~quere, ~si, ~tum **to cast back** [3]fixus ~a, ~um *adj.* **fixed** [4]stabilio ~ire, ~iui, ~itum **to make stable** [5]alioquin *adv.* **otherwise** [6]abeo ~ire, ~ii, ~itum **to go away** [7]sapio ~ere, ~ii **to taste of** [8]intimus ~a, ~um *superl. adj.* **inmost** [9]praeuaricator ~oris *m.* lawyer guilty of collusion (legal); ECCL **apostate** [10]inhaereo ~rere, ~si, ~sum **to cling to** [11]quietus ~a, ~um *adj.* **at rest** [12]asper ~era, ~erum *adj.* rough > **difficult to traverse** [13]suauis ~is, ~e *adj.* **sweet** [14]amarus ~a, ~um *adj.* **bitter** [15]iuste *adv.* **justly** [16]iniuste *adv.* **unjustly** [17]ambulo ~are, ~aui, ~atum **to walk** [18]difficilis ~is, ~e *adj.* **difficult** [19]laboriosus ~a, ~um *adj.* **laborious** [20]requies ~etis *f.* **rest** [21]regio ~onis *f.* **land** [22]descendo ~dere, ~di, ~sum **to descend** [23]occido ~dere, ~di, ~sum **to kill** [24]abundantia ~ae *f.* **abundance** [25]tono ~are, ~ui **to thunder**

ad eum in illud secretum[26] unde processit[27] ad nos, in ipsum primum[28] Virginalem[29] uterum[30] ubi ei nupsit[31] humana creatura, caro mortalis,[32] ne semper mortalis. et inde *uelut sponsus[33] procedens de thalamo[34] suo exultauit[35] ut gigans[36] ad currendam[37] uiam* (Ps 18:6). non enim tardauit,[38] sed cucurrit clamans dictis, factis, morte, uita, descensu,[39] ascensu,[40] clamans ut redeamus ad eum: et discessit[41] ab oculis, ut redeamus ad eum. et discessit ab oculis, ut redeamus ad cor et inueniamus eum. abscessit[42] enim et ecce hic[43] est. noluit nobiscum diu esse et non reliquit nos. illuc[44] enim abscessit unde numquam recessit, *quia mundus per eum factus est, et in hoc mundo erat* (Jn 1:10–11) et *uenit in hunc mundum peccatores[45] saluos facere*[46] (1 Tim 1:15). cui confitetur *anima mea et sanat eam, quoniam peccauit illi* (Ps 40:5). *filii hominum, quo usque[47] graues corde?* (Ps 4:3). numquid et post descensum uitae non uultis ascendere[48] et uiuere? sed quo ascenditis, quando in alto[49] estis et *posuistis in caelo os uestrum* (Ps 72:9)? descendite, ut ascendatis, et ascendatis ad Deum. cecidistis enim ascendendo contra Deum."

Dic eis ista, ut plorent[50] *in conualle[51] plorationis[52]* (Ps 83:7 VL), et sic eos rape tecum ad Deum, quia de Spiritu eius haec dicis eis, si dicis ardens[53] igne caritatis.

---

[26]secretum ~i *neut.* **secret place** [27]procedo ~dere, ~ssi, ~ssum **to come forth** [28]primum *adv.* **first** [29]uirginalis ~is, ~e *adj.* **virginal** [30]uterum ~i *neut.* **womb** [31]nubo ~bere, ~psi, ~ptum **to wed** [32]mortalis ~is, ~e *adj.* **mortal** [33]sponsus ~i *m.* **bridegroom** [34]thalamus, ~os ~i *m.* **chamber** [35]exulto ~are, ~aui **to exult** [36]gigans ~ntis *m.* **giant** [37]curro ~rere, cucurri, ~sum **to run** [38]tardo ~are, ~aui, ~atum **to hold back** [39]descensus ~us *m.* descent; ECCL **descent into Hell** [40]ascensus ~us *m.* ascent; ECCL **Ascension** [41]discedo ~dere, ~ssi, ~ssum **to depart** [42]abscedo ~dere, ~ssi, ~ssum **to go away** [43]hic *adv.* **here** [44]illuc *adv.* **to that place** [45]peccator ~oris *m.* ECCL **sinner** [46]'saluos facere' ECCL **to save (from sin)** [47]quousque *adv. (often as two words)* **how long** [48]ascendo ~dere, ~di, ~sum **to ascend** [49]altum ~i *neut.* **heights** [50]ploro ~are, ~aui, ~atum **to weep aloud** [51]conuallis ~is *f.* **valley** [52]ploratio ~onis *f.* ECCL **tears** [53]ardens ~ntis *adj.* **burning**

A lost work: *The Beautiful and the Fitting*

4.13.20 Haec tunc non noueram, et amabam pulchra inferiora[1] et ibam in profundum,[2] et dicebam amicis meis, "Num[3] amamus aliquid nisi pulchrum? quid est ergo pulchrum? et quid est pulchritudo?[4] quid est

---

[1]inferior ~ior, ~ius *compar. adj.* **lower** [2]profundum ~i *neut.* **depths** [3]num *particle (expects a negative answer)* **surely not..?** [4]pulchritudo ~inis *f.* **beauty**

quod nos allicit[5] et conciliat[6] rebus quas amamus? nisi enim esset in eis decus[7] et species, nullo modo nos ad se mouerent." et animaduertebam[8] et uidebam in ipsis corporibus aliud esse quasi totum et ideo pulchrum, aliud autem quod ideo deceret,[9] quoniam apte[10] adcommodaretur[11] alicui, sicut pars corporis ad uniuersum suum aut calciamentum[12] ad pedem et similia. et ista consideratio[13] scaturriuit[14] in animo meo ex intimo[15] corde meo, et scripsi libros *de Pulchro et Apto*[16] — puto duos aut tres: *tu scis, Deus* (Ps 68:6), nam excidit[17] mihi. non enim habemus eos, sed aberrauerunt[18] a nobis nescio quo modo.

[5]allicio ~icere, ~exi, ~ectum **to attract** [6]concilio ~are, ~aui, ~atum **to win over** [7]decus ~oris *neut.* **grace** [8]animaduerto ~tere, ~ti, ~sum **to pay careful attention** [9]decet ~ere, ~uit **to adorn** [10]apte *adv.* **aptly** [11]adcommodo ~are, ~aui, ~atum **to fit** [12]calciamentum ~i *neut.* **shoe** [13]consideratio ~onis *f.* **consideration** [14]scaturrio ~ire **to gush forth** [15]intimus ~a, ~um *adj.* **inmost** [16]aptus ~a, ~um *ppl. adj.* **fitting** [17]excido ~ere, ~i **to slip away** [18]aberro ~are, ~aui, ~atum **to get away from**

To Hierius, from Augustine

4.14.21 Quid est autem quod me mouit, Domine Deus meus, ut ad Hierium, Romanae urbis oratorem,[1] scriberem illos libros? quem non noueram facie, sed amaueram hominem ex doctrinae fama, quae illi clara erat, et quaedam uerba eius audieram et placuerant mihi. sed magis quia placebat aliis et eum efferebant laudibus,[2] stupentes[3] quod ex homine Syro, docto prius Graecae facundiae,[4] post in Latina etiam dictor[5] mirabilis[6] extitisset[7] et esset scientissimus rerum ad studium sapientiae pertinentium,[8] mihi placebat. laudatur homo et amatur absens. Utrumnam[9] ab ore laudantis intrat in cor audientis amor ille? absit! sed ex amante alio accenditur[10] alius. hinc enim amatur qui laudatur, dum non fallaci[11] corde laudatoris[12] praedicari[13] creditur, id est cum amans eum laudat.

[1]orator ~oris *m.* **orator** [2]'efferebant laudibus' **they used to praise highly** [3]stupeo ~ere, ~ui **to be stunned** [4]facundia ~ae *f.* **ability to speak/write fluently** [5]dictor ~oris *m.* LATE **speaker** [6]mirabilis ~is, ~e *adj.* **marvelous** [7]exsisto ~ere, extiti **to prove to be** [8]pertineo ~ere, ~ui **to pertain to** [9]utrumnam *conj.* LATE *introduces direct question* [10]accendo ~dere, ~di, ~sum **to enkindle** [11]fallax ~acis *adj.* **disingenuous** [12]laudator ~oris *m.* **person who praises** [13]praedico ~are, ~aui, ~atum **to make special mention**

Admiration is contagious

4.14.22 Sic enim tunc amabam homines ex hominum iudicio, non enim ex tuo, Deus meus, in quo nemo fallitur. sed tamen cur non sicut auriga[1] nobilis, sicut uenator[2] studiis popularibus[3] diffamatus,[4] sed longe aliter et grauiter[5] et ita, quemadmodum et me laudari uellem? non autem uellem ita laudari et amari me ut histriones,[6] quamquam eos et ipse laudarem et amarem, sed eligens[7] latere[8] quam ita notus esse et uel haberi odio[9] quam sic amari. ubi distribuuntur[10] ista pondera[11] uariorum[12] et diuersorum[13] amorum in anima una? quid est quod amo in alio quod rursus nisi odissem, non a me detestarer[14] et repellerem,[15] cum sit uterque nostrum homo? non enim sicut equus bonus amatur ab eo qui nollet hoc esse etiamsi posset. hoc et de histrione dicendum est, qui naturae nostrae socius est. ergone amo in homine quod odi esse, cum sim homo? grande profundum[16] est ipse homo, *cuius etiam capillos[17] tu, Domine, numeratos habes* (Mt 10:30) et non minuuntur[18] in te: et tamen capilli eius magis numerabiles[19] quam affectus eius et motus cordis eius.

[1]auriga ~ae *m.* **charioteer** [2]uenator ~oris *m.* **animal-fighter in an arena** [3]popularis ~is, ~e *adj.* **popular** [4]diffamatus ~a, ~um *adj.* **widely known** [5]grauiter *adv.* **seriously** [6]histrio ~onis *f.* **actor** [7]eligo ~igere, ~egi, ~ectum **to choose**; ECCL **to prefer** [8]lateo ~ere, ~ui **to hide** > **to live in obscurity** [9]'haberi odio' **to be regarded with contempt** [10]distribuo ~uere, ~ui, ~utum **to arrange** [11]pondus ~eris *neut.* **weight** [12]uarius ~a, ~um *adj.* **various** [13]diuersus ~a, ~um *adj.* **diverse** [14]detestor ~ari, ~atus **to detest** [15]repello ~ere, reppuli, repulsum **to thrust away** [16]profundum ~i *neut.* **deep** [17]capillus ~i *m.* **hair** [18]minuo ~uere, ~ui, ~utum **to diminish** [19]numerabilis ~is, ~e *adj.* **easy to count**

Getting noticed

4.14.23 At ille rhetor[1] ex eo erat genere quem sic amabam ut uellem esse me talem. et errabam typho[2] *et circumferebar[3] omni uento* (Eph 4:14), et nimis occulte[4] gubernabar[5] abs te. et unde scio et unde certus confiteor tibi quod illum in amore laudantium magis amaueram quam in rebus ipsis de quibus laudabatur? quia si non laudatum uituperarent[6]

[1]rhetor ~oris *m.* **rhetorician** [2]typhus ~i *m.* ECCL **proud vanity** [3]circumfero ~ferre, ~tuli, ~latum **to carry about** [4]occulte *adv.* **secretly** [5]guberno ~are, ~aui, ~atum **to steer** [6]uitupero ~are, ~aui, ~atum **to find fault**

eum idem ipsi et uituperando atque spernendo[7] ea ipsa narrarent, non accenderer[8] in eo et non excitarer,[9] et certe res non aliae forent nec homo ipse alius, sed tantummodo alius affectus narrantium. ecce ubi iacet anima infirma[10] nondum haerens[11] soliditati[12] ueritatis: sicut aurae linguarum flauerint[13] a pectoribus opinantium,[14] ita fertur et uertitur,[15] torquetur[16] ac retorquetur,[17] et obnubilatur[18] ei lumen et non cernitur ueritas, et ecce est ante nos.

Et magnum quiddam mihi erat, si sermo meus et studia mea illi uiro innotescerent.[19] quae si probaret,[20] flagrarem[21] magis; si autem improbaret,[22] sauciaretur[23] cor uanum et inane[24] soliditatis tuae. et tamen pulchrum illud atque aptum,[25] unde ad eum scripseram, libenter[26] animo uersabam[27] ob os[28] contemplationis[29] meae et nullo conlaudatore[30] mirabar.

[7]sperno ~ere, spreui, spretum **to spurn** [8]accendo ~dere, ~di, ~sum **to kindle** [9]excito ~are, ~aui, ~atum **to excite** [10]infirmus ~a, ~um *adj.* **infirm** [11]haereo ~rere, ~si, ~sum **to adhere to** [12]soliditas ~atis *f.* **solidity** [13]flo ~are, ~aui, ~atum **to blow** (of winds) [14]opinor ~ari, ~atus **to express an opinion** [15]uerto ~tere, ~ti, ~sum **to turn > to go to and fro** (pass. in middle sense) [16]torqueo ~quere, ~si, ~tum **to twist** [17]retorqueo ~quere, ~si, ~tum **to twist back around** [18]obnubilo ~are, ~aui, ~atum **to render obscure** [19]innotesco ~escere, ~ui **to become known** [20]probo ~are, ~aui, ~atum **to approve** [21]flagro ~are, ~aui **to burn** (with love) [22]improbo ~are, ~aui, ~atum **to reject** [23]saucio ~are, ~aui, ~atum **to wound** [24]inanis ~is, ~e *adj.* **empty** [25]aptus ~a, ~um *ppl. adj.* **fitting** [26]libenter *adv.* **with pleasure** [27]uerso ~are, ~aui, ~atum **to turn over and over** [28]ob os' **before one's eyes** [29]contemplatio ~onis *f.* **contemplation** [30]conlaudator ~oris *m.* AUG **one who joins in praising**

Tracing God's artistry

4.15.24 Sed tantae rei cardinem[1] in arte tua nondum uidebam, Omnipotens,[2] *qui facis mirabilia[3] solus* (Ps 71:18), et ibat animus per formas corporeas et pulchrum, quod per se ipsum, aptum[4] autem, quod ad aliquid adcommodatum[5] deceret,[6] definiebam[7] et distinguebam[8] et exemplis[9] corporeis adstruebam.[10] et conuerti me ad animi naturam, et non me sinebat falsa opinio[11] quam de spiritalibus habebam uerum

[1]cardo ~inis *m.* **hinge** *or* **axis** [2]omnipotens ~ntis *adj.* **omnipotent** [3]mirabile ~is *neut.* ECCL **wonder** [4]aptus ~a, ~um *ppl. adj.* **fitting** [5]adcommodatus ~a, ~um *adj.* **suitable** [6]decet ~ere, ~uit **to accord with** [7]definio ~ire, ~iui or ~ii, ~itum **to define** [8]distinguo ~guere, ~xi, ~ctum **to distinguish** [9]exemplum ~i *neut.* **example** [10]adstruo ~ere, ~xi, ~ctum to build; LATE **to support** *or* **to prove** [11]opinio ~onis *f.* **opinion**

cernere. et inruebat[12] in oculos ipsa uis ueri, et auertebam[13] palpitantem[14] mentem ab incorporea[15] re ad liniamenta[16] et colores[17] et tumentes[18] magnitudines[19] et, quia non poteram ea uidere in animo, putabam me non posse uidere animum. et cum in uirtute pacem amarem, in uitiositate[20] autem odissem discordiam,[21] in illa unitatem,[22] in ista quandam diuisionem[23] notabam,[24] inque illa unitate mens rationalis[25] et natura ueritatis ac summi boni mihi esse uidebatur, in ista uero diuisione inrationalis[26] uitae nescioquam substantiam et naturam summi mali, quae non solum esset substantia sed omnino uita esset, et tamen abs te non esset, Deus meus, *ex quo sunt omnia* (1 Cor 8:6), miser opinabar.[27] et illam "monadem"[28] appellabam tamquam sine ullo sexu[29] mentem, hanc uero "dyadem,"[30] iram in facinoribus,[31] libidinem in flagitiis,[32] nesciens quid loquerer. non enim noueram neque didiceram nec ullam substantiam malum esse nec ipsam mentem nostram summum atque incommutabile bonum.

[12]inruo ~uere, ~ui **to rush against** [13]auerto ~tere, ~ti, ~sum **to avert** [14]palpito ~are, ~aui **to palpitate** [15]incorporeus ~a, ~um *adj.* **incorporeal** [16]liniamentum ~i *neut.* **line** [17]color ~oris *m.* **color** [18]tumeo ~ere, ~ui **to distend** [19]magnitudo ~inis *f.* **vast space** [20]uitiositas ~atis *f.* **vice** [21]discordia ~ae *f.* **discord** [22]unitas ~atis *f.* **unity** [23]diuisio ~onis *f.* **division** [24]noto ~are, ~aui, ~atum **to note** [25]rationalis ~is, ~e *adj.* **rational** [26]inrationalis ~is, ~e *adj.* **irrational** [27]opinor ~ari, ~atus **to suppose** (to be true) [28]monas ~dis *f.* LATE **"monad"** (unity in Pythagorean phil.) [29]sexus ~us *m.* *(neut.)* **sex** (male or female) [30]dyas, duas ~adis *f.* LATE **"dyad"** (duality in Pythagorean phil.) [31]facinus ~oris *neut.* deed > **crime** [32]flagitium ~ii *neut.* **indecency** (of sexual misconduct)

Inclination determines outcome

4.15.25 Sicut enim facinora[1] sunt, si uitiosus[2] est ille animi motus in quo est impetus et se iactat[3] insolenter[4] ac turbide,[5] et flagitia,[6] si est immoderata[7] illa animae affectio[8] qua carnales[9] hauriuntur[10] uoluptates, ita errores et falsae opiniones[11] uitam contaminant,[12] si rationalis[13] mens ipsa uitiosa est, qualis in me tunc erat nesciente alio lumine illam

[1]facinus ~oris *neut.* deed > **crime** [2]uitiosus ~a, ~um *adj.* **corrupt** [3]iacto ~are, ~aui, ~atum to throw > **to flaunt oneself** (refl.) [4]insolenter *adv.* **insolently** [5]turbide *adv.* **in disorderly fashion** [6]flagitium ~ii *neut.* **indecency** (of sexual misconduct) [7]immoderatus ~a, ~um *adj.* **immoderate** [8]affectio ~onis *f.* **feeling** [9]carnalis ~is, ~e *adj.* ECCL **carnal** [10]haurio ~rire, ~si, ~stum **to drink in** [11]opinio ~onis *f.* **opinion** [12]contamino ~are, ~aui, ~atum **to contaminate** [13]rationalis ~is, ~e *adj.* **rational**

inlustrandam[14] esse, ut sit particeps[15] ueritatis, quia non est ipsa natura ueritatis, *quoniam tu inluminabis lucernam*[16] *meam, Domine. Deus meus, inluminabis tenebras meas* (Ps 17:29), et *de plenitudine*[17] *tua omnes nos accepimus* (Jn 1:16). es enim tu *lumen uerum quod inluminat omnem hominem uenientem in hunc mundum* (Jn 1:9), quia in te *non est transmutatio*[18] *nec momenti*[19] *obumbratio*[20] (Jas 1:17).

[14]inlustro ~are, ~aui, ~atum **to illuminate** [15]particeps ~cipis *adj.* **participating in** (w. gen.) [16]lucerna ~ae *f.* **lamp** [17]plenitudo ~inis *f.* **fullness** [18]transmutatio ~onis *f.* **change** [19]momentum ~i *neut.* **movement** [20]obumbratio ~onis *f.* **shadowing**

Vain attempts to reach God

4.15.26 Sed ego conabar ad te et repellebar[1] abs te, ut saperem[2] mortem, quoniam *superbis resistis* (Jas 4:6). quid autem superbius quam ut adsererem[3] mira dementia[4] me id esse naturaliter[5] quod tu es? cum enim ego essem mutabilis et eo[6] mihi manifestum[7] esset, quod utique ideo sapiens esse cupiebam, ut ex deteriore[8] melior fierem, malebam[9] tamen etiam te opinari[10] mutabilem quam me non hoc esse quod tu es. itaque repellebar et resistebas uentosae[11] ceruici[12] meae, et imaginabar[13] formas corporeas et caro carnem accusabam,[14] et *spiritus ambulans*[15] *nondum reuertebar*[16] (Ps 77:39) ad te et ambulando ambulabam in ea quae non sunt, neque in te neque in me neque in corpore, neque mihi creabantur a ueritate tua, sed a mea uanitate fingebantur[17] ex corpore. et dicebam paruulis fidelibus tuis, ciuibus meis, a quibus nesciens exulabam,[18] dicebam illis garrulus[19] et ineptus,[20] "Cur ergo errat anima quam fecit Deus?" et mihi nolebam dici, "Cur ergo errat Deus?" et contendebam[21] magis incommutabilem tuam substantiam coactam errare quam meam mutabilem sponte[22] deuiasse[23] et poena errare confitebar.

[1]repello ~ere, reppuli, repulsum **to drive back** [2]sapio ~ere, ~ii **to taste** [3]adsero ~ere, ~ui, ~tum **to assert** [4]dementia ~ae *f.* **insanity** [5]naturaliter *adv.* **by nature** [6]eo *adv.* **because** [7]manifestus ~a, ~um *adj.* **obvious** [8]deterior ~ior, ~ius *compar. adj.* **worse** [9]malo ~lle, ~lui **to prefer** [10]opinor ~ari, ~atus **to think** [11]uentosus ~a, ~um *adj.* **puffed up** [12]ceruix ~icis *f.* **neck** (as fig. for the will) [13]imaginor ~ari, ~atus **to imagine** [14]accuso ~are, ~aui, ~atum **to blame** [15]ambulo ~are, ~aui, ~atum **to walk > to go abroad** [16]reuertor, reuor- ~ti, ~sus **to return** [17]fingo ~ngere, ~nxi, ~ctum **to devise** [18]exulo ~are, ~aui, ~atum **to live in exile** [19]garrulus ~a, ~um *adj.* **garrulous** [20]ineptus ~a, ~um *adj.* **inept** [21]contendo ~dere, ~di, ~tum **to contend** [22]spons ~ntis *f.* (abl. only) **will** [23]deuio ~are, ~aui, ~atum in LATE **to turn to evil**

Joyless proud imagination

4.15.27 Et eram aetate annorum fortasse[1] uiginti[2] sex[3] aut septem,[4] cum illa uolumina[5] scripsi, uoluens[6] apud me corporalia figmenta[7] obstrepentia[8] cordis mei auribus, quas intendebam, dulcis Veritas, in interiorem melodiam[9] tuam, cogitans de pulchro et apto,[10] et stare cupiens et audire te et *gaudio gaudere propter uocem sponsi*[11] (Jn 3:29), et non poteram, quia uocibus erroris mei rapiebar foras[12] et pondere[13] superbiae[14] meae in ima[15] decidebam.[16] non enim dabas *auditui*[17] *meo gaudium et laetitiam*, aut *exultabant*[18] *ossa,*[19] *quae humilata*[20] (Ps 50:10) non erant.

[1]fortasse *adv.* **perhaps** [2]uiginti *indecl. adj.* **twenty** [3]sex *indecl. adj.* **six** [4]septem *indecl. adj.* **seven** [5]uolumen ~inis *neut.* **volume** [6]uoluo ~uere, ~ui, ~utum **to revolve** [7]figmentum ~i *neut.* **fiction** [8]obstrepo ~ere, ~ui, ~itum **to clamor** [9]melodia ~ae *f.* LATE **melody** [10]aptus ~a, ~um *ppl. adj.* **fitting** [11]sponsus ~i *m.* **bridegroom** [12]foras *adv.* **outwardly** [13]pondus ~eris *neut.* **weight** [14]superbia ~ae *f.* **pride** [15]imus ~a, ~um *adj.* **the bottom** (*neut. pl.* as noun) [16]decido ~ere, ~i **to sink down** [17]auditus ~us *m.* **hearing** [18]exulto ~are, ~aui **to exult** [19]os ossis *neut.* **bones** (*pl.* esp. as seat of emotion); ECCL soul (fig.) [20]humilo ~are, ~aui, ~atum ECCL **to humble**

Aristotle's *Categories*

4.16.28 Et *quid mihi proderat* (Eccl 2:15) quod annos natus ferme[1] uiginti,[2] cum in manus meas uenissent Aristotelica quaedam, quas appellant *Decem*[3] *Categorias* (quarum nomine, cum eas rhetor[4] Carthaginiensis, magister meus, buccis[5] typho[6] crepantibus[7] commemoraret et alii qui docti habebantur, tamquam in nescio quid magnum et diuinum[8] suspensus[9] inhiabam[10]), legi eas solus et intellexi? quas cum contulissem[11] cum eis qui se dicebant uix eas magistris eruditissimis,[12] non loquentibus tantum sed multa in puluere[13] depingentibus,[14] intellexisse, nihil inde aliud mihi dicere potuerunt quam ego solus apud me ipsum legens cognoueram. et satis aperte[15] mihi uidebantur loquentes de substantiis, sicuti est homo, et quae in illis essent, sicuti est figura[16] hominis, qualis

[1]ferme *adv.* **almost** [2]uiginti *indecl. adj.* **twenty** [3]decem *indecl. adj.* **ten** [4]rhetor ~oris *m.* **rhetorician** [5]bucca ~ae *f.* **cheeks** [6]typhus ~i *m.* ECCL **proud vanity** [7]crepo ~are, ~ui **to rattle on** [8]diuinus ~a, ~um *adj.* **divine** [9]suspensus ~a, ~um *adj.* **in suspense** [10]inhio ~are, ~aui, ~atum **to open one's mouth** (in astonishment) [11]confero ~rre, contuli, conlatum **to confer** [12]eruditus ~a, ~um *adj.* **erudite** [13]puluis ~eris *m.* **dust** (used for drawing diagrams) [14]depingo ~ngere, ~nxi, ~ctum **to draw** [15]aperte *adv.* **clearly** [16]figura ~ae *f.* **figure**

sit, et statura,[17] quot[18] pedum sit, et cognatio,[19] cuius frater sit, aut ubi sit constitutus[20] aut quando natus, aut stet an sedeat,[21] aut calciatus[22] uel armatus[23] sit, aut aliquid faciat aut patiatur aliquid, et quaecumque in his nouem[24] generibus, quorum exempli[25] gratia quaedam posui, uel in ipso substantiae genere innumerabilia[26] reperiuntur.[27]

[17]statura ~ae *f.* **stature** [18]quot *indecl. adj.* **how many** [19]cognatio ~onis *f.* **relationship** [20]constituo ~uere, ~ui, ~utum **to place** [21]sedeo ~ere, sedi, sessum **to be seated** [22]calcio ~are, ~aui, ~atum **to put shoes on** [23]armo ~are, ~aui, ~atum **to arm with weapons** [24]nouem *indecl. adj.* **nine** [25]exemplum ~i *neut.* **example** [26]innumerabilis ~is, ~e *adj.* **innumerable** [27]reperio ~ire, repperi, ~tum **to find**

What good is it being smarter than others?

4.16.29 *Quid hoc mihi proderat* (Eccl 2:15), quando et oberat,[1] cum etiam te, Deus meus, mirabiliter[2] simplicem[3] atque incommutabilem, illis decem[4] praedicamentis[5] putans quidquid esset omnino comprehensum, sic intellegere conarer, quasi et tu subiectus[6] esses magnitudini[7] tuae aut pulchritudini,[8] ut illa essent in te quasi in subiecto sicut in corpore, cum tua magnitudo et tua pulchritudo tu ipse sis, corpus autem non eo[9] sit magnum et pulchrum quo corpus est, quia etsi minus magnum et minus pulchrum esset, nihilominus[10] corpus esset? falsitas[11] enim erat quam de te cogitabam, non ueritas, et figmenta[12] miseriae meae, non firmamenta beatitudinis[13] tuae. iusseras enim, et ita fiebat in me, ut *terra spinas*[14] *et tribulos*[15] *pareret*[16] mihi et *cum labore peruenirem ad panem*[17] *meum* (Gen 3:18–19).

[1]obsum ~esse, ~fui **to be a hindrance** [2]mirabiliter *adv.* **marvelously** [3]simplex ~icis *adj.* **simple** [4]decem *indecl. adj.* **ten** [5]praedicamentum ~i *neut.* AUG **category** [6]subiectus ~a, ~um *adj.* **subordinate** [7]magnitudo ~inis *f.* **greatness** [8]pulchritudo ~inis *f.* **beauty** [9]eo... quo' **for this reason... because** [10]nihilominus *adv.* **none the less** [11]falsitas ~atis *f.* LATE **false opinion** [12]figmentum ~i *neut.* **fiction** [13]beatitudo ~inis *f.* **beatitude** [14]spina ~ae *f.* **thorn** [15]tribulus ~i *m.* **prickly plant** [16]pario ~ere, peperi, ~tum **to bring forth** [17]panis ~is *m.* **bread**

What good is it being self-taught?

4.16.30 *Et quid mihi proderat* (Eccl 2:15) quod omnes libros artium quas "liberales"[1] uocant tunc nequissimus[2] malarum cupiditatum seruus

[1]liberalis ~is, ~e *adj.* **liberal** (of arts, studies, education) [2]nequam *indecl. adj.* **useless**

per me ipsum legi et intellexi, quoscumque[3] legere potui? et gaudebam in eis, et nesciebam unde esset quidquid ibi uerum et certum esset. dorsum[4] enim habebam ad lumen et ad ea quae inluminantur faciem, unde ipsa facies mea, qua inluminata cernebam, non inluminabatur. quidquid de arte loquendi et disserendi,[5] quidquid de dimensionibus[6] figurarum[7] et de musicis[8] et de numeris, sine magna difficultate[9] nullo hominum tradente intellexi. *scis tu, Domine Deus* (Ps 68:6) meus, quia et celeritas[10] intellegendi et dispiciendi[11] acumen[12] donum tuum est. (sed non inde *sacrificabam*[13] *tibi* (Ps 53:8); itaque mihi non ad usum sed ad perniciem[14] magis ualebat, quia tam bonam *partem substantiae* (Lk 15:12) meae sategi[15] habere in potestate et *fortitudinem*[16] *meam* non *ad te custodiebam*[17] (Ps 58:10), sed profectus[18] sum abs te in longinquam[19] regionem,[20] ut eam dissiparem[21] in meretrices[22] cupiditates.) nam quid mihi proderat bona res non utenti bene? non enim sentiebam illas artes etiam ab studiosis[23] et ingeniosis[24] difficillime[25] intellegi, nisi cum eis eadem conabar exponere,[26] et erat ille excellentissimus[27] in eis qui me exponentem non tardius[28] sequeretur.

[3]'omnes... quoscumque' **all __whatsoever** [4]dorsum ~i *neut.* **back** [5]dissero ~ere, ~ui, ~tum **to set out in words** [6]dimensio ~onis *f.* **dimension** [7]figura ~ae *f.* **geometrical figure** [8]musica ~ae *f.* **music** (theory or sounds) [9]difficultas ~atis *f.* **difficulty** [10]celeritas ~atis *f.* **quickness** [11]dispicio ~icere, ~exi, ~ectum **to perceive mentally** [12]acumen ~inis *neut.* **acumen** [13]sacrifico ~are, ~aui, ~atum **to offer as sacrifice** [14]pernicies ~ei *f.* **source of ruin** [15]satago ~agere, ~egi, ~actum **to busy oneself** [16]fortitudo ~inis *f.* **strength** [17]custodio ~ire, ~iui, ~itum **to keep safe** [18]proficiscor ~icisci, ~ectus **to depart** [19]longinquus ~a, ~um *adj.* **far off** [20]regio ~onis *f.* **land** [21]dissipo ~are, ~aui, ~atum **to dissipate** [22]meretrix ~icis *f.* **prostitute** [23]studiosus ~a, ~um *adj.* **studious** [24]ingeniosus ~a, ~um *adj.* **ingenious** [25]difficiliter *adv.* **with difficulty** [26]expono ~onere, ~osui, ~ositum **to explain** [27]excellens ~ntis *adj.* **excellent** [28]tardus ~a, ~um *adj.* **slow**

What good is it being clever?

4.16.31 Sed *quid mihi hoc proderat*, (Eccl 2:15) putanti quod tu, Domine Deus ueritas, corpus esses lucidum[1] et immensum[2] et ego frustum[3] de illo corpore? nimia[4] peruersitas![5] sed sic eram nec erubesco,[6] Deus meus, *confiteri tibi in me misericordias tuas* (Ps 106:8) et inuocare te,

[1]lucidus ~a, ~um *adj.* **shining** [2]immensus ~a, ~um *adj.* **immense** [3]frustum ~i *neut.* **fragment** [4]nimius ~a, ~um *adj.* **excessive** [5]peruersitas ~atis *f.* **perversity** [6]erubesco ~escere, ~ui **to feel ashamed**

qui non erubui tunc profiteri[7] hominibus blasphemias[8] meas et latrare[9] aduersum te. quid ergo tunc mihi proderat ingenium per illas doctrinas agile[10] et nullo adminiculo[11] humani magisterii[12] tot nodosissimi[13] libri enodati,[14] cum deformiter[15] et sacrilega[16] turpitudine[17] in doctrina pietatis errarem? aut quid tantum oberat[18] paruulis tuis longe tardius[19] ingenium, cum a te longe non recederent, ut in nido[20] Ecclesiae tuae tuti plumescerent[21] et alas[22] caritatis alimento[23] sanae[24] fidei nutrirent?[25]

> O Domine Deus noster,
> *in uelamento*[26] *alarum tuarum speremus*[27] (Ps 35:8; 60:5),
> et protege[28] nos et porta[29] nos.
> tu portabis et paruulos
> *et usque ad canos*[30] *tu portabis* (Isa 46:4),
> quoniam firmitas[31] nostra quando tu es, tunc est firmitas,
> cum autem nostra est, infirmitas[32] est.
> uiuit apud te semper bonum nostrum,
> et quia inde auersi[33] sumus, peruersi[34] sumus.
> reuertamur[35] iam, Domine, ut non euertamur,[36]
> quia uiuit apud te sine ullo defectu[37] bonum nostrum,
> quod tu ipse es,
> et non timemus ne non sit quo redeamus, quia nos inde ruimus.[38]
> nobis autem absentibus non ruit domus nostra,
> aeternitas tua.

---

[7]profiteor ~iteri, ~essus **to profess openly** [8]blasphemia ~ae *f.* ECCL **blasphemy** [9]latro ~are, ~aui, ~atum **to bark** [10]agilis ~is, ~e *adj.* **quick** [11]adminiculum ~i *neut.* **reliance** [12]magisterium ~ii *neut.* **teacher** [13]nodosus ~a, ~um *adj.* **knotty** [14]enodo ~are, ~aui, ~atum **to unravel** [15]deformiter *adv.* **hideously** [16]sacrilegus ~a, ~um *adj.* **sacrilegious** [17]turpitudo ~inis *f.* **ugliness** [18]obsum ~esse, ~fui **to hinder** [19]tardus ~a, ~um *adj.* **slow** [20]nidus ~i *m.* **nest** [21]plumesco ~ere **to grow feathers** [22]ala ~ae *f.* **wing** [23]alimentum ~i *neut.* **food** [24]sanus ~a, ~um *adj.* **healthy** [25]nutrio ~ire, ~iui or ~ii, ~itum **to nurture** [26]uelamentum ~i *neut.* **covering** [27]spero ~are, ~aui, ~atum **to hope in** [28]protego ~gere, ~xi, ~ctum **to protect** [29]porto ~are, ~aui, ~atum **to carry** [30]canus ~a, ~um *adj.* **white-haired** (old age) [31]firmitas ~atis *f.* **strength** [32]infirmitas ~atis *f.* **weakness** [33]auerto ~tere, ~ti, ~sum **to turn aside** [34]peruerto ~tere, ~ti, ~sum **to pervert** [35]reuertor ~ti, ~sus **to return** [36]euerto ~tere, ~ti, ~sum **to overturn** [37]defectus ~us *m.* **defect** [38]ruo ~ere, ~i **to fall**

5

LUCKY FAUSTUS

Carthage to Rome, then Milan, 382–383

Confession as sacrifice

5.1.1 Accipe sacrificium[1] confessionum mearum de *manu linguae* (Prov 18:21) meae (quam formasti et excitasti,[2] ut *confiteatur nomini tuo* [Ps 53:8]), et *sana omnia ossa*[3] *mea*, et dicant, *Domine, quis similis tibi?* (Ps 6:3; 34:10). neque enim docet te quid in se agatur qui tibi confitetur, quia oculum tuum non excludit[4] cor clausum[5] nec manum tuam repellit[6] duritia[7] hominum, sed soluis[8] eam cum uoles, aut miserans aut uindicans,[9] *et non est qui se abscondat*[10] *a calore*[11] *tuo* (Ps 18:7).

Sed *te laudet anima mea* (Ps 118:75) ut amet te, et *confiteatur tibi miserationes*[12] *tuas* (Ps 106:8) ut laudet te. non cessat[13] nec tacet laudes tuas uniuersa creatura tua, nec *spiritus omnis* (Ps 150:6) per os conuersum ad te, nec animalia[14] nec corporalia per os considerantium ea, ut exsurgat[15] in te a lassitudine[16] anima nostra, innitens[17] eis quae fecisti et transiens ad te, qui fecisti haec mirabiliter.[18] et ibi refectio[19] et uera fortitudo.[20]

---

[1]sacrificium ~ii *neut.* **sacrifice** [2]excito ~are, ~aui, ~atum **to excite** [3]os ossis *neut.* **bones** (*pl.* esp. as seat of emotion); ECCL **soul** (fig.) [4]excludo ~dere, ~si, ~sum **to keep out** [5]clausus ~a, ~um *adj.* **closed** [6]repello ~ere, reppuli, repulsum **to repel** [7]duritia ~ae *f.* **hardness** [8]soluo ~uere, ~ui, ~utum **to melt** [9]uindico ~are, ~aui, ~atum **to punish** [10]abscondo ~ere, ~i, ~itum **to hide** [11]calor ~oris *m.* **heat** [12]miseratio ~onis *f.* **mercy** [13]cesso ~are, ~aui, ~atum **to cease** [14]animalis ~is, ~e *adj.* **living** [15]exsurgo ~gere, ~rexi **to rise up** [16]lassitudo ~inis *f.* **weariness** [17]innitor ~ti, ~xus **to lean on for support** [18]mirabiliter *adv.* **wonderfully** [19]refectio ~onis *f.* **refreshment** [20]fortitudo ~inis *f.* **strength**

The unrighteous forsake God

5.2.2 Eant et fugiant a te inquieti[1] iniqui.[2] et tu uides eos et distinguis[3] umbras,[4] et ecce pulchra sunt cum eis omnia et ipsi turpes sunt. et quid nocuerunt[5] tibi? aut in quo imperium tuum dehonestauerunt,[6] a caelis usque in nouissima[7] iustum et integrum?[8] quo enim fugerunt, cum fugerent a facie tua? aut ubi tu non inuenis eos? sed fugerunt ut non uiderent te uidentem se atque excaecati[9] in te offenderent,[10] quia non deseris aliquid eorum quae fecisti; in te offenderent iniusti[11] et iuste[12] uexarentur,[13] subtrahentes[14] se lenitati[15] tuae et offendentes in rectitudinem[16] tuam et cadentes in asperitatem[17] tuam. uidelicet[18] nesciunt quod ubique[19] sis, quem nullus circumscribit[20] locus, et solus es praesens etiam his qui longe fiunt a te.

> Conuertantur ergo et quaerant te,
> quia non, sicut ipsi deseruerunt creatorem suum,
> ita tu deseruisti creaturam tuam:
> ipsi conuertantur.
>
> et ecce ibi es in corde eorum, in corde confitentium tibi
> et proicientium[21] se in te et plorantium[22] in sinu tuo
> post uias suas difficiles.[23]
> et tu facilis *terges*[24] *lacrimas eorum* (Rev 7:17),
> et magis plorant et gaudent in fletibus,[25]
> quoniam tu, Domine, non aliquis homo, caro et sanguis,
> sed tu, Domine, qui fecisti,
> reficis[26] et consolaris[27] eos.

Et ubi ego eram, quando te quaerebam? et tu eras ante me, ego autem et a me discesseram[28] nec me inueniebam: quanto minus te!

---

[1]inquietus ~a, ~um *adj.* **restless** [2]iniquus, ~os ~a *adj.* unfair; ECCL **unrighteous** (as noun) [3]distinguo ~guere, ~xi, ~ctum **to distinguish** [4]umbra ~ae *f.* shadow > **shadowy outline** [5]noceo ~ere, ~ui, ~itum **to injure** [6]dehonesto ~are, ~aui, ~atum **to dishonor** [7]nouissimus ~a, ~um *superl. adj.* **farthest point** (*neut. pl.* as noun) [8]integer ~gra, ~grum *adj.* **intact** [9]excaeco ~are, ~aui, ~atum **to blind** [10]offendo ~dere, ~di, ~sum **to stumble** [11]iniustus ~a, ~um *adj.* **unjust** [12]iuste *adv.* **justly** [13]uexo ~are, ~aui, ~atum **to vex** [14]subtraho ~here, ~xi, ~ctum **to withdraw** [15]lenitas ~atis *f.* **gentleness** [16]rectitudo ~inis *f.* straightness; LATE **uprightness** [17]asperitas ~atis *f.* **severity** [18]uidelicet *adv.* **it is plain to see** [19]ubique *adv.* **everywhere** [20]circumscribo ~bere, ~psi, ~ptum **to circumscribe** [21]proicio ~icere, ~ieci, ~iectum **to fling** (refl.) [22]ploro ~are, ~aui, ~atum **to weep aloud** [23]difficilis ~is, ~e *adj.* **difficult** [24]tergo ~gere **to wipe** [25]fletus ~us *m.* **weeping** [26]reficio ~icere, ~eci, ~ectum **to remake** [27]consolor ~ari, ~atus **to console** [28]discedo ~dere, ~ssi, ~ssum **to depart**

Faustus in Carthage

5.3.3 Proloquar[1] in conspectu Dei mei annum illum undetricensimum[2] aetatis meae.

Iam uenerat Carthaginem quidam Manichaeorum episcopus,[3] Faustus nomine, magnus *laqueus*[4] *diaboli*[5] (1 Tim 3:7, 2 Tim 2:26), et multi implicabantur[6] in eo per inlecebram[7] suauiloquentiae.[8] quam ego iam tametsi[9] laudabam, discernebam tamen a ueritate rerum quarum discendarum auidus[10] eram, nec quali uasculo[11] sermonis, sed quid mihi scientiae comedendum[12] apponeret[13] nominatus apud eos ille Faustus intuebar. fama enim de illo praelocuta[14] mihi erat quod esset honestarum[15] omnium doctrinarum peritissimus[16] et apprime[17] disciplinis[18] liberalibus[19] eruditus.[20]

Et quoniam multa philosophorum[21] legeram memoriaeque mandata[22] retinebam,[23] ex eis quaedam comparabam[24] illis Manichaeorum longis fabulis,[25] et mihi probabiliora[26] ista uidebantur quae dixerunt illi qui *tantum potuerunt ualere ut possent aestimare*[27] *saeculum,* quamquam *eius Dominum minime*[28] *inuenerint* (Wis 13:9). quoniam *magnus es, Domine, et humilia*[29] *respicis,*[30] *excelsa*[31] *autem a longe cognoscis* (Ps 137:6), nec propinquas[32] nisi obtritis[33] corde nec inueniris a superbis, nec si illi curiosa[34] peritia[35] numerent stellas[36] et harenam[37] et dimetiantur[38] sidereas[39] plagas[40] et uestigent[41] uias astrorum.[42]

---

[1]proloquor ~qui, ~cutus **to speak out** [2]undetricesimus ~a, ~um *adj.* **twenty-ninth** [3]episcopus ~i *m.* ECCL **bishop** [4]laqueus ~i *m.* **snare** [5]diabolus ~i *m.* ECCL **the Devil** [6]implico ~are, ~aui, ~atum or ~itum **to entangle** [7]inlecebra ~ae *f.* **attraction** [8]suauiloquentia ~ae *f.* **agreeableness of speech** [9]tametsi *conj.* **even though** [10]auidus ~a, ~um *adj.* **eager** [11]uasculum ~i *neut.* **vessel** [12]comedo ~edere, ~edi, ~esum **to eat up** [13]appono ~ere, apposui, appositum **to serve** (food) [14]praeloquor ~qui, ~cutus to **preface;** ECCL **to make known beforehand** [15]honestus ~a, ~um *adj.* **honorable** [16]peritus ~a, ~um *adj.* **skilled** [17]apprime *adv.* **especially** [18]disciplina ~ae *f.* **teaching** [19]liberalis ~is, ~e *adj.* **liberal** (of arts, studies, education) [20]eruditus ~a, ~um *adj.* **erudite** [21]philosophus ~i *m.* **philosopher** [22]mandatum ~i *neut.* **instruction** [23]retineo ~ere, ~ui, retentum **to retain** [24]comparo ~are, ~aui, ~atum **to compare** [25]fabula ~ae *f.* **fictitious story** [26]probabilis ~is, ~e *adj.* **probable** [27]aestimo ~are, ~aui, ~atum **to judge** [28]minime *superl. adv.* **in the least degree** [29]humilis ~is, ~e *adj.* **humble** [30]respicio ~icere, ~exi, ~ectum **to take notice** [31]excelsus ~a, ~um *adj.* **lofty** (in rank or reputation) [32]propinquo ~are, ~aui **to draw near** [33]obtero ~terere, ~triui, ~tritum **to crush** [34]curiosus ~a, ~um *adj.* **painstaking** [35]peritia ~ae *f.* **expertise** [36]stella ~ae *f.* **star** [37]harena ~ae *f.* **grains of sand** [38]dimetior ~tiri, ~nsus **to measure distance** [39]sidereus ~a, ~um *adj.* **starry** [40]plaga ~ae *f.* **open expanse of sky** [41]uestigo ~are, ~aui, ~atum **to track** [42]astrum ~i *neut.* **planet**

Pride of natural philosophers

5.3.4 Mente sua enim quaerunt ista et ingenio quod tu dedisti eis et multa inuenerunt et praenuntiauerunt[1] ante multos annos defectus[2] luminarium[3] solis et lunae,[4] quo die, qua hora, quanta ex parte futuri essent, et non eos fefellit numerus. et ita factum est ut praenuntiauerunt, et scripserunt regulas[5] indagatas,[6] et leguntur hodie[7] atque ex eis praenuntiatur quo anno et quo mense[8] anni et quo die mensis et qua hora diei et quota parte[9] luminis sui defectura[10] sit luna uel sol: et ita fiet ut praenuntiatur. et mirantur haec homines et stupent[11]qui nesciunt ea, et exultant[12] atque extolluntur[13] qui sciunt, et per impiam[14] superbiam[15] recedentes et deficientes a lumine tuo tanto ante solis defectum futurum praeuident,[16] et in praesentia[17] suum non uident (non enim religiose[18] quaerunt unde habeant ingenium quo ista quaerunt), et inuenientes quia tu fecisti eos, non ipsi se dant tibi, se ut serues quod fecisti, et quales se ipsi fecerant occidunt[19] se tibi, et trucidant[20] exaltationes[21] suas sicut uolatilia,[22] et curiositates[23] suas sicut pisces[24] maris quibus perambulant[25] secretas[26] semitas[27] abyssi, et luxurias[28] suas sicut pecora[29] campi, ut tu, *Deus, ignis edax*[30] (Heb 12:29) consumas[31] mortuas curas eorum, recreans[32] eos immortaliter.[33]

[1]praenuntio ~are, ~aui, ~atum **to predict** [2]defectus ~us *m.* **eclipse** [3]luminare ~is *neut.* lamp; ECCL **luminary** (sun and moon) [4]luna ~ae *f.* **moon** [5]regula ~ae *f.* **rule** [6]indago ~are, ~aui, ~atum to track down > **to ascertain by investigation** [7]hodie *adv.* **today** [8]mensis ~is *m.* **month** [9]'quota parte' **what proportion of the whole** [10]deficio ~icere, ~eci, ~ectum **to eclipse** [11]stupeo ~ere, ~ui **to be stupefied** [12]exulto ~are, ~aui **to exult** [13]extollo ~ere **to admire** [14]impius ~a, ~um *adj.* **impious** [15]superbia ~ae *f.* **pride** [16]praeuideo ~idere, ~idi, ~isum **to foresee** [17]praesentia ~ae *f.* **present time** [18]religiose *adv.* **reverently** [19]occido ~dere, ~di, ~sum **to kill** [20]trucido ~are, ~aui, ~atum **to slaughter** [21]exaltatio ~onis *f.* LATE raising up; ECCL **conceit** [22]uolatilis ~is, ~e *adj.* flying; **bird** (as noun) [23]curiositas ~atis *f.* **curiosity** (usu. in a bad sense) [24]piscis ~is *m.* **fish** [25]perambulo ~are, ~aui, ~atum **to roam** [26]secretus ~a, ~um *adj.* **secret** [27]semita ~ae *f.* **path** [28]luxuria ~ae *f.* **willful behavior** [29]pecus ~oris *neut.* **beast** [30]edax ~acis *adj.* **devouring** [31]consumo ~ere, ~psi, ~ptum **to consume** [32]recreo ~are, ~aui, ~atum **to recreate** [33]immortaliter *adv.* (coll.) **immortally**

Foolish hearts darkened

5.3.5 Sed non nouerunt *Viam* (Jn 14:6), Verbum tuum, *per quod fecisti ea* (Jn 1:3) quae numerant et ipsos qui numerant, et sensum quo cernunt quae numerant et mentem de qua numerant: *et sapientiae tuae non est* *numerus*[1] (Ps 146:5). ipse autem Unigenitus[2] *factus est nobis sapientia et iustitia et sanctificatio*[3] (1 Cor 1:30), et numeratus est inter nos, et soluit[4] *tributum*[5] *Caesari* (Mt 22:21). non nouerunt hanc Viam qua descendant[6] ad illum a se et per eum ascendant[7] ad eum. non nouerunt hanc Viam, et putant se excelsos[8] esse cum sideribus et lucidos,[9] et ecce ruerunt[10] in terram, *et obscuratum*[11] *est insipiens*[12] *cor eorum* (Rom 1:21). et multa uera de creatura dicunt et ueritatem, creaturae artificem,[13] non pie[14] quaerunt, et ideo non inueniunt, aut si inueniunt, *cognoscentes Deum non sicut Deum honorant*[15] *aut gratias agunt, et euanescunt*[16] *in cogitationibus suis, et dicunt se esse sapientes* (Rom 1:21–22) sibi tribuendo[17] quae tua sunt, ac per hoc student[18] peruersissima[19] caecitate[20] etiam tibi tribuere quae sua sunt, mendacia[21] scilicet[22] in te conferentes,[23] qui Veritas es, *et immutantes*[24] *gloriam incorrupti*[25] *Dei in similitudinem*[26] *imaginis corruptibilis*[27] *hominis et uolucrum*[28] *et quadrupedum*[29] *et serpentium*[30] (Rom 1:23), et *conuertunt ueritatem tuam in mendacium, et colunt et seruiunt creaturae potius quam creatori* (Rom 1:25).

[1]numerus ~i *m.* number > **reckoning** [2]unigenitus ~a, ~um *adj.* ECCL **only-begotten** [3]sanctificatio ~onis *f.* ECCL **sanctification** [4]soluo ~uere, ~ui, ~utum **to pay** [5]tributum ~i *neut.* **tribute** [6]descendo ~dere, ~di, ~sum **to descend** [7]ascendo ~dere, ~di, ~sum **to ascend** [8]excelsus ~a, ~um *adj.* **lofty** [9]lucidus ~a, ~um *adj.* **shining** [10]ruo ~ere, ~i **to rush blindly** [11]obscuro ~are, ~aui, ~atum **to obscure** [12]insipiens ~ntis *adj.* **foolish** [13]artifex ~ficis *m.* **maker** [14]pie *adv.* **piously** [15]honoro ~are, ~aui, ~atum **to honor** [16]euanesco ~escere, ~ui **to vanish**; ECCL **to become empty/foolish** [17]tribuo ~uere, ~ui, ~utum **to attribute** [18]studeo ~ere, ~ui **to devote oneself (to)** [19]peruersus ~a, ~um *adj.* **perverse** [20]caecitas ~atis *f.* **blindness** [21]mendax ~acis *adj.* **lying** [22]scilicet *adv.* **that is to say** (as epexegetic *particle*) [23]confero ~rre, contuli, conlatum **to ascribe** [24]immuto ~are, ~aui, ~atum **to change** [25]incorruptus ~a, ~um *adj.* **incorruptible** [26]similitudo ~inis *f.* **likeness** [27]corruptibilis ~is ~e *adj.* ECCL **corruptible** [28]uolucer ~cris *m.* **birds** [29]quadrupes ~edis *adj.* **four-footed creature** (as noun) [30]serpens ~ntis *f. m.* **serpent**

Incoherent Mani

5.3.6 Multa tamen ab eis ex ipsa creatura uera dicta retinebam,[1] et occurrebat mihi ratio per numeros et ordinem temporum et uisibiles attestationes[2] siderum, et conferebam[3] cum dictis Manichaei, quae de his rebus multa scripsit copiosissime[4] delirans,[5] et non mihi occurrebat

[1]retineo ~ere, ~ui, retentum **to retain** [2]attestatio ~onis *f.* **attestation** [3]confero ~rre, contuli, conlatum **to compare** [4]copiose *adv.* **copiously** [5]deliro ~are **to speak deliriously**

ratio nec solistitiorum[6] et aequinoctiorum[7] nec defectuum[8] luminarium[9] nec quidquid tale in libris saecularis[10] sapientiae didiceram. ibi autem credere iubebar, et ad illas rationes numeris et oculis meis exploratas[11] non occurrebat, et longe diuersum[12] erat.

[6]solstitium ~ii *neut.* **solstice** [7]aequinoctium ~ii *neut.* **equinox** [8]defectus ~us *m.* **eclipse** [9]luminare ~is *neut.* lamp; ECCL **luminary** (sun and moon) [10]saecularis ~is, ~e *adj.* ECCL **secular** [11]exploratus ~a, ~um *adj.* **known for certain** [12]diuersus ~a, ~um *adj.* **different**

The Great Bear

5.4.7 Numquid, *Domine Deus ueritatis* (Ps 30:6), quisquis nouit ista, iam placet tibi? infelix[1] enim homo qui scit illa omnia, te autem nescit; beatus autem qui te scit, etiamsi illa nesciat. qui uero et te et illa nouit, non propter illa beatior, sed propter te solum beatus est, si cognoscens te sicut te glorificet[2] et gratias agat, et non euanescat[3] in cogitationibus suis. sicut enim melior est qui nouit possidere[4] arborem et de usu eius tibi gratias agit, quamuis nesciat uel quot[5] cubitis[6] alta sit uel quanta latitudine[7] diffusa,[8] quam ille qui eam metitur et omnes ramos[9] eius numerat et neque possidet eam neque creatorem eius nouit aut diligit, sic fidelis homo, cuius *totus mundus diuitiarum*[10] *est* (Prov 17:6 VL) et *quasi nihil habens omnia possidet* (2 Cor 6:10) inhaerendo[11] tibi, cui seruiunt omnia, quamuis nec saltem[12] septentrionum[13] gyros[14] nouerit, dubitare[15] stultum[16] est, quin[17] utique melior sit quam mensor[18] caeli et numerator[19] siderum et pensor[20] elementorum[21] et neglegens[22] tui, qui *omnia in mensura*[23] *et numero et pondere*[24] *disposuisti*[25] (Wis 11:21).

[1]infelix ~icis *adj.* **unhappy** [2]glorifico ~are, ~aui, ~atus ECCL **to glorify** [3]euanesco ~escere, ~ui to vanish; ECCL **to become empty/foolish** [4]possideo ~idere, ~edi, ~essum **to possess** [5]quot *indecl. adj.* **how many** [6]cubitum ~i *neut.* **cubit** (about 18") [7]latitudo ~inis *f.* **wide** [8]diffusus ~a, ~um *adj.* **spreading** [9]ramus ~i *m.* **branch** [10]diuitiae ~arum *f. pl.* **wealth** [11]inhaereo ~rere, ~si, ~sum **to cling to** [12]saltem *adv.* **even** [13]septentriones ~um *m. pl.* **Ursa Major** (the Great Bear) [14]gyrus ~i *m.* **circuit** [15]dubito ~are, ~aui, ~atum **to be in doubt** [16]stultus ~a, ~um *adj.* **foolish** [17]quin *conj.* **(but) that** (expr. absence of doubt) [18]mensor ~oris *m.* **measurer** [19]numerator ~oris *m.* AUG **numberer** [20]pensor ~oris *m.* AUG **one who weighs or considers** [21]elementum ~i *neut.* **element** (of matter) [22]neglego ~gere, ~xi, ~ctum **to neglect** [23]mensura ~ae *f.* **measure** [24]pondus ~eris *neut.* **weight** [25]dispono ~onere, ~osui, ~ositum **to arrange in order**

Mani claims to be the Holy Spirit

5.5.8 Sed tamen quis quaerebat Manichaeum nescio quem etiam ista scribere, sine quorum peritia[1] pietas disci poterat? dixisti enim homini, *Ecce pietas est sapientia* (Job 28:28). quam ille ignorare posset, etiamsi ista perfecte[2] nosset; ista uero quia non nouerat, impudentissime[3] audens docere, prorsus[4] illam nosse non posset. uanitas est enim mundana[5] ista etiam nota profiteri,[6] pietas autem tibi confiteri. unde ille deuius[7] ad hoc ista multum locutus est, ut conuictus[8] ab eis qui ista uere didicissent, quis esset eius sensus in ceteris quae abditiora[9] sunt manifeste[10] cognosceretur. non enim parui se aestimari[11] uoluit, sed Spiritum Sanctum, consolatorem[12] et ditatorem[13] fidelium tuorum, auctoritate plenaria[14] personaliter[15] in se esse persuadere[16] conatus est. itaque cum de caelo ac stellis[17] et de solis ac lunae[18] motibus falsa dixisse deprehenderetur,[19] quamuis ad doctrinam religionis[20] ista non pertineant,[21] tamen ausus[22] eius sacrilegos[23] fuisse satis emineret,[24] cum ea non solum ignorata sed etiam falsa tam uesana[25] superbiae[26] uanitate diceret, ut ea tamquam diuinae[27] personae[28] tribuere[29] sibi niteretur.[30]

[1]peritia ~ae *f.* **expertise** [2]perfecte *adv.* **perfectly** [3]impudenter *adv.* **impudently** [4]prorsus *adv.* **absolutely** (stregthening 'non') [5]mundanus ~a, ~um *adj.* **worldly** [6]profiteor ~iteri, ~essus **to teach publicly** [7]deuius ~a, ~um *adj.* **deviating** [8]conuinco ~incere, ~ici, ~ictum **to prove wrong** [9]abditus ~a, ~um *adj.* **obscure** [10]manifeste *adv.* **manifestly** [11]aestimo ~are, ~aui, ~atum **to esteem** [12]consolator ~oris *m.* **comforter** [13]ditator ~oris *m.* AUG **enricher** [14]plenarius ~a, ~um *adj.* LATE **fully present** [15]personaliter *adv.* **personally** [16]persuadeo ~dere, ~si, ~sum **to persuade** [17]stella ~ae *f.* **star** [18]luna ~ae *f.* **moon** [19]deprehendo ~dere, ~di, ~sum **to discover** [20]religio ~onis *f.* **religion** [21]pertineo ~ere, ~ui **to pertain to** [22]ausus ~us *m.* **daring** [23]sacrilegus ~a, ~um *adj.* **sacrilegious** [24]emineo ~ere, ~ui **to be obvious** [25]uesanus ~a, ~um *adj.* **crazy** [26]superbia ~ae *f.* **pride** [27]diuinus ~a, ~um *adj.* **divine** [28]persona ~ae *f.* **person** [29]tribuo ~uere, ~ui, ~utum **to attribute** [30]nitor ~ti, ~xus or ~sus **to endeavor**

Innocent ignorance

5.5.9 Cum enim audio Christianum aliquem fratrem illum aut illum[1] ista nescientem et aliud pro alio sentientem, patienter[2] intueor opinantem[3] hominem nec illi obesse[4] uideo, cum de te, Domine *creator omnium* (Hymn 2.1), non credat indigna,[5] si forte situs[6] et habitus[7] creaturae

[1]'illum aut illum' **this or that** [2]patienter *adv.* **patiently** [3]opinor ~ari, ~atus **to express as an opinion** [4]obsum ~esse, ~fui **to harm** [5]indignus ~a, ~um *adj.* **unworthy** [6]situs ~us *m.* **position** [7]habitus ~us *m.* **physical make-up**

corporalis ignoret. obest autem, si hoc ad ipsam doctrinae pietatis formam pertinere[8] arbitretur et pertinacius[9] affirmare[10] audeat quod ignorat. sed etiam talis infirmitas[11] in fidei cunabulis[12] a caritate matre sustinetur,[13] donec adsurgat[14] *nouus homo* (Eph 4:24) in uirum perfectum *et circumferri*[15] *non possit omni uento doctrinae* (Eph 4:13–14).

In illo autem qui doctor,[16] qui auctor,[17] qui dux et princeps eorum quibus illa suaderet,[18] ita fieri ausus est, ut qui eum sequerentur non quemlibet[19] hominem sed Spiritum tuum Sanctum se sequi arbitrarentur, quis tantam dementiam,[20] sicubi[21] falsa dixisse conuinceretur,[22] non detestandam[23] longeque abiciendam[24] esse iudicaret?

Sed tamen nondum liquido[25] compereram[26] utrum etiam secundum eius uerba uicissitudines[27] longiorum et breuiorum dierum atque noctium et ipsius noctis et diei et deliquia[28] luminum et si quid eius modi in aliis libris legeram posset exponi,[29] ut, si forte posset, incertum[30] quidem mihi fieret utrum ita se res haberet an ita, sed ad fidem meam illius auctoritatem propter creditam sanctitatem[31] praeponerem.[32]

---

[8]pertineo ~ere, ~ui **to pertain to** [9]pertinax ~acis *adj.* **obstinate** [10]affirmo ~are, ~aui, ~atum **to affirm** [11]infirmitas ~atis *f.* **weakness** [12]cunabula ~orum *neut. pl.* **cradle** [13]sustineo ~ere, ~ui **to sustain** [14]adsurgo ~gere, ~rexi, ~rectum **to grow up** [15]circumfero ~ferre, ~tuli, ~latum **to carry about** [16]doctor ~oris *m.* **teacher** [17]auctor ~oris *m.* **founder** [18]suadeo ~dere, ~si, ~sum **to seek to persuade** [19]quilibet, quae-, quod- *adj.* **any (not very special)** [20]dementia ~ae *f.* **insanity** [21]sicubi *conj.* **if anywhere** [22]conuinco ~incere, ~ici, ~ictum **to expose** [23]detestor ~ari, ~atus **to detest** [24]abicio ~cere, ~eci, ~ectum **to abandon** [25]liquido *adv.* **clearly** [26]comperio ~ire, ~i, ~tum **to ascertain** [27]uicissitudo ~inis *f.* **vicissitude** [28]deliquium ~ii *neut.* **eclipse (of sun or moon)** [29]expono ~onere, ~osui, ~ositum **to explain** [30]incertus ~a, ~um *adj.* **uncertain** [31]sanctitas ~atis *f.* **holiness** [32]praepono ~onere, ~osui, ~ositum **to prefer**

Nine years adrift

5.6.10 Et per annos ferme[1] ipsos nouem[2] quibus eos animo uagabundus[3] audiui nimis extento desiderio uenturum expectabam istum Faustum. ceteri enim eorum in quos forte incurrissem,[4] qui talium rerum quaestionibus[5] a me obiectibus[6] deficiebant,[7] illum mihi promittebant,[8]

---

[1]ferme *adv.* **nearly** [2]nouem *indecl. adj.* **nine** [3]uagabundus ~a, ~um *adj.* LATE **wandering** [4]incurro ~rere, ~ri, ~sum **to encounter** [5]quaestio ~onis *f.* **question** [6]obicio ~icere, ~ieci, ~iectum **to put before** [7]deficio ~icere, ~eci, ~ectum **to fail** [8]promitto ~ittere, ~isi, ~issum **to promise** > **to vouch for**

cuius aduentu[9] conlatoque[10] conloquio[11] facillime mihi haec et si qua forte maiora quaererem enodatissime[12] expedirentur.[13] ergo ubi uenit, expertus sum hominem gratum et iucundum[14] uerbis et ea ipsa quae illi solent dicere multo suauius[15] garrientem.[16] sed quid ad meam sitim[17] pretiosorum[18] poculorum[19] decentissimus[20] ministrator?[21] iam rebus talibus satiatae[22] erant aures meae, nec ideo mihi meliora uidebantur quia melius dicebantur, nec ideo uera quia diserta,[23] nec ideo sapiens anima quia uultus congruus[24] et decorum[25] eloquium.[26] illi autem qui eum mihi promittebant non boni rerum existimatores[27] erant, et ideo illis uidebatur prudens[28] et sapiens, quia delectabat eos loquens. sensi autem aliud genus hominum etiam ueritatem habere suspectam[29] et ei nolle adquiescere,[30] si compto[31] atque uberi[32] sermone promeretur.[33]

Me autem iam docueras, Deus meus, miris et occultis modis (et propterea[34] credo quod tu me docueris, quoniam uerum est, nec quisquam praeter te alius doctor[35] est ueri, ubicumque[36] et undecumque[37] claruerit[38]), iam ergo abs te didiceram nec eo[39] debere uideri aliquid uerum dici, quia eloquenter[40] dicitur, nec eo falsum, quia incomposite[41] sonant signa labiorum;[42] rursus nec ideo uerum, quia impolite[43] enuntiatur,[44] nec ideo falsum, quia splendidus[45] sermo est, sed perinde[46] esse sapientiam et stultitiam[47] sicut sunt cibi utiles[48] et inutiles,[49] uerbis autem ornatis[50] et inornatis[51] sicut uasis[52] urbanis[53] et rusticanis[54] utrosque cibos posse ministrari.[55]

---

[9]aduentus ~us *m.* **arrival** [10]confero ~rre, contuli, conlatum **to discuss** [11]conloquium ~ii *neut.* **conversation** [12]enodate *adv.* **clearly and thoroughly** [13]expedio ~ire, ~iui, ~itum **to solve** [14]iucundus ~a, ~um *adj.* **pleasant** [15]suauis ~is, ~e *adj.* **agreeable** [16]garrio ~ire, ~iui **to chatter** [17]sitis ~is *f.* **thirst** [18]pretiosus ~a, ~um *adj.* **precious** [19]poculum, -clum ~i *neut.* **cup** [20]decens ~ntis *adj.* **having a pleasing appearance** [21]ministrator ~oris *m.* **waiter** [22]satias (~atis) *f.* **satiety** [23]disertus ~a, ~um *adj.* **skilled in speaking** [24]congruus ~a, ~um *adj.* **agreeable** [25]decorus ~a, ~um *adj.* **elegant** [26]eloquium ~ii *neut.* **eloquence** [27]existimator ~oris *m.* **judge** [28]prudens ~ntis *adj.* **prudent** [29]suspectus ~a, ~um *adj.* **suspect** [30]adquiesco ~escere, ~ei **to acquiesce** [31]comptus ~a, ~um *adj.* **polished** [32]uber ~ris *adj.* **rich (in style)** [33]promo ~mere, ~mpsi, ~mptum **to deliver** (an oration) [34]propterea *adv.* **consequently** [35]doctor ~oris *m.* **teacher** [36]ubicumque *adv.* **in whatever place** [37]undecumque *adv.* **from whatever place** [38]claresco ~escere, ~ui **to shine** [39]eo *adv.* **necessarily** [40]eloquenter *adv.* **eloquently** [41]incomposite *adv.* **in a disorderly manner** [42]labium ~ii *neut.* **lip** [43]impolite *adv.* **without elegance or refinement** [44]enuntio ~are, ~aui, ~atum **to articulate** [45]splendidus ~a, ~um *adj.* **brilliant** [46]perinde *adv.* **to be correlated** [47]stultitia ~ae *f.* **foolishness** [48]utilis ~is, ~e *adj.* **wholesome** [49]inutilis ~is, ~e *adj.* **unwholesome** [50]ornatus ~a, ~um *adj.* **embellished** [51]inornatus ~a, ~um *adj.* **unembellished** [52]uas uasis *neut.* **vessel** [53]urbanus ~a, ~um *adj.* **elegant and sophisticated** [54]rusticanus ~a, ~um *adj.* **rustic and countrified** [55]ministro ~are, ~aui, ~atum **to serve**

Affable Faustus

5.6.11 Igitur auiditas[1] mea, qua illum tanto tempore expectaueram hominem, delectabatur quidem motu affectuque disputantis[2] et uerbis congruentibus[3] atque ad uestiendas[4] sententias facile occurrentibus. delectabar autem et cum multis uel etiam prae multis laudabam ac ferebam, sed moleste habebam[5] quod in coetu[6] audientium non sinerer ingerere[7] illi et partiri[8] cum eo curas quaestionum[9] mearum conferendo[10] familiariter[11] et accipiendo ac reddendo sermonem. quod ubi potui et aures eius cum familiaribus[12] meis eoque tempore occupare coepi quo non dedeceret[13] alternis[14] disserere,[15] et protuli[16] quaedam quae me mouebant, expertus sum prius hominem expertem[17] liberalium[18] disciplinarum[19] nisi grammaticae[20] atque eius ipsius usitato[21] modo. et quia legerat aliquas Tullianas orationes[22] et paucissimos[23] Senecae libros et nonnulla[24] poetarum[25] et suae sectae[26] si qua uolumina[27] Latine atque composite[28] conscripta[29] erant, et quia aderat cotidiana[30] sermocinandi[31] exercitatio,[32] inde suppetebat[33] eloquium,[34] quod fiebat acceptius magisque seductorium[35] moderamine[36] ingenii et quodam lepore[37] naturali.[38]

Itane est, ut recolo, Domine Deus meus, arbiter[39] conscientiae[40] meae? coram te cor meum et recordatio[41] mea, qui me tunc agebas abdito[42] secreto[43] prouidentiae[44] tuae et inhonestos[45] errores meos iam conuertebas ante faciem meam, ut uiderem et odissem.

---

[1]auiditas ~atis *f.* **eagerness** [2]disputo ~are, ~aui, ~atum **to dispute** [3]congruens ~ntis *adj.* **fitting** [4]uestio ~ire, ~iui, ~itum **to clothe** [5]'moleste habebam' **I began getting annoyed** [6]coetus ~us *m.* **company** [7]ingero ~rere, ~ssi, ~stum **to get a person's attention** [8]partior ~iri, ~itus **to share** [9]quaestio ~onis *f.* **question** [10]confero ~rre, contuli, conlatum **to discuss** [11]familiariter *adv.* **on familiar terms** [12]familiaris ~is, ~e *adj.* **friends** (*m.* as noun) [13]dedecet ~ere, ~uit **to be inappropriate** [14]alternis *adv.* **in turns** [15]dissero ~ere, ~ui, ~tum **to set out in words** [16]profero ~ferre, ~tuli, ~latum **to bring up** [17]expers ~rtis *adj.* **devoid of** [18]liberalis ~is, ~e *adj.* **liberal** (of arts, studies, education) [19]disciplina ~ae *f.* **instruction** [20]grammatica ~ae *f.* **grammar** [21]usitatus ~a, ~um *adj.* **usual** [22]oratio ~onis *f.* **speech** [23]paucus ~a, ~um *adj.* **few** [24]nonnullus ~a, ~um *adj.* **a few** [25]poeta ~ae *m.* **poet** [26]secta ~ae *f.* school of philosophy; ECCL **sect** [27]uolumen ~inis *neut.* **volume** [28]composite ~ius *adv.* **well-arranged** [29]conscribo ~bere, ~psi, ~ptum **to write down** [30]cotidianus ~a, ~um *adj.* **daily** [31]sermocinor ~ari, ~atus **to hold conversation** [32]exercitatio ~onis *f.* exercise > **practice** [33]suppeto ~ere, ~iui **to have available** [34]eloquium ~ii *neut.* **eloquence** [35]seductorius ~a, ~um ECCL **seductive** [36]moderamen ~inis *neut.* **control** [37]lepos ~oris *m.* **wit** [38]naturalis ~is, ~e *adj.* **natural** [39]arbiter ~tri *m.* **judge** [40]conscientia ~ae *f.* **conscience** [41]recordatio ~onis *f.* **recollection** [42]abditus ~a, ~um *adj.* **hidden** [43]secretum ~i *neut.* secret > **mysterious process** (transf.) [44]prouidentia ~ae *f.* **providence** [45]inhonestus ~a, ~um *adj.* **shameful**

Ignorant Faustus

5.7.12 Nam posteaquam[1] ille mihi imperitus[2] earum artium quibus eum excellere[3] putaueram satis apparuit, desperare[4] coepi posse mihi eum illa quae me mouebant aperire atque dissoluere;[5] quorum quidem ignarus[6] posset ueritatem tenere pietatis, sed si Manichaeus non esset. libri quippe eorum pleni sunt longissimis fabulis[7] de caelo et sideribus et sole et luna;[8] quae mihi eum, quod utique cupiebam, conlatis[9] numerorum rationibus quas alibi[10] ego legeram, utrum potius ita essent ut Manichaei libris continebantur, an certe uel par etiam inde ratio redderetur,[11] subtiliter[12] explicare[13] posse iam non arbitrabar.

Quae tamen ubi consideranda et discutienda[14] protuli,[15] modeste[16] sane[17] ille nec ausus est subire[18] ipsam sarcinam.[19] nouerat enim se ista non nosse nec eum puduit[20] confiteri. non erat de talibus, quales multos loquaces[21] passus eram, conantes ea me docere et dicentes nihil. iste uero *cor* habebat, etsi *non rectum*[22] *ad te* (Ps 77:37), nec tamen nimis incautum[23] ad se ipsum. non usquequaque[24] imperitus erat imperitiae[25] suae, et noluit se temere[26] disputando[27] in ea coartari[28] unde nec exitus[29] ei ullus nec facilis esset reditus: etiam hinc mihi amplius placuit. pulchrior est enim temperantia[30] confitentis animi quam illa quae nosse cupiebam. et eum in omnibus difficilioribus[31] et subtilioribus[32] quaestionibus[33] talem inueniebam.

---

[1]posteaquam *conj.* **after** [2]imperitus ~a, ~um *adj.* **inexperienced** [3]excello ~ere **to excel** [4]despero ~are, ~aui, ~atum **to despair** [5]dissoluo ~uere, ~ui, ~utum **to unravel** [6]ignarus ~a, ~um *adj.* **ignorant** [7]fabula ~ae *f.* **fictitious story** [8]luna ~ae *f.* **moon** [9]confero ~rre, contuli, conlatum **to compare** [10]alibi *adv.* **elsewhere** [11]'ratio redderetur' **to render an account** [12]subtiliter *adv.* **with precision of argument** [13]explico ~are, ~aui or ~ui, ~atum **to explain** [14]discutio ~tere, ~ssi, ~ssum **to break up; LATE to discuss** [15]profero ~ferre, ~tuli, ~latum **to put forward** [16]modeste *adv.* **modestly** [17]sane *adv.* **quite** (w. *adv.*) [18]subeo ~ire, ~ii, ~itum **to place oneself under** [19]sarcina ~ae *f.* **burden** [20]pudeo ~ere, ~ui **to be ashamed** [21]loquax ~acis *adj.* **loquacious** [22]rectus ~a, ~um *adj.* **right** [23]incautus ~a, ~um *adj.* **incautious** [24]usquequaque *adv.* **altogether** [25]imperitia ~ae *f.* **inexperience** [26]temere *adv.* **rashly** [27]disputo ~are, ~aui, ~atum **to argue** [28]coarto ~are, ~aui, ~atum **to corner** [29]exitus ~us *m.* **a way out** [30]temperantia ~ae *f.* **restraint** [31]difficilis ~is, ~e *adj.* **difficult** [32]subtilis ~is, ~e *adj.* **subtle** [33]quaestio ~onis *f.* **question**

Unwitting Faustus

5.7.13 Refracto[1] itaque studio quod intenderam in Manichaei litteras, magisque desperans[2] de ceteris eorum doctoribus,[3] quando in multis quae me mouebant ita ille nominatus apparuit, coepi cum eo pro studio eius agere uitam, quo ipse flagrabat[4] in eas litteras quas tunc iam rhetor[5] Carthaginis adulescentes[6] docebam, et legere cum eo siue quae ille audita desideraret siue quae ipse tali ingenio apta[7] existimarem.[8] ceterum conatus[9] omnis meus quo proficere[10] in illa secta[11] statueram[12] illo homine cognito prorsus[13] intercidit,[14] non ut ab eis omnino separarer[15] sed, quasi melius quicquam non inueniens, eo, quo iam quoquo modo[16] inrueram,[17] contentus interim[18] esse decreueram,[19] nisi aliquid forte quod magis eligendum[20] esset eluceret.[21]

Ita ille Faustus, qui multis *laqueus*[22] *mortis* (Ps 17:6) extitit,[23] meum quo captus eram relaxare[24] iam coeperat, nec uolens nec sciens. manus enim tuae, Deus meus, in abdito[25] prouidentiae[26] tuae non deserebant animam meam, et de sanguine cordis matris meae per lacrimas eius diebus et noctibus pro me sacrificabatur[27] tibi, et egisti mecum miris modis. tu illud egisti, Deus meus, nam *a Domino gressus*[28] *hominis diriguntur,*[29] *et uiam eius uolet* (Ps 36:23). aut quae procuratio[30] salutis praeter manum tuam reficientem[31] quae fecisti?

---

[1]refringo ~ingere, ~egi, ~actum **to break** [2]despero ~are, ~aui, ~atum **to despair** [3]doctor ~oris *m.* **teacher** [4]flagro ~are, ~aui **to burn with zeal** [5]rhetor ~oris *m.* **rhetorician** [6]adulescens ~ntis *m.* **young man** [7]aptus ~a, ~um *ppl. adj.* **suitable** [8]existimo ~are, ~aui, ~atum **to judge** [9]conatus ~us *m.* **impulse** [10]proficio ~icere, ~eci, ~ectum **to make progress** [11]secta ~ae *f.* **school of philosophy;** ECCL **sect** [12]statuo ~uere, ~ui, ~utum **to decide** [13]prorsus *adv.* **entirely** [14]intercido ~dere, ~di **to fall into oblivion** [15]separo ~are, ~aui, ~atum **to separate** [16]'quoquo modo' **in whatever way** [17]inruo ~uere, ~ui **to fall into** [18]interim *adv.* **for the time being** [19]decerno ~ernere, ~reui, ~retum **to make up one's mind** [20]eligo ~igere, ~egi, ~ectum **to choose** [21]eluceo ~cere, ~xi **to manifest itself** [22]laqueus ~i *m.* **snare** [23]exto ~are, extiti **to prove to be** [24]relaxo ~are, ~aui, ~atum **to loosen** [25]abditus ~a, ~um *adj.* **hidden** [26]prouidentia ~ae *f.* **providence** [27]sacrifico ~are, ~aui, ~atum **to offer as sacrifice** (pass. *impers.*) [28]gressus ~us *m.* **step** [29]dirigo ~igere, ~exi, ~ectum **to direct** [30]procuratio ~onis *f.* concern for; LATE **procuring** [31]reficio ~icere, ~eci, ~ectum **to remake**

To Rome

5.8.14 Egisti ergo mecum ut mihi persuaderetur[1] Romam pergere[2] et potius ibi docere quod docebam Carthagini. et hoc unde mihi persuasum

---

[1]persuadeo ~dere, ~si, ~sum **to persuade** (w. dat. of person) [2]pergo ~gere, ~rexi, ~rectum **to move on**

est non praeteribo confiteri tibi, quoniam et in his altissimi tui recessus[3] et praesentissima in nos misericordia tua cogitanda et praedicanda[4] est.

non ideo Romam pergere uolui, quod maiores quaestus[5] maiorque mihi dignitas[6] ab amicis qui hoc suadebant[7] promittebatur[8] (quamquam et ista ducebant animum tunc meum), sed illa erat causa maxima et paene[9] sola, quod audiebam quietius[10] ibi studere[11] adulescentes[12] et ordinatiore[13] disciplinae[14] cohercitione[15] sedari,[16] ne in eius scholam[17] quo magistro non utuntur passim[18] et proterue[19] inruant,[20] nec eos admitti[21] omnino nisi ille permiserit.[22] contra apud Carthaginem foeda[23] est et intemperans[24] licentia[25] scholasticorum.[26] inrumpunt[27] impudenter[28] et prope furiosa[29] fronte[30] perturbant[31] ordinem quem quisque discipulis[32] ad proficiendum[33] instituerit.[34] multa iniuriosa[35] faciunt mira hebetudine,[36] et punienda[37] legibus nisi consuetudo patrona[38] sit, hoc miseriores eos ostendens, quo iam quasi liceat faciunt quod per tuam aeternam legem numquam licebit, et impune[39] se facere arbitrantur, cum ipsa faciendi caecitate[40] puniantur et incomparabiliter[41] patiantur peiora quam faciunt.

Ergo quos mores cum studerem meos esse nolui, eos cum docerem cogebar perpeti[42] alienos. et ideo placebat ire ubi talia non fieri omnes qui nouerant indicabant.

Verum autem *tu, spes mea et portio*[43] *mea in terra uiuentium* (Ps 141:6), ad mutandum terrarum locum pro salute animae meae, et Carthagini

---

[3]recessus ~us *m.* **recess** [4]praedico ~are, ~aui, ~atum **to make known** [5]quaestus ~us *m.* **income** [6]dignitas ~atis *f.* **importance** [7]suadeo ~dere, ~si, ~sum **to recommend** [8]promitto ~ittere, ~isi, ~issum **to promise** [9]paene *adv.* **practically** [10]quiete *adv.* **quietly** [11]studeo ~ere, ~ui **to study** [12]adulescens ~ntis *m.* **young man** [13]ordinatus ~a, ~um *adj.* **well-ordered** [14]disciplina ~ae *f.* **discipline** [15]cohercitio ~onis *f.* **restraint** [16]sedo ~are, ~aui, ~atum **to keep calm** [17]schola ~ae *f.* **school** [18]passim *adv.* **at random** [19]proterue *adv.* **without constraint** [20]inruo ~uere, ~ui **to rush in** [21]admitto ~ittere, ~isi, ~issum **to admit** [22]permitto ~ittere, ~isi, ~issum **to permit** [23]foedus ~a, ~um *adj.* **loathsome** [24]intemperans ~ntis *adj.* **unrestrained** [25]licentia ~ae *f.* **license** [26]scholasticus ~a, ~um *adj.* **student** (*m.* as noun) [27]inrumpo ~umpere, ~upi, ~uptum **to force one's way into** [28]impudenter *adv.* **impudently** [29]furiosus ~a, ~um *adj.* **frenzied** [30]frons ~ntis *f.* **front** > (mil.) **frontal assault** [31]perturbo ~are, ~aui, ~atum **to throw into confusion** [32]discipulus ~i *m.* **pupil** [33]proficio ~icere, ~eci, ~ectum **to make progress** [34]instituo ~uere, ~ui, ~utum **to establish** [35]iniuriosus ~a, ~um *adj.* **injurious** [36]hebetudo ~inis *f.* LATE **insensitivity** [37]punior, poenior ~iri, ~itus. **to punish** [38]patrona ~ae *f.* **protection** [39]impune *adv.* **with impunity** [40]caecitas ~atis *f.* **blindness** [41]incomparabiliter *adv.* ECCL **incomparably** [42]perpetior ~ti, ~ssus **to tolerate to the full** [43]portio ~onis *f.* **portion**

stimulos[44] quibus inde auellerer[45] admouebas,[46] et Romae inlecebras[47] quibus attraherer[48] proponebas[49] mihi per homines qui diligunt uitam mortuam, hinc insana[50] facientes, inde uana pollicentes,[51] et ad corrigendos[52] *gressus*[53] *meos* (Ps 39:3) utebaris occulte[54] et illorum et mea peruersitate.[55] nam et qui perturbabant otium[56] meum foeda rabie[57] caeci[58] erant, et qui inuitabant[59] ad aliud terram sapiebant,[60] ego autem, qui detestabar[61] hic[62] ueram miseriam, illic falsam felicitatem[63] appetebam.[64]

[44]stimulus ~i *m.* **goad** [45]auello ~ellere, ~elli ~ulsum **to tear away** [46]admoueo ~mouere, ~moui, ~motum **to lead towards** [47]inlecebra ~ae *f.* **allurement** [48]attraho ~here, ~xi, ~ctum to draw > **to attract** (invisibly) [49]propono ~onere, ~osui, ~ositum **to place before** [50]insanus ~a, ~um *adj.* **insane** [51]polliceor ~eri, ~itus **to promise** [52]corrigo ~igere, ~exi, ~ectum **to make straight** [53]gressus ~us *m.* **step** [54]occulte *adv.* **secretly** [55]peruersitas ~atis *f.* **perversity** [56]otium ~ii *neut.* **tranquility** [57]rabies (~ei) *f.* **frenzy** [58]caecus ~a, ~um *adj.* **blind** [59]inuito ~are, ~aui, ~atum **to invite** [60]sapio ~ere, ~ii **to savor of** [61]detestor ~ari, ~atus **to detest** [62]hic *adv.* **here** [63]felicitas ~atis *f.* **happiness** [64]appeto ~ere, ~iui or ~ii, ~itum **to try to reach**

Monica abandoned

5.8.15 Sed quare[1] hinc abirem[2] et illuc[3] irem, tu sciebas, Deus, nec indicabas mihi nec matri, quae me profectum[4] atrociter[5] planxit[6] et usque ad mare secuta est. sed fefelli eam, uiolenter[7] me tenentem ut aut reuocaret[8] aut mecum pergeret.[9] et finxi[10] me amicum nolle deserere donec uento facto nauigaret,[11] et mentitus[12] sum matri, et illi matri. et euasi,[13] quia et hoc dimisisti mihi misericorditer[14] seruans me ab aquis maris, plenum exsecrandis[15] sordibus[16] usque ad aquam gratiae tuae, qua me abluto[17] siccarentur[18] flumina maternorum[19] oculorum, quibus pro me cotidie[20] tibi rigabat[21] terram sub uultu suo.

Et tamen recusanti[22] sine me redire uix persuasi[23] ut in loco qui proximus[24] nostrae naui erat, memoria Beati Cypriani, maneret ea nocte.

[1]quare *adv.* **why?** [2]abeo ~ire, ~ii, ~itum **to go away** [3]illuc *adv.* **there** [4]proficiscor ~icisci, ~ectus **to depart** [5]atrociter *adv.* **with bitter feeling** [6]plango ~gere, ~xi, ~ctum **to beat the breast in grief** [7]uiolenter *adv.* **with violent expressions of feeling** [8]reuoco ~are, ~aui, ~atum **to call upon to return** [9]pergo ~gere, ~rexi, ~rectum **to set out** [10]fingo ~ngere, ~nxi, ~ctum **to pretend** [11]nauigo ~are, ~aui, ~atum **to sail** [12]mentior ~iri, ~itus **to deceive** [13]euado ~dere, ~si, ~sum **to escape** [14]misericorditer *adv.* **mercifully** [15]exsecror ~ari, ~atus **to detest** [16]sordes ~is *f.* **baseness** [17]abluo ~uere, ~ui, ~utum **to wash off** [18]sicco ~are, ~aui, ~atum **to dry up** [19]maternus ~a, ~um *adj.* **mother's** [20]cotidie *adv.* **day by day** [21]rigo ~are, ~aui, ~atum **to soak** [22]recuso ~are, ~aui, ~atum **to refuse** [23]persuadeo ~dere, ~si, ~sum **to persuade** [24]proximus ~a, ~um *superl. adj.* **close by**

sed ea nocte clanculo[25] ego profectus sum, illa autem non; mansit orando[26] et flendo. et quid a te petebat, Deus meus, tantis lacrimis, nisi ut nauigare me non sineres? sed tu alte[27] consulens[28] et exaudiens cardinem[29] desiderii eius non curasti quod tunc petebat, ut me faceres quod semper petebat. flauit[30] uentus et impleuit uela[31] nostra et litus subtraxit[32] aspectibus[33] nostris, in quo mane[34] illa insaniebat[35] dolore, et querellis[36] et gemitu[37] implebat aures tuas contemnentis[38] ista.

Cum et me cupiditatibus meis raperes ad finiendas ipsas cupiditates et illius carnale[39] desiderium iusto dolorum flagello[40] uapularet.[41] amabat enim secum praesentiam[42] meam more matrum, sed multis multo amplius, et nesciebat quid tu illi gaudiorum facturus esses de absentia[43] mea. nesciebat, ideo flebat et eiulabat,[44] atque illis cruciatibus[45] arguebatur[46] in ea reliquiarium[47] *Euae*, cum gemitu quaerens quod cum *gemitu pepererat*[48] (Gen 3:16). et tamen post accusationem[49] fallaciarum[50] et crudelitatis[51] meae conuersa rursus ad deprecandum[52] te pro me abiit ad solita, et ego Romam.

[25]clanculo *adv.* **secretly** [26]oro ~are, ~aui, ~atum **to beseech** [27]alte *adv.* **deeply** [28]consulo ~ere, ~ui, ~tum **to counsel** [29]cardo ~inis *m.* **pivotal point** [30]flo ~are, ~aui, ~atum **to blow** [31]uelum ~i *neut.* **sail** [32]subtraho ~here, ~xi, ~ctum **to withdraw** [33]aspectus ~us *m.* **gaze** [34]mane *indecl. neut.* **morning** [35]insanio ~ire, ~iui or ~ii, ~itum **to be out of one's mind** [36]querella ~ae *f.* **protest** [37]gemitus ~us *m.* **groaning** [38]contemno ~nere, ~psi, ~ptum **to pay no heed** [39]carnalis ~is, ~e *adj.* ECCL **carnal** [40]flagellum ~i *neut.* **scourge** [41]uapulo ~are, ~aui, ~atum **to be thrashed** [42]praesentia ~ae *f.* **presence** [43]absentia ~ae *f.* **absence** [44]eiulo ~are **to wail** [45]cruciatus ~us *m.* **torture** [46]arguo ~uere, ~ui, ~utum **to prove** [47]reliquiarium ~i *neut.* LATE **remnant** *or* **heritage** [48]pario ~ere, peperi, ~tum **to give birth to** [49]accusatio ~onis *f.* **accusation** [50]fallacia ~ae *f.* **deception** [51]crudelitas ~atis *f.* **cruelty** [52]deprecor ~ari, ~atus **to beg in prayer**

Sick to death

5.9.16 Et ecce excipior[1] ibi flagello[2] aegritudinis[3] corporalis, et ibam iam ad inferos[4] portans[5] omnia mala quae commiseram[6] et in te et in me et in alios, multa et grauia super originalis[7] peccati uinculum[8] quo *omnes in Adam morimur* (1 Cor 15:22). non enim quicquam eorum

[1]excipio ~ipere, ~epi, ~eptum **to meet** [2]flagellum ~i *neut.* **scourge** [3]aegritudo ~inis *f.* **sickness** [4]inferus ~a, ~um *adj.* **of the underworld**; ECCL **Hell** [5]porto ~are, ~aui, ~atum **to carry** [6]committo ~ittere, ~isi, ~issum **to commit** [7]originalis ~is, ~e *adj.* **original** [8]uinculum ~i *neut.* **chain**

mihi donaueras[9] in Christo, nec *soluerat*[10] *ille in cruce*[11] *sua inimicitias*[12] (Eph 2:14–16) quas tecum contraxeram[13] peccatis meis. quomodo enim eas solueret in cruce phantasmatis,[14] quod de illo credideram? quam ergo falsa mihi uidebatur mors carnis eius, tam uera erat animae meae, et quam uera erat mors carnis eius, tam falsa uita animae meae, quae id non credebat. et ingrauescentibus[15] febribus[16] iam ibam et peribam. quo enim irem, si hinc tunc abirem,[17] nisi *in ignem* (Mt 25:41) atque tormenta[18] digna factis meis in ueritate ordinis tui?

Et hoc illa nesciebat et tamen pro me orabat[19] absens; tu autem ubique[20] praesens ubi erat exaudiebas eam, et ubi eram miserebaris mei, ut recuperarem[21] salutem corporis adhuc insanus[22] corde sacrilego.[23] neque enim desiderabam in illo tanto periculo baptismum[24] tuum, et melior eram puer, quo illum de materna[25] pietate flagitaui,[26] sicut iam recordatus atque confessus sum. sed in dedecus[27] meum creueram et consilia medicinae[28] tuae demens[29] inridebam, qui non me siuisti talem bis[30] mori. quo uulnere si feriretur[31] cor matris, numquam sanaretur. non enim satis eloquor[32] quid erga[33] me habebat animi, et quanto maiore sollicitudine[34] me parturiebat[35] spiritu quam carne pepererat.[36]

[9]dono ~are, ~aui, ~atum **to forgive** [10]soluo ~uere, ~ui, ~utum **to set free** [11]crux ~ucis *f.* **cross** [12]inimicitia ~ae *f.* **enmity** [13]contraho ~ahere, ~axi, ~actum **to incur** [14]phantasma ~atis *neut.* phantom; LATE **figment of the imagination** [15]ingrauesco ~ere **to grow worse** [16]febris ~is *f.* **fever** [17]abeo ~ire, ~ii, ~itum **to go away** [18]tormentum ~i *neut.* **torment** [19]oro ~are, ~aui, ~atum **to pray** [20]ubique *adv.* **everywhere** [21]recupero ~are, ~aui, ~atum **to recuperate** [22]insanus ~a, ~um *adj.* **insane** [23]sacrilegus ~a, ~um *adj.* **sacrilegious** [24]baptismus ~i *m.* (~um ~i *neut.*) ECCL **baptism** [25]maternus ~a, ~um *adj.* **mother's** [26]flagito ~are, ~aui, ~atum **to ask repeatedly** [27]dedecus ~oris *neut.* **shame** [28]medicina ~ae *f.* **medicine** [29]demens ~ntis *adj.* **out of one's mind** [30]bis *adv.* **doubly** [31]ferio ~ire **to deal a blow** [32]eloquor ~qui, ~cutus **to speak** [33]erga *prep. acc.* **for** (of feelings) [34]sollicitudo ~inis *f.* **anxiety** [35]parturio ~ire, ~iui **to be in labor** (giving birth) [36]pario ~ere, peperi, ~tum **to give birth to**

Faithful Monica

5.9.17 Non itaque uideo quomodo sanaretur, si mea talis illa mors transuerberasset[1] uiscera[2] dilectionis[3] eius. et ubi essent tantae preces,[4] et tam crebrae[5] *sine intermissione*[6] (1 Thess 5:17)? nusquam[7] nisi ad te.

[1]transuerbero ~are, ~aui, ~atum **to transfix** [2]uiscus ~eris *neut.* internal organs > **innermost heart** (*pl.*) [3]dilectio ~onis *f.* ECCL **love** [4]preces ~um *f. pl.* **prayer** [5]creber ~bra, ~brum *adj.* **frequent** [6]intermissio ~onis *f.* **intermission** [7]nusquam *adv.* **nowhere**

an uero tu, *Deus misericordiarum* (1 Cor 1:3), sperneres[8] *cor contritum*[9] *et humilatum*[10] (Ps 50:19) uiduae[11] castae[12] ac sobriae,[13] frequentantis[14] elemosynas,[15] obsequentis[16] atque seruientis sanctis tuis, nullum diem praetermittentis[17] oblationem[18] ad altare[19] tuum, bis[20] die, mane[21] et uespere,[22] ad ecclesiam tuam sine ulla intermissione uenientis, non ad uanas fabulas[23] et aniles[24] loquacitates,[25] sed ut te audiret in tuis sermonibus et tu illam in suis orationibus?[26] huiusne tu lacrimas, quibus non a te aurum et argentum[27] petebat, nec aliquod nutabile[28] aut uolubile[29] bonum, sed salutem animae filii sui, tu, cuius munere talis erat, contemneres[30] et repelleres[31] ab auxilio[32] tuo? nequaquam,[33] Domine. immo uero[34] aderas et exaudiebas et faciebas ordine quo praedestinaueras[35] esse faciendum. absit ut tu falleres eam in illis uisionibus[36] et responsis tuis, quae iam commemoraui et quae non commemoraui, quae illa fideli pectore tenebat et semper orans[37] tamquam chirographa[38] tua ingerebat[39] tibi. dignaris[40] enim, *quoniam in saeculum*[41] *misericordia tua* (Ps 117:1), eis quibus omnia debita dimittis, etiam promissionibus[42] debitor[43] fieri.

---

[8]sperno ~ere, spreui, spretum **to spurn** [9]contero ~terere, ~triui, ~tritum to crush, grind; ECCL *ppl. adj.* **contrite** [10]humilo ~are, ~aui, ~atum ECCL **to humble** [11]uiduus ~a, ~um *adj.* **widow** (*f.* as noun) [12]castus ~a, ~um *adj.* **chaste** [13]sobrius ~ia, ~ium *adj.* **sober** [14]frequento ~are, ~aui, ~atum **to perform assiduously** [15]elemosyna ~ae *f.* ECCL **almsgiving** [16]obsequens ~ntis *adj.* **obedient** [17]praetermitto ~ittere, ~isi, ~issum **to neglect** [18]oblatio ~onis *f.* offering ECCL **oblation (of the Mass)** [19]altaria ~ium *neut. pl.*, (*sg. nom.* ~e) **altar** [20]bis *adv.* **twice** [21]mane *indecl. neut.* **morning** [22]uesper *m.* (~era ~erae *f.*) **evening** [23]fabula ~ae *f.* **fictitious story** [24]anilis ~is, ~e *adj.* **characteristic of an old woman** [25]loquacitas ~atis *f.* **talkativeness** [26]oratio ~onis *f.* speech; ECCL **prayer** [27]argentum ~i *neut.* **silver** [28]nutabilis ~is, ~e *adj.* **frail** [29]uolubilis ~is, ~e *adj.* spinning > **unstable** (transf.) [30]contemno ~nere, ~psi, ~ptum **to despise** [31]repello ~ere, reppuli, repulsum **to reject** [32]auxilium ~ii *neut.* **help** [33]nequaquam *adv.* **by no means** [34]'immo uero' **no, in fact...** [35]praedestino ~are, ~aui, ~atum ECCL **to predestine** [36]uisio ~onis *f.* **vision** [37]oro ~are, ~aui, ~atum **to pray** [38]chirographum ~i *neut.* handwriting > **written promise** [39]ingero ~rere, ~ssi, ~stum to heap on > **to say repeatedly** [40]digno ~are, ~aui, ~atum **to deign (to)** [41]'in saeculum' **forever** [42]promissio ~onis *f.* **promise** [43]debitor ~oris *m.* **debtor**

Restored to health

5.10.18 Recreasti[1] ergo me ab illa aegritudine[2] et saluum[3] fecisti *filium ancillae*[4] *tuae* (Ps 115:16) tunc interim[5] corpore, ut esset cui salutem meliorem atque certiorem dares.

---

[1]recreo ~are, ~aui, ~atum **to revive** [2]aegritudo ~inis *f.* **illness** [3]saluus ~a, ~um *adj.* **well** [4]ancilla ~ae *f.* **handmaid** [5]interim *adv.* **for the time being**

Et iungebar⁶ etiam tunc Romae falsis illis atque fallentibus Sanctis, non enim tantum Auditoribus⁷ eorum, quorum e numero erat etiam is in cuius domo aegrotaueram⁸ et conualueram,⁹ sed eis etiam quos "Electos"¹⁰ uocant. adhuc enim mihi uidebatur non esse nos qui peccamus, sed nescio quam aliam in nobis peccare naturam, et delectabat superbiam¹¹ meam extra¹² culpam¹³ esse et, cum aliquid mali fecissem, non confiteri me fecisse, ut *sanares animam meam, quoniam peccabat tibi* (Ps 40:5), sed excusare¹⁴ me amabam et accusare¹⁵ nescio quid aliud quod mecum esset et ego non essem. uerum autem totum ego eram et aduersus me impietas¹⁶ mea me diuiserat,¹⁷ et id erat peccatum insanabilius,¹⁸ quo me peccatorem¹⁹ non esse arbitrabar.

Et execrabilis²⁰ iniquitas, te, Deus omnipotens,²¹ te in me ad perniciem²² meam, quam me a te ad salutem malle²³ superari.²⁴ nondum ergo *posueras custodiam²⁵ ori meo et ostium²⁶ continentiae²⁷ circum²⁸ labia²⁹ mea* (Ps 140:3), ut *non declinaret³⁰ cor meum in uerba mala ad excusandas excusationes³¹ in peccatis cum hominibus operantibus³² iniquitatem* (Ps 140:4), et ideo adhuc combinabam³³ *cum electis eorum* (Ps 140:4), sed tamen iam desperans³⁴ in ea falsa doctrina me posse proficere,³⁵ eaque ipsa quibus, si nihil melius reperirem,³⁶ contentus esse decreueram³⁷ iam remissius³⁸ neglegentiusque³⁹ retinebam.⁴⁰

---

⁶iungo ~gere, ~xi, ~ctum **to join** ⁷auditor ~oris *m.* **hearer** (lower order of Manichee) ⁸aegroto ~are, ~aui, ~atum **to be ill** ⁹conualesco ~escere, ~ui **to convalesce** ¹⁰electus ~a, ~um *adj.* **"elect"** (high ranking Manichee) ¹¹superbia ~ae *f.* **pride** ¹²extra *prep. acc.* **beyond** ¹³culpa ~ae *f.* **blame** ¹⁴excuso ~are, ~aui, ~atum **to excuse** ¹⁵accuso ~are, ~aui, ~atum **to accuse** ¹⁶impietas ~atis *f.* **impiety** ¹⁷diuido ~idere, ~isi, ~isum **to divide** ¹⁸insanabilis ~is, ~e *adj.* **incurable** ¹⁹peccator ~oris *m.* ECCL **sinner** ²⁰execrabilis ~is, ~e *adj.* **detestable** ²¹omnipotens ~ntis *adj.* **omnipotent** ²²pernicies ~ei *f.* **ruin** ²³malo ~lle, ~lui **to prefer** ²⁴supero ~are, ~aui, ~atum **to overcome** ²⁵custodia ~ae *f.* **guard** ²⁶ostium ~ii *neut.* **gate** ²⁷continentia ~ae *f.* **continence** ²⁸circum *prep. acc.* **round about** ²⁹labium ~ii *neut.* **lip** ³⁰declino ~are, ~aui, ~atum **to sink** ³¹excusatio ~onis *f.* **excuse** ³²operor ~ari, ~atus **to be at work** ³³combino ~are, ~aui, ~atum ECCL **to join with** ³⁴despero ~are, ~aui, ~atum **to despair** ³⁵proficio ~icere, ~eci, ~ectum **to make progress** ³⁶reperio ~ire, repperi, ~tum **to discover** ³⁷decerno ~ernere, ~reui, ~retum **to decide** ³⁸remisse *adv.* **half-heartedly** ³⁹neglegenter *adv.* **carelessly** ⁴⁰retineo ~ere, ~ui, retentum to hold fast > **to continue to adhere**

Cicero's *Academics*

5.10.19 Etenim[1] suborta[2] est etiam mihi cogitatio, prudentiores[3] illos ceteris fuisse philosophos[4] quos "Academicos" appellant, quod de omnibus dubitandum[5] esse censuerant[6] nec aliquid ueri ab homine comprehendi posse decreuerant.[7] ita enim et mihi liquido[8] sensisse uidebantur, ut uulgo[9] habentur, etiam illorum intentionem[10] nondum intellegenti. nec dissimulaui[11] eundem hospitem[12] meum reprimere[13] a nimia[14] fiducia[15] quam sensi eum habere de rebus fabulosis[16] quibus Manichaei libri pleni sunt. amicitia[17] tamen eorum familiarius[18] utebar quam ceterorum hominum qui in illa haeresi[19] non fuissent. nec eam defendebam[20] pristina[21] animositate,[22] sed tamen familiaritas[23] eorum (plures enim eos Roma occultat[24]) pigrius[25] me faciebat aliud quaerere, praesertim[26] desperantem[27] in Ecclesia tua, *Domine caeli et terrae* (Mt 11:25), *creator omnium* (Hymn 2.1) *uisibilium et inuisibilium* (Col 1:16), posse inueniri uerum, unde me illi auerterant,[28] multumque mihi turpe uidebatur credere figuram[29] te habere humanae carnis et membrorum nostrorum liniamentis[30] corporalibus terminari,[31] et quoniam cum de Deo meo cogitare uellem, cogitare nisi moles corporum non noueram (neque enim uidebatur mihi esse quicquam quod tale non esset), ea maxima et prope sola causa erat ineuitabilis[32] erroris mei.

[1]etenim *conj.* **for** [2]suborior ~iri, ~tus **to spring up** [3]prudens ~ntis *adj.* **prudent** [4]philosophus ~i *m.* **philosopher** [5]dubito ~are, ~aui, ~atum **to be in doubt** [6]censeo ~ere, ~ui, ~um **to suppose** [7]decerno ~ernere, ~reui, ~retum **to determine** [8]liquidus ~a, ~um *adj.* **clear** [9]uulgo *adv.* **commonly** [10]intentio ~onis *f.* **intention** [11]dissimulo ~are, ~aui, ~atum to disguise > **to turn a blind eye** [12]hospes ~itis *m.* **host** [13]reprimo ~imere, ~essi, ~essum **to restrain** [14]nimius ~a, ~um *adj.* **excessive** [15]fiducia ~ae *f.* **confidence** [16]fabulosus ~a, ~um *adj.* **fantastical** [17]amicitia ~ae *f.* **friendship** [18]familiaris ~is, ~e *adj.* **intimate** [19]haeresis ~is *f.* philosophical sect; ECCL **heresy** [20]defendo ~dere, ~di, ~sum **to defend** [21]pristinus ~a, ~um *adj.* **previous** [22]animositas ~tatis *f.* animosity; LATE **ardor** [23]familiaritas ~atis *f.* **close friendship** [24]occulto ~are, ~aui, ~atum **to conceal**; LATE **to harbor** [25]pigre *adv.* **reluctantly** [26]praesertim *adv.* **especially** [27]despero ~are, ~aui, ~atum **to despair** [28]auerto ~tere, ~ti, ~sum **to turn away** [29]figura ~ae *f.* **form** [30]liniamentum ~i *neut.* **outline** [31]termino ~are, ~aui, ~atum **to limit** [32]ineuitabilis ~is, ~e *adj.* **inevitable**

Evil imagined as a substance

5.10.20 Hinc enim et mali substantiam quandam credebam esse talem et habere suam molem taetram[1] et deformem[2] et crassam,[3] quam terram dicebant, siue tenuem[4] atque subtilem,[5] sicuti est aeris[6] corpus, quam malignam[7] mentem per illam terram repentem[8] imaginantur.[9] et quia Deum bonum nullam malam naturam creasse qualiscumque[10] me pietas credere cogebat, constituebam[11] ex aduerso[12] sibi duas moles, utramque infinitam, sed malam[13] angustius,[14] bonam grandius, et ex hoc initio[15] pestilentioso[16] me cetera sacrilegia[17] sequebantur. cum enim conaretur animus meus recurrere[18] in Catholicam fidem, repercutiebar,[19] quia non erat Catholica fides quam esse arbitrabar. et magis pius mihi uidebar, si te, Deus meus, cui *confitentur ex me miserationes*[20] *tuae* (Ps 106:8), uel ex ceteris partibus infinitum crederem, quamuis ex una, qua tibi moles mali opponebatur,[21] cogerer finitum fateri,[22] quam si ex omnibus partibus in corporis humani forma te opinarer[23] finiri. et melius mihi uidebar credere nullum malum te creasse (quod mihi nescienti non solum aliqua substantia sed etiam corporea uidebatur, quia et mentem cogitare non noueram nisi eam subtile corpus esse, quod tamen per loci spatia diffunderetur[24]) quam credere abs te esse qualem putabam naturam mali.

Ipsumque Saluatorem[25] nostrum, Unigenitum[26] tuum, tamquam de massa[27] lucidissimae[28] molis tuae porrectum[29] ad nostram salutem ita putabam, ut aliud de illo non crederem nisi quod possem uanitate imaginari. talem itaque naturam eius nasci non posse de Maria Virgine arbitrabar, nisi carni concerneretur.[30] concerni autem et non inquinari[31]

---

[1]taeter ~tra, ~trum *adj.* **foul** [2]deformis ~is, ~e *adj.* **deformed** [3]crassus ~a, ~um *adj.* **dense** [4]tenuis ~is, ~e *adj.* **thin** [5]subtilis ~is, ~e *adj.* **composed of fine particles** [6]aer aeris *m.* (*f.*) **air** [7]malignus ~a, ~um *adj.* **malignant** [8]repo ~ere, ~si **to creep** [9]imaginor ~ari, ~atus **to imagine** [10]qualiscumque ~iscumque, ~ecumque *adj.* **such as it was** [11]constituo ~uere, ~ui, ~utum **to suppose** [12]'ex aduerso' **opposite** [13]mala ~ae *f.* **evil** [14]angustus ~a, ~um *adj.* **small** [15]initium ~ii *neut.* **starting point** [16]pestilentiosus ~a, ~um *adj.* **diseased** [17]sacrilegium ~ii *neut.* **sacrilege** [18]recurro ~rrere, ~rri, ~rsum **to have recourse to** [19]repercutio ~tere, ~ssi, ~ssum **to repel** [20]miseratio ~onis *f.* **compassion** [21]oppono ~onere, ~osui, ~ositum **to oppose** [22]fateor ~eri, fassus **to concede** [23]opinor ~ari, ~atus **to think** [24]diffundo ~undere, ~udi, ~usum **to diffuse** [25]saluator ~oris *m.* ECCL **Savior** [26]unigenitus ~a, ~um *adj.* ECCL **only-begotten** [27]massa ~ae *f.* **mass** [28]lucidus ~a, ~um *adj.* **shining** [29]porrigo ~igere, ~exi, ~ectum **to spread out** [30]concerno ~ere ECCL **to intermingle** [31]inquino ~are, ~aui, ~atum **to debase**

non uidebam, quod mihi tale figurabam.[32] metuebam itaque credere in carne natum, ne credere cogerer ex carne inquinatum.[33] nunc spiritales tui blande[34] et amanter[35] ridebunt[36] me, si has confessiones meas legerint, sed tamen talis eram.

[32]figuro ~are, ~aui, ~atum **to figure** [33]inquinatus ~a, ~um *adj.* **debased** [34]blande *adv.* **gently** [35]amanter *adv.* **affectionately** [36]rideo ~dere, ~si, ~sum **to laugh at**

Elpidius the apologist

5.11.21 Deinde quae illi in scripturis tuis reprehenderant[1] defendi[2] posse non existimabam,[3] sed aliquando sane[4] cupiebam cum aliquo illorum librorum doctissimo conferre[5] singula et experiri quid inde sentiret. iam enim Elpidii cuiusdam aduersus eosdem Manichaeos coram loquentis et disserentis[6] sermones etiam apud Carthaginem mouere me coeperant, cum talia de scripturis proferret[7] quibus resisti non facile posset. et inbecilla[8] mihi responsio[9] uidebatur istorum, quam quidem non facile palam[10] promebant[11] sed nobis secretius,[12] cum dicerent scripturas Noui Testamenti[13] falsatas[14] fuisse a nescio quibus, qui Iudaeorum legem inserere[15] Christianae fidei uoluerunt, atque ipsi incorrupta[16] exemplaria[17] nulla proferrent.

Sed me maxime captum et offocatum[18] quodam modo deprimebant[19] corporalia cogitantem moles illae, sub quibus anhelans[20] in auram tuae ueritatis liquidam[21] et simplicem[22] respirare[23] non poteram.

[1]reprehendo ~dere, ~di, ~sum **to find fault** [2]defendo ~dere, ~di, ~sum **to defend** [3]existimo ~are, ~aui, ~atum **to hold the opinion** [4]sane *adv.* **certainly** [5]confero ~rre, contuli, conlatum **to confer** [6]dissero ~ere, ~ui, ~tum **to discuss** [7]profero ~ferre, ~tuli, ~latum **to adduce** [8]inbecillus ~a, ~um *adj.* **weak** [9]responsio ~onis *f.* **response** [10]palam *adv.* **publicly** [11]promo ~mere, ~mpsi, ~mptum **to set forth** [12]secreto *adv.* **in private** [13]testamentum ~i *neut.* **testament** [14]falso ~are, ~aui, ~atum **to falsify** [15]insero ~erere, ~eui, ~itum to plant > **to implant** [16]incorruptus ~a, ~um *adj.* **uncorrupted** [17]exemplar ~aris *neut.* **copy** [18]offoco ~are, ~aui, ~atum **to choke** [19]deprimo ~imere, ~essi, ~essum **to hold down** [20]anhelo ~are, ~aui, ~atum **to gasp** [21]liquidus ~a, ~um *adj.* **clear** [22]simplex ~icis *adj.* **simple** [23]respiro ~are, ~aui, ~atum **to breathe**

Teaching in Rome

5.12.22 Sedulo[1] ergo agere coeperam, propter quod ueneram, ut docerem Romae artem rhetoricam,[2] et prius domi congregare[3] aliquos quibus et per quos innotescere[4] coeperam. et ecce cognosco alia Romae fieri, quae non patiebar in Africa. nam re uera illas euersiones[5] a perditis[6] adulescentibus[7] ibi non fieri manifestatum[8] est mihi: "Sed subito,"[9] inquiunt, "ne mercedem[10] magistro reddant, conspirant[11] multi adulescentes et transferunt[12] se ad alium, desertores[13] fidei et quibus prae pecuniae[14] caritate iustitia uilis[15] est." oderat etiam istos cor meum, quamuis non *perfecto odio*[16] (Ps 138:22). quod enim ab eis passurus eram magis oderam fortasse[17] quam eo quod[18] cuilibet[19] inlicita[20] faciebant. certe tamen turpes sunt tales et *fornicantur*[21] *abs te* (Ps 72:27) amando uolatica[22] ludibria[23] temporum et *lucrum*[24] *luteum*[25] (Tit 1:7), quod cum apprehenditur[26] manum inquinat,[27] et amplectendo[28] mundum fugientem, contemnendo[29] te manentem et reuocantem[30] et ignoscentem[31] redeunti ad te meretrici[32] animae humanae. et nunc tales odi prauos[33] et distortos,[34] quamuis eos corrigendos[35] diligam, ut pecuniae doctrinam ipsam quam discunt praeferant,[36] ei uero te Deum ueritatem et ubertatem[37] certi boni et pacem castissimam.[38] sed tunc magis eos pati nolebam malos propter me, quam fieri propter te bonos uolebam.

---

[1]sedulo *adv.* **earnestly** [2]rhetoricus ~a, ~um *adj.* **rhetorical** [3]congrego ~are, ~aui, ~atum **to gather together** [4]innotesco ~escere, ~ui **to become known** [5]euersio ~onis *f.* **wrecking (havoc)** [6]perditus ~a, ~um *adj.* **abandoned** (morally) [7]adulescens ~ntis *m.* **young man** [8]manifesto ~are, ~aui, ~atum **to make clear** [9]subito *adv.* **suddenly** [10]merces ~edis *f.* **payment** [11]conspiro ~are, ~aui, ~atum **to conspire** [12]transfero ~ferre, ~tuli, ~latum **to transfer** (from one person to another) [13]desertor ~oris *m.* **deserter** [14]pecunia ~ae *f.* **money** [15]uilis ~is, ~e *adj.* **worthless** [16]odium ~i *neut.* **hatred** [17]fortasse *adv.* **perhaps** [18]eo quod' **for the reason that** [19]quilibet, quae-, quod- *pron.* **anyone whatever** [20]inlicitus ~a, ~um *adj.* **unlawfully** [21]fornico ~are, ~aui, ~atum ECCL **to commit adultery/idolatry** [22]uolaticus ~a, ~um *adj.* **flying**; LATE **fleeting** [23]ludibrium ~ii *neut.* **plaything** [24]lucrum ~i *neut.* **lucre** [25]luteus ~a, ~um *adj.* **filthy** [26]apprehendo ~dere, ~di, ~sum **to lay hold of** [27]inquino ~are, ~aui, ~atum **to pollute** [28]amplector ~cti, ~xus **to embrace affectionately** [29]contemno ~nere, ~psi, ~ptum **to regard with contempt** [30]reuoco ~are, ~aui, ~atum **to call upon to return** [31]ignosco ~oscere, ~oui, ~otum **to forgive** (w. dat.) [32]meretrix ~icis *f.* **prostitute** [33]prauus ~a, ~um *adj.* **corrupt** [34]distortus ~a, ~um *adj.* **twisted** [35]corrigo ~igere, ~exi, ~ectum **to straighten out** [36]praefero ~ferre, ~tuli, ~latum **to prefer** x (acc.) **to** y (dat.) [37]ubertas ~atis *f.* **abundance** [38]castus ~a, ~um *adj.* **chaste**

Symmachus sends Augustine to Ambrose

5.13.23 Itaque posteaquam[1] missum est a Mediolanio Romam ad praefectum[2] urbis, ut illi ciuitati rhetoricae[3] magister prouideretur,[4] impertita[5] etiam euectione publica,[6] ego ipse ambiui[7] per eos ipsos Manichaeis uanitatibus ebrios[8] (quibus ut carerem[9] ibam, sed utrique nesciebamus) ut dictione[10] proposita[11] me probatum[12] praefectus tunc Symmachus mitteret.

Et ueni Mediolanium ad Ambrosium episcopum,[13] in optimis notum orbi terrae,[14] pium cultorem[15] tuum, cuius tunc eloquia[16] strenue[17] ministrabant[18] *adipem*[19] *frumenti*[20] (Ps 80:17) tui et *laetitiam olei*[21] (Ps 44:8) et *sobriam*[22] *uini*[23] *ebrietatem*[24] (Hymn 7.23–24) populo tuo. ad eum autem ducebar abs te nesciens, ut per eum ad te sciens ducerer.

Suscepit[25] me paterne[26] ille *homo Dei* (2 Tim 3:17) et peregrinationem[27] meam satis episcopaliter[28] dilexit. et eum amare coepi, primo[29] quidem non tamquam doctorem[30] ueri, quod in ecclesia tua prorsus[31] desperabam,[32] sed tamquam hominem benignum[33] in me. et studiose[34] audiebam disputantem[35] in populo, non intentione[36] qua debui, sed quasi explorans[37] eius facundiam,[38] utrum conueniret[39] famae suae an maior minorue proflueret[40] quam praedicabatur,[41] et uerbis eius suspendebar[42] intentus, rerum autem incuriosus[43] et contemptor[44] adstabam.[45] et delectabar suauitate[46] sermonis, quamquam eruditioris,[47] minus tamen

---

[1]posteaquam *conj.* after [2]praefectus ~i *m.* prefect [3]rhetoricus ~a, ~um *adj.* rhetoric (*f.* as noun) [4]prouideo ~idere, ~idi, ~isum to provide [5]impertio ~ire, ~iui, ~itum to share in [6]'euectione publica' LATE order allowing travel by the state post [7]ambio ~ire, ~iui, ~itum to solicit for support [8]ebrius ~a, ~um *adj.* intoxicated [9]careo ~ere, ~ui, ~itum to be free from [10]dictio ~onis *f.* speech [11]propono ~onere, ~osui, ~ositum to propose [12]probo ~are, ~aui, ~atum to approve > **to give official approval** [13]episcopus ~i *m.* ECCL bishop [14]orbis terrae' the world [15]cultor ~oris *m.* worshipper [16]eloquium ~ii *neut.* eloquence [17]strenue *adv.* energetically [18]ministro ~are, ~aui, ~atum to serve; ECCL to minister to [19]adips ~ipis *m. f.* animal fat; ECCL fatness of grain [20]frumentum ~i *neut.* wheat [21]oleum ~i *neut.* olive oil [22]sobrius ~ia, ~ium *adj.* sober [23]uinum ~i *neut.* wine [24]ebrietas ~atis *f.* intoxication [25]suscipio ~ipere, ~epi, ~eptum to receive [26]paterne *adv.* AUG like a father [27]peregrinatio ~onis *f.* residing abroad (i.e., in Milan) [28]episcopaliter *adv.* AUG in a manner worthy of a bishop [29]primo *adv.* at first [30]doctor ~oris *m.* teacher [31]prorsus *adv.* entirely [32]despero ~are, ~aui, ~atum to despair [33]benignus ~a, ~um *adj.* kind [34]studiose *adv.* enthusiastically [35]disputo ~are, ~aui, ~atum to debate; ECCL to preach [36]intentio ~onis *f.* intention [37]exploro ~are, ~aui, ~atum **to put to the test** [38]facundia ~ae *f.* ability to speak eloquently [39]conuenio ~enire, ~eni, ~entum to be consistent [40]profluo ~uere, ~uxi to flow easily (of speech) [41]praedico ~are, ~aui, ~atum to declare > **to describe as** [42]suspendo ~dere, ~di, ~sum to keep in suspense [43]incuriosus ~a, ~um *adj.* indifferent [44]contemptor ~oris *m.* despiser [45]adsto ~are, ~iti **to stand by** [46]suauitas ~atis *f.* sweetness [47]eruditus ~a, ~um *adj.* erudite

hilarescentis[48] atque mulcentis[49] quam Fausti erat, quod attinet[50] ad dicendi modum. ceterum rerum ipsarum nulla comparatio:[51] nam ille per Manichaeas fallacias[52] aberrabat,[53] ille autem saluberrime[54] docebat salutem. sed *longe est a peccatoribus*[55] *salus* (Ps 118:155), qualis ego tunc aderam, et tamen propinquabam[56] sensim[57] et nesciens.

[48]hilaresco, -isco ~ere **to be light-hearted** [49]mulceo ~ere, mulsi, mulsum **to soothe** [50]attineo ~ere, ~ui, attentum **to concern** (w. 'ad') [51]comparatio ~onis *f.* **comparison** [52]fallacia ~ae *f.* **deceit** [53]aberro ~are, ~aui, ~atum **to wander off** [54]salubriter *adv.* **in a wholesome way** [55]peccator ~oris *m.* ECCL **sinner** [56]propinquo ~are, ~aui **to draw near** [57]sensim *adv.* **gradually**

Ambrose makes Catholicism respectable

5.14.24 Cum enim non satagerem[1] discere quae dicebat, sed tantum quemadmodum dicebat audire (ea mihi quippe iam desperanti[2] ad te uiam patere[3] homini inanis[4] cura remanserat[5]), ueniebant in animum meum simul cum uerbis quae diligebam res etiam quas neglegebam,[6] neque enim ea dirimere[7] poteram. et dum cor aperirem ad excipiendum[8] quam diserte[9] diceret, pariter[10] intrabat et quam uere diceret, gradatim[11] quidem. nam primo[12] etiam ipsa defendi[13] posse mihi iam coeperunt uideri, et fidem Catholicam, pro qua nihil posse dici aduersus oppugnantes[14] Manichaeos putaueram, iam non impudenter[15] adseri[16] existimabam,[17] maxime audito uno atque altero et saepius aenigmate[18] soluto[19] de scriptis ueteribus,[20] ubi, cum ad *litteram*[21] acciperem, *occidebar*[22] (2 Cor 3:6). spiritaliter[23] itaque plerisque[24] illorum librorum locis expositis[25] iam reprehendebam[26] desperationem[27] meam, illam dumtaxat[28] qua credideram legem et prophetas[29] detestantibus[30] atque

[1]satago ~agere, ~egi, ~actum **to trouble oneself** [2]despero ~are, ~aui, ~atum **to despair** [3]pateo ~ere, ~ui **to be open** [4]inanis ~is, ~e *adj.* **empty** [5]remaneo ~ere, ~si **to remain** [6]neglego ~gere, ~xi, ~ctum **to neglect** [7]dirimo ~imere, ~emi, ~emptum **to separate** [8]excipio ~ipere, ~epi, ~eptum **to take in** [9]diserte *adv.* **with skillful expression** [10]pariter *adv.* **together** [11]gradatim *adv.* **gradually** [12]primo *adv.* **at first** [13]defendo ~dere, ~di, ~sum **to defend** [14]oppugno ~are, ~aui, ~atum **to oppose** [15]impudenter *adv.* **impudently** [16]adsero ~ere, ~ui, ~tum **to assert** [17]existimo ~are, ~aui, ~atum **to judge** [18]aenigma ~atis *neut.* **allegory** [19]soluo ~uere, ~ui, ~utum **to resolve** [20]'scriptis ueteribus' ECCL i.e., **Old Testament** [21]'ad litteram' according to the letter, i.e., **literally** [22]occido ~idere, ~idi, ~asum **to die** [23]spiritaliter *adv.* ECCL **spiritually** [24]plerusque ~aque, ~umque *adj.* **many of** [25]expono ~onere, ~osui, ~ositum **to explain** [26]reprehendo ~dere, ~di, ~sum **to find fault** [27]desperatio ~onis *f.* **despair** [28]dumtaxat *adv.* **at least** [29]propheta ~ae *m.* ECCL **prophet** [30]detestor ~ari, ~atus **to detest**

inridentibus resisti omnino non posse. nec tamen iam ideo mihi Catholicam uiam tenendam esse sentiebam, quia et ipsa poterat habere doctos adsertores[31] suos, qui copiose[32] et non absurde[33] obiecta[34] refellerent,[35] nec ideo iam damnandum[36] illud quod tenebam quia defensionis[37] partes aequabantur.[38] ita enim Catholica non mihi uicta uidebatur, ut nondum etiam uictrix[39] appareret.

[31]adsertor ~oris *m.* **defender** [32]copiose *adv.* **eloquently** [33]absurde *adv.* **absurdly** [34]obiectum ~i *neut.* accusation; LATE **objection** [35]refello ~ere, ~i **to refute** [36]damno ~are, ~aui, ~atum **to renounce** [37]defensio ~onis *f.* **defense** [38]aequo ~are, ~aui, ~atum **to equal** [39]uictrix ~icis *f. adj.* **victorious** (of a woman)

From Manichee to catechumen

5.14.25 Tum uero fortiter[1] intendi animum, si quo modo possem certis aliquibus documentis[2] Manichaeos conuincere[3] falsitatis.[4] quod si possem spiritalem substantiam cogitare, statim[5] machinamenta[6] illa omnia soluerentur[7] et abicerentur[8] ex animo meo: sed non poteram. uerum tamen de ipso mundi huius corpore omnique natura quam sensus carnis attingeret[9] multo probabiliora[10] plerosque[11] sensisse philosophos[12] magis magisque considerans atque comparans[13] iudicabam. itaque Academicorum more, sicut existimantur,[14] dubitans[15] de omnibus atque inter omnia fluctuans,[16] Manichaeos quidem relinquendos esse decreui,[17] non arbitrans eo[18] ipso tempore dubitationis[19] meae in illa secta[20] mihi permanendum[21] esse cui iam nonnullos[22] philosophos praeponebam.[23] quibus tamen philosophis, quod sine salutari[24] nomine Christi essent, curationem[25] languoris[26] animae meae committere[27] omnino

[1]fortiter *adv.* **resolutely** [2]documentum ~i *neut.* **example** [3]conuinco ~incere, ~ici, ~ictum **to convict** [4]falsitas ~atis *f.* LATE **error** [5]statim *adv.* **immediately** [6]machinamentum ~i *neut.* **device** [7]soluo ~uere, ~ui, ~utum **to fall into pieces** [8]abicio ~cere, ~eci, ~ectum **to discard** [9]attingo ~tingere, ~tigi, ~tactum **to attain to** [10]probabilis ~is, ~e *adj.* **probable** [11]plerusque ~aque, ~umque *adj.* **many of** [12]philosophus ~i *m.* **philosopher** [13]comparo ~are, ~aui, ~atum **to compare** [14]existimo ~are, ~aui, ~atum **to suppose** [15]dubito ~are, ~aui, ~atum **to be in doubt** [16]fluctuo ~are, ~aui, ~atum **to waver** [17]decerno ~ernere, ~reui, ~retum **to decide** [18]eo *adv.* **consequently** [19]dubitatio ~onis *f.* **doubt** [20]secta ~ae *f.* **school of philosophy**; ECCL **sect** [21]permaneo ~ere, ~si, ~sum **to persist** [22]nonnullus ~a, ~um *adj.* **some** [23]praepono ~onere, ~osui, ~ositum **to prefer** [24]salutaris ~is, ~e *adj.* **life-giving** [25]curatio ~onis *f.* **treatment** [26]languor ~oris *m.* **illness** [27]committo ~ittere, ~isi, ~issum **to commit**

recusabam.[28] statui[29] ergo tamdiu[30] esse catechumenus[31] in Catholica Ecclesia mihi a parentibus commendata,[32] donec aliquid certi[33] eluceret[34] quo cursum dirigerem.[35]

[28]recuso ~are, ~aui, ~atum **to refuse** [29]statuo ~uere, ~ui, ~utum **to determine** [30]tamdiu *adv.* **for the time** [31]catechumenus ~i *m.* ECCL **catechumen** [32]commendo ~are, ~aui, ~atum **to commend** [33]certum ~i *neut.* **certainty** [34]eluceo ~cere, ~xi **to manifest itself** [35]dirigo ~igere, ~exi, ~ectum **to direct**

6

AMBROSE, ALYPIUS, AND AMBITION

Milan, 385

Monica in Milan

6.1.1 *Spes mea a iuuentute[1] mea* (Ps 71:5), ubi mihi eras et quo recesse-
ras? an uero non tu feceras me et *discreueras me a quadrupedibus[2] et a
uolatilibus[3] caeli sapientiorem me feceras* (Job 35:11 VL)? et ambulabam[4]
per *tenebras et lubricum[5]* (Ps 34:6) et quaerebam te foris[6] a me, et non
inueniebam *Deum cordis mei* (Ps 72:26). et ueneram *in profundum[7]
maris* (Ps 67:23), et diffidebam[8] et desperabam[9] de inuentione[10] ueri.

Iam uenerat ad me mater pietate fortis, *terra marique* me *sequens*
(Aen. 9.492) et in periculis omnibus de te secura.[11] nam et per marina[12]
discrimina[13] ipsos nautas[14] consolabatur,[15] a quibus rudes[16] abyssi uiato-
res,[17] cum perturbantur,[18] consolari solent, pollicens[19] eis peruentionem[20]
cum salute, quia hoc ei tu per uisum pollicitus eras. et inuenit me,
periclitantem[21] quidem grauiter[22] desperatione[23] indagandae[24] ueritatis,
sed tamen ei cum indicassem non me quidem iam esse Manichaeum,
sed neque Catholicum Christianum, non quasi inopinatum[25] aliquid

---

[1]iuuentus ~utis *f.* **youth** [2]quadrupes ~edis *adj.* **four-footed creature** (as noun) [3]uolatilis ~is, ~e *adj.*
flying; **bird** (as noun) [4]ambulo ~are, ~aui, ~atum **to walk** [5]lubricus ~a, ~um *adj.* **slippery place**
(*neut.* as noun) [6]foris *adv.* **outside** [7]profundum ~i *neut.* **depths** [8]diffido ~dere, ~sus **to despair**
[9]despero ~are, ~aui, ~atum **to give up as hopeless** [10]inuentio ~onis *f.* **discovery** [11]securus ~a, ~um
adj. **safe** [12]marinus ~a, ~um *adj.* **at sea** [13]discrimen ~inis *neut.* **peril** [14]nauta ~ae *m.* **sailor** [15]consolor
~ari, ~atus **to comfort** [16]rudis ~is, ~e *adj.* **inexperienced** [17]uiator ~oris *m.* **traveler** [18]perturbo
~are, ~aui, ~atum **to upset** [19]polliceor ~eri, ~itus **to promise** [20]peruentio ~onis *f.* AUG **arrival**
[21]periclitor ~ari, ~atus **to be in danger** [22]grauiter *adv.* **deeply** [23]desperatio ~onis *f.* **despair** [24]indago
~are, ~aui, ~atum **to ascertain** [25]inopinatus ~a, ~um *adj.* **unforeseen**

audierit, exiliuit²⁶ laetitia, cum iam secura fieret ex ea parte miseriae meae in qua me tamquam mortuum sed resuscitandum²⁷ tibi flebat, et feretro²⁸ cogitationis offerebat²⁹ ut diceres filio uiduae,³⁰ *Iuuenis, tibi dico, surge*³¹ (Lk 7:14), et reuiuesceret³² et inciperet loqui et traderes illum matri suae. nulla ergo turbulenta³³ exultatione³⁴ trepidauit³⁵ cor eius, cum audisset ex tanta parte iam factum quod tibi cotidie³⁶ plangebat³⁷ ut fieret, ueritatem me nondum adeptum³⁸ sed falsitati³⁹ iam ereptum. immo uero⁴⁰ quia certa erat et quod restabat⁴¹ te daturum, qui totum promiseras,⁴² placidissime⁴³ et pectore pleno fiduciae⁴⁴ respondit mihi credere se in Christo quod priusquam de hac uita emigraret⁴⁵ me uisura esset fidelem Catholicum.

Et hoc quidem mihi. tibi autem, fons misericordiarum, preces⁴⁶ et lacrimas densiores,⁴⁷ ut *accelerares*⁴⁸ *adiutorium*⁴⁹ *tuum* (Ps 69:2) et *inluminares tenebras meas* (Ps 17:29), et studiosius⁵⁰ ad ecclesiam currere⁵¹ et in Ambrosii ora suspendi,⁵² ad *fontem salientis*⁵³ *aquae in uitam aeternam* (Jn 4:14). diligebat autem illum uirum *sicut angelum Dei* (Gal 4:14), quod per illum cognouerat me interim⁵⁴ ad illam ancipitem⁵⁵ fluctuationem⁵⁶ iam esse perductum⁵⁷ per quam transiturum me ab aegritudine⁵⁸ ad sanitatem,⁵⁹ intercurrente⁶⁰ artiore⁶¹ periculo quasi per accessionem⁶² quam "criticam"⁶³ medici⁶⁴ uocant, certa praesumebat.⁶⁵

---

²⁶exilio ~ire, ~ui **to leap up** ²⁷resuscito ~are **to reawaken**; ECCL **to raise from the dead** ²⁸feretrum ~i *neut.* **funeral bier** ²⁹offero ~rre, obtuli, oblatum **to offer** ³⁰uiduus ~a, ~um *adj.* **widow** (*f.* as noun) ³¹surgo ~rgere, ~rrexi, ~rrectum **to rise** ³²reuiuesco ~escere, reuixi, reuictum **to revive** ³³turbulentus ~a, ~um *adj.* **turbulent** ³⁴exultatio ~onis *f.* **exultation** ³⁵trepido ~are, ~aui, ~atum **to tremble** ³⁶cotidie *adv.* **day by day** ³⁷plango ~gere, ~xi, ~ctum **to bewail** ³⁸adipiscor ~ipisci, ~eptus **to obtain** ³⁹falsitas ~atis *f.* LATE **error** ⁴⁰'immo uero' **no, in fact...** ⁴¹resto ~are, ~iti **to remain to be done** ⁴²promitto ~ittere, ~isi, ~issum **to promise** ⁴³placide *adv.* **calmly** ⁴⁴fiducia ~ae *f.* **trust** ⁴⁵emigro ~are, ~aui, ~atum **to move on** ⁴⁶preces ~um *f. pl.* **prayer** ⁴⁷densus ~a, ~um *adj.* **frequently** ⁴⁸accelero ~are, ~aui, ~atum **to hasten** ⁴⁹adiutorium ~ii *neut.* **help** ⁵⁰studiose *adv.* **eagerly** ⁵¹curro ~rere, cucurri, ~sum **to run** ⁵²suspendo ~dere, ~di, ~sum **to hang on** ⁵³saliens ~ntis *adj.* **gushing** ⁵⁴interim *adv.* **for the time being** ⁵⁵anceps ~ipitis *adj.* **wavering** ⁵⁶fluctuatio ~onis *f.* **uncertainty** ⁵⁷perduco ~cere, ~xi, ~ctum **to conduct** ⁵⁸aegritudo ~inis *f.* **sickness** ⁵⁹sanitas ~atis *f.* **health** ⁶⁰intercurro ~rrere, ~rri, ~rsum **to intervene** ⁶¹artus ~a, ~um *adj.* **critical** ⁶²accessio ~onis *f.* **addition** > **complication** (medical) ⁶³criticus ~a, ~um *adj.* LATE **decisive moment** (medical) ⁶⁴medicus ~i *m.* **physician** ⁶⁵praesumo ~ere, ~si, ~ptum **to take for granted**

Shrines of the Martyrs

6.2.2 Itaque cum ad memorias sanctorum, sicut in Africa solebat, pul-
tes[1] et panem[2] et merum[3] attulisset[4] atque ab ostiario[5] prohiberetur,[6]
ubi hoc episcopum[7] uetuisse[8] cognouit, tam pie[9] atque oboedienter[10]
amplexa[11] est ut ipse mirarer quam facile accusatrix[12] potius consuetudinis suae quam disceptatrix[13] illius prohibitionis[14] effecta[15] sit. non enim
obsidebat[16] spiritum eius uinulentia[17] eamque stimulabat[18] in odium[19]
ueri amor uini,[20] sicut plerosque[21] mares[22] et feminas qui ad canticum[23]
sobrietatis[24] sicut ad potionem[25] aquatam[26] madidi[27] nausiant,[28] sed illa
cum attulisset canistrum[29] cum sollemnibus[30] epulis[31] praegustandis[32]
atque largiendis,[33] plus etiam quam unum pocillum[34] pro suo palato[35]
satis sobrio[36] temperatum,[37] unde dignationem[38] sumeret, non ponebat,
et si multae essent quae illo modo uidebantur honorandae[39] memoriae
defunctorum,[40] idem ipsum unum, quod ubique[41] poneret, circumfere-
bat,[42] quo iam non solum aquatissimo sed etiam tepidissimo[43] cum suis
praesentibus per sorbitiones[44] exiguas[45] partiretur,[46] quia pietatem ibi
quaerebat, non uoluptatem.

Itaque ubi comperit[47] a praeclaro[48] praedicatore[49] atque antistite[50]
pietatis praeceptum[51] esse ista non fieri nec ab eis qui sobrie[52] facerent,
ne ulla occasio[53] se ingurgitandi[54] daretur ebriosis,[55] et quia illa quasi

---

[1]puls ~ltis *f.* **porridge** [2]panis ~is *m.* **bread** [3]merum ~i *neut.* **undiluted wine** [4]affero ~rre, attuli, allatum **to bring** [5]ostiarius ~ii *m.* gatekeeper; ECCL **sacristan** [6]prohibeo ~ere, ~ui, ~itum **to prohibit**
[7]episcopus ~i *m.* ECCL **bishop** [8]ueto ~are, ~ui, ~itum **to forbid** [9]pie *adv.* **piously** [10]oboedienter
adv. **obediently** [11]amplector ~cti, ~xus **to embrace** [12]accusatrix ~icis *f.* **accuser** [13]disceptatrix ~icis
f. **arbitrator** [14]prohibitio ~onis *f.* **prohibition** [15]efficio ~icere, ~eci, ~ectum **to become** [16]obsideo
~idere, ~edi, ~essum **to beset** [17]uinulentia ~ae *f.* **excessive drinking** [18]stimulo ~are, ~aui, ~atum
to incite [19]odium ~i *neut.* **hatred** [20]uinum ~i *neut.* **wine** [21]plerusque ~aque, ~umque *adj.* **many**
[22]mas maris *m.* **male** [23]canticum ~i *neut.* **song** [24]sobrietas ~atis *f.* **sobriety** [25]potio ~onis *f.* **drink**
[26]aquatus ~a, ~um *adj.* **diluted** [27]madidus ~a, ~um *adj.* **inebriated** [28]nausio ~are, ~aui **to feel
nauseated** [29]canistrum ~i *neut.* **basket** [30]sollemnis ~is, ~e *adj.* **festal** [31]epulae ~arum *f. pl.* **banquet
foods** [32]praegusto ~are, ~aui, ~atum **to eat or drink a little** [33]largior ~iri, ~itus **to give generously**
[34]pocillum ~i *neut.* **small cup** [35]palatum ~i *neut.* **palate** [36]sobrius ~ia, ~ium *adj.* **sober** [37]temperatus
~a, ~um *adj.* **moderate** [38]dignatio ~onis *f.* **respect** [39]honoro ~are, ~aui, ~atum **to honor** [40]defunctus
~a, ~um *adj.* **dead** [41]ubique *adv.* **everywhere** [42]circumfero ~ferre, ~tuli, ~latum **to carry about**
[43]tepidus ~a, ~um *adj.* **tepid** [44]sorbitio ~onis *f.* **draught** [45]exiguus ~a, ~um *adj.* **scanty** [46]partior
~iri, ~itus **to share** [47]comperio ~ire, ~i, ~tum **to find out** [48]praeclarus ~a, ~um *adj.* **illustrious**
[49]praedicator ~oris *m.* ECCL **preacher** [50]antistes ~titis *m.* **priest > patron** [51]praeceptum ~i *neut.*
precept [52]sobrie *adv.* **soberly** [53]occasio ~onis *f.* **occasion** [54]ingurgito ~are, ~aui, ~atum **to souse
in liquor** [55]ebriosus ~a, ~um *adj.* **addicted to alcohol**

parentalia[56] superstitioni[57] gentilium[58] essent simillima, abstinuit[59] se libentissime,[60] et pro canistro pleno terrenis[61] fructibus plenum purgatioribus[62] uotis pectus ad memorias martyum[63] afferre didicerat, ut et quod posset daret egentibus[64] et sic communicatio[65] Dominici[66] Corporis illic celebraretur,[67] cuius passionis[68] imitatione[69] immolati[70] et coronati[71] sunt martyres.

Sed tamen uidetur mihi, Domine Deus meus (et ita est *in conspectu tuo* de hac re *cor meum* [Ps 18:15]), non facile fortasse[72] de hac amputanda[73] consuetudine matrem meam fuisse cessuram si ab alio prohiberetur quem non sicut Ambrosium diligebat. quem propter salutem meam maxime diligebat, eam uero ille propter eius religiosissimam[74] conuersationem,[75] qua *in bonis operibus* (1 Tim 5:10) tam *feruens*[76] *spiritu* (Rom 12:11) frequentabat[77] ecclesiam, ita ut saepe erumperet,[78] cum me uideret, in eius praedicationem[79] gratulans[80] mihi, quod talem matrem haberem, nesciens qualem illa me filium, qui dubitabam[81] de illis omnibus et inueniri posse *uiam uitae* (Ps 15:10) minime[82] putabam.

[56]parentalia ~ium *neut. pl.* **Parentalia** (Roman festival for ancestors) [57]superstitio ~onis *f.* **superstition** [58]gentilis ~is *m. adj.* ECCL **Gentile** (pagan) [59]abstineo ~ere, ~ui, abstentum **to abstain** [60]libenter *adv.* **willingly** [61]terrenus ~a, ~um *adj.* **earthly** [62]purgatus ~a, ~um *adj.* **purged** [63]martyr ~is *m. f.* ECCL **martyr** [64]egens ~ntis *adj.* **needy** [65]communicatio ~onis *f.* sharing; ECCL **participation** [66]dominicus ~a, ~um *adj.* ECCL **of the LORD** [67]celebro ~are, ~aui, ~atum **to celebrate** [68]passio ~onis *f.* passion; ECCL **Passion** (suffering) [69]imitatio ~onis *f.* **imitation** (of an example) [70]immolo ~are, ~aui, ~atum **to offer as sacrifice** [71]corono ~are, ~aui, ~atum **to crown** [72]fortasse *adv.* **perhaps** [73]amputo ~are, ~aui, ~atum **to cut off** [74]religiosus ~a, ~um *adj.* **religious** [75]conuersatio ~onis *f.* **manner of life** [76]feruens ~ntis *adj.* **fervid** [77]frequento ~are, ~aui, ~atum **to frequent** [78]erumpo ~umpere, ~upi, ~uptum **to break out** [79]praedicatio ~onis *f.* **special mention** [80]gratulor ~ari, ~atus **to congratulate** (w dat.) [81]dubito ~are, ~aui, ~atum **to be in doubt** [82]minime *superl. adv.* **by no means**

Inaccessible Ambrose

6.3.3 Nec iam ingemescebam[1] orando[2] ut subuenires[3] mihi, sed ad quaerendum intentus et ad disserendum[4] inquietus[5] erat animus meus, ipsumque Ambrosium felicem quendam hominem secundum saeculum opinabar,[6] quem sic tantae potestates honorarent;[7] caelibatus[8] tantum

[1]ingemesco ~escere, ~ui **to begin to groan** [2]oro ~are, ~aui, ~atum **to pray** [3]subuenio ~enire, ~eni, ~entum **to bring relief** [4]dissero ~ere, ~ui, ~tum **to discuss** [5]inquietus ~a, ~um *adj.* **restless** [6]opinor ~ari, ~atus **to think** [7]honoro ~are, ~aui, ~atum **to honor** [8]caelibatus ~us *m.* **celibacy**

eius mihi laboriosus[9] uidebatur. quid autem ille spei gereret, et aduersus ipsius excellentiae[10] temptamenta[11] quid luctaminis[12] haberet quidue solaminis[13] in aduersis,[14] et occultum os eius, quod erat in corde eius, quam sapida[15] gaudia de pane[16] tuo ruminaret,[17] nec conicere[18] noueram nec expertus eram.

Nec ille sciebat aestus[19] meos nec foueam[20] periculi mei. non enim quaerere ab eo poteram quod uolebam, sicut uolebam, secludentibus[21] me ab eius aure atque ore cateruis[22] negotiosorum[23] hominum, quorum infirmitatibus[24] seruiebat. cum quibus quando non erat, quod perexiguum[25] temporis erat, aut corpus reficiebat[26] necessariis[27] sustentaculis[28] aut lectione[29] animum. sed cum legebat, oculi ducebantur per paginas[30] et cor intellectum[31] rimabatur,[32] uox autem et lingua quiescebant.[33] saepe cum adessemus (non enim uetabatur[34] quisquam ingredi[35] aut ei uenientem nuntiari[36] mos erat), sic eum legentem uidimus tacite[37] et aliter numquam, sedentesque[38] in diuturno[39] silentio[40] (quis enim tam intento esse oneri[41] auderet?) discedebamus[42] et coniectabamus[43] eum paruo ipso tempore quod reparandae[44] menti suae nanciscebatur,[45] feriatum[46] ab strepitu[47] causarum alienarum, nolle in aliud auocari[48] et cauere[49] fortasse[50] ne, auditore[51] suspenso[52] et intento, si qua obscurius[53] posuisset ille quem legeret, etiam exponere[54] esset necesse[55] aut de aliquibus difficilioribus[56] dissertare[57] quaestionibus,[58] atque huic operi

---

[9]laboriosus ~a, ~um *adj.* **painful** [10]excellentia ~ae *f.* **excellence** [11]temptamentum ~i *neut.* **test, trial;** ECCL **temptation** [12]luctamen ~inis *neut.* **struggle** [13]solamen ~inis *neut.* **source of comfort** [14]aduersus ~i *m.* **adversity** [15]sapidus ~a, ~um *adj.* **savory** [16]panis ~is *m.* **bread** [17]rumino ~are, ~aui, ~atum **to ruminate/meditate** [18]conicio ~icere, ~ieci, ~iectum **to conjecture** [19]aestus ~us *m.* **perplexity** [20]fouea ~ae *f.* **pitfall** [21]secludo ~dere, ~si, ~sum **to shut out** [22]caterua ~ae *f.* **crowd** [23]negotiosus ~a, ~um *adj.* **occupied with business** [24]infirmitas ~atis *f.* **weakness** [25]perexiguus ~a, ~um *adj.* **very brief** [26]reficio ~icere, ~eci, ~ectum **to refresh** [27]necessarius ~a, ~um *adj.* **necessary** [28]sustentaculum ~i. *neut.* LATE **nourishment** [29]lectio ~onis *f.* **reading** [30]pagina ~ae *f.* **page** [31]intellectus ~us *m.* **meaning** [32]rimor ~ari, ~atus **to examine carefully** [33]quiesco ~ere, quieui, quietum **to rest** [34]ueto ~are, ~ui, ~itum **to forbid** [35]ingredior ~di, ~ssus **to enter** [36]nuntio ~are, ~aui, ~atum **to announce** [37]tacite *adv.* **silently** [38]sedeo ~ere, sedi, sessum **to sit** [39]diuturnus ~a, ~um *adj.* **long** (of time) [40]silentium ~ii *neut.* **silence** [41]onus ~eris *neut.* **nuisance** [42]discedo ~dere, ~ssi, ~ssum **to depart** [43]coniecto ~are, ~aui, ~atum **to conjecture** [44]reparo ~are, ~aui, ~atum **to recover > to reinvigorate** [45]nanciscor ~i, nactus **to get an opportunity** [46]feriatus ~a, ~um *adj.* **at rest** [47]strepitus ~us *m.* **din** [48]auoco ~are, ~aui, ~atum **to distract** [49]caueo ~ere, caui, ~tum **to be cautious** [50]fortasse *adv.* **perhaps** [51]auditor ~oris *m.* **listener** [52]suspensus ~a, ~um *adj.* **in suspense** [53]obscurus ~a, ~um *adj.* **obscure** [54]expono ~onere, ~osui, ~ositum **to explain** [55]necesse *adv.* **it would be necessary** (w. 'esset') [56]difficilis ~is, ~e *adj.* **difficult** [57]disserto ~are, ~aui, ~atum **to deal with** [58]quaestio ~onis *f.* **question**

temporibus impensis[59] minus quam uellet uoluminum[60] euolueret,[61] quamquam et causa seruandae uocis, quae illi facillime obtundebatur,[62] poterat esse iustior tacite legendi. quolibet[63] tamen animo id ageret, bono utique ille uir agebat.

[59]impendo ~dere, ~di, ~sum **to expend** [60]uolumen ~inis *neut.* papyrus roll, i.e., **book** [61]euoluo ~uere, ~ui, ~utum to unroll, i.e., **to read** [62]obtundo ~undere, ~udi, ~usum **to grow hoarse** [63]quolibet *adv.* **whatever**

Catholic faith not as imagined

6.3.4 Sed certe mihi nulla dabatur copia sciscitandi[1] quae cupiebam de tam sancto oraculo[2] tuo, pectore illius, nisi cum aliquid breuiter[3] esset audiendum. aestus[4] autem illi mei otiosum[5] eum ualde cui refunderentur[6] requirebant[7] nec umquam inueniebant. et eum quidem in populo *uerbum ueritatis recte[8] tractantem[9]* (2 Tim 2:15) omni die Dominico[10] audiebam, et magis magisque mihi confirmabatur[11] omnes uersutarum[12] calumniarum[13] nodos[14] quos illi deceptores[15] nostri aduersus diuinos[16] libros innectebant[17] posse dissolui.[18] ubi uero etiam comperi[19] *ad imaginem tuam hominem* (Gen 1:26) a te factum ab spiritalibus Filiis tuis, quos de Matre Catholica per gratiam regenerasti,[20] non sic intellegi ut humani corporis forma te determinatum[21] crederent atque cogitarent (quamquam quomodo se haberet spiritalis substantia, ne quidem tenuiter[22] atque *in aenigmate*[23] (1 Cor 13:12) suspicabar[24]), tamen gaudens erubui[25] non me tot annos aduersus Catholicam fidem, sed contra carnalium[26] cogitationum figmenta[27] latrasse.[28] eo[29] quippe

[1]sciscitor ~ari, ~atus **to ask questions** [2]oraculum ~i *neut.* **oracle** [3]breuiter *adv.* **briefly** [4]aestus ~us *m.* heat > **swell of the sea** (fig.) [5]otiosus ~a, ~um *adj.* **at leisure** [6]refundo ~undere, ~udi, ~usum **to pour out** [7]requiro ~rere, ~siui, ~situm **to require** [8]recte *adv.* **rightly** [9]tracto ~are, ~aui, ~atum **to handle** [10]dominicus ~a, ~um *adj.* ECCL **LORD's** [11]confirmo ~are, ~aui, ~atum **to confirm** [12]uersutus ~a, ~um *adj.* **cunning** (in a bad sense) [13]calumnia ~ae *f.* **calumny** [14]nodus ~i *m.* knot > **knotty problem** [15]deceptor ~oris *m.* **deceiver** [16]diuinus ~a, ~um *adj.* **divine** [17]innecto ~ctere, ~xui, ~xum **to weave** [18]dissoluo ~uere, ~ui, ~utum **to unravel** [19]comperio ~ire, ~i, ~tum **to find out** [20]regenero ~are **to reproduce**; ECCL to **regenerate** [21]determino ~are, ~aui, ~atum **to delimit** [22]tenuiter *adv.* **feebly** [23]'in aenigmate' **obscurely** [24]suspicor ~ari, ~atus **to form an idea** [25]erubesco ~escere, ~ui **to feel ashamed** [26]carnalis ~is, ~e *adj.* ECCL **carnal** [27]figmentum ~i *neut.* **fiction** [28]latro ~are, ~aui, ~atum **to bark at** [29]eo *adv.* **to such a degree**

temerarius[30] et impius[31] fueram, quod ea quae debebam quaerendo discere accusando[32] dixeram.

Tu enim, altissime et proxime,[33] secretissime[34] et praesentissime, cui membra non sunt alia maiora et alia minora, sed ubique[35] totus es et nusquam[36] locorum es, non es utique forma ista corporea, tamen fecisti hominem ad imaginem tuam, et ecce ipse a capite usque ad pedes in loco est.

[30]temerarius ~a, ~um *adj.* **rash** [31]impius ~a, ~um *adj.* **impious** [32]accuso ~are, ~aui, ~atum **to find fault** [33]proximus ~a, ~um *superl. adj.* **most near** [34]secretus ~a, ~um *adj.* **apart** [35]ubique *adv.* **everywhere** [36]nusquam *adv.* **nowhere**

A no-nonsense Church

6.4.5 Cum ergo nescirem quomodo haec subsisteret[1] imago tua, *pulsans*[2] (Mt 7:7) proponerem[3] quomodo credendum esset, non insultans[4] opponerem[5] quasi ita creditum esset. tanto igitur acrior[6] cura rodebat[7] intima[8] mea, quid certi[9] retinerem,[10] quanto me magis pudebat[11] tam diu inlusum[12] et deceptum[13] promissione[14] certorum puerili[15] errore et animositate[16] tam multa incerta[17] quasi certa garrisse.[18] quod enim falsa essent, postea mihi claruit;[19] certum tamen erat quod incerta essent et a me aliquando pro certis habita fuissent, cum Catholicam tuam caecis[20] contentionibus[21] accusarem,[22] etsi nondum compertam[23] uera docentem, non tamen ea docentem quae grauiter[24] accusabam.

Itaque confundebar[25] et conuertebar, et gaudebam, Deus meus, quod *ecclesia* unica,[26] *corpus* (Col 1:18, 24) Unici tui, in qua mihi nomen

[1]subsisto ~istere, ~titi **to remain**; LATE **to subsist** [2]pulso ~are, ~aui, ~atum **to knock** [3]propono ~onere, ~osui, ~ositum **to propose a question** [4]insulto ~are, ~aui, ~atum **to insult** [5]oppono ~onere, ~osui, ~ositum **to oppose** [6]acer acris, acre *adj.* **sharp** [7]rodo ~dere, ~si, ~sum **to gnaw** [8]intimus ~a, ~um *superl. adj.* **inmost self** (*neut. pl.* as noun) [9]certum ~i *neut.* **certainty** [10]retineo ~ere, ~ui, ~tentum **to hold fast to** [11]pudeo ~ere, ~ui **to make ashamed** (*impers.* w. acc.) [12]inludo ~dere, ~si, ~sum **to dupe** [13]decipio ~ipere, ~epi, ~eptum **to deceive** [14]promissio ~onis *f.* **promise** [15]puerilis ~is, ~e *adj.* **childish** [16]animositas ~tatis *f.* **animosity**; LATE **enthusiasm** [17]incertus ~a, ~um *adj.* **uncertainty** (*neut.* as noun) [18]garrio ~ire, ~iui **to talk nonsense** [19]claresco ~escere, ~ui **to become clear** [20]caecus ~a, ~um *adj.* **blind** [21]contentio ~onis *f.* **contention** [22]accuso ~are, ~aui, ~atum **to accuse** [23]comperio ~ire, ~i, ~tum **to find out** [24]grauiter *adv.* **seriously** [25]confundo ~undere, ~udi, ~usum **to confound** [26]unicus ~a, ~um *adj.* **one and only**

Christi infanti[27] est inditum,[28] non saperet[29] infantiles[30] nugas[31] neque hoc haberet *in doctrina sua sana*[32] (Tit 1:9), quod *te creatorem omnium* (Hymn 2.1) in spatium loci quamuis summum et amplum,[33] tamen undique[34] terminatum[35] membrorum humanorum figura[36] contruderet.[37]

---

[27]infans ~ntis *m. f.* **infant** [28]indo ~ere, ~idi, ~itum **to place on** [29]sapio ~ere, ~ii **to have a taste for** [30]infantilis ~is, ~e *adj.* **infantile** [31]nugae ~arum *f. pl.* **nonsense** [32]sanus ~a, ~um *adj.* **sound** [33]amplus ~a, ~um *adj.* **spacious** [34]undique *adv.* **on every side** [35]termino ~are, ~aui, ~atum **to limit** [36]figura ~ae *f.* **form** [37]contrudo ~dere, ~si, ~sum **to cram**

Ambrose and allegorical interpretation

6.4.6 Gaudebam etiam quod uetera scripta legis et prophetarum[1] iam non illo oculo mihi legenda proponerentur[2] quo antea[3] uidebantur absurda,[4] cum arguebam[5] tamquam ita sentientes sanctos tuos, uerum autem non ita sentiebant. et tamquam regulam[6] diligentissime commendaret,[7] saepe in popularibus[8] sermonibus suis dicentem Ambrosium laetus audiebam: *Littera occidit,*[9] *Spiritus autem uiuificat*[10] (2 Cor 3:6), cum ea quae ad litteram peruersitatem[11] docere uidebantur, remoto[12] *mystico*[13] *uelamento*[14] (2 Cor 3:14–16), spiritaliter[15] aperiret, non dicens quod me offenderet,[16] quamuis ea diceret quae utrum uera essent adhuc ignorarem. tenebam enim cor meum ab omni adsensione[17] timens praecipitium,[18] et suspendio[19] magis necabar.[20] uolebam enim eorum quae non uiderem ita me certum fieri ut certus essem quod septem[21] et tria decem[22] sint. neque enim tam insanus[23] eram ut ne hoc quidem putarem posse comprehendi, sed sicut hoc, ita cetera cupiebam, siue corporalia, quae coram sensibus meis non adessent, siue spiritalia, de quibus cogitare nisi corporaliter[24] nesciebam. et sanari credendo

---

[1]propheta ~ae *m.* ECCL **prophet** [2]propono ~onere, ~osui, ~ositum **to place before** [3]antea *adv.* **in the past** [4]absurdus ~a, ~um *adj.* **absurd** [5]arguo ~uere, ~ui, ~utum **to argue** [6]regula ~ae *f.* **rule** [7]commendo ~are, ~aui, ~atum **to recommend** [8]popularis ~is *m.* **people of the community** [9]occido ~dere, ~di, ~sum **to kill** [10]uiuifio ~are, ~aui, ~atum ECCL **to make alive** [11]peruersitas ~atis *f.* **something unreasonable** [12]remoueo ~ouere, ~oui, ~otum **to remove** [13]mysticus ~a, ~um *adj.* mysterious; ECCL **mystical** [14]uelamentum ~i *neut.* **veil** [15]spiritaliter *adv.* ECCL **spiritually** [16]offendo ~dere, ~di, ~sum **to cause difficulty** [17]adsensio ~onis *f.* **assent** [18]praeceps ~ipitis *neut.* **headlong fall** [19]suspendium ~i *neut.* **hanging oneself (in suspense)** [20]neco ~are, ~aui, ~atum **to put to death** [21]septem *indecl. adj.* **seven** [22]decem *indecl. adj.* **ten** [23]insanus ~a, ~um *adj.* **insane** [24]corporaliter *adv.* **corporeally**

poteram, ut purgatior[25] acies mentis[26] meae dirigeretur[27] aliquo modo in *ueritatem tuam semper manentem* (Ps 116:2) et ex nullo deficientem.[28] sed sicut euenire[29] adsolet,[30] ut malum medicum[31] expertus etiam bono timeat se committere,[32] ita erat ualetudo[33] animae meae, quae utique nisi credendo sanari non poterat et, ne falsa crederet, curari recusabat,[34] *resistens manibus tuis* (Ps 16:8), qui medicamenta[35] fidei confecisti[36] et sparsisti[37] super morbos[38] orbis terrarum[39] et tantam illis auctoritatem tribuisti.[40]

[25]purgatus ~a, ~um *adj.* **purged** [26]'acies mentis' **gaze of the mind** (phil.) [27]dirigo ~igere, ~exi, ~ectum **to direct** [28]deficio ~icere, ~eci, ~ectum **to fail** [29]euenio ~enire, ~eni, ~entum **to happen** [30]adsoleo ~ere *impers.* **it is usual** [31]medicus ~i *m.* **physician** [32]committo ~ittere, ~isi, ~issum **to commit** [33]ualetudo ~inis *f.* **health** [34]recuso ~are, ~aui, ~atum **to refuse** [35]medicamentum ~i *neut.* **medicine** [36]conficio ~icere, ~eci, ~ectum **to manufacture** [37]spargo ~gere, ~si, ~sum **to distribute widely** [38]morbus ~i *m.* **disease** [39]'orbis terrarum' **of the world** [40]tribuo ~uere, ~ui, ~utum **to endow**

A moderate Church

6.5.7 Ex hoc tamen quoque iam[1] praeponens[2] doctrinam Catholicam, modestius[3] ibi minimeque[4] fallaciter[5] sentiebam iuberi ut crederetur quod non demonstrabatur[6] (siue esset quid, sed cui forte non esset, siue nec quid esset), quam illic[7] temeraria[8] pollicitatione[9] scientiae credulitatem[10] inrideri et postea tam multa fabulosissima[11] et absurdissima,[12] quia demonstrari non poterant, credenda imperari.

Deinde paulatim[13] tu, Domine, manu mitissima[14] et misericordissima[15] pertractans[16] et componens cor meum, consideranti quam innumerabilia[17] crederem quae non uiderem neque cum gererentur adfuissem, sicut tam multa in historia[18] gentium, tam multa de locis atque urbibus quae non uideram, tam multa amicis, tam multa medicis,[19] tam multa hominibus aliis atque aliis, quae nisi crederentur, omnino in hac uita

[1]'quoque iam' **even then** [2]praepono ~onere, ~osui, ~ositum **to prefer** [3]modeste *adv.* **modestly** [4]minime *superl. adv.* **not at all** [5]fallaciter *adv.* **deceitfully** [6]demonstro ~are, ~aui, ~atum **to demonstrate** [7]illic *adv.* **in that situation** (i.e., among the Manichees) [8]temerarius ~a, ~um *adj.* **rash** [9]pollicitatio ~onis *f.* **promise** [10]credulitas ~atis *f.* **credulity** [11]fabulosus ~a, ~um *adj.* **fantastical** [12]absurdus ~a, ~um *adj.* **absurd** [13]paulatim *adv.* **little by little** [14]mitis ~is, ~e *adj.* **mild** [15]misericors ~rdis *adj.* **merciful** [16]pertracto ~are, ~aui, ~atum **to work on** [17]innumerabilis ~is, ~e *adj.* **innumerable** [18]historia ~ae *f.* **history** [19]medicus ~i *m.* **doctor**

nihil ageremus, postremo[20] quam inconcusse[21] fixum[22] fide retinerem[23] de quibus parentibus ortus[24] essem, quod scire non possem nisi audiendo credidissem.

Persuasisti[25] mihi non qui crederent libris tuis, quos tanta in omnibus fere[26] gentibus auctoritate fundasti,[27] sed qui non crederent esse culpandos[28] nec audiendos esse, si qui forte mihi dicerent, "Unde scis illos libros unius ueri et ueracissimi[29] Dei Spiritu esse humano generi ministratos?"[30] idipsum[31] enim maxime credendum erat, quoniam nulla pugnacitas[32] calumniosarum[33] quaestionum[34] per tam multa quae legeram inter se confligentium[35] philosophorum[36] extorquere[37] mihi potuit ut aliquando non crederem te *esse* quidquid esses, quod ego nescirem, aut *administrationem*[38] *rerum humanarum* (N.D. 2.3) ad te pertinere.[39]

[20]postremo *adv.* **lastly** [21]inconcusse *adv.* ECCL **unshakably** [22]fixus ~a, ~um *adj.* **unwavering** [23]retineo ~ere, ~ui, retentum **to retain** [24]orior ~iri, ~tus **to be born** [25]persuadeo ~dere, ~si, ~sum **to persuade** (w. dat. of person) [26]fere *adv.* **almost** [27]fundo ~are, ~aui, ~atum **to establish** [28]culpo ~are, ~aui, ~atum **to blame** [29]uerax ~acis *adj.* **truthful** [30]ministro ~are, ~aui, ~atum **to furnish** [31]idipsum *pron.* ECCL **very thing** [32]pugnacitas ~atis *f.* **contentiousness** [33]calumniosus ~a, ~um *adj.* **calumnious** [34]quaestio ~onis *f.* **question** [35]configo ~gere, ~xi, ~ctum **to disagree** [36]philosophus ~i *m.* **philosopher** [37]extorqueo ~quere, ~si, ~tum to wrench away > **to force one to admit** [38]administratio ~onis *f.* **governance** [39]pertineo ~ere, ~ui **to be of concern**

Scripture not absurd

6.5.8 Sed id credebam aliquando robustius,[1] aliquando exilius,[2] semper tamen credidi et esse te et curam nostri gerere, etiamsi ignorabam uel quid sentiendum esset de substantia tua uel quae uia duceret aut reduceret[3] ad te. ideoque cum *essemus infirmi*[4] (Rom 5:6) ad inueniendam liquida[5] ratione ueritatem et ob hoc nobis opus esset auctoritate sanctarum litterarum, iam credere coeperam nullo modo te fuisse tributurum[6] tam excellentem[7] illi scripturae per omnes iam terras auctoritatem, nisi et per ipsam tibi credi et per ipsam te quaeri uoluisses.

Iam enim absurditatem[8] quae me in illis litteris solebat offendere,[9] cum multa ex eis probabiliter[10] exposita[11] audissem, ad sacramentorum

[1]robustus ~a, ~um *adj.* **robust** [2]exilis ~is, ~e *adj.* **flimsy** [3]reduco ~cere, ~xi, ~ctum **to lead back** [4]infirmus ~a, ~um *adj.* **powerless** [5]liquidus ~a, ~um *adj.* **clear** [6]tribuo ~uere, ~ui, ~utum **to confer** [7]excellens ~ntis *adj.* **outstanding** [8]absurditas ~tatis *f.* AUG **absurdity** [9]offendo ~dere, ~di, ~sum **to give offense** [10]probabiliter *adv.* **plausibly** [11]expono ~onere, ~osui, ~ositum **to explain**

altitudinem[12] referebam[13] eoque mihi illa uenerabilior[14] et sacrosancta[15] fide dignior apparebat auctoritas, quo et omnibus ad legendum esset in promptu[16] et secreti[17] sui dignitatem[18] in intellectu[19] profundiore[20] seruaret, uerbis apertissimis et humillimo[21] genere loquendi se cunctis praebens[22] et exercens[23] intentionem[24] eorum qui non *sunt leues corde* (Sir 19:4), ut exciperet[25] omnes populari[26] sinu et *per angusta[27] foramina[28]* (Mt 7:13; 19:24) paucos[29] ad te traiceret,[30] multo tamen plures quam si nec tanto apice[31] auctoritatis emineret[32] nec turbas gremio[33] sanctae humilitatis[34] hauriret.[35]

Cogitabam haec et aderas mihi, suspirabam et audiebas me, fluctuabam[36] et gubernabas[37] me, ibam per uiam saeculi latam[38] nec deserebas.

[12]altitudo ~inis *f.* **loftiness** [13]refero ~rre, rettuli, relatum **to refer to** [14]uenerabilis ~is, ~e *adj.* **venerable** [15]sacrosanctus ~a, ~um *adj.* **sacred** [16]'in promptu' **within easy reach** [17]secretum ~i *neut.* **secret** [18]dignitas ~atis *f.* **dignity** [19]intellectus ~us *m.* **meaning** [20]profundus ~a, ~um *adj.* **profound** [21]humilis ~is, ~e *adj.* **lowly** [22]praebeo ~ere, ~ui, ~itum **to put within reach** [23]exerceo ~ere, ~ui, ~itum **to exercise** [24]intentio ~onis *f.* **mental effort** [25]excipio ~ipere, ~epi, ~eptum **to give shelter** [26]popularis ~is, ~e *adj.* popular; LATE **welcoming** [27]angustus ~a, ~um *adj.* **narrow** [28]foramen ~inis *neut.* **opening** [29]paucus ~a, ~um *adj.* **few** [30]traicio ~icere, ~ieci, ~iectum **to convey** [31]apex ~icis *m.* **peak** [32]emineo ~ere, ~ui **to tower above** [33]gremium ~ii *neut.* **lap** [34]humilitas ~atis *f.* **humility** [35]haurio ~rire, ~si, ~stum **to draw in** [36]fluctuo ~are, ~aui, ~atum **to grope** [37]guberno ~are, ~aui, ~atum **to guide** [38]latus ~a, ~um *adj.* **broad**

The happy beggar

6.6.9 Inhiabam[1] honoribus, lucris,[2] coniugio,[3] et *tu inridebas* (Ps 2:4). patiebar in eis cupiditatibus amarissimas[4] difficultates,[5] te propitio[6] tanto magis, quanto minus sinebas mihi dulcescere[7] quod non eras tu. uide cor meum, Domine, qui uoluisti ut hoc recordarer et confiterer tibi. nunc *tibi inhaereat[8] anima mea* (Ps 62:9), quam de uisco[9] tam tenaci[10] mortis exuisti.[11] quam misera erat! et sensum uulneris tu pungebas,[12] ut *relictis omnibus* (Lk 5:11) *conuerteretur ad te* (Ps 50:15), *qui es super omnia* (Rom 9:5) et sine quo nulla essent omnia, *conuerteretur et sanaretur* (Isa 6:10, Mt 13:15).

[1]inhio ~are, ~aui, ~atum **to be avid for** [2]lucrum ~i *neut.* **profit** [3]coniugium ~ii *neut.* **marriage** [4]amarus ~a, ~um *adj.* **bitter** [5]difficultas ~atis *f.* **difficulty** [6]propitius ~a, ~um *adj.* **propitious** [7]dulcesco ~ere **to become sweet** [8]inhaereo ~rere, ~si, ~sum **to cling to** [9]uiscum ~i *neut.* **birdlime** [10]tenax ~acis *adj.* **gripping** [11]exuo ~uere, ~ui, ~utum **to release** [12]pungo ~gere, pupugi, ~ctum **to prick**

Quam ergo miser eram, et quomodo egisti ut sentirem miseriam meam die illo quo, cum pararem recitare[13] imperatori[14] laudes, quibus plura mentirer[15] et mentienti faueretur[16] ab scientibus, easque curas anhelaret[17] cor meum et cogitationum tabificarum[18] febribus[19] aestuaret,[20] transiens per quendam uicum[21] Mediolanensem animaduerti[22] pauperem[23] mendicum,[24] iam, credo, saturum,[25] iocantem[26] atque laetantem.[27] et ingemui[28] et locutus sum cum amicis qui mecum erant multos dolores insaniarum[29] nostrarum, quia omnibus talibus conatibus[30] nostris, qualibus tunc laborabam,[31] sub stimulis[32] cupiditatum trahens[33] infelicitatis[34] meae sarcinam[35] et trahendo exaggerans,[36] nihil uellemus aliud nisi ad securam[37] laetitiam peruenire, quo nos mendicus ille iam praecessisset[38] numquam illuc[39] fortasse[40] uenturos. quod enim iam ille pauculis[41] et emendicatis[42] nummulis[43] adeptus[44] erat, ad hoc ego tam aerumnosis[45] anfractibus[46] et circuitibus[47] ambiebam,[48] ad laetitiam scilicet[49] temporalis[50] felicitatis.[51] non enim uerum gaudium habebat, sed et ego illis ambitionibus[52] multo falsius quaerebam. et certe ille laetabatur, ego anxius[53] eram, securus ille, ego trepidus.[54] et si quisquam percontaretur[55] me utrum mallem[56] exultare[57] an metuere, responderem: "Exultare"; rursus si interrogaret utrum me talem mallem qualis ille, an qualis ego tunc essem, me ipsum curis timoribusque[58] confectum[59] eligerem,[60] sed peruersitate[61] — numquid ueritate? neque enim eo[62]

---

[13]recito ~are, ~aui, ~atum **to recite** [14]imperator ~oris *m.* **emperor** (spec. Valentinian II) [15]mentior ~iri, ~itus **to tell a lie** [16]faueo ~ere, faui, ~tum **to admire** [17]anhelo ~are, ~aui, ~atum **to gasp** [18]tabificus ~a, ~um *adj.* **causing decay** [19]febris ~is *f.* **fever** [20]aestuo ~are, ~aui, ~atum **to burn up** [21]uicus ~i *m.* **street** [22]animaduerto ~tere, ~ti, ~sum **to notice** [23]pauper ~eris *adj.* **poor** [24]mendicus ~i *m.* **beggar** [25]satur ~ra, ~rum, ~rior *adj.* **well-fed** [26]iocor ~ari, ~atus **to joke around** [27]laetor ~ari, ~atus **to be cheerful** [28]ingemesco ~escere, ~ui **to begin to groan** [29]insania ~ae *f.* **insanity** [30]conatus ~us *m.* **endeavor** [31]laboro ~are, ~aui, ~atum **to work at** [32]stimulus ~i *m.* **goad** [33]traho ~here, ~xi, ~ctum **to drag** [34]infelicitas ~atis *f.* **unhappiness** [35]sarcina ~ae *f.* **load** [36]exaggero ~are, ~aui, ~atum **to heap or pile up** [37]securus ~a, ~um *adj.* **untroubled** [38]praecedo ~edere, ~essi, ~essum **to arrive before** [39]illuc *adv.* **there** [40]fortasse *adv.* **perhaps** [41]pauculus ~a, ~um *adj.* **a few** [42]emendico ~are, ~aui, ~atum **to obtain by begging** [43]nummulus ~i *m.* **coin** [44]adipiscor ~ipisci, ~eptus **to gain** [45]aerumnosus ~a, ~um *adj.* **stressful** [46]anfractus ~us *m.* **circular motion** [47]circuitus ~us *m.* **cycle** [48]ambio ~ire, ~iui, ~itum **to go in circles** [49]scilicet *adv.* **I mean** [50]temporalis ~is, ~e *adj.* **temporal** [51]felicitas ~atis *f.* **happiness** [52]ambitio ~onis *f.* **ambition** [53]anxius ~a, ~um *adj.* **anxious** [54]trepidus ~a, ~um *adj.* **apprehensive** [55]percontor ~ari, ~atus **to question** [56]malo ~lle, ~lui **to prefer** [57]exulto ~are, ~aui **to be exhilarated** [58]timor ~oris *m.* **fear** [59]conficio ~icere, ~eci, ~ectum **to finish** > **to overwhelm** [60]eligo ~igere, ~egi, ~ectum **to choose** [61]peruersitas ~atis *f.* **wrong-headedness** [62]eo *adv.* **consequently**

me praeponere[63] illi debebam, quo doctior eram, quoniam non inde gaudebam, sed placere inde quaerebam hominibus, non ut eos docerem, sed tantum ut placerem. propterea[64] et tu *baculo[65]* (Ps 22:4) disciplinae[66] *tuae confringebas[67] ossa[68] mea* (Ps 41:11).

[63]praepono ~onere, ~osui, ~ositum **to prefer** x (acc.) **to** y (dat.) [64]propterea *adv.* **for this reason** [65]baculum ~i *neut.* **rod** [66]disciplina ~ae *f.* **discipline** [67]confringo ~ingere, ~egi, ~actum **to break** [68]os ossis *neut.* **bones** (*pl.* esp. as seat of emotion); ECCL **soul** (fig.)

False glory, real happiness

6.6.10 Recedant ergo ab anima mea qui dicunt ei, "Interest[1] unde quis gaudeat. gaudebat mendicus[2] ille uinulentia,[3] tu gaudere cupiebas gloria." *qua gloria, Domine* (1 Cor 1:31), quae non est in te? nam sicut uerum gaudium non erat, ita nec illa uera gloria et amplius uertebat[4] mentem meam. et ille ipsa nocte digesturus[5] erat ebrietatem[6] suam, ego cum mea dormieram[7] et surrexeram[8] et dormiturus et surrecturus eram, uide quot[9] dies! interest uero unde quis gaudeat, scio, et gaudium spei fidelis incomparabiliter[10] distat[11] ab illa uanitate, sed et tunc distabat inter nos. nimirum[12] quippe ille felicior erat, non tantum quod hilaritate[13] perfundebatur,[14] cum ego curis euiscerarer,[15] uerum etiam quod ille bene optando adquisiuerat[16] uinum,[17] ego mentiendo[18] quaerebam typhum.[19]

Dixi tunc multa in hac sententia caris[20] meis, et saepe aduertebam[21] in his quomodo mihi esset, et inueniebam male[22] mihi esse et dolebam et conduplicabam[23] ipsum male et, si quid adrisisset[24] prosperum,[25] taedebat[26] apprehendere,[27] quia paene[28] priusquam teneretur auolabat.[29]

[1]intersum ~esse, ~fui **to make a difference** (*impers.*) [2]mendicus ~i *m.* **beggar** [3]uinulentia ~ae *f.* **excessive drinking** [4]uerto ~tere, ~ti, ~sum **to turn > to subvert** [5]digero ~rere, ~ssi, ~stum **to digest,** i.e., **sleep off** [6]ebrietas ~atis *f.* **intoxication** [7]dormio ~ire, ~iui, ~itum **to fall asleep** [8]surgo ~rgere, ~rrexi, ~rrectum **to get up from bed** [9]quot *indecl. adj.* **how many** [10]incomparabiliter *adv.* ECCL **incomparably** [11]disto ~are **to be different** [12]nimirum *particle* **without a doubt** [13]hilaritas ~atis *f.* **light-heartedness** [14]perfundo ~undere, ~udi, ~usum **to drench** [15]euiscero ~are, ~aui, ~atum **to eviscerate** [16]adquiro ~rere, ~siui, ~situm **to acquire** [17]uinum ~i *neut.* **wine** [18]mentior ~iri, ~itus **to lie** [19]typhus ~i *m.* ECCL **proud vanity** [20]carus ~a, ~um *adj.* **friend** (as noun) [21]aduerto ~tere, ~ti, ~sum **to notice** [22]'male... esse' **to be distressing** (w. dat.) [23]conduplico ~are, ~aui, ~atum **to double** [24]adrideo ~dere, ~si, ~sum **to smile at** [25]prosperus ~a, ~um *adj.* **success** (*neut.* as noun) [26]taedet ~dere, ~sum est **to be sick of** (w inf.) [27]apprehendo ~dere, ~di, ~sum **to seize** [28]paene *adv.* **almost** [29]auolo ~are, ~aui, ~atum **to fly away**

Alypius and the circus

6.7.11 Congemescebamus[1] in his qui simul amice[2] uiuebamus, et maxime ac familiarissime[3] cum Alypio et Nebridio ista conloquebar.[4] quorum Alypius ex eodem quo ego eram ortus[5] municipio,[6] parentibus primatibus[7] municipalibus,[8] me minor natu. nam et studuerat[9] apud me, cum in nostro oppido[10] docere coepi, et postea Carthagini, et diligebat multum, quod ei bonus et doctus uiderer, et ego illum propter magnam uirtutis indolem,[11] quae in non magna aetate satis eminebat.[12] gurges[13] tamen morum Carthaginiensium, quibus nugatoria[14] feruent[15] spectacula,[16] absorbuerat[17] eum in insaniam[18] circensium.[19] sed cum in eo miserabiliter[20] uolueretur,[21] ego autem rhetoricam[22] ibi professus[23] publica[24] schola[25] uterer, nondum me audiebat ut magistrum propter quandam simultatem[26] quae inter me et patrem eius erat exorta.[27] et compereram[28] quod circum[29] exitiabiliter[30] amaret, et grauiter[31] angebar,[32] quod tantam spem perditurus[33] uel etiam perdidisse mihi uidebatur. sed monendi[34] eum et aliqua cohercitione[35] reuocandi[36] nulla erat copia uel amicitiae[37] beniuolentia[38] uel iure magisterii.[39] putabam enim eum de me cum patre sentire, ille uero non sic erat. itaque postposita[40] in hac re patris uoluntate salutare[41] me coeperat ueniens in auditorium[42] meum et audire aliquid[43] atque abire.[44]

---

[1]congemesco ~are, ~aui, ~atum ECCL **to sigh together** [2]amice *adv.* **as friends** [3]familiariter *adv.* **on the most intimate terms** [4]conloquor ~qui, ~cutus **to discuss** [5]orior ~iri, ~tus **to be born** [6]municipium ~ii *neut.* **municipality** [7]primas ~atis *adj.* **of the highest rank** [8]municipalis ~is, ~e *adj.* **of a municipality** [9]studeo ~ere, ~ui **to study** [10]oppidum ~i *neut.* **town** [11]indoles ~is *f.* **innate good qualities** [12]emineo ~ere, ~ui **to be evident** [13]gurges ~itis *m.* **whirlpool** [14]nugatorius ~ia, ~ium *adj.* **worthless** [15]feruo ~ere, ferbui **to be enthusiastic** [16]spectaculum ~i *neut.* spectacle > **public show** [17]absorbeo ~bere, ~bui, ~ptum **to absorb** [18]insania ~ae *f.* **insanity** [19]circensis ~is, ~e *adj.* **of the circus** (spec. games) [20]miserabiliter *adv.* **miserably** [21]uoluo ~uere, ~ui, ~utum **to toss about** [22]rhetoricus ~a, ~um *adj.* **rhetoric** (*f.* as noun) [23]profiteor ~iteri, ~essus **to teach professionally** [24]publicus ~a, ~um *adj.* public > **state-sponsored** [25]schola ~ae *f.* **school** [26]simultas ~atis *f.* **quarrel** [27]exorior ~iri, ~tus **to arise** [28]comperio ~ire, ~i, ~tum **to find out** [29]circus ~i *m.* **circus** (where public games were held) [30]exitiabiliter *adv.* AUG **fatally** [31]grauiter *adv.* **deeply** [32]ango ~gere, ~xi, ~ctum **to distress** [33]perdo ~ere, ~idi, ~itum **to lose** > **to squander** [34]moneo ~ere, ~ui, ~itum **to warn** [35]cohercitio ~onis *f.* **restraint** [36]reuoco ~are, ~aui, ~atum **to call upon to return** [37]amicitia ~ae *f.* **friendship** [38]beniuolentia ~ae *adj.* **goodwill** [39]magisterium ~ii *neut.* **teacher** [40]postpono ~onere, ~osui, ~ositum **to treat as secondary** [41]saluto ~are, ~aui, ~atum **to greet** [42]auditorium ~ii *neut.* **lecture room** [43]aliquid *adv.* **to some extent** [44]abeo ~ire, ~ii, ~itum **to depart**

Alypius and the unintended rebuke

6.7.12 Sed enim de memoria mihi lapsum[1] erat agere cum illo, ne uanorum ludorum[2] caeco[3] et praecipiti[4] studio tam bonum interimeret[5] ingenium, uerum autem, Domine, tu, qui praesides[6] gubernaculis[7] omnium quae creasti, non eum oblitus eras futurum inter filios tuos antistitem[8] sacramenti tui et, ut aperte[9] tibi tribueretur[10] eius correctio,[11] per me quidem illam sed nescientem operatus[12] es. nam quodam die cum sederem[13] loco solito et coram me adessent discipuli,[14] uenit, salutauit,[15] sedit atque in ea quae agebantur intendit animum. et forte lectio[16] in manibus erat, quam dum exponerem[17] opportune[18] mihi adhibenda[19] uideretur similitudo[20] circensium,[21] quo illud quod insinuabam[22] et iucundius[23] et planius[24] fieret cum inrisione[25] mordaci[26] eorum quos illa captiuasset[27] insania.[28] *scis tu, Deus* (Ps 68:6) noster, quod tunc de Alypio ab illa peste[29] sanando non cogitauerim. at ille in se rapuit meque illud non nisi propter se dixisse credidit et quod alius acciperet ad suscensendum[30] mihi, accepit honestus[31] adulescens[32] ad suscensendum sibi et ad me ardentius[33] diligendum. dixeras enim tu iam olim[34] et innexueras[35] litteris tuis, *Corripe*[36] *sapientem, et amabit te* (Prov 9:8 VL). at ego illum non corripueram, sed utens tu omnibus et scientibus et nescientibus ordine quo nosti (et ille ordo iustus est) de corde et lingua mea carbones[37] ardentes[38] operatus es, quibus mentem spei bonae adureres[39] tabescentem[40] ac sanares.

---

[1]labor ~bi, ~psus **to slip** [2]ludus ~i *m.* game > **public games at the circus** [3]caecus ~a, ~um *adj.* **blind** [4]praeceps ~ipitis *adj.* **headlong** [5]interimo ~imere, ~emi, ~emptum **to put an end to** [6]praesideo ~idere, ~edi **to govern** [7]gubernaculum ~i *neut.* **steering** [8]antistes ~titis *m.* **high priest; ECCL priest/bishop** [9]aperte *adv.* **clearly** [10]tribuo ~uere, ~ui, ~utum **to attribute** [11]correctio ~onis *f.* **correction** [12]operor ~ari, ~atus **to be at work** [13]sedeo ~ere, sedi, sessum **to be seated** [14]discipulus ~i *m.* **student** [15]saluto ~are, ~aui, ~atum **to greet** [16]lectio ~onis *f.* **reading** [17]expono ~onere, ~osui, ~ositum **to explain** [18]opportune *adv.* **opportunely** [19]adhibeo ~ere, ~ui, ~itum **to cite or make use of** [20]similitudo ~inis *f.* **analogy** [21]circenses ~ium *m. pl.* **games in the circus** [22]insinuo ~are, ~aui, ~atum **to convey** (an idea) [23]iucunde *adv.* **pleasantly** [24]plane *adv.* **plainly** [25]inrisio ~onis *f.* **derision** [26]mordax ~acis *adj.* **caustic** [27]captiuo ~are, ~aui, ~atum LATE **to take into captivity** [28]insania ~ae *f.* **insanity** [29]pestis ~is *f.* **deadly disease** [30]suscenseo, succ- ~ere, ~ui **to be angry with** (dat.) [31]honestus ~a, ~um *adj.* **honorable** [32]adulescens ~ntis *m.* **young man** [33]ardenter *adv.* **ardently** [34]'iam olim' **long time past** [35]innecto ~ctere, ~xui, ~xum **to weave** (w. dat.) [36]corripio ~ipere, ~ipui, ~eptum **to rebuke** [37]carbo ~onis *m.* **coal** [38]ardens ~ntis *adj.* **burning** [39]aduro ~urere, ~ussi, ~ustum **to cauterize** (medical) [40]tabesco ~escere, ~ui **to waste away**

Taceat laudes tuas qui miserationes[41] tuas non considerat, quae tibi de medullis[42] meis confitentur. etenim[43] uero ille post illa uerba proripuit[44] se ex fouea[45] tam alta, qua libenter[46] demergebatur[47] et cum mira uoluptate caecabatur,[48] et excussit[49] animum forti temperantia,[50] et resiluerunt[51] omnes circensium[52] sordes[53] ab eo ampliusque illuc[54] non accessit.[55] deinde patrem reluctantem[56] euicit[57] ut me magistro uteretur; cessit ille atque concessit.[58]

Et audire me rursus incipiens illa mecum superstitione[59] inuolutus[60] est, amans in Manichaeis ostentationem[61] continentiae,[62] quam ueram et germanam[63] putabat. erat autem illa uecors[64] et seductoria,[65] *pretiosas[66] animas captans[67]* (Prov 6:26) nondum uirtutis altitudinem[68] scientes tangere[69] et superficie[70] decipi[71] faciles, sed tamen adumbratae[72] simulataeque[73] uirtutis.

[41]miseratio ~onis *f.* **mercy** [42]medulla ~ae *f.* marrow > **depths of the heart** (transf.) [43]etenim *conj.* **for** [44]proripio ~ipere, ~ipui, ~eptum **to burst out** (refl.) [45]fouea ~ae *f.* **pitfall** [46]libenter *adv.* **willingly** [47]demergo ~gere, ~si, ~sum **to be swallowed** [48]caeco ~are, ~aui, ~atum **to make blind** [49]excutio ~tere, ~ssi, ~ssum **to shake out** [50]temperantia ~ae *f.* **self-control** [51]resilio ~ire, ~ui **to be forced back** [52]circensis ~is, ~e *adj.* **of the circus** [53]sordes ~is *f.* **filth** [54]illuc *adv.* **there** [55]accedo ~dere, ~ssi, ~ssum **to go near** [56]reluctor ~ari, ~atus **to show reluctance** [57]euinco ~incere, ~ici, ~ictum **to prevail over** [58]concedo ~dere, ~ssi, ~ssum **to give in** [59]superstitio ~onis *f.* **superstition** [60]inuoluo ~uere, ~ui, ~utum **to wrap oneself up** (in) [61]ostentatio ~onis *f.* **ostentatious display** [62]continentia ~ae *f.* **continence** [63]germanus ~a, ~um *adj.* **genuine** [64]uecors uecordis *adj.* **demented** [65]seductorius ~a, ~um ECCL **seductive** [66]pretiosus ~a, ~um *adj.* **precious** [67]capto ~are, ~aui, ~atum **to entrap** [68]altitudo ~inis *f.* **depth** [69]tango ~ere, tetigi, tactum **to touch** [70]superficies ~iei *f.* **surface**; LATE **superficiality** [71]decipio ~ipere, ~epi, ~eptum **to deceive** [72]adumbratus ~a, ~um *adj.* **sketchy** [73]simulo ~are, ~aui, ~atum **to pretend**

Alypius and the gladiators

6.8.13 Non sane[1] relinquens incantatam[2] sibi a parentibus terrenam[3] uiam, Romam praecesserat[4] ut ius disceret, et ibi gladiatorii[5] spectaculi[6] hiatu[7] incredibili[8] et incredibiliter[9] abreptus[10] est. cum enim auersaretur[11] et detestaretur[12] talia, quidam eius amici et condiscipuli,[13] cum forte

[1]sane *adv.* **certainly** [2]incanto ~are, ~aui, ~atum **to enchant** (w. dat.) [3]terrenus ~a, ~um *adj.* **of-this-world** [4]praecedo ~edere, ~essi, ~essum **to go before** [5]gladiator ~oris *m.* **gladiatorial show** (*pl.*) [6]spectaculum ~i *neut.* **spectacle** [7]hiatus ~us *m.* **greedy desire** [8]incredibilis ~is, ~e *adj.* **incredible** [9]incredibiliter *adv.* **to an incredible degree** [10]abripio ~ipere, ~ipui, ~eptum **to snatch away** [11]auersor ~ari, ~atus **to turn away in disgust** [12]detestor ~ari, ~atus **to detest** [13]condiscipulus ~i *m.* **fellow-student**

de prandio[14] redeuntibus peruium[15] esset, recusantem[16] uehementer[17] et resistentem familiari[18] uiolentia[19] duxerunt in amphitheatrum[20] crudelium[21] et funestorum[22] ludorum[23] diebus, haec dicentem: "Si corpus meum in locum illum trahitis[24] et ibi constituitis,[25] numquid et animum et oculos meos in illa spectacula potestis intendere? adero itaque absens ac sic et uos et illa superabo."[26] quibus auditis illi nihilo setius[27] eum adduxerunt[28] secum, idipsum[29] forte explorare[30] cupientes utrum posset efficere.[31] quo ubi uentum est et sedibus quibus potuerunt locati[32] sunt, feruebant[33] omnia immanissimis[34] uoluptatibus. ille clausis foribus[35] oculorum interdixit[36] animo ne in tanta mala procederet.[37] atque utinam[38] et aures obturauisset![39] nam quodam pugnae[40] casu, cum clamor[41] ingens[42] totius populi uehementer eum pulsasset,[43] curiositate[44] uictus et quasi paratus,[45] quidquid illud esset, etiam uisum contemnere[46] et uincere, aperuit oculos. et percussus[47] est grauiore uulnere in anima quam ille in corpore quem cernere concupiuit,[48] ceciditque miserabilius[49] quam ille quo cadente factus est clamor. qui per eius aures intrauit et reserauit[50] eius lumina, ut esset qua[51] feriretur[52] et deiceretur[53] audax[54] adhuc potius quam fortis animus, et eo[55] infirmior[56] quo *de se prae-sumserat,*[57] *qui debuit de te* (Jdt 6:15). ut enim uidit illum sanguinem, immanitatem simul ebibit[58] et non se auertit,[59] sed fixit[60] aspectum[61] et hauriebat[62] furias[63] et nesciebat, et delectabatur scelere[64] certaminis[65]

---

[14]prandium ~ii *neut.* **luncheon** [15]peruius ~a, ~um *adj.* **open to entry** [16]recuso ~are, ~aui, ~atum **to refuse** [17]uehementer *adv.* **vehemently** [18]familiaris ~is, ~e *adj.* **congenial** [19]uiolentia ~ae *f.* **violence** [20]amphitheatrum ~i *neut.* **amphitheater** [21]crudelis ~is, ~e *adj.* **cruel** [22]funestus ~a, ~um *adj.* **deadly** [23]ludus ~i *m.* **public games** (*pl.*) [24]traho ~here, ~xi, ~ctum **to drag** [25]constituo ~uere, ~ui, ~utum **to place** [26]supero ~are, ~aui, ~atum **to prevail over** [27]'nihilo setius' **none the less** [28]adduco ~cere, ~xi, ~ctum **to bring along** [29]idipsum *pron.* ECCL **very thing** [30]exploro ~are, ~aui, ~atum **to test** [31]efficio ~icere, ~eci, ~ectum **to accomplish** [32]loco ~are, ~aui, ~atum **to settle in** [33]feruo ~ere, ferbui **to seethe** [34]immanis ~is, ~e *adj.* **brutal** [35]foris ~is *f.* **entrance** [36]interdico ~cere, ~xi, ~ctum **to forbid** (w. dat. of person and 'ne') [37]procedo ~dere, ~ssi, ~ssum **to emerge** [38]utinam *particle* **if only** [39]obturo ~are, ~aui, ~atum **to plug** [40]pugna ~ae *f.* **fight** [41]clamor ~oris *m.* **shouting and applause** [42]ingens ~ntis *adj.* **very great** [43]pulso ~are, ~aui, ~atum **to strike** [44]curiositas ~atis *f.* **curiosity** (usu. in a bad sense) [45]paratus ~a, ~um *adj.* **prepared** [46]contemno ~nere, ~psi, ~ptum **to regard with contempt** [47]percutio ~tere, ~ssi, ~ssum **to strike forcibly** [48]concupisco ~iscere, ~iui, ~itum **to desire lustfully** [49]miserabiliter *adv.* **miserably** [50]resero ~are, ~aui, ~atum **to unbar** [51]qua *adv.* **by which route** [52]ferio ~ire **to strike down** [53]deicio ~icere, ~ieci, ~iectum **to throw down** [54]audax ~acis *adj.* **bold** [55]eo *adv.* **for that reason** [56]infirmus ~a, ~um *adj.* **weak** [57]praesumo ~ere, ~si, ~ptum to assume; ECCL **to presume** [58]ebibo ~ere, ~i, ~itum **to drink up** [59]auerto ~tere, ~ti, ~sum **to avert** [60]figo ~gere, ~xi, ~xum **to fix** [61]aspectus ~us *m.* **gaze** [62]haurio ~rire, ~si, ~stum **to drink in** [63]furia ~ae *f.* **madness** (*pl.*) [64]scelus ~eris *neut.* **wicked** [65]certamen ~inis *neut.* **contest**

et cruenta⁶⁶ uoluptate inebriabatur.⁶⁷ et non erat iam ille qui uenerat sed unus de turba ad quam uenerat, et uerus eorum socius a quibus adductus⁶⁸ erat. quid plura!⁶⁹ spectauit, clamauit, exarsit,⁷⁰ abstulit inde secum insaniam⁷¹ qua stimularetur⁷² redire non tantum cum illis a quibus prius abstractus⁷³ est, sed etiam prae illis et alios trahens.

Et inde tamen manu ualidissima⁷⁴ et misericordissima⁷⁵ eruisti⁷⁶ eum tu, et docuisti *non sui habere sed tui fiduciam*⁷⁷ (Prov 3:5), sed longe postea.

⁶⁶cruentus ~a, ~um *adj.* **bloody** ⁶⁷inebrio ~are, ~aui, ~atum **to intoxicate** ⁶⁸adduco ~cere, ~xi, ~ctum **to bring along** ⁶⁹'quid plura' **why say more?** ⁷⁰exardesco ~descere, ~si **to be enflamed** ⁷¹insania ~ae *f.* **insanity** ⁷²stimulo ~are, ~aui, ~atum **to incite** ⁷³abstraho ~here, ~xi, ~ctum **to carry away** ⁷⁴ualidus ~a, ~um *adj.* **strong** ⁷⁵misericors ~rdis *adj.* **merciful** ⁷⁶eruo ~uere, ~ui, ~utum **to pluck out; ECCL to rescue** ⁷⁷fiducia ~ae *f.* **trust**

Alypius the thief

6.9.14 Verum tamen iam hoc ad medicinam¹ futuram in eius memoria reponebatur.² nam et illud quod, cum adhuc studeret³ iam me audiens apud Carthaginem et medio die⁴ cogitaret in foro⁵ quod recitaturus⁶ erat, sicut exerceri⁷ scholastici⁸ solent, siuisti eum comprehendi ab aeditimis⁹ fori tamquam furem,¹⁰ non arbitror aliam ob causam¹¹ te permisisse,¹² Deus noster, nisi ut ille uir tantus futurus iam inciperet discere quam non facile in cognoscendis causis homo ab homine damnandus¹³ esset temeraria¹⁴ credulitate.¹⁵

Quippe ante tribunal¹⁶ deambulabat¹⁷ solus cum tabulis¹⁸ ac stilo,¹⁹ cum ecce adulescens²⁰ quidam ex numero scholasticorum, fur uerus, securim²¹ clanculo²² apportans,²³ illo non sentiente ingressus²⁴ est ad

¹medicina ~ae *f.* **medicine** ²repono ~onere, ~osui, ~ositum **to store away** ³studeo ~ere, ~ui **to study** ⁴'medio die' **midday** ⁵forum ~i *neut.* **forum** ⁶recito ~are, ~aui, ~atum **to recite** ⁷exerceo ~ere, ~ui, ~itum **to train by practice** ⁸scholasticus ~a, ~um *adj.* **student of rhetoric** (*m.* as noun) ⁹aeditimus ~i *m.* **sacristan** ¹⁰fur ~ris *m.* **burglar** ¹¹'aliam ob causam' **for any other reason** ¹²permitto ~ittere, ~isi, ~issum **to permit** ¹³damno ~are, ~aui, ~atum **to condemn** ¹⁴temerarius ~a, ~um *adj.* **rash** ¹⁵credulitas ~atis *f.* **credulity** ¹⁶tribunal ~alis *neut.* **judicial platform** ¹⁷deambulo ~are, ~aui, ~atum **to go for a walk** ¹⁸tabula ~ae *f.* **wooden writing tablet** ¹⁹stilus ~i *m.* **stylus** ²⁰adulescens ~ntis *m.* **young man** ²¹securis ~is *f.* **axe** ²²clanculo *adv.* **secretly** ²³apporto ~are, ~aui, ~atum **to bring with one** ²⁴ingredior ~di, ~ssus **to go into**

cancellos[25] plumbeos[26] qui uico[27] argentario[28] desuper[29] praeminent[30] et praecidere[31] plumbum[32] coepit. sono autem securis audito submurmurauerunt[33] argentarii qui subter[34] erant, et miserunt qui apprehenderent[35] quem forte inuenissent. quorum uocibus auditis relicto instrumento[36] ille discessit[37] timens, ne cum eo teneretur. Alypius autem, qui non uiderat intrantem, exeuntem[38] sensit et celeriter[39] uidit abeuntem[40] et, causam scire cupiens, ingressus est locum et inuentam securim stans atque admirans[41] considerabat, cum ecce illi qui missi erant reperiunt[42] eum solum ferentem ferrum cuius sonitu[43] exciti[44] uenerant. tenent, attrahunt,[45] congregatis[46] inquilinis[47] fori tamquam furem manifestum[48] se comprehendisse gloriantur,[49] et inde offerendus[50] iudiciis ducebatur.

[25]cancellus ~i *m.* **barrier** *or* **grating** [26]plumbeus ~a, ~um *adj.* **made of lead** [27]uicus ~i *m.* **quarter** *or* **street** [28]argentarius ~ii *m.* **silver-smith** [29]desuper *adv.* **from overhead** [30]praemineo ~ere **to protrude** [31]praecido ~dere, ~di, ~sum **to cut away** [32]plumbum ~i *neut.* **lead** [33]submurmuro ~are **to murmur softly** [34]subter *adv.* **below** [35]apprehendo ~dere, ~di, ~sum **to lay hold of** [36]instrumentum ~i *neut.* **tool** [37]discedo ~dere, ~ssi, ~ssum **to run away** [38]exeo ~ire, ~iui or ~ii, ~itum **to come out** [39]celeriter *adv.* **quickly** [40]abeo ~ire, ~ii, ~itum **to go away** [41]admiror ~ari, ~atus **to marvel or wonder (at)** [42]reperio ~ire, repperi, ~tum **to discover** [43]sonitus ~us *m.* **sound** [44]excio, ~ieo ~ire, ~iui, ~itum **to stir to action** [45]attraho ~here, ~xi, ~ctum **to drag with force** [46]congrego ~are, ~aui, ~atum **to come together** [47]inquilinus ~i *m.* **tenant** [48]manifestus ~a, ~um *adj.* **caught in the act** (of crime) [49]glorior ~ari, ~atus **to boast** [50]offero ~rre, obtuli, oblatum **to bring before**

Alypius the innocent

6.9.15 Sed hactenus[1] docendus fuit. statim[2] enim, Domine, subuenisti[3] innocentiae,[4] *cuius testis*[5] *eras tu* (Wis 1:6) solus. cum enim duceretur uel ad custodiam[6] uel ad supplicium,[7] fit eis obuiam[8] quidam architectus,[9] cuius maxima erat cura publicarum[10] fabricarum.[11] gaudent illi eum potissimum[12] occurrisse, cui solebant in suspicionem[13] uenire ablatarum rerum quae perissent de foro,[14] ut quasi tandem iam ille cognosceret a quibus haec fierent. uerum autem uiderat homo saepe Alypium in domo cuiusdam senatoris[15] ad quem salutandum[16] uentitabat,[17] statimque

[1]hactenus *adv.* **this far (and no farther)** [2]statim *adv.* **immediately** [3]subuenio ~enire, ~eni, ~entum **to bring relief** (w. dat.) [4]innocentia ~ae *f.* **innocence** [5]testis ~is *m.* **witness** [6]custodia ~ae *f.* **custody** [7]supplicium ~ii *neut.* **punishment** [8]obuiam *adv.* **on the way (so as to meet)** [9]architectus ~i *m.* **architect** [10]publicus ~a, ~um *adj.* **public** [11]fabrica ~ae *f.* **building** [12]potissimum *adv.* **especially** [13]suspicio ~onis *f.* **suspicion** [14]forum ~i *neut.* **forum** [15]senator ~oris *m.* **senator** [16]saluto ~are, ~aui, ~atum **to greet** [17]uentito ~are, ~aui, ~atum **to visit frequently**

cognitum manu apprehensa[18] semouit[19] a turbis et tanti mali causam quaerens, quid gestum esset audiuit omnesque tumultuantes[20] qui aderant et minaciter[21] frementes[22] iussit uenire secum.

Et uenerunt ad domum illius adulescentis[23] qui rem commiserat.[24] puer uero erat ante ostium,[25] et tam paruus erat ut nihil exinde[26] domino suo metuens facile posset totum indicare; cum eo quippe in foro fuit pedisequus.[27] quem posteaquam[28] recoluit Alypius, architecto intimauit.[29] at ille securim[30] demonstrauit[31] puero, quaerens ab eo cuius esset. qui confestim[32] "Nostra" inquit; deinde interrogatus aperuit cetera.

Sic in illam domum translata[33] causa confusisque[34] turbis quae de illo triumphare[35] iam coeperant, futurus dispensator[36] uerbi tui et multarum in ecclesia tua causarum examinator[37] experientior instructiorque[38] discessit.[39]

---

[18]apprehendo ~dere, ~di, ~sum **to lay hold of** [19]semoueo ~ouere, ~oui, ~otum **to remove** [20]tumultuor ~ari, ~atus **to make a commotion** [21]minaciter *adv.* **menacingly** [22]fremo ~ere, ~ui, ~itum **to hum, buzz** (of crowd noise) [23]adulescens ~ntis *m.* **young man** [24]committo ~ittere, ~isi, ~issum **to commit** [25]ostium ~ii *neut.* **door** [26]exinde *adv.* **for that reason** [27]pedisequus ~i *m.* **servant boy** [28]posteaquam *conj.* **after which** [29]intimo ~are, ~aui, ~atum **to make known** (w. dat.) [30]securis ~is *f.* **axe** [31]demonstro ~are, ~aui, ~atum **to show** [32]confestim *adv.* **without delay** [33]transfero ~ferre, ~tuli, ~latum **to transfer** [34]confundo ~undere, ~udi, ~usum **to be embarrassed** [35]triumpho ~are, ~aui, ~atum **to march in triumph** [36]dispensator ~oris *m.* administrator; ECCL **dispenser** [37]examinator ~oris *m.* LATE **judge** [38]instructus ~a, ~um *adj.* **equipped** [39]discedo ~dere, ~ssi, ~ssum **to depart**

Alypius the assessor

6.10.16 Hunc ergo Romae inueneram, et adhaesit[1] mihi fortissimo uinculo[2] mecumque Mediolanium profectus[3] est, ut nec me desereret et de iure quod didicerat aliquid ageret secundum uotum magis parentum quam suum. et ter[4] iam adsederat[5] mirabili[6] continentia[7] ceteris, cum ille magis miraretur eos qui aurum innocentiae[8] praeponerent.[9]

---

[1]adhaereo ~rere, ~si, ~sum **to cling (to)** [2]uinculum ~i *neut.* **bond** (of friendship) [3]proficiscor ~icisci, ~ectus **to set out** [4]ter *adv.* **three times** [5]adsideo ~idere, ~edi, ~essum **to assist as assessor** [6]mirabilis ~is, ~e *adj.* **astonishing** [7]continentia ~ae *f.* **continence** [8]innocentia ~ae *f.* innocence > **integrity** [9]praepono ~onere, ~osui, ~ositum **to prefer** x (acc.) **to** y (dat.).

Temptata[10] est quoque eius indoles[11] non solum inlecebra[12] cupiditatis sed etiam stimulo[13] timoris.[14] Romae adsidebat comiti[15] Largitionum[16] Italicianarum. erat eo tempore[17] quidam potentissimus senator[18] cuius et beneficiis[19] obstricti[20] multi et terrori[21] subditi[22] erant. uoluit sibi licere nescio quid ex more potentiae[23] suae quod esset per leges inlicitum;[24] restitit[25] Alypius. promissum[26] est praemium;[27] inrisit animo. praeten-tae[28] minae;[29] calcauit,[30] mirantibus omnibus inusitatam[31] animam, quae hominem tantum et innumerabilibus[32] praestandi[33] nocendique[34] modis ingenti[35] fama celebratum[36] uel amicum non optaret uel non formida-ret[37] inimicum. ipse autem iudex[38] cui consiliarius[39] erat, quamuis et ipse fieri nollet, non tamen aperte[40] recusabat,[41] sed in istum causam transferens[42] ab eo se non permitti[43] adserebat,[44] quia et re uera, si ipse faceret, iste discederet.[45]

Hoc solo autem paene[46] iam inlectus[47] erat studio litterario,[48] ut pre-tiis[49] praetorianis[50] codices[51] sibi conficiendos[52] curaret, sed consulta[53] iustitia deliberationem[54] in melius uertit, utiliorem[55] iudicans aequita-tem[56] qua prohibebatur[57] quam potestatem qua sinebatur. paruum est hoc, sed *qui in paruo fidelis est et in magno fidelis est*, nec ullo modo erit inane[58] quod tuae Veritatis ore processit:[59] *Si in iniusto[60] mammona[61]*

---

[10]tempto ~are, ~aui, ~atum **to test** [11]indoles ~is *f.* **innate quality** [12]inlecebra ~ae *f.* **allurement** [13]stimulus ~i *m.* **goad** [14]timor ~oris *m.* **fear** [15]comes ~itis *m.* companion; LATE **Count (imperial official)** [16]largitio ~onis *f.* largess; LATE **treasury** [17]'eo tempore' **at that time** [18]senator ~oris *m.* **senator** [19]beneficium ~ii *neut.* kindness > **political favor** [20]obstringo ~ngere, ~nxi, ~ctum **to obligate** [21]terror ~oris *m.* **terror** [22]subdo ~ere, ~idi, ~itum **to make subject** [23]potentia ~ae *f.* **power over others** [24]inlicitus ~a, ~um *adj.* **forbidden** [25]resto ~are, ~iti **to resist** [26]promitto ~ittere, ~isi, ~issum **to promise** [27]praemium ~ii *neut.* **payment** [28]praetendo ~dere, ~di, ~tum **to hold out** [29]minae ~arum *f. pl.* **threats** [30]calco ~are, ~aui, ~atum **to trample** [31]inusitatus ~a, ~um *adj.* **unusual** [32]innumerabilis ~is, ~e *adj.* **innumerable** [33]praesto ~are, ~iti, ~itum **to offer benefits** [34]noceo ~ere, ~ui, ~itum **to injure** [35]ingens ~ntis *adj.* very great > **influential** [36]celebratus ~a, ~um *adj.* **widely known** [37]formido ~are, ~aui, ~atum **to dread** [38]iudex ~icis *m.* **judge** [39]consiliarius ~ii *m.* **assessor** [40]aperte *adv.* **openly** [41]recuso ~are, ~aui, ~atum **to refuse** [42]transfero ~ferre, ~tuli, ~latum **to transfer** [43]permitto ~ittere, ~isi, ~issum **to permit** [44]adsero ~ere, ~ui, ~tum **to claim** [45]discedo ~dere, ~ssi, ~ssum **to separate company** [46]paene *adv.* **nearly** [47]inlecto ~are **to allure** [48]litterarius ~ia, ~ium *adj.* **literary** [49]pretium ~ii *neut.* **price** [50]praetorianus ~a, ~um *adj.* AUG **of the praetor** [51]codex ~icis *m.* **book** [52]conficio ~icere, ~eci, ~ectum **to copy out** (books) [53]consulto ~are, ~aui, ~atum **to consult** [54]deliberatio ~onis *f.* **deliberation** [55]utilis ~is, ~e *adj.* **profitable** [56]aequitas ~atis *f.* **fairness** [57]prohibeo ~ere, ~ui, ~itum **to prohibit** [58]inanis ~is, ~e *adj.* **empty** [59]procedo ~dere, ~ssi, ~ssum **to proceed** [60]iniustus ~a, ~um *adj.* **unjust** [61]mammonas *m.* ECCL **riches**

fideles non fuistis, uerum quis dabit uobis? et si in alieno fideles non fuistis, uestrum quis dabit uobis? (Lk 16:11–12).

Talis ille tunc inhaerebat[62] mihi mecumque nutabat[63] in consilio, quisnam[64] esset tenendus uitae modus.

[62]inhaereo ~rere, ~si, ~sum **to cling to** [63]nuto ~are, ~aui, ~atum **to waver** [64]quisnam quae-, quid- *adj.* **what kind of**

Keen-minded Nebridius

6.10.17 Nebridius etiam, qui relicta patria uicina[1] Carthagini atque ipsa Carthagine, ubi frequentissimus[2] erat, relicto *paterno*[3] *rure*[4] (Ep. 2.3) optimo, relicta domo et non secutura matre, nullam obaliam causam[5] Mediolanium uenerat, nisi ut mecum uiueret in flagrantissimo[6] studio ueritatis atque sapientiae, pariter[7] suspirabat pariterque fluctuabat,[8] batae uitae inquisitor[9] ardens[10] et quaestionum[11] difficillimarum[12] scrutator[13] acerrimus.[14] et erant ora trium egentium[15] et inopiam[16] suam sibimet inuicem[17] anhelantium[18] et ad te expectantium, ut *dares eis escam*[19] *in tempore opportuno*[20] (Ps 103:27). et in omni amaritudine[21] quae nostros saeculares[22] actus[23] de misericordia tua sequebatur, intuentibus nobis finem cur ea pateremur, occurrebant tenebrae, et auersabamur[24] gementes[25] et dicebamus, "Quamdiu[26] haec?" et hoc crebro[27] dicebamus, et dicentes non relinquebamus ea, quia non elucebat[28] certum[29] aliquid quod illis relictis apprehenderemus.[30]

[1]uicinus ~a, ~um *adj.* **in the vicinity of** (w. dat.) [2]frequens ~ntis *adj.* **regularly** (*quasi-adv.*) [3]paternus ~a, ~um *adj.* **father's** [4]rus ruris *neut.* **country estate** [5]'nullam ob aliam causam' **for no other reason than** [6]flagrans ~ntis *adj.* **enthusiastic** [7]pariter *adv.* **together** [8]fluctuo ~are, ~aui, ~atum **to waver** [9]inquisitor ~oris *m.* **investigator** [10]ardens ~ntis *adj.* **passionate** [11]quaestio ~onis *f.* **question** [12]difficilis ~is, ~e *adj.* **difficult** [13]scrutator ~oris *m.* **inquirer** [14]acer acris, acre *adj.* sharp > **keen** [15]egeo ~ere, ~ui *intr.* **to go without** [16]inopia ~ae *f.* **poverty** [17]inuicem *adv.* **in each one's turn** [18]anhelo ~are, ~aui, ~atum **to gasp out one's life** (hyperb.) [19]esca ~ae *f.* **food** [20]'in tempore opportuno' **in due season** [21]amaritudo ~inis *f.* **bitterness** [22]saecularis ~is, ~e *adj.* ECCL **worldly** [23]actus ~us *m.* movement > **doing** [24]auersor ~ari, ~atus **to turn away in disgust** [25]gemo ~ere, ~ui, ~itum **to groan** [26]quamdiu *adv.* **for how long?** [27]crebro *adv.* **repeatedly** [28]eluceo ~cere, ~xi **to manifest itself** [29]certum ~i *neut.* **certainty** [30]apprehendo ~dere, ~di, ~sum **to lay hold of**

Thirty years old and stuck

6.11.18 Et ego maxime mirabar, satagens[1] et recolens quam longum tempus esset ab undeuicensimo[2] anno aetatis meae, quo feruere[3] coeperam studio sapientiae, disponens[4] ea inuenta relinquere omnes uanarum cupiditatum spes inanes[5] et *insanias*[6] *mendaces*[7] (Ps 39:5). et ecce iam tricenariam[8] aetatem gerebam, *in eodem luto*[9] *haesitans*[10] (Ph. 780) auiditate[11] fruendi[12] praesentibus fugientibus et dissipantibus[13] me, dum dico, "Cras[14] inueniam. ecce manifestum[15] apparebit, et tenebo.

"Ecce Faustus ueniet et exponet[16] omnia.

"O magni uiri Academici! *nihil* ad agendam uitam certi[17] *comprehendi potest* (Ac. 2.18). immo[18] quaeramus diligentius[19] et non desperemus.[20] ecce iam non sunt absurda[21] in libris Ecclesiasticis[22] quae absurda uidebantur, et possunt aliter atque honeste[23] intellegi. figam[24] pedes in eo gradu[25] in quo puer a parentibus positus eram, donec inueniatur perspicua[26] ueritas.

"Sed ubi quaeretur? quando quaeretur? non uacat[27] Ambrosio, non uacat legere. ubi ipsos codices[28] quaerimus? unde aut quando comparamus?[29] a quibus sumimus?[30]

"Deputentur[31] tempora, distribuantur[32] horae pro salute animae. magna spes oborta[33] est: non docet Catholica fides quod putabamus et uani accusabamus.[34] nefas[35] habent docti eius credere Deum figura[36]

---

[1]satago ~agere, ~egi, ~actum **to be hard pressed** [2]undeuicensimus ~a, ~um *adj.* **nineteenth** [3]ferueo ~ere, ferbui **to be fired up** [4]dispono ~onere, ~osui, ~ositum **to plan out** [5]inanis ~is, ~e *adj.* **empty** [6]insania ~ae *f.* **insanity** [7]mendax ~acis *adj.* **lying** [8]tricenarius ~a, ~um *adj.* **thirty (years old)** [9]'in eodem luto' **in the same sticky situation** [10]haesito ~are, ~aui, ~atum **to be stuck** [11]auiditas ~atis *f.* **with keen thirst** (abl. as *adv.*) [12]fruor ~i, ~ctus **to enjoy** (w. abl.) [13]dissipo ~are, ~aui, ~atum **to disintegrate** [14]cras *adv.* **tomorrow** [15]manifestus ~a, ~um *adj.* **manifestly obvious** [16]expono ~onere, ~osui, ~ositum **to explain** [17]certum ~i *neut.* **certainty** [18]immo *particle* **rather** [19]diligenter *adv.* **diligently** [20]despero ~are, ~aui, ~atum **to despair** [21]absurdus ~a, ~um *adj.* **absurd** [22]ecclesiasticus ~a, ~um *adj.* **ECCL of the Church** [23]honeste *adv.* **creditably** [24]figo ~gere, ~xi, ~xum **to place firmly** [25]gradus ~us *m.* **step** [26]perspicuus ~a, ~um *adj.* **clear** [27]uaco ~are, ~aui, ~atum **to have opportunity** (w. dat.) [28]codex ~icis *m.* **book** [29]comparo ~are, ~aui, ~atum **to secure** [30]sumo ~mere, ~mpsi, ~mptum **to take** > **to borrow** [31]deputo ~are, ~aui, ~atum **to appoint** [32]distribuo ~uere, ~ui, ~utum **to divide up** [33]oborior ~iri, ~tus **to arise** > **to spring up suddenly** [34]accuso ~are, ~aui, ~atum **to accuse** [35]nefas *indecl. neut.* **sacrilege** [36]figura ~ae *f.* **form**

humani corporis terminatum.[37] et dubitamus[38] *pulsare,*[39] quo *aperiantur* (Mt 7:7–8) cetera? antemeridianis[40] horis discipuli[41] occupant: ceteris quid facimus? cur non id agimus?

"Sed quando salutamus[42] amicos maiores, quorum suffragiis[43] opus habemus? quando praeparamus[44] quod emant[45] scholastici?[46] quando reparamus[47] nos ipsos relaxando[48] animo ab intentione[49] curarum?"

[37]termino ~are, ~aui, ~atum **to limit** [38]dubito ~are, ~aui, ~atum **to hesitate** [39]pulso ~are, ~aui, ~atum **to knock** [40]antemeridianus ~a, ~um *adj.* **morning** [41]discipulus ~i *m.* **student** [42]saluto ~are, ~aui, ~atum **to call on a patron** [43]suffragium ~ii *neut.* **favorable influence** [44]praeparo ~are, ~aui, ~atum **to prepare** [45]emo emere, emi, emptum **to buy** [46]scholasticus ~a, ~um *adj.* **rhetoric student** (*m.* as noun) [47]reparo ~are, ~aui, ~atum **to reinvigorate** [48]relaxo ~are, ~aui, ~atum **to relax** [49]intentio ~onis *f.* **mental effort**

Contemplating renunciation

6.11.19 "Pereant omnia et dimittamus haec uana et inania:[1] conferamus[2] nos ad solam inquisitionem[3] ueritatis. uita misera est, mors incerta[4] est. subito[5] obrepat:[6] quomodo hinc exibimus?[7] et ubi nobis discenda sunt quae hic[8] neglegimus?[9] ac non potius huius neglegentiae[10] supplicia[11] luenda?[12]

"Quid si mors ipsa omnem curam cum sensu amputabit[13] et finiet? ergo et hoc quaerendum.

"Sed absit ut ita sit. non uacat,[14] non est inane, quod tam eminens[15] culmen[16] auctoritatis Christianae fidei toto orbe diffunditur.[17] numquam tanta et talia pro nobis diuinitus[18] agerentur, si morte corporis etiam uita animae consumeretur.[19] quid cunctamur[20] igitur relicta spe saeculi conferre nos totos ad quaerendum Deum et uitam beatam?

[1]inanis ~is, ~e *adj.* **empty** [2]confero ~rre, contuli, conlatum **to devote** (refl.) [3]inquisitio ~onis *f.* **search** [4]incertus ~a, ~um *adj.* **uncertain** [5]subito *adv.* **unexpectedly** [6]obrepo ~ere, ~si, ~tum **to creep up stealthily** [7]exeo ~ire, ~iui or ~ii, ~itum **to pass away** [8]hic *adv.* **here** [9]neglego ~gere, ~xi, ~ctum **to neglect** [10]neglegentia ~ae *f.* **negligence** [11]supplicium ~ii *neut.* **punishment** [12]luo ~ere, ~i **to suffer** [13]amputo ~are, ~aui, ~atum **to cut off** [14]uaco ~are, ~aui, ~atum **to be empty** [15]emineo ~ere, ~ui **to be pre-eminent** [16]culmen ~inis *neut.* **exalted position** [17]diffundo ~undere, ~udi, ~usum **to spread** [18]diuinitus *adv.* **by divine agency** [19]consumo ~ere, ~psi, ~ptum **to extinguish** [20]cunctor ~ari, ~atus **to delay**

"Sed expecta: iucunda[21] sunt etiam ista, habent non paruam dulcedi-nem[22] suam; non facile ab eis praecidenda[23] est intentio,[24] quia turpe est ad ea rursum redire. ecce iam quantum est ut impetretur[25] aliquis honor. et quid amplius in his desiderandum? suppetit[26] amicorum maiorum copia: ut nihil aliud[27] et multum festinemus,[28] uel praesidatus[29] dari potest. et ducenda uxor[30] cum aliqua pecunia,[31] ne sumptum[32] nostrum grauet,[33] et ille erit modus cupiditatis. multi magni uiri et imitatione[34] dignissimi sapientiae studio cum coniugibus dediti[35] fuerunt."

[21]iucundus ~a, ~um *adj.* **delightful** [22]dulcedo ~inis *f.* **sweetness** [23]praecido ~dere, ~di, ~sum **to break away** [24]intentio ~onis *f.* **attention** [25]impetro ~are, ~aui, ~atum **to succeed in obtaining** [26]suppeto ~ere, ~iui **to be available** [27]'nihil aliud' **if nothing else** [28]festino ~are, ~aui, ~atum **to act quickly** [29]praesidatus ~us *m.* LATE **governorship** [30]uxor ~oris *f.* **wife** [31]pecunia ~ae *f.* **wealth** [32]sumptus ~us *m.* **expenses** [33]grauo ~are, ~aui, ~atum **to weigh heavy on** [34]imitatio ~onis *f.* **imitation** [35]deditus ~a, ~um *adj.* **devoted**

Conversion postponed

6.11.20 Cum haec dicebam et alternabant[1] hi uenti et impellebant[2] huc atque illuc[3] cor meum, transibant tempora et *tardabam[4] conuerti ad Dominum, et differebam[5] de die in diem* (Sir 5:8) iuuere in te et non differebam cotidie[6] in memet ipso mori. amans beatam uitam timebam illam in sede sua et ab ea fugiens quaerebam eam. putabam enim me miserum fore nimis si feminae priuarer[7] amplexibus,[8] et medicinam[9] *misericordiae tuae ad eandem infirmitatem[10] sanandam* (Ps 102:3–4) non cogitabam, quia expertus non eram, et propriarum[11] uirium cre-debam esse continentiam,[12] quarum mihi non eram conscius,[13] cum tam stultus[14] essem ut nescirem, sicut scriptum est, *neminem posse esse continentem nisi tu dederis* (Wis 8:21). utique dares, si gemitu[15] interno[16] pulsarem[17] aures tuas et fide solida[18] in *te iactarem[19] curam meam* (Ps 54:23).

[1]alterno ~are, ~aui, ~atum **to sway** [2]impello ~ellere, ~uli, ~ulsum **to impel** [3]'huc... illuc' **this way and that** [4]tardo ~are, ~aui, ~atum **to delay** [5]differo ~rre, distuli, dilatum **to defer** [6]cotidie *adv.* **daily** [7]priuo ~are, ~aui, ~atum **to deprive of** (w. dat.) [8]amplexus ~us *m.* **embrace** [9]medicina ~ae *f.* **medicine** [10]infirmitas ~atis *f.* **infirmity** [11]proprius ~a, ~um *adj.* **one's own** [12]continentia ~ae *f.* **continence** [13]conscius ~a, ~um *adj.* **conscious** [14]stultus ~a, ~um *adj.* **foolish** [15]gemitus ~us *m.* **groaning** [16]internus ~a, ~um *adj.* **internal** [17]pulso ~are, ~aui, ~atum **to knock** [18]solidus ~a, ~um *adj.* **solid** [19]iacto ~are, ~aui, ~atum **to cast**

Alypius discourages marriage

6.12.21 Prohibebat[1] me sane[2] Alypius ab uxore[3] ducenda, cantans nullo modo nos posse securo[4] otio[5] simul in amore sapientiae uiuere, sicut iam diu desideraremus, si id fecissem. erat enim ipse in ea re etiam tunc castissimus,[6] ita ut mirum esset, quia uel experientiam[7] concubitus[8] ceperat in ingressu[9] adulescentiae[10] suae, sed non haeserat[11] magisque doluerat et spreuerat[12] et deinde iam continentissime uiuebat. ego autem resistebam illi exemplis[13] eorum qui coniugati[14] coluissent sapientiam et *promeruissent*[15] *Deum* (Heb 13:16) et habuissent fideliter[16] ac dilexissent amicos. a quorum ego quidem granditate[17] animi longe aberam et deligatus[18] morbo[19] carnis mortifera[20] suauitate[21] trahebam[22] catenam[23] meam, solui[24] timens et quasi concusso[25] uulnere repellens[26] uerba bene suadentis[27] tamquam manum soluentis. insuper[28] etiam per me ipsi quoque Alypio *loquebatur serpens*[29] (Gen 3:1), et innectebat[30] atque spargebat[31] per linguam meam dulces *laqueos*[32] *in uia eius* (Ps 141:4), quibus illi honesti[33] et expediti[34] pedes implicarentur.[35]

[1]prohibeo ~ere, ~ui, ~itum **to keep from** [2]sane *adv.* **at any rate** [3]uxor ~oris *f.* wife [4]securus ~a, ~um *adj.* **untroubled** [5]otium ~ii *neut.* **leisure** [6]castus ~a, ~um *adj.* **chaste** [7]experientia ~ae *f.* **experience** [8]concubitus ~us *m.* **sexual intercourse** [9]ingressus ~us *m.* **onset** [10]adulescentia ~ae *f.* **adolescence** [11]haereo ~rere, ~si, ~sum **to continue** [12]sperno ~ere, spreui, spretum **to spurn** [13]exemplum ~i *neut.* **example** [14]coniugo ~are, ~aui, ~atum **to join in marriage** [15]promereo ~ere, ~ui, ~itum **to please** [16]fideliter *adv.* **loyally** [17]granditas ~atis *f.* **grandeur** [18]deligo ~are, ~aui, ~atum **to tie down** [19]morbus ~i *m.* **disease** [20]mortiferus ~era, ~erum *adj.* **deadly** [21]suauitas ~atis *f.* **sweetness** [22]traho ~here, ~xi, ~ctum **to drag** [23]catena ~ae *f.* **chain** [24]soluo ~uere, ~ui, ~utum **to untie** [25]concutio ~tere, ~ssi, ~ssum **to strike** [26]repello ~ere, reppuli, repulsum **to thrust away** [27]suadeo ~dere, ~si, ~sum **to urge** [28]insuper *adv.* **over and above** [29]serpens ~ntis *f. m.* **serpent** [30]innecto ~ctere, ~xui, ~xum **to devise** [31]spargo ~gere, ~si, ~sum **to scatter** [32]laqueus ~i *m.* **trap** [33]honestus ~a, ~um *adj.* **honorable** [34]expeditus ~a, ~um *adj.* **unencumbered** [35]implico ~are, ~aui, ~atum or ~itum **to entangle**

Alypius the curious

6.12.22 Cum enim me ille miraretur, quem non parui penderet,[1] ita haerere[2] uisco[3] illius uoluptatis ut me adfirmarem,[4] quotienscumque[5] inde inter nos quaereremus, caelibem[6] uitam nullo modo posse degere[7]

[1]pendo ~ere, pependi, ~sum **to regard as** [2]haereo ~rere, ~si, ~sum **to stick** [3]uiscum ~i *neut.* **birdlime** [4]adfirmo ~are, ~aui, ~atum **to assert** [5]quotienscumque *adv.* **every time that** [6]caelebs, ~eps ~ibis *adj.* **unmarried** [7]dego ~ere **to spend one's life**

atque ita me defenderem,[8] cum illum mirantem uiderem, ut dicerem multum interesse[9] inter illud quod ipse raptim[10] et furtim[11] expertus esset, quod paene[12] iam ne meminisset quidem atque ideo nulla molestia[13] facile contemneret,[14] et delectationes[15] consuetudinis meae, ad quas si accessisset[16] honestum[17] nomen matrimonii,[18] non eum mirari oportere[19] cur ego illam uitam nequirem[20] spernere,[21] coeperat et ipse desiderare coniugium,[22] nequaquam[23] uictus libidine talis uoluptatis sed curiositatis.[24] dicebat enim scire se cupere quidnam[25] esset illud sine quo uita mea, quae illi sic placebat, non mihi uita sed poena uideretur. stupebat[26] enim liber[27] ab illo uinculo[28] animus seruitutem[29] meam et stupendo ibat in experiendi cupidinem,[30] uenturus in ipsam experientiam[31] atque inde fortasse[32] lapsurus[33] in eam quam stupebat seruitutem, quoniam *sponsionem*[34] *uolebat facere cum morte* (Wis 1:16; Isa 28:18), et *qui amat periculum incidet*[35] *in illud* (Sir 3:27). neutrum[36] enim nostrum, si quod[37] est coniugale[38] decus[39] in officio[40] regendi[41] matrimonii et suscipiendorum[42] liberorum,[43] ducebat nisi tenuiter.[44] magna autem ex parte atque uehementer[45] consuetudo satiandae[46] insatiabilis[47] concupiscentiae[48] me captum excruciabat,[49] illum autem admiratio[50] capiendum trahebat.[51]

Sic eramus, donec *tu, Altissime* (Ps 9:3), non deserens humum[52] nostram miseratus miseros subuenires[53] miris et occultis modis.

---

[8]defendo ~dere, ~di, ~sum **to defend** [9]intersum ~esse, ~fui **to make a difference** (*impers.*) [10]raptim *adv.* **hurriedly** [11]furtim *adv.* **secretly** [12]paene *adv.* **all but** [13]molestia ~ae *f.* **trouble** [14]contemno ~nere, ~psi, ~ptum **to condemn** [15]delectatio ~onis *f.* **pleasure** [16]accedo ~dere, ~ssi, ~ssum **to attach to** [17]honestus ~a, ~um *adj.* **honorable** [18]matrimonium ~ii *neut.* **marriage** [19]oportet ~ere, ~uit *impers.* **it is right** [20]nequeo ~ire, ~iui or ~ii **to be unable (to)** [21]sperno ~ere, spreui, spretum **to spurn** [22]coniugium ~ii *neut.* **marriage** [23]nequaquam *adv.* **not at all** [24]curiositas ~atis *f.* **curiosity** (usu. in a bad sense) [25]quisnam quae-, quid- *pron* **what a thing** [26]stupeo ~ere, ~ui **to be stupefied** [27]liber ~era, ~erum *adj.* **free** [28]uinculum ~i *neut.* **chain** [29]seruitus ~utis *f.* **servitude** [30]cupido ~inis *f. m.* **desire** [31]experientia ~ae *f.* **experience** [32]fortasse *adv.* **perhaps** [33]labor ~bi, ~psus **to sink down** [34]sponsio ~onis *f.* **pact** [35]incido ~ere, ~i **to fall into** [36]neuter ~tra, ~trum *adj.* **neither** [37]'si quod' **whatever** [38]coniugalis ~is, ~e *adj.* **conjugal** [39]decus ~oris *neut.* **dignity** [40]officium ~ii *neut.* **one's duty or obligations** [41]rego ~gere, ~xi, ~ctum **to guide into the right way** [42]suscipio ~ipere, ~epi, ~eptum **to raise** [43]liberi ~orum *m. pl.* **children** [44]tenuiter *adv.* **with little force** [45]uehementer *adv.* **vehemently** [46]satio ~are, ~aui, ~atum **to satiate** [47]insatiabilis ~is, ~e *adj.* **insatiable** [48]concupiscentia ~ae *f.* ECCL **concupiscence** [49]excrucio ~are, ~aui, ~atum **to torture** [50]admiratio ~onis *f.* **wonder** [51]traho ~here, ~xi, ~ctum **to lure on** [52]humum ~i *neut.* **clay** [53]subuenio ~enire, ~eni, ~entum **to bring relief**

Monica plans a wedding

6.13.23 Et instabatur[1] impigre[2] ut ducerem uxorem.[3] iam petebam, iam promittebatur[4] maxime matre dante operam,[5] quo me iam coniugatum[6] baptismus[7] salutaris[8] ablueret,[9] quo me in dies[10] gaudebat aptari[11] et uota sua ac promissa[12] tua in mea fide compleri[13] animaduertebat.[14] cum sane[15] et rogatu[16] meo et desiderio suo forti clamore[17] cordis abs te deprecaretur[18] cotidie[19] ut ei per uisum ostenderes aliquid de futuro matrimonio[20] meo, numquam uoluisti. et uidebat quaedam uana et phantastica,[21] quo cogebat impetus de hac re satagentis[22] humani spiritus, et narrabat mihi non cum fiducia[23] qua solebat, cum tu demonstrabas[24] ei, sed contemnens[25] ea. dicebat enim discernere se nescio quo sapore,[26] quem uerbis explicare[27] non poterat, quid interesset[28] inter reuelantem[29] te et animam suam somniantem.[30]

Instabatur tamen, et puella petebatur, cuius aetas ferme[31] biennio[32] minus quam nubilis[33] erat, et quia ea placebat, exspectabatur.

[1]insto ~are, ~iti **to be pressing** [2]impigre *adv.* **actively** [3]uxor ~oris *f.* **wife** [4]promitto ~ittere, ~isi, ~issum **to promise** [5]'operam dante' **by devoting (her) attention** [6]coniugo ~are, ~aui, ~atum **to join in marriage** [7]baptismus ~i *m.* ECCL **baptism** [8]salutaris ~is, ~e *adj.* **life-giving** [9]abluo ~uere, ~ui, ~utum **to wash**; ECCL **to wash (from sin)** [10]'in dies' **daily** [11]apto ~are, ~aui, ~atum **to make ready** [12]promissum ~i *neut.* **promise** [13]compleo ~ere, ~eui, ~etum **to fulfill** [14]animaduerto ~tere, ~ti, ~sum **to remark upon** [15]sane *adv.* **certainly** [16]rogatus ~us *m.* **request** [17]clamor ~oris *m.* **cry** [18]deprecor ~ari, ~atus **to beg** (w. 'ab' of person) [19]cotidie *adv.* **daily** [20]matrimonium ~ii *neut.* **marriage** [21]phantasticus ~a, ~um *adj.* LATE **imaginary** [22]satago ~agere, ~egi, ~actum **to busy oneself** [23]fiducia ~ae *f.* **confidence** [24]demonstro ~are, ~aui, ~atum **to reveal** [25]contemno ~nere, ~psi, ~ptum **to disregard** [26]sapor ~oris *m.* **smell** *or* taste > **distinctive quality** [27]explico ~are, ~aui *or* ~ui, ~atum **to explain** [28]intersum ~esse, ~fui **to make a difference** (*impers.*) [29]reuelo ~are, ~aui, ~atum **to reveal** [30]somnio ~are, ~aui, ~atus **to dream** [31]ferme *adv.* **almost** [32]biennium ~ii *neut.* **two years** [33]nubilis ~is, ~e *adj.* **of an age suitable for marriage**

Augustine plans a retreat

6.14.24 Et multi amici agitaueramus[1] animo et conloquentes[2] ac detestantes[3] turbulentas[4] humanae uitae molestias[5] paene[6] iam firmaueramus[7] remoti[8] a turbis otiose[9] uiuere, id otium[10] sic moliti[11] ut, si quid[12]

[1]agito ~are, ~aui, ~atum **to stir up** (emotions) [2]conloquor ~qui, ~cutus **to converse** [3]detestor ~ari, ~atus **to detest** [4]turbulentus ~a, ~um *adj.* **turbulent** [5]molestia ~ae *f.* **distress** [6]paene *adv.* **practically** [7]firmo ~are, ~aui, ~atum **to confirm**; LATE **to resolve** [8]remotus ~a, ~um *adj.* **removed** [9]otiose *adv.* **at one's leisure** [10]otium ~ii *neut.* **leisure** [11]molio ~ire, ~itus **to bring about** [12]'si quid' **whatever**

habere possemus, conferremus[13] in medium[14] unamque rem familiarem[15] conflaremus[16] ex omnibus, ut per amicitiae[17] sinceritatem[18] non esset aliud huius et aliud illius, sed quod ex cunctis fieret unum et uniuersum singulorum esset et omnia omnium, cum uideremur nobis esse posse decem[19] ferme[20] homines in eadem societate[21] essentque inter nos praediuites,[22] Romanianus maxime communiceps[23] noster, quem tunc graues aestus[24] negotiorum[25] suorum ad comitatum[26] attraxerant,[27] ab ineunte aetate[28] mihi familiarissimus. qui maxime instabat[29] huic rei et magnam in suadendo[30] habebat auctoritatem, quod ampla[31] res eius multum ceteris anteibat.[32] et placuerat nobis ut bini[33] annui[34] tamquam magistratus[35] omnia necessaria[36] curarent ceteris quietis.[37]

Sed posteaquam[38] coepit cogitari utrum hoc mulierculae[39] sinerent, quas et alii nostrum iam habebant et nos habere uolebamus, totum illud placitum, quod bene formabamus, dissiluit[40] in manibus atque confractum[41] et abiectum[42] est. inde ad suspiria[43] et gemitus[44] et gressus[45] ad sequendas *latas[46] et tritas[47] uias saeculi* (Mt 7:13), quoniam *multae cogitationes erant in corde* (Prov 19:21) nostro, *consilium autem tuum manet in aeternum* (Ps 32:11). ex quo consilio deridebas[48] nostra et tua praeparabas[49] nobis, *daturus escam[50] in opportunitate[51]* et *aperturus manum atque impleturus animas nostras benedictione[52]* (Ps 144:15–16).

---

[13]confero ~rre, contuli, conlatum **to contribute** [14]'in medium' **to be held in common** [15]'rem familiarem' **household property** [16]conflo ~are, ~aui, ~atum **to make by combining** [17]amicitia ~ae *f.* **friendship** [18]sinceritas ~atis *f.* **sincerity** [19]decem *indecl. adj.* **ten** [20]ferme *adv.* **about** [21]societas ~atis *f.* **community** [22]praediues ~itis *adj.* **outstandingly rich** [23]communiceps ~cipis *m.* **fellow townsman** [24]aestus ~us *m.* **anxiety** [25]negotium ~ii *neut.* **business interests** (pl.) [26]comitatus ~us *m.* retinue; LATE **imperial court** [27]attraho ~here, ~xi, ~ctum **to compel to come** [28]'ineunte aetate' beginning of life, i.e., **childhood** [29]insto ~are, ~iti **to insist** [30]suadeo ~dere, ~si, ~sum **to urge** [31]amplus ~a, ~um *adj.* **large** [32]anteeo ~ire, ~iui, ~itum **to surpass** [33]bini ~ae, ~a *adj.* **a pair** [34]annuus ~a, ~um *adj.* **annual** [35]magistratus ~us *m.* **officer** [36]necessarius ~a, ~um *adj.* **necessary** [37]quiesco ~ere, quieui, quietum **to be undisturbed** [38]posteaquam *conj.* **afterwards** [39]muliercula ~ae *f.* **little woman** [40]dissilio ~ire, ~ui **to burst apart** [41]confringo ~ingere, ~egi, ~actum **to undo** [42]abicio ~cere, ~eci, ~ectum **to throw away** [43]suspirium ~ii *neut.* **sigh** (of longing) [44]gemitus ~us *m.* **groaning** [45]gressus ~us *m.* **step** [46]latus ~a, ~um *adj.* **broad** [47]tritus ~a, ~um *adj.* **well-trodden** [48]derideo ~dere, ~si, ~sum **to laugh at** [49]praeparo ~are, ~aui, ~atum **to prepare** [50]esca ~ae *f.* **food** [51]opportunitas ~atis *f.* **in season** [52]benedictio ~onis *f.* ECCL **blessing**

The unnamed partner sent home

6.15.25 Interea[1] *mea peccata multiplicabantur*[2] (Sir 23:3), et auulsa[3] a latere meo tamquam impedimento[4] coniugii[5] cum qua cubare[6] solitus eram, cor, ubi adhaerebat,[7] concisum[8] et uulneratum[9] mihi erat et trahebat[10] sanguinem. et illa in Africam redierat, uouens[11] tibi alium se uirum nescituram, relicto apud me naturali[12] ex illa filio meo. at ego infelix[13] nec feminae imitator,[14] dilationis[15] impatiens,[16] tamquam post biennium[17] accepturus eam quam petebam, quia non amator[18] coniugii sed libidinis seruus eram, procuraui[19] aliam, non utique coniugem, quo tamquam sustentaretur[20] et perduceretur[21] uel integer[22] uel auctior[23] morbus[24] animae meae satellitio[25] perdurantis[26] consuetudinis in regnum uxorium.[27]

Nec sanabatur uulnus illud meum quod prioris praecisione[28] factum erat, sed post feruorem[29] doloremque acerrimum[30] putrescebat,[31] et quasi frigidius[32] sed desperatius[33] dolebat.

[1]interea *adv.* **meanwhile** [2]multiplico ~are, ~aui, ~atum **to multiply** [3]auello ~ellere, ~elli ~ulsum **to tear away** [4]impedimentum ~i *neut.* **obstacle** [5]coniugium ~ii *neut.* **marriage** [6]cubo ~are, ~ui, ~itum **to lie with** (for sexual intercourse) [7]adhaereo ~rere, ~si, ~sum **to cling to** [8]concido ~dere, ~di, ~sum **to cut to pieces** [9]uulnero ~are, ~aui, ~atum **to wound** [10]traho ~here, ~xi, ~ctum to drag > **to leave as a trail** [11]uoueo ~uere, uoui, uotum **to vow** [12]naturalis ~is, ~e *adj.* **natural-born** [13]infelix ~icis *adj.* **unhappy** [14]imitator ~oris *m.* **imitator** [15]dilatio ~onis *f.* **delay** [16]impatiens ~ntis *adj.* **impatient (of)** [17]biennium ~ii *neut.* **two years** [18]amator ~oris *m.* **lover** [19]procuro ~are, ~aui, ~atum to take care of; LATE **to procure** [20]sustento ~are, ~aui, ~atum **to sustain** [21]perduco ~cere, ~xi, ~ctum **to extend** [22]integer ~gra, ~grum *adj.* **unimpaired** [23]auctus ~a, ~um *adj.* **intensified** [24]morbus ~i *m.* **disease** [25]satellitium ~ii *neut.* LATE **support** *or* **escort** [26]perduro ~are, ~aui, ~atum **to persist** [27]uxorius ~a, ~um *adj.* **wifely** [28]praecisio ~onis *f.* **amputation** [29]feruor ~oris *m.* **fever** [30]acer acris, acre *adj.* **sharp** > **acute** [31]putresco ~ere **to putrefy** [32]frigidus ~a, ~um *adj.* **numbing** [33]desperate *adv.* AUG **desperately**

Cicero's *de Finibus Bonorum et Malorum*

6.16.26 Tibi laus, tibi gloria, fons misericordiarum! ego fiebam miserior et tu propinquior.[1] aderat iam iamque[2] dextera tua raptura me de caeno[3] et ablutura,[4] et ignorabam. nec me reuocabat[5] a profundiore[6] uoluptatum carnalium[7] gurgite[8] nisi metus mortis et futuri iudicii

[1]propinquus ~a, ~um *adj.* **near** [2]'iam iamque' **at any time now** [3]caenum ~i *neut.* **slime** [4]abluo ~uere, ~ui, ~utum **to wash off** [5]reuoco ~are, ~aui, ~atum **to call upon to return** [6]profundus ~a, ~um *adj.* **very deep** [7]carnalis ~is, ~e *adj.* ECCL **carnal** [8]gurges ~itis *m.* **whirlpool**

tui, qui per uarias[9] quidem opiniones[10] numquam tamen recessit de pectore meo. et disputabam[11] cum amicis meis Alypio et Nebridio *de Finibus Bonorum et Malorum* (Fin. 1.40): Epicurum accepturum fuisse palmam[12] in animo meo, nisi ego credidissem post mortem restare[13] animae uitam et tractus[14] meritorum,[15] quod Epicurus credere noluit. et quaerebam si essemus immortales[16] et in perpetua[17] corporis uoluptate sine ullo amissionis[18] terrore[19] uiueremus, cur non essemus beati aut quid aliud quaereremus, nesciens idipsum[20] ad magnam miseriam pertinere[21] quod ita demersus[22] et caecus[23] cogitare non possem lumen honestatis[24] et gratis amplectendae[25] pulchritudinis[26] quam non uidet oculus carnis, et uidetur ex intimo.[27] nec considerabam miser ex qua uena[28] mihi manaret[29] quod ista ipsa foeda[30] tamen cum amicis dulciter[31] conferebam,[32] nec esse sine amicis poteram beatus, etiam secundum sensum quem tunc habebam in quantalibet[33] affluentia[34] carnalium uoluptatum. quos utique amicos gratis diligebam uicissimque[35] ab eis me diligi gratis sentiebam.

O tortuosas[36] uias! uae[37] animae audaci[38] quae sperauit,[39] si a te recessisset, se aliquid melius habituram! uersa et reuersa[40] in tergum et in latera et in uentrem,[41] et dura sunt omnia, et tu solus requies.[42] et ecce ades et liberas[43] a miserabilibus[44] erroribus et constituis[45] nos in uia tua et consolaris[46] et dicis: *Currite*[47] (1 Cor 9:24), *ego feram et ego perducam*[48] *et ibi ego feram* (Isa 46:4).

---

[9]uarius ~a, ~um *adj.* **various** [10]opinio ~onis *f.* **belief** [11]disputo ~are, ~aui, ~atum **to reason out** [12]palma ~ae *f.* **palm** (awarded in a particular contest) [13]resto ~are, ~iti **to remain** [14]tractus ~us *m.* **continuation** [15]meritum ~i *neut.* **due reward** [16]immortalis ~is, ~e *adj.* **immortal** [17]perpetuus ~a, ~um *adj.* **perpetual** [18]amissio ~onis *f.* **loss** [19]terror ~oris *m.* **terror** [20]idipsum *pron.* ECCL **the very thing** [21]pertineo ~ere, ~ui **to pertain to** [22]demergo ~gere, ~si, ~sum **to submerge** [23]caecus ~a, ~um *adj.* **blind** [24]honestas ~atis *f.* **excellence** [25]amplector ~cti, ~xus **to embrace** [26]pulchritudo ~inis *f.* **beauty** [27]intimus ~a, ~um *superl. adj.* **inmost self** (*neut.* as noun) [28]uena ~ae *f.* **vein** [29]mano ~are, ~aui **to flow** [30]foedus ~a, ~um *adj.* **foul** [31]dulciter *adv.* **delightfully** [32]confero ~rre, contuli, conlatum **to discuss** [33]quantuslibet ~alibet, ~umlibet *adj.* **however great** [34]affluentia ~ae *f.* **extravagance** [35]uicissim *adv.* **in turn** [36]tortuosus ~a, ~um *adj.* **winding** [37]uae *interj.* [a cry of pain, anger, sorrow] **woe!** [38]audax ~acis *adj.* **audacious** [39]spero ~are, ~aui, ~atum **to hope** [40]reuertor, reuor- ~ti, ~sus **to turn over** [41]uenter ~tris *m.* **stomach** [42]requies ~etis *f.* **rest** [43]libero ~are, ~aui, ~atum **to free** (a slave) [44]miserabilis ~is, ~e *adj.* **miserable** [45]constituo ~uere, ~ui, ~utum **to establish** [46]consolor ~ari, ~atus **to comfort** [47]curro ~rere, cucurri, ~sum **to run** [48]perduco ~cere, ~xi, ~ctum **to bring through**

7

NEOPLATONISM AND THE INCARNATION

Milan, 385–386

Corporeal ideas of God

7.1.1 Iam mortua erat adulescentia[1] mea mala et nefanda,[2] et ibam in iuuentutem,[3] quanto aetate maior, tanto uanitate turpior, qui cogitare aliquid substantiae nisi tale non poteram, quale per hos oculos uideri solet. non te cogitabam, Deus, in figura[4] corporis humani; ex quo audire aliquid de sapientia coepi, semper hoc fugi et gaudebam me hoc repperisse[5] in fide spiritalis matris nostrae, Catholicae tuae, sed quid te aliud cogitarem non occurrebat. et conabar cogitare te, homo et talis homo, summum et *solum et uerum Deum* (Jn 17:3).

Et te incorruptibilem[6] et inuiolabilem[7] et incommutabilem totis medullis[8] credebam, quia nesciens unde et quomodo, plane[9] tamen uidebam et certus eram id quod corrumpi[10] potest deterius[11] esse quam id quod non potest, et quod uiolari[12] non potest incunctanter[13] praeponebam[14] uiolabili,[15] et quod nullam patitur mutationem[16] melius esse

---

[1]adulescentia ~ae *f.* **young adulthood** (age 16–30) [2]nefandus ~a, ~um *adj.* **wicked** [3]iuuentus ~utis *f.* **early manhood** [4]figura ~ae *f.* **form** [5]reperio ~ire, repperi, ~tum **to discover** [6]incorruptibilis ~is, ~e *adj.* ECCL **incorruptible** [7]inuiolabilis ~is, ~e *adj.* **inviolable** [8]medulla ~ae *f.* **depths of the heart** [9]plane *adv.* **plainly** [10]corrumpo ~umpere, ~upi, ~uptum **to corrupt** [11]deterior ~ior, ~ius *compar. adj.* **worse** [12]uiolo ~are, ~aui, ~atum **to injure** [13]incunctanter *adv.* **without hesitation** [14]praepono ~onere, ~osui, ~ositum **to prefer** x (acc.) **to** y (dat.) [15]uiolabilis ~is, ~e *adj.* **susceptible to injury** [16]mutatio ~onis *f.* **change**

quam id quod mutari potest. clamabat uiolenter[17] cor meum aduersus omnia phantasmata[18] mea, et hoc uno ictu[19] conabar abigere[20] *circumuolantem*[21] *turbam immunditiae*[22] (Aen. 3.233) ab acie mentis[23] meae, et uix dimota[24] *in ictu oculi*[25] (1 Cor 15:52), ecce conglobata[26] rursus aderat et inruebat[27] in aspectum[28] meum et obnubilabat[29] eum, ut quamuis non forma humani corporis, corporeum tamen aliquid cogitare cogerer per spatia locorum, siue infusum[30] mundo siue etiam extra[31] mundum per infinita diffusum,[32] etiam ipsum incorruptibile et inuiolabile et incommutabile quod corruptibili[33] et uiolabili et commutabili[34] praeponebam, quoniam quidquid priuabam[35] spatiis talibus nihil mihi esse uidebatur, sed prorsus[36] nihil, ne inane[37] quidem, tamquam si corpus auferatur loco et maneat locus omni corpore uacuatus[38] et terreno[39] et humido[40] et aerio[41] et caelesti,[42] sed tamen sit locus inanis tamquam spatiosum[43] nihil.

[17]uiolenter *adv.* **with violent feelings** [18]phantasma ~àtis *neut.* phantom; LATE **figment of the imagination** [19]ictus ~us *m.* **blow** (from a fist or weapon) [20]abigo ~igere, ~egi, ~actum **to drive away** [21]circumuolo ~are, ~aui **to fly encircling** [22]immunditia ~ae *f.* **uncleanness** [23]'acie mentis' **gaze of the mind** (phil.) [24]dimoueo ~ouere, ~oui, ~otum **to disperse** [25]'ictu oculi' ECCL **twinkling of an eye** [26]conglobo ~are, ~aui, ~atum **to crowd together** [27]inruo ~uere, ~ui **to charge at with hostile intent** [28]aspectus ~us *m.* **sight** [29]obnubilo ~are, ~aui, ~atum **to becloud** [30]infundo ~undere, ~udi, ~usum **to infuse** [31]extra *prep. acc.* **beyond** [32]diffundo ~undere, ~udi, ~usum **to diffuse** [33]corruptibilis ~is ~e *adj.* ECCL **corruptible** [34]commutabilis ~is, ~e *adj.* **changeable** [35]priuo ~are, ~aui, ~atum **to deprive (of)** [36]prorsus *adv.* **entirely** [37]inane ~is *neut.* **emptiness** [38]uacuo ~are, ~aui, ~atum **to empty** [39]terrenus ~a, ~um *adj.* **of the earth** [40]humidus ~a, ~um *adj.* **of water** [41]aerius ~ia, ~ium *adj.* **of air** [42]caelestis ~is, ~e *adj.* **of heaven** [43]spatiosus ~a, ~um *adj.* **spacious**

Incorporeality must be nothing

7.1.2 Ego itaque *incrassatus*[1] *corde* (Mt 13:15) nec mihimet ipsi uel ipse conspicuus,[2] quidquid non per aliquanta[3] spatia tenderetur[4] uel diffunderetur[5] uel conglobaretur[6] uel tumeret[7] uel tale aliquid caperet aut capere posset, nihil prorsus[8] esse arbitrabar. per quales enim formas ire solent oculi mei, per tales imagines ibat cor meum, nec uidebam

[1]incrasso ~are, ~aui, ~atus ECCL **to become dull (unfeeling)** [2]conspicuus ~a, ~um *adj.* conspicuous; LATE **understandable** [3]aliquantus ~a, ~um *adj.* **certain amount of** [4]tendo ~dere, tetendi, ~tum or ~sum **to extend** [5]diffundo ~undere, ~udi, ~usum **to diffuse** [6]conglobo ~are, ~aui, ~atum **to form into a mass** [7]tumeo ~ere, ~ui **to distend** [8]prorsus *adv.* **absolutely**

hanc eandem intentionem[9] qua illas ipsas imagines formabam non esse tale aliquid, quae tamen ipsas non formaret nisi esset magnum aliquid.

Ita etiam te, Vita uitae meae, grandem per infinita spatia undique[10] cogitabam penetrare[11] totam mundi molem et extra[12] eam quaquauersum[13] per immensa[14] sine termine,[15] ut haberet te terra, haberet caelum, haberent omnia et illa finirentur in te, tu autem nusquam.[16] sicut autem luci solis non obsisteret[17] aeris[18] corpus, aeris huius qui supra[19] terram est, quominus[20] per eum traiceretur[21] penetrans eum, non dirrumpendo[22] aut concidendo[23] sed implendo eum totum, sic tibi putabam non solum caeli et aeris et maris sed etiam terrae corpus peruium[24] et ex omnibus maximis minimisque[25] partibus penetrabile[26] ad capiendam praesentiam[27] tuam, occulta inspiratione[28] intrinsecus[29] et extrinsecus[30] administrantem[31] omnia quae creasti.

Ita suspicabar,[32] quia cogitare aliud non poteram; nam falsum erat. illo enim modo maior pars terrae maiorem tui partem haberet et minorem minor, atque ita te plena essent omnia ut amplius tui caperet elephanti[33] corpus quam passeris,[34] quo esset isto grandius grandioremque occuparet locum, atque ita frustatim[35] partibus mundi magnis magnas, breuibus breues partes tuas praesentes faceres. non est autem ita, sed nondum *inluminaueras tenebras meas* (Ps 17:29).

---

[9]intentio ~onis *f.* **mental effort** [10]undique *adv.* **from all sides** [11]penetro ~are, ~aui, ~atum **to penetrate** [12]extra *prep.* **beyond** [13]quaquauersum *adv.* LATE **on all sides** [14]immensus ~a, ~um *adj.* **immeasurable** [15]termen ~inis *neut.* **limit** [16]nusquam *adv.* **never** [17]obsisto ~sistere, ~stiti, ~stitum **to block** (w. dat) [18]aer aeris *m.* **air** [19]supra *prep.* **above** [20]quominus *conj.* **that not** (after verb of preventing) [21]traicio ~icere, ~ieci, ~iectum **to travel through** [22]dirrumpo ~umpere, ~upi, ~uptum **to break apart** [23]concido ~ere, ~i **to split** [24]peruiam (est) *adv.* **there is a way through** [25]minimus ~a, ~um *superl. adj.* **smallest** [26]penetrabilis ~is, ~e *adj.* **penetrable** [27]praesentia ~ae *f.* **presence** [28]inspiratio ~onis *f.* LATE **breathing in**; ECCL **inspiration** [29]intrinsecus *adv.* **internally** [30]extrinsecus *adv.* **externally** [31]administro ~are, ~aui, ~atum **to operate** [32]suspicor ~ari, ~atus **to guess** [33]elephantus ~nti *m.* **elephant** [34]passer ~eris *m.* **sparrow** [35]frustatim *adv.* **piecemeal**

Nebridius' silver bullet

7.2.3 Sat erat mihi, Domine, aduersus[1] illos deceptos[2] deceptores[3] et loquaces[4] mutos,[5] quoniam non ex eis sonabat uerbum tuum —

---

[1]aduersus ~a, ~um *adj.* **contrary to** [2]decipio ~ipere, ~epi, ~eptum **to deceive** [3]deceptor ~oris *m.* **deceiver** [4]loquax ~acis *adj.* **loquacious** [5]mutus ~a, ~um *adj.* **mute** (*neut. pl.* as noun)

sat erat ergo illud quod iam diu[6] ab usque Carthagine a Nebridio proponi[7] solebat et omnes qui audieramus concussi[8] sumus: quid erat tibi factura nescio qua gens tenebrarum, quam ex aduersa mole solent opponere,[9] si tu cum ea pugnare[10] noluisses? si enim responderetur aliquid[11] fuisse nocituram,[12] uiolabilis[13] tu et corruptibilis[14] fores. si autem nihil ea nocere potuisse diceretur, nulla afferretur[15] causa pugnandi, et ita pugnandi ut quaedam portio[16] tua et membrum tuum uel proles[17] de ipsa substantia tua misceretur aduersis potestatibus et non a te creatis naturis, atque in tantum ab eis corrumperetur[18] et commutaretur[19] in deterius[20] ut a beatitudine[21] in miseriam uerteretur et indigeret[22] auxilio[23] quo erui[24] purgarique[25] posset, et hanc esse animam cui tuus Sermo seruienti liber[26] et contaminatae[27] purus[28] et corruptae[29] integer[30] subueniret,[31] sed et ipse corruptibilis, quia ex una eademque substantia.

Itaque si te, quidquid es, id est substantiam tuam qua es, incorruptibilem[32] dicerent, falsa esse illa omnia et exsecrabilia;[33] si autem corruptibilem, idipsum[34] iam falsum et prima uoce[35] abominandum.[36] sat erat ergo istuc[37] aduersus eos omni modo euomendos[38] a pressura pectoris, quia non habebant qua exirent[39] sine horribili[40] sacrilegio[41] cordis et linguae sentiendo de te ista et loquendo.

---

[6]'iam diu' **for a long time back then** [7]propono ~onere, ~osui, ~ositum **to propose** [8]concutio ~tere, ~ssi, ~ssum **to shock** [9]oppono ~onere, ~osui, ~ositum **to oppose** [10]pugno ~are, ~aui, ~atum **to fight** [11]aliquid *adv.* **somewhat** [12]noceo ~ere, ~ui, ~itum **to injure** [13]uiolabilis ~is, ~e *adj.* **able to be wounded** [14]corruptibilis ~is ~e *adj.* ECCL **corruptible** [15]affero ~rre, attuli, allatum **to bring (with hostile intent)** [16]portio ~onis *f.* **part** [17]proles ~is *f.* **offspring** [18]corrumpo ~umpere, ~upi, ~uptum **to corrupt** [19]commuto ~are, ~aui, ~atum **to change** [20]deterior ~ior, ~ius *compar. adj.* **worse** [21]beatitudo ~inis *f.* **beatitude** [22]indigeo ~ere, ~ui **to need** [23]auxilium ~ii *neut.* **help** [24]eruo ~uere, ~ui, ~utum **to pluck out**; ECCL **to rescue** [25]purgo ~are, ~aui, ~atum **to purge** [26]liber ~era, ~erum *adj.* **free** [27]contaminatus ~a, ~um *adj.* **polluted** [28]purus ~a, ~um *adj.* **pure** [29]corruptus ~a, ~um *adj.* **corrupt** [30]integer ~gra, ~grum *adj.* **intact** [31]subuenio ~enire, ~eni, ~entum **to bring help** (w. dat) [32]incorruptibilis ~is, ~e *adj.* ECCL **incorruptible** [33]execrabilis ~is, ~e *adj.* **detestable** [34]idipsum *pron.* ECCL **the thing itself** [35]'prima uoce' **when first spoken aloud** [36]abominor ~ari, ~atus **to abhor** [37]istic ~aec, ~uc *pron.* **that just mentioned** [38]euomo ~ere, ~ui, ~itum **to vomit out** (fig.) [39]exeo ~ire, ~iui or ~ii, ~itum **to escape** [40]horribilis ~is, ~e *adj.* **horrible** [41]sacrilegium ~ii *neut.* **sacrilege**

God necessarily immutable

7.3.4 Sed et ego adhuc, quamuis incontaminabilem[1] et inconuertibilem[2] et nulla ex parte mutabilem dicerem firmeque[3] sentirem Deum nostrum, Deum uerum, qui fecisti non solum animas nostras sed etiam corpora, nec tantum nostras animas et corpora sed omnes et omnia, non tenebam explicatam[4] et enodatam[5] causam mali. quaecumque tamen esset, sic eam quaerendam uidebam, ut non per illam constringerer[6] Deum incommutabilem mutabilem credere, ne ipse fierem quod quaerebam. itaque securus[7] eam quaerebam, et certus non esse uerum quod illi dicerent quos toto animo fugiebam, quia uidebam quaerendo unde *malum repletos*[8] *malitia*[9] (Rom 1:29), qua[10] opinarentur[11] tuam potius substantiam male pati[12] quam suam male facere.[13]

[1]incontaminabilis ~is, ~e *adj.* ECCL **undefilable** [2]inconuertibilis ~is, ~e *adj.* ECCL **unchangeable** [3]firme *adv.* **firmly** [4]explico ~are, ~aui, ~atum **to explain** [5]enodo ~are, ~aui, ~atum **to unravel** [6]constringo ~ngere, ~nxi, ~ctum **to constrain** [7]securus ~a, ~um *adj.* **untroubled** [8]repletus ~a, ~um *adj.* **full of** (w. abl.) [9]malitia ~ae *f.* **wicked character** [10]qua *adv.* **inasmuch as** [11]opinor ~ari, ~atus **to think** [12]'male pati' **to be subject to evil** [13]'male facere' **to do what is evil**

Free will the cause of evil?

7.3.5 Et intendebam ut cernerem quod audiebam, liberum[1] uoluntatis arbitrium[2] causam esse ut male faceremus[3] *et rectum*[4] *iudicium tuum* (Ps 118:137) ut pateremur, et eam liquidam[5] cernere non ualebam. itaque aciem mentis[6] de profundo[7] educere[8] conatus mergebar[9] iterum,[10] et saepe conatus mergebar iterum atque iterum. subleuabat[11] enim me in lucem tuam quod tam sciebam me habere uoluntatem quam me uiuere. itaque cum aliquid uellem aut nollem, non alium quam me uelle ac nolle certissimus eram, et ibi esse causam peccati mei iam iamque[12] animaduertebam.[13] quod autem inuitus[14] facerem, pati me potius quam

[1]liber ~era, ~erum *adj.* **free** [2]arbitrium ~ii *neut.* **choice** [3]'male faceremus' **we act wickedly** [4]rectus ~a, ~um *adj.* **right** [5]liquidus ~a, ~um *adj.* **clear** [6]'aciem mentis' **gaze of the mind** (phil.) [7]profundum ~i *neut.* **depths** [8]educo ~cere, ~xi, ~ctum **to raise** [9]mergo ~gere, ~si, ~sum **to sink** [10]iterum *adv.* **again** [11]subleuo ~are, ~aui, ~atum **to assist to rise** [12]'iam iamque' **now all but—** [13]animaduerto ~tere, ~ti, ~sum **to become aware** [14]inuitus ~a, ~um *adj.* **unwilling**

facere uidebam, et id non culpam[15] sed poenam esse iudicabam, qua me non iniuste[16] plecti[17] te iustum cogitans cito[18] fatebar.[19] sed rursus dicebam, "Quis fecit me? nonne Deus meus, non tantum bonus sed ipsum Bonum? unde igitur mihi male uelle et bene nolle? ut esset cur iuste[20] poenas luerem?[21] quis in me hoc posuit et inseuit[22] mihi plantarium[23] amaritudinis,[24] cum totus fierem a dulcissimo Deo meo? si diabolus[25] auctor,[26] unde ipse diabolus? quod si et ipse peruersa[27] uoluntate ex bono angelo diabolus factus est, unde et in ipso uoluntas mala qua diabolus fieret, quando totus angelus a conditore[28] optimo factus esset?"

His cogitationibus deprimebar[29] iterum et suffocabar,[30] sed non usque ad illum infernum[31] subducebar[32] erroris ubi nemo tibi confitetur, dum tu potius mala pati quam homo facere putatur.

[15]culpa ~ae *f.* **fault** [16]iniuste *adv.* **unjustly** [17]plecto ~ere **to punish** [18]cito *adv.* **quickly** [19]fateor ~eri, fassus **to confess** [20]iuste *adv.* **justly** [21]luo ~ere, ~i **to suffer a punishment** [22]insero ~erere, ~eui, ~itum **to implant** [23]plantarium ~ii *neut.* **cuttings** (hort.) [24]amaritudo ~inis *f.* **bitterness** [25]diabolus ~i *m.* ECCL **the Devil** [26]auctor ~oris *m.* **originator** [27]peruersus ~a, ~um *adj.* **perverse** [28]conditor ~oris *m.* founder; ECCL **creator** [29]deprimo ~imere, ~essi, ~essum **to be pulled down by force** (pass.) [30]suffoco ~are, ~aui, ~atum to suffocate > **to drown** [31]infernus ~i *m.* ECCL **Hell** [32]subduco ~cere, ~xi, ~ctum **to pull down from below**

Indestructible necessarily superior to destructible

7.4.6 Sic enim nitebar[1] inuenire cetera, ut iam inueneram melius esse incorruptibile[2] quam corruptibile,[3] et ideo te, quidquid esses, esse incorruptibilem confitebar. neque enim ulla anima umquam potuit poteritue cogitare aliquid quod sit te melius, qui summum et optimum bonum es. cum autem uerissime atque certissime[4] incorruptibile corruptibili praeponatur,[5] sicut iam ego praeponebam, poteram iam cogitatione aliquid attingere[6] quod esset melius Deo meo, nisi tu esses incorruptibilis.

Ubi igitur uidebam incorruptibile corruptibili esse praeferendum,[7] ibi te quaerere debebam atque inde aduertere[8] ubi sit malum, id est unde

[1]nitor ~ti, ~xus or ~sus **to direct one's efforts** [2]incorruptibilis ~is, ~e *adj.* ECCL **incorruptible** [3]corruptibilis ~is ~e *adj.* ECCL **corruptible** [4]certo *adv.* **certainly** [5]praepono ~onere, ~osui, ~ositum **to prefer** x (acc.) **to** y (dat.) [6]attingo ~tingere, ~tigi, ~tactum to touch > **'put one's finger on'** (fig.) [7]praefero ~ferre, ~tuli, ~latum **to give precedence to** x (acc.) **over** y (dat.) [8]aduerto ~tere, ~ti, ~sum to turn towards > **to ascertain**

sit ipsa corruptio,[9] qua uiolari[10] substantia tua nullo modo potest. nullo enim prorsus[11] modo uiolat corruptio Deum nostrum, nulla uoluntate, nulla necessitate,[12] nullo improuiso[13] casu, quoniam ipse est Deus, et quod sibi uult bonum est, et ipse est idem bonum; corrumpi[14] autem non est bonum. nec cogeris inuitus[15] ad aliquid, quia uoluntas tua non est maior quam potentia[16] tua. esset autem maior, si te ipso tu ipse maior esses: uoluntas enim et potentia Dei Deus ipse est. et quid improuisum tibi, qui nosti omnia? et nulla natura est nisi quia nosti eam. et ut quid[17] multa dicimus cur non sit corruptibilis substantia quae Deus est, quando, si hoc esset, non esset Deus?

[9]corruptio ~onis *f.* **corruption** [10]uiolo ~are, ~aui, ~atum **to violate** [11]prorsus *adv.* **absolutely** [12]necessitas ~atis *f.* **necessity** [13]improuisus ~a, ~um *adj.* **unforeseen** [14]corrumpo ~umpere, ~upi, ~uptum **to corrupt** [15]inuitus ~a, ~um *adj.* **unwilling** [16]potentia ~ae *f.* **power** [17]'ut quid' ECCL = quid (*adv.*) **why?**

Where does evil come from?

7.5.7 Et quaerebam unde malum, et male[1] quaerebam, et in ipsa inquisitione[2] mea non uidebam malum. et constituebam[3] *in conspectu* spiritus *mei* (Ps 15:8) uniuersam creaturam, quidquid in ea cernere possumus, sicuti est terra et mare et aer[4] et sidera et arbores et animalia[5] mortalia,[6] et quidquid in ea non uidemus, sicut firmamentum caeli insuper[7] et omnes angelos et cuncta spiritalia eius, sed etiam ipsa, quasi corpora essent, locis et locis ordinauit[8] imaginatio[9] mea. et feci unam massam[10] grandem distinctam[11] generibus corporum, creaturam tuam, siue re uera[12] quae corpora erant, siue quae ipse pro spiritibus finxeram,[13] et eam feci grandem, non quantum erat, quod scire non poteram, sed quantum libuit,[14] undiqueuersum[15] sane[16] finitam, te autem, Domine, ex omni parte ambientem[17] et penetrantem[18] eam, sed usquequaque[19]

[1]male *adv.* **in an evil way** [2]inquisitio ~onis *f.* **search** [3]constituo ~uere, ~ui, ~utum **to draw up** [4]aer aeris *m.* (*f.*) **sky** [5]animal ~alis *neut.* **living creature** [6]mortalis ~is, ~e *adj.* **mortal** [7]insuper *adv.* **above** [8]ordino ~are, ~aui, ~atum **to arrange** [9]imaginatio ~onis *f.* **imagination** [10]massa ~ae *f.* **mass** [11]distinguo ~guere, ~xi, ~ctum **to distinguish** [12]'re uera' **in reality** [13]fingo ~ngere, ~nxi, ~ctum **to contrive** [14]libet ~ere, ~uit or ~itum est *impers.* **it is pleasing** [15]undiqueuersum *adv.* **on all sides** [16]sane *adv.* **certainly** [17]ambio ~ire, ~iui, ~itum **to surround** [18]penetro ~are, ~aui, ~atum **to penetrate** [19]usquequaque *adv.* **in every possible respect**

infinitum, tamquam si mare esset ubique[20] et undique[21] per immensa[22] infinitum solum mare et haberet intra[23] se spongiam[24] quamlibet[25] magnam, sed finitam tamen, plena esset utique spongia illa ex omni sua parte ex immenso mari.

Sic creaturam tuam finitam te infinito plenam putabam et dicebam, "Ecce Deus et ecce quae creauit Deus, et bonus Deus atque his ualidissime[26] longissimeque praestantior;[27] sed tamen bonus bona creauit, et ecce quomodo ambit atque implet ea. ubi ergo malum et unde et qua[28] huc inrepsit?[29] quae radix[30] eius et quod semen[31] eius? an omnino non est? cur ergo timemus et cauemus[32] quod non est? aut si inaniter[33] timemus, certe uel timor[34] ipse malum est, quo incassum[35] stimulatur[36] et excruciatur[37] cor, et tanto grauius malum, quanto non est, quod timeamus, et timemus. idcirco[38] aut est malum quod timemus, aut hoc malum est quia timemus. unde est igitur, quoniam Deus fecit haec omnia bonus bona? maius quidem et summum bonum minora fecit bona, sed tamen et creans et *creata bona sunt omnia* (Gen 1:31). unde est malum? an unde fecit ea, materies aliqua mala erat et formauit atque ordinauit eam, sed reliquit aliquid in illa quod in bonum non conuerteret? cur et hoc? an impotens[39] erat totam uertere et commutare,[40] ut nihil mali remaneret,[41] cum sit omnipotens?[42] postremo[43] cur inde aliquid facere uoluit ac non potius eadem omnipotentia[44] fecit, ut nulla esset omnino? aut uero exsistere[45] poterat contra eius uoluntatem? aut si aeterna erat, cur tam diu per infinita retro[46] spatia temporum sic eam siuit esse ac tanto post placuit aliquid ex ea facere? aut iam, si aliquid subito[47] uoluit agere, hoc potius ageret omnipotens, ut illa non esset atque ipse solus esset totum uerum et summum et infinitum bonum? aut si non erat bene, ut non aliquid boni etiam fabricaretur[48]

---

[20]ubique *adv.* **everywhere** [21]undique *adv.* **in all directions** [22]immensus ~a, ~um *adj.* **immeasurable** [23]intra *prep.* **inside** [24]spongia ~iae *f.* **sponge** [25]quamlibet *adv.* **however** [26]ualide *adv.* **powerfully** [27]praestans ~ntis *adj.* **outstanding** [28]qua *adv.* **how?** [29]inrepo ~pere, ~psi **to worm one's way in** [30]radix ~icis *f.* **root** [31]semen ~inis *neut.* **seed** [32]caueo ~ere, caui, ~tum **to guard against** [33]inaniter *adv.* **groundlessly** [34]timor ~oris *m.* **fear** [35]incassum *adv.* **to no purpose** [36]stimulo ~are, ~aui, ~atum **to goad** [37]excrucio ~are, ~aui, ~atum **to torture** [38]idcirco *adv.* **for that reason** [39]impotens ~ntis *adj.* **powerless** [40]commuto ~are, ~aui, ~atum **to change** [41]remaneo ~ere, ~si **to remain** [42]omnipotens ~ntis *adj.* **omnipotent** [43]postremo *adv.* **finally** [44]omnipotentia ~ae *f.* LATE **omnipotence** [45]exsisto ~ere, extiti **to come into being** [46]retro *adv.* **back to the beginning** [47]subito *adv.* **suddenly** [48]fabrico ~are, ~aui, ~atum **to fashion**

et conderet⁴⁹ qui bonus erat, illa sublata⁵⁰ et ad nihilum⁵¹ redacta⁵² materie quae mala erat, bonam ipse institueret⁵³ unde omnia craret? non enim esset omnipotens si condere non posset aliquid boni nisi ea quam non ipse condiderat adiuuaretur⁵⁴ materia."

Talia uoluebam⁵⁵ pectore misero, ingrauidato⁵⁶ curis mordacissimis⁵⁷ de timore mortis et non inuenta ueritate; stabiliter⁵⁸ tamen haerebat⁵⁹ in corde meo in Catholica Ecclesia fides Christi tui, *Domini et Saluatoris*⁶⁰ *nostri* (2 Pet 2:20), in multis quidem adhuc informis et praeter doctrinae normam⁶¹ fluitans,⁶² sed tamen non eam relinquebat animus, immo⁶³ in dies⁶⁴ magis magisque inbibebat.⁶⁵

⁴⁹condo ~ere, ~idi, ~itum to establish; ECCL **to create** ⁵⁰tollo ~ere, sustuli, sublatum **to take away** ⁵¹nihilum ~i *neut.* **nothing** ⁵²redigo ~igere, ~egi, ~actum **to reduce** ⁵³instituo ~uere, ~ui, ~utum **to bring into existence** ⁵⁴adiuuo ~iuuare, ~iuui, ~iutum **to help** ⁵⁵uoluo ~uere, ~ui, ~utum **to turn over in the mind** ⁵⁶ingrauido ~are, ~aui, ~atum LATE **to impregnate**; ECCL **to weigh down** ⁵⁷mordax ~acis *adj.* **biting** ⁵⁸stabiliter *adv.* **steadfastly** ⁵⁹haereo ~rere, ~si, ~sum **to cling to** ⁶⁰saluator ~oris *m.* ECCL **Savior** ⁶¹norma ~ae *f.* **norm** ⁶²fluito ~are, ~aui **to drift** ⁶³immo *particle* **rather** ⁶⁴'in dies' **as the days go by** ⁶⁵inbibo ~ere, ~i, ~itum **to drink in**

Firminus inadvertently debunks astrology

7.6.8 Iam etiam mathematicorum¹ fallaces² diuinationes³ et impia⁴ deliramenta⁵ reieceram.⁶ *confiteantur* etiam hinc tibi de intimis⁷ uisceribus⁸ animae meae *miserationes⁹ tuae* (Ps 106:8), Deus meus! tu enim, tu omnino (nam quis alius a morte omnis erroris reuocat¹⁰ nos nisi Vita quae mori nescit, et Sapientia mentes indigentes¹¹ inluminans, nullo indigens lumine, qua mundus administratur¹² usque ad arborum uolatica¹³ folia?¹⁴), tu procurasti¹⁵ peruicaciae¹⁶ meae, qua obluctatus¹⁷ sum Vindiciano acuto¹⁸ seni¹⁹ et Nebridio adulescenti²⁰ mirabilis²¹ animae, illi uehementer²² adfirmanti,²³ huic cum dubitatione²⁴ quidem aliqua

¹mathematicus ~i *m.* **astrologer** ²fallax ~acis *adj.* **deceitful** ³diuinatio ~onis *f.* **divination** (foreseeing the future) ⁴impius ~a, ~um *adj.* **impious** ⁵deliramentum ~i *neut.* **nonsense** ⁶reicio ~icere, ~ieci, ~iectum **to reject** ⁷intimus ~a, ~um *superl. adj.* **inmost** ⁸uiscus ~eris *neut.* **innermost self** ⁹miseratio ~onis *f.* **mercy** ¹⁰reuoco ~are, ~aui, ~atum **to call back** ¹¹indigeo ~ere, ~ui **to be needy** (absol.) ¹²administro ~are, ~aui, ~atum **to manage** ¹³uolaticus ~a, ~um *adj.* **flying, i.e., falling** ¹⁴folium ~ii *neut.* **leaf** ¹⁵procuro ~are, ~aui, ~atum **to take care of** ¹⁶peruicacia ~ae *f.* **obstinacy** ¹⁷obluctor ~ari, ~atus **to contend with** (w. dat.) ¹⁸acutus ~a, ~um *adj.* **shrewd** ¹⁹senex ~is, senior *m. adj.* **old man** ²⁰adulescens ~ntis *m.* **young man** ²¹mirabilis ~is, ~e *adj.* **remarkable** ²²uehementer *adv.* **with mental vigor** ²³adfirmo ~are, ~aui, ~atum **to affirm** ²⁴dubitatio ~onis *f.* **hesitation**

sed tamen crebro[25] dicenti non esse illam artem futura praeuidendi,[26] coniecturas[27] autem hominum habere saepe uim sortis[28] et multa dicendo dici pleraque[29] uentura, nescientibus eis qui dicerent sed in ea non tacendo incurrentibus[30] — procurasti[31] ergo tu hominem amicum, non quidem segnem[32] consultorem[33] mathematicorum nec eas litteras bene callentem[34] sed, ut dixi, consultorem curiosum[35] et tamen scientem aliquid quod a patre suo se audisse dicebat: quod quantum ualeret ad illius artis opinionem[36] euertendam[37] ignorabat.

Is ergo uir nomine Firminus, liberaliter[38] institutus[39] et excultus[40] eloquio,[41] cum me tamquam carissimum de quibusdam suis rebus, in quas saecularis[42] spes eius intumuerat,[43] consuleret,[44] quid mihi secundum suas quas constellationes[45] appellant uideretur, ego autem, qui iam de hac re in Nebridii sententiam flecti[46] coeperam, non quidem abnuerem[47] conicere[48] ac dicere quod nutanti[49] occurrebat, sed tamen subicerem[50] prope iam esse mihi persuasum[51] ridicula[52] illa esse et inania.[53]

Tum ille mihi narrauit patrem suum fuisse librorum talium curiosissimum et habuisse amicum aeque[54] illa simulque sectantem.[55] qui pari studio et conlatione[56] flatabant[57] in eas nugas[58] ignem cordis sui, ita ut mutorum[59] quoque animalium,[60] si quae domi parerent,[61] obseruarent[62] momenta[63] nascentium atque ad ea caeli positionem[64] notarent,[65] unde illius quasi artis experimenta[66] conligerent. itaque dicebat audisse se a patre quod, cum eundem Firminum praegnans[67] mater esset, etiam

---

[25]crebro *adv.* **repeatedly** [26]praeuideo ~idere, ~idi, ~isum **to foresee** [27]coniectura ~ae *f.* **conjecture** [28]sors ~rtis *f.* **chance** [29]plerusque ~aque, ~umque *adj.* **a great number** (as noun) [30]incurro ~rere, ~ri, ~sum **to run into** [31]procuro ~are, ~aui, ~atum to take care of; LATE **to provide** [32]segnis ~is, ~e *adj.* **lazy** [33]consultor ~oris *m.* **seeker** [34]calleo ~ere **to be skilled or experienced** [35]curiosus ~a, ~um *adj.* **curious** [36]opinio ~onis *f.* **belief** [37]euerto ~tere, ~ti, ~sum **to overthrow** [38]liberaliter *adv.* **in the liberal arts** [39]instituo ~uere, ~ui, ~utum to establish > **to train** [40]excolo ~olere, ~olui, ~ultum **to polish** [41]eloquium ~ii *neut.* **eloquence** [42]saecularis ~is, ~e *adj.* ECCL **worldly** [43]intumesco ~escere, ~ui **to rise** [44]consulo ~ere, ~ui, ~tum **to consult** [45]constellatio ~onis *f.* LATE **position of the stars at birth** [46]flecto ~ctere, ~xi, ~xum **to incline to** [47]abnueo ~ere, ~i **to decline** [48]conicio ~icere, ~ieci, ~iectum **to conjecture** [49]nuto ~are, ~aui, ~atum **to doubt** [50]subicio ~icere, ~ieci, ~iectum **to suggest an idea** [51]persuadeo ~dere, ~si, ~sum **to persuade** [52]ridiculus ~a, ~um *adj.* **ridiculous** [53]inanis ~is, ~e *adj.* **illusory** [54]aeque *adv.* **equally** [55]sector ~ari, ~atus **to pursue** [56]conlatio ~onis *f.* combination; LATE **discussion** [57]flato ~are, ~aui, ~atum LATE **to blow** [58]nugae ~arum *f. pl.* **nonsense** [59]mutus ~a, ~um *adj.* **dumb** [60]animal ~alis *neut.* **animal** [61]pario ~ere, peperi, ~tum **to give birth to** [62]obseruo ~are, ~aui, ~atum **to observe** [63]momentum ~i *neut.* **moment** [64]positio ~onis *f.* **position** [65]noto ~are, ~aui, ~atum **to mark** [66]experimentum ~i *neut.* **experiment** [67]praegnans ~ntis *adj.* **pregnant**

illius paterni[68] amici famula[69] quaedam pariter[70] utero[71] grandescebat,[72] quod latere[73] non potuit dominum, qui etiam canum[74] suarum partus[75] examinatissima[76] diligentia nosse curabat; atque ita factum esse, ut cum iste coniugis,[77] ille autem ancillae[78] dies et horas minutioresque[79] horarum articulos[80] cautissima[81] obseruatione[82] numerarent, enixae[83] essent ambae[84] simul, ita ut easdem constellationes usque ad easdem minutias[85] utrique nascenti facere cogerentur, iste filio, ille seruulo.[86]

Nam cum mulieres[87] parturire[88] coepissent, indicauerunt sibi ambo quid sua cuiusque domo ageretur, et parauerunt quos ad se inuicem[89] mitterent, simul ut natum quod parturiebatur esset cuique nuntiatum:[90] quod tamen ut continuo[91] nuntiaretur, tamquam in regno[92] suo facile effecerant.[93] atque ita qui ab alterutro[94] missi sunt tam ex paribus domorum interuallis[95] sibi obuiam[96] factos esse dicebat, ut aliam positionem siderum aliasque particulas[97] momentorum neuter[98] eorum notare sineretur. et tamen Firminus amplo[99] apud suos loco natus dealbatiores[100] uias saeculi cursitabat,[101] augebatur[102] diuitiis,[103] sublimabatur[104] honoribus, seruus autem ille conditionis[105] iugo nullatenus[106] relaxato[107] dominis seruiebat, ipso indicante qui nouerat eum.

---

[68]paternus ~a, ~um *adj.* father's [69]famula ~ae *f.* female slave [70]pariter *adv.* at the same time [71]uterum ~i *neut.* womb [72]grandesco ~ere to swell in size [73]lateo ~ere, ~ui to hide [74]canis, ~es ~is *m.* dog [75]partus ~us *m.* giving birth [76]examinatus ~a, ~um *ppl. adj.* LATE scrupulous [77]coniugium ~ii *neut.* wife [78]ancilla ~ae *f.* handmaid [79]minutus ~a, ~um *adj.* short (in length) [80]articulus ~i *m.* point of time [81]cautus ~a, ~um *adj.* careful [82]obseruatio ~onis *f.* observation [83]enitor ~ti, ~xus to give birth [84]ambo ~ae, ~o *pl. pron.* both [85]minutia ~ae *f.* smallness; LATE minutiae [86]seruulus ~i *m.* (dimin.) little slave [87]mulier ~eris *f.* woman [88]parturio ~ire, ~iui to be in labor (giving birth) [89]'se inuicem' to each other [90]nuntio ~are, ~aui, ~atum to report [91]continuo *adv.* without delay [92]regnum ~i *neut.* dominion > place (domain) [93]efficio ~icere, ~eci, ~ectum to bring about [94]alteruter ~tra, ~trum *adj.* one or the other [95]interuallum ~i *neut.* distance [96]obuiam *adv.* so as to meet [97]particula ~ae *f.* small part [98]neuter ~tra, ~trum *adj.* neither [99]amplus ~a, ~um *adj.* distinguished [100]dealbatus ~a, ~um *ppl. adj.* LATE whitewashed [101]cursito ~are, ~aui to run about [102]augeo ~gere, ~xi, ~ctum to increase [103]diuitiae ~arum *f. pl.* wealth [104]sublimo ~are, ~aui, ~atum to elevate to a position [105]condicio ~onis *f.* condition i.e., plight [106]nullatenus *adv.* LATE in no way [107]relaxo ~are, ~aui, ~atum to relax

One horoscope, two fates

7.6.9 His itaque auditis et creditis (talis quippe narrauerat) omnis illa reluctatio[1] mea resoluta[2] concidit,[3] et primo[4] Firminum ipsum conatus sum ab illa curiositate[5] reuocare,[6] cum dicerem, constellationibus[7] eius inspectis[8] ut uera pronuntiarem,[9] debuisse me utique uidere ibi parentes inter suos esse primarios,[10] nobilem familiam[11] propriae[12] ciuitatis, natales[13] ingenuos,[14] honestam[15] educationem[16] liberalesque[17] doctrinas; at si me ille seruus ex eisdem constellationibus (quia et illius ipsae essent) consuluisset,[18] ut eidem quoque uera proferrem,[19] debuisse me rursus ibi uidere abiectissimam[20] familiam, conditionem[21] seruilem[22] et cetera longe a prioribus aliena[23] longeque distantia.[24] unde autem fieret ut eadem inspiciens diuersa[25] dicerem, si uera dicerem, si autem eadem dicerem, falsa dicerem, inde certissime[26] conlegi ea quae uera consideratis constellationibus dicerentur non arte dici sed sorte,[27] quae autem falsa, non artis imperitia[28] sed sortis mendacio.

[1]reluctatio ~onis *f.* LATE **resistance** [2]resoluo ~uere, ~ui, ~utum **to weaken** [3]concido ~ere, ~i **to collapse** [4]primo *adv.* **first** [5]curiositas ~atis *f.* **curiosity** (usu. in a bad sense) [6]reuoco ~are, ~aui, ~atum **to call back** [7]constellatio ~onis *f.* LATE **position of the stars at birth** [8]inspicio ~icere, ~exi, ~ectum **to inspect** [9]pronuntio ~are, ~aui, ~atum to announce; ECCL **to predict** [10]primarius ~a, ~um *adj.* **of the highest station** [11]familia ~ae *f.* **family** [12]proprius ~a, ~um *adj.* **one's own** [13]natalis ~is *m.* **parentage** (*pl.*) [14]ingenuus ~a, ~um *adj.* **freeborn status** [15]honestus ~a, ~um *adj.* **distinguished** [16]educatio ~onis *f.* **upbringing** [17]liberalis ~is, ~e *adj.* **liberal** (of arts, studies, education) [18]consulo ~ere, ~ui, ~tum **to consult** [19]profero ~ferre, ~tuli, ~latum **to make known** [20]abiectus ~a, ~um *adj.* **abject** [21]condicio ~onis *f.* **condition** [22]seruilis ~is, ~e *adj.* **servile** [23]alienus ~a, ~um *adj.* **different** [24]distantia ~ae *f.* **distance** [25]diuersus ~a, ~um *adj.* **opposite** [26]certo *adv.* **certainly** [27]sors ~rtis *f.* **chance** [28]imperitia ~ae *f.* **lack of skill**

The case of twins

7.6.10 Hinc autem accepto aditu,[1] ipse mecum talia ruminando,[2] ne quis eorundem delirorum[3] qui talem quaestum[4] sequerentur, quos iam iamque[5] inuadere[6] atque inrisos refellere[7] cupiebam, mihi ita resisteret, quasi aut Firminus mihi aut illi pater falsa narrauerit, intendi considerationem[8]

[1]aditus ~us *m.* **approach** [2]rumino ~are, ~aui, ~atum **to ruminate** [3]delirus ~a, ~um *adj.* **having a deranged mind** [4]quaestus ~us *m.* **occupation** [5]'iam iamque' **now all but** [6]inuado ~dere, ~si, ~sum **to assault** [7]refello ~ere, ~i **to refute** [8]consideratio ~onis *f.* **consideration**

in eos qui gemini[9] nascuntur, quorum plerique[10] ita post inuicem[11] funduntur[12] ex utero[13] ut paruum ipsum temporis interuallum,[14] quantamlibet[15] uim in rerum natura habere contendant,[16] conligi tamen humana obseruatione[17] non possit litterisque signari[18] omnino non ualeat quas mathematicus[19] inspecturus[20] est ut uera pronuntiet.[21] et non erunt uera, quia easdem litteras inspiciens eadem debuit dicere de Esau et de Iacob, sed non eadem utrique acciderunt.[22] falsa ergo diceret aut, si uera diceret, non eadem diceret: at eadem inspiceret. non ergo arte sed sorte[23] uera diceret.

Tu enim, Domine, iustissime moderator[24] uniuersitatis,[25] consulentibus[26] consultisque nescientibus occulto instinctu[27] agis ut, dum quisque consulit, hoc audiat quod eum oportet[28] audire occultis meritis[29] animarum ex abysso iusti iudicii tui. cui non dicat homo, *Quid est hoc? Ut quid hoc?*[30] (Sir 39:26). non dicat, non dicat; homo est enim.

[9]geminus ~a, ~um *adj.* **twin** [10]plerusque ~aque, ~umque *adj.* **most of** [11]inuicem *adv.* **each in turn** [12]fundo ~ere, fudi, fusum to pour out > **to give birth** [13]uterum ~i *neut.* **womb** [14]interuallum ~i *neut.* **interval** [15]quantuslibet ~alibet, ~umlibet *adj.* **however great** [16]contendo ~dere, ~di, ~tum **to allege** [17]obseruatio ~onis *f.* **observation** [18]signo ~are, ~aui, ~atum **to mark with a sign** [19]mathematicus ~i *m.* **astrologer** [20]inspicio ~icere, ~exi, ~ectum **to inspect** [21]pronuntio ~are, ~aui, ~atum ECCL **to predict** [22]accido ~ere, ~i **to happen to** [23]sors ~rtis *f.* **chance** [24]moderator ~oris *m.* **ruler** [25]uniuersitas ~atis *f.* **the universe** [26]consulo ~ere, ~ui, ~tum **to consult** [27]instinctus ~us *m.* **inspiration** [28]oportet ~ere, ~uit *impers.* **it is right** [29]meritum ~i *neut.* **merit** [30]'ut quid hoc' ECCL = 'quid hoc' **what does this mean?**

The happy mean

7.7.11 Iam itaque me, *adiutor*[1] *meus* (Ps 17:3), illis uinculis[2] solueras,[3] et quaerebam unde malum, et non erat exitus.[4] sed me non sinebas ullis fluctibus cogitationis auferri ab ea fide qua credebam et esse te et esse incommutabilem substantiam tuam et esse de hominibus curam et iudicium tuum et in Christo, Filio tuo, Domino nostro, atque scripturis sanctis quas Ecclesiae tuae Catholicae commendaret[5] auctoritas, uiam

[1]adiutor ~oris *m.* **helper** [2]uinculum ~i *neut.* **chain** [3]soluo ~uere, ~ui, ~utum **to set free** [4]exitus ~us *m.* **exit** [5]commendo ~are, ~aui, ~atum **to commend** (for instruction)

te posuisse salutis humanae ad eam uitam quae post hanc mortem futura est. his itaque saluis[6] atque inconcusse[7] roboratis[8] in animo meo, quaerebam aestuans[9] unde sit malum.

Quae illa tormenta[10] parturientis[11] cordis mei, qui gemitus,[12] Deus meus! et ibi erant aures tuae nesciente me. et cum in silentio[13] forti- ter[14] quaererem, magnae uoces erant ad misericordiam tuam tacitae contritiones[15] animi mei. tu sciebas quid patiebar, et nullus hominum. quantum enim erat quod inde digerebatur[16] per linguam meam in aures familiarissimorum[17] meorum! numquid totus tumultus[18] animae meae, cui nec tempora nec os meum sufficiebat,[19] sonabat eis? totum tamen ibat in auditum[20] tuum quod *rugiebam*[21] *a gemitu cordis mei, et ante te erat desiderium meum, et lumen oculorum meorum non erat mecum* (Ps 37:9–11). intus enim erat, ego autem foris,[22] nec in loco illud. at ego intendebam in ea quae locis continentur, et non ibi inueniebam locum ad requiescendum, nec recipiebant me ista ut dicerem, "Sat est et bene est," nec dimittebant redire ubi mihi satis esset bene. superior[23] enim eram istis, te uero inferior,[24] et tu gaudium uerum mihi subdito[25] tibi et tu mihi subieceras[26] quae infra[27] me creasti. et hoc erat rectum[28] tem- peramentum[29] et media regio[30] salutis meae, ut manerem ad imaginem tuam et tibi seruiens dominarer[31] corpori. sed cum superbe[32] contra te surgerem[33] et currerem[34] aduersus Dominum *in ceruice*[35] *crassa*[36] *scuti*[37] *mei* (Job 15:26 VL), etiam ista infima[38] supra[39] me facta sunt et premebant, et nusquam[40] erat laxamentum[41] et respiramentum.[42] ipsa

---

[6]saluus ~a, ~um *adj.* **secure** [7]inconcusse *adv.* ECCL **unshakably** [8]roboro ~are, ~aui, ~atum **to strengthen** [9]aestuo ~are, ~aui, ~atum **to be feverish** [10]tormentum ~i *neut.* **torment** [11]parturio ~ire, ~iui **to be in labor giving birth** (fig. of the mind) [12]gemitus ~us *m.* **groaning** [13]silentium ~ii *neut.* **silence** [14]fortiter *adv.* **vigorously** [15]contritio ~onis *f.* **grief**; ECCL **contrition** [16]digero ~rere, ~ssi, ~stum **to enumerate** [17]familiaris ~is, ~e *adj.* **intimate friend** (as noun) [18]tumultus ~us *m.* **tumult** [19]sufficio ~icere, ~eci, ~ectum **to be sufficient** [20]auditus ~us *m.* **hearing** [21]rugio ~ire in [onomat.] **to bellow** [22]foris *adv.* **outside** [23]superior ~or, ~us *compar. adj.* **higher** [24]inferior ~ior, ~ius *compar. adj.* **lower** [25]subditus ~a, ~um *adj.* **subject to** (w. dat.) [26]subicio ~icere, ~ieci, ~iectum **to place x** (acc.) **below y** (dat.) [27]infra *prep. acc.* **below** [28]rectus ~a, ~um *adj.* **right** [29]temperamentum ~i *neut.* **balance** [30]regio ~onis *f.* **region** [31]dominor ~ari, ~atus **to master** [32]superbe *adv.* **proudly** [33]surgo ~rgere, ~rrexi, ~rrectum **to rise** [34]curro ~rere, cucurri, ~sum **to run** [35]ceruix ~icis *f.* **neck** [36]crassus ~a, ~um *adj.* **thick** [37]scutum ~i *neut.* **heavy infantry shield** [38]infimus ~a, ~um *superl. adj.* **lowest** [39]supra *prep.* **above** [40]nusquam *adv.* **nowhere** [41]laxamentum ~i *neut.* **relaxation** [42]respiramentum ~i *neut.* AUG **room to breathe**

occurrebant undique[43] aceruatim[44] et conglobatim[45] cernenti, cogitanti autem imagines corporum ipsae opponebantur[46] redeunti, quasi diceretur, "Quo is, indigne[47] et sordide?"[48] et haec de uulnere meo creuerant, quia *humilasti[49] tamquam uulneratum[50] superbum* (Ps 88:11), et tumore[51] meo separabar[52] abs te et nimis inflata[53] facies claudebat oculos meos.

[43]undique *adv.* **from all sides** [44]aceruatim *adv.* **on a large scale** [45]conglobatim *adv.* AUG **in a heap** [46]oppono ~onere, ~osui, ~ositum **to place in the way** [47]indignus ~a, ~um *adj.* **unworthy** [48]sordidus ~a, ~um *adj.* **sordid condition** [49]humilo ~are, ~aui, ~atum ECCL **to humble** [50]uulnero ~are, ~aui, ~atum **to wound** [51]tumor ~oris *m.* **swollen** [52]separo ~are, ~aui, ~atum **to separate** [53]inflatus ~a, ~um *adj.* **puffed up**

Re-forming deformity

7.8.12 *Tu uero, Domine, in aeternum manes* (Ps 101:13) et *non in aeternum irasceris[1] nobis* (Ps 84:6), quoniam miseratus es *terram et cinerem[2]* (Job 42:6 VL). et placuit *in conspectu tuo* (Ps 18:15) reformare[3] deformia[4] mea, et *stimulis[5] internis[6] agitabas[7]* (Aen. 11.337) me ut impatiens[8] essem donec mihi per interiorem aspectum[9] certus esses. et residebat[10] tumor[11] meus ex occulta manu medicinae[12] tuae aciesque[13] conturbata[14] et contenebrata[15] mentis meae acri[16] collyrio[17] salubrium[18] dolorum *de die in diem* (Ps 60:9) sanabatur.

[1]irascor ~i, iratus sum **to be angry** [2]cinis ~eris *m.* **ashes** [3]reformo ~are, ~aui, ~atum **to give new form** [4]deformis ~is, ~e *adj.* **deformity** (*neut.* as noun) [5]stimulus ~i *m.* **goad** [6]internus ~a, ~um *adj.* **internal** [7]agito ~are, ~aui, ~atum **to move** [8]impatiens ~ntis *adj.* **impatient** [9]aspectus ~us *m.* **vision** [10]resido ~ere, resedi **to shrink** [11]tumor ~oris *m.* **swelling** [12]medicina ~ae *f.* **medicine** [13]'acies... mentis' **gaze of the mind** (phil.) [14]conturbo ~are, ~aui, ~atum **to disquiet** [15]contenebro ~are, ~aui, ~atus ECCL **to darken** [16]acer acris, acre *adj.* **stinging** [17]collyrium ~ii *neut.* **eye ointment** [18]saluber ~bris, ~bre *adj.* **health-giving**

Books of the (Neo)Platonists

7.9.13 Et primo[1] uolens ostendere mihi *quam resistas superbis, humilibus[2] autem des gratiam* (1 Pet 5:5), et quanta misericordia tua demonstrata[3] sit hominibus uia humilitatis,[4] quod *Verbum tuum caro factum est et habitauit[5] inter* (Jn 1:14) homines, procurasti[6] mihi per quendam

[1]primo *adv.* **first** [2]humilis ~is, ~e *adj.* **humble** [3]demonstro ~are, ~aui, ~atum **to point out** [4]humilitas ~atis *f.* **humility** [5]habito ~are, ~aui, ~atum **to dwell** [6]procuro ~are, ~aui, ~atum **to take care of** LATE **to provide**

hominem immanissimo[7] typho[8] turgidum[9] quosdam Platonicorum libros ex Graeca lingua in Latinam uersos,[10] et ibi legi, non quidem his uerbis sed hoc idem omnino multis et multiplicibus[11] suaderi[12] rationibus, quod *in principio erat Verbum et Verbum erat apud Deum et Deus erat Verbum. hoc erat in principio apud Deum. omnia per ipsum facta sunt, et sine ipso factum est nihil. quod factum est in eo uita est, et uita erat lux hominum; et lux in tenebris lucet,*[13] *et tenebrae eam non comprehenderunt.* et quia hominis anima, quamuis *testimonium perhibeat*[14] *de lumine, non est tamen ipsa lumen,* sed Verbum Deus est *lumen uerum, quod inluminat omnem hominem uenientem in hunc mundum.* et quia *in hoc mundo erat, et mundus per eum factus est, et mundus eum non cognouit.* quia uero *in sua propria*[15] *uenit et sui eum non receperunt, quotquot*[16] *autem receperunt eum, dedit eis potestatem filios Dei fieri credentibus in nomine eius,* (Jn 1:1–12) non ibi legi.

[7]immanis ~is, ~e *adj.* **immense** [8]typhus ~i *m.* ECCL **proud vanity** [9]turgidus ~a, ~um *adj.* **swollen** [10]uerto ~tere, ~ti, ~sum to turn > **to translate** [11]multiplex ~icis *adj.* **varied** [12]suadeo ~dere, ~si, ~sum **to urge** [13]luceo ~ere, luxi **to shine** [14]'testimonium perhibeat' **he may bear witness** [15]proprius ~a, ~um *adj.* **one's own** [16]quotquot *indecl. adj.* **however many**

The Word found in the Neoplatonists

7.9.14 Item[1] legi ibi quia Verbum, Deus, *non ex carne, non ex sanguine non ex uoluntate uiri neque ex uoluntate carnis, sed ex Deo natus est* (Jn 1:13); sed quia *Verbum caro factum est et habitauit*[2] *in nobis* (Jn 1:14), non ibi legi. indagaui[3] quippe in illis litteris uarie[4] dictum et multis modis quod *sit Filius in forma patris, non rapinam*[5] *arbitratus*[6] *esse aequalis*[7] *Deo* (Phil 2:6–11), quia naturaliter[8] *idipsum*[9] est, sed quia *semet ipsum exinaniuit*[10] *formam serui accipiens, in similitudinem*[11] *hominum factus et habitu*[12] *inuentus ut homo, humilauit*[13] *se factus oboediens*[14] *usque ad mortem, mortem autem crucis:*[15] *propter quod Deus eum exaltauit*[16]

[1]item *adv.* **similarly** [2]habito ~are, ~aui, ~atum **to dwell** [3]indago ~are, ~aui, ~atum **to ascertain** [4]uarie *adv.* **variously** [5]rapina ~ae *f.* **plundering** [6]arbitro ~are, ~aui, ~atum **to think** [7]aequalis ~is, ~e *adj.* **equal** [8]naturaliter *adv.* **by nature** [9]idipsum *pron.* ECCL **self-same** [10]exinanio ~ire, ~iui, ~itum **to empty** [11]'in similitudinem' **in the likeness of** (w. gen.) [12]habitus ~us *m.* **condition** [13]humilo ~are, ~aui, ~atum ECCL **to humble** [14]oboediens ~ntis *adj.* **obedient** [15]crux ~ucis *f.* **cross** [16]exalto ~are, ~aui, ~atum **to raise**

a mortuis *et donauit*[17] *ei nomen quod est super omne nomen, ut in nomine Iesu omne genu*[18] *flectatur*[19] *caelestium*[20] *terrestrium*[21] *et infernorum,*[22] *et omnis lingua confiteatur quia Dominus Iesus in gloria est Dei Patris,* non habent illi libri.

Quod enim ante omnia tempora et supra[23] omnia tempora incommutabiliter[24] manet unigenitus[25] Filius tuus coaeternus tibi, et quia *de plenitudine*[26] *eius accipiunt* (Jn 1:16) animae ut beatae sint, et quia participatione[27] manentis in se Sapientiae renouantur[28] ut sapientes sint, est ibi; quod autem *secundum tempus pro impiis*[29] *mortuus est* (Rom 5:6), et *Filio tuo unico*[30] *non pepercisti, sed pro nobis omnibus tradidisti eum* (Rom 8:32), non est ibi. *abscondisti*[31] enim *haec a sapientibus et reuelasti*[32] *ea paruulis* (Mt 11:25), ut *uenirent ad eum laborantes*[33] *et onerati*[34] *et reficeret*[35] *eos, quoniam mitis*[36] *est et humilis*[37] *corde* (Mt 11:28–29), et *diriget*[38] *mites in iudicio et docet mansuetos*[39] *uias suas* (Ps 24:9), *uidens humilitatem*[40] *nostram et laborem nostrum et dimittens omnia peccata nostra* (Ps 24:18). qui autem cothurno[41] tamquam doctrinae sublimioris[42] elati[43] non audiunt dicentem, *Discite a me quoniam mitis sum et humilis corde, et inuenietis requiem*[44] *animabus uestris* (Mt 11:29), etsi *cognoscunt Deum, non sicut Deum glorificant*[45] *aut gratias agunt, sed euanescunt*[46] *in cogitationibus suis et obscuratur*[47] *insipiens*[48] *cor eorum; dicentes se esse sapientes stulti*[49] *facti sunt* (Rom 1:21–22).

---

[17]dono ~are, ~aui, ~atum **to grant** x (acc.) **to** y (dat.) [18]genu ~us *neut.* **knee** [19]flecto ~ctere, ~xi, ~xum **to bend** [20]caelestis ~is, ~e *adj.* **celestial** [21]terrestris ~is, ~e *adj.* **terrestrial** [22]infernus ~a, ~um *adj.* **infernal** [23]supra *prep. acc.* **above** [24]incommutabiliter *adv.* AUG **unchangeably** [25]unigenitus ~a, ~um *adj.* ECCL **only-begotten** [26]plenitudo ~inis *f.* **fullness** [27]participatio ~onis *f.* **participation** [28]renouo ~are, ~aui, ~atum **to renew** [29]impius ~a, ~um *adj.* **impious** [30]unicus ~a, ~um *adj.* **one and only** [31]abscondo ~ere, ~i, ~itum **to hide** [32]reuelo ~are, ~aui, ~atum **to reveal** [33]laboro ~are, ~aui, ~atum **to labor** [34]onero ~are, ~aui, ~atum **to overwhelm** [35]reficio ~icere, ~eci, ~ectum **to remake** [36]mitis ~is, ~e *adj.* **meek** [37]humilis ~is, ~e *adj.* **humble** [38]dirigo ~igere, ~exi, ~ectum **to guide** [39]mansuetus ~a, ~um *adj.* **gentle** [40]humilitas ~atis *f.* **humble condition** [41]cothurnus ~i *m.* actor's high heeled boots; LATE **haughtiness** [42]sublimis ~is, ~e *adj.* **sublime** [43]effero ~rre, extuli, elatum **to lift** [44]requies ~etis *f.* **rest** [45]glorifico ~are, ~aui, ~atus ECCL **to glorify** [46]euanesco ~escere, ~ui to vanish; ECCL **to become vain** [47]obscuro ~are, ~aui, ~atum **to darken** [48]insipiens ~ntis *adj.* **foolish** [49]stultus ~a, ~um *adj.* **fool** (*m.* as noun)

Romans 1:23

7.9.15 Et ideo legebam ibi etiam *immutatam[1] gloriam incorruptionis[2] tuae* in idola[3] et uaria[4] simulacra,[5] *in similitudinem[6] imaginis corruptibilis[7] hominis et uolucrum[8] et quadrupedum[9] et serpentium[10]* (Rom 1:23), uidelicet[11] Aegyptium cibum quo *Esau perdidit primogenita[12] sua* (Gen 25:33–34), quoniam caput quadrupedis pro te honorauit[13] populus primogenitus,[14] *conuersus corde in Aegyptum* (Acts 7:39) et curuans[15] imaginem tuam, animam suam, ante *imaginem uituli[16] manducantis[17] faenum[18]* (Ps 105:20).

Inueni haec ibi et non manducaui. placuit enim tibi, Domine, auferre opprobrium[19] diminutionis[20] *ab Iacob, ut maior seruiret minori* (Rom 9:12), et uocasti *Gentes[21] in hereditatem[22] tuam* (Ps 78:1). et ego ad te ueneram ex Gentibus et intendi in *aurum quod ab Aegypto uoluisti ut auferret populus tuus* (Ex 3:22), quoniam tuum erat, ubicumque[23] erat. et dixisti Atheniensibus per apostolum[24] tuum quod *in te uiuimus et mouemur et sumus, sicut et quidam secundum eos dixerunt* (Acts 17:28), et utique inde erant illi libri. et non attendi in idola Aegyptiorum, quibus de auro tuo ministrabant[25] qui *transmutauerunt[26] ueritatem Dei in mendacium, et coluerunt et seruierunt creaturae potius quam creatori* (Rom 1:25).

---

[1]immuto ~are, ~aui, ~atum **to change** [2]incorruptio ~onis *f.* ECCL **incorruptibility** [3]idolum ~i *neut.* ECCL **idol** [4]uarius ~a, ~um *adj.* **various** [5]simulacrum ~i *neut.* **image** (usu. of a god) [6]similitudo ~inis *f.* **likeness** [7]corruptibilis ~is ~e *adj.* ECCL **corruptible** [8]uolucer ~cris *m.* **bird** [9]quadrupes ~edis *adj.* **four-footed animal** (as noun) [10]serpens ~ntis *f. m.* **serpent** [11]uidelicet *adv.* **namely** (as *particle*) [12]primogenita, ~orum *neut.* LATE **rights of the first-born** [13]honoro ~are, ~aui, ~atum **to honor** [14]primogenitus ~a, ~um *adj.* LATE **first-born** [15]curuo ~are, ~aui, ~atum **to bow down** [16]uitulus ~i *m.* **calf** [17]manduco ~are, ~aui, ~atum **to chew** [18]faenum ~i *neut.* **hay** [19]opprobrium ~ii *neut.* **reproach** [20]diminutio ~onis *f.* **being less** [21]gens ~tis *f.* **people;** ECCL **Gentiles** [22]hereditas ~atis *f.* **inheritance** [23]ubicumque *adv.* **wherever** [24]apostolus ~i *m.* ECCL **apostle** (St. Paul) [25]ministro ~are, ~aui, ~atum **to serve** [26]transmuto ~are, ~aui, ~atum **to change** x **into** y

The Region of Unlikeness

7.10.16 Et inde admonitus[1] redire ad memet ipsum, intraui in intima[2] mea duce te, et potui, quoniam *factus es adiutor[3] meus* (Ps 29:11).

---

[1]admoneo ~ere, ~ui, ~itum **to admonish** [2]intimus ~a, ~um *superl. adj.* **inmost self** (*neut.* as noun) [3]adiutor ~oris *m.* **helper**

intraui et uidi qualicumque[4] oculo animae meae supra[5] eundem oculum animae meae, supra mentem meam, lucem incommutabilem, non hanc uulgarem[6] et conspicuam[7] omni carni, nec quasi ex eodem genere grandior erat, tamquam si ista multo multoque[8] clarius[9] claresceret[10] totumque occuparet magnitudine.[11] non hoc illa erat sed aliud, aliud ualde ab istis omnibus. nec ita erat supra mentem meam, sicut oleum[12] super aquam nec sicut caelum super terram, sed superior,[13] quia ipsa fecit me, et ego inferior,[14] quia factus ab ea. qui nouit ueritatem, nouit eam, et qui nouit eam, nouit aeternitatem; caritas nouit eam.

O aeterna Veritas et uera Caritas et cara Aeternitas, *tu es Deus meus* (Ps 42:2), tibi suspiro *die ac nocte* (Ps 41:4)! et cum te primum[15] cognoui, tu *adsumpsisti*[16] *me* (Ps 26:10) ut uiderem esse quod uiderem, et nondum me esse qui uiderem. et reuerberasti[17] infirmitatem[18] aspectus[19] mei, radians[20] in me uehementer,[21] et contremui[22] amore et horrore.[23] et inueni longe me esse a te *in regione*[24] *dissimilitudinis*[25] (Plot. 1.8.13), tamquam audirem uocem tuam de excelso:[26] "Cibus sum grandium: cresce et manducabis[27] me. nec tu me in te mutabis sicut cibum carnis tuae, sed tu mutaberis in me." et cognoui quoniam *pro iniquitate erudisti*[28] *hominem, et tabescere*[29] *fecisti sicut araneam*[30] *animam* (Ps 38:12 VL) meam, et dixi, "Numquid nihil est ueritas, quoniam neque per finita neque per infinita locorum spatia diffusa[31]est?" et clamasti de longinquo,[32] "Immo[33] uero *ego sum qui sum*." (Ex 3:14).

Et audiui, sicut auditur in corde, et non erat prorsus[34] unde dubitarem,[35] faciliusque dubitarem uiuere me quam non esse ueritatem, *quae per ea quae facta sunt intellecta conspicitur*[36] (Rom 1:20).

---

[4]qualiscumque *adj.* **as it were** [5]supra *prep. acc.* **above** or **beyond** [6]uulgaris ~is, ~e *adj.* **ordinary** [7]conspicuus ~a, ~um *adj.* **conspicuous** [8]'multo multoque' **far and away** (w. *compar. adv.*) [9]clare *adv.* **distinctly** [10]claresco ~escere, ~ui **to shine** [11]magnitudo ~inis *f.* **intensity** [12]oleum ~i *neut.* **oil** [13]superior ~or, ~us *compar. adj.* **higher** [14]inferior ~ior, ~ius *compar. adj.* **lower** [15]primum *adv.* **first** [16]adsumo ~ere, ~psi, ~ptum **to take to oneself; ECCL to lift up** [17]reuerbero ~are, ~aui, ~atum **to repel violently** [18]infirmitas ~atis *f.* **weakness** [19]aspectus ~us *m.* **gaze** [20]radio ~are **to radiate light** [21]uehementer *adv.* **energetically** [22]contremesco ~escere, ~ui **to tremble** [23]horror ~oris *m.* **dread** [24]regio ~onis *f.* **region** [25]dissimilitudo ~inis *f.* **unlikeness** [26]excelsus ~a, ~um *adj.* **high** [27]manduco ~are, ~aui, ~atum **to eat** [28]erudio ~ire, ~ii or ~iui, ~itum **to train; ECCL to reprove** [29]tabesco ~escere, ~ui **to waste away** [30]aranea ~ae *f.* **spider's web** [31]diffundo ~undere, ~udi, ~usum **to diffuse** [32]longinquus ~a, ~um *adj.* **far off** [33]immo *particle* **no, indeed** (contradictory) [34]prorsus *adv.* **entirely** [35]dubito ~are, ~aui, ~atum **to be in doubt** [36]conspicio ~icere, ~exi, ~ectum **to see > to perceive**

Real but unreal

7.11.17 Et inspexi[1] cetera infra[2] te et uidi nec omnino esse nec omnino non esse: esse quidem, quoniam abs te sunt, non esse autem, quoniam id quod es non sunt. id enim uere est quod incommutabiliter[3] manet. *mihi autem inhaerere[4] Deo bonum est* (Ps 72:28), quia, si non manebo in illo, nec in me potero. ille autem *in se manens innouat[5] omnia* (Wis 7:27), et *Dominus meus es, quoniam bonorum meorum non eges[6]* (Ps 15:2).

[1]inspicio ~icere, ~exi, ~ectum **to observe** [2]infra *prep. acc.* **below** [3]incommutabiliter *adv.* AUG **unchangeably** [4]inhaereo ~rere, ~si, ~sum **to cling to** [5]innouo ~are, ~aui, ~atum **to renew** [6]egeo ~ere, ~ui **to need**

Relative goods

7.12.18 Et manifestatum[1] est mihi quoniam bona sunt quae corrumpuntur,[2] quae neque si summa bona essent neque nisi bona essent corrumpi possent; quia si summa bona essent, incorruptibilia[3] essent, si autem nulla bona essent, quid in eis corrumperetur non esset. nocet[4] enim corruptio[5] et, nisi bonum minueret,[6] non noceret. aut igitur nihil nocet corruptio, quod fieri non potest, aut, quod certissimum est, omnia quae corrumpuntur priuantur[7] bono. si autem omni bono priuabuntur, omnino non erunt. si enim erunt et corrumpi iam non poterunt, meliora erunt, quia incorruptibiliter[8] permanebunt.[9] et quid monstrosius[10] quam ea dicere omni bono amisso facta meliora? ergo si omni bono priuabuntur, omnino nulla erunt: ergo quamdiu[11] sunt, bona sunt.

Ergo quaecumque sunt, bona sunt, malumque illud quod quaerebam unde esset non est substantia, quia si substantia esset, bonum esset. aut enim esset incorruptibilis substantia, magnum utique bonum, aut substantia corruptibilis[12] esset, quae nisi bona esset, corrumpi non posset.

[1]manifesto ~are, ~aui, ~atum **to make clear** [2]corrumpo ~umpere, ~upi, ~uptum **to corrupt** [3]incorruptibilis ~is, ~e *adj.* ECCL **incorruptible** [4]noceo ~ere, ~ui, ~itum **to harm** [5]corruptio ~onis *f.* **corrupt condition** [6]minuo ~uere, ~ui, ~utum **to diminish** [7]priuo ~are, ~aui, ~atum **to deprive** [8]incorruptibiliter *adv.* AUG **incorruptibly** [9]permaneo ~ere, ~si, ~sum **to continue to exist** [10]monstrosus ~a, ~um *adj.* **monstrous** [11]quamdiu *adv.* **as long as** [12]corruptibilis ~e *adj.* ECCL **corruptible**

Itaque uidi et manifestatum est mihi quia omnia bona tu fecisti et prorsus[13] nullae substantiae sunt quas tu non fecisti. et quoniam non aequalia[14] omnia fecisti, ideo sunt omnia, quia singula bona sunt, et simul omnia ualde bona, quoniam *fecit Deus* noster *omnia bona ualde* (Gen 1:31).

[13]prorsus *adv.* **at all** [14]aequalis ~is, ~e *adj.* **equal**

Evil has no being

7.13.19 Et tibi omnino non est malum, non solum tibi sed nec uniuersae creaturae tuae, quia extra[1] non est aliquid quod inrumpat[2] et corrumpat[3] ordinem quem imposuisti ei. in partibus autem eius quaedam quibusdam quia non conueniunt,[4] mala putantur; et eadem ipsa conueniunt aliis et bona sunt et in semet ipsis bona sunt. et omnia haec, quae sibimet inuicem[5] non conueniunt, conueniunt inferiori[6] parti rerum, quam terram dicimus, habentem caelum suum nubilosum[7] atque uentosum[8] congruum[9] sibi. et absit iam ut dicerem, "Non essent ista," quia etsi sola ista cernerem, desiderarem quidem meliora, sed iam etiam de solis istis laudare te deberem, quoniam laudandum te ostendunt *de terra draco-nes*[10] *et omnes abyssi, ignis, grando,*[11] *nix,*[12] *glacies,*[13] *spiritus tempestatis,*[14] *quae faciunt uerbum tuum, montes et omnes colles,*[15] *ligna*[16] *fructifera*[17] *et omnes cedri,*[18] *bestiae*[19] *et omnia pecora,*[20] *reptilia*[21] *et uolatilia*[22] *pin-nata.*[23] *reges terrae et omnes populi, principes et omnes iudices*[24] *terrae, iuuenes et uirgines, seniores*[25] *cum iunioribus*[26] *laudent nomen tuum* (Ps 148:7–12). cum uero etiam *de caelis te laudent, laudent te,* Deus noster. *in excelsis*[27] *omnes angeli tui, omnes uirtutes*[28] *tuae, sol et luna,*[29] *omnes*

[1]extra *adv.* **outside** [2]inrumpo ~umpere, ~upi, ~uptum **to burst into** [3]corrumpo ~umpere, ~upi, ~uptum **to corrupt** [4]conuenio ~enire, ~eni, ~entum **to fit in** [5]inuicem *adv.* **mutually** [6]inferior ~ior, ~ius *compar. adj.* **lower** [7]nubilosus ~a, ~um *adj.* **cloudy** [8]uentosus ~a, ~um *adj.* **windy** [9]congruus ~a, ~um *adj.* **fitting** [10]draco ~onis *m.* **dragon** [11]grando ~inis *f.* **hail** [12]nix niuis *f.* **snow** [13]glacies ~ei *f.* **ice** [14]tempestas ~atis *f.* **storm** [15]collis ~is *m.* **hill** [16]lignum ~i *neut.* **wood (tree)** [17]fructifer ~era, ~erum *adj.* **fruit-bearing** [18]cedrus ~i *f.* **cedar** *or* **juniper** [19]bestia ~ae *f.* **beast** [20]pecus ~oris *neut.* **sheep** [21]reptilis ~is ~e *adj.* ECCL **creeping; reptile** (as noun) [22]uolatilis ~is, ~e *adj.* **flying; bird** (as noun) [23]pinnatus ~a, ~um *adj.* **winged** [24]iudex ~icis *m.* **judge** [25]senex ~is, senior *m. adj.* **old man** [26]iuniores ~um *m. pl.* **younger men** [27]excelsus ~a, ~um *adj.* **lofty;** ECCL **heavens** (*neut. pl.*) [28]uirtus ~utis *f.* **virtue;** ECCL **host (of angels)** [29]luna ~ae *f.* **moon**

stellae[30] *et lumen, caeli caelorum et aquae quae super caelos sunt laudent nomen tuum* (Ps 148:1–5). non iam desiderabam meliora, quia omnia cogitabam, et meliora quidem superiora[31] quam inferiora, sed meliora omnia quam sola superiora iudicio saniore[32] pendebam.[33]

[30]stella ~ae *f.* **star** [31]superior ~or, ~us *compar. adj.* **higher** [32]sanus ~a, ~um *adj.* **sensible** [33]pendo ~ere, pependi, ~sum to weigh > **to regard as**

Idolatry in the imagination

7.14.20 *Non est sanitas*[1] (Ps 37:4) eis quibus displicet aliquid creaturae tuae, sicut mihi non erat cum displicerent multa quae fecisti. et quia non audebat anima mea ut ei displiceret Deus meus, nolebat esse tuum quidquid ei displicebat. et inde ierat in opinionem[2] duarum substantiarum, et non requiescebat, et aliena loquebatur. et inde rediens fecerat sibi deum per infinita spatia locorum omnium et eum putauerat esse te et eum *conlocauerat*[3] *in corde suo* (Ezek 14:7), et facta erat rursus templum idoli[4] sui abominandum[5] tibi, sed posteaquam[6] fouisti[7] caput nescientis et clausisti *oculos meos, ne uiderent uanitatem* (Ps 118:37). cessaui[8] de me paululum,[9] et consopita[10] est insania[11] mea, et euigilaui[12] in te et uidi te infinitum aliter, et uisus[13] iste non a carne trahebatur.[14]

[1]sanitas ~atis *f.* **soundness of mind** [2]opinio ~onis *f.* **belief** [3]conloco ~are, ~aui, ~atum **to put in place** [4]idolum ~i *neut.* ECCL **idol** [5]abominandus ~a, ~um *adj.* **abominable** [6]posteaquam *conj.* **afterward** [7]foueo ~ere, foui, fotum **to treat** (medical) [8]cesso ~are, ~aui, ~atum **to rest** [9]paululum *adv.* **somewhat** [10]consopio ~ire, ~iui, ~itum **to lull to sleep** [11]insania ~ae *f.* **insanity** [12]euigilo ~are, ~aui, ~atum **to wake up** [13]uisus ~us *m.* **vision** [14]traho ~here, ~xi, ~ctum to haul > **to derive** (from a source)

A place for everything, everything in its place

7.15.21 Et respexi[1] alia, et uidi tibi debere quia sunt et in te cuncta finita, sed aliter, non quasi in loco, sed quia tu es omnitenens[2] manu ueritate, et omnia uera sunt in quantum[3] sunt, nec quicquam est falsitas,[4] nisi cum putatur esse quod non est. et uidi quia non solum locis

[1]respicio ~icere, ~exi, ~ectum **to turn one's gaze upon** [2]omnitenens ~ntis *adj.* ECCL **who holds all** [3]'in quantum' **to the degree** [4]falsitas ~atis *f.* LATE **falsity**

sua quaeque suis conueniunt[5] sed etiam temporibus et quia tu, qui solus aeternus es, non post innumerabilia[6] spatia temporum coepisti operari,[7] quia omnia spatia temporum, et quae praeterierunt et quae praeteribunt, nec abirent[8] nec uenirent nisi te operante et manente.

[5]conuenio ~enire, ~eni, ~entum **to fit** [6]innumerabilis ~is, ~e *adj.* **innumerable** [7]operor ~ari, ~atus **to be at work** [8]abeo ~ire, ~ii, ~itum **to go away**

Evil is a perversity of will

7.16.22 Et sensi expertus non esse mirum quod palato[1] non sano[2] poena est et panis[3] qui sano suauis[4] est, et oculis aegris[5] odiosa[6] lux quae puris[7] amabilis.[8] et iustitia tua displicet iniquis,[9] nedum[10] uipera[11] et uermiculus,[12] quae bona creasti, apta[13] inferioribus[14] creaturae tuae partibus, quibus et ipsi iniqui apti sunt, quanto dissimiliores[15] sunt tibi, apti autem superioribus,[16] quanto similiores fiunt tibi.

Et quaesiui quid esset iniquitas et non inueni substantiam, sed a summa substantia, te Deo, detortae[17] in infima[18] uoluntatis peruersitatem,[19] *proicientis[20] intima[21] sua* (Sir 10:10) et tumescentis[22] foras.[23]

[1]palatum ~i *neut.* **palate** [2]sanus ~a, ~um *adj.* **healthy** [3]panis ~is *m.* **bread** [4]suauis ~is, ~e *adj.* **pleasant** [5]aeger ~gra, ~grum *adj.* **ailing** [6]odiosus ~a, ~um *adj.* **hateful** [7]purus ~a, ~um *adj.* **clear** [8]amabilis ~is, ~e *adj.* **causing pleasure** [9]iniquus, ~os ~a *adj.* **unfair**; ECCL **unrighteous** (as noun) [10]nedum *conj.* **much less** [11]uipera ~ae *f.* **viper** [12]uermiculus ~i *m.* **maggot** [13]aptus ~a, ~um *ppl. adj.* **fitted** [14]inferior ~ior, ~ius *compar. adj.* **lower** [15]dissimilis ~is, ~e *adj.* **dissimilar** [16]superior ~or, ~us *compar. adj.* **higher** [17]detorqueo ~quere, ~si, ~tum **to twist or distort** [18]infimus ~a, ~um *superl. adj.* **lowest** [19]peruersitas ~atis *f.* **perversity** [20]proicio ~icere, ~ieci, ~iectum **to throw away** [21]intimus ~a, ~um *superl. adj.* **inmost self** (*neut. pl.* as noun) [22]tumesco ~ere **to become swollen with pride** [23]foras *adv.* **outwardly**

Neoplatonic ecstasy

7.17.23 Et mirabar quod iam te amabam, non pro te phantasma,[1] et non stabam frui[2] Deo meo, sed rapiebar ad te decore[3] tuo moxque diripiebar[4] abs te pondere[5] meo, et ruebam[6] in ista cum gemitu;[7]

[1]phantasma ~atis *neut.* **phantom**; LATE **figment of the imagination** [2]fruor ~i, ~ctus **to enjoy** (w. abl.) [3]decus ~oris *neut.* **beauty** [4]diripio ~ipere, ~ipui, ~eptum **to tear away** [5]pondus ~eris *neut.* **weight** [6]ruo ~ere, ~i **to tumble down** [7]gemitus ~us *m.* **groan**

et pondus hoc consuetudo carnalis.[8] sed mecum erat memoria tui, neque ullo modo dubitabam[9] esse cui cohaererem,[10] sed nondum me esse qui cohaererem, *quoniam corpus quod corrumpitur*[11] *adgrauat*[12] *animam et deprimit*[13] *terrena*[14] *inhabitatio*[15] *sensum multa cogitantem* (Wis 9:15), eramque certissimus quod *inuisibilia tua a constitutione*[16] *mundi per ea quae facta sunt intellecta conspiciuntur,*[17] *sempiterna*[18] *quoque uirtus et diuinitas*[19] *tua* (Rom 1:20). quaerens enim unde approbarem[20] pulchri-tudinem[21] corporum, siue caelestium[22] siue terrestrium,[23] et quid mihi praesto[24] esset integre[25] de mutabilibus iudicanti et dicenti, "Hoc ita esset debet, illud non ita" — hoc ergo quaerens, unde iudicarem cum ita iudicarem, inueneram incommutabilem et ueram ueritatis aeternitatem supra[26] mentem meam commutabilem.[27]

Atque ita gradatim[28] a corporibus ad sentientem per corpus animam atque inde ad eius interiorem uim, cui sensus corporis exteriora[29] nun-tiaret,[30] et quousque[31] possunt bestiae.[32]

Atque inde rursus ad ratiocinantem[33] potentiam[34] ad quam refertur[35] iudicandum quod sumitur a sensibus corporis. quae se quoque in me comperiens[36] mutabilem erexit[37] se ad intellegentiam[38] suam et abduxit[39] *cogitationem a consuetudine* (Tusc. 1.38), subtrahens[40] se contradicen-tibus[41] turbis phantasmatum, ut inueniret quo lumine aspergeretur,[42] cum sine ulla dubitatione[43] clamaret incommutabile praeferendum[44] esse mutabili unde nosset ipsum incommutabile (quod nisi aliquo modo nosset, nullo modo illud mutabili certa praeponeret[45]).

---

[8]carnalis ~is, ~e *adj.* ECCL **carnal** [9]dubito ~are, ~aui, ~atum **to be in doubt** [10]cohaereo ~rere, ~si, ~sum **to cling to** (w. dat.) [11]corrumpo ~umpere, ~upi, ~uptum **to corrupt** [12]adgrauo ~are, ~aui, ~atum **to weigh down** [13]deprimo ~imere, ~essi, ~essum **to sink** [14]terrenus ~a, ~um *adj.* **earthly** [15]inhabitatio ~onis *neut.* ECCL **dwelling** [16]constitutio ~onis *f.* **arrangement** [17]conspicio ~icere, ~exi, ~ectum **to perceive** [18]sempiternus ~a, ~um *adj.* **eternal** [19]diuinitas ~atis *f.* **divinity** [20]approbo ~are, ~aui, ~atum **to approve** [21]pulchritudo ~inis *f.* **beauty** [22]caelestis ~is, ~e *adj.* **celestial** [23]terre-stris ~is, ~e *adj.* **terrestrial** [24]praesto *adv.* **ready at hand** [25]integre *adv.* **honestly** [26]supra *prep. acc.* **above** [27]commutabilis ~is, ~e *adj.* **changeable** [28]gradatim *adv.* **by stages** [29]exter ~era, ~erum *adj.* **external** [30]nuntio ~are, ~aui, ~atum **to report** [31]quousque *adv.* **to the degree that** [32]bestia ~ae *f.* **beast** [33]ratiocinor ~ari, ~atus **to reason** [34]potentia ~ae *f.* **capacity** [35]refero ~rre, rettuli, relatum **to refer to** [36]comperio ~ire, ~i, ~tum **to ascertain** [37]erigo ~igere, ~exi, ~ectum **to raise oneself** (refl.) [38]intellegentia ~ae *f.* **intelligence** [39]abduco ~cere, ~xi, ~ctum **to withdraw** [40]subtraho ~here, ~xi, ~ctum **to drag away** [41]contradico ~icere, ~ixi, ~ictum **to object;** ECCL **to oppose** [42]aspergo ~gere, ~si, ~sum **to sprinkle** [43]dubitatio ~onis *f.* **hesitation** [44]praefero ~ferre, ~tuli, ~latum **to prefer** x (acc.) **to** y (dat.) [45]praepono ~onere **to put** x (acc.) **before** y (dat.).

Et peruenit ad ID QUOD EST in ictu[46] trepidantis[47] aspectus.[48] tunc uero *inuisibilia tua per ea quae facta sunt intellecta conspexi* (Rom 1:20), sed aciem[49] figere[50] non eualui,[51] et repercussa[52] infirmitate[53] redditus solitis non mecum ferebam nisi amantem memoriam et quasi olefacta[54] desiderantem quae comedere[55] nondum possem.

[46]ictus ~us *m.* **impact** [47]trepido ~are, ~aui, ~atum **to tremble** [48]aspectus ~us *m.* **glance** [49]acies ~ei *f.* **gaze** [50]figo ~gere, ~xi, ~xum **to fix** [51]eualesco ~escere, ~ui **to have sufficient strength** [52]repercutio ~tere, ~ssi, ~ssum **to repel** [53]infirmitas ~atis *f.* **weakness** [54]olefacio ~acere, ~eci, ~actum **to catch a whiff** [55]comedo ~edere, ~edi, ~esum **to eat**

I need a mediator

7.18.24 Et quaerebam uiam comparandi[1] roboris[2] quod esset idoneum[3] ad fruendum[4] te, nec inueniebam donec amplecterer[5] *mediatorem[6] Dei et hominum, hominem Christum Iesum* (1 Tim 2:5), *qui est super omnia Deus benedictus[7] in saecula* (Rom 9:5), uocantem et dicentem, *Ego sum Via et Veritas et Vita* (Jn 14:6), et cibum, cui capiendo inualidus[8] eram, miscentem carni, quoniam *Verbum caro factum est* (Jn 1:14) ut infantiae[9] nostrae lactesceret[10] Sapientia tua, per quam creasti omnia. non enim tenebam Deum meum Iesum, humilis[11] humilem, nec cuius rei magistra[12] esset eius infirmitas[13] noueram. Verbum enim tuum, aeterna Veritas, superioribus[14] creaturae tuae partibus supereminens[15] subditos[16] erigit[17] ad se ipsam, in inferioribus[18] autem *aedificauit[19] sibi humilem domum* (Prov 9:1) de limo[20] nostro, per quam subdendos[21] deprimeret[22] a seipsis[23] et ad se traiceret,[24] sanans tumorem[25] et nutriens[26] amorem, ne fiducia[27] sui progrederentur[28] longius, sed potius infirmarentur,[29]

[1]comparo ~are, ~aui, ~atum **to muster** [2]robur ~oris *neut.* **strength** [3]idoneus ~a, ~um *adj.* **adequate** [4]fruor ~i, ~ctus **to enjoy** (w. abl) [5]amplector ~cti, ~xus **to embrace affectionately** [6]mediator ~oris *m.* **mediator** [7]benedictus ~a, ~um *adj.* ECCL **blessed** [8]inualidus ~a, ~um *adj.* **powerless** [9]infantia ~ae *f.* **infancy** [10]lactesco ~ere **to produce milk** [11]humilis ~is, ~e *adj.* **humble** [12]magistra ~ae *f.* **teacher** [13]infirmitas ~atis *f.* **weakness** [14]superior ~or, ~us *compar. adj.* **higher** [15]supereminus ~ere **to stand out above** [16]subditus ~a, ~um *adj.* **subject to** [17]erigo ~igere, ~exi, ~ectum **to lift up** [18]inferior ~ior, ~ius *compar. adj.* **lower** [19]aedifico ~are, ~aui, ~atum **to build** [20]limus ~i *m.* **mud** [21]subdo ~ere, ~idi, ~itum **to make subject** [22]deprimo ~imere, ~essi, ~essum **to draw down** [23]seipse ~a, ~um *pron.* ECCL **they themselves** [24]traicio ~icere, ~ieci, ~iectum **to transfer** [25]tumor ~oris *m.* **swollen condition** [26]nutrio ~ire, ~iui or ~ii, ~itum **to nourish** [27]fiducia ~ae *f.* trust > **in reliance on** (abl., w. gen.) [28]progredior ~di, ~ssus **to proceed** [29]infirmo ~are, ~aui, ~atum **to weaken**

uidentes ante pedes suos infirmam[30] Diuinitatem[31] ex participatione[32] *tunicae*[33] *pelliciae*[34] *nostrae* (Gen 3:21), et lassi[35] prosternerentur[36] in eam, illa autem surgens[37] leuaret[38] eos.

[30]infirmus ~a, ~um *adj.* **weak** [31]diuinitas ~atis *f.* **divinity** [32]participatio ~onis *f.* **participation** [33]tunica ~ae *f.* **coat** [34]pellicius ~a, ~um *adj.* **made of skins** [35]lassus ~a, ~um *adj.* tired > **mentally fatigued** [36]prosterno ~ernere, ~raui, ~ratum **to lay prostrate** [37]surgo ~rgere, ~rrexi, ~rrectum **to rise up** [38]leuo ~are, ~aui, ~atum **to lift up**

Christ viewed as merely a man

7.19.25 Ego uero aliud putabam tantumque sentiebam de Domino Christo meo, quantum de excellentis[1] sapientiae uiro cui nullus posset aequari,[2] praesertim[3] quia mirabiliter[4] natus ex uirgine, ad exemplum[5] contemnendorum[6] temporalium[7] prae adipiscenda[8] immortalitate,[9] diuina[10] pro nobis cura tantam auctoritatem magisterii[11] meruisse[12] uidebatur. quid autem sacramenti haberet *Verbum caro factum* (Jn 1:14), ne suspicari[13] quidem poteram. tantum cognoueram ex his quae de illo scripta traderentur quia manducauit[14] et bibit,[15] dormiuit,[16] ambulauit,[17] exhilaratus[18] est, contristatus[19] est, sermocinatus[20] est, non haesisse[21] carnem illam Verbo tuo nisi cum anima et mente humana. nouit hoc omnis qui nouit incommutabilitatem[22] Verbi tui, quam ego iam noueram, quantum poteram, nec omnino quicquam inde dubitabam.[23] etenim[24] nunc mouere membra corporis per uoluntatem, nunc non mouere, nunc aliquo affectu affici,[25] nunc non affici, nunc proferre[26] per signa sapientes sententias, nunc esse in silentio,[27] propria[28] sunt mutabilitatis[29] animae et mentis. quae si falsa de illo scripta essent, etiam omnia

[1]excellens ~ntis, *adj.* **excellent** [2]aequo ~are, ~aui, ~atum **to be equal** [3]praesertim *adv.* **first and foremost** [4]mirabiliter *adv.* **amazingly** [5]exemplum ~i *neut.* **example** [6]contemno ~nere, ~psi, ~ptum **to despise** [7]temporalis ~is, ~e *adj.* **temporal** [8]adipiscor ~ipisci, ~eptus **to win** [9]immortalitas ~atis *f.* **immortality** [10]diuinus ~a, ~um *adj.* **divine** [11]magisterium ~ii *neut.* **teacher** [12]mereo ~ere, ~ui, ~itum **to merit** [13]suspicor ~ari, ~atus **to imagine** [14]manduco ~are, ~aui, ~atum **to eat** [15]bibo ~ere, ~i **to drink** [16]dormio ~ire, ~iui, ~itum **to sleep** [17]ambulo ~are, ~aui, ~atum **to walk** [18]exhilaro ~are, ~aui, ~atum **to gladden** [19]contristo ~are, ~aui, ~atum **to sadden** [20]sermocinor ~ari, ~atus **to have a conversation** [21]haereo ~rere, ~si, ~sum **to unite** [22]incommutabilitas ~tatis *f.* AUG **unchangeableness** [23]dubito ~are, ~aui, ~atum **to be in doubt** [24]etenim *conj.* **for** [25]afficio ~icere, ~eci, ~ectum **to affect** [26]profero ~ferre, ~tuli, ~latum **to give voice to** [27]silentium ~ii *neut.* **silence** [28]proprius ~a, ~um *adj.* **peculiar to** [29]mutabilitas ~atis *f.* **mutability**

periclitarentur[30] mendacio neque in illis litteris ulla fidei salus generi humano remaneret.[31] quia itaque uera scripta sunt, totum hominem in Christo agnoscebam, non corpus tantum hominis aut cum corpore sine mente animum, sed ipsum hominem, non persona[32] ueritatis, sed magna quadam naturae humanae excellentia et perfectiore participatione[33] sapientiae praeferri[34] ceteris arbitrabar.

Alypius autem Deum carne indutum[35] ita putabat credi a Catholicis ut praeter Deum et carnem non esset in Christo, animam mentemque hominis non existimabat[36] in eo praedicari.[37] et quoniam bene persuasum[38] tenebat ea quae de illo memoriae mandata[39] sunt sine uitali[40] et rationali[41] creatura non fieri, ad ipsam Christianam fidem pigrius[42] mouebatur. sed postea haereticorum[43] Apollinaristarum hunc errorem esse cognoscens Catholicae fidei conlaetatus[44] et contemperatus[45] est.

Ego autem aliquanto[46] posterius[47] didicisse me fateor,[48] in eo quod *Verbum caro factum est*, quomodo Catholica ueritas a Photini falsitate[49] dirimatur.[50] improbatio[51] quippe haereticorum facit eminere[52] quid Ecclesia tua sentiat et quid habeat *sana*[53] *doctrina* (1 Tim 1:10). *oportuit*[54] *enim et haereses*[55] *esse, ut probati*[56] *manifesti*[57] *fierent* (1 Cor 11:19) inter *infirmos*[58] (Rom 14:1).

---

[30]periclitor ~ari, ~atus to endanger [31]remaneo ~ere, ~si to remain [32]persona ~ae *f.* persona [33]participatio ~onis *f.* participation [34]praefero ~ferre, ~tuli, ~latum to prefer (w dat.) [35]induo ~uere, ~ui, ~utum to assume *or* put on [36]existimo ~are, ~aui, ~atum to think [37]praedico ~are, ~aui, ~atum to predicate; ECCL to preach [38]persuadeo ~dere, ~si, ~sum to persuade [39]memoriae mandata' committed to record [40]uitalis ~is, ~e *adj.* living [41]rationalis ~is, ~e *adj.* rational [42]pigre *adv.* reluctantly [43]haereticus ~i *m.* ECCL heretic [44]conlaetor ~ari, ~atum ECCL to rejoice with [45]contempero ~are, ~aui, ~atum to temper; LATE to conform to [46]aliquanto *adv.* somewhat [47]posterius *compar. adv.* later [48]fateor ~eri, fassus to confess [49]falsitas ~atis *f.* LATE false opinion [50]dirimo ~imere, ~emi, ~emptum to divide; LATE to distinguish [51]improbatio ~onis *f.* discrediting [52]emineo ~ere, ~ui to stand out in relief [53]sanus ~a, ~um *adj.* sound [54]oportet ~ere, ~uit *impers.* it is necessary [55]haeresis ~is *f.* philosophical sect; ECCL heresy [56]probo ~are, ~aui, ~atum to approve (as noun) [57]manifestus ~a, ~um *adj.* evident [58]infirmus ~a, ~um *adj.* weak

Invisible perceived through visible

7.20.26 Sed tunc, lectis Platonicorum illis libris, posteaquam[1] inde admonitus[2] quaerere incorpoream[3] ueritatem, *inuisibilia tua per ea*

---

[1]posteaquam *conj.* ever since [2]admoneo ~ere, ~ui, ~itum to admonish [3]incorporeus ~a, ~um *adj.* incorporeal

quae facta sunt intellecta conspexi[4] (Rom 1:20) et repulsus[5] sensi quid per tenebras animae meae contemplari[6] non sinerer, certus esse[7] te et infinitum esse nec tamen per locos finitos infinitosue diffundi[8] et uere te esse, qui semper *idem ipse esses* (Ps 101:28), ex nulla parte nulloque motu alter aut aliter, cetera uero ex te esse omnia, hoc solo firmissimo[9] documento[10] quia sunt, certus quidem in istis eram, nimis tamen infirmus[11] ad fruendum[12] te. garriebam[13] plane[14] quasi peritus[15] et, nisi in *Christo, Saluatore*[16] *nostro* (Tit 1:4), uiam tuam quaererem, non peritus sed periturus essem. iam enim coeperam uelle uideri sapiens plenus poena mea et non flebam, insuper[17] et *inflabar*[18] *scientia* (1 Cor 8:1). ubi enim erat illa aedificans[19] *caritas* (1 Cor 13:4) a *fundamento*[20] *humilitatis,*[21] *quod est Christus Iesus* (1 Cor 3:11)? aut quando illi libri me docerent eam? in quos me propterea,[22] priusquam scripturas tuas considerarem, credo uoluisti incurrere,[23] ut imprimeretur[24] memoriae meae quomodo ex eis affectus[25] essem et, cum postea in libris tuis mansuefactus[26] essem et curantibus digitis[27] tuis contrectarentur[28] uulnera mea, discernerem atque distinguerem[29] quid interesset[30] inter praesumptionem[31] et confessionem, inter uidentes quo eundum sit nec uidentes qua,[32] et Viam ducentem ad beatificam[33] patriam non tantum cernendam sed et habitandam.[34] nam si primo[35] sanctis tuis litteris informatus[36] essem et in earum familiaritate[37] obdulcuisses[38] mihi, et post in illa uolumina[39] incidissem,[40] fortasse[41] aut abripuissent[42] me a

---

[4]conspicio ~icere, ~exi, ~ectum to see > **to perceive** [5]repello ~ere, reppuli, repulsum **to rebuff** [6]contemplor ~ari, ~atus **to contemplate** [7]'certus esse' **being certain (that)** [8]diffundo ~undere, ~udi, ~usum **to diffuse** [9]firmus ~a, ~um *adj.* **reliable** [10]documentum ~i *neut.* **example** [11]infirmus ~a, ~um *adj.* **weak** [12]fruor ~i, ~ctus **to enjoy** (w. abl) [13]garrio ~ire, ~iui **to chatter** [14]plane *adv.* **clearly** [15]peritus ~a, ~um *adj.* **expert** [16]saluator ~oris *m.* ECCL **Savior** [17]insuper *adv.* **besides** [18]inflo ~are, ~aui, ~atum **to inflate** [19]aedifico ~are, ~aui, ~atum **to build** [20]fundamentum ~i *neut.* **foundation** [21]humilitas ~atis *f.* **humility** [22]propterea *adv.* **consequently** [23]incurro ~rere, ~ri, ~sum **to stumble over** [24]imprimo ~imere, ~essi, ~essum **to imprint** [25]afficio ~icere, ~eci, ~ectum **to affect** [26]mansuefacio ~facere, ~feci, ~factum **to tame** [27]digitus ~i *m.* **finger** [28]contrecto ~are, ~aui, ~atum **to touch gently** [29]distinguo ~guere, ~xi, ~ctum **to distinguish** [30]intersum ~esse, ~fui **to make a difference** (*impers.*) [31]praesumptio ~onis *f.* **presumption** [32]qua *adv.* **by what road** [33]beatificus ~a, ~um *adj.* **blessed** [34]habito ~are, ~aui, ~atum **to dwell** [35]primo *adv.* **at first** [36]informo ~are, ~aui, ~atum **to form** (by instruction) [37]familiaritas ~atis *f.* **familiarity** [38]obdulcesco ~ere AUG **to become sweet** [39]uolumen ~inis *neut.* **volume** (papyrus roll [lit.]) [40]incido ~ere, ~i **to come by chance** [41]fortasse *adv.* **perhaps** [42]abripio ~ipere, ~ipui, ~eptum **to snatch away**

solidamento[43] pietatis, aut si in affectu quem salubrem[44] inbiberam[45] perstitissem,[46] putarem etiam ex illis libris eum posse concipi,[47] si eos solos quisque didicisset.

[43]solidamentum ~i *neut.* LATE **solid foundation** [44]saluber ~bris, ~bre *adj.* **healthful** [45]inbibo ~ere, ~i, ~itum **to drink in** [46]persto ~are, ~iti, ~atum **to continue resolutely** [47]concipio ~ipere, ~epi, ~eptum **to form an idea**

The Apostle

7.21.27 Itaque auidissime[1] arripui[2] uenerabilem[3] stilum[4] Spiritus tui, et prae ceteris apostolum[5] Paulum, et perierunt illae quaestiones[6] in quibus mihi aliquando uisus est aduersari[7] sibi et non congruere[8] testimoniis[9] legis et prophetarum[10] textus[11] sermonis eius, et apparuit mihi una facies *eloquiorum[12] castorum[13]* (Ps 11:7), *et exultare[14] cum tremore[15]* (Ps 2:11) didici.

Et coepi et inueni, quidquid illac[16] uerum legeram, hac[17] cum commendatione[18] gratiae tuae dici, ut qui uidet non sic glorietur,[19] quasi non acceperit non solum id quod uidet, sed etiam ut uideat (*quid enim habet quod non accepit?* [1 Cor 4:7]) et ut te, qui *es semper idem* (Ps 101:28), non solum admoneatur[20] ut uideat, sed etiam sanetur ut teneat, et qui de longinquo[21] uidere non potest, uiam tamen ambulet[22] qua ueniat et uideat et teneat, quia, etsi condelectetur[23] homo legi Dei secundum interiorem hominem, quid faciet de *alia lege in membris suis repugnante[24] legi mentis suae et se captiuum[25] ducente in lege peccati, quae est in membris eius* (Rom 7:23)? quoniam *iustus es, Domine* (Ps 118:37), nos autem *peccauimus, inique[26] fecimus, impie[27] gessimus* (1 Kgs 8:47),

[1]auide *adv.* **eagerly** [2]arripio ~ere, ~ui, arreptum **to seize** [3]uenerabilis ~is, ~e *adj.* **venerable** [4]stilus ~i *m.* stylus; ECCL **writing** [5]apostolus ~i *m.* ECCL **apostle** [6]quaestio ~onis *f.* **difficulty** [7]aduersor ~ari, ~atus **to contradict** [8]congruo ~ere, ~ui **to agree** [9]testimonium ~ii *neut.* **testimony** [10]propheta ~ae *m.* ECCL **prophet** [11]textus ~us *m.* fabric; LATE **text** [12]eloquium ~ii *neut.* **utterance** [13]castus ~a, ~um *adj.* **chaste** [14]exulto ~are, ~aui **to exult** [15]tremor ~oris *m.* **trembling** [16]illac *adv.* **there** [17]hac *adv.* **here** [18]commendatio ~onis *f.* **approval** [19]glorior ~ari, ~atus **to boast** [20]admoneo ~ere, ~ui, ~itum **to urge** [21]longinquus ~a, ~um *adj.* **far off** [22]ambulo ~are, ~aui, ~atum **to walk** [23]condelector ~ari, ~atum ECCL **to delight in** [24]repugno ~are, ~aui, ~atum **to rebel against** [25]captiuus ~i *m.* **captive** [26]inique *adv.* ECCL **wickedly** [27]impie *adv.* **impiously**

et *grauata*[28] *est super nos manus tua* (Ps 31:4), et iuste[29] traditi sumus *antiquo*[30] *peccatori,*[31] *praeposito*[32] *mortis* (Heb 2:14), quia persuasit[33] uoluntati nostrae similitudinem[34] uoluntatis suae, qua *in ueritate tua non stetit* (Jn 8:44).

Quid faciet *miser homo? quis eum liberabit*[35] *de corpore mortis huius, nisi gratia tua per Iesum Christum Dominum nostrum* (Rom 7:24–25), quem genuisti[36] coaeternum et creasti *in principio uiarum tuarum* (Prov 8:22), in quo *princeps huius mundi* (Jn 14:30) non inuenit quicquam morte dignum, et occidit[37] eum? et euacuatum[38] est *chirographum*[39] *quod erat contrarium*[40] *nobis* (Col 2:14).

Hoc illae litterae non habent: non habent illae paginae[41] uultum pietatis huius, lacrimas confessionis, *sacrificium*[42] *tuum, spiritum contribulatum,*[43] *cor contritum*[44] *et humilatum*[45] (Ps 50:19), populi salutem, *sponsam*[46] *ciuitatem* (Rev 21:2), *arram*[47] *Spiritus Sancti* (2 Cor 1:22), poculum[48] pretii[49] nostri. nemo ibi cantat, *Nonne Deo subdita*[50] *erit anima mea? ab ipso enim salutare*[51] *meum: etenim*[52] *ipse Deus meus et salutaris meus, susceptor*[53] *meus: non mouebor amplius* (Ps 61:2–3). nemo ibi audit uocantem: *Venite ad me, qui laboratis.*[54] dedignantur[55] ab eo discere *quoniam mitis*[56] *est et humilis*[57] *corde* (Mt 11:28–29). *abscondisti*[58] *enim haec a sapientibus et prudentibus*[59] *et reuelasti*[60] *ea paruulis* (Mt 11:25).

Et aliud est de siluestri[61] cacumine[62] uidere patriam pacis et iter ad eam non inuenire et frustra[63] conari per inuia[64] circum[65] obsidentibus[66]

---

[28]grauo ~are, ~aui, ~atum **to be heavy** [29]iuste *adv.* **justly** [30]antiquus ~a, ~um *adj.* **ancient** [31]peccator ~oris *m.* ECCL **sinner** [32]praepositus ~i *m.* **person placed in charge** [33]persuadeo ~dere, ~si, ~sum **to induce** (w. dat.) [34]similitudo ~inis *f.* **after the manner of** (w. gen.) [35]libero ~are, ~aui, ~atum **to free** (a slave) [36]gigno ~ere, genui, genitum **to beget** [37]occido ~dere, ~di, ~sum **to kill** [38]euacuo ~are **to empty**; ECCL **to make void** [39]chirographum ~i *neut.* **handwritten bond** [40]contrarius ~a, ~um *adj.* **hostile** [41]pagina ~ae *f.* **page** [42]sacrificium ~ii *neut.* **sacrificial offering** [43]contribulo ~are ~atum ECCL **to crush** [44]contero ~terere, ~triui, ~tritum to crush, grind ECCL *ppl. adj.* **contrite** [45]humilo ~are, ~aui, ~atum ECCL **to humble** [46]sponsa ~ae *f.* **promised bride** [47]arra ~ae *f.* **deposit** [48]poculum, -clum ~i *neut.* **cup** [49]pretium ~ii *neut.* **ransom** [50]subdo ~ere, ~idi, ~itum **to subject** [51]salutare ~is *neut.* ECCL **salvation** [52]etenim *conj.* **for** [53]susceptor ~oris *m.* ECCL **protector** [54]laboro ~are, ~aui, ~atum **to labor** [55]dedignor ~ari, ~atus **to reject with contempt** [56]mitis ~is, ~e *adj.* **gentle** [57]humilis ~is, ~e *adj.* **humble** [58]abscondo ~ere, ~i, ~itum **to hide** [59]prudens ~ntis *adj.* **prudent** [60]reuelo ~are, ~aui, ~atum **to reveal** [61]siluestris ~tris, ~tre *adj.* **wooded** [62]cacumen ~inis *neut.* **height** [63]frustra *adv.* **in vain** [64]inuius ~a, ~um *adj.* **impassable path** (*neut.* as noun) [65]circum *adv.* **round about** [66]obsideo ~idere, ~edi, ~essum **to obstruct**

et insidiantibus[67] fugitiuis[68] desertoribus[69] cum principe suo *leone*[70] *et dracone*[71] (Ps 90:13), et aliud tenere uiam illuc[72] ducentem cura caelestis[73] imperatoris[74] munitam,[75] ubi non latrocinantur[76] qui caelestem militiam[77] deseruerunt; uitant[78] enim eam sicut supplicium.[79]

Haec mihi inuiscerabantur[80] miris modis, cum *minimum*[81] *apostolorum* (1 Cor 15:9) tuorum legerem, et *consideraueram opera tua et expaueram*[82] (Hab 3:2 VL).

[67]insidior ~ari, ~atus **to lie in wait** [68]fugitiuus ~a, ~um *adj.* **fugitive** (of runaway slaves) [69]desertor ~oris *m.* **deserter** [70]leo ~onis *m.* **lion** [71]draco ~onis *m.* **dragon** [72]illuc *adv.* **there** [73]caelestis ~is, ~e *adj.* **heavenly** [74]imperator ~oris *m.* **emperor** [75]munitus ~a, ~um *adj.* **well-protected** [76]latrocinor ~ari, ~atus **to engage in brigandage** [77]militia ~ae *f.* **army** [78]uito ~are, ~aui, ~atum **to avoid** [79]supplicium ~ii *neut.* **torment** [80]inuiscero ~are, ~aui, ~atum LATE **to implant deeply** [81]minimus ~a, ~um *superl. adj.* **least** [82]expauesco ~auescere, ~aui **to be terrified at**

8

"TOLLE, LEGE"

Milan, 386

A visit to Simplicianus

8.1.1 Deus meus, recorder in gratiarum actione[1] tibi et confitear *misericordias tuas super me* (Ps 85:13). perfundantur[2] *ossa*[3] *mea* dilectione[4] tua et *dicant: Domine, quis similis tibi?* (Ps 34:10). *dirupisti*[5] *uincula*[6] *mea: sacrificem*[7] *tibi sacrificium*[8] *laudis* (Ps 115:16–17). quomodo dirupisti ea narrabo, et dicent omnes qui adorant[9] te, cum audiunt haec, *Benedictus*[10] *Dominus* (Ps 71:18) *in caelo et in terra* (Ps 134:6); *magnum et mirabile*[11] *nomen eius* (Ps 75:2; 8:2).

Inhaeserant[12] praecordiis[13] meis uerba tua, et undique[14] circumuallabar[15] abs te. de uita tua aeterna certus eram, quamuis eam *in aenigmate*[16] et quasi *per speculum*[17] (1 Cor 13:12) uideram; dubitatio[18] tamen omnis de incorruptibili[19] substantia, quod ab illa esset omnis substantia, ablata mihi erat, nec certior de te sed stabilior[20] in te esse cupiebam. de mea uero temporali[21] uita nutabant[22] omnia et mundandum[23] erat cor a

---

[1]'gratiarum actione' **expression of thanks** [2]perfundo ~undere, ~udi, ~usum **to wash over** (pass.) [3]os ossis *neut.* **bones** (*pl.* esp. as seat of emotion); ECCL soul (fig.) [4]dilectio ~onis *f.* ECCL **love** [5]dirrumpo ~umpere, ~upi, ~uptum **to break** [6]uinculum ~i *neut.* **chain** [7]sacrifico ~are, ~aui, ~atum **to offer in sacrifice** [8]sacrificium ~ii *neut.* **sacrificial offering** [9]adoro ~are, ~aui, ~atum **to worship** [10]benedictus ~a, ~um *adj.* ECCL **blessed** [11]mirabilis ~is, ~e *adj.* **marvelous** [12]inhaereo ~rere, ~si, ~sum **to implant** [13]praecordia ~orum *neut. pl.* **deepest affections** [14]undique *adv.* **on every side** [15]circumuallo ~are, ~aui, ~atum **to surround** [16]'in aenigmate' **obscurely** [17]speculum ~i *neut.* **mirror** [18]dubitatio ~onis *f.* **doubt** [19]incorruptibilis ~is, ~e *adj.* ECCL **incorruptible** [20]stabilis ~is, ~e *adj.* **firmly established** [21]temporalis ~is, ~e *adj.* **temporal** [22]nuto ~are, ~aui, ~atum to nod > **to remain in doubt** [23]mundo ~are, ~aui, ~atum **to make clean**

fermento[24] *ueteri* (1 Cor 5:7). et placebat Via ipse Saluator,[25] et ire *per eius angustias*[26] (Mt 7:14) adhuc pigebat.[27]

Et immisisti[28] in mentem meam uisumque est bonum in conspectu meo pergere[29] ad Simplicianum, qui mihi bonus apparebat seruus tuus et lucebat[30] in eo gratia tua. audieram etiam quod a iuuentute[31] sua deuotissime[32] tibi uiueret; iam uero[33] tunc senuerat[34] et longa aetate in tam bono studio sectandae[35] uitae tuae multa expertus, multa edoctus[36] mihi uidebatur: et uere sic erat. unde mihi ut proferret[37] uolebam conferenti[38] secum aestus[39] meos quis esset aptus[40] modus sic affecto[41] ut ego eram ad *ambulandum*[42] *in uia tua* (Ps 127:1).

[24]fermentum ~i *neut.* **leaven** [25]saluator ~oris *m.* ECCL **Savior** [26]angustia ~ae *f.* **narrowness** [27]piget ~ere, ~uit, ~itum **to irk** [28]immitto ~ittere, ~isi, ~issum **to send** [29]pergo ~gere, ~rexi, ~rectum **to make one's way** [30]luceo ~ere, luxi **to shine** [31]iuuentus ~utis *f.* **early adulthood** [32]deuote *adv.* LATE **devoutly** [33]'iam uero' **what is more** [34]senesco ~escere, ~ui **to grow old** [35]sector ~ari, ~atus **to follow** [36]edoceo ~ere, ~ui, ~tum **to instruct thoroughly** [37]profero ~ferre, ~tuli, ~latum **to propose** [38]confero ~rre, contuli, conlatum **to confer** [39]aestus ~us *m.* ebb and flow > **perplexity** [40]aptus ~a, ~um *ppl. adj.* **suitable** [41]affectus ~a, ~um *adj.* **disposed** (w. *adv.*) [42]ambulo ~are, ~aui, ~atum to walk; ECCL **to live**

One Church, many vocations

8.1.2 Videbam enim plenam Ecclesiam, et *alius sic ibat, alius autem sic* (1 Cor 7:7), mihi autem displicebat quod agebam in saeculo et oneri[1] mihi erat ualde, non iam inflammantibus[2] cupiditatibus, ut solebant, spe honoris et pecuniae[3] ad tolerandam[4] illam seruitutem[5] tam grauem. iam enim me illa non delectabant prae dulcedine[6] tua et *decore*[7] *domus tuae,* quam *dilexi* (Ps 25:8), sed adhuc tenaciter[8] conligabar ex femina, nec me prohibebat[9] apostolus[10] coniugari,[11] quamuis exhortaretur[12] ad melius, maxime *uolens omnes homines sic esse ut ipse erat* (1 Cor 7:7). sed ego infirmior[13] eligebam[14] molliorem locum et propter hoc unum uoluebar,[15] in ceteris languidus[16] et tabescens[17] curis marcidis,[18] quod et

[1]onus ~eris *neut.* **burden** [2]inflammo ~are, ~aui, ~atum **to set on fire** (fig. desire) [3]pecunia ~ae *f.* **possessions** [4]tolero ~are, ~aui, ~atum **to tolerate** [5]seruitus ~utis *f.* **servitude** [6]dulcedo ~inis *f.* **sweetness** [7]decus ~oris *neut.* **beauty** [8]tenaciter *adv.* **tenaciously** [9]prohibeo ~ere, ~ui, ~itum **to forbid** [10]apostolus ~i *m.* ECCL **the apostle** (St. Paul) [11]coniugo ~are, ~aui, ~atum **to marry** [12]exhortor ~ari, ~atum **to exhort** [13]infirmus ~a, ~um *adj.* **weak** [14]eligo ~igere, ~egi, ~ectum **to choose** [15]uoluo ~uere, ~ui, ~utum **to roll along** [16]languidus ~a, ~um *adj.* **losing interest** [17]tabesco ~escere, ~ui **to waste away** [18]marcidus ~a, ~um *adj.* withered; LATE **withering**

in aliis rebus quas nolebam pati congruere[19] cogebar uitae coniugali,[20] cui deditus[21] obstringebar.[22] audieram ex ore Veritatis esse *spadones*[23] *qui se ipsos absciderunt*[24] *propter regnum caelorum*, sed *Qui potest*, inquit, *capere, capiat* (Mt 19:12).

Vani sunt certe omnes homines quibus non inest[25] *Dei scientia, nec de his quae uidentur bona potuerunt inuenire Eum Qui Est* (Wis 13:1–3). at ego iam non eram in illa uanitate. transcenderam[26] eam et contestante[27] uniuersa creatura inueneram te creatorem nostrum et Verbum tuum apud te Deum tecumque unum Deum, per quod creasti omnia. et est aliud genus impiorum,[28] qui *cognoscentes Deum non sicut Deum glorificauerunt*[29] *aut gratias egerunt* (Rom 1:21). in hoc quoque incideram,[30] *et dextera tua suscepit*[31] *me* (Ps 17:36) et inde ablatum posuisti ubi conualescerem,[32] quia dixisti homini, *Ecce pietas est sapientia* (Job 28:28 VL), et, *Noli uelle uideri sapiens* (Sir 7:5), *quoniam dicentes se esse sapientes stulti*[33] *facti sunt* (Rom 1:22). et inueneram iam *bonam margaritam*[34] (Mt 13:46), et *uenditis*[35] omnibus quae haberem *emenda*[36] erat, et dubitabam.[37]

---

[19]congruo ~ere, ~ui **to adapt to** [20]coniugalis ~is, ~e *adj.* **conjugal** [21]deditus ~a, ~um *adj.* **given over** [22]obstringo ~ngere, ~nxi, ~ctum **to obligate** [23]spado ~onis *m.* **eunuch** [24]abscido ~dere, ~di, ~sum **to cut off** [25]insum inesse, infui **to be possessed of** [26]transcendo ~dere, ~di, ~sum **to transcend** [27]contestor ~ari, ~atus **to call to witness; ECCL to testify** [28]impius ~a, ~um *adj.* **impious** [29]glorifico ~are, ~aui, ~atus ECCL **to glorify** [30]incido ~ere, ~i **to fall into** [31]suscipio ~ipere, ~epi, ~eptum **to save from being lost** [32]conualesco ~escere, ~ui **to recover health** [33]stultus ~a, ~um *adj.* **foolish** [34]margarita ~ae *f.* **pearl** [35]uendo ~ere, ~idi, ~itum **to sell** [36]emo emere, emi, emptum **to buy** [37]dubito ~are, ~aui, ~atum **to hesitate**

Simplicianus on Victorinus

8.2.3 Perrexi[1] ergo ad Simplicianum, patrem in accipienda gratia tunc episcopi[2] Ambrosii et quem uere ut patrem diligebat. narraui ei circuitus[3] erroris mei. ubi autem commemoraui legisse me quosdam libros Platonicorum, quos Victorinus, quondam[4] rhetor[5] urbis Romae, quem Christianum defunctum[6] esse audieram, in Latinam linguam

---

[1]pergo ~gere, ~rexi, ~rectum **to make one's way** [2]episcopus ~i *m.* ECCL **bishop** [3]circuitus ~us *m.* **cycle** [4]quondam *adv.* **at one time** [5]rhetor ~oris *m.* **rhetorician** [6]defungor ~gi, ~ctus **to have died** (perf.)

transtulisset,[7] gratulatus[8] est mihi quod non in aliorum philosophorum[9] scripta incidissem[10] plena fallaciarum[11] et deceptionum[12] *secundum elementa*[13] *huius mundi* (Col 2:8), in istis autem omnibus modis insinuari[14] Deum et eius Verbum.

Deinde, ut me exhortaretur[15] ad humilitatem[16] Christi *sapientibus absconditam*[17] *et reuelatam*[18] *paruulis* (Mt 11:25), Victorinum ipsum recordatus est, quem Romae cum esset familiarissime[19] nouerat, deque illo mihi narrauit quod non silebo.[20]

Habet enim magnam laudem gratiae tuae confitendam tibi, quemadmodum ille doctissimus senex[21] et omnium liberalium[22] doctrinarum peritissimus[23] quique philosophorum tam multa legerat et diiudicauerat,[24] doctor[25] tot nobilium senatorum,[26] qui etiam ob insigne[27] praeclari[28] magisterii,[29] quod ciues huius mundi eximium[30] putant, statuam[31] Romano Foro[32] meruerat[33] et acceperat, usque ad illam aetatem uenerator[34] idolorum[35] sacrorumque[36] sacrilegorum[37] particeps,[38] quibus tunc tota fere[39] Romana nobilitas[40] inflata,[41] inspirabat[42] populo etiam

et omnigenum[43] *deum monstra*[44] *et Anubem latratorem,*[45]
quae aliquando
contra Neptunum et Venerem contraque Mineruam
tela tenuerant (Aen. 8.698–700).

---

[7]transfero ~ferre, ~tuli, ~latum to convey > **to translate** [8]gratulor ~ari, ~atus **to congratulate** [9]philosophus ~i *m.* **philosopher** [10]incido ~ere, ~i **to fall into** [11]fallacia ~ae *f.* **deceit** [12]deceptio ~onis *f.* ECCL **deception** [13]elementum ~i *neut.* **elements** [14]insinuo ~are, ~aui, ~atum **to convey** (an idea) [15]exhortor ~ari, ~atum **to encourage** [16]humilitas ~atis *f.* **humility** [17]absconditus ~a, ~um *adj.* **hidden** [18]reuelo ~are, ~aui, ~atum **to reveal** [19]familiariter *adv.* **as a close friend** [20]sileo ~ere, ~ui **to be silent** [21]senex ~is, senior *m. adj.* **old man** [22]liberalis ~is, ~e *adj.* **liberal** (of arts, studies, education) [23]peritus ~a, ~um *adj.* **skilled** [24]diiudico ~are, ~aui, ~atum **to distinguish** [25]doctor ~oris *m.* **teacher** [26]senator ~oris *m.* **senator** [27]insigne ~is *neut.* **outward mark of honor** [28]praeclarus ~a, ~um *adj.* **outstanding** [29]magisterium ~ii *neut.* **office** [30]eximius ~a, ~um *adj.* **exceptional** [31]statua ~ae *f.* **statue** [32]'Romano Foro' **in the Roman Forum** [33]mereo ~ere, ~ui, ~itum **to deserve** [34]uenerator ~oris *m.* **venerator** [35]idolum ~i *neut.* ECCL **idol** [36]sacrum ~i *neut.* **sacred rite or festival** [37]sacrilegus ~a, ~um *adj.* **sacrilegious** [38]particeps ~cipis *adj.* **participating (in)** [39]fere *adv.* **almost** [40]nobilitas ~atis *f.* **nobility** [41]inflo ~are, ~aui, ~atum **to inflate** [42]inspiro ~are, ~aui, ~atum **to inspire** (LATE w. dat.) [43]omnigenus ~a, ~um *adj.* **of every kind** [44]monstrum ~i *neut.* **monster** [45]latrator ~oris *m.* **to bark**

Et a se uictis iam Roma supplicabat,[46] quae iste senex Victorinus tot annos ore terricrepo[47] defensitauerat,[48] non erubuerit[49] esse puer Christi tui et infans[50] fontis tui, subiecto[51] collo[52] ad humilitatis iugum et edomita[53] fronte[54] ad crucis[55] opprobrium.[56]

[46]supplico ~are, ~aui, ~atum **to supplicate** [47]terricrepus ~a, ~um *adj.* AUG **sounding terrifying** [48]defensito ~are, ~aui, ~atum **to defend habitually** [49]erubesco ~escere, ~ui **to feel ashamed** [50]infans ~ntis *m. f.* **infant** [51]subicio ~icere, ~ieci, ~iectum **to make subject** [52]collum ~i *neut.* **neck** (fig. for the will) [53]edomo ~are, ~ui, ~itum **to subjugate** [54]frons ~ntis *f.* **brow** [55]crux ~ucis *f.* **cross** [56]opprobrium ~ii *neut.* **reproach**

An inside joke: do walls make Christians?

8.2.4 O Domine, Domine, qui *inclinasti[1] caelos et descendisti,[2] tetigisti[3] montes et fumigauerunt[4]* (Ps 143:5), quibus modis te insinuasti[5] illi pectori? legebat, sicut ait Simplicianus, sanctam scripturam omnesque Christianas litteras inuestigabat[6] studiosissime[7] et perscrutabatur,[8] et dicebat Simpliciano, non palam[9] sed secretius[10] et familiarius,[11] "Noueris me iam esse Christianum." et respondebat ille, "Non credam nec deputabo[12] te inter Christianos, nisi in Ecclesia Christi uidero." ille autem inridebat dicens, "Ergo parietes[13] faciunt Christianos?" et hoc saepe dicebat, iam se esse Christianum, et Simplicianus illud saepe respondebat, et saepe ab illo parietum inrisio[14] repetebatur.[15]

Amicos enim suos reuerebatur[16] offendere,[17] superbos daemonico-las,[18] quorum ex culmine[19] *Babylonicae* (Rev 17:5) dignitatis[20] quasi ex *cedris[21] Libani*, quas nondum *contriuerat[22] Dominus* (Ps 28:5), grauiter[23] ruituras[24] in se inimicitias[25] arbitrabatur. sed posteaquam[26] legendo et

[1]inclino ~are, ~aui, ~atum **to bend down** [2]descendo ~dere, ~di, ~sum **to descend** [3]tango ~ere, tetigi, tactum **to touch** [4]fumigo ~are, ~aui, ~atum **to make smoke** [5]insinuo ~are, ~aui, ~atum **to instill > to convey** [6]inuestigo ~are, ~aui, ~atum **to search out** [7]studiose *adv.* **intensively** [8]perscrutor ~ari, ~atus **to study carefully** [9]palam *adv.* **publicly** [10]secreto *adv.* **in private** [11]familiariter *adv.* **intimately** [12]deputo ~are, ~aui, ~atum **to regard as** [13]paries ~etis *m.* **wall** [14]inrisio ~onis *f.* **jest** [15]repeto ~ere, ~iui or ~ii, ~itum **to repeat** [16]reuereor ~eri, ~itus **to feel abashed before** [17]offendo ~dere, ~di, ~sum **to give offense (to)** [18]daemonicola ~ae *m.* AUG **worshipper of demons** [19]culmen ~inis *neut.* **height** [20]dignitas ~atis *f.* **standing** [21]cedrus ~i *f.* **cedar** *or* **juniper** [22]contero ~terere, ~triui, ~tritum **to grind down** [23]grauiter *adv.* **grievously** [24]ruo ~ere, ~i **to rush down uncontrollably** [25]inimicitia ~ae *f.* **enmity** [26]posteaquam *conj.* **after that**

inhiando²⁷ hausit²⁸ firmitatem²⁹ timuitque *negari* a Christo *coram angelis sanctis*, si eum timeret *coram hominibus confiteri* (Lk 12:8–9), reusque³⁰ sibi magni criminis apparuit erubescendo³¹ de sacramentis humilitatis³² Verbi tui et non erubescendo de sacris³³ sacrilegis³⁴ superborum daemoniorum,³⁵ quae imitator³⁶ superbus acceperat, depuduit³⁷ uanitati et erubuit ueritati subitoque³⁸ et inopinatus³⁹ ait Simpliciano, ut ipse narrabat, "Eamus in ecclesiam: Christianus uolo fieri."

At ille non se capiens laetitia perrexit⁴⁰ cum eo. ubi autem imbutus⁴¹ est primis instructionis⁴² sacramentis, non multo post etiam nomen dedit ut per baptismum⁴³ regeneraretur,⁴⁴ mirante Roma, gaudente Ecclesia. superbi uidebant et irascebantur,⁴⁵ *dentibus⁴⁶ suis stridebant⁴⁷ et tabescebant⁴⁸* (Ps 111:10). seruo autem tuo *Dominus Deus erat spes eius, et non respiciebat⁴⁹ in uanitates et insanias⁵⁰ mendaces⁵¹* (Ps 39:5).

²⁷inhio ~are, ~aui, ~atum **to long for** ²⁸haurio ~rire, ~si, ~stum **to drink in** ²⁹firmitas ~atis *f.* **strength** ³⁰reus ~i *m.* **one guilty of** (w. gen) ³¹erubesco ~escere, ~ui **to feel ashamed** ³²humilitas ~atis *f.* **humility** ³³sacrum ~i *neut.* **sacred rite or festival** ³⁴sacrilegus ~a, ~um *adj.* **sacrilegious** ³⁵daemonium ~i *neut.* ECCL **demon** ³⁶imitator ~oris *m.* **imitator** ³⁷depudesco ~escere, ~ui **to become shameless** ³⁸subito *adv.* **suddenly** ³⁹inopinatus ~a, ~um *adj.* **unforeseen** ⁴⁰pergo ~gere, ~rexi, ~rectum **to make one's way** ⁴¹imbuo ~uere, ~ui, ~utum **to give initial instruction** ⁴²instructio ~onis *f.* **instruction** ⁴³baptismus ~i *m.* (~um ~i *neut.*) ECCL **baptism** ⁴⁴regenero ~are **to reproduce; ECCL to regenerate** ⁴⁵irascor ~i, iratus sum **to be angry** ⁴⁶dens ~ntis *m.* **tooth** ⁴⁷strido ~ere, ~i [onomat.] **to hiss** *or* **to gnash** ⁴⁸tabesco ~escere, ~ui **to waste away** ⁴⁹respicio ~icere, ~exi, ~ectum **to look back at** ⁵⁰insania ~ae *f.* **insanity** ⁵¹mendax ~acis *adj.* **lying**

Victorinus, Victorinus!

8.2.5 Denique¹ ut uentum est ad horam profitendae² fidei, quae uerbis certis conceptis³ retentisque⁴ memoriter⁵ de loco eminentiore⁶ in conspectu populi fidelis Romae reddi solet ab eis qui accessuri⁷ sunt ad gratiam tuam, oblatum⁸ esse dicebat Victorino a presbyteris⁹ ut secretius¹⁰ redderet, sicut nonnullis¹¹ qui uerecundia¹² trepidaturi¹³ uidebantur offerri¹⁴ mos erat; illum autem maluisse¹⁵ salutem suam in

¹denique *adv.* **at last** ²profiteor ~iteri, ~essus **to profess openly** ³'uerbis conceptis' **in a solemn or formal utterance** ⁴retineo ~ere, ~ui, retentum **to retain in memory** ⁵memoriter *adv.* **accurately** (remembered) ⁶eminens ~ntis *adj.* **prominent** ⁷accedo ~dere, ~ssi, ~ssum **to approach** ⁸offero ~rre, obtuli, oblatum **to offer** ⁹presbyter ~i *m.* ECCL **priest** ¹⁰secreto *adv.* **in private** ¹¹nonnullus ~a, ~um *adj.* **not a few** ¹²uerecundia ~ae *f.* **modesty > oversensitivity** ¹³trepido ~are, ~aui, ~atum **to feel anxious** ¹⁴offero ~rre, obtuli, oblatum **to occur** ¹⁵malo ~lle, ~lui **to prefer**

conspectu sanctae multitudinis[16] profiteri. non enim erat salus quam docebat in rhetorica,[17] et tamen eam publice[18] professus erat. quanto minus ergo uereri[19] debuit mansuetum[20] gregem[21] tuum pronuntians[22] uerbum tuum, qui non uerebatur in uerbis suis turbas insanorum?[23]

Itaque ubi ascendit[24] ut redderet, omnes sibimet inuicem,[25] quisque ut eum nouerat, instrepuerunt[26] nomen eius strepitu[27] gratulationis[28] (quis autem ibi non eum nouerat?) et sonuit presso[29] sonitu[30] per ora cunctorum conlaetantium,[31] "Victorinus, Victorinus." cito[32] sonuerunt exultatione,[33] quia uidebant eum, et cito siluerunt[34] intentione,[35] ut audirent eum. pronuntiauit ille fidem ueracem[36] praeclara[37] fiducia,[38] et uolebant eum omnes rapere intro[39] in cor suum. et rapiebant amando et gaudendo: hae rapientium manus erant.

[16]multitudo ~inis *f.* **congregation** [17]rhetoricus ~a, ~um *adj.* **rhetoric** (*f.* as noun) [18]publice *adv.* **publicly** [19]uereor ~eri, ~itus **to be afraid of** [20]mansuetus ~a, ~um *adj.* **gentle** [21]grex ~egis *m.* **flock** [22]pronuntio ~are, ~aui, ~atum **to speak publicly** [23]insanus ~a, ~um *adj.* **frenzied** [24]ascendo ~dere, ~di, ~sum **to mount** [25]inuicem *adv.* **each in turn** [26]instrepo ~ere, ~ui, ~itum **to utter loudly** [27]strepitus ~us *m.* **clamor** [28]gratulatio ~onis *f.* **thanksgiving** [29]pressus ~a, ~um *adj.* **low** [30]sonitus ~us *m.* **sound** [31]conlaetor ~ari, ~atum ECCL **to rejoice together** [32]cito *adv.* **spontaneously** [33]exultatio ~onis *f.* **exultation** [34]sileo ~ere, ~ui **to be silent** [35]intentio ~onis *f.* **attention** [36]uerax ~acis *adj.* **spoken truthfully** [37]praeclarus ~a, ~um *adj.* **brilliant** [38]fiducia ~ae *f.* **confidence** [39]intro *adv.* **inwardly**

Lost and found

8.3.6 Deus bone, quid agitur in homine, ut plus gaudeat de salute desperatae[1] animae et de maiore periculo liberatae[2] quam si spes ei semper adfuisset aut periculum minus fuisset? etenim[3] tu quoque, misericors[4] Pater, *plus gaudes de uno paenitente*[5] *quam de nonaginta*[6] *nouem*[7] *iustis quibus non opus est paenitentia*[8] (Lk 15:7). et nos cum magna iucunditate[9] audimus, cum audimus quam exultantibus[10] *pastoris*[11] *umeris*[12] *reportetur*[13] *ouis*[14] *quae errauerat* (Lk 15:4–5), et *drachma*[15] (Lk 15:8–9) referatur[16] in thesauros[17] tuos conlaetantibus[18] uicinis[19] mulieri[20]

[1]desperatus ~a, ~um *adj.* **desperate** [2]libero ~are, ~aui, ~atum **to liberate** [3]etenim *conj.* **for** [4]misericors ~rdis *adj.* **merciful** [5]paeniteo ~ere, ~ui **to regret**; ECCL **to repent** [6]nonaginta *indecl. adj.* **ninety** [7]nouem *indecl. adj.* **nine** [8]paenitentia ~ae *f.* **regret**; ECCL **regret for sin** [9]iucunditas ~atis *f.* **agreeableness**; ECCL **joyfulness** [10]exulto ~are, ~aui **to exult** [11]pastor ~oris *m.* **shepherd** [12]umerus ~i *m.* **shoulder** [13]reporto ~are, ~aui, ~atum **to carry back** [14]ouis ~is *f.* **sheep** [15]drachma ~ae *f.* **(Greek silver) coin** [16]refero ~rre, rettuli, relatum **to return** [17]thesaurus ~i *m.* **treasure box** [18]conlaetor ~ari, ~atum ECCL **to rejoice with** [19]uicinus ~a, ~um *adj.* **neighbor** (as noun) [20]mulier ~eris *f.* **woman**

quae inuenit, et lacrimas excutit[21] gaudium sollemnitatis[22] domus tuae, cum legitur in domo tua de minore filio tuo quoniam *mortuus erat et reuixit,*[23] *perierat et inuentus est* (Lk 15:32). gaudes quippe in nobis et in angelis tuis sancta caritate sanctis. nam tu semper idem, qui ea quae non semper nec eodem modo sunt eodem modo semper nosti omnia.

[21]excutio ~tere, ~ssi, ~ssum **to cause to flow** [22]sollemnitas ~atis *f.* ritual observance; ECCL **solemnity** (Eucharist) [23]reuiuesco ~escere, reuixi **to come to life again**

Pleasure results from distress

8.3.7 Quid ergo agitur in anima, cum amplius delectatur inuentis aut redditis rebus quas diligit quam si eas semper habuisset? contestantur[1] enim et cetera et plena sunt omnia testimoniis[2] clamantibus, "Ita est." triumphat[3] uictor imperator,[4] et non uicisset nisi pugnauisset,[5] et quanto maius periculum fuit in proelio, tanto est gaudium maius in triumpho.[6] iactat[7] tempestas[8] nauigantes[9] minaturque[10] naufragium:[11] omnes *futura morte pallescunt*[12] (Aen. 4.644): tranquillatur[13] caelum et mare, et exultant[14] nimis, quoniam timuerunt nimis. aeger[15] est carus[16] et uena[17] eius malum renuntiat:[18] omnes qui eum saluum[19] cupiunt aegrotant[20] simul animo: fit ei recte[21] et nondum ambulat[22] pristinis[23] uiribus, et fit iam tale gaudium quale non fuit cum antea[24] saluus et fortis ambularet.

Easque ipsas uoluptates humanae uitae etiam non inopinatis[25] et praeter uoluntatem inruentibus,[26] sed institutis[27] et uoluntariis[28] molestiis[29] homines adquirunt.[30] edendi[31] et bibendi[32] uoluptas nulla est, nisi

[1]contestor ~ari, ~atus **to call to witness**; ECCL **to testify** [2]testimonium ~ii *neut.* **testimony** [3]triumpho ~are, ~aui, ~atum **to celebrate a triumph** [4]imperator ~oris *m.* **emperor** [5]pugno ~are, ~aui, ~atum **to fight** [6]triumphus ~i *m.* **victory parade** [7]iacto ~are, ~aui, ~atum **to toss** [8]tempestas ~atis *f.* **tempest** [9]nauigo ~are, ~aui, ~atum **to sail** [10]minor ~ari, ~atus **to threaten** [11]naufragium ~ii *neut.* **shipwreck** [12]pallesco ~escere, ~ui **to turn pale** [13]tranquillo ~are, ~aui, ~atum **to make calm** [14]exulto ~are, ~aui **to rejoice** [15]aeger ~gra, ~grum *adj.* **ailing** [16]carus ~a, ~um *adj.* **dear one** (as noun) [17]uena ~ae *f.* **vein > pulse** (of an artery) [18]renuntio ~are, ~aui, ~atum **to tell** [19]saluus ~a, ~um *adj.* **in good health** [20]aegroto ~are, ~aui, ~atum **to be ill** [21]'fit recte' **it turns out right** [22]ambulo ~are, ~aui, ~atum **to walk** [23]pristinus ~a, ~um *adj.* **former** [24]antea *adv.* **before this** [25]inopinatus ~a, ~um *adj.* **unforeseen** [26]inruo ~uere, ~ui **to rush in** [27]instituo ~uere, ~ui, ~utum **to plan** [28]uoluntarius ~a, ~um *adj.* **voluntarily undertaken** [29]molestia ~ae *f.* **discomfort** [30]adquiro ~rere, ~siui, ~situm **to acquire** [31]edo esse, edi, esum **to eat** [32]bibo ~ere, ~i **to drink**

praecedat[33] esuriendi[34] et sitiendi[35] molestia. et ebriosi[36] quaedam salsiuscula[37] comedunt,[38] quo fiat molestus[39] ardor,[40] quem dum exstinguit[41] potatio,[42] fit delectatio.[43] et institutum[44] est ut iam pactae[45] sponsae[46] non tradantur statim,[47] ne uile[48] habeat maritus[49] datam quam non suspirauerit sponsus[50] dilatam.[51]

[33]praecedo ~edere, ~essi, ~essum **to precede** [34]esurio, ess- ~ire, ~itum **to be hungry** [35]sitio ~ire **to be thirsty** [36]ebriosus ~a, ~um *adj.* **drunk** (as noun) [37]salsiusculus ~a ~um *adj. dim.* AUG **rather salty** [38]comedo ~edere, ~edi, ~esum **to eat up** [39]molestus ~a, ~um *adj.* **burning** [40]ardor ~oris *m.* **desire, i.e., thirst** [41]exstinguo ~guere, ~xi, ~ctum **to extinguish** [42]potatio ~onis *f.* **drinking party** [43]delectatio ~onis *f.* **enjoyment** [44]instituo ~uere, ~ui, ~utum **to establish** (as custom) [45]pactus ~a, ~um *adj.* **pledged** [46]sponsa ~ae *f.* **woman promised in marriage** [47]statim *adv.* **immediately** [48]uilis ~is, ~e *adj.* **cheap** [49]maritus ~a, ~um *adj.* **married** [50]sponsus ~i *m.* **bridegroom** [51]differo ~rre, distuli, dilatum **to keep waiting**

Our proper mode of being

8.3.8 Hoc in turpi et exsecranda[1] laetitia, hoc in ea quae concessa[2] et licita[3] est, hoc in ipsa sincerissima[4] honestate[5] amicitiae,[6] hoc in eo *qui mortuus erat et reuixit,*[7] *perierat et inuentus est* (Lk 15:32): ubique[8] maius gaudium molestia[9] maiore praeceditur.[10] quid est hoc, Domine Deus meus, cum tu aeternum[11] tibi, tu ipse, sis gaudium, et quaedam de te circa[12] te semper gaudeant? quid est quod[13] haec rerum pars alternat[14] defectu[15] et profectu,[16] offensionibus[17] et conciliationibus?[18] an is est modus earum et tantum dedisti eis, cum a summis caelorum usque ad ima[19] terrarum, ab initio[20] usque in finem saeculorum, ab angelo usque ad uermiculum,[21] a motu primo usque ad extremum, omnia genera bonorum et omnia iusta opera tua suis quaeque sedibus locares[22] et suis quaeque temporibus ageres?

[1]exsecrandus ~a, ~um *ppl. adj.* LATE **detestable** [2]concessus ~a, ~um *adj.* **permitted** [3]licitus ~a, ~um *adj.* **legitimate** [4]sincerus ~a, ~um *adj.* **sincere** [5]honestas ~atis *f.* **honorable** [6]amicitia ~ae *f.* **friendship** [7]reuiuesco ~escere, reuixi **to come to life again** [8]ubique *adv.* **everywhere** [9]molestia ~ae *f.* **distress** [10]praecedo ~edere, ~essi, ~essum **to precede** [11]aeternum *adv.* **eternally** [12]circa *prep. acc.* **in the company of** [13]'quid est quod' **why is it that..?** [14]alterno ~are, ~aui, ~atum **to alternate** [15]defectus ~us *m.* **fading** [16]profectus ~us *m.* **advancing** [17]offensio ~onis *f.* **conflict** [18]conciliatio ~onis *f.* **reconciliation** [19]imus ~a, ~um *adj.* **lowest place** (*neut. pl.* as noun) [20]initium ~ii *neut.* **beginning** [21]uermiculus ~i *m.* **little worm** [22]loco ~are, ~aui, ~atum **to assign**

Ei mihi,²³ quam excelsus²⁴ es in excelsis²⁵ et quam profundus²⁶ in profundis!²⁷ et nusquam²⁸ recedis, et uix redimus ad te.

²³'ei mihi' **ah me!** (expr. anguish) ²⁴excelsus ~a, ~um *adj.* **lofty** ²⁵excelsum ~i *neut.* height; ECCL **heavens** (*neut. pl.*) ²⁶profundus ~a, ~um *adj.* **very deep** ²⁷profundum ~i *neut.* **depths** ²⁸nusquam *adv.* **nowhere**

Celebrating famous conversions

8.4.9 Age, Domine, fac, excita¹ et reuoca² nos, accende³ et rape, flagra,⁴ dulcesce:⁵ amemus, curramus.⁶ nonne multi ex profundiore⁷ Tartaro caecitatis⁸ quam Victorinus redeunt ad te et *accedunt⁹ et inluminantur* (Ps 33:6) recipientes lumen? quod *si qui recipiunt, accipiunt a te potestatem ut filii tui fiant* (Jn 1:12). sed si minus noti sunt populis, minus de illis gaudent etiam qui nouerunt eos. quando enim cum multis gaudetur, et in singulis uberius¹⁰ est gaudium, quia feruefaciunt¹¹ se et inflammantur¹² ex alterutro.¹³ deinde quod multis noti, multis sunt auctoritati ad salutem et multis praeeunt¹⁴ secuturis, ideoque multum de illis et qui eos praecesserunt¹⁵ laetantur,¹⁶ quia non de solis laetantur.

Absit enim ut in tabernaculo¹⁷ tuo *prae pauperibus*¹⁸ *accipiantur personae*¹⁹ *diuitum*²⁰ (Jas 2:1–9) aut prae ignobilibus²¹ nobiles, quando potius *infirma*²² *mundi elegisti*²³ *ut confunderes*²⁴ *fortia, et ignobilia huius mundi elegisti et contemptibilia,*²⁵ *et ea quae non sunt tamquam sint, ut ea quae sunt euacuares*²⁶ (1 Cor 1:27–28). et tamen idem ipse *minimus*²⁷ *apostolorum*²⁸ (1 Cor 15:9) tuorum, per cuius linguam tua ista uerba sonuisti, cum *Paulus proconsul*²⁹ (Acts 13:7–12) per eius militiam³⁰

¹excito ~are, ~aui, ~atum **to stir up** ²reuoco ~are, ~aui, ~atum **to call upon to return** ³accendo ~dere, ~di, ~sum **to set on fire** ⁴flagro ~are ~aui **to burn** ⁵dulcesco ~ere **to become sweet** ⁶curro ~rere, cucurri, ~sum **to run** ⁷profundus ~a, ~um *adj.* **deep** ⁸caecitas ~atis *f.* **blindness** ⁹accedo ~dere, ~ssi, ~ssum **to approach** ¹⁰uber ~ris *adj.* **full** ¹¹feruefacio ~facere, ~feci, ~factum **to make red-hot** ¹²inflammo ~are, ~aui, ~atum **to be in flames** (pass.) ¹³alteruter ~tra, ~trum *adj.* **one another** (as *pron.*) ¹⁴praeeo ~ire, ~iui **to lead the way** ¹⁵praecedo ~edere, ~essi, ~essum **to go before** ¹⁶laetor ~ari, ~atus **to rejoice** ¹⁷tabernaculum ~i. *neut.* tent; ECCL **church** (metaphorically) ¹⁸pauper ~eris *adj.* **poor** ¹⁹persona ~ae *f.* **personage** ²⁰diues ~itis, ~itior, ~itissimus *adj.* **rich** ²¹ignobilis ~is, ~e *adj.* **undistinguished** ²²infirma ~a, ~um *adj.* **weak** ²³eligo ~igere, ~egi, ~ectum **to choose** ²⁴confundo ~undere, ~udi, ~usum **to confound** ²⁵contemptibilis ~is, ~e *adj.* **contemptible** ²⁶euacuo ~are **to make void**; ECCL **to make void** ²⁷minimus ~a, ~um *superl. adj.* **least** ²⁸apostolus ~i *m.* ECCL **apostle** ²⁹proconsul ~lis *m.* **proconsul** ³⁰militia ~ae *f.* (military) **campaign**

debellata[31] *superbia*[32] (Aen. 6.853) *sub lene*[33] *iugum Christi* (Mt 11:30) tui missus esset, regis magni prouincialis[34] effectus,[35] ipse quoque ex priore "Saulo" "Paulus" uocari amauit ob tam magnae insigne[36] uictoriae.[37] plus enim hostis uincitur in eo quem plus tenet et de quo plures tenet. plus autem superbos tenet nomine nobilitatis[38] et de his plures nomine auctoritatis.

Quanto igitur gratius[39] cogitabatur Victorini pectus, quod tamquam inexpugnabile[40] receptaculum[41] diabolus[42] obtinuerat,[43] Victorini lingua, quo telo grandi et acuto[44] multos peremerat,[45] abundantius[46] exultare[47] oportuit[48] filios tuos, quia Rex noster *alligauit*[49] *fortem* (Mt 12:29), et uidebant uasa[50] eius erepta mundari[51] et aptari[52] in honorem tuum et fieri utilia[53] *Domino ad omne opus bonum* (2 Tim 2:21).

[31]debello ~are, ~aui, ~atum **to beat into subjection** [32]superbia ~ae *f.* **pride** [33]lenis ~is, ~e *adj.* **light** [34]prouincialis ~is *m.* **provincial** [35]efficio ~icere, ~eci, ~ectum **to become** (pass.) [36]insigne ~is *neut.* **badge of honor** [37]uictoria ~ae *f.* **victory in a contest** [38]nobilitas ~atis *f.* **nobility of rank or birth** [39]grate *adv.* **gladly** [40]inexpugnabilis ~is, ~e *adj.* **impregnable** [41]receptaculum ~i *neut.* **stronghold** [42]diabolus ~i *m.* ECCL **the Devil** [43]obtineo ~inere, ~inui, ~entum **to keep in one's power** [44]acutus ~a, ~um *adj.* **sharp** [45]perimo ~imere, ~emi, ~emptum **to destroy** [46]abundanter *adv.* **abundantly** [47]exulto ~are, ~aui **to exult** [48]oportet ~ere, ~uit *impers.* **it is right** [49]alligo ~are, ~aui, ~atum **to bind** [50]uas uasis *neut.* **vessel** [51]mundo ~are, ~aui, ~atum **to clean** [52]apto ~are, ~aui, ~atum **to make fit** [53]utilis ~is, ~e *adj.* **useful**

Aspiring to imitate Victorinus

8.5.10 Sed ubi mihi homo tuus Simplicianus de Victorino ista narrauit, exarsi[1] ad imitandum:[2] ad hoc enim et ille narrauerat. posteaquam[3] uero et illud addidit, quod Imperatoris[4] Iuliani temporibus lege data prohibiti[5] sunt Christiani docere litteraturam[6] et oratoriam.[7] quam legem ille amplexus,[8] loquacem[9] scholam[10] deserere maluit[11] quam uerbum tuum, quo *linguas infantium*[12] *facis disertas*[13] (Wis 10:21). non mihi fortior quam felicior uisus est, quia inuenit occasionem[14] uacandi[15] tibi, cui rei ego

[1]exardesco ~descere, ~si **to be inflamed** (with desire) [2]imitor ~ari, ~atus **to imitate** [3]posteaquam *conj.* **after this** [4]imperator ~oris *m.* **emperor** [5]prohibeo ~ere, ~ui, ~itum **to forbid** [6]litteratura ~ae *f.* **literature** [7]oratorius ~a, ~um *adj.* **oratory** (*f.* as noun) [8]amplector ~cti, ~xus **to pay attention to** [9]loquax ~acis *adj.* **loquacious** [10]schola ~ae *f.* **school** [11]malo ~lle, ~lui **to prefer** [12]infans ~ntis *m. f.* **infant** [13]disertus ~a, ~um *adj.* **skilled in speaking** [14]occasio ~onis *f.* **opportunity** [15]uaco ~are, ~aui, ~atum **to be free to** (w. dat. of purpose)

suspirabam, ligatus[16] non ferro alieno sed mea ferrea[17] uoluntate. uelle meum tenebat inimicus et inde mihi catenam[18] fecerat et constrinxerat[19] me. quippe ex uoluntate peruersa[20] facta est libido, et dum seruitur libidini, facta est consuetudo, et dum consuetudini non resistitur, facta est necessitas.[21] quibus quasi ansulis[22] sibimet innexis[23] (unde catenam appellaui) tenebat me obstrictum[24] dura seruitus.[25]

Voluntas autem noua quae mihi esse coeperat, ut *te gratis colerem* (Job 1:9 VL) fruique[26] te uellem, Deus, sola certa iucunditas,[27] nondum erat idonea[28] ad superandam[29] priorem uetustate[30] roboratam.[31] ita duae uoluntates meae, *una uetus, alia noua* (Col 3:9–10), illa carnalis,[32] illa spiritalis, confligebant[33] inter se atque discordando[34] dissipabant[35] animam meam.

---

[16]ligo ~are, ~aui, ~atum **to bind** [17]ferreus ~a, ~um *adj.* **iron** (transf.) [18]catena ~ae *f.* **chain** [19]constringo ~ngere, ~nxi, ~ctum **to control** [20]peruersus ~a, ~um *adj.* **perverse** [21]necessitas ~atis *f.* **compulsion** [22]ansula ~ae *f.* **ring** [23]innecto ~ctere, ~xui, ~xum **to be interconnected** (pass.) [24]obstringo ~ngere, ~nxi, ~ctum **to obligate** [25]seruitus ~utis *f.* **servitude** [26]fruor ~i, ~ctus **to enjoy** (w. abl) [27]iucunditas ~atis *f.* **charm** [28]idoneus ~a, ~um *adj.* **able** [29]supero ~are, ~aui, ~atum **to prevail over** [30]uetustas ~atis *f.* **age** [31]roboro ~are, ~aui, ~atum **to strengthen** [32]carnalis ~is, ~e *adj.* ECCL **carnal** [33]confligo ~gere, ~xi, ~ctum **to fight** [34]discordo ~ore **to be in conflict** [35]dissipo ~are, ~aui, ~atum **to disintegrate**

Flesh against spirit

8.5.11 Sic intellegebam me ipso experimento[1] id quod legeram, quomodo *caro concupisceret[2] aduersus spiritum et spiritus aduersus carnem* (Gal 5:17), ego quidem in utroque, sed magis ego in eo quod in me approbabam[3] quam in eo quod in me improbabam.[4] ibi enim magis *iam non ego* (Rom 7:17), quia ex magna parte id patiebar inuitus[5] quam faciebam uolens, sed tamen consuetudo aduersus me pugnacior[6] ex me facta erat, quoniam uolens quo nollem peruueneram. et quis iure[7] contradiceret,[8] cum peccantem iusta poena sequeretur?

---

[1]experimentum ~i *neut.* **experience** [2]concupisco ~iscere, ~iui, ~itum **to lust** [3]approbo ~are, ~aui, ~atum **to approve** [4]improbo ~are, ~aui, ~atum **to disapprove** [5]inuitus ~a, ~um *adj.* **unwillingly** (*quasi-adv.*) [6]pugnax ~acis *adj.* **eager to fight** [7]iure *adv.* **justly** [8]contradico ~icere, ~ixi, ~ictum **to protest**

Et non erat iam illa excusatio[9] qua uideri mihi solebam propterea[10] me nondum contempto[11] saeculo seruire tibi, quia incerta[12] mihi esset perceptio[13] ueritatis: iam enim et ipsa certa erat. ego autem adhuc terra obligatus[14] militare[15] tibi recusabam[16] et impedimentis[17] omnibus sic timebam expediri,[18] quemadmodum impediri[19] timendum est.

[9]excusatio ~onis *f.* **excuse** [10]propterea *adv.* **on that account** [11]contemno ~nere, ~psi, ~ptum **to regard with contempt** [12]incertus ~a, ~um *adj.* **uncertain** [13]perceptio ~onis *f.* **perception** [14]obligo ~are, ~aui, ~atum **to fetter** [15]milito ~are, ~aui, ~atum **to serve as a soldier** [16]recuso ~are, ~aui, ~atum **to refuse** [17]impedimentum ~i *neut.* **hindrance** [18]expedio ~ire, ~iui, ~itum **to disentangle** [19]impedio ~ire, ~iui, ~itum **to hinder**

Too slow to follow

8.5.12 Ita sarcina[1] saeculi, uelut somno adsolet,[2] dulciter[3] premebar, et cogitationes quibus *meditabar*[4] *in te* (Ps 62:7) similes erant conatibus[5] expergisci[6] uolentium, qui tamen superati[7] soporis[8] altitudine[9] remerguntur.[10] et sicut nemo est qui dormire[11] semper uelit omniumque sano[12] iudicio uigilare[13] praestat,[14] differt[15] tamen plerumque[16] homo somnum excutere[17] cum grauis torpor[18] in membris est, eumque iam displicentem carpit[19] libentius[20] quamuis surgendi[21] tempus aduenerit:[22] ita certum[23] habebam esse melius tuae caritati me dedere[24] quam meae cupiditati cedere, sed illud placebat et uincebat, hoc libebat[25] et uinciebat.[26] non enim erat quod tibi responderem dicenti mihi, *Surge qui dormis et exsurge*[27] *a mortuis, et inluminabit te Christus* (Eph 5:14), et undique[28] ostendenti uera te dicere, non erat omnino quid responderem ueritate

[1]sarcina ~ae *f.* **burden** (fig.) [2]adsoleo ~ere **it is usual** (*impers.*) [3]dulciter *adv.* **delightfully** [4]meditor ~ari, ~atus **to meditate** [5]conatus ~us *m.* **attempt** [6]expergiscor ~i, experrectus **to rouse oneself** [7]supero ~are, ~aui, ~atum **to prevail over** [8]sopor ~oris *m.* **deep sleep** [9]altitudo ~inis *f.* **depths** [10]remergo ~gere, ~si, ~sum AUG (fig.) **to plunge again** [11]dormio ~ire, ~iui, ~itum **to sleep** [12]sanus ~a, ~um *adj.* **sane** [13]uigilo ~are, ~aui, ~atum **to be awake** [14]praesto ~are, ~iti, ~itum **to be preferable** (w. inf.) [15]differo ~rre, distuli, dilatum **to delay** [16]plerumque *adv.* **generally** [17]excutio ~tere, ~ssi, ~ssum **to shake off** [18]torpor ~oris *m.* **lethargy** [19]carpo ~ere, ~si, ~tum **to seize** (with 'somnum') [20]libenter *adv.* **willingly** [21]surgo ~rgere, ~rrexi, ~rrectum **to rise** [22]aduenio ~uenire, ~ueni, ~uentum **to come** [23]certum ~i *neut.* **certainty** [24]dedo ~ere, ~idi, ~itum **to devote oneself to** (refl.) [25]libet ~ere, ~uit or ~itum est *impers.* **it is pleasing** [26]uincio ~cire, ~xi, ~ctum **to chain** [27]exsurgo ~gere, ~rexi **to rise** [28]undique *adv.* **from all directions**

conuictus,[29] nisi tantum uerba lenta[30] et somnolenta:[31] "Modo," "Ecce modo," "Sine paululum."[32] sed "Modo et modo" non habebat modum et "Sine paululum" in longum ibat.

Frustra[33] *condelectabar*[34] *legi tuae secundum interiorem hominem,* cum *alia lex in membris meis repugnaret*[35] *legi mentis meae et captiuum*[36] *me duceret in lege peccati quae in membris meis erat* (Rom 7:22–23). lex enim peccati est uiolentia[37] consuetudinis, qua trahitur[38] et tenetur etiam inuitus[39] animus eo[40] merito[41] quo in eam uolens inlabitur.[42] *miserum* ergo *me quis liberaret*[43] *de corpore mortis huius nisi gratia tua per Iesum Christum, Dominum nostrum?* (Rom 7:24–25).

[29]conuinco ~incere, ~ici, ~ictum **to convict** [30]lentus ~a, ~um *adj.* **sluggish** [31]somnolentus ~a, ~um *adj.* **drowsy** [32]paululum *adv.* **for a short while** [33]frustra *adv.* **in vain** [34]condelector ~ari, ~atum ECCL **to delight in** [35]repugno ~are, ~aui, ~atum **to fight back** [36]captiuus ~i *m.* **captive** [37]uiolentia ~ae *f.* **overwhelming force** [38]traho ~here, ~xi, ~ctum **to drag** [39]inuitus ~a, ~um *adj.* **unwillingly** (*quasi-adv.*) [40]eo *adv.* **because** [41]merito *adv.* **deservedly** [42]inlabor ~bi, ~psus **to fall into** [43]libero ~are, ~aui, ~atum **to set free** (a slave)

Verecundus

8.6.13 Et de uinculo[1] quidem desiderii concubitus,[2] quo artissimo[3] tenebar, et saecularium[4] negotiorum[5] seruitute[6] quemadmodum me exemeris,[7] narrabo et *confitebor nomini tuo* (Ps 53:8), *Domine, adiutor*[8] *meus et redemptor*[9] *meus* (Ps 18:15).

Agebam solita, crescente anxitudine,[10] et cotidie[11] suspirabam tibi. frequentabam[12] ecclesiam tuam, quantum uacabat[13] ab eis negotiis sub quorum pondere[14] gemebam.[15] mecum erat Alypius otiosus[16] ab opere iuris peritorum[17] post adsessionem[18] tertiam,[19] expectans quibus iterum[20] consilia uenderet,[21] sicut ego uendebam dicendi facultatem,[22]

[1]uinculum ~i *neut.* **chain** [2]concubitus ~us *m.* **sex** [3]artus ~a, ~um *adj.* **firm** [4]saecularis ~is, ~e *adj.* ECCL **secular** [5]negotium ~ii *neut.* **concern** [6]seruitus ~utis *f.* **servitude** [7]eximo ~imere, ~emi, ~emptum **to extract** [8]adiutor ~oris *m.* **helper** [9]redemptor ~oris *m.* ransomer; ECCL **redeemer** [10]anxitudo ~inis *f.* **anxiety** [11]cotidie *adv.* **daily** [12]frequento ~are, ~aui, ~atum **to frequent** [13]uaco ~are, ~aui, ~atum **to be free from** (w. 'ab') [14]pondus ~eris *neut.* **weight** [15]gemo ~ere, ~ui, ~itum **to groan** [16]otiosus ~a, ~um *adj.* **at leisure** [17]'iuris peritorum' **legal consultant** [18]adssessio ~onis *f.* sitting beside; LATE **duty of assessor** [19]tertius ~a, ~um *adj.* **third** [20]iterum *adv.* **again** [21]uendo ~ere, ~idi, ~itum **to sell** (services) [22]facultas ~atis *f.* **skill**

si qua[23] docendo praestari[24] potest. Nebridius autem amicitiae[25] nostrae cesserat, ut omnium nostrum familiarissimo[26] Verecundo, Mediolanensi et ciui et grammatico,[27] subdoceret,[28] uehementer[29] desideranti et familiaritatis[30] iure flagitanti[31] de numero nostro fidele adiutorium,[32] quo indigebat[33] nimis. non itaque Nebridium cupiditas commodorum[34] eo traxit[35] (maiora enim posset, si uellet, de litteris agere) sed officio[36] beniuolentiae[37] petitionem[38] nostram contemnere[39] noluit, amicus dulcissimus et mitissimus.[40] agebat autem illud prudentissime[41] cauens[42] innotescere[43] personis[44] *secundum hoc saeculum* (Eph 2:2) maioribus, deuitans[45] in eis omnem inquietudinem[46] animi, quem uolebat habere liberum[47] et quam multis posset horis feriatum[48] ad quaerendum aliquid uel legendum uel audiendum de sapientia.

[23]qua *adv.* **in any way** [24]praesto ~are, ~iti, ~itum **to excel** [25]amicitia ~ae *f.* **friendship** [26]familiaris ~is, ~e *adj.* **intimate** [27]grammaticus ~i *m.* **grammar teacher** [28]subdoceo ~ere **to assistant teach** [29]uehementer *adv.* **in an impassioned manner** [30]familiaritas ~atis *f.* **close friendship** [31]flagito ~are, ~aui, ~atum **to ask repeatedly** [32]adiutorium ~ii *neut.* **help** [33]indigeo ~ere, ~ui **to need** [34]commodum ~i *neut.* **salary** [35]traho ~here, ~xi, ~ctum to draw > **to derive** [36]officium ~ii *neut.* **obligation** [37]beniuolentia ~ae *f.* **goodwill** [38]petitio ~onis *f.* **request** [39]contemno ~nere, ~psi, ~ptum **to disregard** [40]mitis ~is, ~e *adj.* **kind** [41]prudenter *adv.* **discreetly** [42]caueo ~ere, caui, ~tum **to be cautious** [43]innotesco ~escere, ~ui **to become known** [44]persona ~ae *f.* **personage** [45]deuito ~are, ~aui, ~atum **to avoid** [46]inquietudo ~inis *f.* **disturbance**; LATE **disquiet** [47]liber ~era, ~erum *adj.* **free** [48]feriatus ~a, ~um *adj.* **unemployed**

Ponticianus relates the conversion of St. Antony

8.6.14 Quodam igitur die (non recolo causam qua[1] erat absens Nebridius) cum ecce ad nos domum uenit ad me et Alypium Ponticianus quidam, ciuis noster in quantum Afer, praeclare[2] in palatio[3] militans:[4] nescio quid a nobis uolebat. et consedimus[5] ut conloqueremur.[6] et forte supra[7] mensam[8] lusoriam[9] quae ante nos erat attendit codicem.[10] tulit, aperuit, inuenit apostolum[11] Paulum, inopinate[12] sane:[13] putauerat enim aliquid de libris quorum professio[14] me conterebat.[15] tum uero arridens[16] meque

[1]causam qua' **for what reason** [2]praeclare *adv.* **conspicuously successful** [3]palatium ~i *neut.* palace; LATE **imperial court** [4]milito ~are, ~aui, ~atum to serve in the military; LATE **to serve in government** [5]consido ~sidere, ~sedi **to sit down** [6]conloquor ~qui, ~cutus **to talk together** [7]supra *prep. acc.* **on top** [8]mensa ~ae *f.* **table** [9]lusorius ~a, ~um *adj.* **used for games** [10]codex ~icis *m.* **book** [11]apostolus ~i *m.* ECCL **apostle** [12]inopinate *adv.* LATE **unexpectedly** [13]sane *adv.* **quite** [14]professio ~onis *f.* **profession** [15]contero ~terere, ~triui, ~tritum **to exhaust** [16]arrideo ~dere, ~si, ~sum **to smile at**

intuens gratulatorie[17] miratus est, quod eas et solas prae oculis meis litteras repente[18] comperisset.[19] Christianus quippe et fidelis erat, et saepe tibi, Deo nostro, prosternebatur[20] in ecclesia crebris[21] et diuturnis[22] orationibus.[23] cui ego cum indicassem illis me scripturis curam maximam impendere,[24] ortus[25] est sermo ipso narrante de Antonio Aegyptio mona-cho,[26] cuius nomen excellenter[27] clarebat[28] apud seruos tuos, nos autem usque in illam horam latebat.[29] quod ille ubi comperit,[30] immoratus[31] est in eo sermone, insinuans[32] tantum uirum ignorantibus et admirans[33] eandem nostram ignorantiam.[34] stupebamus[35] autem audientes tam recenti[36] memoria et prope nostris temporibus testatissima[37] *mirabilia*[38] *tua* (Ps 144:5) in fide recta[39] et Catholica Ecclesia. omnes miraba-mur, et nos, quia tam magna erant, et ille, quia inaudita[40] nobis erant.

---

[17]gratulatorie *adv.* AUG **in a congratulatory manner** [18]repente *adv.* **suddenly** [19]comperio ~ire, ~i, ~tum **to find out** [20]prosterno ~ernere, ~raui, ~ratum **to prostrate** [21]creber ~bra, ~brum *adj.* **frequent** [22]diuturnus ~a, ~um *adj.* **long** [23]oratio ~onis *f.* **speech**; ECCL **prayer** [24]impendo ~dere, ~di, ~sum **to devote** (with 'curam') [25]orior ~iri, ~tus **to arise** [26]monachus ~i *m.* ECCL **monk** [27]excellenter *adv.* **outstandingly** [28]clareo ~ere **to be famous** [29]lateo ~ere, ~ui **to escape notice** [30]comperio ~ire, ~i, ~tum **to find out** [31]immoror ~ari, ~atus **to linger over a topic** [32]insinuo ~are, ~aui, ~atum **to introduce** [33]admiror ~ari, ~atus **to marvel (at)** [34]ignorantia ~ae *f.* **ignorance** [35]stupeo ~ere, ~ui **to be stupefied** [36]recens ~ntis *adj.* **recent** [37]testatus ~a, ~um *adj.* **well attested** [38]mirabile ~is *neut.* ECCL **wondrous work** [39]rectus ~a, ~um *adj.* **right** [40]inauditus ~a, ~um *adj.* **unheard of**

Ponticianus relates a conversion at Trier

8.6.15 Inde sermo eius deuolutus[1] est ad monasteriorum[2] greges[3] et mores suaueolentiae[4] tuae et ubera[5] deserta heremi,[6] quorum nos nihil sciebamus. et erat monasterium Mediolanii plenum bonis fratribus[7] extra[8] urbis moenia[9] sub Ambrosio nutritore,[10] et non noueramus.

Pertendebat[11] ille et loquebatur adhuc, et nos intenti tacebamus. unde incidit[12] ut diceret nescio quando[13] se et tres alios contuberna-les[14] suos, nimirum[15] apud Treueros, cum imperator[16] promeridiano[17]

---

[1]deuoluo ~uere, ~ui, ~utum **to roll down**; ECCL **to turn (of conversation)** [2]monasterium ~i *neut.* ECCL **monastery** [3]grex ~egis *m.* **flock**; ECCL **congregation** [4]suaueolentia ~ae *f.* LATE **sweet fragrance** [5]uber ~ris *adj.* **frutiful** [6]heremus ~i *m.* ECCL **desert** [7]frater ~tris *m.* **brother**; ECCL **brethren** (*pl.*) [8]extra *prep. acc.* **outside** [9]moenia ~ium *neut. pl.* **walls** [10]nutritor ~oris *m.* **nurse**; LATE **patron** [11]pertendo ~dere, ~di **to continue on** [12]incido ~ere, ~i **to occur to a person** [13]'nescio quando' **at some time or other** [14]contubernalis ~is *m.* **fellow agent** [15]nimirum *particle* **as a matter of fact** [16]imperator ~oris *m.* **emperor** [17]promeridianus ~a, ~um *adj.* AUG **morning**

circensium[18] spectaculo[19] teneretur, exisse[20] deambulatum[21] in hortos[22] muris[23] contiguos[24] atque illic, ut forte combinati[25] spatiabantur,[26] unum secum seorsum[27] et alios duos itidem[28] seorsum pariterque[29] digressos;[30] sed illos uagabundos[31] inruisse[32] in quandam casam[33] ubi habitabant[34] quidam serui tui *spiritu pauperes,*[35] *qualium est regnum caelorum* (Mt 5:3), et inuenisse ibi codicem[36] in quo scripta erat *Vita Antonii.* quam legere coepit unus eorum et mirari et accendi,[37] et inter[38] legendum meditari[39] arripere[40] talem uitam et relicta militia[41] saeculari[42] seruire tibi. erant autem ex eis quos dicunt agentes in rebus.[43] tum subito[44] repletus[45] amore sancto et sobrio[46] pudore,[47] iratus[48] sibi, coniecit[49] oculos in amicum et ait illi, "Dic, quaeso[50] te, omnibus istis laboribus nostris quo ambimus[51] peruenire? quid quaerimus? cuius rei causa militamus?[52] maiorne esse poterit spes nostra in palatio[53] quam ut Amici Imperatoris simus? et ibi quid non fragile[54] plenumque periculis? et per quot[55] pericula peruenitur ad grandius periculum? et quando istuc[56] erit? *amicus* autem *Dei* (Jas 2:23), si uoluero, ecce nunc fio."

Dixit hoc et turbidus[57] parturitione[58] nouae uitae reddidit oculos paginis.[59] et legebat et mutabatur intus, ubi tu uidebas, et exuebatur[60] mundo mens eius, ut mox apparuit. namque[61] dum legit et uoluit[62] fluctus cordis sui, infremuit[63] aliquando et discreuit decreuitque[64]

---

[18]circenses ~ium *m. pl.* **circus** [19]spectaculum ~i *neut.* **performance** [20]exeo ~ire, ~iui or ~ii, ~itum **to go out** [21]deambulo ~are, ~aui, ~atum **to go for a walk** [22]hortus ~i *m.* **garden** [23]murus ~i *m.* **city wall** [24]contiguus ~a, ~um *adj.* **adjacent** [25]combino ~are, ~aui, ~atum ECCL **to join up** [26]spatior ~ari, ~atus **to stroll** [27]seorsum *adv.* **apart from the rest** [28]itidem *adv.* **likewise** [29]pariter *adv.* **together** [30]digredior ~di, ~ssus **to go off** [31]uagabundus ~a, ~um *adj.* LATE **wandering** [32]inruo ~uere, ~ui **to happen upon** [33]casa ~ae *f.* **small cottage** [34]habito ~are, ~aui, ~atum **to dwell** [35]pauper ~eris *adj.* **poor** [36]codex ~icis *m.* **book** [37]accendo ~dere, ~di, ~sum **to arouse the feelings** [38]inter *prep. acc.* **in the middle of** [39]meditor ~ari, ~atus **to meditate** [40]arripio ~ere, ~ui, arreptum **to seize eagerly** [41]militia ~ae *f.* military service; LATE **government service** [42]saecularis ~is, ~e *adj.* ECCL **secular** [43]agentes in rebus' **special agents** [44]subito *adv.* **suddenly** [45]repletus ~a, ~um *adj.* **filled with** (w. abl.) [46]sobrius ~ia, ~ium *adj.* **sober** [47]pudor ~oris *m.* **shame** [48]irascor ~i, iratus sum **to become angry** [49]conicio ~icere, ~ieci, ~iectum **to direct** [50]quaeso ~ere **please** (w. imp.) [51]ambio ~ire, ~iui, ~itum **to strive** [52]milito ~are, ~aui, ~atum **to serve in the military**; LATE **to serve in government** [53]palatium ~i *neut.* **palace**; LATE **imperial court** [54]fragilis ~is, ~e *adj.* **fragile** [55]quot *indecl. adj.* **how many** [56]istic ~aec, ~uc *pron.* **that very thing** [57]turbidus ~a, ~um *adj.* **troubled in expression** [58]parturitio ~onis *f.* LATE **travail** [59]pagina ~ae *f.* **page** [60]exuo ~uere, ~ui, ~utum **to strip from** [61]namque *conj.* **for** [62]uoluo ~uere, ~ui, ~utum **to roll** (of waves) [63]infremo ~ere, ~ui **to utter a confused cry of joy** [64]decerno ~ernere, ~reui, ~retum **to decide on**

meliora, iamque tuus ait amico suo, "Ego iam abrupi[65] me ab illa spe nostra et Deo seruire statui,[66] et hoc ex hac hora, in hoc loco aggredior.[67] te si piget[68] imitari,[69] noli aduersari."[70] respondit ille adhaerere[71] se socium tantae mercedis[72] tantaeque militiae. et ambo[73] iam tui *aedificabant*[74] *turrem*[75] *sumptu*[76] (Lk 14:28) idoneo[77] *relinquendi omnia sua et sequendi te* (Lk 5:11).

Tunc Ponticianus et qui cum eo per alias horti partes deambulabat, quaerentes eos, deuenerunt[78] in eundem locum et inuenientes admonuerunt[79] ut redirent, quod iam declinasset[80] dies. at illi, narrato placito et proposito[81] suo quoque modo in eis talis uoluntas orta[82] esset atque firmata,[83] petiuerunt ne sibi molesti essent[84] si adiungi[85] recusarent.[86] isti autem nihilo[87] mutati a pristinis[88] fleuerunt se tamen, ut dicebat, atque illis pie[89] congratulati[90] sunt, et commendauerunt[91] se orationibus[92] eorum et trahentes[93] cor in terra abierunt[94] in palatium, illi autem affigentes[95] cor caelo manserunt in casa. et habebant ambo sponsas[96] quae, posteaquam[97] hoc audierunt, dicauerunt[98] etiam ipsae uirginitatem[99] tibi.

[65]abrumpo ~umpere, ~upi, ~uptum **to detach oneself** [66]statuo ~uere, ~ui, ~utum **to determine** [67]aggredior ~di, ~ssus **to set oneself to a task** [68]piget ~ere, ~uit, ~itum *impers.* **to displease** [69]imitor ~ari, ~atus **to imitate** [70]aduersor ~ari, ~atus **to oppose** [71]adhaereo ~rere, ~si, ~sum **to attach oneself** [72]merces ~edis *f.* **reward** [73]ambo ~ae, ~o *pl. pron.* **both** [74]aedifico ~are, ~aui, ~atum **to build** [75]turris ~is *f.* **tower** [76]sumptus ~us *m.* **cost** [77]idoneus ~a, ~um *adj.* **fit** [78]deuenio ~enire, ~eni, ~entum **to turn up at** [79]admoneo ~ere, ~ui, ~itum **to urge** [80]declino ~are, ~aui, ~atum **to end** [81]propositum ~i *neut.* intention > **chosen way of life** [82]orior ~iri, ~tus **to rise** [83]firmo ~are, ~aui, ~atum **to make firm** [84]'molesti essent' **be troublesome** [85]adiungo ~gere, ~xi, ~ctum **to join** [86]recuso ~are, ~aui, ~atum **to refuse** [87]nihilum ~i *neut.* **by no degree** (abl.) [88]pristinus ~a, ~um *adj.* **former state** (*neut.* as noun) [89]pie *adv.* **piously** [90]congratulor ~ari, ~atus sum **to congratulate** [91]commendo ~are, ~aui, ~atum **to commend** [92]oratio ~onis *f.* **speech**; ECCL **prayer** [93]traho ~here, ~xi, ~ctum **to drag** [94]abeo ~ire, ~ii, ~itum **to go away** [95]affigo ~gere, ~xi, ~xum **to fix** [96]sponsa ~ae *f.* **woman promised in marriage** [97]posteaquam *conj.* **after** [98]dico ~are, ~aui, ~atum **to devote** [99]uirginitas ~atis *f.* **virginity**

Pulled inward as Ponticianus talks on

8.7.16 Narrabat haec Ponticianus. tu autem, Domine, inter uerba eius retorquebas[1] me ad me ipsum, auferens me a dorso[2] meo, ubi me posueram

[1]retorqueo ~quere, ~si, ~tum **to wrench backwards** [2]dorsum ~i *neut.* **back**

dum nollem me attendere, et constituebas³ me ante faciem meam, ut
uiderem quam turpis essem, quam distortus⁴ et sordidus,⁵ maculosus⁶
et ulcerosus.⁷ et uidebam et horrebam,⁸ et quo a me fugerem non erat.
sed si conabar auertere⁹ a me aspectum,¹⁰ narrabat ille quod narrabat,
et tu me rursus opponebas¹¹ mihi et impingebas¹² me in oculos meos,
ut inuenirem iniquitatem meam et odissem (Ps 35:3). noueram eam, sed
dissimulabam¹³ et cohibebam¹⁴ et obliuiscebar.

³constituo ~uere, ~ui, ~utum **to set down** ⁴distortus ~a, ~um *adj.* **distorted** ⁵sordidus ~a, ~um
adj. **filthy** ⁶maculosus ~a, ~um *adj.* **stained** ⁷ulcerosus ~a, ~um *adj.* **ulcerous** ⁸horreo ~ere, ~ui
to shudder (with fear) ⁹auerto ~tere, ~ti, ~sum **to avert** ¹⁰aspectus ~us *m.* **gaze** ¹¹oppono ~onere,
~osui, ~ositum **to place in the way** ¹²impingo ~ingere, ~egi, ~actum **to force** ¹³dissimulo ~are,
~aui, ~atum **to pretend** ¹⁴cohibeo ~ere, ~ui, ~itum **to suppress**

Loathing twelve wasted years

8.7.17 Tunc uero quanto ardentius¹ amabam illos de quibus audiebam salubres² affectus, quod se totos tibi sanandos dederunt, tanto
exsecrabilius³ me comparatum⁴ eis oderam, quoniam multi mei anni
mecum effluxerant⁵ (forte duodecim⁶ anni) ex quo ab undeuicensimo⁷
anno aetatis meae, lecto Ciceronis *Hortensio,* excitatus⁸ eram studio
sapientiae et differebam⁹ contempta¹⁰ felicitate¹¹ terrena¹² ad eam inue-
stigandam¹³ uacare,¹⁴ cuius non inuentio¹⁵ sed uel sola inquisitio¹⁶ iam
praeponenda¹⁷ erat etiam inuentis thesauris¹⁸ regnisque gentium et ad
nutum¹⁹ circumfluentibus²⁰ corporis uoluptatibus. at ego adulescens²¹
miser ualde, miser in exordio²² ipsius adulescentiae,²³ etiam petieram
a te castitatem²⁴ et dixeram, "Da mihi castitatem et continentiam,²⁵

¹ardenter *adv.* **ardently** ²saluber ~bris, ~bre *adj.* **healthful** ³exsecrabiliter *adv.* **detestably** ⁴comparo
~are, ~aui, ~atum **to compare** ⁵effluo ~uere, ~uxi **to flow away** > **to slip out of one's grasp** (fig. of
time) ⁶duodecim *indecl. adj.* **twelve** ⁷undeuicensimus ~a, ~um *adj.* **nineteenth** ⁸excito ~are, ~aui,
~atum **to excite** ⁹differo ~rre, distuli, dilatum **to delay** ¹⁰contemno ~nere, ~psi, ~ptum **to despise**
¹¹felicitas ~atis *f.* **happiness** ¹²terrenus ~a, ~um *adj.* **earthly** ¹³inuestigo ~are, ~aui, ~atum **to inve-
stigate** ¹⁴uaco ~are, ~aui, ~atum **to be free to** (w. 'ad') ¹⁵inuentio ~onis *f.* **discovery** ¹⁶inquisitio
~onis *f.* **search** ¹⁷praepono ~onere, ~osui, ~ositum **to prefer** ¹⁸thesaurus ~i *m.* **treasury** ¹⁹nutus
~us *m.* (merely a) **nod** ²⁰circumfluo ~ere, ~xi **to be abundantly supplied** (w. abl.) ²¹adulescens
~ntis *m.* **young man** ²²exordium ~i *neut.* **beginning** ²³adulescentia ~ae *f.* **young adulthood** (age
16–30) ²⁴castitas ~atis *f.* **chastity** ²⁵continentia ~ae *f.* **continence**

sed noli modo." timebam enim ne me cito[26] exaudires et cito sanares a morbo[27] concupiscentiae,[28] quem malebam[29] expleri[30] quam exstingui.[31] et ieram *per uias prauas*[32] (Sir 2:16) superstitione[33] sacrilega,[34] non quidem certus in ea sed quasi praeponens eam ceteris, quae non pie[35] quaerebam sed inimice[36] oppugnabam.[37]

[26]cito *adv.* **quickly** [27]morbus ~i *m.* **disease** [28]concupiscentia ~ae *f.* ECCL **concupiscence** [29]malo ~lle, ~lui **to prefer** [30]expleo ~ere, ~eui, ~etum **to satisfy an appetite** [31]exstinguo ~guere, ~xi, ~ctum **to extinguish** [32]prauus ~a, ~um *adj.* **crooked** [33]superstitio ~onis *f.* **superstition** [34]sacrilegus ~a, ~um *adj.* **sacrilegious** [35]pie *adv.* **piously** [36]inimice *adv.* **with hostility** [37]oppugno ~are, ~aui, ~atum **to oppose**

Excuse of uncertainty taken away

8.7.18 Et putaueram me propterea[1] *differre*[2] *de die in diem* (Sir 5:8) contempta[3] spe saeculi te solum sequi, quia non mihi apparebat certum[4] aliquid quo dirigerem[5] cursum meum. et uenerat dies quo nudarer[6] mihi et increparet[7] in me conscientia[8] mea: "Ubi est lingua? nempe[9] tu dicebas propter incertum[10] uerum nolle te abicere[11] sarcinam[12] uanitatis. ecce iam certum est, et illa te adhuc premit, umerisque[13] liberioribus[14] pinnas[15] recipiunt qui neque ita in quaerendo attriti[16] sunt nec decennio[17] et amplius ista meditati."[18]

Ita rodebar[19] intus et confundebar[20] pudore[21] horribili[22] uehementer,[23] cum Ponticianus talia loqueretur. terminato[24] autem sermone et causa qua uenerat, abiit[25] ille, et ego ad me.

Quae non in me dixi? quibus sententiarum uerberibus[26] non flagellaui[27] animam meam, ut sequeretur me conantem post te ire? et renitebatur,[28] recusabat,[29] et non se excusabat.[30] consumpta[31] erant et

[1]propterea *adv.* **consequently** [2]differo ~rre, distuli, dilatum **to defer** [3]contemno ~nere, ~psi, ~ptum **to regard with contempt** [4]certum ~i *neut.* **certainty** [5]dirigo ~igere, ~exi, ~ectum **to steer** [6]nudo ~are, ~aui, ~atum **to strip bare** [7]increpo ~are, ~ui, ~itum **to reproach violently** [8]conscientia ~ae *f.* **conscience** [9]nempe *particle* **without a doubt** [10]incertus ~a, ~um *adj.* **uncertain** [11]abicio ~cere, ~eci, ~ectum **to throw off** [12]sarcina ~ae *f.* **burden** [13]umerus ~i *m.* **shoulder** [14]liber ~era, ~erum *adj.* **free** [15]pinna ~ae *f.* **wing** [16]attero ~terere, ~triui, ~tritum **to waste** [17]decennium ~ii *neut.* **decade** [18]meditor ~ari, ~atus **to ponder** [19]rodo ~dere, ~si, ~sum **to gnaw** [20]confundo ~undere, ~udi, ~usum **to dismay** [21]pudor ~oris *m.* **shame** [22]horribilis ~is, ~e *adj.* **horrible** [23]uehementer *adv.* **overpoweringly** [24]termino ~are, ~aui, ~atum **to bring to a close** [25]abeo ~ire, ~ii, ~itum **to go away** [26]uerber ~ris *neut.* **whip** [27]flagello ~are, ~aui, ~atum **to flog** [28]reniteo ~ere **to hold in check** [29]recuso ~are, ~aui, ~atum **to refuse** [30]excuso ~are, ~aui, ~atum **to excuse** [31]consumo ~ere, ~psi, ~ptum **to exhaust**

conuicta[32] argumenta[33] omnia. remanserat[34] muta[35] trepidatio[36] et quasi mortem reformidabat[37] restringi[38] a fluxu[39] consuetudinis, quo tabescebat[40] in mortem.

[32]conuiuo ~uere, ~xi, ~ctum **to refute** [33]argumentum ~i *neut.* **argument** [34]remaneo ~ere, ~si **to remain** [35]mutus ~a, ~um *adj.* **mute** [36]trepidatio ~onis *f.* **trepidation** [37]reformido ~are, ~aui, ~atum **to shrink from in fear** [38]restringo ~ngere, ~nxi, ~ctum **to restrain** [39]fluxus ~us *m.* **flow** [40]tabesco ~escere, ~ui **to wither away**

A small garden

8.8.19 Tum in illa grandi rixa[1] interioris domus meae, quam fortiter[2] excitaueram[3] cum anima mea *in cubiculo[4] nostro* (Mt 6:6), corde meo, tam uultu quam mente turbatus[5] inuado[6] Alypium: exclamo,[7] "Quid patimur? quid est hoc? quid audisti? surgunt[8] indocti[9] et *caelum rapiunt* (Mt 11:12), et nos cum doctrinis nostris sine corde, ecce ubi uolutamur[10] in *carne et sanguine* (1 Cor 15:50)! an quia praecesserunt,[11] pudet[12] sequi et non pudet nec saltem[13] sequi?" dixi nescio qua talia,[14] et abripuit[15] me ab illo aestus[16] meus, cum taceret attonitus[17] me intuens. neque enim solita sonabam. plus loquebantur animum meum frons,[18] genae,[19] oculi, color,[20] modus uocis quam uerba quae promebam.[21]

Hortulus[22] quidam erat hospitii[23] nostri, quo nos utebamur sicut tota domo: nam hospes[24] ibi non habitabat,[25] dominus domus. illuc[26] me abstulerat tumultus[27] pectoris, ubi nemo impediret[28] ardentem[29] litem[30] quam mecum aggressus[31] eram, donec exiret[32] — qua[33] tu sciebas, ego autem non: sed tantum insaniebam[34] salubriter[35] et moriebar uitaliter,[36]

[1]rixa ~ae *f.* **noisy quarrel** [2]fortiter *adv.* **powerfully** [3]excito ~are, ~aui, ~atum **to stir up** [4]cubiculum ~i *neut.* **inner room** [5]turbatus ~a, ~um *adj.* **troubled** [6]inuado ~dere, ~si, ~sum **to seize upon** [7]exclamo ~are, ~aui, ~atum **to exclaim** [8]surgo ~rgere, ~rrexi, ~rrectum **to rise up** [9]indoctus ~a, ~um *adj.* **uneducated** [10]uoluto ~are, ~aui, ~atum **to roll** > **to wallow** [11]praecedo ~edere, ~essi, ~essum **to go ahead** [12]pudeo ~ere, ~ui **to make ashamed** [13]saltem *adv.* **even** [14]nescio quo talia' **in some unaccountable way** [15]abripio ~ipere, ~ipui, ~eptum **to snatch away** [16]aestus ~us *m.* **heat** > **passion** > **feverish state** [17]attonitus ~a, ~um *adj.* **astounded** [18]frons ~ntis *f.* **forehead** [19]gena ~ae *f.* **cheek** [20]color ~oris *m.* **color** [21]promo ~mere, ~mpsi, ~mptum **to bring into the open** [22]hortulus ~i *m.* **garden** [23]hospitium ~(i)i *neut.* **lodgings** [24]hospes ~itis *m.* **host** [25]habito ~are, ~aui, ~atum **to live** [26]illuc *adv.* **there** [27]tumultus ~us *m.* **tumult** [28]impedio ~ire, ~iui, ~itum **to hinder** [29]ardens ~ntis *adj.* **burning** [30]lis litis *f.* **dispute** [31]aggredior ~di, ~ssus **to undertake** [32]exeo ~ire, ~iui or ~ii, ~itum **to pass** [33]qua *adv.* **how** [34]insanio ~ire, ~iui or ~ii, ~itum **to act crazily** [35]salubriter *adv.* **salubriously** [36]uitaliter *adv.* **so as to endow with life**

gnarus[37] quid mali essem et ignarus[38] quid boni post paululum[39] futurus essem. abscessi[40] ergo in hortum, et Alypius pedem post pedem. neque enim secretum[41] meum non erat, ubi ille aderat. aut quando me sic affectum[42] desereret? sedimus[43] quantum potuimus remoti[44] ab aedibus.[45] ego *fremebam*[46] *spiritu* (Jn 11:33), indignans[47] indignatione[48] turbulentissima[49] quod non irem in placitum et pactum[50] tecum, Deus meus, in quod eundum esse *omnia ossa*[51] *mea clamabant* (Ps 34:10) et in caelum tollebant[52] laudibus. et non illuc ibatur nauibus aut quadrigis[53] aut pedibus, quantum saltem de domo in eum locum ieram ubi sedebamus. nam non solum ire uerum etiam peruenire illuc nihil erat aliud quam uelle ire, sed uelle fortiter et integre,[54] non semisauciam[55] hac atque hac[56] uersare[57] et iactare[58] uoluntatem parte adsurgente[59] cum alia parte cadente[60] luctantem.[61]

[37]gnarus ~a, ~um *adj.* **knowing** [38]ignarus ~a, ~um *adj.* **not knowing** [39]'post paululum' **after a little while** [40]abscedo ~dere, ~ssi, ~ssum **to go away** [41]secretum ~i *neut.* **privacy** [42]afficio ~icere, ~eci, ~ectum **to affect** [43]sedeo ~ere, sedi, sessum **to sit** [44]remotus ~a, ~um *adj.* **removed** [45]aedis ~is *f.* **house** (*pl.*) [46]fremo ~ere, ~ui, ~itum **to make inarticulate sounds** [47]indignor ~ari, ~atus **to be indignant** [48]indignatio ~onis *f.* **indignation** [49]turbulentus ~a, ~um *adj.* **violently disturbed** [50]pactum ~i *neut.* **pact** [51]os ossis *neut.* **bones** (*pl.* esp. as seat of emotion); ECCL soul (fig.) [52]tollo ~ere, sustuli, sublatum **to raise** (**to heaven**) [53]quadriga ~ae *f.* **chariot** [54]integre *adv.* **uncompromisingly** [55]semisaucius ~a, ~um *adj.* AUG **half-wounded** (fig.) [56]'hac... hac' **this way... that way** [57]uerso ~are, ~aui, ~atum **to spin** [58]iacto ~are, ~aui, ~atum **to toss** [59]adsurgo ~gere, ~rexi, ~rectum **to stand up** [60]cado ~ere, cecidi, casum **to collapse** [61]luctor ~ari, ~atus **to struggle**

Spastic nonverbal: spiritual contractions

8.8.20 Denique[1] tam multa faciebam corpore in ipsis cunctationis[2] aestibus,[3] quae aliquando uolunt homines et non ualent, si aut ipsa membra non habeant aut ea uel conligata uinculis[4] uel resoluta[5] languore[6] uel quoquo modo[7] impedita[8] sint. si uulsi[9] capillum,[10] si percussi[11] frontem,[12] si consertis[13] digitis[14] amplexatus[15] sum genu,[16] quia uolui,

[1]denique *adv.* **at length** [2]cunctatio ~onis *f.* **hesitation** [3]aestus ~us *m.* **heat > passion > feverish state** [4]uinculum ~i *neut.* **chain** [5]resoluo ~uere, ~ui, ~utum **to go limp** [6]languor ~oris *m.* **faintness** [7]'quoquo modo' **in any way whatever** [8]impedio ~ire, ~iui, ~itum **to impede** [9]uello ~ere, uulsi, uulsum **to pull out** [10]capillus ~i *m.* **hair** [11]percutio ~tere, ~ssi, ~ssum **to strike forcibly** [12]frons ~ntis *f.* **forehead** [13]consero ~ere, ~ui, ~tum **to join together** [14]digitus ~i *m.* **finger** [15]amplexor ~ari, ~atus **to hug** [16]genu ~us *neut.* **knee**

feci. potui autem uelle et non facere, si mobilitas[17] membrorum non obsequeretur.[18] tam multa ergo feci, ubi non hoc erat uelle quod posse: et non faciebam quod et incomparabili[19] affectu amplius mihi placebat, et mox ut[20] uellem possem, quia mox ut uellem, utique uellem. ibi enim facultas[21] ea, quae uoluntas, et ipsum uelle iam facere erat; et tamen non fiebat, faciliusque obtemperabat[22] corpus tenuissimae[23] uoluntati animae, ut ad nutum[24] membra mouerentur, quam ipsa sibi anima ad uoluntatem suam magnam in sola uoluntate perficiendam.

[17]mobilitas ~atis *f.* **mobility** [18]obsequor ~qui, ~cutus **to follow the promptings** [19]incomparabilis ~is, ~e *adj.* **incomparable** [20]'mox ut' **as soon as** [21]facultas ~atis *f.* **faculty** [22]obtempero ~are, ~aui, ~atum **to obey** (w. dat.) [23]tenuis ~is, ~e *adj.* **slight** [24]nutus ~us *m.* **nod > assent** *or* **command**

Conflict: willing and unwilling

8.9.21 Unde hoc monstrum?[1] et quare istuc?[2] luceat[3] misericordia tua, et interrogem, si forte mihi respondere possint latebrae[4] poenarum hominum et tenebrosissimae[5] contritiones[6] filiorum Adam. unde hoc monstrum? et quare istuc? imperat animus corpori, et paretur[7] statim;[8] imperat animus sibi, et resistitur. imperat animus ut moueatur manus, et tanta est facilitas[9] ut uix a seruitio[10] discernatur imperium: et animus animus est, manus autem corpus est. imperat animus ut uelit animus, nec alter est nec facit tamen. unde hoc monstrum? et quare istuc, inquam, ut uelit qui non imperaret nisi uellet, et non facit quod imperat?

Sed non ex toto uult: non ergo ex toto imperat. nam in tantum imperat, in quantum uult, et in tantum non fit quod imperat, in quantum non uult, quoniam uoluntas imperat ut sit uoluntas, nec alia, sed ipsa. non itaque plena imperat; ideo non est quod imperat. nam si plena esset, nec imperaret ut esset, quia iam esset.

[1]monstrum ~i *neut.* **unnatural situation** [2]'quare istuc' **to what end?** [3]luceo ~ere, luxi **to shine** [4]latebra ~ae *f.* **hidden recess** [5]tenebrosus ~a, ~um *adj.* **dark** [6]contritio ~onis *f.* **despondency** [7]pareo ~ere, ~ui, ~itum **to obey** [8]statim *adv.* **immediately** [9]facilitas ~atis *f.* **ease** [10]seruitium ~ii *neut.* **servility**

Non igitur monstrum partim[11] uelle, partim nolle, sed aegritudo[12] animi est, quia non totus adsurgit[13] ueritate consuetudine praegrauatus.[14] et ideo sunt duae uoluntates, quia una earum tota non est et hoc adest alteri quod deest alteri.

[11]partim *adv.* **in part** [12]aegritudo ~inis *f.* **sickness** [13]adsurgo ~gere, ~rexi, ~rectum **to rise** [14]praegrauo ~are, ~aui, ~atum **to weigh down**

Manichee psychology refuted

8.10.22 *Pereant a facie tua* (Ps 67:3), Deus, sicuti pereunt, *uaniloqui*[1] *et mentis seductores*[2] (Tit 1:10) qui, cum duas uoluntates in deliberando[3] animaduerterint,[4] duas naturas duarum mentium esse adseuerant,[5] unam bonam, alteram malam. ipsi uere mali sunt, cum ista mala sentiunt, et idem ipsi boni erunt, si uera senserint uerisque consenserint,[6] ut dicat eis apostolus[7] tuus, *Fuistis aliquando tenebrae, nunc autem lux in Domino* (Eph 5:8). illi enim dum uolunt esse lux, non in Domino sed in se ipsis, putando animae naturam hoc esse quod Deus est, ita facti sunt densiores[8] tenebrae, quoniam longius a te recesserunt horrenda[9] arrogantia,[10] *a te uero lumine inluminante omnem hominem uenientem in hunc mundum* (Jn 1:9). attendite quid dicatis, et erubescite[11] et *accedite*[12] *ad eum et inluminamini, et uultus uestri non erubescent* (Ps 33:6 VL).

Ego cum deliberabam ut iam *seruirem Domino Deo* (Mt 4:10) meo, sicut diu disposueram,[13] ego eram qui uolebam, ego qui nolebam: ego eram. nec plene[14] uolebam nec plene nolebam. ideo mecum contendebam[15] et dissipabar[16] a me ipso, et ipsa dissipatio[17] me inuito[18] quidem fiebat, nec tamen ostendebat naturam mentis alienae sed poenam meae. et ideo *non iam ego operabar*[19] illam, *sed quod habitabat*[20] *in me peccatum* (Rom 7:20) de supplicio[21] liberioris[22] peccati, quia eram filius Adam.

[1]uaniloquus ~a, ~um *adj.* **speaking grandiosely** [2]seductor ~oris *m.* ECCL **seducer** [3]delibero ~are, ~aui, ~atum **to deliberate** [4]animaduerto ~tere, ~ti, ~sum to pay attention > **to observe** [5]adseuero ~are, ~aui, ~atum **to assert emphatically** [6]consentio ~tire, ~si, ~sum **to consent** [7]apostolus ~i *m.* ECCL **apostle** (St. Paul) [8]densus ~a, ~um *adj.* **dense** [9]horrendus ~a, ~um *adj.* **fearful** [10]arrogantia ~ae *f.* **arrogance** [11]erubesco ~escere, ~ui **to feel ashamed** [12]accedo ~dere, ~ssi, ~ssum **to draw near** [13]dispono ~onere, ~osui, ~ositum to distribute > **to intend** [14]plene *adv.* **entirely** [15]contendo ~dere, ~di, ~tum **to contend** [16]dissipo ~are, ~aui, ~atum **to disintegrate** [17]dissipatio ~onis *f.* **disintegration** [18]inuitus ~a, ~um *adj.* **unwillingly** (*quasi-adv.*) [19]operor ~ari, ~atus **to perform** [20]habito ~are, ~aui, ~atum **to dwell** [21]supplicium ~ii *neut.* **punishment** [22]liber ~era, ~erum *adj.* **free**

Contrary desires are not separate natures

8.10.23 Nam si tot[1] sunt contrariae[2] naturae quot[3] uoluntates sibi resistunt, non iam duae sed plures erunt. si deliberet[4] quisquam utrum ad conuenticulum[5] eorum pergat[6] an ad theatrum,[7] clamant isti, "Ecce duae naturae, una bona hac[8] ducit, altera mala illac[9] reducit,[10] nam unde ista cunctatio[11] sibimet aduersantium[12] uoluntatum?" ego autem dico ambas[13] malas, et quae ad illos ducit et quae ad theatrum reducit. sed non credunt nisi bonam esse qua itur ad eos.

Quid si ergo quisquam noster deliberet et secum altercantibus[14] duabus uoluntatibus fluctuet,[15] utrum ad theatrum pergat an ad ecclesiam nostram, nonne et isti quid respondeant fluctuabunt? aut enim fatebuntur[16] quod nolunt, bona uoluntate pergi in ecclesiam nostram, sicut in eam pergunt qui sacramentis eius imbuti[17] sunt atque detinentur,[18] aut duas malas naturas et duas malas mentes in uno homine confligere[19] putabunt, et non erit uerum quod solent dicere, unam bonam, alteram malam, aut conuertentur ad uerum et non negabunt, cum quisque deliberat, animam unam diuersis[20] uoluntatibus aestuare.[21]

[1]tot *indecl. adj.* **as many** (w. *correl.* 'quot') [2]contrarius ~a, ~um *adj.* **opposing** [3]quot *indecl. adj.* **as** [4]delibero ~are, ~aui, ~atum **to deliberate** [5]conuenticulum ~i *neut.* **small assembly** [6]pergo ~gere, ~rexi, ~rectum **to go** [7]theatrum ~i *neut.* **theatre** [8]hac *adv.* **in this direction** [9]illac *adv.* **in that direction** [10]reduco ~cere, ~xi, ~ctum **to lead back** [11]cunctatio ~onis *f.* **hesitation** [12]aduersor ~ari, ~atus **to be opposed** [13]ambo ~ae, ~o *pl. adj. pron.* **both** [14]altercor ~ari, ~atus **to argue** [15]fluctuo ~are, ~aui, ~atum **to vacillate** [16]fateor ~eri, fassus **to admit** [17]imbuo ~uere, ~ui, ~utum **to initiate** [18]detineo ~inere, ~inui, ~entum **to detain** [19]confligo ~gere, ~xi, ~ctum **to be in conflict** [20]diuersus ~a, ~um *adj.* **divergent** [21]aestuo ~are, ~aui, ~atum to burn > **to be unsettled**

Not two minds in one person

8.10.24 Iam ergo non dicant, cum duas uoluntates in homine uno aduersari[1] sibi sentiunt, duas contrarias[2] mentes de duabus contrariis substantiis et de duobus contrariis principiis contendere,[3] unam bonam, alteram malam. nam tu, *Deus uerax*[4] (Jn 3:33), improbas[5] eos et redarguis[6] atque conuincis[7] eos, sicut in utraque mala uoluntate, cum quisque

[1]aduersor ~ari, ~atus **to be opposed** [2]contrarius ~a, ~um *adj.* **opposing** [3]contendo ~dere, ~di, ~tum **to contend** [4]uerax ~acis *adj.* **truthful** [5]improbo ~are, ~aui, ~atum **to reject** [6]redarguo ~ere, ~i **to prove untrue** [7]conuinco ~incere, ~ici, ~ictum **to convict of error**

deliberat[8] utrum hominem ueneno[9] interimat[10] an ferro, utrum fundum[11] alienum illum an illum inuadat,[12] quando utrumque non potest, utrum emat[13] uoluptatem luxuria[14] an pecuniam[15] seruet auaritia,[16] utrum ad circum[17] pergat[18] an ad theatrum,[19] si uno die utrumque exhibeatur;[20] addo etiam tertium,[21] an ad furtum[22] de domo aliena, si subest[23] occasio;[24] addo et quartum,[25] an ad committendum[26] adulterium,[27] si et inde simul facultas[28] aperitur; si omnia concurrant[29] in unum articulum[30] temporis pariterque[31] cupiantur omnia quae simul agi nequeunt,[32] discerpunt[33] enim animum sibimet aduersantibus quattuor[34] uoluntatibus uel etiam pluribus in tanta copia rerum quae appetuntur,[35] nec tamen tantam multitudinem[36] diuersarum[37] substantiarum solent dicere.

Ita et in bonis uoluntatibus. nam quaero ab eis utrum bonum sit delectari lectione[38] apostoli[39] et utrum bonum sit delectari psalmo[40] sobrio[41] et utrum bonum sit euangelium[42] disserere.[43] respondebunt ad singula: "Bonum." quid si ergo pariter delectent omnia simulque uno tempore, nonne diuersae uoluntates distendunt[44] cor hominis, dum deliberatur quid potissimum[45] arripiamus?[46] et omnes bonae sunt et certant[47] secum, donec eligatur[48] unum quo feratur tota uoluntas una, quae in plures diuidebatur.[49] ita etiam cum aeternitas delectat superius[50]

---

[8]delibero ~are, ~aui, ~atum **to deliberate** [9]uenenum ~i *neut.* **poison** [10]interimo ~imere, ~emi, ~emptum **to take a life** [11]fundus ~i *m.* **estate** [12]inuado ~dere, ~si, ~sum **to invade > to seize control of** [13]emo emere, emi, emptum **to buy** [14]luxuria ~ae *f.* **luxury** [15]pecunia ~ae *f.* **wealth** [16]auaritia ~ae *f.* **avarice** [17]circus ~i *m.* **circus** (place for public games) [18]pergo ~gere, ~rexi, ~rectum **to go** [19]theatrum ~i *neut.* **theatre** [20]exhibeo ~ere, ~ui, ~itum **to put on a show** [21]tertius ~a, ~um *adj.* **third** [22]furtum ~i *neut.* **theft** [23]subsum ~esse, suffui **to be close at hand** [24]occasio ~onis *f.* **occasion** [25]quartus ~a, ~um *adj.* **fourth** [26]committo ~ittere, ~isi, ~issum **to commit** [27]adulterium ~ii *neut.* **adultery** [28]facultas ~atis *f.* **opportunity** [29]concurro ~rere, ~ri, ~sum **to coincide** [30]articulus ~i *m.* **point of time** [31]pariter *adv.* **together** [32]nequeo ~ire, ~iui or ~ii **to be unable (to)** [33]discerpo ~pere, ~psi, ~ptum **to tear in pieces** [34]quattuor *indecl. adj.* **four** [35]appeto ~ere, ~iui or ~ii, ~itum **to desire** [36]multitudo ~inis *f.* **large number** [37]diuersus ~a, ~um *adj.* **different** [38]lectio ~onis *f.* **reading** [39]apostolus ~i *m.* ECCL **the apostle** (St. Paul) [40]psalmus ~i, *m.* ECCL **psalm** [41]sobrius ~ia, ~ium *adj.* **sober** [42]euangelium ~i *neut.* ECCL **the Gospel(s)** [43]dissero ~ere, ~ui, ~tum **to discuss** [44]distendo ~dere, ~di, ~tum **to strain** [45]potissimum *adv.* **especially** [46]arripio ~ere, ~ui, arreptum **to avail oneself of** [47]certo ~are, ~aui, ~atum **to rival** [48]eligo ~igere, ~egi, ~ectum **to choose** [49]diuido ~idere, ~isi, ~isum **to divide** [50]superius *adv.* **from above**

et temporalis[51] boni uoluptas retentat[52] inferius,[53] eadem anima est non tota uoluntate illud aut hoc uolens et ideo discerpitur graui molestia,[54] dum illud ueritate praeponit,[55] hoc familiaritate[56] non ponit.

[51]temporalis ~is, ~e *adj.* **temporal** [52]retento ~are **to keep hold of** [53]inferius *compar. adv.* **from below** [54]molestia ~ae *f.* **distress** [55]praepono ~onere, ~osui, ~ositum **to prefer** [56]familiaritas ~atis *f.* **familiarity**

A severe mercy

8.11.25 Sic aegrotabam[1] et excruciabar,[2] accusans[3] memet ipsum solito acerbius[4] nimis ac uoluens[5] et uersans[6] me in uinculo[7] meo, donec abrumperetur[8] totum, quo iam exiguo[9] tenebar, sed tenebar tamen. et instabas[10] tu in occultis meis, Domine, seuera[11] misericordia, flagella[12] ingeminans[13] timoris[14] et pudoris,[15] ne rursus cessarem[16] et non abrumperetur idipsum[17] exiguum et tenue[18] quod remanserat,[19] et reualesceret[20] iterum[21] et me robustius[22] alligaret.[23] dicebam enim apud me intus, "Ecce modo fiat, modo fiat," et cum uerbo iam ibam in placitum. iam paene[24] faciebam et non faciebam, nec relabebar[25] tamen in pristina[26] sed de proximo[27] stabam et respirabam.[28] et item[29] conabar, et paulo minus[30] ibi eram et paulo minus, iam iamque[31] attingebam[32] et tenebam. et non ibi eram nec attingebam nec tenebam, haesitans[33] mori morti et uitae uiuere, plusque in me ualebat deterius[34] inolitum[35] quam melius insolitum,[36] punctumque ipsum temporis[37] quo aliud

[1]aegroto ~are, ~aui, ~atum **to be sick** [2]excrucio ~are, ~aui, ~atum **to torment** [3]accuso ~are, ~aui, ~atum **to accuse** [4]acerbe *adv.* **bitterly** [5]uoluo ~uere, ~ui, ~utum **to roll** [6]uerso ~are, ~aui, ~atum **to spin** [7]uinculum ~i *neut.* **chain** [8]abrumpo ~umpere, ~upi, ~uptum **to burst apart** [9]exiguus ~a, ~um *adj.* **by a little** (abl.) [10]insto ~are, ~iti **to press (a person)** [11]seuerus ~a, ~um *adj.* **severe** [12]flagellum ~i *neut.* **whip** [13]ingemino ~are, ~aui, ~atum **to increase in intensity** [14]timor ~oris *m.* **fear** [15]pudor ~oris *m.* **shame** [16]cesso ~are, ~aui, ~atum **to do nothing** [17]idipsum *pron.* ECCL **self-same** [18]tenuis ~is, ~e *adj.* **slender** [19]remaneo ~ere, ~si **to remain** [20]reualesco ~escere, ~ui **to regain one's strength** [21]iterum *adv.* **again** [22]robuste *adv.* **forcefully** [23]alligo ~are, ~aui, ~atum **to bind** [24]paene *adv.* **almost** [25]relabor ~bi, ~psus **to slip** [26]pristinus ~a, ~um *adj.* **former state of things** (*neut.* as noun) [27]'de proximo' **close by** [28]respiro ~are, ~aui, ~atum **to catch one's breath** [29]item *adv.* **similarly** [30]'paulo minus' **all but** [31]'iam iamque' **at any time now** [32]attingo ~tingere, ~tigi, ~tactum **to touch** [33]haesito ~are, ~aui, ~atum **to falter** [34]deterior ~ior, ~ius *compar. adj.* **worse** [35]inolesco ~escere, ~eui, ~itum **to implant** [36]insolitus ~a, ~um *adj.* **unfamiliar** [37]'punctum... temporis' **point in time**

futurus eram, quanto propius admouebatur,[38] tanto ampliorem[39] incu-
tiebat[40] horrorem.[41] sed non recutiebat[42] retro[43] nec auertebat,[44] sed
suspendebat.[45]

[38]admoueo ~mouere, ~moui, ~motum **to draw near** [39]amplus ~a, ~um *adj.* **intense** (w. abstract
noun) [40]incutio ~tere, ~ssi, ~ssum **to instill** [41]horror ~oris *m.* **feeling of dread** [42]recutio ~tere,
~ssi, ~ssum **to strike and cause recoil** [43]retro *adv.* **backwards** [44]auerto ~tere, ~ti, ~sum **to turn
aside** [45]suspendo ~dere, ~di, ~sum **to keep in suspense**

Psychomachia: Antiquae Amicae

8.11.26 Retinebant[1] nugae[2] nugarum et *uanitates uanitantium*[3] (Eccl
1:2), Antiquae[4] Amicae[5] meae, et succutiebant[6] uestem meam carneam[7]
et submurmurabant,[8] "Dimittisne nos?" et "A momento[9] isto non
erimus tecum ultra[10] in aeternum" et "A momento isto non tibi licebit
hoc et illud ultra in aeternum." et quae suggerebant[11] in eo quod dixi
"hoc et illud," quae suggerebant, Deus meus, auertat[12] ab anima serui
tui misericordia tua! quas sordes[13] suggerebant, quae dedecora![14] et
audiebam eas iam longe minus quam dimidius,[15] non tamquam libere[16]
contradicentes[17] eundo in obuiam,[18] sed uelut a dorso[19] mussitantes[20] et
discedentem[21] quasi furtim[22] uellicantes,[23] ut respicerem.[24] tardabant[25]
tamen cunctantem[26] me abripere[27] atque excutere[28] ab eis et transilire[29]
quo uocabar, cum diceret mihi consuetudo uiolenta,[30] "Putasne sine
istis poteris?"

[1]retineo ~ere, ~ui, retentum **to hold tight** [2]nugae ~arum *f. pl.* **trifles** [3]uanitantes ~ium *pl.* AUG
vain people [4]antiquus ~a, ~um *adj.* **long-standing** [5]amica ~ae *f.* **mistress** [6]succutio ~tere, ~ssi,
~ssum to **jolt from below;** LATE **to pluck softly** [7]carneus ~a, ~um *adj.* ECCL **fleshly** [8]submur-
muro ~are **to murmur softly** [9]momentum ~i *neut.* **moment** [10]ultra *adv.* **any longer** [11]suggero ~rere,
~ssi, ~stum **to suggest** [12]auerto ~tere, ~ti, ~sum **to avert** [13]sordes ~is *f.* **filth** [14]dedecus ~oris *neut.*
disgraceful acts (*pl.*) [15]dimidius ~a, ~um *adj.* **half** [16]libere *adv.* **openly** [17]contradico ~icere, ~ixi,
~ictum **to object;** ECCL **to oppose** [18]'eundo in obuiam' **facing head-on** [19]dorsum ~i *neut.* **back**
[20]mussito ~are, ~aui, ~atum **to talk in subdued tones** [21]discedo ~dere, ~ssi, ~ssum **to part company**
[22]furtim *adv.* **stealthily** [23]uellico ~are, ~aui, ~atum **to tear away bit by bit** [24]respicio ~icere, ~exi,
~ectum **to look back at** [25]tardo ~are, ~aui, ~atum **to slow down** [26]cunctor ~ari, ~atus **to move
slowly** [27]abripio ~ipere, ~ipui, ~eptum **to snatch away** [28]excutio ~tere, ~ssi, ~ssum **to shake off**
[29]transilio ~ire, ~ui **to leap across** [30]uiolentus ~a, ~um *adj.* **aggressive**

Psychomachia: Continentia

8.11.27 Sed iam tepidissime[1] hoc dicebat. aperiebatur enim ab ea parte qua intenderam faciem et quo transire trepidabam[2] casta[3] dignitas[4] Continentiae,[5] serena[6] et non dissolute[7] hilaris,[8] honeste[9] blandiens[10] ut uenirem neque dubitarem,[11] et extendens ad me suscipiendum[12] et amplectendum[13] pias manus plenas gregibus[14] bonorum exemplorum.[15] ibi tot pueri et puellae, ibi iuuentus[16] multa et omnis aetas, et graues uiduae[17] et uirgines anus,[18] et in omnibus ipsa Continentia nequaquam[19] sterilis,[20] sed fecunda[21] *mater filiorum gaudiorum* (Ps 112:9) de Marito[22] te, Domine. et inridebat me inrisione[23] hortatoria,[24] quasi diceret, "Tu non poteris quod isti, quod istae? an uero isti et istae in se ipsis possunt ac non in Domino Deo suo? Dominus Deus eorum me dedit eis. quid in te stas et non stas? proice[25] te in eum! noli metuere. non se subtrahet[26] ut cadas: proice te securus!"[27] excipiet[28] et sanabit te." et erubescebam[29] nimis, quia illarum nugarum[30] murmura[31] adhuc audiebam, et cunctabundus[32] pendebam.[33] et rursus illa, quasi diceret, "Obsurdesce[34] aduersus immunda[35] illa *membra tua super terram, ut mortificentur*[36] (Col 3:5). *narrant tibi delectationes,*[37] *sed non sicut lex Domini Dei tui.*" (Ps 118:85 VL).

Ista controuersia[38] in corde meo non nisi de me ipso aduersus me ipsum. at Alypius affixus[39] lateri meo inusitati[40] motus mei exitum[41] tacitus opperiebatur.[42]

---

[1]tepide *adv.* **tepidly** [2]trepido ~are, ~aui, ~atum **to tremble** [3]castus ~a, ~um *adj.* **chaste** [4]dignitas ~atis *f.* **dignity** [5]continentia ~ae *f.* **continence** (personified) [6]serenus ~a, ~um *adj.* **serene** [7]dissolute *adv.* carelessly; LATE **dissolutely** [8]hilaris ~is, ~e. *adj.* **light-hearted** [9]honeste *adv.* **becomingly** [10]blandior ~iri, ~itus **to coax** (w. 'ut' + subj.) [11]dubito ~are, ~aui, ~atum **to hesitate** [12]suscipio ~ipere, ~epi, ~eptum **to support** [13]amplector ~cti, ~xus **to embrace affectionately** [14]grex ~egis *m.* flock > **troop** [15]exemplum ~i *neut.* **example** [16]iuuentus ~utis *f.* **youth** [17]uiduus ~a, ~um *adj.* **widow** (*f.* as noun) [18]anus ~us *f.* **old woman** [19]nequaquam *adv.* **not at all** [20]sterilis ~is, ~e *adj.* **sterile** [21]fecundus ~a, ~um *adj.* **fruitful** [22]maritus ~i *m.* **bridegroom** [23]inrisio ~onis *f.* **mockery** [24]hortatorius ~a, ~um *adj.* ECCL **cheering** [25]proicio ~icere, ~ieci, ~iectum **to fling oneself forth** [26]subtraho ~here, ~xi, ~ctum **to withdraw** [27]securus ~a, ~um *adj.* **free from anxiety** [28]excipio ~ipere, ~epi, ~eptum **to care for** [29]erubesco ~escere, ~ui **to feel ashamed** [30]nugae ~arum *f. pl.* **trifles** [31]murmur ~uris *neut.* [onomat.] **murmur** [32]cunctabundus ~a, ~um *adj.* **hesitating** [33]pendeo ~ere, pependi **to hang in suspense** [34]obsurdesco ~escere, ~ui **to become deaf** [35]immundus ~a, ~um *adj.* **unclean** [36]mortifico ~are, ~aui, ~atum ECCL to put to death; **to mortify** [37]delectatio ~onis *f.* **delight** [38]controuersia ~ae *f.* **controversy** [39]affigo ~gere, ~xi, ~xum **to attach** [40]inusitatus ~a, ~um *adj.* **unusual** [41]exitus ~us *m.* **outcome** [42]opperior ~iri, ~tus **to wait for**

Weeping under the fig tree

8.12.28 Ubi uero a fundo[1] arcano[2] alta[3] consideratio[4] traxit[5] et congessit[6] totam miseriam meam in conspectu cordis mei, oborta[7] est procella[8] ingens[9] ferens ingentem imbrem[10] lacrimarum. et ut totum effunderem[11] cum uocibus suis, surrexi[12] ab Alypio (solitudo[13] mihi ad negotium[14] flendi aptior[15] suggerebatur[16]) et secessi[17] remotius[18] quam ut posset mihi onerosa[19] esse etiam eius praesentia.[20] sic tunc eram, et ille sensit: nescio quid[21] enim, puto, dixeram in quo apparebat sonus uocis meae iam fletu[22] grauidus,[23] et sic surrexeram. mansit ergo ille ubi sedebamus[24] nimie[25] stupens.[26] ego sub quadam *fici*[27] *arbore* (Gen 3:7, Mt 21:19, Jn 1:47–48) straui[28] me nescio quomodo,[29] et dimisi habenas[30] lacrimis, et proruperunt[31] flumina oculorum meorum, *acceptabile*[32] *sacrificium*[33] *tuum* (Ps 50:19), et non quidem his uerbis, sed in hac sententia multa dixi tibi: *Et tu, Domine, usquequo?*[34] (Ps 6:4). *usquequo, Domine, irasceris*[35] *in finem? ne memor*[36] *fueris iniquitatum nostrarum antiquarum*[37] (Ps 78:5, 8). sentiebam enim eis me teneri. iactabam[38] uoces miserabiles:[39] "Quamdiu,[40] quamdiu, 'Cras[41] et cras'? quare[42] non modo? quare non hac hora finis turpitudinis[43] meae?"

---

[1]fundus ~i *m.* **the depths** [2]arcanus ~a, ~um *adj.* **secret** [3]altus ~a, ~um *adj.* **profound** [4]consideratio ~onis *f.* **contemplation** [5]traho ~here, ~xi, ~ctum **to drag** [6]congero ~rere, ~ssi, ~stum **to make into a heap** [7]oborior ~iri, ~tus **to spring up** (of tears) [8]procella ~ae *f.* **violent storm** [9]ingens ~ntis *adj.* **vast** [10]imber ~bris *m.* **stream** [11]effundo ~undere, ~udi, ~usum **to pour out** [12]surgo ~rgere, ~rrexi, ~rrectum **to rise to one's feet** [13]solitudo ~inis *f.* **solitude** [14]negotium ~ii *neut.* **business** [15]aptus ~a, ~um *ppl. adj.* **suitable** [16]suggero ~rere, ~ssi, ~stum **to suggest** [17]secedo ~dere, ~ssi, ~ssum **to withdraw to a private place** [18]remote *adv.* **farther away** (*compar.*) [19]onerosus ~a, ~um *adj.* **burdensome** [20]praesentia ~ae *f.* **presence** [21]'nescio quid' **something or other** (of slight importance) [22]fletus ~us *m.* **weeping** [23]grauidus ~a, ~um *adj.* **laden** [24]sedeo ~ere, sedi, sessum **to sit** [25]nimie *adv.* LATE **exceedingly** [26]stupeo ~ere, ~ui **to be dazed** [27]ficus ~i **fig** [28]sterno ~ere, straui, stratum **to throw oneself prostrate** [29]'nescio quomodo' **in some unaccountable way** [30]habena ~ae *f.* **reins; restraint** (fig.) [31]prorumpo ~umpere, ~upi, ~uptum **to burst forth** [32]acceptabilis ~e *adj.* ECCL **acceptable** [33]sacrificium ~ii *neut.* **sacrificial offering** [34]usquequo *adv.* ECCL = quousque **how long?** [35]irascor ~i, iratus sum **to be angry** [36]memor ~oris *adj.* **mindful** [37]antiquus ~a, ~um *adj.* **former** [38]iacto ~are, ~aui, ~atum **to vent** [39]miserabilis ~is, ~e *adj.* **miserable** [40]quamdiu *adv.* **for how long?** [41]cras *adv.* **tomorrow** [42]quare *adv.* **why?** [43]turpitudo ~inis *f.* **ugliness**

Tolle, lege: St. Paul

8.12.29 Dicebam haec et flebam amarissima[1] *contritione*[2] *cordis* (Ps 50:19) mei. et ecce audio uocem de uicina[3] domo cum cantu dicentis et crebro[4] repetentis,[5] quasi pueri an puellae, nescio: "Tolle[6] lege, tolle lege." statimque[7] mutato uultu intentissimus cogitare coepi utrumnam[8] solerent pueri in aliquo genere ludendi[9] cantitare[10] tale aliquid. nec occurrebat omnino audisse me uspiam,[11] repressoque[12] impetu lacrimarum surrexi,[13] nihil aliud interpretans[14] diuinitus[15] mihi iuberi nisi ut aperirem codicem[16] et legerem quod primum caput inuenissem. audieram enim *de Antonio* (Vita 2) quod ex euangelica[17] lectione[18] cui forte superuenerat[19] admonitus[20] fuerit, tamquam sibi diceretur quod legebatur: *Vade,*[21] *uende*[22] *omnia quae habes, et da pauperibus*[23] *et habebis thesaurum*[24] *in caelis; et ueni, sequere me* (Mt 19:21), et tali oraculo[25] confestim[26] *ad te esse conuersum* (Ps 50:15). itaque concitus[27] redii in eum locum ubi sedebat[28] Alypius: ibi enim posueram codicem apostoli[29] cum inde surrexeram. arripui,[30] aperui, et legi in silentio[31] capitulum[32] quo primum coniecti[33] sunt oculi mei: *Non in comessationibus*[34] *et ebrietatibus,*[35] *non in cubilibus*[36] *et impudicitiis,*[37] *non in contentione*[38] *et aemulatione,*[39] *sed induite*[40] *Dominum Iesum Christum et carnis prouidentiam*[41] *ne feceritis*

---

[1]amarus ~a, ~um *adj.* **bitter** [2]contritio ~onis *f.* grief; ECCL **contrition** [3]uicinus ~a, ~um *adj.* **neighboring** [4]crebro *adv.* **frequently** [5]repeto ~ere, ~iui, ~itum **to repeat** [6]tollo ~ere, sustuli, sublatum **to pick up** [7]statim *adv.* **at that moment** [8]utrumnam *conj.* LATE **whether** [9]ludo ~dere, ~si, ~sum **to play** [10]cantito ~are, ~aui, ~atum **to sing repeatedly** [11]uspiam *adv.* **anywhere** [12]reprimo ~imere, ~essi, ~essum **to hold in check** [13]surgo ~rgere, ~rrexi, ~rrectum **to rise to one's feet** [14]interpretor ~ari, ~atus **to interpret** [15]diuinitus *adv.* **by divine agency or inspiration** [16]codex ~icis *m.* **book** [17]euangelicus ~a, ~um ECCL **of the Gospel** [18]lectio ~onis *f.* **reading** [19]superuenio ~enire, ~eni, ~entum **to happen upon** [20]admonitus ~us *m.* **admonition** [21]uado ~ere **to go** (esp. with purpose) [22]uendo ~ere, ~idi, ~itum **to sell** [23]pauper ~eris *adj.* **poor** [24]thesaurus ~i *m.* **treasure** [25]oraculum ~i *neut.* **oracle** [26]confestim *adv.* **immediately** [27]concitus ~a, ~um *adj.* **incited to action** [28]sedeo ~ere, sedi, sessum **to sit** [29]apostolus ~i *m.* ECCL **the apostle** (St. Paul) [30]arripio ~ere, ~ui, arreptum **to seize eagerly** [31]silentium ~ii *neut.* **silence** [32]capitulum ~i *neut.* capital; LATE **chapter** [33]conicio ~icere, ~ieci, ~iectum **to cast** [34]comessatio ~onis *f.* **revelry** [35]ebrietas ~atis *f.* **drunkenness** [36]cubile ~is *neut.* bed > **sexual relations** [37]impudicitia ~ae *f.* **sexual indecency** [38]contentio ~onis *f.* **quarrel** [39]aemulatio ~onis *f.* **jealous rivalry** [40]induo ~uere, ~ui, ~utum **to put on** [41]prouidentia ~ae *f.* **provision for** (w. gen.)

in concupiscentiis[42] (Rom 13:13–14). nec ultra[43] uolui legere nec opus erat. statim quippe cum fine huiusce[44] sententiae quasi luce securitatis[45] infusa[46] cordi meo omnes dubitationis[47] tenebrae diffugerunt.[48]

[42]concupiscentia ~ae *f.* ECCL **concupiscence** [43]ultra *adv.* **any longer** [44]'huiusce' **of this very** [45]securitas ~atis *f.* **calmness** [46]infundo ~undere, ~udi, ~usum **to pour in** > **to instill** [47]dubitatio ~onis *f.* **doubt** [48]diffugio ~ugere, ~ugi **to disperse**

Make room for Alypius

8.12.30 Tum interiecto[1] aut digito[2] aut nescio quo alio[3] signo codicem[4] clausi et tranquillo[5] iam uultu indicaui Alypio. at ille quid in se ageretur (quod ego nesciebam) sic indicauit. petit uidere quid legissem. ostendi, et attendit etiam ultra[6] quam ego legeram. et ignorabam quid sequeretur. sequebatur uero: *Infirmum*[7] *autem in fide recipite* (Rom 14:1). quod ille ad se rettulit[8] mihique aperuit. sed tali admonitione[9] firmatus[10] est placitoque ac proposito bono[11] et congruentissimo[12] suis moribus, quibus a me in melius iam olim[13] ualde longeque distabat,[14] sine ulla turbulenta[15] cunctatione[16] coniunctus[17] est.

Inde ad matrem ingredimur,[18] indicamus: gaudet. narramus quemadmodum gestum sit: exultat[19] et triumphat[20] et benedicebat[21] tibi, *qui potens es ultra quam petimus et intellegimus facere* (Eph 3:20), quia tanto amplius sibi a te concessum[22] de me uidebat quam petere solebat miserabilibus[23] flebilibusque[24] gemitibus.[25] *conuertisti enim me ad te* (Ps 50:15), ut nec uxorem[26] quaererem nec aliquam spem saeculi huius, stans in ea regula[27] fidei in qua me ante[28] tot annos ei reuelaueras,[29]

[1]intericio ~icere, ~ieci, ~iectum **to insert** [2]digitus ~i *m.* **finger** [3]'nescio quo alio' **by some such other** [4]codex ~icis *m.* **book** [5]tranquillus ~a, ~um *adj.* **calm** [6]ultra *prep. acc.* **beyond** [7]infirmus ~a, ~um *adj.* **weak** [8]refero ~rre, rettuli, relatum **to refer** [9]admonitio ~onis *f.* **admonition** [10]firmo ~are, ~aui, ~atum **to confirm** [11]'proposito bono' **with a good intention** [12]congruens ~ntis *adj.* **fitting** [13]olim *adv.* **for a long time** [14]disto ~are **to be different** [15]turbulentus ~a, ~um *adj.* **disordered** [16]cunctatio ~onis *f.* **hesitation** [17]coniungo ~gere, ~xi, ~ctum **to join together** [18]ingredior ~di, ~ssus **to go into** [19]exulto ~are, ~aui **to exult** [20]triumpho ~are, ~aui, ~atum **to celebrate triumphantly** [21]benedico ~cere, ~xi, ~ctum; ECCL **to bless** [22]concedo ~dere, ~ssi, ~ssum **to grant** [23]miserabilis ~is, ~e *adj.* **pitiable** [24]flebilis ~is, ~e *adj.* **tearful** [25]gemitus ~us *m.* **groaning** [26]uxor ~oris *f.* **wife** [27]regula ~ae *f.* **ruler** [28]ante *adv.* **before** [29]reuelo ~are, ~aui, ~atum **to reveal**

et *conuertisti luctum*[30] *eius in gaudium* (Ps 29:12) multo uberius[31] quam uoluerat, et multo carius[32] atque castius[33] quam de nepotibus[34] carnis meae requirebat.[35]

---

[30]luctus ~us *m.* **mourning** [31]uberius *compar. adv.* **in greater abundance** [32]care *adv.* **lovingly** [33]caste *adv.* **chastely** [34]nepos ~otis *m.* **grandchild** [35]requiro ~rere, ~siui, ~situm **to long for**

9

SAINT MONICA

Cassiciacum (Cassago Brianza), Milan, and Ostia, 386–387

I will what you will

9.1.1 *O Domine, ego seruus tuus, ego seruus tuus et filius ancillae[1] tuae: dirupisti[2] uincula[3] mea, tibi sacrificabo[4] hostiam[5] laudis* (Ps 115:16–17). laudet te cor meum et lingua mea, *et omnia ossa[6] mea dicant, Domine, quis similis tibi?* (Ps 34:10). dicant, et responde mihi et *dic animae meae, Salus tua ego sum* (Ps 34:3).

Quis ego et qualis ego? quid non mali aut facta mea aut, si non facta, dicta mea aut, si non dicta, uoluntas mea fuit? *tu autem, Domine, bonus et misericors[7]* (Ps 85:15), et dextera tua respiciens[8] profunditatem[9] mortis meae et a fundo[10] cordis mei exhauriens[11] abyssum corruptionis.[12] et hoc erat totum, nolle quod uolebam et uelle quod uolebas. sed ubi erat tam annoso[13] tempore et de quo imo[14] altoque secreto[15] euocatum[16] est in momento[17] liberum arbitrium[18] meum, quo subderem[19] ceruicem[20] leni[21] *iugo tuo et umeros[22] leui sarcinae[23] tuae* (Mt 11:30), Christe Iesu, *adiutor[24] meus*

---

[1]ancilla ~ae *f.* **handmaid** [2]dirrumpo ~umpere, ~upi, ~uptum **to burst** [3]uinculum ~i *neut.* **chain** [4]sacrifico ~are, ~aui, ~atum **to offer as sacrifice** [5]hostia ~ae *f.* **offering** [6]os ossis *neut.* **bones** (*pl.* esp. as seat of emotion); ECCL soul (fig.) [7]misericors ~rdis *adj.* **merciful** [8]respicio ~icere, ~exi, ~ectum **to show concern for** [9]profunditas ~tatis *f.* LATE **depth** [10]fundus ~i *m.* **the depths** [11]exhaurio ~rire, ~si, ~stum **to drain** [12]corruptio ~onis *f.* **corruption** [13]annosus ~a, ~um *adj.* **long** (of time) [14]imus ~a, ~um *adj.* **lowest part** (*neut.* as noun) [15]secretum ~i *neut.* **secret** [16]euoco ~are, ~aui, ~atum **to call out** [17]momentum ~i *neut.* **moment** [18]'liberum arbitrium' **free will** [19]subdo ~ere, ~idi, ~itum **to place under** (a yoke) [20]ceruix ~icis *f.* **neck** [21]lenis ~is, ~e *adj.* **gentle** [22]umerus ~i *m.* **shoulder** [23]sarcina ~ae *f.* **load** [24]adiutor ~oris *m.* **helper**

et redemptor[25] *meus* (Ps 18:15)? quam suaue[26] mihi subito[27] factum est carere[28] suauitatibus[29] nugarum,[30] et quas amittere metus fuerat iam dimittere gaudium erat. eiciebas[31] enim eas a me, uera tu et summa suauitas, eiciebas et intrabas pro eis omni uoluptate dulcior, sed *non carni et sanguini* (Gal 1:16), omni luce clarior, sed omni secreto interior, omni honore sublimior,[32] sed non sublimibus in se. iam liber erat animus meus a curis mordacibus[33] ambiendi[34] et adquirendi[35] et uolutandi[36] atque scalpendi[37] scabiem[38] libidinum, et garriebam[39] tibi, claritati[40] meae et diuitiis[41] meis et saluti meae, Domino Deo meo.

[25]redemptor ~oris *m.* ransomer; ECCL **redeemer** [26]suauis ~is, ~e *adj.* **pleasant** [27]subito *adv.* **suddenly** [28]careo ~ere, ~ui, ~itum **to do without** [29]suauitas ~atis *f.* **pleasantness** [30]nugae ~arum *f. pl.* **trifles** [31]eicio eicere, eieci, eiectum **to cast off** [32]sublimis ~is, ~e *adj.* **sublime** [33]mordax ~acis *adj.* **biting** [34]ambio ~ire, ~iui, ~itum to go round > **to self-promote** [35]adquiro ~rere, ~siui, ~situm **to acquire** [36]uoluto ~are, ~aui, ~atum to roll > **to wallow** [37]scalpo ~pere, ~psi, ~ptum **to scratch** [38]scabies ~ei *f.* **itch, scab** [39]garrio ~ire, ~iui **to chatter** [40]claritas ~atis *f.* **fame** [41]diuitiae ~arum *f. pl.* **riches**

Harvest

9.2.2 Et placuit mihi *in conspectu tuo* (Ps 18:15) non tumultuose[1] abripere[2] sed leniter[3] subtrahere[4] ministerium[5] linguae meae nundinis[6] loquacitatis,[7] ne ulterius[8] pueri *meditantes*[9] non *legem tuam* (Ps 118:70), non pacem tuam, sed insanias[10] mendaces[11] et bella forensia,[12] mercarentur[13] ex ore meo arma furori suo. et opportune[14] iam paucissimi[15] dies supererant[16] ad uindemiales[17] ferias,[18] et statui[19] tolerare[20] illos, ut sollemniter[21] abscederem[22] et redemptus[23] a te iam non redirem uenalis.[24]

Consilium ergo nostrum erat coram te, coram hominibus autem nisi nostris non erat. et conuenerat[25] inter nos ne passim[26] cuiquam

[1]tumultuose *adv.* **in a noisy way** [2]abripio ~ipere, ~ipui, ~eptum **to bring to an end** [3]leniter *adv.* **gently** [4]subtraho ~here, ~xi, ~ctum **to withdraw** [5]ministerium ~ii *neut.* **employment** [6]nundinae ~arum *f. pl.* **marketplace** (pejorative) [7]loquacitas ~atis *f.* **talkativeness** [8]ulterius *adv.* **any longer** [9]meditor ~ari, ~atus **to contemplate** [10]insania ~ae *f.* **insanity** [11]mendax ~acis *adj.* **lying** [12]forensis ~is, ~e *adj.* **of the law courts** [13]mercor ~ari, ~atus **to buy** [14]opportune *adv.* **opportunely** [15]paucus ~a, ~um *adj.* **few** [16]supersum ~esse, ~fui **to remain** [17]uindemialis ~is, ~e *adj.* **of the vintage festival** (23 Aug–15 Oct) [18]feriae ~arum *f. pl.* **holiday** [19]statuo ~uere, ~ui, ~utum **to resolve (to)** [20]tolero ~are, ~aui, ~atum **to tolerate** [21]sollemniter *adv.* **with proper formality** [22]abscedo ~dere, ~ssi, ~ssum **to go away** [23]redimo ~imere, ~emi, ~emptum **to redeem** [24]uenalis ~is, ~e *adj.* **for sale** [25]conuenio ~enire, ~eni, ~entum **to agree together** [26]passim *adv.* all over the place > **indiscriminately**

effunderetur,²⁷ quamquam tu nobis a *conualle*²⁸ *plorationis*²⁹ (Ps 83:7) ascendentibus³⁰ et cantantibus *canticum*³¹ *graduum*³² (Ps 119–133) dederas *sagittas*³³ *acutas*³⁴ et *carbones*³⁵ *uastatores*³⁶ *aduersus linguam subdolam*³⁷ (Ps 119:3–4), uelut³⁸ consulendo³⁹ contradicentem⁴⁰ et, sicut cibum adsolet,⁴¹ amando consumentem.⁴²

---

²⁷effundo ~undere, ~udi, ~usum **to spread** ²⁸conuallis ~is *f.* **valley** ²⁹ploratio ~onis *f.* ECCL **tears** ³⁰ascendo ~dere, ~di, ~sum **to ascend** ³¹canticum ~i *neut.* **song;** ECCL **psalm** ³²gradus ~us *m.* **step** ³³sagitta ~ae *f.* **arrows** ³⁴acutus ~a, ~um *adj.* **sharp** ³⁵carbo ~onis *m.* **burning coal** ³⁶uastator ~oris *m.* **one that lays waste** ³⁷subdolus ~a, ~um *adj.* **treacherous** ³⁸uelut *adv.* **as though** (indicating pretense) ³⁹consulo ~ere, ~ui, ~tum **to show concern** ⁴⁰contradico ~icere, ~ixi, ~ictum to object; ECCL **to oppose** ⁴¹adsoleo ~ere *impers.* **it is usual** ⁴²consumo ~ere, ~psi, ~ptum to consume > **to devour**

Hearts on fire

9.2.3 Sagittaueras¹ tu cor nostrum caritate tua et gestabamus² uerba tua transfixa³ uisceribus.⁴ et exempla⁵ seruorum tuorum, quos de nigris⁶ lucidos⁷ et de mortuis uiuos feceras, congesta⁸ in sinum cogitationis nostrae urebant⁹ et absumebant¹⁰ grauem torporem,¹¹ ne in ima¹² uergeremus,¹³ et accendebant¹⁴ nos ualide,¹⁵ ut omnis ex *lingua subdola*¹⁶ (Ps 119:2) contradictionis¹⁷ flatus¹⁸ inflammare¹⁹ nos acrius²⁰ posset, non extinguere.²¹

Verum tamen quia propter nomen tuum, quod sanctificasti²² per terras, etiam laudatores²³ utique haberet uotum et propositum²⁴ nostrum, iactantiae²⁵ simile uidebatur non opperiri²⁶ tam proximum²⁷ feriarum²⁸ tempus, sed de publica²⁹ professione³⁰ atque ante oculos³¹ omnium sita ante³²

---

¹sagitto ~are, ~aui, ~atum LATE **to shoot with an arrow** ²gesto ~are, ~aui, ~atum **to carry about** ³transfigo ~gere, ~xi, ~xum **to pierce** ⁴uiscus ~eris *neut.* **innermost part; heart** (fig.) ⁵exemplum ~i *neut.* **example** ⁶niger ~gra *adj.* **dark** ⁷lucidus ~a, ~um *adj.* **shining** ⁸congero ~rere, ~ssi, ~stum **to crowd together** ⁹uro ~ere, ussi, ustum **to burn up** ¹⁰absumo ~ere, ~psi, ~ptum **to consume** (with fire) ¹¹torpor ~oris *m.* **lethargy** ¹²imus ~a, ~um *adj.* **the bottom** (*neut. pl.* as noun) ¹³uergo ~ere **to sink** ¹⁴accendo ~dere, ~di, ~sum **to set on fire** ¹⁵ualide *adv.* **intensely** ¹⁶subdolus ~a, ~um *adj.* **treacherous** ¹⁷contradictio ~onis *f.* **speaking in opposition** ¹⁸flatus ~us *m.* **gust of wind; boasting** (fig.) ¹⁹inflammo ~are, ~aui, ~atum **to inflame** (the mind) ²⁰acriter *adv.* **keenly** ²¹extinguo ~guere, ~xi, ~ctum **to extinguish** ²²sanctifico ~are, ~aui, ~atum ECCL **to hallow** ²³laudator ~oris *m.* **admirer** ²⁴propositum ~i *neut.* intention > **chosen way of life** ²⁵iactantia ~ae *f.* **ostentation** ²⁶opperior ~iri, ~tus **to wait for** ²⁷proximus ~a, ~um *superl. adj.* **close at hand** ²⁸feriae ~arum *f. pl.* **holiday** ²⁹publicus ~a, ~um *adj.* **public** ³⁰professio ~onis *f.* **profession** ³¹'ante oculos' **in full view of** (w. gen.) ³²ante *adv.* **beforehand**

discedere,[33] ut conuersa in factum meum ora cunctorum, intuentium quam uicinum[34] uindemialium[35] diem praeuenire[36] uoluerim, multa dicerent, quod quasi appetissem[37] magnus uideri. et quo mihi erat istuc,[38] ut putaretur et disputaretur[39] de animo meo et *blasphemaretur*[40] *bonum nostrum* (Rom 14:16)?

[33]discedo ~dere, ~ssi, ~ssum **to give up** (an occupation) [34]uicinus ~a, ~um *adj.* **imminent** [35]uinde-mialis ~is, ~e *adj.* **of the vintage festival** (23 Aug–15 Oct) [36]praeuenio ~enire, ~eni, ~entum **to anticipate** [37]appeto ~ere, ~iui or ~ii, ~itum **to seek to** [38]'quo mihi erat istuc' **what was that to me?** (rhet.) [39]disputo ~are, ~aui, ~atum **to debate** [40]blasphemo ~are, ~aui ~atum ECCL **to speak evil of**

It's getting hard to breathe

9.2.4 Quin[1] etiam quod ipsa aestate[2] litterario[3] labori nimio[4] pulmo[5] meus cedere[6] coeperat et difficulter[7] trahere[8] suspiria[9] doloribusque pectoris testari[10] se saucium[11] uocemque clariorem[12] productioremue[13] recusare,[14] primo[15] perturbauerat[16] me quia magisterii[17] illius sarcinam[18] paene[19] iam necessitate[20] deponere[21] cogebat aut, si curari et conuale-scere[22] potuissem, certe intermittere.[23] sed ubi plena uoluntas *uacandi*[24] *et uidendi quoniam tu es Dominus* (Ps 45:11) oborta[25] mihi est atque firmata[26] (nosti, Deus meus), etiam gaudere coepi quod haec quoque suberat[27] non mendax[28] excusatio,[29] quae offensionem[30] hominum temperaret,[31] qui propter liberos[32] suos me liberum[33] esse numquam uolebant. plenus igitur tali gaudio tolerabam[34] illud interuallum[35] temporis donec decurreret[36] (nescio utrum uel uiginti[37] dies erant), sed tamen fortiter[38] tolerabantur

[1]quin *adv.* **in fact** [2]aestas ~atis *f.* **summer** [3]litterarius ~ia, ~ium *adj.* **literary** [4]nimius ~a, ~um *adj.* **excessive** [5]pulmo ~onis *m.* **lungs** [6]cedo ~dere, ~ssi, ~ssum **to give out** [7]difficulter *adv.* **with diffi-culty** [8]traho ~here, ~xi, ~ctum **to draw (in)** [9]suspirium ~ii *neut.* **deep or labored breath** [10]testor ~ari, ~atus **to give evidence** [11]saucius ~a, ~um *adj.* **distressed** [12]clarus ~a, ~um *adj.* **clear > loud** [13]productus ~a, ~um *adj.* **extended** [14]recuso ~are, ~aui, ~atum **to refuse** [15]primo *adv.* **at first** [16]perturbo ~are, ~aui, ~atum **to upset** [17]magisterium ~ii *neut.* **teacher** [18]sarcina ~ae *f.* **burden > responsibility** (fig.) [19]paene *adv.* **practically** [20]necessitas ~atis *f.* **necessity** [21]depono ~onere, ~osui, ~ostum **to lay down** [22]conualesco ~escere, ~ui **to recover health** [23]intermitto ~ittere, ~isi, ~issum **to leave off temporarily** [24]uaco ~are, ~aui, ~atum **to take a rest** [25]oborior ~iri, ~tus **to arise** [26]firmo ~are, ~aui, ~atum **to make strong** [27]subsum ~esse, suffui to be under > **to be the underlying cause** [28]mendax ~acis *adj.* **untruthful** [29]excusatio ~onis *f.* **excuse** [30]offensio ~onis *f.* **offense** [31]tempero ~are, ~aui, ~atum **to appease** [32]liberi ~orum *m. pl.* **children** [33]liber ~era, ~erum *adj.* **free** [34]tolero ~are, ~aui, ~atum **to tolerate** [35]interuallum ~i *neut.* **interval** [36]decurro ~rrere, ~rri, ~rsum to run downhill > **to run its course** (fig.) [37]uiginti *indecl. adj.* **twenty** [38]fortiter *adv.* **resolutely**

quia recesserat cupiditas, quae mecum solebat ferre graue negotium,[39] et ego premendus[40] remanseram[41] nisi patientia[42] succederet.[43]

Peccasse me in hoc quisquam seruorum tuorum, fratrum[44] meorum, dixerit, quod iam pleno corde militia[45] tua passus me fuerim uel una hora sedere[46] in cathedra[47] mendacii, at ego non contendo.[48] sed tu, Domine misericordissime,[49] nonne et hoc peccatum cum ceteris horrendis[50] et funereis[51] in aqua sancta ignouisti[52] et remisisti[53] mihi?

[39]negotium ~ii *neut.* **business** [40]premo ~mere, ~ssi, ~ssum to press > **to overwhelm** [41]remaneo ~ere, ~si **to continue** [42]patientia ~ae *f.* **patient endurance** [43]succedo ~dere, ~ssi, ~ssum **to replace** [44]frater ~tris *m.* brother; ECCL **brethren** (*pl.*) [45]militia ~ae *f.* **service** [46]sedeo ~ere, sedi, sessum **to sit** [47]cathedra ~ae *f.* **chair** [48]contendo ~dere, ~di, ~tum **to argue** [49]misericors ~rdis *adj.* **merciful** [50]horrendus ~a, ~um *adj.* **horrendous** [51]funereus ~a, ~um *adj.* **deadly** [52]ignosco ~oscere, ~oui, ~otum **to pardon** [53]remitto ~ittere, ~isi, ~issum **to forgive**

Requiem for Verecundus

9.3.5 Macerabatur[1] anxitudine[2] Verecundus de isto nostro bono, quod propter uincula[3] sua, quibus tenacissime[4] tenebatur, deseri se nostro consortio[5] uidebat. nondum Christianus, coniuge fideli, ea ipsa tamen artiore[6] prae ceteris compede[7] ab itinere quod aggressi[8] eramus retardabatur,[9] nec Christianum esse alio modo se uelle dicebat quam illo quo non poterat. benigne[10] sane[11] obtulit[12] ut, quamdiu[13] ibi essemus, in re eius essemus. retribues[14] illi, Domine, *in resurrectione*[15] *iustorum* (Lk 14:14), quia iam ipsam sortem[16] retribuisti ei. quamuis enim absentibus nobis, cum Romae iam essemus, corporali aegritudine[17] correptus[18] et in ea Christianus et fidelis factus ex hac uita emigrauit.[19] ita misertus es non solum eius sed etiam nostri, ne cogitantes egregiam[20] erga[21] nos amici humanitatem[22] nec eum in grege[23] tuo numerantes dolore

[1]macero ~are, ~aui, ~atum **to be vexed** (pass.) [2]anxitudo ~inis *f.* **anxiety** [3]uinculum ~i *neut.* **bond** [4]tenaciter *adv.* **with a firm hold** [5]consortium ~ii *neut.* **communal life** [6]artus ~a, ~um *adj.* **firm** [7]compes ~edis *f.* **fetters** [8]aggredior ~di, ~ssus **to undertake** [9]retardo ~are, ~aui, ~atum **to hinder** [10]benigne *adv.* **readily** [11]sane *adv.* **very** [12]offero ~rre, obtuli, oblatum **to offer** [13]quamdiu *adv.* **as long as** [14]retribuo ~uere, ~ui, ~utum **to repay** [15]resurrectio ~onis *f.* ECCL **resurrection** [16]sors ~rtis *f.* **lot** [17]aegritudo ~inis *f.* **sickness** [18]corripio ~ipere, ~ipui, ~eptum **to seize hold of** [19]emigro ~are, ~aui, ~atum **to depart** [20]egregius ~ia, ~ium *adj.* **first-rate** [21]erga *prep. acc.* **towards** [22]humanitas ~atis *f.* **kindness** [23]grex ~egis *m.* **flock**

intolerabili[24] cruciaremur.[25] gratias tibi, Deus noster! tui sumus. indicant hortationes[26] et consolationes[27] tuae: fidelis promissor[28] reddis Verecundo pro rure[29] illo eius Cassiciaco, ubi ab aestu[30] saeculi requieuimus in te, amoenitatem[31] sempiterne[32] uirentis[33] paradisi[34] tui, quoniam dimisisti ei peccata super terram in monte incaseato,[35] *monte tuo, monte uberi*[36] (Ps 67:16).

[24]intolerabilis ~is, ~e *adj.* **intolerable** [25]crucio ~are, ~aui, ~atum to torment > **to cause mental anguish** [26]hortatio ~onis *f.* **encouragement** [27]consolatio ~onis *f.* **consolation** [28]promissor ~oris *m.* **promisor** [29]rus ruris *neut.* **country estate** [30]aestus ~us *m.* heat > **ebb and flow** [31]amoenitas ~atis *f.* **pleasantness** [32]sempiterne *adv.* **everlastingly** [33]uireo ~ere, ~ui **to be in full bloom** [34]paradisus ~i *m.* ECCL **paradise** (heaven) [35]incaseatus ~a, ~um LATE fattened, i.e., **flowing with milk** [36]uber ~ris *neut.* **plenty**

Requiem for Nebridius

9.3.6 Angebatur[1] ergo tunc ipse, Nebridius autem conlaetabatur.[2] quamuis enim et ipse nondum Christianus in illam foueam[3] perniciosissimi[4] erroris inciderat[5] ut ueritatis Filii tui carnem phantasma[6] crederet, tamen inde emergens[7] sic sibi erat,[8] nondum imbutu[9] ullis ecclesiae tuae sacramentis, sed inquisitor[10] ardentissimus[11] ueritatis.

Quem non multo post conuersionem[12] nostram et regenerationem[13] per baptismum[14] tuum ipsum etiam fidelem Catholicum, castitate[15] perfecta atque continentia[16] tibi seruientem in Africa apud suos, cum tota domus eius per eum Christiana facta esset, carne soluisti.[17] et nunc ille uiuit *in sinu Abraham* (Lk 16:22). quidquid illud est quod illo significatur[18] "sinu," ibi Nebridius meus uiuit, dulcis amicus meus, tuus autem, Domine, adoptiuus[19] ex liberto[20] filius: ibi uiuit. nam quis alius tali animae locus? ibi uiuit unde me multa interrogabat homuncionem[21] inexpertum.[22] iam non ponit aurem ad os meum sed spiritale os ad

[1]ango ~gere, ~xi, ~ctum **to be distressed** [2]conlaetor ~ari, ~atum ECCL **to share in joy** [3]fouea ~ae *f.* **pitfall** [4]perniciosus ~a, ~um *adj.* **deadly** [5]incido ~ere, ~i **to fall into** [6]phantasma ~atis *neut.* **apparition** [7]emergo ~gere, ~si, ~sum **to emerge** [8]'sic sibi erat' **he found himself** [9]imbuo ~uere, ~ui, ~utum **to receive initial instruction** [10]inquisitor ~oris *m.* **searcher** [11]ardens ~ntis *adj.* **enthusiastic** [12]conuersio ~onis *f.* turning; ECCL **conversion** [13]regeneratio ~onis *f.* ECCL **regeneration** [14]baptismus ~i *m.* (~um ~i *neut.*) ECCL **baptism** [15]castitas ~atis *f.* **chastity** [16]continentia ~ae *f.* **continence** [17]soluo ~uere, ~ui, ~utum **to release** [18]significo ~are, ~aui, ~atum **to signify** [19]adoptiuus ~a, ~um *adj.* **adopted** [20]libertus ~i *m.* **freedman** [21]homuncio ~onis *m.* **puny human** [22]inexpertus ~a, ~um *adj.* **inexperienced**

fontem tuum, et bibit[23] quantum potest sapientiam pro auiditate[24] sua sine fine felix. nec eum sic arbitror inebriari[25] ex ea ut obliuiscatur mei, cum tu, Domine, quem potat[26] ille, nostri sis memor.[27]

Sic ergo eramus, Verecundum consolantes[28] tristem salua[29] amicitia[30] de tali conuersione nostra et exhortantes[31] ad fidem gradus[32] sui, uitae scilicet[33] coniugalis,[34] Nebridium autem opperientes,[35] quando sequeretur, quod de tam proximo[36] poterat. et erat iam iamque[37] facturus, cum ecce euoluti[38] sunt dies illi tandem. nam longi et multi uidebantur prae amore libertatis otiosae[39] ad cantandum de medullis[40] omnibus: *tibi dixit cor meum, Quaesiui uultum tuum; uultum tuum, Domine, requiram*[41] (Ps 26:8).

[23]bibo ~ere, ~i **to drink** [24]auiditas ~atis *f.* **with keen thirst** (abl. as *adv.*) [25]inebrio ~are, ~aui, ~atum **to intoxicate** [26]poto ~are, ~aui, ~atum **to drink** [27]memor ~oris *adj.* **mindful** (w. gen.) [28]consolor ~ari, ~atus **to comfort** [29]saluus ~a, ~um *adj.* **secure** [30]amicitia ~ae *f.* **friendship** [31]exhortor ~ari, ~atum **to encourage** [32]gradus ~us *m.* **position** [33]scilicet *adv.* **that is to say** (as epexegetic *particle*) [34]coniugalis ~is, ~e *adj.* **married** [35]opperior ~iri, ~tus **to wait for** [36]proximus ~a, ~um *superl. adj.* **close at hand** [37]'iam iamque' **now all but** [38]euoluo ~uere, ~ui, ~utum **to roll away** [39]otiosus ~a, ~um *adj.* **at leisure** [40]medulla ~ae *f.* marrow > **depths of the heart** (transf.) [41]requiro ~rere, ~siui, ~situm **to seek**

Cassiciacum retreat: dialogues

9.4.7 Et uenit dies quo etiam actu[1] soluerer[2] a professione[3] rhetorica,[4] unde iam cogitatu[5] solutus eram, et factum est. eruisti[6] linguam meam unde iam erueras cor meum, et benedicebam[7] tibi gaudens, profectus[8] in uillam[9] cum meis omnibus. ibi quid egerim in litteris iam quidem seruientibus tibi, sed adhuc superbiae[10] scholam[11] tamquam in pausatione[12] anhelantibus,[13] testantur[14] libri disputati[15] cum praesentibus et cum ipso me solo coram te; quae autem cum absente *Nebridio*, testantur *epistulae*[16] (ep. 3, 4).

[1]actus ~us *m.* **duty** [2]soluo ~uere, ~ui, ~utum **to release** [3]professio ~onis *f.* **profession** [4]rhetoricus ~a, ~um *adj.* **rhetorical** [5]cogitatus ~us *m.* **thinking** [6]eruo ~uere, ~ui, ~utum to remove forcefully; ECCL **to rescue** [7]benedico ~cere, ~xi, ~ctum to commend; ECCL **to bless** [8]proficiscor ~icisci, ~ectus **to set out for** [9]uilla ~ae *f.* **villa** [10]superbia ~ae *f.* **pride** [11]schola ~ae *f.* **school** [12]pausatio ~onis *f.* LATE **pause** (for breath) [13]anhelo ~are, ~aui, ~atum **to pant** [14]testor ~ari, ~atus **to testify** [15]disputo ~are, ~aui, ~atum **to dialogue** [16]epistula ~ae *f.* **personal letter**

Et quando mihi sufficiat[17] tempus commemorandi omnia magna erga[18] nos beneficia tua in illo tempore, praesertim[19] ad alia maiora properanti?[20] reuocat[21] enim me recordatio[22] mea, et dulce mihi fit, Domine, confiteri tibi quibus internis[23] me stimulis[24] perdomueris,[25] et quemadmodum me complanaueris,[26] *humiliatis*[27] *montibus et collibus*[28] (Isa 40:4, Lk 3:5) cogitationum mearum et tortuosa[29] mea direxeris[30] et aspera[31] lenieris,[32] quoque modo ipsum etiam Alypium, fratrem cordis mei, subegeris[33] nomini Unigeniti[34] tui, Domini et Saluatoris[35] nostri Iesu Christi, quod primo[36] dedignabatur[37] inseri[38] litteris nostris. magis enim eas uolebat redolere[39] gymnasiorum[40] *cedros,*[41] *quas iam contriuit*[42] *Dominus* (Ps 28:5), quam salubres[43] herbas[44] Ecclesiasticas[45] aduersas[46] serpentibus.[47]

---

[17]sufficio ~icere, ~eci, ~ectum **to suffice** (w. dat.) [18]erga *prep. acc.* **towards** [19]praesertim *adv.* **especially** [20]propero ~are, ~aui, ~atum **to hurry** [21]reuoco ~are, ~aui, ~atum **to call back** [22]recordatio ~onis *f.* **recollection** [23]internus ~a, ~um *adj.* **internal** [24]stimulus ~i *m.* **goad** [25]perdomo ~are, ~ui, ~itum **to tame** [26]complano ~are, ~aui, ~atum **to pull down** [27]humilio ~are, ~aui, ~atum LATE **to humble** [28]collis ~is *m.* **hill** [29]tortuosus ~a, ~um *adj.* **tortuous** [30]dirigo ~igere, ~exi, ~ectum **to direct** [31]asper ~era, ~erum *adj.* **harsh** [32]lenio ~ire, ~iui or ~ii, ~itum **to soften** [33]subigo ~igere, ~egi, ~actum **to subdue** [34]unigenitus ~a, ~um *adj.* ECCL **only-begotten** [35]saluator ~oris *m.* ECCL **Savior** [36]primo *adv.* **at first** [37]dedignor ~ari, ~atus **to refuse scornfully** [38]insero ~ere, ~ui, ~tum **to insert** [39]redoleo ~ere **to smell of** [40]gymnasium ~ii *neut.* **school for Greek philosophy** [41]cedrus ~i *f.* **cedar** *or* **juniper** [42]contero ~terere, ~triui, ~tritum **to crush** [43]saluber ~bris, ~bre *adj.* **health giving** [44]herba ~ae *f.* **medicinal herb** [45]ecclesiasticus ~a, ~um *adj.* ECCL **of the Church** [46]aduersus ~a, ~um *adj.* **inimical** [47]serpens ~ntis *f. m.* **serpent**

Cassiciacum retreat: Psalm 4:2

9.4.8 Quas tibi, Deus meus, uoces dedi, cum legerem psalmos[1] Dauid, cantica[2] fidelia, sonos pietatis excludentes[3] turgidum[4] spiritum, rudis[5] in germano[6] amore tuo, catechumenus[7] in uilla[8] cum catechumeno Alypio feriatus,[9] matre adhaerente[10] nobis muliebri[11] habitu,[12] uirili[13] fide, anili[14] securitate,[15] materna[16] caritate, Christiana pietate! quas tibi uoces dabam in psalmis illis, et quomodo in te inflammabar[17] ex eis et

---

[1]psalmus ~i, *m.* ECCL **psalm** [2]canticum ~i *neut.* **hymn** [3]excludo ~dere, ~si, ~sum **to keep out** [4]turgidus ~a, ~um *adj.* **swollen** [5]rudis ~is, ~e *adj.* **untaught** [6]germanus ~a, ~um *adj.* **genuine** [7]catechumenus ~i *m.* ECCL **catechumen** [8]uilla ~ae *f.* **villa** [9]feriatus ~a, ~um *adj.* **on holiday** [10]adhaereo ~rere, ~si, ~sum **to join** [11]muliebris ~is, ~e *adj.* **womanly** [12]habitus ~us *m.* **demeanor** [13]uirilis ~is, ~e *adj.* **proper to a man** [14]anilis ~is, ~e *adj.* **proper to an old woman** [15]securitas ~atis *f.* **calmness of manner** [16]maternus ~a, ~um *adj.* **motherly** [17]inflammo ~are, ~aui, ~atum **to inflame** (fig. the mind)

accendebar[18] eos recitare,[19] si possem, toto orbi terrarum[20] aduersus typhum[21] generis humani! et tamen toto orbe cantantur, et *non est qui se abscondat[22] a calore[23] tuo* (Ps 18:7). quam uehementi[24] et acri[25] dolore indignabar[26] Manichaeis et miserabar eos rursus, quod illa sacramenta, illa medicamenta[27] nescirent et insani[28] essent aduersus antidotum[29] quo sani[30] esse potuissent! uellem ut alicubi[31] iuxta[32] essent tunc et, me nesciente quod ibi essent, intuerentur faciem meam et audirent uoces meas quando legi quartum[33] psalmum in illo tunc otio.[34] quid de me fecerit ille psalmus (*Cum inuocarem, exaudiuit me Deus iustitiae meae; in tribulatione[35] dilatasti[36] mihi. miserere mei, Domine, et exaudi orationem[37] meam* [Ps 4:2]) audirent ignorante me utrum audirent, ne me propter se illa dicere putarent quae inter haec uerba dixerim, quia et re uera nec ea dicerem nec sic ea dicerem, si me ab eis audiri uiderique sentirem, nec, si dicerem, sic acciperent quomodo mecum et mihi coram te de familiari[38] affectu animi mei.

---

[18]accendo ~dere, ~di, ~sum **to fan the flame (of feelings)** [19]recito ~are, ~aui, ~atum **to recite** [20]'orbi terrarum' **(to) the world** [21]typhus ~i *m.* ECCL **proud vanity** [22]abscondo ~ere, ~i, ~itum **to hide** [23]calor ~oris *m.* **heat** [24]uehemens ~ntis *adj.* **severe** [25]acer acris, acre *adj.* **bitter** [26]indignor ~ari, ~atus **to be indignant** (w. dat.) [27]medicamentum ~i *neut.* **medicine** [28]insanus ~a, ~um *adj.* **insane** [29]antidotum ~i *neut.* **antidote** [30]sanus ~a, ~um *adj.* **sane** [31]alicubi *adv.* **somewhere** [32]iuxta *adv.* **nearby** [33]quartus ~a, ~um *adj.* **fourth** [34]otium ~ii *neut.* **leisure** [35]tribulatio ~onis *f.* ECCL **tribulation** [36]dilato ~are, ~aui, ~atum **to enlarge** [37]oratio ~onis *f.* speech; ECCL **prayer** [38]familiaris ~is, ~e *adj.* **intimate**

Cassiciacum retreat: Psalm 4:3–4

9.4.9 Inhorrui[1] timendo ibidemque[2] inferbui[3] sperando[4] et *exultando[5] in tua misericordia* (Ps 30:8), Pater. et haec omnia exibant[6] per oculos et uocem meam, cum conuersus ad nos *Spiritus tuus bonus* (Ps 142:10) ait nobis, *Filii hominum, quousque[7] graues corde? ut quid diligitis uanitatem et quaeritis mendacium?* (Ps 4:3). dilexeram enim uanitatem et quaesieram mendacium, et tu, Domine, iam *magnificaueras[8] sanctum tuum* (Ps 4:4), *suscitans[9] eum a mortuis et conlocans[10] ad dexteram tuam* (Eph 1:20),

---

[1]inhorresco ~escere, ~ui **to begin to shudder** [2]ibidem *adv.* **in the same moment** [3]inferueo ~uere, ~bui **to come to a boil**; ECCL **to be kindled** [4]spero ~are, ~aui, ~atum **to hope in** [5]exulto ~are, ~aui **to exult** [6]exeo ~ire, ~iui or ~ii, ~itum **to flow out** [7]quousque *adv.* **how long?** [8]magnifico ~are, ~aui, ~atum **to magnify** [9]suscito ~are, ~aui, ~atum **to raise** [10]conloco ~are, ~aui, ~atum **to place**

unde mitteret ex alto[11] promissionem[12] suam, *Paracletum, Spiritum ueri-tatis* (Jn 14:16–17). et miserat eum iam, sed ego nesciebam. miserat eum, quia *iam* magnificatus *erat resurgens*[13] *a mortuis* (Rom 6:9) et ascendens[14] in caelum. ante[15] autem *Spiritus nondum erat datus, quia Iesus nondum erat clarificatus*[16] (Jn 7:39). et clamat prophetia,[17] *Quousque graues corde? ut quid diligitis uanitatem et quaeritis mendacium? et scitote quoniam Dominus magnificauit Sanctum suum* (Ps 4:3–4). clamat *Quousque,* clamat *Scitote,* et ego tamdiu nesciens uanitatem dilexi et mendacium quaesiui, et ideo *audiui et contremui*[18] (Hab 3:16), quoniam talibus dicitur qualem me fuisse reminiscebar.[19] in phantasmatis[20] enim quae pro ueritate tenueram uanitas erat et mendacium. et insonui[21] multa grauiter[22] ac fortiter[23] in dolore recordationis[24] meae. quae utinam[25] audissent qui adhuc usque diligunt uanitatem et quaerunt mendacium: forte conturbarentur[26] et euomuissent[27] illud, et exaudires eos cum clamarent ad te, quoniam uera morte carnis *mortuus est pro nobis qui te interpellat*[28] *pro nobis* (Rom 8:34).

[11]altum ~i *neut.* **on high** [12]promissio ~onis *f.* **promise** [13]resurgo ~rgere, ~rrexi, ~rrectum **to rise (again)** [14]ascendo ~dere, ~di, ~sum **to ascend** [15]ante *adv.* **before** [16]clarifico ~are, ~aui, ~atum ECCL **to glorify** [17]prophetia ~ae, *f.* ECCL **prophecy** [18]contremesco ~escere, ~ui **to tremble with fear** [19]reminiscor ~i **to recollect** [20]phantasma ~atis *neut.* phantom; LATE **figment of the imagination** [21]insono ~are, ~ui **to cry out loud** [22]grauiter *adv.* **with depth of feeling** [23]fortiter *adv.* **loudly** [24]recordatio ~onis *f.* **recollection** [25]utinam *particle* **if only** [26]conturbo ~are, ~aui, ~atum **to dismay** [27]euomo ~ere, ~ui, ~itum **to vomit or spew out** [28]interpello ~are, ~aui, ~atum **to interpose;** ECCL **to intercede**

Cassiciacum retreat: Psalm 4:5–7

9.4.10 Legebam, *Irascimini*[1] *et nolite peccare* (Ps 4:5), et quomodo mouebar, Deus meus, qui iam didiceram irasci mihi de praeteritis, ut de cetero non peccarem, et merito[2] irasci, quia non alia natura gentis tenebrarum de me peccabat, sicut dicunt qui sibi non irascuntur et *thesaurizant*[3] *sibi iram in die irae et reuelationis*[4] *iusti iudicii tui* (Rom 2:5)!

[1]irascor ~i, iratus sum **to be angry** [2]merito *adv.* **with good cause** [3]thesaurizo ~are, ~aui, ~atum ECCL **to store up** [4]reuelatio ~onis *f.* ECCL **revelation**

Nec iam bona mea foris[5] erant nec oculis carneis[6] in isto sole quaerebantur. uolentes enim gaudere forinsecus[7] facile uanescunt[8] et effunduntur[9] in *ea quae uidentur et temporalia*[10] *sunt* (2 Cor 4:18), et imagines eorum famelica[11] cogitatione lambiunt.[12] et o si fatigentur[13] inedia[14] et dicant, *Quis ostendet nobis bona?* (Ps 4:6). et dicamus, et audiant, *Signatum*[15] *est in nobis lumen uultus tui, Domine* (Ps 4:7). non enim *lumen* nos sumus *quod inluminat omnem hominem* (Jn 1:9), sed inluminamur a te ut, *qui fuimus aliquando tenebrae, simus lux in te* (Eph 5:8). o si uiderent internum[16] aeternum, quod ego quia gustaueram,[17] frendebam,[18] quoniam non eis poteram ostendere, si afferent[19] ad me cor in oculis suis foris a te et dicerent, *Quis ostendet nobis bona?* ibi enim ubi mihi iratus eram, *intus in cubili*[20] *ubi com-punctus*[21] *eram* (Ps 4:5), ubi sacrificaueram[22] mactans[23] uetustatem[24] meam et inchoata[25] meditatione[26] renouationis[27] meae sperans[28] in te, ibi mihi dulcescere[29] coeperas et *dederas laetitiam in corde meo* (Ps 4:7).

Et exclamabam[30] legens haec foris et agnoscens intus, nec uolebam multiplicari[31] terrenis[32] bonis, deuorans[33] tempora et deuoratus tem-poribus, cum haberem in aeterna simplicitate[34] aliud *frumentum*[35] *et uinum*[36] *et oleum*[37] (Ps 4:8).

---

[5]foris *adv.* **outside** [6]carneus ~a, ~um *adj.* ECCL **carnal** [7]forinsecus *adv.* **on the outside** [8]uanesco ~ere **to vanish** [9]effundo ~undere, ~udi, ~usum **to pour out** [10]temporalis ~is, ~e *adj.* **temporal** [11]famelicus ~a, ~um *adj.* **famished** [12]lambio ~ere, ~i LATE **to lick** [13]fatigo ~are, ~aui, ~atum **to weary** [14]inedia ~ae *f.* **starvation** [15]signo ~are, ~aui, ~atum **to mark with a sign** [16]internus ~a, ~um *adj.* **within** [17]gusto ~are, ~aui, ~atum **to taste** [18]frendo ~ere, fresum **to gnash one's teeth** [19]affero ~rre, attuli, allatum **to bring** [20]cubile ~is *neut.* **chamber** [21]compunnctus ~a, ~um *ppl. adj.* LATE **stung by one's conscience** [22]sacrifico ~are, ~aui, ~atum **to offer sacrifice** [23]macto ~are, ~aui, ~atum **to slay sacrificially** [24]uetustas ~atis *f.* **past** [25]inchoo ~are, ~aui, ~atum **to enter upon** [26]meditatio ~onis *f.* **meditation** [27]renouatio ~onis *f.* **renewal** [28]spero ~are, ~aui, ~atum **to hope in** [29]dulcesco ~ere **to become sweet** [30]exclamo ~are, ~aui, ~atum **to cry out** [31]multiplico ~are, ~aui, ~atum to multiply; ECCL **to enrich** [32]terrenus ~a, ~um *adj.* **earthly** [33]deuoro ~are, ~aui, ~atum **to devour** [34]simplicitas ~atis *f.* **simplicity** [35]frumentum ~i *neut.* **wheat** [36]uinum ~i *neut.* **wine** [37]oleum ~i *neut.* **oil**

Cassiciacum retreat: Psalm 4:9-10

9.4.11 Et clamabam in consequenti[1] uersu[2] clamore[3] alto[4] cordis mei, "O *in pace*! o *in Idipsum*!"[5] o quid dixit? *Obdormiam*[6] *et somnum capiam* (Ps 4:9)! quoniam quis resistet nobis, cum fiet sermo qui scriptus est, *Absorpta*[7] *est mors in uictoriam*[8] (1 Cor 15:54)? et tu es Idipsum ualde, qui non mutaris, et in te requies[9] obliuiscens laborum omnium, quoniam nullus alius tecum nec ad alia multa adipiscenda[10] quae non sunt quod tu, sed tu, *Domine, singulariter*[11] *in spe constituisti*[12] *me* (Ps 4:10).

Legebam et ardebam,[13] nec inueniebam quid facerem surdis[14] mortuis ex quibus fueram, pestis,[15] latrator[16] amarus[17] et caecus[18] aduersus litteras de melle[19] caeli melleas[20] et de lumine tuo luminosas,[21] *et super inimicis scripturae huius tabescebam*[22] (Ps 138:21).

[1]consequens ~ntis *adj.* **next** [2]uersus ~us *m.* **verse** [3]clamor ~oris *m.* **cry** [4]altum ~i *neut.* **the deep > depths of the soul** (fig.) [5]idipsum *pron.* ECCL **self-same**; AUG **Being Itself** [6]obdormio ~ire, ~iui or ~ii, ~itum **to fall asleep** [7]absorbeo ~bere, ~bui, ~ptum **to swallow** [8]uictoria ~ae *f.* **victory** [9]requies ~etis *f.* **rest** [10]adipiscor ~ipisci, ~eptus **to acquire** [11]singulariter *adv.* **singly**; ECCL **with single purpose** [12]constituo ~uere, ~ui, ~utum **to establish** [13]ardeo ~dere, ~si **to burn > to burn with zeal** [14]surdus ~a, ~um *adj.* **deaf** [15]pestis ~is *f.* **instrument of death** [16]latrator ~oris *m.* **barker, i.e., shouting salesman** [17]amarus ~a, ~um *adj.* **harsh** [18]caecus ~a, ~um *adj.* **blind** [19]mel mellis *neut.* **honey** [20]melleus ~a, ~um *adj.* **honey-sweet** [21]luminosus ~a, ~um *adj.* **luminous** [22]tabesco ~escere, ~ui **to pine away**

Cassiciacum retreat: miracle cure

9.4.12 Quando recordabor omnia dierum illorum feriatorum?[1] sed nec oblitus sum nec silebo[2] flagelli[3] tui asperitatem[4] et misericordiae tuae mirabilem[5] celeritatem.[6] dolore dentium[7] tunc excruciabas[8] me, et cum in tantum ingrauesceret[9] ut non ualerem loqui, *ascendit*[10] *in cor* (1 Cor 2:9) meum admonere[11] omnes meos qui aderant ut deprecarentur[12] te pro me, Deum salutis omnimodae.[13] et scripsi hoc in cera[14] et dedi ut eis legeretur. mox ut[15] genua[16] supplici[17] affectu fiximus,[18] fugit dolor

[1]feriatus ~a, ~um *adj.* **on holiday** [2]sileo ~ere, ~ui **to be silent** [3]flagellum ~i *neut.* **scourge** [4]asperitas ~atis *f.* **severity** [5]mirabilis ~is, ~e *adj.* **marvelous** [6]celeritas ~atis *f.* **quickness** [7]dens ~ntis *m.* **tooth** [8]excrucio ~are, ~aui, ~atum **to torment** [9]ingrauesco ~ere **to become oppressive** [10]ascendo ~dere, ~di, ~sum **to rise** [11]admoneo ~ere, ~ui, ~itum **to urge** [12]deprecor ~ari, ~atus **to pray** [13]omnimodus ~a, ~um *adj.* **of every sort** [14]cera ~ae *f.* **writing tablet coated with wax** [15]'mox ut' **as soon as** [16]genu ~us *neut.* **knee** [17]supplex ~icis *adj.* **suppliant** [18]figo ~gere, ~xi, ~xum to fix > **to set down**

ille. sed quis dolor? aut quomodo fugit? expaui,[19] fateor,[20] *Domine meus Deus meus* (Jn 20:28). nihil enim tale ab ineunte aetate[21] expertus fueram, et insinuati[22] sunt mihi in profundo[23] nutus[24] tui. et gaudens in fide *laudaui nomen tuum* (Ps 144:2), et ea fides me securum[25] esse non sinebat de praeteritis peccatis meis, quae mihi per baptismum[26] tuum remissa[27] nondum erant.

[19]expauesco ~auescere, ~aui to become frightened [20]fateor ~eri, fassus to confess [21]'ab ineunte aetate' from the beginning of my life [22]insinuo ~are, ~aui, ~atum to instill [23]profundus ~a, ~um *adj.* profound [24]nutus ~us *m.* nod (as symbol of absolute power) [25]securus ~a, ~um *adj.* untroubled [26]baptismus ~i *m.* (~um ~i *neut.*) ECCL baptism [27]remitto ~ittere, ~isi, ~issum to remit

A letter from Ambrose

9.5.13 Renuntiaui[1] peractis[2] uindemialibus[3] ut scholasticis[4] suis Mediolanenses uenditorem[5] uerborum alium prouiderent,[6] quod et tibi ego seruire delegissem[7] et illi professioni[8] prae difficultate[9] spirandi[10] ac dolore pectoris non sufficerem.[11] et insinuaui[12] per litteras antistiti[13] tuo, uiro sancto Ambrosio, pristinos[14] errores meos et praesens uotum meum, ut moneret[15] quid mihi potissimum[16] de libris tuis legendum esset, quo percipiendae[17] tantae gratiae paratior[18] aptiorque[19] fierem. at ille iussit Esaiam prophetam,[20] credo, quod prae ceteris euangelii[21] uocationisque[22] gentium[23] sit praenuntiator[24] apertior. uerum tamen ego primam huius lectionem[25] non intellegens totumque talem arbitrans[26] distuli[27] repetendum[28] exercitatior[29] in Dominico[30] eloquio.[31]

[1]renuntio ~are, ~aui, ~atum to formally announce [2]perago ~agere, ~egi, ~actum to complete [3]uindemialis ~is, ~e *adj.* of the vintage festival (23 Aug–15 Oct) [4]scholasticus ~a, ~um *adj.* student in school of rhetoric (*m.* as noun) [5]uenditor ~oris *m.* vendor [6]prouideo ~idere, ~idi, ~isum to make provision [7]deligo ~igere, ~egi, ~ectum to choose [8]professio ~onis *f.* profession [9]difficultas ~atis *f.* difficulty [10]spiro ~are, ~aui, ~atum to breathe [11]sufficio ~icere, ~eci, ~ectum to have capacity [12]insinuo ~are, ~aui, ~atum to make an introduction [13]antistes ~titis *m.* high priest; ECCL priest/bishop [14]pristinus ~a, ~um *adj.* previous [15]moneo ~ere, ~ui, ~itum to recommend [16]potissimum *adv.* especially [17]percipio ~ipere, ~epi, ~eptum to reap [18]paratus ~a, ~um *adj.* prepared [19]aptus ~a, ~um *ppl. adj.* suited [20]propheta ~ae *m.* ECCL prophet [21]euangelium ~i *neut.* ECCL the Gospel(s) [22]uocatio ~onis *f.* invitation; ECCL calling [23]gens ~tis *f.* nation; ECCL Gentile [24]praenuntiator ~oris *m.* AUG one who announces beforehand [25]lectio ~onis *f.* reading [26]arbitro ~are, ~aui, ~atum to decide [27]differo ~rre, distuli, dilatum to postpone [28]repeto ~ere, ~iui or ~ii, ~itum to return to [29]exercitatus ~a, ~um *adj.* proficient [30]dominicus ~a, ~um *adj.* ECCL of the LORD [31]eloquium ~ii *neut.* mode of speaking

Baptism... and requiem for Adeodatus

9.6.14 Inde ubi tempus aduenit[1] quo me nomen dare oporteret,[2] relicto rure[3] Mediolanium remeauimus.[4] placuit et Alypio renasci[5] in te mecum iam *induto*[6] *humilitate*[7] (Col 3:12) sacramentis tuis congrua[8] et fortissimo domitori[9] corporis, usque ad Italicum solum[10] glaciale[11] nudo pede[12] obterendum[13] insolito[14] ausu.[15] adiunximus[16] etiam nobis puerum Adeodatum ex me natum carnaliter[17] de peccato meo. tu bene feceras eum. annorum erat ferme[18] quindecim[19] et ingenio praeueniebat[20] multos graues et doctos uiros. munera tua tibi confiteor, Domine Deus meus, *creator omnium* (Hymn 2.1) et multum potens formare nostra deformia,[21] nam ego in illo puero praeter delictum[22] non habebam. quod enim et nutriebatur[23] a nobis in disciplina[24] tua, tu inspiraueras[25] nobis, nullus alius. munera tua tibi confiteor. est liber noster qui inscribitur[26] *de Magistro*: ipse ibi mecum loquitur. tu scis illius esse sensa omnia quae inseruntur[27] ibi ex persona[28] conlocutoris[29] mei, cum esset in annis sedecim.[30] multa eius alias mirabiliora[31] expertus sum: horrori[32] mihi erat illud ingenium. et quis praeter te talium miraculorum[33] opifex?[34] cito[35] de terra abstulisti uitam eius, et securior[36] eum recordor non timens quicquam pueritiae[37] nec adulescentiae[38] nec omnino homini illi. sociauimus[39] eum coaeuum[40] nobis in gratia tua, educandum[41] in disciplina tua.

[1]aduenio ~uenire, ~ueni, ~uentum **to arrive** [2]oportet ~ere, ~uit *impers.* **it is requisite** [3]rus ruris *neut.* **countryside** [4]remeo ~are, ~aui, ~atum **to return (home)** [5]renascor ~asci, ~atus **to be reborn** [6]induo ~uere, ~ui, ~utum **to put on, clothe** [7]humilitas ~atis *f.* **humility** [8]congruus ~a, ~um *adj.* **in accord** [9]domitor ~oris *m.* **tamer** [10]solum ~i *neut.* **ground** [11]glacialis ~is, ~e *adj.* **frozen** [12]'nudo pede' **barefoot** [13]obtero ~terere, ~triui, ~tritum **to trample; LATE to tread** [14]insolitus ~a, ~um *adj.* **unusual** [15]ausus ~us *m.* **daring** [16]adiungo ~gere, ~xi, ~ctum **to include with** (a group) [17]carnaliter *adv.* ECCL **carnally** [18]fere, ferme *adv.* **almost** [19]quindecim *indecl. adj.* **fifteen** [20]praeuenio ~enire, ~eni, ~entum **to surpass** [21]deformis ~is, ~e *adj.* **deformed** [22]delictum ~i *neut.* **offense; ECCL sin** [23]nutrio ~ire, ~iui or ~ii, ~itum **to nurture** [24]disciplina ~ae *f.* **instruction** [25]inspiro ~are, ~aui, ~atum **to inspire** (LATE w. dat.) [26]inscribo ~bere, ~psi, ~ptum **to entitle** (a book) [27]insero ~ere, ~ui, ~tum **to introduce** [28]persona ~ae *f.* **character** [29]conlocutor ~oris *m.* LATE **conversation partner** [30]sedecim *indecl. adj.* **sixteen** [31]mirabilis ~is, ~e *adj.* **marvelous** [32]horror ~oris *m.* **awe** [33]miraculum ~i *neut.* **prodigy** [34]opifex ~icis *m.* **artificer** [35]cito *adv.* **soon** [36]securus ~a, ~um *adj.* **untroubled** [37]pueritia ~ae *f.* **boyhood** (age 2–11) [38]adulescentia ~ae *f.* **young adulthood** (age 16–30) [39]socio ~are, ~aui, ~atum **to bring in as a partner** [40]coaeuus ~a, ~um *adj.* ECCL **of the same age** [41]educo ~are, ~aui, ~atum **to raise**

Et baptizati[42] sumus et fugit a nobis sollicitudo[43] uitae praeteritae. nec satiabar[44] illis diebus dulcedine[45] mirabili considerare altitudinem[46] consilii tui super salutem generis humani. quantum fleui in *hymnis*[47] *et canticis*[48] (Eph 5:19) tuis, suaue[49] sonantis Ecclesiae tuae uocibus commotus[50] acriter![51] uoces illae influebant[52] auribus meis, et eliquabatur[53] ueritas in cor meum, et exaestuabat[54] inde affectus pietatis, et currebant[55] lacrimae, et bene mihi erat cum eis.

[42]baptizo ~are, ~aui, ~atum ECCL **to baptize** [43]sollicitudo ~inis *f.* **anxiety** [44]satio ~are, ~aui, ~atum **to satisfy** (appetites) [45]dulcedo ~inis *f.* **sweetness** [46]altitudo ~inis *f.* highness > profundity > **inscrutability** [47]hymnus ~i, *m.*, ECCL **hymn** [48]canticum ~i *neut.* **chant** [49]suauis ~is, ~e *adj.* **sweet** [50]commoueo ~ouere, ~oui, ~otum **to move (emotionally)** [51]acriter *adv.* **keenly** [52]influo ~uere, ~uxi, ~uxum **to flow in** [53]eliquo ~are, ~aui, ~atum **to flow clearly** [54]exaestuo ~are, ~aui, ~atum **to surge** [55]curro ~rere, cucurri, ~sum to run > **to flow continuously**

Monica: the vigil against Empress Justina

9.7.15 Non longe coeperat Mediolanensis ecclesia genus hoc consolationis[1] et exhortationis[2] celebrare[3] magno studio fratrum[4] concinentium[5] uocibus et cordibus. nimirum[6] annus erat aut non multo amplius, cum Iustina, Valentiniani regis pueri[7] mater, hominem tuum Ambrosium persequeretur[8] haeresis[9] suae causa, qua fuerat seducta[10] ab Arrianis. excubabat[11] pia plebs[12] in ecclesia, mori parata[13] cum episcopo[14] suo, seruo tuo. ibi mea mater, ancilla[15] tua, sollicitudinis[16] et uigiliarum[17] primas tenens, orationibus[18] uiuebat. nos adhuc frigidi[19] a calore[20] Spiritus tui excitabamur[21] tamen ciuitate attonita[22] atque turbata.[23]

[1]consolatio ~onis *f.* **consolation** [2]exhortatio ~onis *f.* **exhortation** [3]celebro ~are, ~aui, ~atum **to celebrate** (the liturgy) [4]frater ~tris *m.* brother; ECCL **brethren** (*pl.*) [5]concino ~ere, ~ui **to sing** (antiphonally) [6]nimirum *particle* **evidently** [7]'regis pueri' (**of**) **the boy-emperor** [8]persequor ~qui, ~cutus to pursue; ECCL **to persecute** [9]haeresis ~is *f.* philosophical school or sect; ECCL **heresy** [10]seduco ~cere, ~xi, ~ctum to draw aside; ECCL **to seduce** [11]excubo ~are, ~ui, ~itum **to keep watch** [12]plebs ~ebis *f.* body (of people); ECCL **congregation** [13]paratus ~a, ~um *adj.* **prepared** [14]episcopus ~i *m.* ECCL **bishop** [15]ancilla ~ae *f.* **handmaid** [16]sollicitudo ~inis *f.* **anxiety** [17]uigilia ~ae *f.* **night vigil** [18]oratio ~onis *f.* speech; ECCL **prayer** [19]frigidus ~a, ~um *adj.* **frigid** [20]calor ~oris *m.* **heat** [21]excito ~are, ~aui, ~atum **to excite** [22]attonitus ~a, ~um *adj.* **stricken with calamity** [23]turbatus ~a, ~um *adj.* **in a state of turmoil**

Tunc *hymni*[24] *et psalmi*[25] (Col 3:16) ut canerentur[26] secundum morem orientalium partium,[27] ne populus maeroris[28] taedio[29] contabesceret,[30] institutum[31] est, ex illo in hodiernum[32] retentum[33] multis iam ac paene[34] omnibus gregibus[35] tuis et per cetera orbis imitantibus.[36]

[24]hymnus ~i, *m.*, ECCL **hymn** [25]psalmus ~i, *m.* ECCL **psalm** [26]cano ~ere, cecini **to chant** (songs, etc.) [27]'orientalium partium' **of the Eastern part (of the Church)** [28]maeror ~oris *m.* **sorrow** [29]taedium ~ii *neut.* **being weary (with)** [30]contabesco ~escere, ~ui **to be consumed** [31]instituo ~uere, ~ui, ~utum **to institute** [32]hodiernus ~a, ~um *adj.* **today** (*m.* as noun) [33]retineo ~ere, ~ui, retentum **to hold fast** [34]paene *adv.* **practically** [35]grex ~egis *m.* **flock**; ECCL **congregation** [36]imitor ~ari, ~atus **to imitate**

Martyrs: Protasius and Gervasius

9.7.16 Tunc memorato[1] antistiti[2] tuo per uisum aperuisti quo loco laterent[3] martyrum[4] corpora Protasii et Geruasii, quae per tot annos incorrupta[5] in thesauro[6] secreti[7] tui reconderas,[8] unde opportune[9] promeres[10] ad cohercendam[11] rabiem[12] femineam[13] sed regiam.[14] cum enim propalata[15] et effossa[16] digno[17] cum honore transferrentur[18] ad Ambrosianam basilicam,[19] non solum quos immundi[20] uexabant[21] spiritus confessis eisdem daemonibus[22] sanabantur, uerum etiam quidam plures annos caecus[23] ciuis ciuitatique notissimus, cum populi tumultuante[24] laetitia causam quaesisset atque audisset, exiliuit[25] eoque[26] se ut duceret suum ducem rogauit,[27] quo perductus[28] impetrauit[29] admitti[30] ut sudario[31] tangeret[32] feretrum[33] *pretiosae*[34] *in conspectu tuo mortis sanctorum tuorum* (Ps 115:15); quod ubi fecit atque admouit[35] oculis, confestim[36] aperti

[1]memoratus ~a, ~um *adj.* **renowned**; LATE **above-mentioned** [2]antistes ~titis *m.* **high priest**; ECCL **priest/bishop** [3]lateo ~ere, ~ui **to lie hidden** [4]martyr ~is *m. f.* ECCL **martyr** [5]incorruptus ~a, ~um *adj.* **uncorrupted** [6]thesaurus ~i *m.* **treasure chamber** [7]secretus ~a, ~um *adj.* **secret** [8]recondo ~ere, ~idi, ~itum **to store away** [9]opportune *adv.* **opportunely** [10]promo ~mere, ~mpsi, ~mptum **to bring forth** [11]coherceo ~ere, ~ui, ~itum **to check** [12]rabies (~ei) *f.* **ferocity** [13]femineus ~a, ~um *adj.* **of a woman** [14]regius ~a, ~um *adj.* **royal** [15]propalo ~are LATE **to make public** [16]effodio ~odere, ~odi, ~ossum **to dig up** [17]digno *adv.* LATE **worthily** [18]transfero ~ferre, ~tuli, ~latum **to transport** [19]basilica ~ae *f.* **basilica** [20]immundus ~a, ~um *adj.* **unclean** [21]uexo ~are, ~aui, ~atum **to afflict** [22]daemon ~onis *m.* ECCL **demon** [23]caecus ~a, ~um *adj.* **blind** [24]tumultuor ~ari, ~atus **to make a commotion** [25]exilio ~ire, ~ui **to leap up** [26]eo *adv.* **to that place** [27]rogo ~are, ~aui, ~atum **to ask** [28]perduco ~cere, ~xi, ~ctum **to bring** [29]impetro ~are, ~aui, ~atum **to have one's request granted** [30]admitto ~ittere, ~isi, ~issum **to allow** [31]sudarium ~ii *neut.* **handkerchief** [32]tango ~ere, tetigi, tactum **to touch** [33]feretrum ~i *neut.* **bier** [34]pretiosus ~a, ~um *adj.* **precious** [35]admoueo ~mouere, ~moui **to bring into contact** [36]confestim *adv.* **immediately**

sunt. inde fama discurrens,[37] inde laudes tuae feruentes,[38] lucentes,[39] inde illius inimicae animus etsi ad credendi sanitatem[40] non applicatus,[41] a persequendi[42] tamen furore compressus[43] est. gratias tibi, Deus meus!

Unde et quo duxisti recordationem[44] meam, ut haec etiam confiterer tibi, quae magna oblitus praeterieram? et tamen tunc, cum ita fragraret[45] *odor*[46] *unguentorum*[47] *tuorum,* non *currebamus*[48] *post te* (Cant 1:3). ideo plus flebam inter cantica[49] hymnorum[50] tuorum, olim[51] suspirans tibi et tandem respirans,[52] quantum patet[53] aura in domo faenea.[54]

---

[37]discurro ~rrere, ~rri, ~rsum **to run in all directions** [38]ferueo ~ere, ferbui **to be fervent** [39]luceo ~ere, luxi **to be clearly known or felt** [40]sanitas ~atis *f.* **soundness of mind** [41]applico ~are, ~aui, ~atum **to bring near** [42]persequor ~qui, ~cutus to pursue; ECCL **to persecute** [43]comprimo ~imere, ~essi, ~essum **to hold back** [44]recordatio ~onis *f.* **recollection** [45]fragro ~are, ~aui **to be fragrant** [46]odor ~oris *m.* **smell** [47]unguentum ~i *neut.* **ointment** [48]curro ~rere, cucurri, ~sum **to run** [49]canticum ~i *neut.* **chant** [50]hymnus ~i, *m.*, ECCL **hymn** [51]olim *adv.* **once** [52]respiro ~are, ~aui, ~atum **to breathe in** [53]pateo ~ere, ~ui **to spread out** [54]faeneus ~a, ~um *adj.* **made of straw**

Monica: childhood

9.8.17 *Qui habitare*[1] *facis unanimes*[2] *in domo* (Ps 67:7), consociasti[3] nobis et Euodium iuuenem ex nostro municipio.[4] qui cum agens in rebus[5] militaret,[6] prior nobis *ad te conuersus est* (Ps 50:15) et baptizatus[7] et relicta militia[8] saeculari[9] accinctus[10] in tua. simul eramus, simul habitaturi placito sancto. quaerebamus quisnam[11] locus nos utilius[12] haberet seruientes tibi; pariter[13] remeabamus[14] in Africam. et cum apud *Ostia Tiberina* (Aen. 1.13–14) essemus, mater defuncta[15] est.

Multa praetereo, quia multum festino:[16] accipe confessiones meas et gratiarum actiones,[17] Deus meus, de rebus innumerabilibus[18] etiam in silentio.[19] sed non praeteribo quidquid mihi anima parturit[20] de illa famula[21] tua, quae me parturiuit et carne, ut in hanc temporalem,[22] et

---

[1]habito ~are, ~aui, ~atum **to dwell** [2]unanimis ~is, ~e *adj.* **of one mind** [3]consocio ~are, ~aui, ~atum **to join in association** [4]municipium ~ii *neut.* **town** [5]agens in rebus' **special agent** [6]milito ~are, ~aui, ~atum **to serve in the military**; LATE **to serve in government** [7]baptizo ~are, ~aui, ~atum ECCL **to baptize** [8]militia ~ae *f.* **military service**; LATE **government service** [9]saecularis ~is, ~e *adj.* ECCL **secular** [10]accingo ~gere, ~xi, ~ctum **to get ready (for action)** [11]quisnam quae-, quid- *adj.* **what** [12]utiliter *adv.* **usefully** [13]pariter *adv.* **together** [14]remeo ~are, ~aui, ~atum **to return (home)** [15]defungor ~gi, ~ctus **to have died** (pf. tense) [16]festino ~are, ~aui, ~atum **to move quickly** [17]gratiarum actiones' **expressions of thanks** [18]innumerabilis ~is, ~e *adj.* **innumerable** [19]silentium ~ii *neut.* **silence** [20]parturio ~ire, ~iui **to give birth** (fig. from the mind) [21]famula ~ae *f.* **handmaid** [22]temporalis ~is, ~e *adj.* **temporal**

corde, ut in aeternam lucem nascerer. non eius sed tua dicam dona in
eam, neque enim se ipsa fecerat aut educauerat[23] se ipsam. tu creasti
eam (nec pater nec mater sciebat qualis ex eis fieret) et erudiuit[24] eam
in timore[25] *tuo* (Ps 5:8) *uirga*[26] Christi *tui* (Ps 22:4), regimen[27] Unici[28]
tui, in domo fideli, bono membro Ecclesiae tuae. nec tantam erga[29]
suam disciplinam[30] diligentiam[31] matris praedicabat[32] quantam famulae
cuiusdam decrepitae,[33] quae patrem eius infantem[34] portauerat,[35] sicut
dorso[36] grandiuscularum[37] puellarum paruuli portari solent. cuius rei
gratia et propter senectam[38] ac mores optimos in domo Christiana satis
a dominis honorabatur.[39] unde etiam curam dominicarum[40] filiarum
commissam[41] diligenter[42] gerebat et erat in eis cohercendis,[43] cum
opus esset, sancta seueritate[44] uehemens[45] atque in docendis sobria[46]
prudentia.[47] nam eas, praeter illas horas quibus ad mensam[48] parentum
moderatissime[49] alebantur,[50] etiamsi exardescerent[51] siti,[52] nec aquam
bibere[53] sinebat, praecauens[54] consuetudinem malam et addens uerbum
sanum:[55] "Modo aquam bibitis, quia in potestate uinum[56] non habetis;
cum autem ad maritos[57] ueneritis factae dominae[58] apothecarum[59] et
cellariorum,[60] aqua sordebit,[61] sed mos potandi[62] praeualebit."[63] hac
ratione praecipiendi[64] et auctoritate imperandi frenabat[65] auiditatem[66]
tenerioris aetatis et ipsam puellarum sitim formabat ad honestum[67]
modum, ut iam nec liberet[68] quod non deceret.[69]

---

[23]educo ~are, ~aui, ~atum **to bring up** [24]erudio ~ire, ~ii or ~iui, ~itum **to train** [25]timor ~oris *m.*
fear [26]uirga ~ae *f.* **rod** (as instrument of discipline) [27]regimen ~inis *neut.* **guidance** [28]unicus ~a,
~um *adj.* **one and only** [29]erga *prep.* **with regard to** [30]disciplina ~ae *f.* **instruction** [31]diligentia ~ae *f.*
diligence [32]praedico ~are, ~aui, ~atum **to make special mention** [33]decrepitus ~a, ~um *adj.* **worn
out** (with age) [34]infans ~ntis *m. f.* **infant** [35]porto ~are, ~aui, ~atum **to carry** [36]dorsum ~i *neut.* **back**
[37]grandiusculus ~a, ~um *adj. dim.* AUG **mostly grown up** [38]senecta ~ae *f.* **old age** [39]honoro ~are,
~aui, ~atum **to honor** [40]dominicus ~a, ~um *adj.* **the master's** [41]committo ~ittere, ~isi, ~issum
to commit [42]diligenter *adv.* **carefully** [43]coherceo ~ere, ~ui, ~itum **to restrain** [44]seueritas ~atis *f.*
severity [45]uehemens ~ntis *adj.* **strongly expressive** [46]sobrius ~ia, ~ium *adj.* **sensible** [47]prudentia
~ae *f.* **practical wisdom** [48]mensa ~ae *f.* **table** [49]moderate *adv.* **moderately** [50]alo ~ere, ~ui, ~tum
to feed [51]exardesco ~descere, ~si (~sum) **to burn** [52]sitis ~is *f.* **thirst** [53]bibo ~ere, ~i **to drink**
[54]praecaueo ~auere, ~aui, ~autum **to take precaution** [55]sanus ~a, ~um *adj.* **wholesome** [56]uinum
~i *neut.* **wine** [57]maritus ~i *m.* **married life** (*pl.*) [58]domina ~ae *f.* **mistress** (head of a household)
[59]apotheca ~ae *f.* **storeroom** (esp. for wine) [60]cellarium ~ii *neut.* **cellar** [61]sordeo ~ere **to seem not
good enough** [62]poto ~are, ~aui, ~atum or ~um **to drink** (wine) [63]praeualeo ~ere, ~ui **to prevail**
[64]praecipio ~ipere, ~epi, ~eptum **to instruct proactively** [65]freno ~are, ~aui, ~atum **to restrain**
[66]auiditas ~atis *f.* **greed** [67]honestus ~a, ~um *adj.* **respectable** [68]libet ~ere, ~uit *impers.* **it is pleasing**
[69]decet ~ere, ~uit *impers.* **it is proper**

Monica: a providential insult

9.8.18 Et subrepserat[1] tamen, sicut mihi filio famula[2] tua narrabat, subrepserat ei uinulentia.[3] nam cum de more tamquam puella sobria[4] iuberetur a parentibus de cupa[5] uinum[6] depromere,[7] submisso[8] poculo[9] qua[10] desuper[11] patet,[12] priusquam in lagunculam[13] funderet[14] merum,[15] primoribus labris[16] sorbebat[17] exiguum,[18] quia non poterat amplius sensu recusante.[19] non enim ulla temulenta[20] cupidine[21] faciebat hoc, sed quibusdam superfluentibus[22] aetatis excessibus,[23] qui ludicris[24] motibus ebulliunt[25] et in puerilibus[26] animis maiorum pondere[27] premi solent. itaque ad illud modicum[28] cotidiana[29] modica addendo (quoniam *qui modica spernit,*[30] *paulatim*[31] *decidit*[32] [Sir 19:1]) in eam consuetudinem lapsa[33] erat ut prope[34] iam plenos mero caliculos[35] inhianter[36] hauriret.[37]

Ubi tunc sagax[38] anus[39] et uehemens[40] illa prohibitio?[41] numquid ualebat aliquid aduersus latentem[42] morbum,[43] nisi tua medicina,[44] Domine, uigilaret[45] super nos? absente patre et matre et nutritoribus[46] tu praesens, qui creasti, qui uocas, qui etiam per praepositos[47] homines boni aliquid agis ad animarum salutem. quid tunc egisti, Deus meus? unde curasti? unde sanasti? nonne protulisti[48] durum et acutum[49] ex altera anima conuicium[50] tamquam medicinale[51] ferrum ex occultis prouisionibus[52] tuis et uno ictu[53] putredinem[54] illam praecidisti?[55]

---

[1]subrepo ~ere, ~si, ~tum **to creep in** [2]famula ~ae *f.* **handmaid** [3]uinulentia ~ae *f.* **excessive drinking** [4]sobrius ~ia, ~ium *adj.* **sober** [5]cupa ~ae *f.* **cask** [6]uinum ~i *neut.* **wine** [7]depromo ~ere, ~psi, ~ptum **to fetch** [8]submitto ~ittere, ~isi, ~issum **to dip** [9]poculum, -clum ~i *neut.* **cup** [10]qua *adv.* **where** [11]desuper *adv. prep.* **from above** [12]pateo ~ere, ~ui **to be open** [13]laguncula ~ae *f.* **small flask or bottle** [14]fundo ~ere, fudi, fusum **to pour out** [15]merum ~i *neut.* **wine unmixed with water** [16]primoribus labris' **very lightly on the lips** [17]sorbeo ~ere, ~ui, ~itum **to drink in** [18]exiguum ~i *neut.* **small amount** [19]recuso ~are, ~aui, ~atum **to refuse** [20]temulentus ~a, ~um *adj.* **drunken** [21]cupido ~inis *f. m.* **particular desire** [22]superfluo ~uere, ~uxi **to overflow** [23]excessus ~us *m.* departure; LATE **excess** [24]ludicrum ~i *neut.* **fun** [25]ebullio ~ire, ~ii or ~iui **to burst out** [26]puerilis ~is, ~e *adj.* **childish** [27]pondus ~eris *neut.* **weight (authority)** [28]modicum ~i *neut.* **modest amount** [29]cotidianus ~a, ~um *adj.* **daily** [30]sperno ~ere, spreui, spretum **to spurn** [31]paulatim *adv.* **little by little** [32]decido ~ere, ~i **to fall or lapse** [33]labor ~bi, ~psus **to fall into** [34]prope *adv.* practically > **pretty well** (hyperbole) [35]caliculus ~i *m.* **small cup** [36]inhianter *adv.* AUG **eagerly** [37]haurio ~rire, ~si, ~stum **to swallow** [38]sagax ~acis *adj.* **perceptive** [39]anus ~us *f.* **old woman** [40]uehemens ~ntis *adj.* **stern** [41]prohibitio ~onis *f.* **prohibition** [42]latens ~ntis *adj.* **hidden** [43]morbus ~i *m.* **disease** [44]medicina ~ae *f.* **medicine** [45]uigilo ~are, ~aui, ~atum **to be watchful** [46]nutritor ~oris *m.* **nurse** [47]praepositus ~i *m.* **person placed in charge** [48]profero ~ferre, ~tuli, ~latum **to bring forth** [49]acutus ~a, ~um *adj.* **sharp** [50]conuicium ~ii *neut.* **abusive insult** [51]medicinalis ~is, ~e *adj.* **medical** [52]prouisio ~onis *f.* foresight; LATE **provision** [53]ictus ~us *m.* **cut** [54]putredo ~inis *f.* **putrefaction** [55]praecido ~dere, ~di, ~sum **to cut or sever**

ancilla[56] enim, cum qua solebat accedere[57] ad cupam, litigans[58] cum domina[59] minore, ut fit, sola cum sola, obiecit[60] hoc crimen amarissima[61] insultatione[62] uocans "meribibulam."[63] quo illa stimulo[64] percussa[65] respexit[66] foeditatem[67] suam confestimque[68] damnauit[69] atque exuit.[70]

Sicut amici adulantes[71] peruertunt,[72] sic inimici litigantes plerumque[73] corrigunt.[74] nec tu quod per eos agis, sed quod ipsi uoluerunt, retribuis[75] eis. illa enim irata[76] exagitare[77] appetiuit[78] minorem dominam, non sanare, et ideo clanculo,[79] aut quia ita eas inuenerat locus et tempus litis,[80] aut ne forte et ipsa periclitaretur,[81] quod tam sero[82] prodidisset.[83] at tu, Domine, rector[84] caelitum[85] et terrenorum,[86] ad usus tuos contorquens[87] profunda[88] torrentis,[89] fluxum[90] saeculorum ordinate[91] turbulentum,[92] etiam de alterius animae insania[93] sanasti alteram, ne quisquam cum hoc aduertit,[94] potentiae[95] suae tribuat,[96] si uerbo eius alius corrigatur quem uult corrigi.

[56]ancilla ~ae *f.* **handmaid** [57]accedo ~dere, ~ssi, ~ssum **to go** [58]litigo ~are, ~aui, ~atum **to quarrel** [59]domina ~ae *f.* **mistress** (head of a household) [60]obicio ~icere, ~ieci, ~iectum **to lay to one's charge** [61]amarus ~a, ~um *adj.* **bitter** [62]insultatio ~onis *f.* **insult** [63]meribibula ~ae *f.* AUG 'the little lush' [64]stimulus ~i *m.* **sting** [65]percutio ~tere, ~ssi, ~ssum to strike > **to affect grievously** (transf.) [66]respicio ~icere, ~exi, ~ectum **to take heed of** [67]foeditas ~atis *f.* **foulness** [68]confestim *adv.* **at once** [69]damno ~are, ~aui, ~atum **to condemn** [70]exuo ~uere, ~ui, ~utum **throw off** [71]adulans ~ntis *adj.* **flattering** [72]peruerto ~tere, ~ti, ~sum **to pervert** [73]plerumque *adv.* **generally** [74]corrigo ~igere, ~exi, ~ectum **to make straight** [75]retribuo ~uere, ~ui, ~utum **to repay** [76]irascor ~i, iratus sum **to be angry** [77]exagito ~are, ~aui, ~atum **to stir up feelings** [78]appeto ~ere, ~iui or ~ii, ~itum **to seek** [79]clanculo *adv.* **secretly** [80]lis litis *f.* **quarrel** [81]periclitor ~ari, ~atus **to expose to danger** [82]sero *adv.* **too late** [83]prodo ~ere, ~idi, ~itum **to reveal** [84]rector ~oris *m.* **governor** [85]caeles ~itis *adj.* **in heaven** [86]terrenus ~a, ~um *adj.* **on earth** [87]contorqueo ~quere, ~si, ~tum **to turn in another direction** [88]profundum ~i *neut.* **depths** [89]torrens ~ntis *m.* **torrent** [90]fluxus ~us *m.* **flux** [91]ordinate *adv.* **in an orderly manner** [92]turbulentus ~a, ~um *adj.* **haphazard** [93]insania ~ae *f.* **insanity** [94]aduerto ~tere, ~ti, ~sum **to take notice** [95]potentia ~ae *f.* **power** [96]tribuo ~uere, ~ui, ~utum **to credit**

Monica: wife

9.9.19 Educata[1] itaque pudice[2] ac sobrie[3] potiusque a te subdita[4] parentibus quam a parentibus tibi, ubi *plenis annis nubilis[5] facta est* (Aen. 7.53), tradita *uiro seruiuit ueluti domino* (Eph 5:22) et sategit[6] *eum lucrari[7] tibi* (1 Pet 3:1), loquens te illi moribus suis, quibus eam pulchram faciebas

[1]educo ~are, ~aui, ~atum **to raise** [2]pudice *adv.* **decently** [3]sobrie *adv.* **sensibly** [4]subditus ~a, ~um *adj.* **subject** (to authority) [5]nubilis ~is, ~e *adj.* **of an age suitable for marriage** [6]satago ~agere, ~egi, ~actum **to busy oneself** [7]lucror ~ari, ~atus **to win**

et reuerenter[8] amabilem[9] atque mirabilem[10] uiro. ita autem tolerauit[11] cubilis[12] iniurias ut nullam de hac re cum marito[13] haberet umquam simultatem.[14] *expectabat enim misericordiam tuam super eum* (Jude 21; Ps 85:13), ut in te credens castificaretur.[15] erat uero ille praeterea[16] sicut beniuolentia[17] praecipuus,[18] ita ira feruidus.[19] sed nouerat haec non resistere irato[20] uiro, non tantum facto sed ne uerbo quidem. iam uero[21] refractum[22] et quietum[23] cum opportunum[24] uiderat, rationem facti sui reddebat, si forte ille inconsideratius[25] commotus[26] fuerat. denique[27] cum matronae[28] multae, quarum uiri mansuetiores[29] erant, plagarum[30] uestigia[31] etiam dehonestata[32] facie gererent, inter amica[33] conloquia[34] illae arguebant[35] maritorum uitam, haec earum linguam, ueluti per iocum[36] grauiter[37] admonens,[38] ex quo illas tabulas quae matrimoniales[39] uocantur recitari[40] audissent, tamquam instrumenta[41] quibus ancillae[42] factae essent deputare[43] debuisse; proinde[44] memores[45] condicionis[46] superbire[47] aduersus dominos non oportere.[48] cumque[49] mirarentur illae, scientes quam ferocem[50] coniugem sustineret,[51] numquam fuisse auditum aut aliquo indicio[52] claruisse[53] quod Patricius ceciderit[54] uxorem[55] aut quod a se inuicem[56] uel unum diem domestica[57] lite[58] dissenserint,[59] et causam familiariter[60] quaererent, docebat illa

[8]reuerenter *adv.* **considerately** [9]amabilis ~is, ~e *adj.* **worthy to be loved** [10]mirabilis ~is, ~e *adj.* **causing wonder** [11]tolero ~are, ~aui, ~atum **to endure** [12]cubile ~is *neut.* **marriage bed** [13]maritus ~i *m.* **husband** [14]simultas ~atis *f.* **animosity** [15]castifico ~are, ~aui, ~atum ECCL **to make chaste** [16]praeterea *adv.* **moreover** [17]beniuolentia ~ae *f.* **kindness** [18]praecipuus ~a, ~um *adj.* **exceptional** [19]feruidus ~a, ~um *adj.* **hot-blooded** [20]iratus ~a, ~um *adj.* **enraged** (esp. w. dat. of person) [21]'iam uero' **what is more** [22]refringo ~ingere, ~egi, ~actum **to check** [23]quietus ~a, ~um *adj.* **calm > peaceable** [24]opportunus ~a, ~um *adj.* **favorably disposed** [25]inconsiderate *adv.* **thoughtlessly** [26]commoueo ~ouere, ~oui, ~otum **to agitate** [27]denique *adv.* **in point of fact** [28]matrona ~ae *f.* **married woman** [29]mansuetus ~a, ~um *adj.* **mild-mannered** [30]plaga ~ae *f.* **blow** [31]uestigium ~ii *neut.* **visible trace** [32]dehonesto ~are, ~aui, ~atum **to dishonor** [33]amicus ~a, ~um *adj.* **among friends** [34]conloquium ~ii *neut.* **conversation** [35]arguo ~uere, ~ui, ~utum to allege > **to criticize** [36]iocus ~i *m.* **jest** [37]grauiter *adv.* **seriously** [38]admoneo ~ere, ~ui, ~itum **to give advice** [39]tabulas matrimonialis' ECCL **marriage contract** [40]recito ~are, ~aui, ~atum to recite > **to read aloud** [41]instrumentum ~i *neut.* **basis** (legal) [42]ancilla ~ae *f.* **handmaid** [43]deputo ~are, ~aui, ~atum **to regard as** [44]proinde *adv.* **accordingly** [45]memor ~oris *adj.* **mindful** (w. gen.) [46]condicio ~onis *f.* marriage contract > **legal position** [47]superbio ~ire **to be haughty** [48]oportet ~ere, ~uit *impers.* **it is right** [49]cumque *adv.* **whenever** [50]ferox ~ocis *adj.* **violent** [51]sustineo ~ere, ~ui **to face** [52]indicium ~ii *neut.* **sign** [53]claresco ~escere, ~ui **to make obvious** [54]caedo ~dere, cecidi, ~sum **to beat** [55]uxor ~oris *f.* **wife** [56]inuicem *adv.* **mutually** [57]domesticus ~a, ~um *adj.* **domestic** [58]lis litis *f.* **quarrel** [59]dissentio ~tire, ~si, ~sum **to disagree with each other** [60]familiariter *adv.* **as a close friend**

institutum⁶¹ suum, quod supra⁶² memoraui.⁶³ quae obseruabant,⁶⁴ exper-
tae gratulabantur;⁶⁵ quae non obseruabant, subiectae⁶⁶ uexabantur.⁶⁷

⁶¹institutum ~i *neut.* practice > **mode of life** ⁶²supra *adv.* **above** (higher up on the page) ⁶³memoro ~are, ~aui, ~atum **to mention** ⁶⁴obseruo ~are, ~aui, ~atum **to observe in practice** ⁶⁵gratulor ~ari, ~atus **to be glad** (w/o dat. of person) ⁶⁶subicio ~icere, ~ieci, ~iectum **to subjugate** ⁶⁷uexo ~are, ~aui, ~atum **to treat roughly**

Monica: daughter-in-law

9.9.20 Socrum¹ etiam suam primo² susurris³ malarum ancillarum⁴
aduersus se inritatam⁵ sic uicit obsequiis,⁶ perseuerans⁷ tolerantia⁸ et
mansuetudine,⁹ ut illa ultro¹⁰ filio suo medias¹¹ linguas famularum¹²
proderet,¹³ quibus inter se et nurum¹⁴ pax domestica¹⁵ turbabatur,¹⁶
expeteretque¹⁷ uindictam.¹⁸ itaque posteaquam¹⁹ ille et matri obtem-
perans²⁰ et curans familiae²¹ disciplinam²² et concordiae²³ suorum
consulens²⁴ proditas ad prodentis arbitrium²⁵ uerberibus²⁶ cohercuit,²⁷
promisit²⁸ illa talia de se praemia²⁹ sperare³⁰ debere, quaecumque de sua
nuru sibi, quo placeret, mali aliquid loqueretur, nullaque iam audente
memorabili³¹ inter se beniuolentiae³² suauitate³³ uixerunt.

¹socrus ~us *f.* **mother-in-law** ²primo *adv.* **at first** ³susurrus ~i *m.* [onomat.] **whisper** ⁴ancilla ~ae *f.* **handmaid** ⁵inrito ~are, ~aui, ~atum **to provoke anger** ⁶obsequium ~ii *neut.* **deference** ⁷perseuerans ~ntis *adj.* **persevering** ⁸tolerantia ~ae *f.* **patient endurance** ⁹mansuetudo ~inis *f.* **mildness** ¹⁰ultro *adv.* **on one's own initiative** ¹¹medius ~a, ~um *adj.* coming between; LATE **meddling** ¹²famula ~ae *f.* **servant girl** ¹³prodo ~ere, ~idi, ~itum **to reveal** ¹⁴nurus ~us *f.* **daughter-in-law** ¹⁵domesticus ~a, ~um *adj.* **domestic** ¹⁶turbo ~are, ~aui, ~atum **to disturb** ¹⁷expeto ~ere, ~iui, ~itum **to ask for** ¹⁸uindicta ~ae *f.* **punishment** ¹⁹posteaquam *conj.* **after that** ²⁰obtempero ~are, ~aui, ~atum **to comply** (w. dat.) ²¹familia ~ae *f.* **family** ²²disciplina ~ae *f.* **discipline** ²³concordia ~ae *f.* **state of peace** ²⁴consulo ~ere, ~ui, ~tum **to consult** ²⁵arbitrium ~ii *neut.* **judgment** ²⁶uerber ~ris *neut.* **flogging** ²⁷coherceo ~ere, ~ui, ~itum **to punish** ²⁸promitto ~ittere, ~isi, ~issum **to promise** ²⁹praemium ~ii *neut.* **reward** ³⁰spero ~are, ~aui, ~atum **to expect** ³¹memorabilis ~is, ~e *adj.* **memorable** ³²beniuolentia ~ae *f.* **goodwill** ³³suauitas ~atis *f.* **pleasantness**

Monica: peacemaker

9.9.21 Hoc quoque illi bono mancipio¹ tuo, in cuius utero² me creasti,
Deus meus, misericordia mea (Ps 58:18), munus grande donaueras,³ quod
inter dissidentesque⁴ atque discordes⁵ quaslibet⁶ animas, ubi poterat,

¹mancipium ~ii *neut.* **slave** ²uterum ~i *neut.* **womb** ³dono ~are, ~aui, ~atum **to endow** ⁴dissideo ~idere, ~edi **to disagree** ⁵discors ~rdis *adj.* **discordant** ⁶quilibet, quae-, quod- *adj.* **any whatever**

tam se praebebat[7] pacificam[8] ut cum ab utraque[9] multa de inuicem[10] audiret amarissima,[11] qualia solet eructare[12] turgens[13] atque indigesta[14] discordia,[15] quando praesenti amicae[16] de absente inimica per acida[17] conloquia[18] cruditas[19] exhalatur[20] odiorum,[21] nihil tamen alteri de altera proderet[22] nisi quod ad eas reconciliandas[23] ualeret. paruum hoc bonum mihi uideretur, nisi turbas[24] innumerabiles[25] tristis experirer (nescio qua horrenda[26] pestilentia[27] peccatorum latissime[28] peruagante[29]) non solum iratorum[30] inimicorum iratis inimicis dicta prodere, sed etiam quae non dicta sunt addere, cum contra homini humano parum esse debeat inimicitias[31] hominum nec excitare[32] nec augere[33] male[34] loquendo, nisi eas etiam extinguere[35] bene loquendo studuerit:[36] qualis illa erat docente te magistro intimo[37] in schola[38] pectoris.

[7]praebeo ~ere, ~ui, ~itum **to put oneself forward** (refl.) [8]pacificus ~a, ~um *adj.* **tending to make peace** [9]utraque *adv.* **on both sides** [10]inuicem *adv.* **each in turn** [11]amarus ~a, ~um *adj.* **bitter** [12]eructo ~are, ~aui, ~atum **to disgorge noisily** [13]turgeo ~ere, tursi **to swell** [14]indigestus ~a, ~um *adj.* disorderly; LATE **undigested** [15]discordia ~ae *f.* **discord** [16]amica ~ae *f.* **friend** [17]acidus ~a, ~um *adj.* **acid** [18]conloquium ~ii *neut.* **talk** [19]cruditas ~atis *f.* **indigestion** [20]exhalo, exal- ~are, ~aui, ~atum **to belch** [21]odium ~i *neut.* **hatred** [22]prodo ~ere, ~idi, ~itum **to reveal to** (w. dat.) [23]reconcilio ~are, ~aui, ~atum **to reconcile** [24]turba ~ae *f.* **crowd** > **hordes** (contemptuous) [25]innumerabilis ~is, ~e *adj.* **innumerable** [26]horrendus ~a, ~um *adj.* **horrendous** [27]pestilentia ~ae *f.* **epidemic** [28]latus ~a, ~um *adj.* **extensive** [29]peruagor ~ari, ~atus **to pervade** [30]iratus ~a, ~um *adj.* **angry** [31]inimicitia ~ae *f.* **enmity** [32]excito ~are, ~aui, ~atum **to stir up** [33]augeo ~gere, ~xi, ~ctum **to increase** [34]male *adv.* **wrongfully** [35]extinguo ~guere, ~xi, ~ctum **to extinguish** [36]studeo ~ere, ~ui **to devote oneself (to)** [37]intimus ~a, ~um *superl. adj.* **inmost** [38]schola ~ae *f.* **school**

Monica: servant of your servants

9.9.22 Denique[1] etiam uirum suum iam in extrema uita temporali[2] eius lucrata[3] est tibi, nec in eo iam fideli planxit[4] quod in nondum fideli tolerauerat:[5] erat etiam serua[6] seruorum tuorum. quisquis eorum nouerat eam, multum in ea laudabat et honorabat[7] et diligebat te, quia sentiebat praesentiam[8] tuam in corde eius *sanctae conuersationis*[9] (2 Pet 3:11) fructibus testibus.[10] fuerat enim *unius uiri uxor*[11] (1 Tim 5:9),

[1]denique *adv.* **at last** [2]temporalis ~is, ~e *adj.* **temporal** [3]lucror ~ari, ~atus **to win** [4]plango ~gere, ~xi, ~ctum **to mourn for** [5]tolero ~are, ~aui, ~atum **to tolerate** [6]serua ~ae *f.* **servant** [7]honoro ~are, ~aui, ~atum **to honor** [8]praesentia ~ae *f.* **presence** [9]conuersatio ~onis *f.* **manner of life** [10]testis ~is *m.* **witness** [11]uxor ~oris *f.* **wife**

mutuam[12] *uicem*[13] *parentibus reddiderat, domum suam pie*[14] *tractauerat*[15] (1 Tim 5:4), *in operibus bonis testimonium*[16] *habebat* (1 Tim 5:10). nutrierat[17] *filios,* totiens[18] *eos parturiens*[19] (Gal 4:19) quotiens[20] abs te deuiare[21] cernebat. postremo[22] nobis, Domine, omnibus, quia ex munere tuo sinis loqui, seruis tuis, qui ante dormitionem[23] eius in te iam consociati[24] uiuebamus percepta[25] gratia baptismi[26] tui, ita curam gessit quasi omnes genuisset,[27] ita seruiuit quasi ab omnibus genita fuisset.

[12]mutuus ~a, ~um *adj.* **debt** (as noun) [13]uicis *genitive f.* **repayment** [14]pie *adv.* **dutifully** [15]tracto ~are, ~aui, ~atum **to deal with** [16]testimonium ~ii *neut.* **testimony** [17]nutrio ~ire, ~iui or ~ii, ~itum **to bring up** [18]totiens *adv.* **so often** [19]parturio ~ire, ~iui **to be in labor** (giving birth) [20]quotiens, -ies *adv.* **as often** [21]deuio ~are, ~aui, ~atum in LATE **to deviate** [22]postremo *adv.* **finally** [23]dormitio ~onis *f.* **sleep** (euphem. **death**) [24]consociatus ~a, ~um *adj.* **as a companion** [25]percipio ~ipere, ~epi, ~eptum **to acquire** [26]baptismus ~i *m.* (~um ~i *neut.*) ECCL **baptism** [27]gigno ~ere, genui, genitum **to give birth**

Monica: conversation partner

9.10.23 Impendente[1] autem die quo ex hac uita erat exitura[2] (quem diem tu noueras ignorantibus nobis), prouenerat,[3] ut credo, procurante[4] te occultis tuis modis, ut ego et ipsa soli staremus, incumbentes[5] ad quandam fenestram[6] unde hortus[7] intra[8] domum quae nos habebat prospectabatur,[9] illic apud *Ostia Tiberina* (Aen. 1.13–14), ubi remoti[10] a turbis post longi itineris laborem instaurabamus[11] nos nauigationi.[12] conloquebamur[13] ergo soli ualde dulciter[14] et, *praeterita obliuiscentes in ea quae ante*[15] *sunt extenti* (Phil 3:13), quaerebamus inter nos apud praesentem ueritatem, quod tu es, qualis futura esset uita aeterna sanctorum, quam *nec oculus uidit nec auris audiuit nec in cor hominis ascendit*[16] (1 Cor 2:9). sed inhiabamus[17] ore cordis in superna[18] fluenta[19] fontis tui, *fontis uitae, qui est apud te* (Ps 35:10), ut inde pro captu[20] nostro aspersi[21] quoquo modo[22] rem tantam cogitaremus.

[1]impendeo ~dere, ~sum **to be impending** [2]exeo ~ire, ~iui or ~ii, ~itum **to go out** [3]prouenio ~enire, ~eni, ~entum **to turn out** [4]procuro ~are, ~aui, ~atum to take care of LATE **to provide** [5]incumbo ~umbere, ~ubui **to lean** [6]fenestra ~ae *f.* **window** [7]hortus ~i *m.* **garden** [8]intra *prep.* **inside** [9]prospecto ~are, ~aui, ~atum **to afford a view of** [10]remotus ~a, ~um *adj.* **removed** [11]instauro ~are, ~aui, ~atum **to refresh** [12]nauigatio ~onis *f.* **voyage by ship** [13]conloquor ~qui, ~cutus **to discuss** [14]dulciter *adv.* **sweetly** [15]ante *adv.* **ahead** [16]ascendo ~dere, ~di, ~sum **to climb** [17]inhio ~are, ~aui, ~atum **to stand gaping** [18]supernus ~a, ~um *adj.* **celestial** [19]fluentum ~i *neut.* **stream** [20]captus ~us *m.* **capacity** [21]aspergo ~gere, ~si, ~sum **to sprinkle** [22]'quoquo modo' **in whatever measure possible**

242

Monica: co-mystic

9.10.24 Cumque ad eum finem sermo perduceretur,[1] ut carnalium[2] sensuum delectatio[3] quantalibet,[4] in quantalibet luce corporea, prae illius uitae iucunditate[5] non comparatione[6] sed ne commemoratione[7] quidem digna uideretur, erigentes[8] nos ardentiore[9] affectu *in Idipsum*[10] (Ps 4:9), perambulauimus[11] gradatim[12] cuncta corporalia et ipsum caelum, unde sol et luna[13] et stellae[14] lucent[15] super terram. et adhuc ascendebamus[16] interius[17] cogitando et loquendo et mirando opera tua. et uenimus in mentes nostras et transcendimus[18] eas, ut attingeremus[19] regionem[20] ubertatis[21] indeficientis,[22] ubi *pascis Israhel* (Ps 79:2 VL) in aeternum ueritate pabulo,[23] et ibi Vita Sapientia est, per quam fiunt omnia ista, et quae fuerunt et quae futura sunt, et ipsa non fit, sed sic est ut fuit, et sic erit semper. quin[24] potius "fuisse" et "futurum esse" non est in ea, sed esse solum, quoniam aeterna est: nam fuisse et futurum esse non est aeternum. et dum loquimur et inhiamus[25] illi, attingimus eam modice[26] toto ictu[27] cordis. et suspirauimus et reliquimus ibi religatas[28] *primitias*[29] *spiritus* (Rom 8:23) et remeauimus[30] ad strepitum[31] oris nostri, ubi uerbum et incipitur et finitur. et quid simile Verbo tuo, Domino nostro, *in se permanenti*[32] sine uetustate[33] atque *innouanti*[34] *omnia*? (Wis 7:27).

---

[1]perduco ~cere, ~xi, ~ctum **to bring** [2]carnalis ~is, ~e *adj*. ECCL **carnal** [3]delectatio ~onis *f.* **delight** [4]quantuslibet ~alibet, ~umlibet *adj*. **no matter how great** [5]iucunditas ~atis *f.* **enjoyment** [6]comparatio ~onis *f.* **comparison** [7]commemoratio ~onis *f.* **mention** [8]erigo ~igere, ~exi, ~ectum **to lift up** [9]ardens ~ntis *adj*. **ardent** [10]idipsum *pron*. ECCL self-same; AUG **Being Itself** [11]perambulo ~are, ~aui, ~atum **to walk about** [12]gradatim *adv*. **progressively** [13]luna ~ae *f.* **moon** [14]stella ~ae *f.* **star** [15]luceo ~ere, luxi **to shine** [16]ascendo ~dere, ~di, ~sum **to ascend** [17]interius *adv*. **inwardly** [18]transcendo ~dere, ~di, ~sum **to transcend** [19]attingo ~tingere, ~tigi, ~tactum **to arrive at** [20]regio ~onis *f.* **land** [21]ubertas ~atis *f.* **fruitfulness** [22]indeficiens ~ntis *adj*. ECCL **unfailing** [23]pabulum ~i *neut.* fodder; **food** (fig.) [24]quin *adv*. (makes emphatic 'potius') [25]inhio ~are, ~aui, ~atum **to gaze with astonishment** [26]modice *adv*. **slightly** [27]ictus ~us *m.* **beat** [28]religo ~are, ~aui, ~atum **to bind** [29]primitiae ~arum *f. pl.* **first-fruits** [30]remeo ~are, ~aui, ~atum **to return** (home) [31]strepitus ~us *m.* **noise** [32]permaneo ~ere, ~si, ~sum **to abide** [33]uetustas ~atis *f.* **old age** [34]innouo ~are, ~aui, ~atum **to renew**

Poem of the beatific vision

9.10.25 Dicebamus ergo,

"Si cui sileat[1] tumultus[2] carnis,
sileant phantasiae[3] terrae et aquarum et aeris,[4]
sileant et poli,[5]
et ipsa sibi anima sileat
et transeat se non se cogitando,
sileant somnia[6] et imaginariae[7] reuelationes,[8]
omnis lingua et omne signum, et quidquid transeundo fit
si cui sileat omnino
— quoniam si quis audiat, dicunt haec omnia,
'*non ipsa nos fecimus,*
sed fecit nos qui manet in aeternum' (Ps 99:3; 32:11) —
his dictis si iam taceant,
quoniam erexerunt[9] aurem in eum qui fecit ea,
et loquatur ipse solus
non per ea sed per se ipsum,
ut audiamus *Verbum eius* (Jn 1:1),
non per linguam carnis neque per uocem angeli
nec per *sonitum*[10] *nubis*[11] (Ps 76:18)
nec per aenigma[12] *similitudinis*[13] (Num 12:7, 1 Cor 13:12),
sed ipsum quem in his amamus,
ipsum sine his audiamus
sicut nunc extendimus nos et rapida[14] cogitatione
attingimus[15] aeternam sapientiam super omnia manentem,
si continuetur[16] hoc
et subtrahantur[17] aliae uisiones[18] longe imparis[19] generis

[1]sileo ~ere, ~ui **to be silent** [2]tumultus ~us *m.* **tumult** [3]phantasia ~ae *f.* **fantasy** [4]aer aeris *m.* (*f.*) **sky** [5]polus ~i *m.* **pole** (axis of heavenly sphere) [6]somnium ~ii *neut.* **dream** [7]imaginarius ~a, ~um *adj.* **in the imagination** [8]reuelatio ~onis *f.* ECCL **revelation** [9]erexerunt aurem' **they had pricked up the ear** [10]sonitus ~us *m.* **thunder** [11]nubes ~is *f.* **cloud** [12]aenigma ~atis *neut.* **riddle** [13]similitudo ~inis *f.* **similarity** > **simile** [14]rapidus ~a, ~um *adj.* **swift flowing** [15]attingo ~tingere, ~tigi, ~tactum **to touch** [16]continuo ~are, ~aui, ~atum **to continue** [17]subtraho ~here, ~xi, ~ctum **to take away** [18]uisio ~onis *f.* **vision** [19]impar ~ris *adj.* **unequal**

et haec una rapiat et absorbeat[20]
et recondat[21] in interiora gaudia spectatorem[22] suum,
ut talis sit sempiterna[23] uita
quale fuit hoc momentum[24] intellegentiae[25] cui suspirauimus,
nonne hoc est: *intra in gaudium Domini tui* (Mt 25:21)?
et istud quando?
an cum *omnes resurgimus,*[26]
sed non omnes immutabimur[27] (1 Cor 15:51)?"

[20]absorbeo ~bere, ~bui, ~ptum **to engulf** [21]recondo ~ere, ~idi, ~itum **to hide away** [22]spectator ~oris *m.* **one who watches** [23]sempiternus ~a, ~um *adj.* **eternal** [24]momentum ~i *neut.* **moment** [25]intellegentia ~ae *f.* **understanding** [26]resurgo ~rgere, ~rrexi, ~rrectum **to rise again** [27]immuto ~are, ~aui, ~atum **to change form**

Monica: mission accomplished

9.10.26 Dicebam talia, etsi non isto modo et his uerbis, tamen, *Domine, tu scis* (Jn 21:15), quod illo die, cum talia loqueremur et mundus iste nobis inter uerba uilesceret[1] cum omnibus delectationibus[2] suis, tunc ait illa, "Fili, quantum ad me attinet,[3] nulla re iam delector in hac uita. quid hic[4] faciam adhuc et cur hic sim, nescio, iam consumpta[5] spe huius saeculi. unum erat propter quod in hac uita aliquantum[6] immorari[7] cupiebam, ut te Christianum Catholicum uiderem priusquam morerer. cumulatius[8] hoc mihi Deus meus praestitit,[9] ut te etiam contempta[10] felicitate[11] terrena[12] seruum eius uideam. quid hic facio?"

[1]uilesco ~ere, ~ui LATE **to become worthless** [2]delectatio ~onis *f.* **delight** [3]attineo ~ere, ~ui, attentum **to concern** (w. 'ad') [4]hic *adv.* **here** [5]consumo ~ere, ~psi, ~ptum **to exhaust** [6]aliquantum *adv.* **a little** [7]immoror ~ari, ~atus **to linger** [8]cumulate *adv.* **abundantly** [9]praesto ~are, ~iti, ~itum **to fulfill** [10]contemno ~nere, ~psi, ~ptum **to regard with contempt** [11]felicitas ~atis *f.* **happiness** [12]terrenus ~a, ~um *adj.* **earthly**

Monica: final illness

9.11.27 Ad haec ei quid responderim non satis recolo, cum interea[1] uix intra[2] quinque[3] dies aut non multo amplius decubuit[4] febribus.[5]

[1]interea *adv.* **in the meantime** [2]intra *prep. acc.* **within** [3]quinque *indecl. adj.* **five** [4]decubo ~are, ~aui, ~atum **to get down**; LATE **to fall ill** [5]febris ~is *f.* **attack of fever**

et cum aegrotaret,[6] quodam die defectum animae[7] passa est et paululum[8] subtracta[9] a praesentibus. nos concurrimus,[10] sed cito[11] reddita est sensui et aspexit astantes[12] me et fratrem meum, et ait nobis quasi quaerenti similis,[13] "Ubi eram?" deinde nos intuens maerore[14] attonitos:[15] "Ponitis hic"[16] inquit "matrem uestram." ego silebam[17] et fletum[18] frenabam,[19] frater autem meus quiddam locutus est, quo eam non in peregre,[20] sed in patria defungi[21] tamquam felicius optaret. quo audito illa uultu anxio[22] reuerberans[23] eum oculis, quod talia saperet,[24] atque inde me intuens: "Vide" ait "quid dicit." et mox ambobus:[25] "Ponite" inquit "hoc corpus ubicumque.[26] nihil uos eius cura conturbet.[27] tantum illud uos rogo,[28] ut ad Domini altare[29] memineritis mei, ubiubi[30] fueritis." cumque hanc sententiam uerbis quibus poterat explicasset,[31] conticuit[32] et ingrauescente[33] morbo[34] exercebatur.[35]

---

[6]aegroto ~are, ~aui, ~atum **to be ill** [7]'defectum animae' **faintness** [8]paululum *adv.* **for a short while** [9]subtraho ~here, ~xi, ~ctum **to withdraw** [10]concurro ~rere, ~ri, ~sum **to hurry together** [11]cito *adv.* **readily** [12]asto ~are, ~iti **to stand by** [13]simile ~is *neut.* **like** [14]maeror ~oris *m.* **grief** [15]attonitus ~a, ~um *adj.* **overwhelmed** [16]hic *adv.* **here** [17]sileo ~ere, ~ui **to be silent** [18]fletus ~us *m.* **weeping** [19]freno ~are, ~aui, ~atum **to restrain** [20]peregre *adv.* **abroad** [21]defungor ~gi, ~ctus **to die** [22]anxius ~a, ~um *adj.* **anxious** [23]reuerbero ~are, ~aui, ~atum **to repel**; LATE **to reproach** [24]sapio ~ere, ~ii **to feel** [25]ambo ~ae, ~o *pl.* *pron.* **both** [26]ubicumque *adv.* **wherever** [27]conturbo ~are, ~aui, ~atum **to upset** [28]rogo ~are, ~aui, ~atum **to ask** [29]altaria ~ium *neut. pl., sg. nom.* ~e **altar** [30]ubiubi *conj.* **wherever** [31]explico ~are, ~aui or ~ui, ~atum **to explain** [32]conticesco ~escere, ~ui **to fall silent** [33]ingrauesco ~ere **to grow worse** [34]morbus ~i *m.* **illness** [35]exerceo ~ere, ~ui, ~itum to exercise > **to trouble**

Monica: set free

9.11.28 Ego uero cogitans dona tua, *Deus inuisibilis* (Col 1:15), quae immittis[1] in corda fidelium tuorum, et proueniunt[2] inde fruges[3] admirabiles,[4] gaudebam et gratias tibi agebam, recolens quod noueram, quanta cura semper aestuasset[5] de sepulchro[6] quod sibi prouiderat[7] et praeparauerat[8] iuxta[9] corpus uiri sui. quia enim ualde concorditer[10] uixerant, id etiam uolebat, ut est animus humanus minus capax[11]

---

[1]immitto ~ittere, ~isi, ~issum **to send to** [2]prouenio ~enire, ~eni, ~entum **to produce** [3]frux ~ugis *f.* **fruit** [4]admirabilis ~is, ~e *adj.* **admirable** [5]aestuo ~are, ~aui, ~atum **to feel strongly** [6]sepulchrum ~i *neut.* **grave** [7]prouideo ~idere, ~idi, ~isum **to provide** [8]praeparo ~are, ~aui, ~atum **to prepare** [9]iuxta *prep. acc.* **next to** [10]concorditer *adv.* **harmoniously** [11]capax ~acis *adj.* **capable of understanding**

diuinorum,[12] adiungi[13] ad illam felicitatem[14] et commemorari ab hominibus, concessum[15] sibi esse post transmarinam[16] peregrinationem[17] ut coniuncta[18] terra amborum[19] coniugum terra tegeretur. quando autem ista inanitas[20] plenitudine[21] bonitatis[22] tuae coeperat in eius corde non esse, nesciebam et laetabar,[23] admirans[24] quod sic mihi apparuisset (quamquam et in illo sermone nostro ad fenestram,[25] cum dixit, "Iam quid hic[26] facio?" non apparuit desiderare in patria mori). audiui etiam postea quod iam cum Ostiis essemus cum quibusdam amicis meis materna[27] fiducia[28] conloquebatur[29] quodam die de contemptu[30] uitae huius et bono mortis, ubi ipse non aderam, illisque stupentibus[31] uirtutem feminae (quoniam tu dederas ei) quaerentibusque utrum non formidaret[32] tam longe a sua ciuitate corpus relinquere, "Nihil" inquit "longe est Deo, neque timendum est, ne ille non agnoscat in fine saeculi unde me resuscitet."[33]

Ergo die nono[34] aegritudinis[35] suae, quinquagesimo[36] et sexto[37] anno aetatis suae, tricesimo[38] et tertio[39] aetatis meae, anima illa religiosa[40] et pia corpore soluta[41] est.

[12]diuinus ~a, ~um *adj.* **divine** [13]adiungo ~gere, ~xi, ~ctum **to add** [14]felicitas ~atis *f.* **happiness** [15]concedo ~dere, ~ssi, ~ssum **to pass away** [16]transmarinus ~a, ~um *adj.* **overseas** [17]peregrinatio ~onis *f.* **travel abroad** [18]coniunctus ~a, ~um *adj.* **connected** [19]ambo ~ae, ~o *pl. adj. pron.* **both** [20]inanitas ~atis *f.* **empty concern** [21]plenitudo ~inis *f.* **plenitude** [22]bonitas ~atis *f.* **goodness** [23]laetor ~ari, ~atus **to be glad** [24]admiror ~ari, ~atus **to wonder at** [25]fenestra ~ae *f.* **window** [26]hic *adv.* **here** [27]maternus ~a, ~um *adj.* **motherly** [28]fiducia ~ae *f.* **confidence** [29]conloquor ~qui, ~cutus **to discuss** [30]contemptus ~us *m.* **contempt** [31]stupeo ~ere, ~ui **to be stunned** [32]formido ~are, ~aui, ~atum **to dread** [33]resuscito ~are **to reawaken**; ECCL **to raise from the dead** [34]nonus ~a, ~um *adj.* **ninth** [35]aegritudo ~inis *f.* **sickness** [36]quinquagesimus ~a, ~um *adj.* **fiftieth** [37]sextus ~a, ~um *adj.* **sixth** [38]tricesimus ~a, ~um *adj.* **thirtieth** [39]tertius ~a, ~um *adj.* **third** [40]religiosus ~a, ~um *adj.* **religious** [41]soluo ~uere, ~ui, ~utum **to set free**

Monica: a grief restrained

9.12.29 Premebam[1] oculos eius, et confluebat[2] in praecordia[3] mea maestitudo[4] ingens[5] et transfluebat[6] in lacrimas, ibidemque[7] oculi mei uiolento[8] animi imperio resorbebant[9] fontem suum usque ad siccitatem,[10]

[1]premo ~mere, ~ssi, ~ssum to press > **to close** [2]confluo ~ere, ~xi **to flood** [3]praecordia ~orum *neut. pl.* **depths of the heart** [4]maestitudo ~inis *f.* **grief** [5]ingens ~ntis *adj.* **enormous** [6]transfluo ~ere to flow across; LATE **to flow over** [7]ibidem *adv.* **at that very instant** [8]uiolentus ~a, ~um *adj.* **violent** [9]resorbeo ~ere **to swallow down** [10]siccitas ~atis *f.* **dryness**

et in tali luctamine[11] ualde male[12] mihi erat. tum uero ubi efflauit[13] extremum, puer Adeodatus exclamauit[14] in planctu[15] atque ab omnibus nobis cohercitus[16] tacuit. hoc modo etiam meum quiddam puerile,[17] quod labebatur[18] in fletus,[19] iuuenali[20] uoce cordis cohercebatur et tacebat. neque enim decere[21] arbitrabamur funus[22] illud questibus[23] lacrimo-sis[24] gemitibusque[25] celebrare,[26] quia his plerumque[27] solet deplorari[28] quaedam miseria morientium aut quasi omnimoda[29] extinctio.[30] at illa nec misere[31] moriebatur nec omnino moriebatur. hoc et documentis[32] morum eius *et fide non ficta*[33] (1 Tim 1:5) rationibusque certis tenebamus.

[11]luctamen ~inis *neut.* **struggle** [12]male *adv.* **painfully** [13]efflo ~are, ~aui, ~atum **to breathe** [14]exclamo ~are, ~aui, ~atum **to cry out** [15]planctus ~us *m.* **unrestrained grief** [16]coherceo ~ere, ~ui, ~itum **to restrain** [17]puerilis ~is, ~e *adj.* **childish** [18]labor ~bi, ~psus **to slip into** [19]fletus ~us *m.* **weeping** [20]iuuenalis ~is, ~e *adj.* **youthful** [21]decet ~ere, ~uit *impers.* **it is becoming** [22]funus ~eris *neut.* **death** [23]questus ~us *m.* **plaintive crying** [24]lacrimosus ~a, ~um *adj.* **tearfully** [25]gemitus ~us *m.* **groaning** [26]celebro ~are, ~aui, ~atum **to observe** [27]plerumque *adv.* **most of the time** [28]deploro ~are, ~aui, ~atum **to lament** [29]omnimodus ~a, ~um *adj.* of every sort; LATE **total** [30]extinctio ~onis *f.* **extinction** [31]misere *adv.* **in misery** [32]documentum ~i *neut.* **example** [33]fictus ~a, ~um *adj.* **insincere**

Separation is the cause of grief

9.12.30 Quid erat ergo quod intus mihi grauiter[1] dolebat, nisi ex consuetudine simul uiuendi, dulcissima et carissima, repente[2] dirupta[3] uulnus recens?[4] gratulabar[5] quidem testimonio[6] eius, quod in ea ipsa ultima aegritudine[7] obsequiis[8] meis interblandiens[9] appellabat me pium et commemorabat grandi dilectionis[10] affectu numquam se audisse ex ore meo iaculatum[11] in se durum aut contumeliosum[12] sonum. sed tamen quid tale, Deus meus, qui *fecisti nos* (Ps 99:3), quid comparabile[13] habebat honor a me delatus[14] illi et seruitus[15] ab illa mihi? quoniam itaque deserebar tam magno eius solacio,[16] sauciabatur[17] anima et quasi dilaniabatur[18] uita, quae una facta erat ex mea et illius.

[1]grauiter *adv.* **deeply** [2]repente *adv.* **suddenly** [3]dirrumpo ~umpere, ~upi, ~uptum **to disrupt** [4]recens ~ntis *adj.* recent > **new** [5]gratulor ~ari, ~atus **to be glad** [6]testimonium ~ii *neut.* **testimony** [7]aegritudo ~inis *f.* **sickness** [8]obsequium ~ii *neut.* **attentiveness** [9]interblandior ~iri, ~itus AUG **to respond with a caress** [10]dilectio ~onis *f.* ECCL **love** [11]iaculor ~ari, ~atus **to throw > to snipe at** (fig.) [12]contumeliosus ~a, ~um *adj.* **rude** [13]comparabilis ~is, ~e *adj.* **comparable** [14]defero ~rre, detuli, delatum **to render** [15]seruitus ~utis *f.* **servitude** [16]solacium ~ii *neut.* **consolation** [17]saucio ~are, ~aui, ~atum **to wound** [18]dilanio ~are, ~aui, ~atum **to tear to pieces**

Monica: a grief suppressed

9.12.31 Cohibito[1] ergo a fletu[2] illo puero, psalterium[3] arripuit[4] Euodius et cantare coepit psalmum.[5] cui respondebamus omnis domus: *Misericordiam et iudicium cantabo tibi, Domine* (Ps 100:1). audito autem quid ageretur, conuenerunt[6] multi fratres[7] ac religiosae[8] feminae et, de more illis quorum officium[9] erat funus[10] curantibus, ego in parte, ubi decenter[11] poteram, cum eis qui me non deserendum esse censebant,[12] quod erat tempori congruum[13] disputabam[14] eoque fomento[15] ueritatis mitigabam[16] cruciatum[17] tibi notum, illis ignorantibus et intente[18] audientibus et sine sensu doloris me esse arbitrantibus. at ego in auribus tuis, ubi eorum nullus audiebat, increpabam[19] mollitiam[20] affectus mei et constringebam[21] fluxum[22] maeroris,[23] cedebatque mihi paululum.[24] rursusque impetu suo ferebatur non usque ad eruptionem[25] lacrimarum nec usque ad uultus mutationem,[26] sed ego sciebam quid corde premerem.[27] et quia mihi uehementer[28] displicebat tantum in me posse haec humana, quae ordine debito et sorte[29] conditionis[30] nostrae accidere[31] necesse[32] est, alio dolore dolebam dolorem et duplici[33] tristitia[34] macerabar.[35]

[1]cohibeo ~ere, ~ui, ~itum **to hold back** [2]fletus ~us *m.* **weeping** [3]psalterium ~i, *neut.* ECCL **psalter** [4]arripio ~ere, ~ui, arreptum **to take hold of** [5]psalmus ~i, *m.* ECCL **psalm** [6]conuenio ~enire, ~eni, ~entum **to gather** [7]frater ~tris *m.* brother; ECCL **brethren** (*pl.*) [8]religiosus ~a, ~um *adj.* **religious** [9]officium ~ii *neut.* **office (duty)** [10]funus ~eris *neut.* **burial** [11]decenter *adv.* **decently** [12]censeo ~ere, ~ui, ~um **to suppose** [13]congruus ~a, ~um *adj.* **fitting** [14]disputo ~are, ~aui, ~atum **to discuss** [15]fomentum ~i *neut.* remedy > **balm** (fig.) [16]mitigo ~are, ~aui, ~atum **to alleviate** [17]cruciatus ~us *m.* **torment** [18]intente *adv.* **intently** [19]increpo ~are, ~ui, ~itum **to chide** [20]mollitia ~ae *f.* **softness** [21]constringo ~ngere, ~nxi, ~ctum **to confine** [22]fluxus ~us *m.* **flow** [23]maeror ~oris *m.* **grief** [24]paululum *adv.* **somewhat** [25]eruptio ~onis *f.* **eruption** [26]mutatio ~onis *f.* **change** [27]premo ~mere, ~ssi, ~ssum **to press > to suppress** [28]uehementer *adv.* **immensely** [29]sors ~rtis *f.* **lot** [30]condicio ~onis *f.* **condition** [31]accido ~ere, ~i **to happen to** [32]necesse *adv.* **it is necessary** (w. 'est') [33]duplex ~icis *adj.* **double** [34]tristitia ~ae *f.* **despondency** [35]macero ~are, ~aui, ~atum **to wear down**

Monica: Deus Creator Omnium

9.12.32 Cum ecce corpus elatum[1] est, imus, redimus sine lacrimis. nam neque in eis precibus[2] quas tibi fudimus,[3] cum offerretur[4] pro ea

[1]effero ~rre, extuli, elatum **to carry away** [2]preces ~um *f. pl.* **prayers** [3]fundo ~ere, fudi, fusum **to pour out** [4]offero ~rre, obtuli, oblatum **to offer**

sacrificium[5] pretii[6] nostri iam iuxta[7] sepulchrum,[8] posito cadauere[9] priusquam deponeretur,[10] sicut illic fieri solet, nec in eis ergo precibus fleui, sed toto die grauiter[11] in occulto maestus[12] eram et mente turbata[13] rogabam[14] te, ut poteram, quo sanares dolorem meum, nec faciebas, credo commendans[15] memoriae meae uel hoc uno documento[16] omnis consuetudinis uinculum[17] etiam aduersus mentem, quae iam non fallaci[18] uerbo pascitur.

Visum etiam mihi est ut irem lauatum,[19] quod audieram inde balneis[20] nomen inditum[21] quia Graeci "βαλανεῖον" dixerint, quod anxietatem[22] pellat[23] ex animo. ecce et hoc confiteor misericordiae tuae, *Pater orphanorum*[24] (Ps 67:6), quoniam laui et talis eram qualis priusquam lauissem, neque enim exudauit[25] de corde meo maeroris[26] amaritudo.[27] deinde dormiui[28] et euigilaui,[29] et non parua ex parte mitigatum[30] inueni dolorem meum atque, ut eram in lecto[31] meo solus, recordatus sum ueridicos[32] uersus[33] Ambrosii tui. tu es enim,

> *Deus, creator omnium*
> *polique[34] rector[35] uestiens[36]*
> *diem decoro[37] lumine,*
> *noctem sopora[38] gratia,*
>
> *artus[39] solutos[40] ut quies[41]*
> *reddat laboris usui*
> *mentesque fessas[42] alleuet[43]*
> *luctuque[44] soluat[45] anxios.[46]*
> (Hymn 2.1–8)

---

[5]sacrificium ~ii *neut.* **sacrificial offering** [6]pretium ~ii *neut.* price; ECCL **redemption** [7]iuxta *prep. acc.* **beside** [8]sepulchrum ~i *neut.* **sepulchre** [9]cadauer ~eris *neut.* **corpse** [10]depono ~onere, ~osui, ~ostum **to lay to rest** [11]grauiter *adv.* **grievously** [12]maestus ~a, ~um *adj.* **mournful** [13]turbo ~are, ~aui, ~atum **to disturb** [14]rogo ~are, ~aui, ~atum **to ask** [15]commendo ~are, ~aui, ~atum **to commit (for instruction)** [16]documentum ~i *neut.* **example** [17]uinculum ~i *neut.* **chain** [18]fallax ~acis *adj.* **deceitful** [19]lauo ~are, laui, ~atum **to wash up** [20]balneum ~i *neut.* **public bath** [21]indo ~ere, ~idi, ~itum **to attach** (a name) [22]anxietas ~atis *f.* **anxiety** [23]pello ~ere, pepuli, pulsum **to drive** [24]orphanus ~i *m.* ECCL **orphan** [25]exudo ~are, ~aui, ~atum **to sweat out** [26]maeror ~oris *m.* **sorrow** [27]amaritudo ~inis *f.* **bitterness** [28]dormio ~ire, ~iui, ~itum **to sleep** [29]euigilo ~are, ~aui, ~atum **to wake up** [30]mitigo ~are, ~aui, ~atum **to mitigate** [31]lectus ~i *m.* **bed** [32]ueridicus ~a, ~um *adj.* **truly spoken** [33]uersus ~us *m.* **verse** [34]polus ~i *m.* **sky** [35]rector ~oris *m.* **ruler** [36]uestio ~ire, ~iui, ~itum **to clothe** [37]decorus ~a, ~um *adj.* **glorious** [38]soporus ~a, ~um *adj.* **drowsy** [39]artus ~us *m.* **limb** [40]solutus ~a, ~um *adj.* **loose > limp** [41]quies ~etis *f.* **rest** [42]fessus ~a, ~um *adj.* **weary** [43]alleuo ~are, ~aui, ~atum **to alleviate** [44]luctus ~us *m.* **grief** [45]soluo ~uere, ~ui, ~utum **to release** [46]anxius ~a, ~um *adj.* **worried**

Monica: a grief observed

9.12.33 Atque inde paulatim[1] reducebam[2] in pristinum[3] sensum ancillam[4] tuam conuersationemque[5] eius piam in te et sancte[6] in nos blandam[7] atque morigeram,[8] qua subito[9] destitutus[10] sum, et libuit[11] flere *in conspectu tuo* (Ps 18:15) de illa et pro illa, de me et pro me. et dimisi lacrimas quas continebam, ut effluerent[12] quantum uellent, substernens[13] eas cordi meo. et requieuit in eis, quoniam ibi erant aures tuae, non cuiusquam hominis superbe[14] interpretantis[15] ploratum[16] meum.

Et nunc, Domine, confiteor tibi in litteris: legat qui uolet, et interpretetur ut uolet, et si peccatum inuenerit, fleuisse me matrem exigua[17] parte horae, matrem oculis meis interim[18] mortuam quae me multos annos fleuerat ut oculis tuis uiuerem, non inrideat sed potius, si est grandi caritate, pro peccatis meis fleat ipse ad te, Patrem omnium fratrum[19] Christi tui.

[1]paulatim *adv.* **gradually** [2]reduco ~cere, ~xi, ~ctum **to come back** [3]pristinus ~a, ~um *adj.* **previous** [4]ancilla ~ae *f.* **handmaid** [5]conuersatio ~onis *f.* **manner of life** [6]sancte *adv.* **religiously** [7]blandus ~a, ~um *adj.* **sweet** [8]morigerus ~a, ~um *adj.* **indulgent** [9]subito *adv.* **suddenly** [10]destituo ~uere, ~ui, ~utum **to deprive** [11]libet ~ere, ~uit or ~itum est *impers.* **it is pleasing** [12]effluo ~uere, ~uxi **to flow** [13]substerno ~ernere, ~raui, ~ratum **to spread out as a bed** [14]superbe *adv.* **haughtily** [15]interpretor ~ari, ~atus **to interpret** [16]ploratus ~us *m.* **weeping** [17]exiguus ~a, ~um *adj.* **small** [18]interim *adv.* **meanwhile** [19]frater ~tris *m.* brother; ECCL **brethren** (*pl.*)

Monica: a grief healed

9.13.34 Ego autem, iam sanato corde ab illo uulnere in quo poterat redargui[1] carnalis[2] affectus, fundo[3] tibi, Deus noster, pro illa famula[4] tua longe aliud lacrimarum genus, quod manat[5] de concusso[6] spiritu consideratione[7] periculorum omnis animae quae *in Adam moritur.* quamquam illa *in Christo uiuificata*[8] (1 Cor 15:22) etiam nondum a carne resoluta[9] sic uixerit, ut laudetur nomen tuum in fide moribusque eius, non tamen audeo dicere, ex quo eam *per baptismum*[10] *regenerasti*[11]

[1]redarguo ~ere, ~i **to prove guilty** [2]carnalis ~is, ~e *adj.* ECCL **carnal** [3]fundo ~ere, fudi, fusum **to pour out** [4]famula ~ae *f.* **servant** [5]mano ~are, ~aui **to gush** [6]concussus ~us *m.* **shock** [7]consideratio ~onis *f.* **consideration** [8]uiuifio ~are, ~aui, ~atum ECCL **to make alive** [9]resoluo ~uere, ~ui, ~utum **to release** [10]baptismus ~i *m.* (~um ~i *neut.*) ECCL **baptism** [11]regenero ~are to reproduce; ECCL **to regenerate**

(Tit 3:5), nullum uerbum exisse[12] ab ore eius contra praeceptum[13] tuum. et dictum est a Veritate Filio tuo, *Si quis dixerit fratri suo, fatue,*[14] *reus*[15] *erit gehennae*[16] *ignis* (Mt 5:22); et uae[17] etiam laudabili[18] uitae hominum, si remota[19] misericordia discutias[20] eam! quia uero non exquiris[21] delicta[22] uehementer,[23] fiducialiter[24] speramus[25] aliquem apud te locum. quisquis autem tibi enumerat[26] uera merita[27] sua, quid tibi enumerat nisi munera tua? o si cognoscant se homines homines, et *qui gloriatur,*[28] *in Domino glorietur* (1 Cor 1:31)!

[12]exeo ~ire, ~iui or ~ii, ~itum **to come out** [13]praeceptum ~i *neut.* **precept** [14]fatuus ~a, ~um *adj.* **fool** (as noun) [15]reus ~i *m.* **guilty one** [16]gehenna ~ae, *f.* ECCL **Hell** [17]uae *interj.* [a cry of pain, anger, sorrow] **woe!** [18]laudabilis ~is, ~e *adj.* **praiseworthy** [19]remoueo ~ouere, ~oui, ~otum **to remove** > **to not take into account** [20]discutio ~tere, ~ssi, ~ssum **to break up;** LATE **to examine** [21]exquiro ~rere, ~siui, ~situm **to inquire** [22]delictum ~i *neut.* **offense;** ECCL **sin** [23]uehementer *adv.* **strenuously** [24]fiducialiter *adv.* ECCL **boldly** [25]spero ~are, ~aui, ~atum **to hope for** [26]enumero ~are, ~aui, ~atum **to enumerate** [27]meritum ~i *neut.* **merit** [28]glorior ~ari, ~atus **to boast**

Monica: a prayer for mercy

9.13.35 Ego itaque, *laus mea* (Ps 117:14) et uita mea, *Deus cordis mei* (Ps 72:26), sepositis[1] paulisper[2] bonis eius actibus,[3] pro quibus tibi gaudens gratias ago, nunc pro peccatis matris meae deprecor[4] te. *exaudi me* (Ps 142:1) per medicinam[5] uulnerum nostrorum, *quae pependit*[6] *in ligno*[7] (Gal 3:13) et sedens[8] *ad dexteram tuam te interpellat*[9] *pro nobis* (Rom 8:34). scio misericorditer[10] operatam[11] et *ex corde dimisisse debita debitoribus*[12] *suis* (Mt 18:35). *dimitte illi et tu debita sua* (Mt 6:12), si qua etiam contraxit[13] per tot annos post aquam salutis. dimitte, Domine, *dimitte, obsecro*[14] (Num 14:19), *ne intres cum ea in iudicium* (Ps 142:2). *superexultet*[15] *misericordia iudicio* (Jas 2:13), quoniam eloquia[16] tua uera sunt et *promisisti*[17] *misericordiam misericordibus* (Mt 5:7). quod

[1]sepono ~onere, ~osui, ~ositum **to set to the side** [2]paulisper *adv.* **for a little while** [3]actus ~us *m.* **deed** [4]deprecor ~ari, ~atus **to beg in prayer** [5]medicina ~ae *f.* **medicine** [6]pendeo ~ere, pependi **to hang** [7]lignum ~i *neut.* **tree** [8]sedeo ~ere, sedi, sessum **to sit** [9]interpello ~are, ~aui, ~atum **to interpose;** ECCL **to intercede** [10]misericorditer *adv.* **mercifully** [11]operor ~ari, ~atus **to be at work** [12]debitor ~oris *m.* **debtor** [13]contraho ~ahere, ~axi, ~actum **to contract** [14]obsecro ~are, ~aui, ~atum **to beseech** [15]superexalto ~are, ~aui, ~atum LATE **to exalt above** [16]eloquium ~ii *neut.* **pronouncement** [17]promitto ~ittere, ~isi, ~issum **to promise**

ut essent tu dedisti eis, *qui misereberis cui misertus eris, et misericordiam praestabis*[18] *cui misericors*[19] *fueris* (Rom 9:15).

[18]praesto ~are, ~iti, ~itum **to render** [19]misericors ~rdis *adj.* **merciful**

Monica: Eucharistic devotion

9.13.36 Et credo, iam feceris quod te rogo,[1] sed *uoluntaria*[2] *oris mei approba,*[3] *Domine* (Ps 118:108). namque[4] illa imminente[5] *die resolutionis*[6] *suae* (2 Tim 4:6) non cogitauit suum corpus sumptuose[7] contegi[8] aut condiri[9] aromatis[10] aut monumentum[11] electum[12] concupiuit[13] aut curauit sepulchrum[14] patrium.[15] non ista mandauit[16] nobis, sed tantummodo memoriam sui ad altare[17] tuum fieri desiderauit, cui nullius diei praetermissione[18] seruierat, unde sciret dispensari[19] Victimam[20] sanctam qua *deletum*[21] *est chirographum*[22] *quod erat contrarium*[23] *nobis* (Col 2:14), qua triumphatus[24] est hostis computans[25] delicta[26] nostra et quaerens quid obiciat,[27] et *nihil inueniens in illo* (Lk 23:4), in quo uincimus. quis ei refundet[28] innocentem[29] sanguinem? quis ei restituet[30] *pretium*[31] *quo nos emit*[32] (1 Cor 7:23), ut nos auferat ei?

Ad cuius pretii nostri sacramentum ligauit[33] ancilla[34] tua animam suam uinculo[35] fidei. nemo a protectione[36] tua dirumpat[37] eam; non se interponat[38] nec ui nec insidiis[39] *leo*[40] *et draco*[41] (Ps 90:13). neque enim respondebit illa nihil se debere, ne conuincatur[42] et obtineatur[43]

[1]rogo ~are, ~aui, ~atum **to ask** [2]uoluntarius ~a, ~um *adj.* **voluntary** [3]approbo ~are, ~aui, ~atum **to approve** [4]namque *conj.* **for** [5]immineo ~ere **to be imminent** [6]resolutio ~onis *f.* **release** [7]sumptuose *adv.* **sumptuously** [8]contego ~gere, ~xi, ~ctum **to bury** [9]condio ~ire, ~iui, ~itum **to embalm** [10]aroma ~atis *neut.* **spice** [11]monumentum ~i *neut.* **monument** [12]electus ~a, ~um *adj.* **choice** [13]concupisco ~iscere, ~iui, ~itum **to desire** [14]sepulchrum ~i *neut.* **sepulchre** [15]patrius ~a, ~um *adj.* **homeland** [16]mando ~are, ~aui, ~atum **to command** [17]altaria ~ium *neut. pl., sg. nom.* ~e **altar** [18]praetermissio ~onis *f.* **omission** [19]dispenso ~are, ~aui, ~atum **to dispense** [20]uictima ~ae *f.* **victim** [21]deleo ~ere, ~eui, ~etum **to nullify** [22]chirographum ~i *neut.* **handwriting** > **handwritten debt** [23]contrarius ~a, ~um *adj.* **opposed** [24]triumpho ~are, ~aui, ~atum **to celebrate a triumph** [25]computo ~are, ~aui, ~atum **to count** [26]delictum ~i *neut.* **offense**; ECCL **sin** [27]obicio ~icere, ~ieci, ~iectum **to lay to one's charge** [28]refundo ~undere, ~udi, ~usum **to restore** [29]innocens ~ntis *adj.* **innocent** [30]restituo ~uere, ~ui, ~utum **to pay back** [31]pretium ~ii *neut.* **price** [32]emo emere, emi, emptum **to buy**; ECCL **to redeem** [33]ligo ~are, ~aui, ~atum **to bind together** [34]ancilla ~ae *f.* **handmaid** [35]uinculum ~i *neut.* **chain** [36]protectio ~onis *f.* **protection** [37]dirrumpo ~umpere, ~upi, ~uptum **to break apart** [38]interpono ~ponere, ~posui, ~positum **to come between** [39]insidiae ~arum *f. pl.* **stealth** [40]leo ~onis *m.* **lion** [41]draco ~onis *m.* **dragon** [42]conuinco ~incere, ~ici, ~ictum **to convict** [43]obtineo ~inere, ~inui, ~entum **to hold** > **to hold in one's power**

ab accusatore[44] callido,[45] sed respondebit dimissa debita sua ab eo cui nemo reddet, quod pro nobis non debens reddidit.

[44]accusator ~oris *m.* **accuser** [45]callidus ~a, ~um *adj.* **cunning**

Monica: requiem

9.13.37 Sit ergo in pace cum uiro, ante quem nulli et post quem nulli nupta[1] est, cui seruiuit *fructum tibi afferens*[2] *cum tolerantia*[3] (Lk 8:15), ut eum quoque *lucraretur*[4] *tibi* (1 Pet 3:1). et inspira,[5] *Domine meus, Deus meus* (Jn 20:28), inspira seruis tuis, fratribus[6] meis, filiis tuis, dominis meis, quibus et corde et uoce et litteris seruio, ut quotquot[7] haec legerint, meminerint ad altare[8] tuum Monnicae, famulae[9] tuae, cum Patricio, quondam[10] eius coniuge, per quorum carnem introduxisti[11] me in hanc uitam, quemadmodum nescio. meminerint cum affectu pio parentum meorum in hac luce transitoria,[12] et fratrum meorum sub te patre in matre Catholica, et ciuium meorum in aeterna Hierusalem, cui suspirat peregrinatio[13] populi tui ab exitu[14] usque ad reditum, ut quod a me illa poposcit[15] extremum uberius[16] ei praestetur[17] in multorum orationibus per confessiones quam per orationes[18] meas.

[1]nubo ~bere, ~psi, ~ptum **to marry** [2]affero ~rre, attuli, allatum **to bring forth** [3]tolerantia ~ae *f.* **patience** [4]lucror ~ari, ~atus **to gain** [5]inspiro ~are, ~aui, ~atum **to inspire supernaturally** (w. dat.) [6]frater ~tris *m.* brother; ECCL **brethren** (*pl.*) [7]quotquot *indecl. adj.* **however many** [8]altaria ~ium *neut. pl., sg. nom.* ~e altar [9]famula ~ae *f.* **servant** [10]quondam *adv.* **formerly** [11]introduco ~cere, ~xi, ~ctum **to bring in** [12]transitorius ~a, ~um *adj.* affording passage; ECCL **transitory** [13]peregrinatio ~onis *f.* **sojourn** [14]exitus ~us *m.* **setting out** [15]posco ~ere, poposci **to require** [16]uberius *compar. adv.* **in greater abundance** [17]praesto ~are, ~iti, ~itum **to render** [18]oratio ~onis *f.* speech; ECCL **prayer**

MAIN GLOSSARY

The first 20 words presented in the glossary each occur more than 500 times and account for one out of every three words in the text of *Confessions*. They are treated here in greater detail:

ab, abs, a *prep. abl.* from, away from (with the basic sense of separation), but see the following:

from	place from which
because of	cause
after, since	time
by	agency
in regard to	relation

cum *adv.* introduces various clauses usually with the subjunctive:

when, while, whenever	temporal
because	causal
although, whereas	concessive

cum, -cum *prep. abl.* with, together with, along with

dico ~**cere**, ~**xi**, ~**ctum** (1) to say, speak, tell, name, claim, mean, refer to (2) *ppl. noun* **dictum** ~**i** *neut.* one's words, a saying, precept

ego *pron.* I, me, myself

nom.	ego
gen.	mei
dat.	mihi
acc.	me
abl.	me

et *conj.* and, **et... et** both... and (with the basic sense of connection), but see the following:

and in fact	emphatic
also	reinforcement
but; and yet	slightly adversative
even	= **etiam**
either... or	with other conjunctions

facio ~**ere**, **feci**, **factum** (1) to create, make, do, commit; happen, come about (w. **ut**) (2) *ppl. noun* **factum** ~**i** *neut.* deed, action, misdeed

hic haec, hoc (1) *adj.* this (of what is near in time, place, or thought), **hoc est** that is, namely (2) *pron.* this one, he, she, it

	m.	*f.*	*neut.*	*m.*	*f.*	*neut.*
nom.	hic	haec	hoc	hi	hae	haec
gen.	huius	huius	huius	horum	harum	horum
dat.	huic	huic	huic	his	his	his
acc.	hunc	hanc	hoc	hos	has	haec
abl.	hoc	hac	hoc	his	his	his

ille ~a, ~ud *pron. adj.* that, those (of what is remote); this, these (of what follows); that (time, period), **ille aut ille** this or that; LATE often merely equivalent to **is ea, id**

	m.	*f.*	*neut.*	*m.*	*f.*	*neut.*
nom.	ille	illa	illud	illi	illae	illa
gen.	illius	illius	illius	illorum	illarum	illorum
dat.	illi	illi	illi	illis	illis	illis
acc.	illum	illam	illud	illos	illas	illa
abl.	illo	illa	illo	illis	illis	illis

in *prep.*

(1) *acc.*

into, towards, to, among, upon, against	direction
to, for, for the purpose of	purpose

(2) *abl.*

in, within, among, on, at	place
in, during	time
in the case of, with reference to	other relations
LATE by	instrumental

is ea, id (1) *pron.* he, she, it, they (2) *adj.* this, that, these, those, **id est** that is, that is to say; **id** that (followed by noun clause, relative clause, etc.)

	m.	*f.*	*neut.*	*m.*	*f.*	*neut.*
nom.	is	ea	id	ei	eae	ea
gen.	eius	eius	eius	eorum	earum	eorum
dat.	ei	ei	ei	eis	eis	eis
acc.	eum	eam	id	eos	eas	ea
abl.	eo	ea	eo	eis	eis	eis

meus ~a, ~um (1) *adj.* my, mine; my own (emphatic) (2) *neut. noun* my property, my friends, my family

	m.	*f.*	*neut.*	*m.*	*f.*	*neut.*
nom.	meus	mea	meum	mei	meae	mea
gen.	mei	meae	mei	meorum	mearum	meorum
dat.	meo	meae	meo	meis	meis	meis
acc.	meum	meam	meum	meos	meas	mea
abl.	meo	mea	meo	meis	meis	meis

nec, neque *conj.* not, and not, not even, **nec... nec** neither... nor

non *adv.* not (as the regular negative of a sentence or clause), not (negating an adj., adv., or equivalent phrase); "no" (in answers); occasionally equivalent to **ne** in prohibitions

omnis ~is, ~e (1) *adj. sg.* all, the whole (2) *adj. sg. distributively* every (3) *adj. pl.* any whatever (4) *m. pl. as noun* everyone (5) *neut. sg. as noun* the whole (6) *neut. pl. as noun* everything

	m.	*f.*	*neut.*	*m.*	*f.*	*neut.*
nom.	omnis	omnis	omne	omnes	omnes	omnia
gen.	omnis	omnis	omnis	omnium	omnium	omnium
dat.	omni	omni	omni	omnibus	omnibus	omnibus
acc.	omnem	omnem	omne	omnes	omnes	omnia
abl.	omni	omni	omni	omnibus	omnibus	omnibus

qui quae, quod (1) *rel. pron.* who, which, that, what (2) *interrogative adj.* what? which? what kind? (3) and he, but he (with ref. to antecedent in previous sentence or clause and acting as a connective, **qui** = *et is, sed is,* or similar)

	m.	*f.*	*neut.*	*m.*	*f.*	*neut.*
nom.	qui	quae	quod	qui	quae	quae
gen.	cuius	cuius	cuius	quorum	quarum	quorum
dat.	cui	cui	cui	quibus	quibus	quibus
acc.	quem	quam	quod	quos	quas	quae
abl.	quo	qua	quo	quibus	quibus	quibus

sed *conj.* but, yet, **sed et(iam)** but also, **sed tamen** but nevertheless

sum esse, fui to be, be in existence, be real, live

This is the most frequent verb in *Confessions* and is irregular in its conjugation, however, the majority of its usage is in the present and imperfect, which paradigms follow:

	INDICATIVE		SUBJUNCTIVE	

Present

	sg.	*pl.*	*sg.*	*pl.*
1	sum	sumus	sim	simus
2	es	estis	sis	sitis
3	est	sunt	sit	sint

Imperfect

	sg.	*pl.*	*sg.*	*pl.*
1	eram	eramus	essem	essemus
2	eras	eratis	esses	essetis
3	erat	erant	esset	essent

tu *pron.* you (*sg.*)

nom.	tu
gen.	tui
dat.	tibi
acc.	te
abl.	te

tuus ~a, ~um (1) *adj.* your, yours, dear to you, characteristic of you (2) *neut. as noun* your property, affairs, writings

	m.	*f.*	*neut.*	*m.*	*f.*	*neut.*
nom.	tuus	tua	tuum	tui	tuae	tua
gen.	tui	tuae	tui	tuorum	tuarum	tuorum
dat.	tuo	tuae	tuo	tuis	tuis	tuis
acc.	tuum	tuam	tuum	tuos	tuas	tua
abl.	tuo	tua	tuo	tuis	tuis	tuis

ut (1) *conj. with subjunctive* introduces various clauses:

in order that, that, to	purpose
so that, that	result
although	concession

(2) *adv.* as, just as, when, as soon as; how? (introducing a question)

absum abesse, afui (1) to be away, be absent, be distant; **absit** *interj.* Far be it! God forbid! (2) *ppl. adj.* **absens** ~**ntis** absent

abyssus ~**i** *f.* ECCL abyss, unfathomable depth; the sea; the place of the dead (Hell)

accipio ~**ipere,** ~**epi,** ~**eptum** (1) to take, receive, to take in one's grasp, take charge (2) *ppl adj.* **acceptus** ~**a,** ~**um** acceptable, welcome

ad *prep. acc.* to, towards, near to, at (direction); before, in the presence of (= **apud**); according to (manner); for (LATE end or final purpose, esp. **ad te** for you)

adhuc *adv.* up to the present time, so far, up to that time, still, yet, even

adsum ~**esse,** ~**fui** to be present

aduersus, -um *prep. acc.* against

aetas ~**atis** *f.* one's age, period or time of life (infancy, youth, old age, etc.)

aeternitas ~**atis** *f.* eternity

aeternus ~**a,** ~**um,** ~**ior** (1) *adj.* eternal (2) *adv.* **in aeternum** forever, for all ages

affectus ~**us** *m.* affection, disposition, eagerness, passion

agnosco ~**oscere,** ~**oui,** ~**itum** to recognize, know, identify

ago agere, egi, actum (1) to lead, do, act, perform, accomplish, deal with, behave, give (thanks); to pass, live, spend (time, life); to arrange (w. **cum**); to be done, happen, occur (pass.), to bring it about (pass. w. **ut**); Come! (colloq. imp.)

aio *defective* to say

aliquando *adv.* at some time or other, formerly, once, occasionally, at last

aliqui ~**qua,** ~**quod** *adj.* some, any

aliquis ~**qua,** ~**quid** *pron.* someone, anyone, something, anything

aliter *adv.* otherwise, in another way

alius ~**a,** ~**ud** *adj.* other, another

alius ~**a,** ~**ud** *pron.* another, something different (*neut.*)

alter ~**ra,** ~**rum** (1) *pron.* anyone else, the other (2) *adj.* a second, another, else

amicus ~**i** *m.* friend

amitto ~**ittere,** ~**isi,** ~**issum** to lose

amo ~**are,** ~**aui,** ~**atum** to love, delight in, desire, like, find congenial

amor ~**oris** *m.* love, desire, passion

amplius (1) *adv* more, further, in addition, besides (2) *noun* more

an *particle* or, whether, **utrum... an** whether... or; *introducing direct question* Can it really be that..?

angelus ~**i** *m.* [GRK ἄγγελος] ECCL angel, messenger of God

anima ~**ae** *f.* soul

animus ~**i** *m.* mind, disposition, purpose, intention, courage

annus ~**i** *m.* year, age (in years)

ante *prep. acc.* before, in front of (place or time)

antequam *conj.* before

aperio ~**ire,** ~**ui,** ~**tum** (1) to open, reveal, make known, explain (2) *ppl. adj.* **apertus** ~**a,** ~**um,** ~**ior,** ~**issimus** clear, straightforward

appareo ~**ere,** ~**ui,** ~**itum** (1) to appear, be visible be seen, be found, show itself, occur (2) *ppl. adj.* **apparens** ~**ntis** visible, evident

appello ~**are,** ~**aui,** ~**atum** to call, term, designate, give a name, appeal to a higher authority

apud *prep. acc.* at, near, within, in the presence of (place); in the writings of, "in" (a writer), in (a book); in the practice, habit of

aqua ~**ae** *f.* water

arbitror ~**ari,** ~**atus** (also **o** ~**are**) to think, be of the opinion

ars ~tis *f.* (1) *sg.* art, skill, artistry (2) *pl.* pursuits, studies, the (liberal) arts

at *conj.* but, however, on the other hand

atque, ac (before consonants) *conj.* and, and also; and what is more (emphatic); and yet, yet (slightly adversative)

attendo ~dere, ~di, ~tum to pay attention, look, listen

auctoritas ~atis *f.* authority, power

audio ~ire, ~iui or ~ii, ~itum to hear, hear with understanding; to learn

aufero ~rre, abstuli, ablatum to carry off, remove, kill

auris ~is *f.* (1) *sg.* ear (2) *pl.* sense of hearing

aut *conj.* or, or else (introducing an alternative, usually exclusive); **aut... aut** either... or

autem *particle* (*in second position*) on the other hand, again, furthermore, and in fact (usu. in parenthesis); but (expr. contrast without any adversative sense)

beatus ~a, ~um, ~ior, ~issimus *adj.* blessed, happy

bene, melius, optime *adv.* well, proficiently, better (*compar.*), best (*superl.*)

bonus ~a, ~um, melior, optimus (1) *adj.* good, competent, virtuous, genuine, kind, better (*compar.*, see **melior**), best (*superl.*) (2) *neut. as noun* good thing, blessing, benefit, advantage

breuis ~is, ~e, ~ior, ~issimus *adj.* short, small

caelum ~i *neut.* heaven (as distinct from **terra**); ECCL Heaven, as the created state that participates in God's eternity

canto ~are, ~aui, ~atum to sing, to recite (poetry), to sing in verse, to say or urge repeatedly

cantus ~us *m.* song, singing, tone

capio ~ere, cepi, ~tum (1) to (be able to) contain, have room for, hold, take into the hand, grasp (mentally), to capture (2) *ppl adj.* **captus ~a, ~um** captured, captive (as noun)

caritas ~atis *f.* love, affection; ECCL love, fraternal love (the chief theological virtue)

caro ~nis *f.* also **carnis** *f.* flesh; ECCL the body, the flesh (as adversary to the spirit)

causa ~ae *f.* (1) cause, reason, affair, concern, legal proceedings (2) *prep. abl.* **causa** for the purpose, for the sake of (placed after the gen. it governs)

cerno ~ere, creui, cretum to see, to discern, distinguish

certe *adv.* certainly, surely, at least

certus ~a, ~um, ~ior, ~issimus *adj.* fixed, certain, definite, unmistakable, manifest; assured, confident (of the mind, feelings)

ceterus ~a, ~um (1) *adj.* the rest of, the other (2) *pron.* the others, the rest; (3) *adv.* **ceterum** apart from this, in other respects

cibus ~i *m.* food

clamo ~are, ~aui, ~atum to cry out, to shout the name of, call by name

coaeternus ~a, ~um *adj.* ECCL co-eternal (esp. of the Father and the Son)

coepi ~isse, ~tum (1) to begin to (usu. w infinitive) (2) *ppl. noun* **coeptum ~i** *neut. pl.* undertaking

cogitatio ~onis *f.* thought, reflection

cogito ~are, ~aui, ~atum to think, think about, bear in mind

cognosco ~oscere, ~oui, ~itum to get to know, study, learn, find to be

cogo ~ere, coegi, coactum to compel, force, round up

commemoro ~are, ~aui, ~atum to recall (usu. to someone else; also, to oneself)

comprehendo ~dere, ~di, ~sum to comprehend, understand, express in words, take hold of

confessio ~onis *f.* confession, admission; ECCL (1) praise to God (the normative meaning within the Psalms); confession of sin (the more colloquial sense); admission of a belief (2) *pl.* as the title of the present work and A.'s reference to the work itself

confiteor ~**fiteri,** ~**fessus sum** to admit a fact, confess a crime; ECCL to give praise, to confess sin, to acknowledge gratefully

conligo ~**igere,** ~**egi,** ~**ectum** to gather together, collect, bind, join, unite

conor ~**ari,** ~**atus** to attempt, try; to attempt to go, rise, speak (ellipt.)

considero ~**are,** ~**aui,** ~**atum** to consider closely, think about, bear in mind

conspectus ~**us** *m.* view, vision; sight

consuetudo ~**inis** *f.* a habitual or usual practice, usage, custom, habit

contineo ~**inere,** ~**inui,** ~**entum** (1) to contain (2) *ppl. adj.* **contentus** ~**a,** ~**um,** ~**ior** content, contented, satisfied (3) *ppl. adj.* **continens** ~**ntis,** ~**ntior,** ~**ntissimus** self-restrained, continuous; ECCL continent (chaste)

contra (1) *adv.* in opposition, on the other hand, on the contrary (2) *prep. acc.* against, contrary to

conuerto ~**tere,** ~**ti,** ~**sum** to turn, turn around, turn (one's eyes or face) towards a given object; ECCL to convert, to turn to God in sorrow for sin

cor cordis *neut.* the heart as the center of thought, memory, and other mental processes, the seat of volition, the seat of conscience, the seat of character and emotions; ECCL the soul

coram (1) *prep. abl.* in the presence of, before (2) *adv.* face to face

corporalis ~**is,** ~**e** *adj.* corporeal

corporeus ~**a,** ~**um** *adj.* bodily, material

corpus ~**oris** *neut.* body (as opposed to soul), person, the whole self, structure, object

creator ~**oris** *m.* creator (of the world)

creatura ~**ae** *f.* ECCL creative act, created thing or person, the creation as a whole

credo ~**ere,** ~**idi,** ~**itum** to believe; to have faith or confidence in, trust, rely on (w.

dat.); to think, suppose, imagine; ECCL (1) to have faith in, (often with **in** + acc. or abl.) (2) *ppl. noun* **credens** ~**ntis** *m.* the believing faithful, believers

creo ~**are,** ~**aui,** ~**atum** to create, cause

cresco ~**ere, creui, cretum** to grow, grow up

cuius ~**a,** ~**um** *adj.* of whom, whose, whose?

cupiditas ~**atis** *f.* cupidity, carnal desire

cupio ~**ere,** ~**iui** or ~**ii,** ~**itum** (1) to desire, long for, wish (2) *ppl. adj.* **cupiens** ~**ntis** eager

cur *adv.* why, why?

cura ~**ae** *f.* care, concern, charge

curo ~**are,** ~**aui,** ~**atum** to care for, have concern for, regard anxiously, treat, cure, undertake, see to (a task)

de *prep. abl.* from, down from, away from, out of (position or time); from, of, out of (in partitive sense); on account of, from (cause); concerning, of, in regard to, as to (a subject, thought or speech)

debeo ~**ere,** ~**ui,** ~**itum** (1) to owe; to be bound by (logic, destiny or nature) (2) *ppl. noun* **debitum** ~**i** *neut.* what is owed, debt

delecto ~**are,** ~**aui,** ~**atum** to be delighted, allure; to enjoy oneself (refl.), take pleasure (pass.)

desero ~**ere,** ~**ui,** ~**tum** (1) to desert, leave, forsake, abandon (2) *ppl adj.* **desertus** ~**a,** ~**um** deserted, uninhabited (b) *neut. pl. noun* wilderness

desidero ~**are,** ~**aui,** ~**atum** to desire, long for; to miss someone

desiderium ~**ii** *neut.* desire, longing

dies ~**ei** *m. (f.)* day

diligo ~**igere,** ~**exi,** ~**ectum** (1) to love, have a special regard for (2) *ppl. adj.* **dilectus** ~**a,** ~**um** beloved (3) *ppl. adj.* **diligens** ~**ntis** diligent

dimitto ~**ittere,** ~**isi,** ~**issum** to send away, dismiss, let go, allow to go away; LATE to permit, allow; ECCL to forgive, remit sins

discerno ~**ernere, ~reui, ~retum** to discern; to separate or divide off

disco ~**ere, didici** to learn, get to know

displiceo ~**ere, ~ui, ~itum** to displease, offend

do dare, dedi, datum (1) to give, confer gratuitously, give possession of, make a gift of, grant (2) *ppl. noun* **datum** ~**i** *neut.* gift

doceo ~**ere, ~ui, ~tum** (1) to teach, instruct (2) *ppl. adj.* **doctus** ~**a, ~um, ~ior, ~issimus adj.** learned, educated

doctrina ~**ae** *f.* teaching, instruction, art

doleo ~**ere, ~ui, ~itum** to feel pained, be grieved

dolor ~**oris** *m.* pain, suffering, sorrow, grief

domus ~**us** (~**i**) *f.* house, household, home

donec *conj.* until

donum ~**i** *neut.* gift

duco ~**cere, ~xi, ~ctum** to lead, draw, guide; to obtain (from a source), derive

dulcis ~**is, ~e, ~ior, ~issimus** *adj.* sweet, melodious, delightful, cherished

dum (1) *conj.* while, until, as long as; provided that, if only, in order that (in final sense) (2) *adv.* so long as, yet

duo ~**ae, ~o** *adj.* two

ecce *interj.* look!

ecclesia ~**ae** *f.* [GRK ἐκκλησία] assembly; ECCL the Catholic church, a local church, a church building, the Church as the mystery of salvation revealed in the Scriptures, variously represented as Body of Christ, Spouse, Mother.

enim *particle (in second position)* for, namely, in fact, indeed (introducing the ground or reason for something previously said)

eo ire, ii or iui, itum to go, proceed, make one's way, set out, depart (passive use is always impersonal); ECCL to walk in the way of life

ergo *particle* for that reason, therefore, then, so, accordingly (introducing a resultant event, state of affairs, etc.)

error ~**oris** *m.* error, fault, wandering (fig.)

etiam *particle* still, yet, even now, also, in addition, as well, too, actually

etiamsi, etiam si *conj.* even if, even though

etsi, et si *conj.* even if, although

ex, e *prep. abl.* out of, from, out of (place); of, from (source); from, since (time); from, on account of (cause)

exaudio ~**ire, ~iui, ~itum** to listen or attend to; to heed (a prayer or suppliant)

experior ~**iri, ~tus** (1) to experience, find by experience (a person, thing to be of a given sort), test (2) *ppl. adj.* **expertus** ~**a, ~um, ~issimus** well-proved, tested (3) *ppl. adj.* **experiens** ~**ntis** active; LATE experienced

extendo ~**dere, ~di, ~tum** to extend, stretch forth, stretch out; LATE to long for

facies ~**iei** *f.* face, countenance, form, appearance

facile ~**ius, ~lime** *adv.* easily, willingly, readily, carelessly

fallo ~**ere, fefelli, ~sum** to deceive

falsus ~**a, ~um, ~ior, ~issimus** (1) *adj.* erroneous, untrue, false, not genuine, spurious, unhistorical (2) *neut. as noun* untruth, falsehood, lie

fero ~**rre, tuli, latum** to bear, carry, endure, speak of, tell

fidelis ~**is, ~e, ~ior, ~issimus** *adj.* keeping faith, faithful, constant, loyal, devoted; ECCL *as noun* a baptized Christian, the Faithful (*pl.*)

fides ~**ei** *f.* belief, confidence; ECCL the faith, faith (as one of the three theological virtues)

filius ~**(i)i** *m.* son; ECCL descendant

finio ~**ire, ~iui, ~itum** (1) to limit, end, put an end to (2) *ppl. adj.* **finitus** ~**a, ~um** finite

finis ~is *m.* (*f.*) the end, purpose

fio fieri to take place, occur, arise, produce, to come about (with **ut**, **ne**, etc.)

firmamentum ~i *neut.* support, prop, strengthening, mainstay; LATE the sky, firmament

fleo ~ere, ~eui, ~etum to weep

fons ~ntis *m.* fountain, spring, source

forma ~ae *f.* form, appearance

formo ~are, ~aui, ~atum to form, mold, fashion, shape

forte *adv.* by chance, maybe, perhaps

fortis ~is, ~e, ~ior, ~issimus *adj.* strong, brave

fructus ~us (~i) *m.* enjoyment, useful things, fruit of a tree or plant, produce, profit, reward; ECCL fruit of a good or evil will (fig.)

fugio ~ere, **fugi** to flee, desert, speed away or past, shun

futurus ~a, ~um (1) *adj.* [as future participle of **sum**] what is to be, coming, future, immediately future, impending, imminent (2) *neut. as noun* the future (*sg.*), future events (*pl.*)

gaudeo ~dere, **gauisus** to be happy, be pleased, rejoice

gaudium ~(i)i *neut.* joy

genus ~eris *neut.* race, kind, type, tribe; class (phil.)

grandis ~is, ~e, ~ior, ~issimus *adj.* huge, great, grand, full-grown, mature

gratia ~iae *f.* (1) thanks (w. dat. and ellipsis of verb); ECCL grace as unmerited favor (2) *prep abl.* **gratia** for the sake of (w. gen., usu. placed after its noun) (3) *adv.* **gratis** gratuitously, for its own sake

grauis ~is, ~e, ~ior, ~issimus *adj.* grievous, heavy, oppressive, serious, weighty

habeo ~ere, ~ui, ~itum to hold, possess, consider, regard

hinc *adv.* from this place, from this source, on this account

homo ~inis *m.* human being (of either sex), individual person, the person or individual concerned, the man in question

honor, ~os ~oris *m.* honor, dignity, a (high) public or political office

hora ~ae *f.* hour

humanus ~a, ~um, ~ior, ~issimus (1) *adj.* human (2) *neut. pl. as noun* human affairs, the human fate

iam *adv.* now, already, presently, at this/that stage or point; **non iam** not indeed, no longer (and similarly with other negatives)

ibi *adv.* there, in that place, in that context

idem eadem, idem *pron. adj.* the same (identical with that previously mentioned or under discussion)

ideo *adv.* for that reason, for the reason (that), therefore

igitur *conj.* in that case, so then, accordingly

ignoro ~are, ~aui, ~atum to have no knowledge, be ignorant or unaware of, not know, be unfamiliar with

imago ~inis *f.* image, representation

impero ~are, ~aui, ~atum to command, order; to give orders to (w. dat.)

impleo ~ere, ~eui, ~etum to fill, fulfill

incommutabilis ~is, ~e *adj.* immutable, unchangeable

incompositus ~a, ~um (1) *adj.* not well put together, badly arranged, irregular; disorganized (esp. of speech or writing)

inde *adv.* from that place, from there, from that point; from which (as equivalent to a pronoun, e.g., quo, qua, quibus)

indico ~are, ~aui, ~atum to point out, reveal

infinitus ~a, ~um, ~ior (1) *adj.* infinite (2) *noun* infinitude

informis ~is, ~e, ~ior *adj.* formless, featureless

informitas ~atis *f.* LATE shapelessness, formlessness

inimicus ~a, ~um, ~ior, ~issimus (1) *adj.* unfriendly, ill-disposed, hostile, harmful (2) *noun* personal enemy

iniquitas ~atis *f.* ECCL sin, iniquity (classical usage with basic sense of "unfairness" completely supplanted)

inlumino ~are, ~aui, ~atum to illuminate; ECCL to enlighten

inquam *defective* (1) to say (usu. following direct speech) (2) I mean (in 1st person sg., emphasizing a word, phrase, or sentence)

inrideo ~dere, ~si, ~sum to ridicule, mock, laugh at, scorn

intellego ~gere, ~xi, ~ctum to grasp mentally, understand, realize

intendo ~dere, ~di, ~tum (1) to concentrate, pay attention to (2) *ppl adj.* **intentus** ~a, ~um, ~ior, ~issimus intent, closely listening, closely attentive

inter *prep. acc.* in (or into) the presence of, among, amid, between

interior ~or, ~us (1) *compar. adj.* interior, inner, deeper, hidden, inward (2) *neut. pl. as noun* depths

interrogo ~are, ~aui, ~atum to ask, question, inquire of

intro ~are, ~aui, ~atum to go into, enter

intueor ~eri, ~itus to fix one's gaze upon; to consider, give attention to

intus (1) *adv.* inwardly (2) *prep. gen.* within

inuenio ~enire, ~eni, ~entum to find, come upon, meet, discover

inuisibilis ~is, ~e *adj.* invisible

inuoco ~are, ~aui, ~atum to call upon, invoke, summon for assistance, pray for; ECCL to call into (fig.)

ipse ~a, ~um *pron.* himself (herself, itself, oneself, myself, etc.); LATE sometimes equivalent to **hic**, **ille**, **is** or **idem**

iste ~a, ~ud *pron. adj.* LATE practically equivalent to **hic haec, hoc** and only rarely as in classical second person "that of yours"

ita *adv.* so, thus, in that way; in the same way... as (in comparisons)

itaque *adv.* and so, accordingly, in consequence (expr. result or inference)

iubeo ~bere, ~ssi, ~ssum to order, tell someone to do something, decree

iudicium ~(i)i *neut.* court of law, judgment; ECCL judgment or ordinance of God

iudico ~are, ~aui, ~atum to judge, render a judgment

iustitia ~ae *f.* justice, fairness, equity; ECCL justice, righteousness, as both piety toward God, and justice toward neighbor

iustus ~a, ~um, ~ior, ~issimus *adj.* just, fair; ECCL (1) *adj.* just in giving decrees, impartial in judgment (of God); righteous, as both pious toward God, and charitable toward neighbor (2) *noun* a just person

lacrima ~ae *f.* tears

laetitia ~ae *f.* delight, pleasure, gladness

laudo ~are, ~aui, ~atum to praise, approve, speak well of

laus ~dis *f.* praise

lego ~ere, legi, lectum to read

lex legis *f.* law

liber ~bri *m.* book, volume, roll, a single volume or chapter of a longer work

libido ~inis *f.* lustful desire, whim

lingua ~ae *f.* tongue, speech, utterance, language

littera ~ae *f.* letter of the alphabet, early education, lessons, literary works, personal letters

locus ~i *m.* place, position, a place or passage in a book

longe ~ius, ~issime *adv.* far, a long way, a long while

longus ~a, ~um, ~ior, ~issimus (1) *adj.* long, lengthy (2) *neut. as noun* length (3) *adv.* **longum** long

loquor ~i, locutus to speak, talk, say

lumen ~inis *neut.* light, illumination, eye

lux lucis *f.* light

magis, maxime *adv.* more, rather, to a greater extent; as much... as; not so much... as (w. neg.); especially, most of all (w. *superl.*)

magister ~tri *m.* professional teacher, professor, teacher of rhetoric, grammar, law, etc., schoolmaster, tutor

magnus ~a, ~um, maior, maximus *adj.* great in size or extent, big, vast, great in degree, mighty, distinguished, famous

maior ~or, ~us [*compar.* to **magnus**] (1) *adj.* greater, older, more distinguished, more powerful (2) *m. pl. as noun* elders, grown ups

malus ~a, ~um, peior, pessimus (1) *adj.* bad, evil, wicked, harmful (2) *neut. as noun* trouble, distress, pain, hardship; evil-doing, wickedness

maneo ~ere, ~si, ~sum to remain, abide

manus ~us *f.* hand

mare ~is *neut.* sea

mater ~tris *f.* mother

materia ~ae (~es ~ei) *f.* material, substance, primal matter

melior ~or, ~us [*compar.* of **bonus**] (1) *adj.* better, kinder, more gracious (2) *neut. pl. as noun* better things, a better course

melius *compar. adv.* see **bene**

membrum ~i *neut.* limb, a part of the body

memini ~inisse to remember, recall (perfect used with present force)

memoria ~ae *f.* memory, memorial shrine

mendacium ~ii *neut.* lie, falsehood, deception, illusion

mens ~tis *f.* mind, intellect

-met *enclitic particle* attached for emphasis to certain pronouns

metior ~iri, mensus (metitus) to measure

minor ~or, ~us [*compar.* of **paruus**] *adj.* lesser, smaller, younger

minus *compar. adv.* less, not fully, not perfectly, not adequately (as a mild negative)

miror ~ari, ~atus to marvel, admire, wonder at

mirus ~a, ~um, ~ior, ~issimus (1) *adj.* strange, wonderful (2) wonder, surprise (*neut.* as pred. of various clauses) e.g., it is no wonder that...

miser ~era, ~erum, ~erior, ~errimus (1) *adj.* wretched (2) *m. as noun* wretched one, wretched me

misereor ~eri, ~tus *usu. w. gen.* to take pity on, show compassion, feel pity; also **miseror ~ari, ~atus**

miseria ~ae *f.* wretched or pitiful condition, affliction, distress

misericordia ~ae *f.* compassion, pity, tender-heartedness

mitto ~ere, misi, missum to send, put forth

modus ~i *m.* mode, measure, manner, fashion, way, style, length, number, kind, form, type, mode of being

moles ~is *f.* a large mass, lump

morior ~i, ~tuus (1) to die (2) *ppl. adj.* **mortuus ~a, ~um** dead

mors ~tis *f.* death

mos moris *m.* custom, cultural norms (esp. as a guide to action), character, disposition

motus ~us *m.* movement, motion, emotion, stirring (of the mind), gesture

moueo ~ere, moui, motum to move, distress

multus ~a, ~um (1) *adj.* many, numerous (2) *as noun* many people, many things (3) *adv.* **multo** by far, much (4) *adv.* **multum** greatly (w. verbs), very (w. adj.)

mundus ~i *m.* the earth, the universe, the world (usu. spatial); ECCL the world as a temporal order both evil and passing away (opposed to Heaven and Eternity) esp. **hic mundus** this world

mutabilis ~is, ~e, ~ior *adj.* mutable, changeable, fluctuating, uncertain

muto ~**are,** ~**aui,** ~**atum** to change, modify, alter

nam *particle* for (explanatory), certainly, to be sure; yes (affirmative or assenting)

narro ~**are,** ~**aui,** ~**atum** to tell, relate

nascor ~**i, natus** (1) to be born, come into existence, grow, produce (of fruits and crops) (2) *ppl. adj. indecl.* **natus** aged, so many years old

natura ~**ae** *f.* nature

ne (1) *negative conj.* in order that... not (2) lest (as the negative in prohibitions) (3) *adv.* not

-ne *interrogative enclitic particle* (1) is it so? (introduces direct questions but does not imply anything about the answer expected) (2) or...? (introducing an alternative in a question); **nonne** *interrogative particle* is it not so? (affirmative answer is anticipated)

nemo ~**inis** *m.* nobody, no one

nescio ~**ire,** ~**iui or** ~**ii,** ~**itum** to not know, be unaware, **nescio quis, nescio cuius, etc.** I know not who, what, whose, i.e., someone or other, something or other

nihil (1) *indecl. neut.* nothing (2) *adv.* by no means, not at all

nimis *adv.* too much (w. verbs), too (w. adj.)

nisi *conj.* unless, if not, except; **nisi quia/quod** except that, in so far as

nolo ~**lle,** ~**lui** to be unwilling, to refuse, **noli(te)** Do not —. (2nd person of imp. with infinitive to form a prohibition)

nomen ~**inis** *neut.* name, title, renown, mere name (on pretext of...)

nomino ~**are,** ~**aui,** ~**atum** to name, describe as, call, be celebrated (pass.)

nondum *adv.* not yet

nonne see **-ne**

nos *pron.* we, us

nosco ~**scere, noui, notum** (1) to know, learn (perfect tense often contracted, e.g., 'noram' for 'noueram'; 'nossem' for 'nouissem'; 'nosti' for 'nouisti'; 'noris' for 'noueris') (2) *ppl. adj.* **notus** ~**a,** ~**um,** ~**ior,** ~**issimus** known, well-known

noster ~**tra,** ~**trum** (1) *adj.* our, ours (can be used by an author in ref. to himself) (2) *as noun* our friends, family, things

nox ~**ctis** *f.* night

nullus ~**a,** ~**um** (1) *adj.* not any, no, none (2) *as noun* no one, nothing

numero ~**are,** ~**aui,** ~**atum** to reckon, count, number

numquam *adv.* at no time, never

numquid *interrogative particle* is it really possible that...? (negative answer is anticipated), surely... not? (implying anxiety, caution, incredulity, etc.)

nunc *adv.* now (as the present moment in one's narrative)

o *interj.* oh! (1) in exclamations expr. admiration, pleasure, horror, etc. (2) as a form of address

obliuiscor ~**uisci,** ~**tus** *w. acc. or gen.* to lose remembrance of, forget, forget oneself or one's identity

occultus ~**a,** ~**um,** ~**ior,** ~**issimus** (1) *adj.* hidden (2) *neut. pl. as noun* secrets, secret faults, hidden self

occurro ~**rrere,** ~**rri** ~**rsum** to meet, happen, present itself, occur (to a person, his mind, etc.)

oculus ~**i** *m.* eye, eyesight

odi ~**isse,** ~**osum** to have an aversion to, hate, dislike

omnino *adv.* at all, in any degree, in any circumstances, in every respect, in all circumstances, entirely, absolutely, altogether

optime *superl adv.* see **bene**

optimus ~**a,** ~**um** *superl. adj.* see **bonus**

opus ~**eris** *neut.* work, action, what is needful, **opus esse** to be needed, **opus habere** to have need

ordo ~**inis** *m.* order, arrangement, cycle

os oris *neut.* mouth, face (as implying the gaze)

parens ~**ntis** *m.* parent(s) (usu. *pl.*)

pars ~**tis** *f.* part, degree of a circle; party, side (in opposition to the other)

paruulus, -olus ~**a,** ~**um** (1) *adj.* little, tiny (2) *noun* a child, little one; ECCL child, little one (fig. with respect to humility)

paruus ~**a,** ~**um,** ~**issimus** *adj.* small, young, little, of no consequence, insignificant

pasco ~**cere, paui,** ~**tum** to feed, satisfy, gratify (hunger or another appetite), feed on (pass.)

pater ~**tris** *m.* father

patior ~**ti,** ~**ssus** to suffer, tolerate, bear, undergo

pax pacis *f.* peace

pecco ~**are,** ~**aui,** ~**atum** ECCL (1) to sin (classical usage with basic sense of "to err, make a mistake" completely supplanted) (2) *ppl. neut. noun* peccatum ~**i** sin (classical usage with basic sense of "mistake, error, misdemeanor" completely supplanted)

peior ~**or,** ~**us** *adj.* see **malus**

per *prep. acc.* through, over, across (motion); through, during (time); through, by means of, on account of (agency, means, cause, and manner)

perficio ~**icere,** ~**eci,** ~**ectum** (1) to perfect (2) *ppl adj.* **perfectus** ~**a,** ~**um,** ~**ior,** ~**issimus** perfect, mature, full-grown

pes pedis *m.* foot, step, metrical foot in a verse of poetry

peto ~**ere,** ~**iui,** ~**itum** to ask, seek, request, entreat

pietas ~**atis** *f.* piety, devotion

pius ~**a,** ~**um,** ~**issimus** *adj.* pious, devoted

placeo ~**ere,** ~**ui or** ~**itus** (1) to be pleasing or acceptable, seem good to; to be resolved or agreed (in perfect tense impers.) (2) *ppl. adj.* **placitus** ~**a,** ~**um,** ~**issimus** approved (b) **placitum** ~**i** *neut.* condition

(leg.); LATE convention, agreement, resolution, decision, plan

plenus ~**a,** ~**um,** ~**ior,** ~**issimus** *adj.* full

plus ~**ris** (1) *neut.* more, many (2) *pl. adj.* more (3) *adv.* more, more so

pono ponere, posui, positum to put, place, lay down, bury, set down, state, turn (one's back); to station (mil.)

populus ~**i** *m.* the people; ECCL Christian people

possum posse, potui (1) to be able, be able to (w. infinitive), **potest** it can be done or happen, it is possible (impersonal) (2) *ppl adj.* **potens** ~**ntis,** ~**ntior,** ~**ntissimus** powerful, capable of

post (1) *prep. acc.* after, behind (2) *adv.* after, afterwards, later

postea *adv.* afterwards, later

potestas ~**atis** *f.* (1) power (2) *pl.* higher authorities, the powerful

potius *adv.* rather, more than

prae *prep. abl.* in front of (movement), before (in merit or regard); in comparison with; LATE more than (comparison)

praesens ~**ntis,** ~**ntior,** ~**ntissimus** (1) *adj.* present, face to face, in person (2) *neut. pl. as noun* present transitory things

praeter (1) *prep. acc.* beyond, except (2) *adv.* as well, besides (3) *conj.* besides, apart from, except

praetereo ~**ire,** ~**ii or** ~**iui,** ~**itum** (1) to pass over, omit, to pass (time) (2) **praeteritus** ~**a,** ~**um** (a) *adj.* past, gone by (b) *neut. pl. as noun* the past, one's past

primus ~**a,** ~**um** [*superl.* to **prior**] (1) *adj.* first, foremost (2) *adv.* **primum** first (3) *neut. as noun* first part

principium ~**(i)i** *neut.* beginning

prior ~**or,** ~**us** *compar. adj.* earlier, previous, superior to (w. abl. of comparison)

prius *adv.* **priusquam** *conj.* before, first, earlier

pro *prep. abl.* before, in front of, on behalf of, instead of, in return for, on account of, for the sake of, in comparison with, in proportion to; LATE for (final purpose)

propter (1) *adv.* near (2) *prep. acc.* on account of, because, **propter quod** for which reason

puer ~**eri** *m.* boy, child

pulcher ~**chra,** ~**chrum,** ~**chrior,** ~**cherrimus** (1) *adj.* beautiful (2) *neut. as noun* beauty

puto ~**are,** ~**aui,** ~**atum** to think, suppose, ponder, consider to be, regard as, deem

quaero ~**rere,** ~**si or** ~**siui,** ~**situm** to try to find, search for, seek, ask

qualis ~**is,** ~**e** *adj.* what sort of? of which sort, **talis… qualis** such… as

quam *adv.* how? how, **quam… tam** as much… so much; than (w. *compar.*); as much as possible (w. *superl.*); rather than (with omission of *compar.*); **quam** (used alone to introduce a clause following comparison)

quamquam *rel. adv.* however much, although

quamuis *rel. adv.* however much, although

quando *adv.* when? when, since

quantus ~**a,** ~**um** (1) *adj.* how much? how many? how great, how many, what a (2) *adv.* **quanto** by how much, how much, by as much as, **quanto… tanto** the more… the more; (3) *adv.* **quantum** as much as, to the greatest degree I can (with **possum** or similar)

quasi (1) *conj.* as, as if, as though (2) *adv.* practically, as it were

-**que** *enclitic conj.* and

quemadmodum *adv.* as (for example), in the manner in which, in what way?

quia *conj.* because, since; ECCL that (sometimes introduces indirect discourse in place of infinitive accusative construction)

quidam quaedam, quoddam *adj.* a certain, a kind of, so to speak, as it were

quidam quaedam, quiddam *pron.* a certain one

quidem *particle* certainly, even, at least (placed directly after the word it emphasizes)

quippe *particle* for (explanatory), indeed (confirmatory)

quis quid (1) *interrogative pron. adj.* who? what or which person? what? what or which thing? (2) *rel. pron.* whoever, whatever (3) *adv.* **quid** why?

quis qua or quae, quid (1) *indef. pron.* anybody, anything, **si quis, si quid** anyone who, anything that (2) *adj.* any (**quis** and **quid** only)

quisquam quicquam *pron.* any person, anyone at all, anything, anything whatever

quisque quaeque, quidque, quicque or quodque (1) *pron.* each one, everyone; each person (thing) according as he (it) is more — (w. *compar.*) (2) *adj.* each, every

quisquis quidquid (1) *pron.* anyone who, everyone who, whoever, anything that, all that, whatever (2) *adj.* any — that

quo *interrogative adv.* to what place? where? to what end or purpose? what for?

quo *conj.* on account of which, whence, whereby, thereby (connecting sentences, etc.), the more (esp. with *compar.*)

quod *adv. conj.* because, since, that, as to the fact that; that (to introduce indirect statement after verbs of perceiving, saying, etc)

quomodo, quo modo *adv.* in what way, how, how is it possible that? (in rhet. questions or similar)

quoniam *conj.* in view of the fact that, since, seeing that, inasmuch as (as pure causal conjunction)

quoque *adv.* likewise (correspondence); besides, also (additive); even, indeed, actually (emphatic)

rapio ~ere, ~ui, ~tum to snatch away, to drag off, to attract strongly, to impel; LATE to catch a glimpse of

ratio ~onis *f.* reason, common sense, reckoning, method, manner, way

recedo ~dere, ~ssi, ~ssum to draw back (from a place, someone's presence, etc.), retire, withdraw

recolo ~ere, ~ui, recultum to recall

recordor ~ari, ~atus to call to mind, recollect

reddo ~ere, ~idi, ~itum to repay, to give back, to restore

redeo ~ire, ~ii, ~itum to come or go back, return

relinquo ~inquere, ~iqui, ~ictum to sever one's connection with, forsake, leave

requiesco ~escere, ~eui, ~etum to rest, find repose

res rei *f.* (1) thing, matter, affair, fact, circumstance, undertaking, property (2) *pl.* nature, circumstances

resisto ~istere, ~titi *usu. w. dat.* to resist, oppose, withstand

respondeo ~dere, ~di, ~sum (1) to respond, answer, reply (2) *ppl. noun* **responsum ~i** *neut.* response, answer, reply

rursus ~um *adv.* again, anew, in turn, now again

sacramentum ~i *neut.* solemn obligation, sworn oath; ECCL sacrament, a sacred thing possessing a mysterious character as (1) the theological or doctrinal mysteries of the faith, or (2) the particular rites of the Church esp. baptism and Eucharist

saeculum ~uli *neut.* age, generation, the world (usu. temporal); ECCL this world, the present evil age (as opposed to Heaven and Eternity)

saepe ~ius, ~issime *adv.* often, many times

salus ~utis *f.* safety, deliverance, bodily health; ECCL salvation, health of the soul, deliverance from sin

sanctus ~a, ~um, ~ior, ~issimus (1) *adj.* holy, sacred (2) *m. pl. as noun* ECCL saints, holy ones

sano ~are, ~aui, ~atum to cure physically, heal, restore to health

sapientia ~ae *f.* wisdom, understanding, wisdom as the special study and goal of philosophers

satis, sat (1) *indecl. noun* enough (2) *adv.* sufficiently

scientia ~ae *f.* knowledge

scio ~ire, ~ii or ~iui, ~itum (1) to know, to know what, whether, etc. (with indirect question), to be aware (2) *ppl. adj.* **sciens ~ntis** knowing, aware

scribo ~bere, ~psi, ~ptum (1) to write (2) *ppl. noun* **scriptum ~i** *neut.* writings, written law

scriptura ~ae *f.* writing, a text; ECCL the Sciptures of the Old and New Testament, a passage within Scripture

se, sese *reflexive pron.* himself, herself, itself, themselves (direct reflexive, with ref. to the subject of its clause); **se** he, she, it, they (as pronoun representing subject of verb of speaking, etc., in acc. and infinitive construction); **sese** each other (reciprocal)

secundum *prep. acc.* according to, next, after

semper *adv.* always, forever

sensus ~us *m.* sense (any one of the five physical senses), the faculties of perception (mental and physical), sensation, understanding, consciousness

sententia ~ae *f.* thought, sentiment, opinion, phrase, sentence

sentio ~tire, ~si, ~sum (1) to perceive, feel, see, learn, understand, think, experience sensation, have consciousness (2) *ppl. noun* **sensa ~orum** *neut. pl.* thoughts

sequor ~qui, ~cutus (1) to pursue, follow after (2) *ppl. adj.* **sequens ~ntis** next, following

sermo ~**onis** *m.* speech, conversation, word, sermon

seruio ~**ire, ~iui or ~ii, ~itum** *w. dat.* to serve (a master) in the capacity of slave, wait on, be the servant of, be subject to, be of service to

seruus ~**i** *m.* slave, servant

si *conj.* if, even if (with concessive force)

sic *adv.* in this way, thus, so

sicut, sicuti *conj.* as, such as, as if

signum ~**i** *neut.* sign, symbol, marker

similis ~**is, ~e, ~ior, ~limus** *adj.* similar, like, resembling

simul *adv.* at the same time, as well, together

sine *prep. abl.* without

singuli ~**ae, ~a** *pl. adj.* each one, individual, single, one only

sino sinere, siui, situm (1) to permit, allow (2) *ppl. adj.* **situs** ~**a, ~um** situated

siue, seu *conj.* either... or

sol solis *m.* the sun

soleo ~**ere, ~itus** (1) to be usual, used to, accustomed to (2) *ppl. adj.* **solitus** ~**a, ~um** usual, customary (b) *neut. as noun* usual thing

solus ~**a, ~um** (1) *adj.* alone, only one (2) *adv.* **solum** only, just

sono ~**are (~ere), ~ui, ~itum** (1) to make a sound, utter audibly, echo (2) *ppl. adj.* **sonans** ~**ntis** sonorous, vocalized, noisy

sonus ~**i** *m.* sound, articulate sound, speech

spatium ~**ii** *neut.* space, interval, distance

species ~**ei** *f.* beauty, attractiveness; appearance

spes ~**ei** *f.* hope, prospect; ECCL hope (as one of the three theological virtues)

spiritalis ~**is, ~e** ECCL (1) *adj.* spiritual (as opposed to corporeal or carnal) (2) *noun* spiritual matters, spiritual beings, spiritual ones i.e., sincere, thoughtful Christians

spiritus ~**us** *m.* spirit, soul, breath; ECCL a spirit, spiritual being

sto stare, steti, statum to stand, stand firm, be established

studium ~**(i)i** *neut.* zeal, effort, eagerness, pursuit, study, interest

sub *prep.* (1) *abl.* under (2) *acc.* below

substantia ~**ae** *f.* substance, underlying nature, one's possessions

summus ~**a, ~um** *adj.* highest (in position), uppermost, supreme, highest (in degree)

super *prep.* (1) *acc.* higher than, above, upon; ECCL more than (2) *abl.* on top of, concerning (3) *adv.* over (with verbs of pouring, etc.)

superbus ~**a, ~um, ~ior, ~issimus** (1) *adj.* proud, haughty, disdainful (2) *m. as noun* the proud

superfero ~**ferre, ~tuli, ~latum** to carry over

suspiro ~**are, ~aui, ~atum** to sigh

suus, ~os ~**a, ~um** *adj.* his, her, its, their; his own (in emphatic use)

taceo ~**ere, ~ui, ~itum** (1) to be silent, to say nothing, be silent about, pass over in silence (2) *ppl. adj.* **tacitus** ~**a, ~um** silent, quiet

talis ~**is, ~e** *adj.* of such a character or kind, **talis... qualis** such... as

tam *adv.* so, so much, so very, **quam... tam** as much... so much

tamen *adv.* in spite of what has been said, all the same, nevertheless

tamquam, tan- *conj.* just as (if), as, as though

tantus ~**a, ~um** (1) *adj.* so great, so much (w. **ut**), as great, as much, **tanto** by so much, the more (abl. w. *compar.*), **quanto... tanto** the more... the more (2) *adv.* **tantum, tantummodo** only, merely

temptatio ~**onis** *f.* ECCL temptation (classical usage with basic sense of "attempt, hostile enterprise" completely supplanted)

tempus ~**oris** *neut.* time, point of time, period, the proper time, occasion; at that time (abl. w. demonstrative, rel. or similar e.g., **eo tempore**)

tenebrae ~**arum** *f. pl.* darkness, blindness, obscurity; ECCL darkness (fig.) as effect of sin

teneo ~**ere**, ~**ui**, ~**tum** to have, hold, keep, maintain, embrace, keep in memory; LATE to regard, consider

terra ~**ae** *f.* earth (as distinct from **caelum**), dry land, the ground, dust, clay; ECCL material creation as distinct from the intellectual creation, life lived apart from grace (fig.)

timeo ~**ere**, ~**ui** to fear, dread, be afraid (2) *ppl. adj.* **timens** ~**ntis** *adj.* fearful, afraid (of)

totus ~**a**, ~**um** (1) *adj.* the whole, all, the entire (2) *neut. as noun* the whole thing, the whole world (3) *adv.* **totum** completely, absolutely, utterly

transeo ~**ire**, ~**iui** or ~**ii**, ~**itum** to pass, pass over, cross, cross over; to pass (time)

tres tres, tria *pl. adj.* three

tunc, tum *adv.* at that time, back then, then

ualde ~**ius**, ~**issime** *adv.* in a high degree (w. verbs), extremely, exceedingly (w. adj., adv., or equivalent phrases)

ualeo ~**ere**, ~**ui**, ~**itum** (1) to be strong enough, have the ability, prevail, avail (2) *ppl. adj.* **ualens** ~**ntis** strong, able

uanitas ~**atis** *f.* vanity, emptiness, foolish or empty pride

uanus ~**a**, ~**um**, ~**ior**, ~**issimus** (1) *adj.* vain, empty (2) *neut. pl. noun* vain things, vanities

ubi *adv.* where, where? when; in which (as equivalent to a pronoun, e.g., quo, qua, quibus and similar)

uel *particle* either, or, even, one might go so far as to say, actually, possibly, **uel... uel** either... or; -**ue** *enclitic conj.* or

uenio uenire, ueni, uentum to come

uerbum ~**i** *neut.* word, expression, saying

uere ~**ius**, ~**issime** *adv.* really, truly

ueritas ~**atis** *f.* truth, reality, actuality

uero *adv. particle* in truth, indeed, to be sure, unquestionably, on the other hand, however

uerum *conj.* but only, at the same time, **uerum tamen** but even so, nevertheless

uerus ~**a**, ~**um**, ~**ior**, ~**issimus** (1) *adj.* true, genuine, real, actual (2) *neut. as noun* the truth, fact

uia ~**ae** *f.* way, road, path, course, ways of knowledge (fig.)

uideo uidere, uidi, uisum (1) to see, perceive; to seem, appear, seem best (pass.), to seem to oneself, suppose or imagine that (w. dat. of reflexive) (2) *ppl. noun* **uisum** ~**i** *neut.* dream-vision, the sight (of something)

uir uiri *m.* husband, man

uis uis *f. pl. usu. in the forms* **uires, uirium** also **uim** (acc. sg) strength, force, capacity

uisibilis ~**is**, ~**e** *adj.* visible

uita ~**ae** *f.* life, way of life; ECCL spiritual life

uiuo ~**uere**, ~**xi**, ~**ctum** to be alive, live, make a living; ECCL to live spiritually

uiuus ~**a**, ~**um** (1) *adj.* living, alive; LATE vivid (2) *neut. sg. as noun* the quick

ullus ~**a**, ~**um** (1) *adj.* any at all (in negative constructions) (2) *as noun* anyone, anything, at all, **non ullus** none whatsoever! (emphatic variant of **nullus**)

unde *adv.* from what place? where from? from what source? from the place from which, from which point (in the narrative); from which (as equivalent to a pronoun, e.g., quo, qua, quibus and similar)

uniuersus ~**a**, ~**um** *adj.* the whole of, entire

unus ~**a**, ~**um** (1) *adj.* one (in number), a single, one above all others, only (2) *as noun* one person or thing

uoco ~**are**, ~**aui**, ~**atum** to call, call upon, name

uolo uelle, uolui (1) to want, wish for, desire to have, be willing (2) *ppl adj.* **uolens** ~**ntis** willing, intending

uoluntas ~**atis** *f.* desire, will

uoluptas ~**atis** *f.* pleasure, delight, enjoyment

uos *pron. pl.* you all

uox uocis *f.* voice, cry, sound, word

usque *adv.* all the way to, right up to, as far as, **usque ad** all the way back in time/ space to, **usque ab** ever since the time of

uterque utraque, utrumque (1) *adj.* each... of the two (2) *pron.* each person, each of two things

utique *adv.* absolutely, for certain, necessarily

utor ~**i, usus** *usu. w. abl.* to use, make use of, enjoy

utrum *particle* whether (introducing indirect question), **utrum... an** whether... or (introducing a disjunctive question)

uultus ~**us** *m.* look, facial expression, countenance; ECCL face

APPENDIX A: COMMON LATIN WORDS

This Appendix contains about 200 very common Latin words that Augustine uses infrequently in *Confessions*. While they are low-frequency relative to the rest of the text, they are too familiar to be included in the running glossary.

addo ~ere, ~idi, ~itum to add (to)

ager agri *m.* field

alienus ~a, ~um, ~ior, ~issimus (1) *adj.* not one's own, other's (2) *neut. as noun* others; what belongs to others

altus ~a, ~um, ~ior, ~issimus *adj.* high, tall, deep

arbor ~oris *f.* tree

arma ~orum *neut. pl.* arms, weapons

aspicio ~icere, ~exi, ~ectum to look at, look upon, behold

audeo ~dere, ~sus to dare (to)

aura ~ae *f.* breeze, air

aurum ~i *neut.* gold

bellum ~i *neut.* war, contention

beneficium ~(i)i *neut.* benefit, kindness

cado ~ere, cecidi, casum to fall, fall into

campus ~i *m.* field

caput ~itis *neut.* head, source, chapter

carmen ~inis *neut.* poem, verse, poetry

carus ~a, ~um, ~ior, ~issimus *adj.* dear, beloved

castrum ~i *neut.* camp, army

casus ~us *m.* fall, chance, by chance (abl.)

cedo ~dere, ~ssi, ~ssum to give way, concede, yield

ciuis ~is *m.* fellow citizen, citizen

ciuitas ~atis *f.* city

clarus ~a, ~um, ~ior, ~issimus *adj.* clear; famous, celebrated

claudo ~dere, ~si, ~sum to close, shut, shut in

colo ~ere, ~ui, cultum to worship; to cultivate

comes ~itis *m.* companion

compono ~onere, ~osui, ~ositum to compose, arrange, put in proper order

coniunx ~ugis *m. f.* spouse, wife

consilium ~ii *neut.* counsel, advice, purpose, plan, resolution

copia ~ae *f.* abundance, supply; opportunity (*usu. w. gen.*)

crimen ~inis *neut.* accusation (of), crime

cunctus ~a, ~um (1) *adj.* all (2) *neut. as noun* the whole, all

currus ~us *m.* chariot

cursus ~us *m.* course

deinde *adv.* then, afterwards, in the next place, from then on

desum ~esse, ~fui to be lacking, to fail

dextera ~(e)rae *f.* right hand

dignus ~a, ~um, ~ior, ~issimus *adj.* deserved, deserving, worthy

diu ~utius or **tamdiu** *adv.* long, for a long time

durus ~a, ~um, ~ior, ~issimus *adj.* hard, hard to bear, harsh, unbending

dux ~cis *m.* guide

equus ~i *m.* horse

eripio ~ipere, ~ipui, ~eptum to pluck, seize, snatch (away); to rescue

erro ~are, ~aui, ~atum to wander, err, go astray

exigo ~igere, ~egi, ~actum to demand, require

expecto ~are, ~aui, ~atum Also **exspecto**. to wait for, hope for, expect

extremus ~a, ~um, ~ior (1) *adj.* lowest, last, least, at the end (2) *neut. as noun* one's end, end of life

facilis ~is, ~e, ~ior, ~limus (1) *adj.* easy (2) as *adv.* easily

fama ~ae *f.* fame, reputation, report, news

felix ~icis, ~icior, ~icissimus *adj.* happy

femina ~**ae** *f.* woman, female

ferrum ~**i** *neut.* sword, iron object, iron tool

flamma ~**ae** *f.* flame

fluctus ~**us** *m.* wave (of the sea), also *fig.*

flumen ~**inis** *neut.* torrent, river, stream, flow

frango ~**ngere, fregi,** ~**ctum** to break

frater ~**tris** *m.* brother

fuga ~**ae** *f.* flight, escape

furor ~**oris** *m.* furor, violent madness

gens ~**tis** *f.* race, people, nation

gero ~**rere,** ~**ssi,** ~**stum** to carry out, carry on, perform, do, bear, wage, have

gloria ~**ae** *f.* glory

gratus ~**a,** ~**um,** ~**ior,** ~**issimus** *adj.* pleasant, gracious

hostis ~**is** *m.* enemy

huc *adv.* here, to this place, to this point

iaceo ~**ere,** ~**ui,** ~**itum** to fall, lie, lie helpless; to be brought low (*fig.*)

ignis ~**is** *m.* fire

illic *adv.* there, in that place

imperium ~**ii** *neut.* supreme power, dominion; command

impetus ~**us** *m.* impetus, impulse, rush

impono ~**onere,** ~**osui,** ~**ositum** to impose, place upon

incipio ~**ipere,** ~**epi,** ~**eptum** to begin

ingenium ~**ii** *neut.* intellect, mental powers, natural ability

iniuria ~**ae** *f.* injury, injurious treatment

ira ~**ae** *f.* anger

iter ~**ineris** *neut.* journey, route, way

iugum ~**i** *neut.* yoke

ius iuris *neut.* law, practice of law; prerogative, right

iuuenis ~**is** *m.* youth; young man (30–45 years old)

labor ~**oris** *m.* toilsome labor, struggle, difficulty

laetus ~**a,** ~**um,** ~**ior,** ~**issimus** *adj.* happy, glad

latus ~**eris** *neut.* side, side of the body

leuis ~**is,** ~**e,** ~**ior,** ~**issimus** *adj.* fickle, light-weight, insignificant

libertas ~**atis** *f.* liberty

licet ~**ere,** ~**uit** or ~**itum est** *impers.* it is permitted

litus ~**oris** *neut.* shore

medius ~**a,** ~**um** *adj.* middle, in the middle, between

metuo ~**ere,** ~**i, metutum** (1) to fear, be afraid (2) *ppl. adj.* **metuens** ~**ntis** afraid

metus ~**us** *m.* fear

miles ~**itis** *m.* soldier

mille *indeclinable adj.* thousand

misceo ~**ere,** ~**ui, mixtum** to mix, mingle, concoct

modo *adv.* now, just now, in a moment; only

mollis ~**is,** ~**e,** ~**ior,** ~**issimus** *adj.* soft, easy to bear

mons ~**tis** *m.* mountain

mora ~**ae** *f.* elapsed time, interval, delay, pause

mox *adv.* next, soon

munus ~**eris** *neut.* gift

nauis ~**is** *f.* ship

nego ~**are,** ~**aui,** ~**atum** to deny

nemus ~**oris** *neut.* woods, forest

nobilis ~**is,** ~**e,** ~**ior,** ~**issimus** *adj.* illustrious, distinguished

nouus ~**a,** ~**um,** ~**ior,** ~**issimus** *adj.* new, strange

numerus ~**i** *m.* number, calculation

ob *prep. acc.* because of, on account of, for

occupo ~**are,** ~**aui,** ~**atum** to occupy, cover, engross, hold the attention

ops opis *f.* supply, resources, means

opto ~**are,** ~**aui,** ~**atum** to wish, desire, pray for

orbis ~**is** *m.* world, the world

ostendo ~**dere,** ~**di,** ~**tum** or ~sum to show, indicate, point out

par paris parissimus *adj.* equal, on par with (w. dat.)

parco ~**cere, peperci** to spare, spare from (w. dat.), not condemn

paro ~**are,** ~**aui,** ~**atum** to prepare

parum (1) *indeclinable neut.* a small matter (2) *indeclinable adv.* too little

patria ~ae *f.* homeland, birthplace

pectus ~oris *neut.* breast, chest, heart (soul)

perdo ~ere, ~idi, ~itum to lose

pereo ~ire, ~ii (~iui), ~itum to perish, pass away, vanish, be lost, be ruined

periculum ~i *neut.* danger

peruenio ~enire, ~eni, ~entum to reach, attain, arrive, come to

poena ~ae *f.* punishment

premo ~mere, ~ssi, ~ssum to press, squeeze, hold down, weigh down

princeps ~ipis (1) *m.* chief, prince (2) *adj.* in first place

proelium ~ii *neut.* battle

prope ~ius (1) *adv.* almost, nearly, practically (2) *prep.* near

prosum ~desse, ~fui ~futurum to be useful; to profit

puella ~ae *f.* girl, daughter

quicumque quaecumque, quodcumque *rel. and indef. pron. and adj.* whatever, any whatever, whoever

recipio ~ipere, ~epi, ~eptum to receive

regnum ~i *neut.* kingdom, dominion

rex regis *m.* king

rumpo rumpere, rupi, ruptum to break

sacer ~cra, ~crum, ~cerrimus *adj.* sacred

saeuus ~a, ~um, ~ior, ~issimus *adj.* cruel

sanguis ~inis *m.* blood

sapiens ~ntis, ~ntior, ~ntissimus (1) *adj.* wise (2) *m.* wise man

saxum ~i *neut.* rock

sedes ~is *f.* seat, place to sit, station (in life)

seruo ~are, ~aui, ~atum to keep, preserve

sidus ~eris *neut.* star

silua ~ae *f.* woods

sinus ~us *m.* bosom, embrace; recess, cavity

socius ~ii (1) *m.* companion, associate (2) *adj.* kindred, related

somnus ~i *m.* sleep

specto ~are, ~aui, ~atum to watch, look at

sumo ~mere, ~mpsi, ~mptum to take, take up, take from a source

tandem *adv.* really, at last, in the end, after all

tectum ~i *neut.* roof, shelter

tego ~gere, ~xi, ~ctum to cover, clothe

telum ~i *neut.* spear

templum ~i *neut.* temple

tener ~ra, ~rum, ~rior, ~rrimus *adj.* tender

tergum ~i *neut.* back

tot *indeclinable adj.* so many

trado ~ere, ~idi, ~itum to hand down, hand over, pass on, give in marriage

tristis ~is, ~e, ~ior, ~issimus *adj.* unhappy, sad, saddened

turba ~ae *f.* crowd, commotion, disorder

turpis ~is, ~e, ~ior, ~issimus *adj.* foul, disgusting, repulsive, degraded, shameful

tutus ~a, ~um, ~ior, ~issimus *adj.* safe

uelut *adv.* just as, as though, as if. Also **ueluti** for example

uentus ~i *m.* wind

uerto ~tere, ~ti, ~sum to turn, turn into (w. 'in'), change directions, reverse

uester ~tra, ~trum *adj.* your, your own

uestis ~is *f.* garment, clothing, attire

uetus ~eris, ~erior, ~errimus *adj.* old, ancient

uictor ~oris *m.* victor

uinco ~ere, uici, uictum to win, overcome, defeat, prevail, get the better of

uirgo ~inis *f.* virgin

uirtus ~utis *f.* virtue, power, strength, excellence

uitium ~ii *neut.* depravity, vice

uix *adv.* with difficulty, scarcely, barely

ultimus ~a, ~um *adj.* last

umbra ~ae *f.* shadow, shade (ghost)

umquam *adv.* ever

uotum ~i *neut.* desire, hope, prayer, pious wish

urbs ~bis *f.* city

usus ~us *m.* use

uulnus ~eris *neut.* wound

APPENDIX B: PEOPLE AND PLACES

Abraham *m., usu. indecl.* ECCL Abraham, the first major patriarch of Israel, regarded as the spiritual father of Christians, whose covenant with God was viewed as fulfilled in Christ and the Church. He is represented as welcoming the faithful departed into Paradise in the parable of Lazarus and the rich man.

Academicus ~i *m.* Academic philosophers as popularized by **Cicero** in his book *Academica,* and answered in one of Augustine's first books after his conversion, *Contra Academicos* (written during the retreat to **Cassiciacum**). The Academics espoused the view that certain knowledge of how to live was unattainable. Also, **Academicus** ~a, ~um *adj.*

Adam, Adae *m.* ECCL Adam, the first human being, father of the human race, and humanity's designated representative in Eden along with Eve, whose mutual participation in sin ended Paradise. The Fall introduced sin as a hereditary trait and normative condition for Adam's posterity resulting in societal estrangement from God and personal death. The human race is thus referred to unhappily as "children of Adam."

Adeodatus ~i *m.* Adeodatus, the son of Augustine by the unnamed woman. Adeodatus was present at **Cassiciacum** and was baptized with Augustine by Ambrose (24–25 April 387). Augustine's early work **de Magistro** reports a dialogue between father and son about the nature of knowledge and learning.

Aegyptus, ~os ~i *f.* Egypt, as the land of Jewish captivity, and figurative for pagan achievements in knowledge and culture that can be put into the service of the Church. Also, the home of **Antony** and hermetic monasticism. Also, **Aegyptius** ~a, ~um *adj.*

Aeneas ~ae (*acc.* ~an) *m.* Aeneas, one of the few survivors of the destruction of **Troy** who is reckoned the legendary founder of **Rome** by the poet **Vergil**. In the *Aeneid* he lands at **Carthage** after escaping the wrath of **Juno** at sea, meets and falls in love with Queen **Dido**, then later abandons her to fulfill his quest for **Italy**. His wandering is sometimes understood figuratively for the wandering of the human soul, and is connected to the idea of the prodigal son in Luke's Gospel.

Africa ~ae *f.* North Africa, especially as a **Roman** province and home to the leading city, **Carthage**. North Africa and **Italy** are the two stages upon which the drama of Augustine's spiritual odyssey is played out. Notable locations include **Thagaste**, **Madaura**, and **Carthage**. Augustine's later vocation as priest and bishop was centered in North Africa at Hippo. Also, **Afer Afra, Afrum** *adj.*

Alexandrinus ~a, ~um *adj.* belonging to Alexandria, the city in **Egypt** founded by Alexander the Great, where **Athanasius** was bishop in the 3rd century.

Alypius ~ii *m.* Alypius was Augustine's soulmate and closest associate. As hinted at, he would become the future bishop of their hometown, **Thagaste**. He studied rhetoric under Augustine despite a feud with his father, and followed Augustine into the sect of the **Manichees**. Alypius was a law student in **Rome**, worked three terms as an Assessor in the Treasury (where he proved his integrity) and was present at the great crisis of conversion in the garden, then went on retreat to **Cassiciacum** where he displayed strong feelings about how the Dialogues should be constructed. Alypius ultimately decided to be baptized in **Milan,** Easter, 387 along with Augustine. Alypius and **Monica** are the only two individuals for whom Augustine provides a significant back story.

Ambrosius ~ii *m.* St. Ambrose, the bishop of **Milan** who serves as the counterpoint to **Faustus** the **Manichean** bishop in Augustine's spiritual journey. He is a somewhat inaccessible spiritual mentor to Augustine, although he baptizes Augustine during Easter, 387. Also, **Ambrosianus ~a, ~um** *adj.*

Amici Imperatoris Friends of the Emperor, an unofficial designation for the small upper-class group that formed the inner circle of the Emperor.

Anaximenes *m.* Anaximenes, the pre-Socratic philosopher from Miletus who speculated that air is the essential matter from which all things exist.

Antonius ~ii *m.* St. Antony of **Egypt** (251–356), hermit and founder of desert monasticism. A biography of his life was written by **Athanasius** and almost immediately translated into Latin.

Anubis ~is *m.* Anubis, the **Egyptian** god of the dead, usually represented as a man with the head of a jackal.

Apollinaristae ~arum *f. pl.* [GRK Ἀπολινάριος] ECCL Apollinarians, a heretical movement from the 4th century that denied a real human mind to **Christ**, substituting instead the divine Logos. The movement was condemned at the First Council of **Carthage** in 381.

Aristotelicum ~i *neut.* (books) of or pertaining to Aristotle, the famous philosopher and natural scientist (384–322 BC), tutor to Alexander the Great, and founder of the Lyceum.

Arriani ~orum *m.* the Arians, a heretical party within the **Catholic Church** that maintained, in opposition to Nicene theology, that the Son was a created being, not equal to the Father, and subordinate in divinity. Although condemned and proscribed, strains of Arian theology continued to exercise some influence even during the lifetime of Augustine.

Athanasius ~i *m.* St. Athanasius, the **Greek** Church father and Bishop of **Alexandria** in the 3rd century, who heroically maintained the divinity of Christ against the **Arians.**

Atheniensis ~is, ~e *adj. as noun* Athenian, a citizen of Athens. Those addressed by **Paul** at the Areopagus during his stop in the city in Acts 17.

Babylon ~onis *f.* or **Babylonia ~ae** *f.* Babylon, the ancient capital of the Assyrian Empire as understood in various biblical senses, both historical and figurative; recalling the 70-year captivity of the Jews after the fall of **Jerusalem** in 586 BC; in the book of Revelation as capital of, and synonymous with pagan **Rome** and the world of sin (and therefore the opposite of the heavenly Jerusalem); as source of confusion; as pride; as lust for dominance over others. Also, **Babylonicus ~a, ~um** *adj.*

Caesar ~aris *m.* cognomen for Octavian Augustus (and succeeding emperors), who is referenced in the Gospel of Matthew in a dispute over paying taxes.

Carthago ~inis *f.* Carthage, the modern-day city in Tunisia, contains the archeological site of ancient Carthage, the city as it would have been known to Augustine both historically and in fiction. Carthage was the scene of the love affair between **Aeneas** and **Dido** in the *Aeneid*, and historically the capital of the **Roman** province of **Africa**. During Augustine's lifetime it was one of the largest cities of the Empire. When Augustine went to Carthage to study (165 miles from his home in **Thagaste**) he would have been immersed in a thoroughly Roman and cosmopolitan city. Also, **Carthaginiensis ~is, ~e** *adj.*

Cassiciacum ~i *m.* Cassiciacum, probably modern day Cassago Brianza, about 20 miles north of **Milan**, was the location of the planned philosophical retreat that followed Augustine's dramatic conversion. It took place at the country villa of his friend **Verecundus**. Accompanied by his mother, son, and close friends it was a season of living with the Psalms, and for writing his first extant works: philosophical dialogues in the style of **Cicero**. These were *Soliloquia, Contra Academicos, De beata vita,* and *De ordine.*

Catholica ~ae *f.* [GRK καθολικός] universal, relating to all; ECCL the Catholic Church, a Catholic Christian. Also, **Catholicus ~a, ~um** *adj.*

Catilina ~ae *m.* Catiline, the great **Roman** conspirator during **Cicero**'s consulship, as reported by Sallust, the historian (*c.* 86–35 BC), in his *Bellum Catilinae* (a standard text

in Augustine's secondary education). Catiline is the model of lust for power, and illustrative that every evil action has a motive to obtain some end beyond the evil itself.

Christianus ~i *m.* Christian, generally understood in the *Confessions* as an individual who has passed through the Catechumenate, received Baptism, and receives the Eucharist in communion with the Catholic Church. Also, **Christianus ~a, ~um** *adj.*

Christus ~i *m.* the strictly historical Christ as first attested in Latin by Tacitus and Pliny; ECCL Christ as both historical person and the Son, second person of the Trinity, variously represented and personified as: Aeterna Simplicitas (Eternal Simplicity), Diuinitas (Divinity), Piscis (Fish, i.e., ΙΧΘΥΣ, as raised from the Deep), Principium (First Principle), Sapientia (Wisdom), Sermo (Word), Sponsus (Bridegroom), Unicus (one and only Son), Verbum (Word), Veritas (Truth), Via (Way), Victima (Victim), Virtus (Power).

Cicero ~onis *m.* M. Tullius Cicero (106–43 BC), Roman orator, author, and politician, who along with **Terence, Vergil,** and Sallust would have made up the standard curriculum for an educated boy in the Late Empire. Augustine was schooled in both the philosophical treatises and political speeches of Cicero as is evident by references to both throughout his writings.

Creusa ~ae *f.* Creusa, the wife of **Aeneas** who was lost in the conflagration while fleeing **Troy**. Her ghost appears to Aeneas urging him to continue his flight from the city and fulfill his destiny.

Cyprianus ~i *m.* St. Cyprian, 3rd century Bishop of **Carthage** and martyr, whose lasting influence was keenly felt throughout North **Africa**.

Danae ~es *f.* The Danaans or **Greeks**, especially as taking part in the Trojan War, in either **Homer** or **Vergil**.

Dauid *m. indecl.* ECCL David, the most famous king of Israel, as well as military leader, musician, and author of many of the Psalms. Also, **Dauiticus** ~a, ~um *adj.*

de Magistro The Teacher, a dialogue between Augustine and **Adeodatus** about the nature of knowledge, written sometime after Augustine's conversion and return to **Africa**. It is the only one of Augustine's dialogues identified by name in *Confessions*.

Decem Categoria ~ae, *f.* [GRK κατηγορία] LATE the *(Ten) Categories* of **Aristotle** as translated into Latin by Marius **Victorinus**. Augustine mastered this text without assistance, although it was notoriously difficult to understand.

Deus, Dei *m.* ECCL God, as principally revealed in Scripture, especially **Deus meus** my God (following ecclesiastical usage of nom. for voc. as throughout the Psalms.) Also, **deus** ~i (infreq.) a god

Dido ~onis *f.* Dido, the founder and queen of **Carthage** in the *Aeneid*, who commits suicide when **Aeneas** abandons her for **Italy**.

Dominus ~i *m.* ECCL the Lord, **Dominus Deus** the Lord God. Also **dominus** ~i (infreq.) owner.

Elpidus ~ii *m.* Elpidius, a skilled **Christian** apologist in **Carthage** who participated in public debates with the **Manichees** and proved difficult to refute. His name is **Greek** for "hopeful" and his appearance probably not coincidental in light of the spiritual progress made in book 5.

Epaphroditus ~i *m.* Epaphroditus, the companion of **Paul**, who assisted with financial support and was associated with the churches in **Philippi** and Ephesus.

Epicurus, ~os ~i *m.* Epicurus, a third-century BC Greek thinker, produced a complete system of philosophy that had the aim of attaining happiness through the avoidance of pain. He did not maintain an afterlife for the soul.

Esaias ~ae *m.* ECCL Isaiah, the Old Testament prophet, to whom Augustine was directed by **Ambrose** for spiritual reading prior to his baptism. Augustine struggled to make sense of the meaning of Isaiah and abandoned the attempt in hopes of trying again later when he was more versed in Scripture.

Esau *indecl. m.* ECCL Esau, the son of **Isaac** and jealous brother of **Jacob**, who sold his birthright for a bowl of porridge.

Eua ~ae *f.* ECCL Eve, the first woman and wife of **Adam**, made from Adam's rib. She was his companion, the mother of the human race, and participant in the Fall. Hence, "children of Eve" for the unhappy human race.

Euodias ~ii *m.* Evodius, a friend of Augustine from **Thagaste**, who joins the group in **Milan** as an already baptized Christian with an imperial post. He was present at the death of **Monica.**

Faustus ~i *m.* Faustus of Milevis (about 100 miles from **Thagaste**), the **Manichean** bishop who proved to be such an intense disappointment to Augustine when they finally met. He was reputed to be able to unravel all sorts of difficult questions, but was rather more affable than educated. Augustine tutored Faustus in literature when he realized the limitations of his learning.

Filius ~ii *m.* the Son, the second person of the **Trinity.** See **Christus.**

Firminus ~i *m.* Firminus, who regarded Augustine as a close friend in **Milan,** related his experience with astrology and the precision with which his father and a friend studied the simultaneous birth of two children (Firminus being one of them) while separated by some distance. The story had other than the intended effect, as it fully convinced Augustine of the futility of casting horoscopes.

Galatae ~arum *m. pl.* Galatians, ECCL the Church community found by **Paul** in Galatia, and recipient of the epistle bearing their name.

Genesis ~is *f.* [GRK γένεσις] ECCL Genesis, the first book of the Old Testament, believed to be authored by **Moses,** and a source of intense interest for Augustine, both as a record of cosmological and human origins, and for its value in his debate with the **Manichees.**

Graecus ~a, ~um *adj.* Greek, Greek language. Also, **Graece** *adv.* in Greek.

Hebraeus ~a, ~um *adj.* Hebrew, the language of the Hebrews.

Helias ~ae *m.* ECCL Elijah, the representative Old Testament prophet, but only referenced as it relates to eating.

Hierius ~i *m.* Hierius of **Rome,** a contemporary of Augustine, an acclaimed public orator known to have been outstanding in both philosophy and rhetoric. He was a Syrian trained first in **Greek,** then in **Latin.** Augustine mentions him only once, then never again in any other work.

Hierusalem *neut. indecl.* Jerusalem, variously understood as the historical city and capital of Judea, but especially as figure of the City of God, eternal life, a spiritual homeland, and in a transferred sense the **Catholic** Church.

Hippocrates ~is *m.* Hippocrates, the fifth-century BC **Greek** physician of Cos and author of many medical treatises, which were standard texts for the study of medicine in late antiquity.

Homerus ~i *m.* Homer, the most famous of the **Greek** epic poets whose works, the *Iliad* and *Odyssey,* became standard texts for educating Greek children, and whose stories were later adapted by **Vergil** in the *Aeneid.*

Hortensius ~a, ~um *adj. Hortensius,* a lost dialogue of **Cicero** that recommended the philosophical life. This was a familiar text in Augustine's secondary education and his reading of it marked an early turning point in the journey of conversion. Augustine's explanation of the etymology of "philosophy" as the love of wisdom at 3.4.8 is probably a recollection from *Hortensius.*

Iacob *indecl.* ECCL Jacob, one of the three great patriarchs (**Abraham, Isaac, and** Jacob) that are frequently recalled together as the family line representative of the Old Covenant and the promises to the people of **Israel**. Jacob notoriously filched the birthright from his brother **Esau** and later wrestled unwittingly with God. God changed his name to **Israel**.

Iesus ~us *m.* [GRK Ἰησοῦς] ECCL Jesus the Christ, see **Christus**.

Iohannes ~is *m.* ECCL John the Baptist (not the Evangelist), who was the forerunner of Christ, and is mentioned only in reference to eating and diet.

Iordanes ~is *m.* Jordan River in Palestine, rich with spiritual resonance as the point of crossing into the Promised Land by the ancient Israelites and the location of John's baptism of Jesus, but only referenced figuratively for human mortality.

Ioseph *indecl.* ECCL Jospeh, the favorite son of **Jacob**, who rescues his family from famine in **Egypt** after being sold into slavery by his brothers, and at the end of his life has his sons blessed by his father other than how he had hoped.

Isaac *indecl. m.* ECCL Isaac, one of the three great patriarchs (**Abraham**, Isaac, and **Jacob**) that are frequently recalled together as the family line representative of the Old Covenant and the promises to the people of **Israel**. Isaac's name means "laughter" recalling his mother Sarah's reaction to the news that she, a barren old woman, would conceive a son.

Israhel ~elis, or *indecl.* ECCL Israel, as the people of God and recipient of God's care, particularly in the Psalms.

Italia ~ae *f.* Italy, as the second stage upon which the drama of Augustine's spiritual odyssey is played out. Notable locations include **Rome, Milan,** and **Ostia**. Also, **Italicus** ~a, ~um *adj.*

Italicianarum, Largitionum LATE Italian Treasury, which oversaw collection of taxes for all of Italy.

Iudaeus ~a, ~um *adj.* Jewish, Jew (as noun).

(Imperator) Iulianus ~a, ~um The Emperor Julian, attempted to return the Empire to traditional Roman religion and as part of that program issued the School Edict in 362, which forbade Christians from teaching the classics.

Iuno ~onis *f.* Juno, wife of **Jupiter**, and bitter adversary of **Aeneas**.

Iuppiter *m.* or **Iupiter, Iouis** Jove or Jupiter, father of the gods of Olympus, and husband of **Juno**. Notorious in ancient literature for his infidelity and sexual misadventures.

Iustina ~ae *f.* Empress Justina, mother of the boy-emperor **Valentinian II**, an **Arian** sympathizer and political opponent of **Ambrose**.

Latina ~ae *f.*, Latin, the Latin language. Also, **Latinus** ~a, ~um, ~ior *adj.*, and **Latine** *adv.* in Latin.

(cedrus) Libanus ~i *m.* (Cedar) of Lebanon, an aromatic species of tree in Palestine, referenced in the Psalms and figurative for pride.

Macedonia ~ae *f.* Macedonia, as a field of operation for **Paul** where he was assisted by the **Philippian** church for his mission, and from which region the churches that he planted likewise assisted him in his need.

Madaura ~ae *f.* Madauros (modern-day Mdaourouch in Algeria) was located about 15 miles from Augustine's hometown of Thagaste. It was the birthplace of the **Latin** writer, Apuleius, whose works were well-known to Augustine.

Manichaeus ~i *m.* Mani(chaeus), born in 216, a Persian religious innovator and author of a complex mythology who fused various traditions into a system that challenged the authority of the Catholic Church. This widespread sect was known as **Manicheism**.

Manichaei ~orum *m. pl.* Manichees, the quasi-Christian, quasi-illegal sect to which Augustine was a loose adherent for about nine years. Their books were known for being large and lavish and their cosmology highly elaborate and fantastic. Also, **Manichaeus** ~a, ~um adj.

Maria ~ae *f.* ECCL the Blessed Virgin Mary.

Mars ~tis *m.* Mars, the planet.

Medea ~ae *f.* the Colchian princess and renegade bride of Jason of the Argonauts. The classical model of female villainy: dark sorceress, cunning deceiver, and filicide. Euripides produced the first *Medea* tragedy, and centuries later it was revived in Latin by Seneca, but the story was most likely known to Augustine through Ovid's description of Medea in flight in *Met.* 7.

Mediolanium ~(i)i neut. Milan, the capital of the Western **Roman** Empire in late antiquity and home of **Ambrose** and his basilica, making it the intellectual center of Christianity in northern **Italy** with a **Christian** community heavily influenced by Neoplatonism. Also, **Mediolanensis** ~is, ~e *adj.*

Minerua ~ae *f.* Minerva, the goddess of wisdom.

Monnica ~ae *f.* St. Monica, Augustine's mother, a dominant personality throughout books 1–9 but only identified by name once. Her singular hope was to see Augustine a **Catholic Christian** before her death. She was deeply devoted to **Ambrose** and her piety was praised by him.

Moyses ~is *m.* ECCL Moses, the great **Jewish** law-giver and political deliverer, who led the **Israelites** (descendants of the Patriarchs) out of captivity in **Egypt**, through the Red Sea, and to the Promised Land of Canaan, but his singular importance to Augustine is as the author of **Genesis**, and especially chapter 1.

Nebridius ~ii *m.* Nebridius, childhood friend of Augustine and part of the **Milan** inner circle, devised convincing arguments against both astrology and **Manicheism**. Although a religious seeker capable of making careful distinctions, he was not baptized with Augustine, though later converted.

Neptunus ~i *m.* Neptune, the god of the sea.

Noe *m. indecl.* ECCL Noah, architect of the ark by which a handful of people were saved from the Great Flood. He is referenced incidentally in the matter of food.

Oceanus ~i *m.* The ocean, especially the Atlantic.

Onesiphorus ~i *m.* ECCL friend of **Paul** whose household was in Ephesus, mentioned (presumably after his death) twice in the epistle 2 Timothy. He is noteworthy for the special care he took to find the Apostle and provide for his necessities while he was deserted and imprisoned in Rome.

Orestes ~is *m.* et **Pylades** ~is *m.* Orestes and Pylades, noble friends who appear in Euripides' play *Iphigenia at Tauris.* Augustine would know the reference based on **Cicero's** comments in *de Amicitia* after having watched a performance of the play adapted by his friend Marcus Pacuvius.

Ostia ~ae *f.* **Tiberinus** ~a, ~um *adj.* Ostia on the Tiber (modern Ostia Antica), was the ancient port of Rome, referenced in the opening lines of the *Aeneid,* and the place of death of **Monica.** Monica's abandonment by Augustine in North Africa (see **Dido**) and death at Ostia reinforce the parallels with **Aeneas.** The modern archeological site is spectacular, although as a result of silting it sits about two miles from the coast.

Paracletus ~i *m.* ECCL advocate, defender, comforter; the Holy Spirit.

Pater ~tris *m.* the Father, the first person of the Trinity.

Patricius ~ii *m.* Patricius, Augustine's father, died when he was seventeen. Augustine's recollections of his father are mixed as he lived most of his life as a pagan and consequently exercised no influence over his son's spiritual

or moral development; he only converted to Christianity toward the end of his life.

Paulus ~i *m.* ECCL St. Paul, the apostle to the Gentiles and author of almost two-thirds of the New Testament, the decisive influence in Augustine's conversion and by far the most frequently cited author in *Confessions* (Psalms being the most frequently cited single work). Also, the governor of Cyprus, Sergius Paulus, whom St. Paul converts.

Philippensis ~is, ~e *adj.* Philippians, ECCL the community of believers established by **Paul** in Philippi ca. 49, and recipient of the epistle that bears their name.

Photinus ~i *m.* Photinus, a 4th century **Christian** bishop and heresiarch who denied any sort of existence to **Christ** before the incarnation.

(libros) Platonicus ~a, ~um *adj.* (books) of the Platonists, written by (at least) Porphyry and translated into **Latin** by Marius **Victorinus.** These would have included the *Enneads* of Plotinus. Both Porphyry and Plotinus are referred to as "Neoplatonists," a modern term that they would not have applied to themselves.

Ponticianus ~i *m.* Ponticianus, a native of North **Africa** and member of the Emperor's secret service, who paid a visit to Augustine and **Alypius** in **Milan** and brought to their attention the conversion of **Antony.** He further elaborated on the growth of monasticism, the **Life of Antony,** and the role it played in a colleague's conversion at **Trier.**

Protasius ~ii *m.* et **Geruasius** ~ii *m.* Protasius and Gervasius, two of the earliest martyrs in **Milan**, whose relics were discovered by **Ambrose** in July, 386 and thereby ended the crisis with Empress **Justina**.

Roma ~ae *f.* Rome, a waypoint on Augustine's spiritual journey, where he taught briefly before being awarded the post in **Milan**, and to which he returned briefly after Monica's death. Also, **Romanus** ~a, ~um *adj.*

Romanianus ~i *m.* Romanianus, Augustine's financial benefactor, who was eager to fund the philosophical community envisaged by the **Milan** circle of friends. He had been influenced by Augustine to join the **Manichees**, and became a **Christian** about ten years after Augustine.

Sabbata ~orum *neut. pl.* ECCL Sabbath, as day of rest, and figurative for eternal rest, appropriately marks the end of *Confessions* and the extended allegorical interpretation of the seven days of creation in book thirteen.

Salomon ~onis *m.* Solomon, king of **Israel** after his father, **David**. Famed for his wisdom and the building of the first Temple in **Jerusalem**, he is the traditional author of much of the book of Proverbs.

Saturnus ~i *m.* Saturn, the planet.

Saul ~is *m.* ECCL Saul of Tarsus, the name of **Paul** before his conversion.

Seneca ~ae *m.* L. Annaeus Seneca (died 65 AD), philosopher, playwright and adviser to the young Nero. Seneca authored a dozen philosophical treatises, left behind a large number of letters, and is the sole representative of **Roman** tragedy, of which eight authentic plays survive including a **Medea**.

Simplicianus ~ i *m.* Simplicianus, theological mentor to **Ambrose** and his successor as Bishop of **Milan**, and friend and adviser to Augustine. He was instrumental in the conversions of both Marius **Victorinus** and Augustine, whose conversion stories parallel one another.

Sodomitus ~a, ~um *adj.* Sodomites, the inhabitants of Sodom, the infamous ancient city of vice and crime. The city was destroyed by a divine firestorm after its residents attempted to sexually assault the angelic messengers sent to warn of the city's destruction.

Spiritus ~us *m.* **Spiritus Sanctus** *m.* Holy Spirit, the third person of the Trinity. Variously represented as Consolator, (Comforter), Doctor (Teacher), Donum (Gift), Munus (Gift), Promissio (Promise). See **Paracletus.**

Symmachus ~i *m.* Symmachus, prefect of **Rome**, who recommended and sent Augustine to **Milan** for the post of Master of Rhetoric. Just prior to this encounter, **Ambrose** had prevailed against Symmachus in the dispute over the restoration of the Altar of Victory.

Syrus ~i *m.* Syrian, used only as descriptive of **Hierius.**

Tartarus ~i *m.* Tartarus, the Underworld and realm of the departed dead in classical literature. Also, **Tartareus** ~a, ~um *adj.*

Terentius ~ia, ~ium *adj.* Terence, one of only two surviving **Latin** writers of comedy, whose plays, especially the *Eunuch,* formed the basic curriculum for school boys in the Late **Roman** Empire.

Teucri ~orum *m. pl.* Teucrians, descendants of Teucer, i.e., the Trojans.

Thagastensis ~e *adj.* Thagaste (modern Souk Ahras in Algeria) was the birthplace and early home of Augustine. A number of Augustine's fellow townsfolk from Thagaste factor into his conversion narrative: his best friend **Alypius**, **Evodius**, and **Romanianus**.

Thessalonica ~ae. *f.* Thessalonica, ECCL the location of a church plant by **Paul**, for which the **Philippians** twice helped finance his mission.

Tobias ~ae *m.* ECCL Tobit, a devout blind Jew living in Nineveh, who observes outlawed burial customs and suffers for his faith, is the main character of the deuterocanonical book that bears his name.

Treueri ~rorum *m. pl.* Treveri, a Celtic tribe for whom is named the city Trier, or Treves, which at one time was called Augusta Treverorum, following the Roman conquest. Later, Trier was one of the capitals of the Western Roman Empire.

Trinitas ~atis *f.* ECCL The Blessed Trinity.

Troia ~ae *f.* the city of Troy (modern Hissarlik) about four miles inland from the coast of Turkey. The site of the Trojan War as described by **Homer** in the *Iliad*, and by **Vergil** in the *Aeneid*. **Aeneas** was one of only a few survivors of the destruction of Troy.

Tullianus ~a, ~um *adj.* of **Cicero**; resembling his style.

Valentinianus ~i *m.* Valentinian II (371–392), the boy-emperor who was raised to the throne at age 4 and died when he was scarcely 21 years old, was the recipient of Augustine's panegyric in **Milan**, 385, and was eulogized by **Ambrose**.

Venus ~eris *f.* Venus, as the planet or the goddess.

Verecundus ~i *m.* Verecundus, a schoolmaster in **Milan**, was a married man who wished to be a Christian, but only as a celibate. He was the owner of the country estate at **Cassiciacum** where the spiritual retreat took place. His conversion occurred after the events recorded in *Confessions* and just prior to his death following a serious illness.

Vergilius ~ia, ~ium *adj.* Vergil or Virgil, the poet (70–19 BC), author of the *Georgics* and the *Aeneid*, which especially served as the standard text of schoolboys in the **Roman** Empire.

Victorinus ~i *m.* Marius Victorinus, born in North **Africa**, was an elite rhetorician in **Rome** who defended the Roman gods and only later in life became a **Christian**. He was influenced by **Simplicianus**, who relates the details of his conversion to Augustine. Prior to his conversion he wrote works on logic and rhetoric and translated the **Ten Categories** of **Aristotle** and various **Platonic** books into Latin. His literary output after his conversion included hymns, commentaries, and doctrinal treatises.

Vindicianus ~i *m.* Vindicianus, the physician to Emperor **Valentinian** who attempted to persuade Augustine to abandon all interest in astrology and focus his efforts on making an honest living at rhetoric. Their conversation is related at 4.3.5, but he is not named until 7.6.8.

***Vita Antonii** Life of Antony* by St. **Athanasius,**
existed in two Latin translations, one anon-
ymous, the other by Evagrius, the friend
of Jerome. The translation by Evagrius was
intended for a more genteel Roman audience and is probably the one known to
Ponticianus, who relates its contents to
Augustine.